JAMES STEPHEN HOGG

A Biography

SARAH ANN HOGG   JAMES STEPHEN HOGG

JAMES STEPHEN
HOGG

A Biography

By ROBERT C. COTNER

1959 · AUSTIN
UNIVERSITY OF TEXAS PRESS

Library of Congress Catalog Card No. 58–59849
© 1959 by University of Texas Press

Manufactured in the United States of America
by the Printing Division of the University of Texas

To These Professors of History:

DEAN VERNER W. CRANE, SAMUEL E. MORISON, CLIFFORD K. SHIPTON
who stimulated new interest in colonial frontiers on land and sea

EDWARD C. KIRKLAND, EDWIN GAY, ABBOTT P. USHER
RUDOLPH BIESELE, ARTHUR M. SCHLESINGER, SR.
who related social and economic forces to life

CHARLES W. HACKETT, CARLOS E. CASTAÑEDA
PABLO MARTÍNEZ DEL RÍO, CLARENCE H. HARING
who broadened the scope of Latin-American history

MILTON R. GUTSCH, WILBUR CORTEZ ABBOTT, DAVID OWEN
THAD RIKER, CHARLES MCILWAIN
who linked some major aspects of European culture with the Americas

EUGENE C. BARKER, PAUL BUCK, CARDINAL GOODWIN
E. MERTON COULTER, RUPERT N. RICHARDSON, WALTER P. WEBB
who expanded regional knowledge and interpretation

and especially FREDERICK MERK
for guidance and encouragement

Preface

EACH YEAR thousands of visitors to the rotunda of the Capitol of the State of Texas observe the portraits of the governors which cover the circular walls beneath the great dome. Many linger to ponder the expression of a full, jovial countenance which shows strength, determination, and kindliness, and whose blue eyes reflect candor—they are looking at the likeness of James Stephen Hogg, the man who, because of his interest in the plain people, is known as "The People's Governor." Candidates for public office still find it useful to know what Hogg said on fundamental issues, and many have envied his hold on the hearts and minds of the plain people.

This biography was written to delineate the life of James S. Hogg (1851–1906), a diligent attorney general (1887–1891) and a vigorous Democratic reform governor of Texas (1891–1895), who was also a greatly loved leader of the people. Much has been made of the "Wisconsin Idea" and the part Robert LaFollette played in the Progressive Movement. Ten years earlier, under the leadership of Governor Hogg, Texas had embarked on a reform program which would be studied later in Wisconsin and elsewhere. Jim Hogg emerges from any objective appraisal of his career as a worthy contemporary of the progressive governors, John P. Altgeld, Theodore Roosevelt, and Bob LaFollette, and as a reformer who remained to the end of his life a progressive. This study attempts to correct the view expressed by C. Vann Woodward and James Tinsley that after Hogg made money in oil he became a deserter from the forces of reform.

At least four prominent figures in the public life of Texas are generally recognized as statesmen: Stephen F. Austin, Sam Houston, John H. Reagan, and James S. Hogg. Two, Austin and Houston, have been the subjects of excellent biographies; Reagan left an autobiography; but a record of Hogg's work was to be found only in his official addresses and state papers and three brief essays. As late as 1951 Reinhard H. Luthin in the October issue of the *American Historical Review* erroneously placed him on a list of "demagogues." Despite the name-calling and charges of political expediency from some of the contemporary, large-city papers in Texas, Hogg was not a demagogue. Rather, he chose to espouse the unpopular side of an issue when he felt it was right. He was, however, a man of the people in the sense that he fought for their welfare. He opposed lawlessness, trusts in restraint of trade, many practices of Jay Gould, Huntington's grasping agents, fictitious bond issues, free passes, and permanent lobbying. Trained in the Granger tradition, Hogg offered "no quarter" to Populists, while respecting many individuals who joined the third party. Hogg had faith in democratic processes and deserves to be known as a sincere champion of law enforcement and effective government in the public interest. In an era when the federal government was becoming stronger in many areas of American life, Hogg saw the need for stronger state governments, but he envisioned the work of state and national governments as supplementary to each other rather than as encroaching upon the constitutional functions of each other.

Jim Hogg was not an upstart in politics. He came from a family in which political activity and association with important political figures was usual. Grandfather Thomas Hogg served in the legislatures of Georgia, Alabama, and Mississippi, while Jim's father, General Joseph L. Hogg, was a lawyer-planter who helped draft the Texas constitution of 1845, presided over a railroad convention in 1854, and served in the Mexican and Civil wars. Senators Sam Houston and Thomas J. Rusk visited in the home of Hogg's parents. Jim Hogg was a son of the Old South, but he helped to mold the New Southwest after 1871, when he began his first newspaper to fight Grantism. His second paper was located in a poor, frontier county and became the successful agent of those people who objected to binding themselves to pay a bond subsidy to the Texas and Pacific Railway, which was building into Dallas. The Hepburn railroad regulation act of 1906 reflected many of the things he had worked for over a period of twenty years. While the forces of progress and reaction strained some of the foundations of the federal system of government, Hogg kept a remarkable sense of humor, at the same time giving blow for blow to his political opponents.

During Reconstruction James Hogg joined Reagan in advocating the extension of suffrage to qualified Negroes, ahead of the Fourteenth and Fifteenth amendments. In 1884 Hogg addressed Negro audiences asking them to vote for Cleveland and thus "redeemed" Smith County from the Republicans. In 1892, when the Republicans in Texas were split along racial lines, Hogg appealed to all groups to vote for his reform program. He opposed a poll tax as unnecessary, at the same time voicing opposition to any federal supervision of elections.

Law enforcement had been his task as justice of the peace, district attorney, attorney general, and governor. He instituted suits which, eventually restored to Texas over one million acres of land illegally obtained by railroads for "siding and switches." He drove forty "wildcat" insurance companies from the state, phrased a strong antitrust law in 1889, and championed a strong railroad commission. Oil and railroad interests sponsored candidates against him in 1890 and 1892. Hogg appreciated Alliance and labor support, in addition to lawyer, farmer, businessman, and banker support generally. He was opposed to government subsidies, government ownership, and the subtreasury plan of the Alliance. The Alliance did not elect Hogg in 1890, as Professor William Hesseltine and others have stated. When reactionary George Clark failed to defeat Hogg in 1892, the Railroad Commission was enjoined by a federal court to permanently desist from enforcing its rate schedules, but the Commission was restored to activity in 1894.

By training, Hogg was a progressive conservative, but he founded the reform or liberal tradition in Texas after his victory in 1892 and carried into effect his reform program. Actually, he was a middle-of-the-roader, leading the "vital center." Like Jefferson, he is quoted by both conservatives and liberals. Speaking before the Boston Chamber of Commerce in 1894, Hogg listed his major reforms as: (1) the railroad commission law, (2) the railroad stock and bond law, (3) the alien land law, (4) the county and municipal bond law, and (5) the corporation land law. Hogg failed to bring Rockefeller to Texas to stand trial for violation of the antitrust law, but eventually heavy fines were paid to the state. Having faced declining revenues as a result of the depression, Hogg left the state in debt when his term ended in 1895, but he called for strict tax collection or a tax rate sufficient to restore solvency and to support adequately a longer school term.

Following his voluntary return to private life in 1895, Hogg helped Horace Chilton become United States senator, and both men strengthened the pro-silver forces. By speaking at Tammany Hall in 1899, Hogg helped to gain the renomination of William J. Bryan in 1900, although he disagreed with Bryan's definition of imperialism. From 1901 to 1905, when Hogg was injured in a railroad accident, he was active in oil development. Men like U.S. Senator Joe Bailey and state Representative John Nance Garner thwarted his reform program at the turn of the century, but Tom Connally and Pat Neff came to his support. In 1906

Thomas Campbell was elected governor and he carried on the Hogg reforms. Woodrow Wilson appropriately declared Hogg to be a forerunner of the twentieth-century Progressive Movement.

Hogg came to prominence in the period of transition from the predominantly agrarian era to the industrial (Hogg said "corporate") age—Henry Commager called it the "watershed" decade. Hogg played a large role in molding this change, as he sought steadfastly to retain the best of the old, to temper the evil of both new and old by law, and to build on the best of both the new and the old a progressive, liberal tradition that was secured by the ballots of the people and that would best fit the needs of Texas. Thus, his political philosophy held the public good always first in his mind and fundamental to his actions.

Among the reforms championed by Hogg none was closer to his heart than the improvement of public and private education. The University of Texas benefited from his support while he was governor, and benefactions, including the Hogg Foundation, have continued from his children. Students who pass by his statue on the campus of the University should know that at a meeting in the Main Building in 1892 he told the assembled students:

You can never forget the causes that led Texians to popular education without injustice to a sense of patriotism . . . To preserve the rights and liberties of the people is the purpose . . . Hereafter the great battles to maintain the liberties of the people must be fought in the forum of reason.

He believed that the purpose of education was "to preserve the rights and liberties of the people," and he expected the students to be prepared to maintain these liberties "in the forum of reason." And in 1904 he said:

Send your children to school. Educate them. Teach them that this government is theirs, but that if they expect to keep special privilege free-booters from stealing it they must be vigilant in their political affairs.

Acknowledgments

Many people have given assistance toward the completion of this biography, and I regret that some names may be omitted in the space here available for acknowledgments. Miss Ima Hogg, only daughter of Governor Hogg, graciously permitted use of the Hogg Collection, over 50,000 items in the Archives Collection, Eugene C. Barker Texas History Center of the University of Texas Library. In 1947 she took time from a busy schedule as a member of the Houston School Board and sponsor of the Houston Symphony Orchestra to make a trip through East Texas with my wife and me to help us meet people her family had known and to explain many matters not revealed in books or letters. President T. S. Painter of the University of Texas arranged a leave of absence for me while I was a recipient of the Walter B. Sharp Fellowship from the Rice Institute in 1949–50. President W. V. Houston and Dr. William Masterson of Rice have been helpful in many ways. Appreciation is also expressed to the Rosenwald Fund and the Harvard Graduate School for grants which enabled me to continue my study at Harvard University.

I am particularly indebted to the following friends who have read all or parts of the manuscript: Dr. Eugene C. Barker, Dr. Rupert N. Richardson, Dr. Joseph H. Parks, Dr. James Howard, Dr. Walter P. Webb, Dr. Walter F. McCaleb, Mrs. Howard Calkins, Mrs. Martha Zivley, Mrs. Norris G. Davis, Dean Maude King, Vice-President Harry H. Ransom, Roger H. Porter, and Dave Cheavens. Their suggestions have been stimulating and helpful.

For research assistance I wish to thank the staffs of the Library of Congress and of the public libraries of Denver, Colorado, and El Paso, Fort Worth, Houston, Waco, Austin, and Dallas, Texas. Appreciation is expressed to President Rupert N. Richardson of Hardin-Simmons University and President Charles Seymour of Yale for sharing their superior knowledge of Colonel E. M. House; to Wayne Gard and Sam Acheson of the Dallas *Morning News;* to Professors Jefferson D. Bragg and Guy B. Harrison at Baylor University; to Dr. James Tinsley of the University of Houston for permission to read his dissertation on the Progressive Movement in Texas; and to Dr. Paolo E. Coletta of the United States Naval Academy for references from his biography of William Jennings Bryan. Discussions of early Alabama history with Dr. Thomas P. Abernethy at the University of Virginia during the summer of 1957 will long be cherished.

I express deep appreciation to my colleagues on the University of Texas Library staff, especially Miss Winnie Allen, Director of the Archives Collection, and Miss Llerena Friend, Director of the Texas Collection and biographer of Sam Houston. Miss Allen made the initial arrangements under which I was able to begin this study before World War II, and when I returned to research I found that numerous students on her staff, by means of funds made available by Miss Hogg, had been at work typing the original letter files. These typescripts greatly facilitated the completion of this study. The files of the University of Texas Archives have been especially valuable in making possible a more accurately balanced account of public reaction to Hogg. Many of the files of independent rural newspapers, usually favorable to Hogg, have disappeared. Fortunately, the Hogg scrapbooks contain numerous clippings on both sides and have kept me from some of the errors made by those who have used only the accessible files of the usually anti-Hogg city dailies. Mrs. Hally Bryan Perry interested Mrs. Walter B. Sharp in the project, and Mrs. Sharp and her son Dudley, Houston businessman and Assistant Secretary for Air during the Eisenhower administration, established the oral history project, Pioneers in Texas Oil History. The availability of these tape recordings in the Archives Collection at the University of Texas has been of great value in the development of certain chapters of this biography; the tapes will be more widely useful in future studies. My footnotes will reveal the names of numerous master's and doctor's degree holders to whom I am indebted for quotations from their special studies.

I wish that my parents might have witnessed the completion of this book. To my brother and his wife, Dr. and Mrs. Thomas E. Cotner, Jr., Washington, D. C., and to my wife, Elizabeth, and to Cathy and Robert, Jr., I am indebted for personal assistance about which they know. The work of student assistants like Melvin Mason, Nancy Rush, Susanne Hood, Mary Ann Jones, and Nancy Bivens, as well as that of others who brought in stories, interviews, or reports, deserves recognition.

All the illustrations in this book, with the exception of the maps, the cartoons from the *Texas Farmer* and the Dallas *News* and the photographs listed below, were graciously supplied by the University of Texas Library, from the Hogg Collection, and by Miss Ima Hogg. The photographs obtained from other sources are those of: George W. Clark, a Walter Barnes photograph of the Clark portrait in the offices of the Texas Court of Criminal Appeals, courtesy of Judge W. A. Morrison; Gustav Cook, from L. E. Daniell's *Types of Successful Men;* N. Wright Cuney, from Maude Cuney Hare's *N. Wright Cuney;* Thomas L. Nugent, from Catharine Nugent's *Life Work of Thomas L. Nugent;* John Nance Garner, from portrait by Seymour Stone (gift of Amon G. Carter), courtesy Texas Memorial Museum; Martin M. Crane and William R. Hamby, courtesy of Barker Texas History Center, the University of Texas; Joseph W. Bailey, from Sam Acheson's *Joe Bailey, the Last Democrat;* Horace Chilton, courtesy of Chilton O'Brien; Thomas

ACKNOWLEDGMENTS

M. Campbell, courtesy of William Campbell; Leroy G. Denman, courtesy of the First National Bank, San Antonio; James H. Robertson, courtesy of Margaret and Ben Robertson; Richard H. Harrison, courtesy of Guy B. Harrison; and Walter B. Sharp, courtesy of Mrs. Walter B. Sharp.

The cartoons from the *Texas Farmer* are republished here through the courtesy of the Texas State Archives. They are: "The Clark Boom" (May 7, 1892); "How We Are Ridden" (May 7, 1892); "Kali Klark and His Klan" (August 27, 1892); "Clark's Jeffersonian Democracy" (October 1, 1892); "A Very Little Giant" (October 22, 1892); "Clark and the Blackbirds" (October 29, 1892); "The Fate of Slanderers" (August 4, 1894). Other cartoons, reproduced from scrapbooks in the Hogg Collection, were first published as indicated below: "Jim Gives Charlie Good Advice" (Austin *Daily Statesman,* August 26, 1894); "The Governor Off Duty" (Austin *Daily Statesman,* August 26, 1894); "A Texas Steer" (Minneapolis *Journal,* July 5, 1899); "A Painful Surprise for Poor Richard" (Washington *Star,* July 6, 1899).

This volume is dedicated to those professors at the University of Texas, at Brown University, and at Harvard University who have generously given me encouragement and the benefit of their scholarship and wisdom. I am especially grateful to Dr. Frederick Merk, at Harvard University, who supervised the original research for the biography of James Stephen Hogg.

Permissions to use quoted material as indicated in the footnotes have been granted by these authors and publishers: From *Spindletop,* by James A. Clark and Michel T. Halbouty, copyright 1952 by James A. Clark and Michel T. Halbouty, reprinted by permission of Random House, Inc.; Harper & Brothers, *Garner of Texas,* copyright, 1948, by Bascom N. Timmons; Charles A. Warner, *Texas Oil and Gas Since 1543,* copyright, 1939, by Gulf Publishing Co.; Charles Seymour, *The Intimate Papers of Colonel House,* copyright, 1926, by Houghton Mifflin Company; C. Vann Woodward, *Origins of the New South, 1877–1913,* copyright, 1951, by Louisiana State University Press and the Littlefield Fund for Southern History, the University of Texas; William Morrow and Company, *Cattle Empire,* copyright, 1949, by Lewis Nordyke; Arthur Meier Schlesinger, *The Rise of Modern America, 1865–1951,* copyright, 1951, the Macmillan Company; Alfred H. Kelly and Winfred A. Harbison, *The American Constitution,* copyright, 1948, by W. W. Norton & Company, Inc.; J. Evetts Haley, *Charles Goodnight, Cowman and Plainsman,* copyright, 1949, by the

University of Oklahoma Press; Gordon Hines, *Alfalfa Bill,* copyright, 1932, by the University of Oklahoma Press, permission of the University of Oklahoma Press; Sam Acheson, *Joe Bailey, The Last Democrat,* copyright, 1932, by the Macmillan Company and Sam Acheson; *Autobiography,* copyright, 1935, by William Hawley Atwell; H. Bailey Carroll, editor, *Southwestern Historical Quarterly,* quotation from Rosalind Langston, "The Life of Colonel R. T. Milner," *SHQ,* XLIV (April, 1941); Waring Cuney, *Norris Wright Cuney,* Crisis Publishing Company, copyright by author Maud Cuney Hare, 1913; President Ted Dealey, the Dallas *Morning News, "Colonel Bill,"* 1939, and Tom Finty, Jr., *Anti-Trust Legislation in Texas,* A. H. Belo Company, 1916; Funk & Wagnalls Company, *Mr. House of Texas,* copyright, 1940, by Arthur D. Howden Smith; Dr. Curtice Rosser, *The Crusading Commoner,* Mathis, Van Nort and Company, copyright, 1937, by author Charles M. Rosser, M.D.

Director Robert Sutherland and the staff of the Hogg Foundation have rendered many courtesies. Appreciation for the use of the Horace Chilton diaries is expressed to the Honorable Chilton O'Brien.

ROBERT CRAWFORD COTNER

Austin, Texas
1959

Contents

Illustrations

Letters and Cartoons

xviii

Charts and Maps

Some Archival Sources

A. J. Rose Papers

The Archibald J. Rose Papers, the Archives, E. C. Barker History Center, the University of Texas Library, Austin. This is a rich collection concerning the activities of the Patrons of Husbandry (Grange) in Texas 1870–1900, as well as many personal and business papers of Mr. Rose.

Arch. Tex. St. Lib.

The Archives, the Texas State Library, Austin. The official depository for papers of state offices. It also holds numerous letters to governors and other public officials, newspapers, books relating to Texas, and manuscript materials. Under construction in Austin is a new archives building, which will make the materials more conveniently accessible.

Arch. Un. Tex. Lib.

The Archives Collection, the University of Texas Library, Austin. Located in the E. C. Barker History Center, it is devoted to the collection and preservation of Texas and University items of historical interest. Especially rich in manuscripts.

Att. Gen. File

The Attorney General Files, the Archives, the Texas State Library, Austin.

Att. Gen. Let. Pr.

Attorney General J. S. Hogg Letter Presses, the Hogg Collection, the Archives, the University of Texas Library, Austin. This file is numbered 38–49 for the period from 1887 to September, 1889. These are usually official letters sent out by the Attorney General or a member of his staff.

B. B. Paddock Papers

The Buckley B. Paddock Papers, the Archives, the University of Texas Library, Austin. Paddock was a developer, a railroad builder, a historian, and mayor of Fort Worth. Usually pro-Clark in politics, his business papers are of special import.

Clark Let. Bk.

Governor Edward Clark's Letter Book, the Archives, the Texas State Library, Austin.

David Rusk Papers

The David Rusk Papers. Some of these documents are in the Archives, the University of Texas Library, Austin; others are in the library of the Stephen F. Austin State College, Nacogdoches.

E. M. House Papers

Edward Mandel House Papers, the Ramsdell Microfilm Collection, the E. C. Barker Texas History Center, the University of Texas Library, Austin. The microfilm is of originals in the Yale University Library. The Austin Public Library has other House papers.

Fam. Let.

Family Letters, the Hogg Collection, the Archives, the University of Texas Library, Austin. Unpaged references are to originals. Not all typescripts have been numbered, but the boxes containing originals in chronological order are easy to use.

Geneal. Fol.

Genealogy Folder, the Hogg Collection, the Archives, the University of Texas, Austin.

Gov. Culberson Let. Pr.

Governor Charles A. Culberson's Letter Press, Governor's Letter File, the Archives, Texas State Library.

Gov. Let. Pr.

The Governor's Letter Presses, the Hogg Collection, the Archives, the University of Texas Library, Austin. These titles are numbered 1–6 and run from January, 1891, to January, 1895, but they are not complete and need to be supplemented by Governor's Letters Written.

Gov. Let. Rec.

Governor's Letters Received, the Hogg Collection, the Archives, the University of Texas Library, Austin. These files are numbered I–LIX and run to October 30, 1894, and they supplement the older file of Letters Received. To check typescript references both should be consulted.

Gov. Let. Wr.

Governor's Letters Written, the Hogg Collection, the Archives, the University of Texas Library, Austin. These files are numbered I–IX and run to November 27, 1894. They supplement the Governor's Letter Press and the personal J. S. Hogg Letter Presses.

G. W. Bailey Notes

The George W. Bailey Notes, the Hogg Collection, the Archives, the University of Texas Library, Austin. Bailey was a Dallas *News* reporter during the period in which Hogg was governor, and he often covered the campaign speeches. He reported on the trip to Boston and the Governor's controversial speech before the State Guard in 1894. After many years with the Houston *Post*, he gathered materials, at the request of Hogg's children, for a biography of the Governor. His notes and draft biography are without reference symbols.

H. C.

The James Stephen Hogg Collection, the Archives, the University of Texas Library, Austin. This collection contains 50,000 items ranging from original letters to typescripts of his attorney general and governor letters, written and received, in the Archives, Texas State Library. References in the biography to these original documents in the State Archives are to the typescripts in the Hogg Collection unless otherwise noted. These files are used by special permission. The most important part of this collection is the J. S. Hogg Papers (a subcollection containing several important series).

H. Chilton Diar.

The Horace Chilton Diaries, available at the Archives, the University of Texas Library, by special permission of Honorable Chilton O'Brien of Beaumont. Horace Chilton was one of Governor Hogg's closest friends.

Ima Hogg Fol.

The Ima Hogg Folder, the Hogg Collection, the Archives, the University of Texas Library, Austin. In the Hogg Collection a folder for each member of the Hogg family contains special items relating to this individual. Pictures and various personal mementos may be included.

Interv. Fol.

The Interview Folder, the Hogg Collection, the Archives, the University of Texas Library, Austin. This folder contains reports of numerous interviews related to Governor Hogg and his family.

J. H. Reagan Fol.

The John H. Reagan Folder, the Archives, the Texas State Library. While the collection is spotty, much of value has been preserved.

These papers are filed under the classification "Main Miscellaneous" and in dated folders.

J. H. Reagan Papers

The John H. Reagan Papers, the Archives, the University of Texas Library, Austin. Reagan was a friend of Hogg's father, and his long association with national and state legislation makes his records unique. Through appointment by J. S. Hogg in 1891, he became the first chairman of the Texas Railroad Commission. This collection duplicates in some degree materials in the J. H. Reagan Folder.

J. L. Hogg Fol.

The Joseph Lewis Hogg Folder, the Hogg Collection, the Archives, the University of Texas Library, Austin. The contents of this folder relate to the father of J. S. Hogg.

J. S. Hogg Let. Pr.

The James S. Hogg Letter Presses, the Hogg Collection, the Archives, the University of Texas Library, Austin. These are numbered 1–23 and cover the period from January, 1887, to March, 1905. They are primarily personal letters sent, which may include information on various topics ranging from elections to family business.

J. S. Hogg Let. Rec.

James S. Hogg Letters Received, the Hogg Collection, the Archives, the University of Texas Library, Austin. These are numbered I–XXXVII. The time range is from 1836 to 1906. These files contain some family letters, letters from intimate political advisers, routine requests from officials and private citizens. They should be supplemented by Governor's Letters Received and other series of letters.

J. S. Hogg Misc.

James S. Hogg Miscellaneous Papers, the Hogg Collection, the Archives, the University of Texas Library, Austin. Often notes on speeches are located here.

J. S. Hogg Papers

The James Stephen Hogg Papers, the Hogg Collection, the Archives, the University of Texas Library, Austin. "Papers" is a broad term generally used to denote all written material in the Hogg Collection whether the letter presses are private or public. Typescripts were made at different times and account for overlapping dates. Some of the main divisions are: Attorney General J. S. Hogg Letter Presses, Family Letters, Governor's Letters Received, Governor's Letters Written, Governor's Letter Presses, James S. Hogg Letters Received, James S. Hogg Miscellaneous Papers.

J. S. Hogg Pers. Acc. Bk.

The James S. Hogg Personal Account Book, the Hogg Collection, the Archives, the University of Texas Library, Austin.

J. S. Hogg Scrapbook

The James Stephen Hogg Scrapbooks, the Hogg Collection, the Archives, the University of Texas Library, Austin. About a score of these books contain personal clippings, cartoons, biographical materials on men of the time, and special national and state campaign material.

J. W. Bailey Papers

The Joseph Weldon Bailey Papers, Dallas Historical Society, Hall of State Building, Dallas. The Bailey papers were used effectively by Sam Acheson in his biography, *Joe Bailey.* Bailey seemed to be an ally of the Hogg forces, but he later opposed Hogg and Horace Chilton. These papers are important also for their presentation of different viewpoints on the Waters-Pierce oil controversy.

Let. Biog. J. S. Hogg

Letters for a Biography of J. S. Hogg, the Hogg Collection, the Archives, the University of Texas Library, Austin. A bound volume of letters collected by George Bailey for the Hogg family.

Let. Wr. Sup.

Letters Written Supplementary (1846–1913), the Hogg Collection, the Archives, the University of Texas Library, Austin. This file contains copies of family letters and other very personal materials furnished by the Hogg Estate. They are boxed but not serialized.

"Mount. Home" Fol.

"Mountain Home" Folder, the Hogg Collection, the Archives, the University of Texas Library, Austin. Includes items relative to Hogg's boyhood home.

O. M. Roberts Papers

The Oran M. Roberts Papers, the Archives, the University of Texas Library, Austin. Roberts was an outstanding political leader from 1860 to 1898. He took great interest in Jim Hogg and Hogg frequently sought his advice, as well as that of Reagan and Lubbock. Some typescript items are in the Hogg Collection, the Archives, the University of Texas Library, Austin.

Pion. Tex. Oil Col.

The Pioneers in Texas Oil Collection, the Archives, the University of Texas, Austin. This is a growing collection of tape recordings made possible largely through the generosity of Mrs. Walter B. Sharp and her son, Dudley, who left his numerous business interests in Houston to serve as Assistant Secretary for Air during the Eisenhower administration.

Rec. Sec. State

Records of the Secretary of State, the Archives, the Texas State Library, Austin.

Sallie Ann Hogg Fol.

The Mrs. Sarah (Sallie) Ann (Stinson) Hogg Folder, the Hogg Collection, the Archives, the University of Texas Library, Austin.

Sec. State Elec. Ret. Fol.

Secretary of State, Election Returns Folders, the Archives, the Texas State Library. These folders contain the official election returns.

Terrell Papers

The Alexander W. Terrell Papers, the Archives, the University of Texas Library, Austin. Excellent for the last half of nineteenth-century history of Texas and Austin by a long-time resident and frequent member of the Texas legislature. He was also a minister to Turkey.

T. E. Hogg Fol.

The Thomas Elisha Hogg Folder, the Hogg Collection, the Archives, the University of Texas Library, Austin.

JAMES STEPHEN HOGG

HOGG

A Biography

CHAPTER I

Son of a General

ON THE MORNING of June 10, 1861, rare stir and confusion prevailed in the East Texas town of Rusk, county seat of Cherokee County, as the people of the town and from the outlying farms and plantations converged on the courthouse square in the vicinity of the Thompson Hotel. In front of the hotel a large group of riders wearing somewhat improvised military uniforms had already assembled in a loose semicircle, difficult to maintain as horses caught the excitement and wheeled and pranced. The unusual mélange of noise was compounded of men's voices in sharp command to their snorting, whinnying mounts, the creak of saddles and boots, the clash of metal, the rising and falling buzz of greeting from one arriving neighbor to another, and now and then a yip or halloo from among the swarm of excited schoolchildren, who had been given a special holiday.

When a tall, lean, straight-figured man emerged from the hotel and stood quietly at the top of the steps, the good-natured chaos faltered, then died away. Among the suddenly sobered school boys were two who watched the man on the steps with special and admiring attention. John Hogg, age fourteen, and James Stephen Hogg, age ten, were accustomed to the respect that the presence of Joseph Lewis Hogg usually commanded, both abroad, among his fellow citizens, and at home, where he brooked no nonsense from sons and daughters. The children standing near John and Jim no doubt looked at them with some envy and a new awe as the sons of the man who was directly responsible for today's occasion. During weeks of arduous and necessarily hasty effort, General Hogg had turned his back on his law practice to recruit and train the men now facing him, who, as the Lone Star Defenders under the captaincy of Frank M. Taylor, were departing to join the army of the Confederacy.

Even the horses were quiet as General Hogg began his "formal and very tender" farewell. His sons, though solemnly listening, were puzzled by the note of sadness in his strong, clear voice, for, to them, war was a thrilling idea. Since their early boyhood they had been told enthralling

3

tales of the gallant roles played in bygone wars by their father, their grandfather, and their great-grandfather, and over the past several weeks they had proudly played soldier and importantly run errands for the men in training. Young Lieutenant Samuel B. Barron, a recently qualified attorney of Rusk, understood the sorrow underlying the General's words. General Hogg not only longed to be heading for action with these departing friends, but he also was deeply disturbed that they must leave while they were still not much more than heroically eager civilians, rather than the seasoned soldiers the Confederacy desperately needed—and which he knew they ought to be if they were to win and survive in battle. Barron said of General Hogg in reference to this occasion:

War was not unknown to him for he had been a soldier . . . He was a fine specimen of the best type of Southern manhood, tall, slender, straight as an Indian, and exceedingly dignified in his manner. As brave as "Old Hickory," he often reminded me of the picture I had seen of General Jackson. . . . Among other things, he said, "Don't ever jeer or mock any of your comrades who cannot stand the fire of the enemy. Some of you, perhaps, will find yourselves unable to do so. Some men are thus constituted without knowing it until they are tried."[1]

The speech was not long, and when it was done the stillness held. And then, when the stir of motion and talk began again, it was subdued, with no resemblance to the earlier cheerful confusion. James noted the deep emotion accompanying the quiet farewells, and watched the riders move off slowly by twos toward the Jacksonville road. Just as the last of the column began to disappear over the brow of the little hill, some one of them started a song, soon taken up by all:

> The Lone Star Defenders, a gallant little band,
> On the tenth of June left their native land . . .[2]

Joseph Hogg, a respected lawyer in Rusk, the county seat of Cherokee County, had been a state senator. In the first year of Texas statehood, Senator Hogg had sponsored the creation of the new county from old Nacogdoches County, and, after his return from the Mexican War, had moved, with his wife, Lucanda McMath Hogg, and three children, up

---

[1] Samuel B. Barron, *The Lone Star Defenders* (New York, Neale Publishing Company, 1908), pp. 18–19. J. A. Templeton, who served with Thomas E. Hogg, confirmed the above in an undated letter to Will C. Hogg, in J. L. Hogg Fol. For explanation of symbols for archival sources and of materials contained in such collections, see "Some Archival Sources," pp. xxi–xxvi.

[2] *Ibid.*, p. 19.

the Angelina River to lands along Mud Creek. The children included Martha Frances (b. 1834), Julia Ann (b. 1839), and Thomas Elisha (b. 1842). John Washington (b. 1848) was born soon after they settled in Cherokee County. James Stephen (b. 1851), Joseph Lewis, Jr. (b. 1854), and Richard (b. 1856) were also natives of Cherokee County. Since the earliest known settlement of great-grandfather John Hogg in South Carolina, the family had been settling on lands recently vacated by Indians. Succeeding generations of these pioneers kept up their militia duties and were prepared to defend their constitutional liberties in legislative halls or on the battlefield.

James Stephen Hogg, who was to be affectionately known by later Texans as "The People's Governor," was born on March 24, 1851, in the midst of a spring storm near Rusk, Texas, at "Mountain Home," the plantation house of his parents.

On both the paternal and the maternal side there were pre-Revolutionary forebears in Virginia and Georgia, and Hogg and McMath ancestors in Scotland.[3] In the ancient language of the Scots, "Hog," "Hogg," "Hogge," "Hoge," and "Hoag" were variations of the same name, which meant a young sheep less than a year old. Mentions of the name, in one variation or another, and of the McMath name are found in early Scottish documents. The movements of the Hogg family from Scotland to Ireland to Virginia tend to illustrate what has been referred to as "phases of the border Scottish Odyssey."[4] Throughout the Middle Ages men by the name of Hogg dwelt in the frontier lands, the fought-over lands of Lothian. They lived between the English and the Highland Scots—from the Firth of Forth to the River Tweed.[5] Both the Hoggs and the McMaths early embraced Calvinism, and the Hoggs were swept along in English plans to subdue Ireland. On the new frontier in Ulster they became known as Scotch-Irish.

They were "frontier men" in spirit, and as such sure to be among those who would strike out again and again for new lands where they

[3] The references to family history are supported by data in the Genealogy Folder in the Hogg Collection, the Archives, the University of Texas Library. See also "Joseph Lewis Hogg" in John Livingston's *Sketches of Prominent Americans* (New York, R. Craighead, 1854), pp. 228–229.

[4] Lawrence H. Gipson, *The British Empire before the American Revolution* (New York, A. A. Knopf, 1939), I, 244.

[5] Henry Paton (ed.) *Register of Interments in Greyfriars Burying-Ground Edinburgh, 1658–1700* (Edinburgh, J. Skinner, 1902), Index; Records Office, *The Index to General Register of Sasines, 1701–1720* (Edinburgh, His Majesty's Stationery Office, 1917), p. 420; Andrew Lang, *History of Scotland* (Edinburgh, Blackwood and Sons, 1917), III, 19; IV, 284 ff.

could find what they deemed liberty. James Froude has described causes for the eighteenth-century general exodus from northern Ireland, and the generalization adds meaning to what is later known of the Hogg family in America:

Men of spirit and energy refused to remain in a country where they were held unfit to receive the rights of citizen . . . Vexed with suits in the ecclesiastical courts, forbidden to educate their children in their own faith, treated as dangerous in a state which but for them would have no existence, and associated with Papists in an Act of Parliament which deprived them of their civil rights, the most earnest of them at last abandoned the unthankful service. They saw at last that the liberties for which their fathers had fought were not to be theirs in Ireland.[6]

Sometime prior to 1750 the parents of John Hogg, great-grandfather of James Stephen Hogg, came to Virginia. Letters in the Hogg Collection suggest a possible kinship with Captain Peter Hog (or Hogg), who was with George Washington at Fort Necessity and aided him in building a line of forts from Winchester, Virginia, to the upper branches of the Tennessee River in 1755, and with a James Hogg of North Carolina, who was an agent from the Transylvania Company to the Second Continental Congress and after the Revolution one of the founders of the University of North Carolina.[7] But no direct connections can be traced, because, before the end of the French and Indian War, John Hogg had been left an orphan and his parents are not mentioned by name in available family records. It is known that he had moved to South Carolina by 1767 with members of the Lindsey family, by whom he may have been reared.[8] He had married some time before the move, and by 1768

[6] James A. Froude, *The English in Ireland in the Eighteenth Century* (New York, Scribner's, Armstrong and Company, 1881), I, 136–137. Cf. Charles A. Hanna, *The Scotch-Irish* (New York, G. P. Putnam's Sons, 1902), I, 436, 486 ff.; Seumas MacManus, *The Story of the Irish Race* (New York, Devin-Adair, 1944), pp. 362–367.

[7] Lena Hogg Bray to W. C. Hogg, October 10, 1932; Sue S. Towles to Governor James S. Hogg, August 11, 1892; Edith Henderson to [Mrs. R. M. Kelso], n.d. All in Geneal. Fol. See also Robert A. Brock (ed.), *The Official Records of Robert Dinwiddie* (Richmond, Virginia Historical Society, 1883–1884), III, 470–471, footnote on Peter Hogg's family; "George Washington to Captain Peter Hogg, July 21, 1756," quoted in *ibid.*, IV, 461. Archibald Henderson in *The Campus of the First State University* (Chapel Hill, University of North Carolina Press, 1949), pp. 10–13, discussed James Hogg of the Transylvania Company.

[8] This is the conclusion of Mrs. W. F. (Stephens) Smith, the librarian at New Albany, Mississippi. Personal interview, June, 1849. Her father was Judge Z. M. Stephens, who claimed John Hogg of Newberry among his ancestors, and who was related to Alexander H. Stephens. Cf. Clayton Torrence (compiler) *Virginia Wills*

he was known to have three sons, James, Lewis, and Thomas, the last born in that year.

A land grant issued to John Hogg on November 22, 1771, bears the Great Seal of the Province of South Carolina and the signature "His Excellency, Right Honorable Lord Charles Greville Montague, Captain General, Governor and Commander-in-Chief":

Unto John Hogg his heirs and Assigns, a plantation or Tract of Land containing Two hundred acres (surveyed for him 25th March 1767) Situate in Berkeley County in the Ford of Broad and Saluda Rivers on a smaller Branch of Enoree Bounding North West part on land laid out to Charles King all other sides Vacant land.[9]

The two hundred acres of virgin lands along the Enoree, near King's Creek in "Ninety-six District," enjoyed adequate rainfall, and the long growing season was to enable the next generation to experiment with cotton production. The Hogg cabin on the Enoree was about fifty miles from the villages of the Cherokee Indians. New neighbors acquired in the fall of 1771 included William and Samuel Chandler. Samuel chose land on "a Branch called King's Creek." His daughter Martha later became the wife of Thomas Hogg.

When the American Revolution began, the South Carolina Up-Country was feuding with Charleston and the Low-Country over representation and courts and Indian policy. The area where the Hoggs lived was largely Whig in politics and Baptist and Presbyterian in religion. The Revolutionary leaders, William Henry Drayton and the Reverend William Tennent, testified after a rally at King's Creek Meeting House that they relied on such men as Hogg and his neighbors in the Tyger-Enoree forks to offset the work of the anti-Association men.[10] However,

---

and Administrations, 1632–1800 (Richmond, William Boyd Press, 1931), which lists inventories for "Lewis Hogg" of Frederick County in 1747 and for "Margaret Hogg" of the same county for 1753. There is also one for a "William Hoge" in 1750. James Lindsey, who died in 1764, may have been the father of Margaret (Lindsey) Hogg. John Hogg had sons named James, Thomas, Williams, and Lewis, and a daughter was named Margaret. She married a Durrette, whose descendants are prominent in Tuscaloosa, Alabama.

[9] Deed Record Book A., pp. 29–30, Office of the Secretary of State, South Carolina (Columbia, S. C.), shows the official copy of surveyor's plot.

[10] John Drayton, *Memoirs of the American Revolution* (Charleston, A. E. Miller, 1821), I, 155. The Reverend Mr. William Tennent's Journal for August 22, 1775, is quoted by George Howe, *History of the Presbyterian Church in South Carolina* (Columbia, 1870), p. 286; Leila Sellers, *Charleston Business on the Eve of the American Revolution* (Chapel Hill, University of North Carolina Press, 1934), p. 10; William A. Shaper, "Sectionalism and Representation in South Caro-

later it was the unwise Indian policy of the British which caused many in the Up-Country to become rebels after they heard of the Declaration of Independence. This region experienced real civil war.

John Hogg was a volunteer in the Patriot forces by September, 1776.[11] A son, Lewis, was seriously wounded in one engagement, but lived to marry; his descendants now live in Newberry, South Carolina. Another son, James, died in the Patriot Army. In each succeeding generation one son was usually named James in his memory.

Thomas (1768–1849), a third son of John, and the grandfather of James Stephen Hogg, was too young to join the Patriot Army, but it is known that he helped to hide cattle and grain from the British, including Tarleton's Redcoats. By the time of the first census, 1790, he was farming near Newberry and was the head of a family.[12] He learned to sell his lands on the crest of the booms and to acquire new acres farther south and then farther west for development. The pattern of location, sale, and resettlement was shown in his successful ventures with slaves and lands on Mulberry Fork of the Oconee River of north Georgia and along Indian Creek in middle Georgia before 1818. He moved to Tuscaloosa County, Alabama, in 1818, then sold in the "flush times" of 1836 and moved on to Choctaw County, Mississippi, just after the Indians had been removed to the Indian Territory.

As Major Hogg, Thomas had raised a volunteer force of Georgians for the War of 1812 and had led his men to join General Jackson's Tennesseeans against the Alabama Indians. In 1814 he entered the Georgia legislature, serving until he went to Alabama. He made his living as a planter and a lawyer, soon establishing the planter-politician pattern that was later followed by his sons. Father and sons always kept up their militia duties. After Alabama was admitted to the Union in 1819, Major Hogg was a member of its first legislature; he served on the special committee that welcomed General Jackson to Huntsville. He served also in the House and Senate, and later helped to establish the University of Alabama. After moving to Bellefontaine, Mississippi, in

lina," American Historical Association, *Annual Report for the Year 1900* (Washington, Government Printing Office, 1901), I, 360–361; David D. Wallace, *The History of South Carolina* (New York, American Historical Society, 1934), II, 139.

[11] The Adjutant General's Office to R. C. Cotner, March 23, 1948; Adjutant General's Office to Mrs. R. M. Kelso, August 2, 1916, in Geneal. Fol. shows rank and service record but is not complete.

[12] United States Bureau of the Census, *Heads of Families at the First Census of the United States . . . , 1790, South Carolina,* (Washington, Government Printing Office, 1908), p. 78.

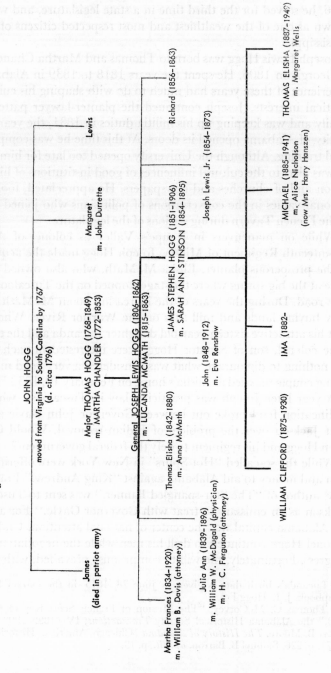

JAMES STEPHEN HOGG GENEALOGY

JOHN HOGG
moved from Virginia to South Carolina by 1767
(d. circa 1796)

Major THOMAS HOGG (1768-1849)
m. MARTHA CHANDLER (1772-1853)

Lewis

Margaret
m. John Durrette

James
(died in patriot army)

General JOSEPH LEWIS HOGG (1806-1862)
m. LUCANDA McMATH (1815-1863)

Martha Frances (1834-1920)
m. William B. Davis (attorney)

Thomas Elisha (1842-1880)
m. Anna McMath

Julia Ann (1839-1896)
m. William W. McDugald (physician)
m. H. C. Ferguson (attorney)

JAMES STEPHEN HOGG (1851-1906)
m. SARAH ANN STINSON (1854-1895)

Richard (1856-1863)

Joseph Lewis Jr. (1854-1873)

John (1848-1912)
m. Eva Renshaw

WILLIAM CLIFFORD (1875-1930)

IMA (1882-

MICHAEL (1885-1941)
m. Alice Nicholson
(now Mrs. Harry Hanszen)

THOMAS ELISHA (1887-194?)
m. Margaret Wells

1836, he served for the third time in a state legislature, and was widely known as one of the wealthiest and most respected citizens of northern Mississippi.

Joseph Lewis Hogg was born to Thomas and Martha Chandler Hogg in Georgia in 1806. He spent the years 1818 to 1839 in Alabama. The experience of these years had much to do with shaping his cultural and political interests. Joseph continued the planter-lawyer pattern of the family and was keeping up his militia duties in 1831, the year the University of Alabama opened its doors. At this time he was completing his legal training. Although the University opened too late for him to enroll, he was alert to the cultural influences of good institutions of higher education and of churches and newspapers. He appreciated, too, the educational values in the conversations of politicians who joined his father at the French Tavern during sessions of the legislature.

While on maneuvers in Roupe's Valley as colonel of Alabama's Seventeenth Regiment of Militia, Joseph Hogg made the acquaintance of the prosperous planter, Elisha McMath, who also owned a general store at the big spring where the stage stopped on the Tuscaloosa-Huntsville road. During the years of the increasing boom McMath had been busy buying lands and mill sites on the Warrior River. When he saw that his attractive sixteen-year-old daughter Lucanda and the tall, handsome colonel, son of Senator Hogg, were interested in each other, he did nothing to discourage what was considered a very good match. The young couple married at Elisha's home on February 10, 1832.[13]

A year later Joseph was practicing law in Tuscaloosa, when a new nullification feud broke out between Governor John Gayle and President Jackson over the problem of Indian removal. Would Gayle call upon Hogg and his regiment to defy the federal government?

While the so-called "Hot Spurs" in New York were offering to raise men and money to aid Alabama against "King Andrew," Francis Scott Key, author of "The Star-spangled Banner," was sent to Tuscaloosa by Jackson as an emissary to treat with Governor Gayle.[14] For a few days the Alabama capital was the center of national attention. Under orders, Colonel Hogg continued to drill his men while the negotiations were in progress. Fortunately, the will to compromise prevailed, with the assist-

[13] Lucanda's birth date is given as June 28, 1815, in the extract from Kelso Scrapbook, J. L. Hogg Fol.

[14] Thomas C. McCorvey, "The Mission of Francis Scott Key to Alabama in 1833," the Alabama Historical Society *Transactions,* IV (1899–1903), 153–165; Albert B. Moore, *The History of Alabama* (Chicago, American Historical Society, 1927), p. 226; Samuel B. Barron, *op. cit.,* p. 19.

ance of the poetically inclined and musically gifted Mrs. Gayle, who carried on in verse a delightful correspondence with Mr. Key. Tuscaloosa society was resplendent at the evening entertainments. The young colonel, tall and slender, with his hair brushed up and back, appearing in a new uniform, reminded many of the guests of young Andrew Jackson. A solution for the Indian problem was found, and for several years serious threats of disunion disappeared.

As Alabama's flush times continued during Jackson's second administration, many crooks and gamblers flocked to Tuscaloosa; by 1835 they had become so numerous and their practices so flagrant that they threatened to rule the town. When, in response to increasing protests, the gamblers refused to move out and, in addition, made threats to burn the town if they were molested, indignant Tuscaloosa citizens called a public meeting at the courthouse, and Joseph Hogg promised to ready the militia to enforce law and order and to protect lives and property. Apparently the young man had acquired a reputation for effective action; not long after the meeting the gamblers finally left town.[15]

Joseph stayed on in Tuscaloosa when his parents moved to Mississippi. The boom was definitely subsiding, however, and by 1839 the effects of the nationwide depression reached into his household and that of his father-in-law. Holding notes and bills of exchange valued at more than seven thousand dollars, Colonel Hogg found it impossible to make collections. About this time Sam Houston came to Tuscaloosa, seeking men and money, in the course of his tour of Alabama to help maintain the independence of Texas. Hogg was interested, but he had recently decided to run for the office of sheriff and was reluctant to abandon the political race. On election day he was one of the top three in the voting count; however, since there was no runoff, the incumbent stayed in. This defeat, his growing debts, and the Whig trend in the county were among the factors that made him consider a move to Texas, where personality still counted more than political party.

Colonel Hogg was thirty-three years old when he and Lucanda and their daughters, Martha Frances, age five, and Julia, an infant in arms, left Alabama. On December 5, 1839, Joseph Lewis Hogg took the oath of allegiance to the Republic of Texas and obtained Second Class Certificate Number 266 for 320 acres of land in the County of Washington.[16] He soon decided, however, that settling in Nacogdoches County

---

[15] Cf. Joseph G. Baldwin, *The Flush Times in Alabama and Mississippi* (New York, D. Appleton & Company, 1861), pp. 126 ff.; John Livingston, *op. cit.*, p. 228.
[16] Original in General Land Office, Austin. Barnes F. Lathrop, *Migration into*

would be wiser. It was doubtful that Washington-on-the-Brazos would remain the site of the capitol. The danger of Mexican or Indian attack was less farther east, and the fact that Nacogdoches was the home of important men such as Thomas J. Rusk, Sam Houston, Colonel John Forbes, Adolphus Sterne, and William B. Ochiltree was an advantage not to be overlooked for a young lawyer with ambitions.

During the next five years Hogg was a supporter of Sam Houston's efforts to have Texas annexed to the United States. He served in the Republic's Eighth Congress, 1843–1844; in 1845 he headed the Judiciary Committee in the Texas State Constitutional Convention. On February 19, 1846, Senators Hogg, Robert Williamson, and Ballard Bagby waited on President Anson Jones to tell him that the people were gathered to hear his final message. Jones, a New Englander who had played a vital part in Texas history, concluded his message thus:

May the Union be perpetual, may it be the means of conferring benefits and blessings upon the people of all the States, is my ardent prayer.[17]

The government of the State of Texas began to function. One of Senator Joseph Hogg's first proposals in the legislature reflected the prolonged depression:

That 200 acres of land not included in a town or city lot, or lots, being the homestead of a family, shall not be subject to forced sale under execution for private debts, nor shall any town or city lot or lots, being the homestead of a family, not to exceed in value two thousand dollars, be subject to forced sale under the execution for private debts.[18]

His bill as passed also provided protection to the library of the lawyer, teacher, or doctor, and to the doctor's surgical instruments, the mechanic's tools, the farmer's provisions for a year, along with some cattle and tools. Thus the revised continuation of the Homestead Law of the Republic was a constructive piece of social legislation protecting families against some of the worst features of depression and debt. Hogg also sponsored the creation of Cherokee County from the old and larger Nacogdoches County (from which over the years nineteen other counties, in whole or part, were also created).

East Texas (Austin, Texas State Historical Association, 1949), pp. 27, 34 ff., gives a careful statistical study of census data showing the heavy migration from Georgia and Alabama. See also Andrew F. Muir, *Texas in 1837* (Austin, University of Texas Press, 1958), pp. 45–48, 170–173.

[17] Texas *Senate Journal* (1846), pp. 12–15; Herbert Gambrell, *Anson Jones* (Garden City, Doubleday, 1948), pp. 418–419.

[18] Texas *Senate Journal* (1846), p. 246.

When war came with Mexico later in 1846, Hogg left his Senate seat to serve in the Second Texas Regiment, commanded by Governor James P. Henderson. Sometime during the march on Monterrey it is probable that he made the acquaintance of Colonel Jefferson Davis of Mississippi. Mustered out with the Texas troops after the victory at Monterrey, he returned to East Texas, and soon afterwards moved his family from the Loco Creek plantation near Nacogdoches to the new estate, "Mountain Home," up the Angelina River near Rusk,[19] the seat of Cherokee County.

Both his law practice in Rusk and the plantation lands along Mud Creek prospered. Joseph and Lucanda's material possessions were further enlarged in 1848 when aging Thomas and Martha Hogg, who had come to live with the younger Hoggs just after Texas became a state, made indenture as follows:

For and in consideration of the natural love and affection . . . give, . . . unto said Joseph L. Hogg and his heirs of his body, the following described Negroes, slaves for life, to wit, Morening, a female slave about sixty-five years of age, Isaac, a male slave about fifty-two years of age, Faty, a female . . . about twenty-five . . . her children, Jim, a boy about 5, Henry, a boy about 3, and Dilcey, a girl child.[20]

The McMaths had given Lucanda some young slaves at the time of her marriage. Others had been acquired by birth or purchase prior to the time of the move to "Mountain Home." The 1848 additions encouraged the acquisition of another tract of land—320 acres about a half mile north of the county courthouse in Rusk. The affluence of the Hogg family continued to increase; by 1860, when James Stephen Hogg was nine years old, his parents owned about twenty slaves and more than twenty-five hundred acres—some nine hundred of them in Limestone County to the west—of both timberland and fertile farmland, bottoms and uplands.

The plantation house at "Mountain Home" did not approach the opulence of the great plantation homes being built along the Mississippi

---

[19] Livingston, *Sketches of Prominent Americans,* p. 229. See also Thomas E. Cotner, *The Military and Political Career of José Joaquín de Herrera* (Austin, University of Texas Press, 1949), being University of Texas *Latin American Studies,* VII, pp. 123–151; Milford P. Norton to David Rusk, June 11, 1846, David Rusk Papers (typescript).

[20] Copy of deed in J. L. Hogg Fol. Deed Record Book R, Tuscaloosa County (Alabama), December 11, 1840, pp. 98–99, shows gift of a Negro girl and two boys, Dick and Robert, from Mr. McMath to Lucanda Hogg. See also Deed Record Book B, Cherokee County (Texas), filed May 4, 1849, pp. 441–442.

River during the prosperous decade of the fifties, but it was well built and comfortable. At first it probably resembled other houses of the region built in the same period (the late 1840's), a typical "double-house" log structure of two main twin wings, with a so-called "dog run" between and a half-story of sleeping rooms above. Soon the logs were covered by siding, and a gallery, again nothing to match the imposing colonnaded verandas of the homes in the older South, was added. Cherokee was still frontier country. The generously proportioned kitchen-vegetable fields may have come close up to the house, as was East Texas custom. Except in the clearing, huge oaks stood all about, from one or more of which the Hogg children probably suspended a long-rope swing. The thick stands of indigenous pine had by 1860 begun to disappear; they had yielded timber for fences and houses and heating, and the sawmills that began to dot the area after 1860 were turning out pine lumber on which some small fortunes would be based. Nevertheless, pine trees were still plentiful, especially on estates such as that of the Hoggs, whose owners knew the value of conservation. Suits over land titles increased lawyer Hogg's legal business. For many years the countryside was one for boys to revel in—cut by many spring branches, creeks, and rivers, with numerous iron-laden hills gentling the landscape and abundant woodland areas supporting a host of small animals and birds.

Colonel Hogg's interest in education was shown in many ways. He donated a site for a school (later known as "College Hill") and arranged for Moses McKnight, from Tennessee, to provide five two-room buildings in which to carry on instruction.[21] When McKnight's health failed and he asked to be released from his contract, Colonel Hogg arranged for Milton P. Tucker, a Georgian, to take over the school. Among Jim Hogg's classmates was Ellie Dickinson, who was to remain his lifelong friend and confidant. Somewhat younger was Tom Campbell, another future governor of Texas. The Hogg children also had private training at home from tutors. A blind musician and poet, Robert McEachern, taught piano to Julia and violin to Martha Frances, Thomas and, later, to James Stephen. McEachern also helped Jim make progress in reading, frequently listening to him read aloud and correcting pronunciation when necessary.

Sometime in 1848 an intelligent young man from Alabama, William B. Davis (a son of a family friend), came to visit the Hoggs. He stayed on in Rusk to study law with Joseph Hogg and later to practice. Before

[21] Hattie J. Roach, *The History of Cherokee County* (Dallas, Southwest Press, 1934), pp. 42–43.

14

long he and Martha Frances Hogg, then about sixteen, attractive, and maturely assertive and accomplished for her years, were in love.

Another young man was of considerable interest to the Hoggs at this time. During the attack on Monterrey, in the Mexican War, Hogg had met an orphan lad named Rufus Chandler. The mother of Colonel Hogg was a Chandler, and, even though kinship was not established, the young man was taken to "Mountain Home" and given a legal education. This freckled-faced Irish lad seems to have set up a law practice and then to have become associated with the gambling element whom Hogg was fighting. Not long after a disagreement at the courthouse, Chandler shot Hogg from ambush and gave him such a bad wound in the hip that for several weeks he was not expected to live. Keeping lights out and using the ruse of sending a trusted Negro to town to order a coffin, the Hogg family played for time. Letters went unclaimed at the post office and Will Davis lived at the house for added protection.

While Joseph was still in his most serious condition, he and Lucanda had a long discussion about Martha Frances and Will Davis, and their romance. Martha was young but knew her mind and after marriage could stay on at "Mountain Home." In 1849 Thomas and John were mere children, and if Colonel Hogg should die there would not be a mature man in the family to look after business matters or the law practice. Will could function as head of the family until Tom should come of age. The parents decided that if the young couple wanted to marry they should go ahead. A home wedding was arranged, with only a few friends in attendance, and the happy pair made their home on the plantation.

Colonel Hogg resigned the office of justice of the peace,[22] and when he recovered sufficiently to sit on a horse, he sent word to Chandler to get out of town or take the consequences. Eventually they had a fatal meeting on the square, which resulted in the death of Chandler. It is evident from the local records and from a letter Sam Houston wrote to his wife November 18, 1850, that Hogg was acquitted for the shooting of Chandler.[23] In his letter Sam Houston wrote of this episode: "I can tell you no news of this section only that my friend Hogg has been acquitted for killing Chandler."

Shortly after his marriage with Martha Frances, Will Davis con-

[22] Joseph L. Hogg to Governor George T. Wood, March 5, 1849, original, Fam. Let.
[23] Amelia W. Williams and Eugene C. Barker (eds.), *The Writings of Sam Houston* (Austin, University of Texas Press, 1938–1943), V (1941), pp. 260–261.

tracted "consumption." Tragically widowed by his early death, Mrs. Davis returned to "Mountain Home," where her son William, Jr., was born in 1852. Having much of her father's Spartan quality, Frances did not repine, and once more she took her accustomed place in the household, helping to supervise the education of her son and younger brothers. She and the gentle Tom were particularly close, both being highly intelligent and interested in music, reading, poetry-writing, and public affairs. As Jim grew older, she coupled him in her affections with her own son and seemed early to sense qualities in him that marked him as outstanding. Jim in his turn was devoted to her, confiding to her his problems and ambitions.

Joseph Hogg was at times a stern father, in that he expected strict obedience and a high quality of performance from his children and would not abide trifling. His own pride was sometimes reflected in his demands on them: he provided the boys with high silk hats to be worn to school, against which even the usually mild Tom finally rebelled by cutting his into shreds one day. Hogg was, however, eminently fair and honorable in his dealings with his children, and on occasion showed unusual tenderness and sensitivity to their needs. For example, he had not planned to give Tom violin lessons. One day he found Tom behind a barn playing his sister's violin. Colonel Hogg told him that if he really wanted to be a good violinist to go into the house and practice under the direction of Julia's music tutor. Mrs. Hogg was the more comfortable parent, being relaxed and kind and endowed with a keen sense of humor. It is interesting to study an 1862 photograph of Mrs. Hogg and a portrait of the General (made later from a photograph also dating from early 1862); characteristics of both faces are repeated in various pictures of their son, from boyhood to late adulthood. However, the mother seems to predominate in the son, and least of all did his face reflect the senior Hogg's appearance of almost fanatical inflexibility.

Lucanda was very proud of her brood and of her husband, and happily abetted the latter in providing the hospitality for which "Mountain Home" became famous. It gave her pleasure that the house was a favorite rendezvous for young people of the Rusk area, as well as for the "great" of Texas who came often to confer with Joseph Hogg on important matters, among them Congressman John Reagan of Palestine, John C. Robertson, Harvard-trained lawyer of Tyler, Oran M. Roberts, from the University of Alabama, Sam Houston, and men interested in the development of railroads to the Gulf and to the Pacific as an aid to the growth of the state. (Colonel Hogg was president of the Railroad

Convention held in Palestine in 1854.) Of the children, James and Tom were usually the most interested in the visits of such men, and nothing pleased James more than to be taken by his father to political gatherings where one of them spoke. One of the most memorable of such occasions to Jim was a speech by United States Senator Sam Houston at the Baptist Church in 1859, when he opposed the "fire-eater" secessionist Governor Hiram Runnels.

On the eve of secession confidence in the future was expressed in many ways, but one example stands out. In the midst of duties connected with the plantation and law office, the drilling of the "Lone Star Defenders," and preparations for the meeting in Austin to discuss secession, James' parents discussed plans for the building of a new Presbyterian church. Both Lucanda and Joseph Hogg maintained active church affiliations, Presbyterian and Baptist. Lucanda wanted to make a substantial contribution to her church, and her husband filed a deed granting to the elders and trustees a half-acre town lot to serve for the church site and other church uses.

Mrs. Hogg had been careful of the religious instruction of her children. She had a happy, singing spirit, and the predestination of her faith never seemed to be a burden to her; her husband was the stoic. Tom accepted his mother's denomination and later became an elder in the Presbyterian church at Denton. James, after the war, decided to follow after his father and joined the Baptist church. As a boy James formed the habit of Bible reading, and he preserved all his life a Bible given to him in 1860 by the mother of Ellie Dickinson.

The prosperous decade of the 1850's had seemed to be a good time for a healthy boy like Jim Hogg to be growing up, but the increasing bitterness of the sectional strife was ominous. Following the election of Abraham Lincoln, early in 1861, Governor Sam Houston, Unionist, was forced to turn over his office to Lieutenant Governor Edward Clark, Confederate. "Mountain Home" was a busier place after Governor Clark appointed Joseph Lewis Hogg one of his aides in charge of recruiting and training for the Fifth Texas Military District, with the rank of brigadier general.

Before the firing on Fort Sumter Joseph Hogg had been one of the few leaders among officials and the public alike to warn of the urgent need for military preparedness and organization. He had gone as a delegate to the "Citizens' Convention" held in Austin at the end of January, 1861. Strongly favoring secession, although this put him in opposition to his good friend Sam Houston, he had nevertheless been one of the

17

leaders who managed to thwart the high-handed efforts of some of the delegates to have Texas join the Confederacy by convention action instead of by vote of the people. On the morning of February 1, he and delegates Richard Coke and George W. Chilton were chosen to escort Governor Houston and the justices of the Texas Supreme Court to chairs from which they could watch the vote that accepted the Ordinance of Secession by 166 to 8.[24] In late March, after the people had voted for the Ordinance, another convention in Austin ratified the Constitution of the Confederacy. General Hogg then candidly called for immediate and adequate military preparation, but those who from the beginning of the crisis had stressed "peaceable secession" did not wish to face the implications of his warning that the South must be ready to wage war. When Fort Sumter fell in mid-April the majority of Texans were dazed and bewildered; they had never accepted war as the inescapable consequence of secession.

For a week after the fall of Sumter, Joseph Hogg restrained himself. On San Jacinto Day (April 21), unable to do so longer, he wrote an urgent letter to Governor Edward Clark, who had stepped up from the office of lieutenant governor when Sam Houston was deposed in March:

The Bombardment and surrender of Ft. Sumter, and the re-enforcement of Ft. Pickens, by Lincoln, and the ordering of troops by our Gov't to Pensacola; and the signs of the times; indicate, that we should organize—and be ready for any hostile emergency. If you will give me authority; I will try to raise at least a regiment of men in Eastern Texas and be ready to march at short notice . . .
There is great anxiety here, as to the manner of raising men. I am not certain what we can do; but feel confident that if there was a call from you . . . it would facilitate the movement.[25]

After Governor Clark put Joseph Hogg in charge of recruiting and training in the Fifth Military District, General Hogg made hurried trips about the district to appoint subordinate enrolling officers. Men came from many nearby towns to offer themselves as recruits. By May 20 five companies were in some shape to march, but they were without arms. Equipment of all kinds was tragically scarce, and the training conse-

24 Ernest W. Winkler (ed.), *Journal of the Secession Convention* (Austin, Austin Printing Company, 1912), pp. 47–49, 235; Llerena B. Friend, *Sam Houston* (Austin, University of Texas Press, 1954), p. 336.
25 Joseph L. Hogg to Governor Edward Clark, April 21, 1861. Original in Clark Let. Bk.

quently even less adequate than it might have been. John and James knew that all of this was a serious matter to their father, and they tackled their chores with high spirits, intensified by the feeling that now their nineteen-year-old brother, Thomas Elisha Hogg, who had left college at Weatherford to become a soldier, was not the only son of General Hogg helping the South.

After the Lone Star Defenders left, General Hogg hastened to complete plans for a large, healthful encampment site. By mid-July Camp Foard, on the Angelina River near Rusk—with the great advantage of a large freestone spring which could afford the best of water for as many as 1,000 men—was in full swing. The boys rode to and from the camp, carrying clothes, food, and messages, and enjoying themselves enormously. But General Hogg was still gallingly hampered by the lack of equipment and a "good drill officer," at one time not even having a copy of Gilham's *Military Manual*. He was further alarmed because some men were listening to Confederate recruiting-agents-at-large and rushing off to the fronts with no training whatsoever. Hogg warned the governor that Texas would not get credit for her quota of eight thousand men if these practices continued.

Despite all the new activity, however, there was still no radical change in the pleasant tenor of the days at "Mountain Home." True, John and Jim and Will Davis, the son of their widowed sister Martha Frances Davis, and even sometimes Joseph Lewis, Jr., who was about seven years old, did more chores than formerly to help about the house and in the fields. The gay, big, but informal parties that had always been a part of life in and around Rusk were things of the past, but neighbors and friends still got together for entertainment on a small scale. The fighting was far away, and for those not as closely concerned with the war as was General Hogg, its actual existence was, for a while, incredible. As August wore on in its overpowering heat, letters from brother Tom, Dr. William Wallace McDugald, the special friend of Jim's pretty sister Julia, and Major James Barker, who had been courting Martha Frances, began to clothe the myth in reality. The inhabitants of "Mountain Home" had always been affectionately close to each other, but now the circle seemed to draw together even more. A letter from Tom, now in the thick of the fighting on the Missouri-Arkansas line, would await reading until everyone—the General and Mrs. Hogg, Martha Frances, Julia, John, Jim, Will, Joseph, Jr., and little Richard—could assemble to hear it. Julia was generous about sharing passages of her letters from

Dr. McDugald, too. A letter from him dated early August, 1861, contained lines that probably made the comfortable room where they sat seem strangely safe:

We arrived at General McCulloch's headquarters about 10:00 A.M. today, tired, dusty, hungry, and sleepy, after a long forced march from Fort Smith, Ark. We are now preparing for our first battle . . . All the boys are busy cooking up three days' rations. If I survive tomorrow's battle I will write a postscript giving the result.

P. S. We captured a lot of pig lead on a raid to Little York. Later . . . General Price's camp was surprised. . . . Lyon has been killed. McCulloch has congratulated us on the victory at Oak Hills.[26]

Letters like this made the General more restless. He had been pleading for an active command in the field, urging that his troops be made into a ranger service, because infantry could not march to Missouri in time to give aid to McCulloch. Not only did he believe a strong cavalry force essential for defense to keep Arkansas and Texas from being invaded, but he counselled offensive action. Hot weather brought more flies, insects, dust, and fever at the camp. Jim would ride out every few days, his pants rolled up to his knees, trying to pick up a little breeze, as he carried mail and fresh clothes. The plantation had never had an overseer, so Jim and John would report on the progress of the crops, the health and work of the slaves, and the requests from the older Negroes for supplies or instructions for making repairs. In this way the boys learned many things about the management of the plantation which normally would be taught at an older age. They were encouraged by their mother to learn all they could, because she knew that the time must come when her husband would be ordered to the front. Meanwhile, tutor Robert McEachern and Sister Frank (Martha Frances) did their best to keep the boys at their books. The striking similarity of Jim's writing to his father's suggests that even the General must have found some time to help James with his penmanship.

In January, 1862, Tom Hogg and Dr. McDugald came home on furlough with the rest of the "Cherokee Boys." Brothers and sisters must have listened wide-eyed to Tom's stories, both because of the things he had to tell and the way he told them. This oldest son of Joseph and Lucanda Hogg had always been interested in words and their power; he wrote poetry and stories and articles that were sometimes published in

[26] Barron, *op. cit.*, pp. 37–41, 60–61.

20

the Rusk newspaper, and whether published or not, highly impressed all the family, especially Jim, to whom Tom was the ideal of everything good and great. "Mountain Home" was a happy place with the circle complete again, and with Julia unable to mask her joy at Wallace Mc-Dugald's nearness. But early in February, much sooner than had been expected, the "Cherokee Boys" were summoned to hurry back to their companies. The Northern advance had begun, and General Earl Van Dorn had sent out a desperate appeal for men.

News censorship was lax, and toward the end of February the increasing havoc of war was made clear to anxious families by such items as this:

The dread conflict of the series of engagements that are likely to make the spring campaign has commenced but at a different point from what has been anticipated. Public attention had been directed to Bowling Green and Columbus . . . No one anticipated that the campaign would be opened at Ft. Donelson, and by an engagement of so serious a character. Yet so it is. Bowling Green, with its frowning fortifications, is abandoned, and an army is in retreat from that point.[27]

"Retreat!" The word was anathema to General Hogg. In March there was more anguishing news. The "Cherokee Boys" had reached northern Arkansas in time to take part in the three-day battle of Pea Ridge (Elk Horn Tavern), fought in bitter cold. Ice and snow covered the ground, and there was little food for the troops. On March 7, the second day of the battle, General Ben McCulloch, going forward alone to learn the enemy's position, had been killed (and the next few weeks would bring a heavy toll among Southern generals). When General Hogg finished reading the article he betrayed little emotion, as was his stoic habit, but his wife and children knew that such news was the more terrible to him because of his own galling inactivity as a trainer, rather than leader, of troops.

A few days later people along the Rusk road saw General Hogg forcing his carriage horse toward "Mountain Home" at a racing pace. For his family, who had assembled fearfully when his swift approach was seen, he had a proud announcement; he had just received word of his appointment by President Jefferson Davis as an active brigadier general with a Confederate command and orders to report to General Van Dorn in eastern Arkansas.

[27] Marshall *Texas Republican,* February 22, 1862.

There was much to be done before his departure, and, when he was reminded that he had missed James' tenth birthday celebration by reason of being absent in Austin on March 24, 1861, for the ratifying of the Confederate Constitution, he decided he could remain at home long enough to celebrate this year's anniversary and still make the rendezvous with Van Dorn on time. During the next few days he took his sons and Will Davis on a tour of the fields and the Negro quarters of his several properties, explaining what he expected of them in his absence, and impressing on John and James that they would now be the men of the house and were to help their mother wherever they were needed. Bob, the son of the Hoggs' coachman, was a twenty-five-year-old Negro, greatly trusted by all the family, and Jim's special friend. (Bob called him "Jeems.") was told to get ready to accompany the General as his personal body servant.

As the time drew near for departure, Joseph Hogg was prevailed upon to write in a "keepsake album" kept by his Julia, just twenty-one. Martha Frances had developed much of her father's stoicism in her ten years of widowhood, and somehow her father knew that she was prepared for whatever might come. But Julia was in love with Dr. McDugald; he, too, was at the front amidst death and disease, and she had never known real sorrow or defeat. Perhaps she needed a final word of encouragement for lonely days ahead, and so he wrote:

Mountain Home
March 21st 1862

Julia Ann,
  Dear Daughter:
. . . I proceed to the field of battle now in full blast, between the usurpationists of the North and our brave patriotic sons of our glorious Confederate States of America, where I hope to find your brother and many or all of our friends alive and battling in defense of the only Government on the globe worth living or dying for. . . .

Should you feel lonely with no one but your Mother, sister and little brothers at our Mountain Home I hope you will be cheerful, when you reflect that you have a Brother and Father battling to keep the latter-day Philistines from Texas. . . .

During this war be courageous, be courteous as you hitherto have been, to the soldiers whom you may see. I depend on the justice of our cause, the bravery of our men, under the auspice of the God of Wars. Thus attended there can surely be no failure. Sooner or later we shall triumph and establish one of the best governments known to man. Then I hope we shall all return home, to meet and greet our friends. Then we can build up one of the greatest, happiest and most wealthy nations on the globe and perpetuate constitutional liberty through all time.

Adieu

Your father

Jos. L. Hogg[28]

Mrs. Davis tried to explain to her son and brothers what had happened when she was a girl and their father had gone away from home to participate in the war with Mexico. However, she and Mrs. Hogg knew that this war was different.

After the birthday celebration Joseph Lewis Hogg bade his family farewell. On April 8, the day after the disastrous battle of Shiloh, he reported to Van Dorn at Des Arc, Arkansas. Shiloh had cost the South 11,000 men, among them the great Texas general, Albert Sidney Johnston. General Hogg was among those who moved at once toward Corinth in an attempt to stem the tide of retreat; his cavalrymen were asked to leave their horses behind, to save space on the boats for men and food and guns.

As Tom told the story later, General Hogg was overworked from the start. The confusion was great, supplies were low, and on Hogg's staff were civilians completely lacking in military experience. At Corinth, Tom Hogg and others of the "Cherokee Boys" came under his command. As Tom's group had pushed east to Corinth from Memphis, the roads and fields along much of the way were strewn with the terrible human consequences of the battle of Shiloh. Transport problems had grown more acute with each mile, especially as westbound trains carried the sick and wounded away from the battle area. General Hogg had become so disturbed over the delays, fearing the Federals would cut the railroad before he reached Corinth, that he had ordered his train to be allowed to pass through. This action almost caused a courtmartial, but, after some questioning, General Beauregard closed the incident. Every officer and man was needed to delay the Yankee advance.

At Corinth sickness began to claim hundreds of lives. Men went torturing days and nights without sleep and were condemned by the lack of supplies to a diet of pickled beef, as easy to swallow "as a piece of skunk," and a "milky looking fluid" called water, which even horses refused to drink. The germ that through centuries of wars has decimated more armies than any battles ever did took over at Corinth, making it a deathtrap for soldiers, of both the North and the South. Dysentery, usually called "flux," struck down General Hogg early in May. On May

[28] Copy in J. L. Hogg Fol.

16, 1862, despite the devoted efforts of Dr. McDugald and Bob, he died. Tom reported to his mother that the grave had been dug near a road at Holly Church, about four miles out of Corinth, and that he had seen the simple wooden marker:

GENERAL J. L. HOGG
RUSK, TEXAS[29]

Thus, not long after his eleventh birthday, James Stephen Hogg was left fatherless, in the midst of events that were to change the family fortunes radically. The first ten years of the boy's life had been extraordinarily happy. In those same ten years following the Compromise of 1850 his parents had greatly prospered, and his father had become a leading citizen, carrying on the family pattern of practicing law, expanding plantation operations, and participating actively in the encouragement of the growth of America. Jim Hogg had reason to be proud of his heritage.

Up to the time of Joseph Hogg's death, "Mountain Home" had been a center of happiness and security. Even now in the midst of the family's grief during the summer of 1862, after the death of General Hogg, the lessening of security was not immediately apparent. Trained by their father to work, John and James Hogg and their nephew Will Davis, labored hard in the fields that summer, trying to produce the crops the Confederate army needed. Tom came home on furlough in time to help with the fall harvest and the sale of cotton, and with him the General's servant, Bob, who was full of stories about the General and about "Marse Tom's" heroism and kindliness to his fellow soldiers. Tom had much to tell about his father and about Major James Barker, Frances' friend, who had been killed during a brave rear-guard action near Corinth and of whose gallantry and "valor, magnanimity, truth, candor, and fidelity," Tom spoke with heartfelt fervor.[30] He told John and James, too, when he was charging them to keep at their studies, how he had filled the weary hours of waiting for orders to attack by studying a small dictionary and a Bible that he always carried.

[29] Barron, *op. cit.*, pp. 82–83; Avery C. Moore, *Destiny's Soldier, General Albert Sidney Johnston* (San Francisco, Fearon Publishers, 1958), pp. 67–77. An account of General J. L. Hogg in the *Confederate Veteran* (1906–1907), p. 379, contains some errors. General Louis Hébert succeeded to the command; later, General Lawrence S. ("Sul") Ross took charge. Ross served as governor of Texas (1887–1891) when James S. Hogg was attorney general.

[30] Sketch of Major James J. A. Barker in "The Last Stand at Corinth" by Captain Thomas E. Hogg (typescript), Th. El. Hogg Fol.

24

There were many business matters to attend to before Tom returned to his command. Mrs. Hogg petitioned for letters of administration, stating that her husband had died without leaving a last will and testament and that she estimated the estate as "probably worth Fifteen-Thousand Dollars." She was appointed administratrix and bonded in September "in the sum of Thirty Thousand Dollars."[31] The inventory and appraisal indicated ownership of fifteen Negroes and over two thousand acres of land, with horses, mules, plows, and other tools needed for plantation work. In November, 1862, a court order provided that Mrs. Hogg should take out five hundred dollars of the "first money that comes into her hands as the law directs in such cases" for a year's support for the widow and children.[32] The family now had special cause to appreciate Joseph Hogg's foresight in incorporating the homestead provision into the state Constitution, for their financial situation now was disturbing. Debts had been incurred in outfitting troops, and some slaves had been sold. Following the Yankee victory at Antietam, Lincoln had issued an Emancipation Proclamation, and it was said that if the South did not lay down its arms by the end of the year all slaves would be freed. To the Hoggs, as to all other Southerners, the loss of slaves meant heavy economic loss, for some families even economic disaster.

To James, age eleven, such matters were remote, and life was still full of exciting moments. The local paper published some of Tom's war stories, and when Tom went to Rusk to talk to Editor Andrew "Whistlin' " Jackson, James was frequently invited to come along. The men would discuss battle maps, while the boy listened closely, probably learning more geography than he ever had in school.

Then came a rumor that a Union invasion was planned through the Indian Territory to support groups northeast of Dallas; supposedly it would be timed with an attack on Galveston, and a possible Trinity River pincers movement from north to south loomed as a sort of second Mississippi campaign to divide the Trans-Mississippi country, which had been furnishing food and men and horses to the Confederates' eastern fronts.[33]

The East Texas crop had been good and had brought high prices, but local consumption was going up, with the influx of refugees to Tyler,

[31] Probate Court Order was issued September 13, 1862. See Probate Minutes, Cherokee County (Texas), Book J, October 21, 1862, pp. 54–56.

[32] Probate Minutes, Book J, p. 56.

[33] Charles Cumberland, "The Confederate Loss and Recapture of Galveston, 1862–1863," *The Southwestern Historical Quarterly,* LI (October, 1947), pp. 109–130.

Marshall and Rusk from Arkansas and especially Louisiana as a result of Union control of lower Louisiana and the danger of further advances up Red River. The new iron works near Rusk were an attempt to meet the needs of the army, as well as to strengthen the economy of the area. Ore was plentiful here, and it was expected that the Negroes could be taught to be foundrymen. Rusk was becoming a supply center, surplus corn now being sold locally instead of through the river ports of Jefferson and Shreveport. One such sale by Mrs. Hogg was made to a Louisiana refugee, a sugar planter from Lafourche Parish.

Recd. Rusk, Texas, Decr. 13th, 1862, of John Williams, one thousand dollars, on account of corn and other articles purchased of me.

Lucanda Hogg, Admx.
By Williams & Williams, Attys.[34]

In the summer of 1863 the fall of Vicksburg and the retreat from Gettysburg weighed heavily on all Southerners as grim implications for the future intensified the strain of the weary present. Lucanda Hogg, Frances, and Julia tried to increase still more their part in the community effort to grow and preserve all food possible and to make bandages and garments for the soldiers.[35] But family sorrows multiplied. Late in the summer Richard, not quite eight years old, died after an illness of several days; soon after his burial, Lucanda, worn out from worry and work and sorrow, took to her bed. Within a few days a new grave was prepared, and the orphaned children laid their mother to rest beside her son and her husband's parents in the little burying ground at "Mountain Home."

Sister Frank, then about thirty years of age, bravely took up the new responsibilities. Her son Will was about eleven, while John was sixteen, James twelve, and Joseph Lewis, Jr. about nine. Donley and Anderson, attorneys, filed her request for appointment as guardian of the minors and of the estates, valued at twenty-five thousand dollars. She was required to make bond for fifty thousand dollars, an increase which indicated the seriousness of inflation. Again James M. Anderson and D. P. Irby, lawyers and former sureties and appraisers, were appointed. An inventory recorded a year later still showed substantial household equipment and tools, as well as two iron safes, cards, three spinning wheels, a

---

[34] Dr. Barnes Lathrop, who is publishing his study of the Pugh Plantation, made available a copy of the original in the Richard L. Pugh Papers.

[35] Roach, *op. cit.*, p. 68.

loom, cattle, sheep, horses, corn, wheat, rye, and 240 pounds of seed cotton, but only six Negroes were listed by name. Some of the Cherokee County land had been sold. (Tradition has it that General Hogg had spent heavily in 1861 to fit out the troops he recruited.) The 925 acres in Limestone County were listed at a value of one dollar per acre.[36] Captain Tom hoped, whatever happened, to retain the law office and eleven and a half acres in Rusk, for he planned to follow in his father's footsteps as a lawyer.

Despite the dismaying war news and the diminishing family fortunes, Martha Frances insisted that the boys must still attend school, and requested appropriations of three hundred dollars each "in Confederate money for the annual support of said minors" as deemed necessary to "keep said wards at school."[37] On November 8, 1864, nine hundred dollars was approved for the year's support and education of John, James, and Joseph, Jr. The diminishing prosperity of the family weighed heavily on Mrs. Davis. As the oldest child, she knew well to what position of responsibility and financial comfort her father had attained, and she knew of the generous inheritance from Thomas and Martha Hogg. Lacking a man to counsel her in the management of the estate, she might lose everything, amid the general inflation and the threatened loss of the slaves. Through it all she kept her sense of humor, her high standards, and her vital and personal religion. She had sometimes resented Joseph Hogg's strictness, but now she realized that strictness was often necessary to rule a home. Rule she did, and Julia and the boys loved and respected her for her efforts.

Captain Thomas Elisha Hogg, lately of Baylor's regiment in Lane's brigade, Texas Division, C.S.A., was mustered out at Winchester, Tennessee, in 1865. He was twenty-two, and soon to be in love. Stopping at Duck Hill, Mississippi, where his cousin Anna Eliza McMath lived, he taught school for a few weeks, making the first money he had ever earned outside of the army.[38] His letters home spoke often of Anna, whom he described affectionately as a brunette with large brown eyes. He had met her while she was in college at Winchester, Tennessee.

Being thus occupied, the Captain was spared the sight of the breaking

---

[36] Probate Minutes, Book J, Cherokee County (Texas), September 26, 1864.

[37] *Ibid.,* Book J, p. 65, and Book F, p. 112.

[38] Mrs. Hermilla Hogg Kelso's account of her father, in Th. E. Hogg Fol. See John Dyer, "Hell in Tennessee," Chap. XII of his *The Gallant Hood* (Indianapolis, Bobbs-Merrill Company, 1950), pp. 271–288.

up of General Edmund Kirby Smith's Trans-Mississippi Department and the temporary suspension of civil government in Texas.[39] When Smith's army disintegrated along the Crockett road James Hogg was one of those who gave food to the tired and defeated soldiers, and he was never to forget his fright and shock at seeing the Sugar Commissary in Rusk looted by crowds of men and women, shouting that the sugar now belonged to them and they would have it before the Yankees arrived.

When Dr. McDugald returned in May, 1865, Mrs. Davis asked him to talk to her overseer, S. T. Mitchell, for things had not been going well on the farms. Reporting back that Mitchell was a sick man and incapable of attending to the plantation as he should, McDugald recommended that she get rid of him, paying him off if she could reach a settlement with him. Further, he believed that the Negro, Bob, who had been sent on home by Captain Hogg, could do a good job of managing the plantation. This was a practical solution to a looming labor problem; with Bob as overseer, the other Negroes might be more inclined to go on working when freedom came.[40]

After May 29, 1865, the newspapers carried President Johnson's amnesty proclamation. When Tom arrived home soon afterwards he and Frances faced together the fact that there might be some question whether they would be included. Tom was the oldest male heir of a family estate valued at over twenty thousand dollars at the last inventory (even though much of the value was a paper one), and Johnson's antipathy for wealthy planters as a class was well known. On June 19, Tom's twenty-third birthday, General Gordon Granger announced from Galveston the restoration of the authority of the United States in Texas and declared that all slaves were now free. All officers and men of the late Confederate army were to be paroled.[41]

During the long summer days James and John again worked in the

---

[39] Joseph H. Parks, *General Edmund Kirby Smith, C.S.A.* (Baton Rouge, Louisiana State University Press, 1954), pp. 457–480; John Q. Anderson (ed.), *Brokenburn: The Journal of Kate Stone, 1861–68* (Baton Rouge, Louisiana State University Press, 1955), pp. 330ff.

[40] Personal interview with Miss Ima Hogg, June, 1946. For copy of overseer agreement see letter from A. C. Jenkins to R. C. Cotner, November 19, 1948, "Mount. Home" Fol.

[41] Rupert N. Richardson, *Texas, the Lone Star State* (New York, Prentice-Hall, Inc., 1942), p. 266; Charles W. Ramsdell, *Reconstruction in Texas*, being *Columbia University Studies in History, Economics, and Public Law*, XXXVI, No. 95 (New York, Columbia University Press, 1911), p. 290; Texas *House Journal* (1870), pp. 4–5.

fields, the sun-baked dirt hot against their bare feet, for shoes had long been lacking. Tom finally managed to get Mitchell to leave. Mitchell's illness soon caused his death, and his brother then involved the Hogg estate in a costly lawsuit over division of the crops. Nevertheless Bob was successfully installed as overseer; however, despite the heroic efforts of everyone concerned to get out the weeds, the crops were short. Owing to demand and scarcity, cotton brought high prices, but the Hogg family was still sorely in need of capital. Southern land values began to tumble. (In the West and North by 1870 there had been land-value increases from 25 to 100 per cent; in the South, with the exception of Missouri, there were decreases up to 70 per cent.)[42]

With the return of the refugee sugar planters to Louisiana and the migration of many local farmers to Texas lands farther west, the market at Rusk for meat and grain rapidly dwindled. The dispersion of the Negroes was a factor in the early closing of one of the Rusk iron furnaces; soon increased Northern competition and taxes closed the others. The dream of Rusk as an industrial center, of which the iron works had been a part, was doomed by 1867, and the plans whereby Rusk citizens Micajah H. Bonner and Charles G. Young hoped to revive railroad building, through an extension of the Houston and Great Northern northward through Cherokee County to Shreveport, were handicapped by the political uncertainty.[43]

In the late fall of 1865 the Hoggs held a family conference, in which Dr. McDugald, now Julia's husband, was included. Capital was sorely needed if they were not to lose more of the estate. It was decided that Mrs. Davis would make a journey to Alabama, in the hope that Mc-Math relatives there might be able to give temporary financial assistance. Will and Jim would go with her, and the McDugalds would look after Joseph at "Mountain Home," where John would also stay to help Tom with the farms.

True to her father's example, on arrival in Alabama Frances saw to it that a school was found for the boys. They boarded and roomed with their teacher, a twenty-two-year-old war veteran, Isaac Wellington McAdory. He was a slender young man, less than five feet ten inches tall, but his keenness of mind was always able to outwit the tactics of even

---

[42] Fred Shannon, *The Farmers' Last Frontier* (New York, Farrar and Rinehart, 1945), p. 80; Hattie L. Roach, *op. cit.,* pp. 67–68.

[43] Roach, *op. cit.,* p. 69; St. Clair G. Reed, *A History of the Texas Railroads* (St. Clair Publishing Company, Houston, 1941), pp. 128–129, 315. See also Probate Minutes Book F, Cherokee County (Texas), dated October 4, 1865, p. 197; March 14, 1866; and subsequent report filed January 5, 1867.

the largest boy bent on trouble. Jim and Will quickly discovered that outside Texas a hearty prejudice existed against all Texans. The initials GTT (Gone to Texas) constituted an Alabama label for thieves, murderers, and deadbeats, and when the visitors were admitted to McAdory's school several local parents objected strenuously, until the young teacher promised, with tongue in cheek, that he would take them under his personal supervision.

In later years James Stephen Hogg was to say that the few months spent at Bucksville under this young man's tutelage constituted one of the most fortunate episodes of his life.[44] McAdory loved boys and girls and he was a born teacher, able to pass on simply and without sentimentality his own philosophy. He found life magnificent, holding such phenomena as the sun, moon, stars, and the sky to be gifts from God. He taught that manual labor was not only honorable but good for the body and the mind. Times, now, he said, were bad, but if men would be content to live simply, even bad times could not hurt too much.

Friday afternoons at the school were reserved for speechmaking. Jim was horrified at first at the idea of standing in front of the still somewhat hostile class, especially since he was self-conscious about being so tall for his age. McAdory, who had noted with interest the boy's fine speaking voice, did not urge him, but suggested that on their walks to and from school Jim might rehearse parts of speeches that he could learn the night before. Gradually assurance came, and before long Jim was enjoying himself, not only when declaiming along the road but also in front of his schoolmates.

Alabama boys remembered that big Jim Hogg was kind and generous, but had some difficulty with fractions. One day at school he had been at the blackboard some time trying to reduce four-fifths of a yard to inches, when Professor McAdory decided to help him. He suggested: "Jim, when you get through school you may go into a drygoods store to clerk. If a lady were to come in and ask you for four-fifths of a yard of cloth, how much would you give her?"

Jim hesitated a moment and then replied, "I would give her a yard and let her go."

Frances took the boys to see such family landmarks as their grandfather Hogg's Baptist church near Big Hurricane Creek, McMath's general store and plantation, and their mother's community church, where Presbyterian, Baptist, or Methodist, but not Unitarian, ministers

[44] See George F. Boyd, "Tribute to a Remarkable Teacher," Birmingham *Age-Herald*, September 22, 1922. Copy in Interv. Fol.

were welcome. On these little journeys Jim also saw the destruction of war, even the charred buildings of the University of Alabama, which his grandfather, Senator Hogg, had labored to build up through legislation. Defeated men and bitter women, whose homes and lands had been ruined, were traveling the roads westward, many among them heading for Texas to make a new start. For the first time, Jim Hogg realized how fortunate his state had been in escaping material devastation; here in Alabama, hope and ambition seemed crippled.

Fannie's mission to obtain money was in the end unsuccessful. She was bitterly disappointed, although she tried to conceal her feelings from the boys. All three, however, were glad to be going home in time to see spring in East Texas. Jim Hogg's horizon had broadened; travel and matching wits with other boys had increased his self-confidence.

In spite of the financial uncertainty, Tom, in the summer of 1866, went to Mississippi to claim Anna McMath as his bride. After the young couple's return in October, it was decided that Tom should become legal guardian for Jim, now fifteen, and Joseph, twelve; Editor Andrew Jackson stood as one of the sureties, William Long, proprietor of Long's Hotel, as the other. Still studying law, Tom started a small school, hoping thus to bring in some cash during the winter, while the family pondered what next must be done.

During the 1866 election campaign Jim went often with Tom to Whistlin' Jackson's *Texas Observer* office, where it was the habit of leading citizens of Rusk to gather for political discussions. Now and then Jackson, who had a great liking for the Hogg brothers, asked Jim to do an odd job around the office, and one day he suggested that the boy try his hand at learning to set type. Jim tackled each job with eager application. Before long he was doing enough work to earn a little money, with which for a time he proudly helped pay his way to Peyton Irving's school. Mr. and Mrs. Irving, fond of Jim and respecting his determination to learn, also found jobs that he could do around the school or at their home to earn some of his tuition.

On a prearranged Friday several boys were scheduled to compete in an oratorical contest, in which Jim was intensely eager to make a good showing. He had memorized his speech and was working on the gestures. Like all great orators he recognized the benefit of practice, which he sought in the woods near the school, where he could be alone. There he felt greater freedom to gesture and speak without restraint. Jim did not know that Ben Wade, a fellow student, was secretly following and learning his speech and mannerisms. When the appointed hour arrived, Ben

31

was called on first. He gave Jim's oration, with all Jim's gestures. Jim was next. He stood up, explained his predicament, proceeded as best he could with an extemporaneous composition, and sat down. He later said that in that experience he learned the advantage of using one's own ideas and phraseology and not relying upon a set speech. He may have vowed never again to plan to deliver an oration created by another man's brain. However, he was not averse to obtaining assistance during the preparation of speeches, and he consulted with others to obtain new viewpoints. He appreciated Tom's assistance with phrasing and sequences, but he always mastered the thoughts in his own forceful vocabulary, and his voice and gestures were already distinctive.

The national election results of 1866 gave the Republicans secure control over both the Senate and the House in Washington, and it was soon apparent that the original moderate plan of reconstruction was going to be changed by the Radical Republicans. Even before the elections John H. Reagan, former Postmaster General of the Confederacy and a prisoner at Fort Warren, Boston (released in the fall of 1865), had written to Governor James Throckmorton, warning of the loss of home rule if some Negroes were not given equal status before the law in matters of suffrage and witnessing in the courts. He doubted that the Texas delegates to Congress would be seated, and he warned that Thaddeus Stevens could be dangerous.[45] In late January, James Hogg brought home from Jackson's office the news that Oran M. Roberts, who had been president of the Texas Secession Convention in 1861, although elected to the U.S. Senate in the fall was still unseated. Also unseated were his New Jersey-born fellow Senator David Burnet, who had opposed secession but lost a son in battle on the Confederate side, and the Texans elected to the House. Roberts had published "The Address of the Texas Delegation" in the Washington, D.C., *National Intelligencer* for January 10, 1867. He argued that Texas had inherited the sectional issue when it entered the Union and had been sucked into the maelstrom of disunion and war; now, having repealed the Ordinance of Secession, thus fully accepting the verdict of war that no state could secede peacefully, Texas requested her right to representation. The unseated Senator went on to state another conviction of his:

To force . . . negro suffrage, by Congressional action, against the almost universal sentiment of the whole State, under the penalty of exclusion or

---

[45] Reagan Papers, 1849–1896 (transcripts) I. See also Reagan's second Fort Warren letter of August 11, 1865, in Walter F. McCaleb (ed.), *Memoirs of John H. Reagan* (New York, Neale Publishing Company, 1906), pp. 286–295.

the destruction of the existing State government, will cause the hearts of men to rankle with injustice, and a feeling of bitterness which will pass from generation to generation. And the negro, from being the subject of kindness, as he is now, may be loathed and hated as the cause—the unconscious victim—of a feeling he had nothing to do with producing.

The restoration of the government upon an enduring basis—and this is what we most heartily desire—ought, as we think, to be upon such terms as the good people of each section can heartily support.[46]

The *Texas Observer* for January 26, 1867, repeated Roberts' "Address." Editor Jackson in his editorial comment warned of the impending destruction of the civil governments, saying that the states might be remanded back to territorial inferiority:

The thanks of the whole State are due to our representatives now at the national Capital . . . Although excluded from seats in Congress, yet by their talent as Statesmen and bearing as gentlemen, they are exerting a moral influence, with the thinking portions of Northern men, more potent than speeches delivered under the sanction of official position.[47]

There is evidence that James Hogg helped to set the type for Roberts' article and the editor's comment. Under Jackson's excellent, realistic tutelage he was learning a trade, perfecting his spelling, developing a pungent prose style, and realizing the importance of a free press (a subject on which Jackson was always ready to expound). Most importantly, he was making a discovery which is one of the necessary passports from childhood to the responsibilities of maturity: in being close to the recording of events, the effects of which he then saw registered on the lives of people in his own community, he began to understand that an event cannot happen in a vacuum; it is, for good or ill, made inevitable by the actions of men. Because of his fortunate association with an editor of the caliber of Whistlin' Jackson, Jim Hogg was better prepared to evaluate the constitutional struggle between President Johnson and Congress as the Radicals gave Reconstruction a new emphasis after the legislation of March 2, 1867.

[46] *National Intelligencer* (Washington, D. C.), January 10, 1867; *Quarterly of the Texas State Historical Association*, XII (October, 1908), 118 ff.
[47] Rusk *Texas Observer*, January 26, 1867.

CHAPTER II

Printer's Devil and Sharecropper, 1867–1870

EDITOR JACKSON hired James Hogg as his full-time printer's devil, early in 1867, and the arrangement included board at Jackson's table and a bed in the *Observer* office. For roommate and co-worker there was a talented boy about James' own age, Charles E. Young; the two boys thus served as fire protection for the owners of the paper, H. W. Newland and Major Jack Davis, a customary device of the day, since newspaper establishments seemed peculiarly vulnerable to blazes.

By his sixteenth birthday in the spring of 1867, Jim had acquired both a capacity for careful attention to his job and an eager interest in mastering the printing trade. Usually too busy to be homesick, he still very much missed the fields and trees and streams at "Mountain Home," the comradeship of his brothers—and most of all his sister Martha Frances, whose loving understanding lifted the spirit of an overgrown boy in the blundering, sometimes painful awkwardnesses of adolescence. As often as he could, he paid visits home, because he needed the faith she continued to express in him. Afterwards, as he walked back to Rusk, he felt renewed, and he did not mind that those he passed on the way might see only a gangling boy, extremely tall, his too-small homespuns sometimes smeared with ineradicable printer's ink and in evident need of replacement.

The print shop was in essence not only an advanced school for Jim Hogg, but possibly the best school he could have attended, given the times and his own needs and developing interests. The small newspaper, run by an intelligent, vigorous editor, furnished an excellent vantage point from which to watch a wounded nation making its convalescent way through the rough and unmapped course of reconstruction. The *Observer* had for its taunting slogan "The World Is Governed Too Much."[1] Its news and forthright editorials brought the boy into direct touch with the issues and thinking of his time. Further, since the *Observer* office ran true to the tradition of small American newspapers in

[1] Rusk *Texas Observer,* January 26, 1867.

doubling as a community club, he heard spirited discussions among the prominent men of the region on the pros and cons of the legislation that was to be the basis for a "New South." He also had the opportunity to read the exchange papers from the North, two of which, *Hearth and Home,* edited by Harriet Beecher Stowe, and later the brilliant Charles Dana's New York *Sun,* he found of never-failing interest. The association with Editor Jackson in itself offered a liberal education, as well as invaluable instruction in the printing craft and the vivid use of the English language.

Whistlin' Jackson, with his pipe upside down, was a Cherokee County institution. Then in the middle of a forty-year period as printer, editor, and owner of papers in Rusk, he had also been a soldier, pioneer, and politician.[2] His editorials were unusually direct and pungent, reflecting both his courage and his wide experience of men and life. Jackson was sincerely interested in all the Hogg boys, and, having found James patient, quick to learn, and possessing a quietly genial sense of humor, was never too busy to help him improve his work as typesetter or to explain a technical or human puzzle. He was a sound and thorough mentor, a worthy successor to young McAdory, whose inspiration had been so important to the boy during the months in Alabama.

Charles Young and Jim Hogg worked side by side, setting type, running off the six to seven hundred copies of the paper—"one side on Wednesday and the other on Friday"—sweeping the office, and hauling water for drinking and for washing off forms. They used an old Hoe hand press, and pulling the lever back was always a struggle. If there was job printing to be done during the day on the Hoe, the boys had to run off the *Observer* copies at night, working by candlelight. On these occasions they often roasted sweet potatoes and then cooked eggs, wrapped in wet pieces of paper, in the hot ashes. The meal was climaxed by ginger cakes bought from an old German baker.

Jim Hogg liked to talk and was never slow to assert his opinions on the basic affairs of town, state, or country. The current difficulties of Reconstruction afforded him an excellent opportunity to study out, just as older heads were trying to do, right from wrong; what he saw personally of the injustice often occasioned by the Scalawags and Carpetbaggers made an impression on his mind which lasted throughout his life. Except for Charles, he seemed to care little about association with other boys his own age and sought instead—though never bumptiously push-

[2] Charles E. Young to George Bailey, February 4, 1923, Let. Biog. J. S. Hogg pp. 39–45.

ing himself forward—the company of men who could talk intelligently to him. He had a sincere reverence for old people. Charles once pointed out a boy who had been disrespectful to an old man on the street, whereupon James rebuked the offender and told him that if "he even bat his eye, he would lick him."[3]

James was usually even-tempered, and Charles "never heard him swear but one time."

Jim was suffering with a large boil on his posterior. At the noon hour he told me to lance it. The printing office was on the second floor and the windows on one side opened next to a roof of an adjoining building, with the eave of this roof terminating directly under the windows. Jim got out on this roof, pulled his clothing down and backed up next to the window in a partly recumbent position. He cautioned me to be careful and even showed me where to put my thumb on the point of the blade of the knife so as to gauge the incision. But when he said, "ready," I popped the blade in the boil about an inch. He gave a yell and shot up to the top of the roof and looked back at me and he cussed me right. He started for me and I started away from him, and I kept at a safe distance from him until he cooled off and the pain left him. The operation was a successful one and I never met Jim afterwards that he did not speak of it.[4]

Among the various items of reading matter at the print shop were a few lawbooks, which belonged to Don Vietch, a cultured, elderly "gentleman of the old school," who sometimes wrote editorials for the paper. In rare moments of spare time Jim dipped into the books, for law as a concept was beginning to take on new meaning to him. Daily, as he set type or clipped the exchanges, he was working with words that, together with the events that went on around him in the town, spelled out the fact that when law was ignored or even technically violated a kind of chaos could result. He knew at first hand the distrust that was sown in the people of Texas when the military removed Governor James Throckmorton from office in the summer of 1867, claiming he was "an impediment to Reconstruction."

On occasional evenings the boys would go to Long's Hotel, a rendezvous for Jackson and his cronies. Here the latest news was heatedly discussed, and in more mellow moments there were abundant tall tales to be heard—from the lips of the self-styled heroes concerned—of Indian fights and thrilling escapes; Mr. Long himself had been famed as an Indian fighter, and nothing pleased him more than to start the yarn ball

[3] *Ibid.*   [4] *Ibid.*

rolling. When the district court was in session, the influx of notable members of the bar of East Texas added new faces to the hotel gatherings, and Jim Hogg was a particularly avid listener at such times. His mental horizon was constantly expanding under the tutelage of his unsuspecting instructors both at the hotel and at Jackson's dinner table. He was also learning the story of Texas—Republic and State—from the men who had made it, their words putting flesh on what he had eagerly read in Henderson Yoakum's *History of Texas*.[5]

The hardships and oppressions of the days of Reconstruction were an unescapable subject of conversation and an ever-present component of daily life. Like all Texans, Jim Hogg deeply resented what proud men were being called upon to undergo. Nevertheless, young as he was, it seemed to him that many of his most bitter neighbors would be better off to cease nourishing their rankling as if it were a thing to be proud of, and try instead to reason about causes, effects, and cures. He had read diligently Reagan's and Roberts' warnings and advice about these times; they had been his father's friends, and he believed they were wise.[6] When newcomers to Texas pointed out that the state was well off in comparison to the rest of the South, he knew they told the truth, for he had seen a little of Alabama's plight. And as he read the northern exchange news at the *Observer* office, he learned that the South had many friends in the North, who freely criticized the present tactics of the administration in Washington and looked ahead to the elections of 1868. These were matters about which Jim often mused aloud, with Charles Young as a willing soundingboard.

Another kind of education that the boys shared was contributed by Robert McEachern, the blind music teacher and poet, who paid frequent evening visits to the office. Jim and Charles would alternate in reading aloud to him, an amply rewarding service by which they learned to know and enjoy *The Arabian Nights* and works of Scott, Byron, Pope, and many other writers, both ancient and modern. They were particularly impressed with a new novel, by John Cooke, *Surrey of Eagle's Nest*, that McEachern brought one night; it was a story of a Virginia staff officer just returned from the war. To Jim, whose turn it

[5] Henderson K. Yoakum published his two-volume *History of Texas* (New York, Redfield) in 1855. His brother, Franklin L. Yoakum, served as president of Larissa College, near Rusk, after 1857.

[6] John H. Reagan, "Fort Warren Letter to the People of Texas, August 11, 1865," quoted in McCaleb (ed.), *Memoirs of John H. Reagan*, pp. 286–295; Oran M. Roberts, "The Address of the Texas Delegation," *National Intelligencer* (Washington, D. C.), January 10, 1867.

was, fell the reading of the opening scene in which Surrey hangs up his "dingy gray uniform and battered old sabre for the inspections of his descendants," saying:

I think those dear, coming grandchildren will take an interest in my adventures. They will belong to the fresh, new generations, and all the jealousies, hatreds, and corroding passions of the present epoch will have disappeared by that time. Simple curiosity will replace the old hatred; the bitter antagonism of the partisan will yield to the philosophic interest of the student . . . How Lee looked, and Stuart spoke—how Jackson lived that wondrous life of his, and Ashby charged upon his milk-white steed—of this the coming generations will talk, and I think they will take more interest in such things than in the most brilliant arguments about secession . . . Come! perhaps as you follow me you will live in the stormy days of a convulsed epoch, breathe its fiery atmosphere, and see its mighty forms as they defile before you, in a long and noble line.[7]

An evening's reading over, the blind man would talk, the boys drinking in the insight of his interpretations. Then they would walk him back to the house where he lived with his mother, who usually had one of her pies waiting for them. One night Jim began chuckling as he and Charles headed back to the office. The reading that night had been from the works of an earlier James Hogg, the Scotch poet, who, due to his father's serious misfortunes had been forced at the age of seven to take employment as a cowherd and later as a shepherd. Jim decided his own lot was not too bad, recalling the amusing account of the poet's plight:

Time after time, I had but two shirts, which grew often so bad, that I was obliged to quit wearing them altogether; for when I put them on, they hung in long tatters as far as my heels. At these times, I certainly made a very grotesque figure; for, on quitting the shirt, I could never induce my breeches to keep up their proper sphere. When the labors of the days were over, I amused myself by playing favorite Scottish tunes on an old violin. My bed being always in stables and cow-houses, I disturbed nobody but myself.[8]

Social life in Rusk, almost completely curtailed during the war years, was slowly resuming in quiet and inexpensive ways. The former "courthouse parties" to which everyone for miles around would be invited for

[7] John Cooke, *Surrey of Eagle's Nest* (New York, Bunce and Huntington, 1866), pp. 9–10.

[8] James Hogg, *Songs of the Ettrick Shepherd* (New York, W. Stoddard, 1832), p. iii; Alan L. Strout, *The Life and Letters of James Hogg* (Lubbock, Texas Tech Press, 1948).

square dancing and other kinds of merrymaking were things of the past, in part because no one now could spend money on nonessentials, but in large part because, with the Reconstruction military personnel omnipresent, people preferred to confine hospitality to "select groups" of their friends. The young people, however, were ingenious at devising ways to have fun, and whenever entertainments were given, the popular Hogg brothers were in demand. Jim especially, in spite of his own feeling of awkwardness, had the reputation of being a "graceful dancer."[9]

Sunday was an occasion to look forward to, for the family always drove to Rusk for church service, where Jim would join them. Afterwards, there would be the pleasant meetings and greetings of friends in front of the church, a town tradition which had become more meaningful in these days, and then Jim would sometimes go back to "Mountain Home" for dinner.

By the end of 1867 the young apprentice had increasingly less time for diversions of any kind. Working hard and faithfully, he had become a first-rate compositor, both in speed and in ability to take responsibility for all the work when Jackson was absent. Further, in the process of handling Jackson's copy and the clippings from the better-edited exchange papers, he had developed a certain amount of writing ability. With these proficiencies, on the occasions when the Rusk shop had hardly enough work to justify feeding two boys who possessed enormous appetites, it was possible for him to journey to this or that nearby town and be sure of a temporary job in its print shop.

One day in the early spring of 1868, while in Palestine setting type for the *Advocate,* he "screwed up his courage" and paid a visit to John H. Reagan, who had returned to his farm outside of Palestine in December, 1865, after his release from imprisonment in Fort Warren. To Jim, Reagan was part of the fabric of Texas history. Born in Tennessee, he had come to Texas in 1839 at the age of twenty-one, serving for a short time in the Republic's army in the Cherokee War. Then, as a surveyor, he had worked for three years through the region from Nacogdoches to Dallas. In 1842 he was elected justice of the peace for Nacogdoches County, later moving to a farm in what became Kaufman County, where he began the study of law. In 1846 he was made county judge and a lieutenant colonel of the Henderson County militia, which he had helped to organize. When he went to Austin in 1847 as a member of the

<hr>

[9] Personal interview with Mrs. Bess (Dickinson) Wrightman, at Rusk, June, 1946, and typescript of interview with Mrs. Mary Ann Reagan, June 19, 1935, Interv. Fol.

Texas legislature, he continued his study of law; after qualifying for practice he became one of the state's leading attorneys. In 1851 he moved to the farm near Palestine, being soon elected district judge for a six-year term. It was characteristic of his integrity that when, in 1856, the district was changed and his salary accordingly raised, he resigned to give the voters a chance to "get a better man"; he was, however, then elected to another six-year term. Later that year he was elected, over his own protests, to the House of Representatives of the United States Congress, and though he vigorously opposed the leaders of the extreme Southern wing of the Democratic Party when they advocated reopening the African slave trade, he was re-elected by a large margin two years later.

In 1861 the Texas Secession Convention, of which he was a member, elected him to the Congress of the Confederacy. President Davis appointed him the Confederacy's Postmaster General and, in the last few weeks of the war, Secretary of the Treasury. Imprisoned at Boston after the war, he addressed the first of his famous "Fort Warren Letters" to President Johnson in the late spring of 1865, counseling the wisdom of leniency toward the South rather than the severe policies then being advocated by the Radical Republicans. In August he wrote the second letter, addressed to the people of Texas, advising them to accept the end of the slave system and to guarantee qualified Negroes some civil rights, including voting, testifying in court, and possibly jury service. The advice was given partly on the basis of his own humanitarian tendencies but largely because he realized that his state by doing otherwise would suffer greater oppressions from the Stevens-Sumner Radicals. Many among the Texas irreconcilables, choosing to misunderstand his motives, condemned him for the letter, some going so far as to say he had been forced to write it by his jailers. Despite his loss of standing among some people in Texas, however, he was a delegate to the convention and cooperated with James Throckmorton in drafting the brief-lived Texas Constitution of 1866.

Jim Hogg knew all of these things, and he also knew that, when Governor Throckmorton was ousted by the military in mid-1867, Reagan had been offered the governorship "by the military satrap then in power. He turned and spurned it."[10] And here on the quiet farm acres, Reagan

---

[10] Quoted from Hogg's description of the visit in a memorial speech in Houston, April 18, 1905, shortly after Reagan's death; for the speech, see Robert C. Cotner (ed.), *Addresses and State Papers of James Stephen Hogg* (Austin, University of Texas Press, 1951), p. 530.

40

(who seemed an old man to the teen-age boy) was making the best of his situation, still looked at askance by some people of his own state and in disfavor with the military government. As he talked to Jim, there was no hint of discouragement or rankling in his words. This was a period of readjustment, he said, and wise men must bide their time, being sure that they kept their minds fresh and unclouded against the day when hopes would again not be in vain. Knowing Reagan's fame as an attorney, Jim spoke of his own dream of some day becoming a lawyer, as his father had been and as Tom Hogg, against the present financial odds, was determined to be, and Reagan gave him kindly advice and encouragement. The profound impression made by Reagan during this visit was to be an influencing factor throughout the rest of Jim Hogg's life.

Not long after returning to Rusk from Palestine, Jim learned that Major Jack Davis had sold his interest in the *Observer* and planned to take his press to one of the rapidly growing prairie towns in Central Texas. Jim quickly decided that he would like to share the adventure. The story of the encounter was later told by the Major to his son, Judge Hugh Barclay Davis of Nacogdoches:

One day shortly before leaving Rusk and when all my belongings were packed for the move, a lad of 17 or 18 approached and sought employment. . . . I was impressed by the lad's earnestness and eagerness to work. I informed him of my financial condition; namely, that I was without funds with which to pay him a salary and that I had a wife and four children to support. He wanted to go along to learn the newspaper business, possibly to see the west. Jim Hogg drove the ox team to Fort Worth. Not finding the legal and newspaper prospects to my liking, I turned southward to the new county of Johnson, and Jim went along to Cleburne.[11]

Before long Davis went back to East Texas, but James Hogg remained a while. Cleburne was in every sense a frontier settlement, even in its vulnerability to Indian raids. Its first house, which later became its first hotel, was built in 1854; the town had acquired its name from a general and had been made the county seat in 1867. J. W. Graves, the proprietor of the Cleburne *Chronicle,* was a hard-working and ambitious man, who apparently demanded the impossible of his employees and gave little indication of understanding the psychology of boys.[12] Jim found his situation here unhappily different from the pleasant days with Whistlin'

[11] Forwarded to the writer by a daughter of Judge Davis, Leilia V. Davis, September 5, 1948.

[12] Scattered copies of the early *Chronicle* are preserved in the Cleburne Public Library, Cleburne, Texas.

Jackson, but, hoping eventually to be able to put aside some money, he decided to stick it out as long as possible. Alonzo C. Scurlock (who by 1892 would be well known as an editor in Fort Worth) soon became his fellow-worker and shop roommate. Among other friends that James Hogg made was a bright young man who also would later be influential in Texas, Martin M. Crane.

However, Hogg's existence in Cleburne was in general not a happy one. Mr. Graves seemed unapproachable, and here on the open black-lands of Central Texas the boy was homesick for the hills and trees of East Texas and for his family. He was about to decide that the situation was hopeless, when a fire conveniently settled the matter by eradicating the print shop. With only fifteen cents in his pocket, he decided to go home.[13] He rode as far as Anderson County with a man as broke as himself. The fifteen cents went to buy three "little sunburst watermelons"; when these were consumed the travelers rode for three days without food.

Graves, who later became an influential Dallas lawyer, was one among many Texans who claimed credit for helping James Stephen Hogg attain the status of a great man. But Hogg never forgot the unhappiness of the Cleburne days. Martin Crane, who was at one time in partnership with Graves in Dallas, told the following story to Hogg's daughter in 1935:

> One day Governor Hogg came into my office and said: "Do you know what? That dad-blamed old partner of yours met me and you don't know what he said to me." Obviously he did not like it. "He said, Governor do you know that you were once in my employ?" "Yes, I remember that very well," said he [Hogg]. "Well, I started a great many young men out in this state—started Ramsey and I started Crane out. . . . But," he said, "you know I never liked you." Your father said he thought at first he would get angry, but it hit his funny bone.[14]

Happy to be home again, James Hogg still felt keenly that it was his responsibility to support himself. Mrs. Davis, determined to provide a medical education for her son Will, had recently gone to Gonzales as a governess for a doctor's family.[15] Tom and his wife Anna, even with John's aid on the farms, had little financial margin, and they were caring for Joseph Lewis, Jr., and planning happily for their first baby. The lack

---

[13] Oscar B. Colquitt, "James Stephen Hogg," in Terrell *Times-Star*, November 4, 1892. Reprint in Dallas *Morning News*, June 24, 1923.

[14] Judge M. M. Crane to Ima Hogg, March 18, 1935, Interv. Fol.

[15] Dr. J. A. King to R. C. Cotner, February 20, 1955.

of adequate farm labor and the consequent decline of production, plus higher taxes and living costs, had forced the sale of more of the family land in the spring of 1868. Like many people with large acreage, they ✓ were "land-poor" and unable to pay taxes; yet land values were so depressed by the large tracts being thrown on the market that a dollar an acre was considered an excellent selling price.

The 925 acres in Limestone County were purchased at 25 cents an acre by Colonel William S. Herndon of Tyler.[16] This rising politician and railroad attorney also bought some of the farming land on Mud Creek at 75 cents an acre, or $240, and paid $200 specie for 8½ acres and a residence, part of the property in Rusk. The probate judge recorded that the sale was made in accordance with the statute for such cases and that "said land brought its fair market value,"[17] a statement that indicated the low tide of economic affairs in Texas. Reluctantly, Tom parted with General Hogg's old law office, which sold for $80 specie; he kept his father's law books, but he was not yet prepared to make a living by law alone. The Hoggs were left with the house at "Mountain Home" and 530 acres.

This was obviously not the time to add another hungry mouth to those already needing to be fed at "Mountain Home," even had Jim's pride allowed him to linger there. The next job for the printer's devil was in Quitman, Wood County, eighty miles north of Rusk. The following version of the debut in Quitman overlooks Hogg's own statement that a friend had paved the way for him to get the job.

Jim: Are you Doc Shuford?
Shuford: I reckon that's me.
Jim: Well, I'm Jim Hogg. . . . I came to work for you.
Shuford: How you know I need somebody?
Jim: Well, Doc, from the looks of this room I'd say you would have been needin' somebody for a long time!
Shuford: All right, son. We'll see just how smart you are. . . . This paper should have been out four days ago, and I ain't had nobody to give me a lift.[18]

The story goes that Jim set the type for the issue of the *Clipper* in a few hours, then printed the paper with the hand-lever press, thereby

[16] Report of Sale filed in Probate Minute Book G, Cherokee County (Texas), March 31, 1868 (unpaged).
[17] *Ibid.*
[18] Great American Life Insurance Company Broadcast, 1938. Transcript of broadcast in H. C.

43

earning the job. Again the wages were board and room, with some odd-job pay to help buy his clothes. Shuford was frequently out of town, and his absence gave Jim, at the age of eighteen, an increasing sense of responsibility. One traditional Wood County tale relates that Shuford once went off to New Orleans and did not return until after the *Clipper's* publication day; his devil is said to have taken firm hold of the situation, printing an edition of the paper that was made up almost wholly of poetry garnered from the exchanges.[19] If a copy could be located, it would be a rare gem.

Quitman had been settled in 1840, becoming the county seat in 1850, but the region around it, not much populated until after 1865, still retained a decided frontier flavor, so that the town had its share of excitement. One day a band of five desperadoes came into town, bent on killing the sheriff. When they managed to corner him in the courthouse, Jim and a friend named Moore borrowed guns and made for Courthouse Square, joined along the way by another man who ran out from his hiding place behind a store. The three of them got the drop on the bad men, who then surrendered and were disarmed.

In the midst of the fracas the sheriff had handed Jim a rifle and told him to guard one of the prisoners while the sheriff went off to round up another man. Hoping to take advantage of Hogg's youth, the ruffian tried to catch Jim off guard. When he attempted to get close enough to grab the rifle, Hogg warned him not to come closer. Thinking he could bluff the youth, he kept inching nearer. When he failed to heed a warning to stop, Jim then felt obliged to hit him with the rifle butt, which quieted him until the sheriff's return. As he revived he swore to get revenge on Jim. After the desperadoes were taken to jail there was more trouble; certain citizens, who had barricaded themselves at the first hint of trouble, emerged and wanted to mob the prisoners.[20] Through all this latter excitement Hogg stood with the sheriff, until order was restored.

Late in the spring of 1869, James left the *Clipper* to become a sharecropper. He cleared ten acres of post-oak land and planted it to cotton for a Dr. Wright, who lived east of town; the ostensible agreement had been that Jim was to have all the proceeds from the first year's planting and share on halves after that. The relationship did not start auspiciously. Instead of being able to live in the home, as he had expected, Jim

19 Judge V. B. Harris, "James Stephen Hogg" (typescript) Interv. Fol., p. 4.
20 *Ibid.*

lived in a small shack away from the house. Grubbing out the roots was hard work, and his shins carried through life the scars of cuts and scratches. The doctor's two daughters enjoyed driving to Quitman in their fancy buggy. On one occasion when Jim was quieting the frisky horse, the doctor suggested that Jim had better drive, whereupon the young ladies haughtily refused to be seen with "a hired hand." Deeply hurt, Jim muttered that someday they would have reason to be proud they had known him.[21] Though subsequently warned that the planter-doctor was a hard trader, he was unprepared for the extent to which "the old scamp would try to swindle" him—paying off Jim's fifty-dollar account at the store and handing him only ten dollars in gold when the crop was laid by after six months of hard work.[22] Cotton sold for 25 cents a pound in November, 1869, a high price; estimating the crop at even the low figure of 250 ginned pounds, or half a bale per acre, Jim's gross should have been $625.[23] A friend in Quitman on hearing the story offered the boy his gun and advised using it, but James declined.

Fortunately, he soon had experiences that revived his faith in human nature. With his ten dollars he took a short course at Mr. Baggett's school, four miles east of Quitman, and there he met Sarah Ann (Sallie) Stinson, the daughter of Colonel James Stinson, a prosperous sawmill owner and scientific farmer. The dark-haired, vivacious, intelligent girl, just over five feet tall, made an indelible impression on James Hogg. Then he had the further good fortune of hearing that Chris Haines, founder of Hainesville, needed help with his cotton. Knocking on the door of the house around twilight one day, he was greeted by Mrs. Haines, who, although just informed by her husband that he needed no more workers, liked the boy immediately and asked him to wait. At her urging, Haines came to the door and invited Jim to come in for supper and to spend the night, since it soon would be too dark for traveling. Before the evening was over, Jim had a new job. He was made one of the household, provided with a homemade walnut desk, and given access to the family library. After the long working hours at

[21] *Ibid.*, p. 5. Story retold by Mrs. J. F. Haines and daughters of Mr. Gunstream in personal interview, June, 1946.

[22] Colquitt, "James Stephen Hogg," Terrell *Times-Star,* November 4, 1892. Typescript of clipping in H.C.

[23] Galveston *Daily News,* November 20 and 30, 1869; Harris, "James Stephen Hogg," p. 5; Colquitt, "James Stephen Hogg," Terrell *Times-Star,* November 4, 1892; Oscar B. Colquitt to George M. Bailey, July 12, 1923, Let. Biog. J. S. Hogg, pp. 257–258. Typescript of clipping in H.C.

the steam-operated ginhouse, he spent his evenings eagerly reading books on history, manners, religion, and government.[24]

He worked for Haines until the ginning season was over, making twenty dollars in gold per month. Then he invited his brother John to join him, and, with what James had saved and some credit, they rented a little tract of unfenced farmland near the Sabine River in the southwest corner of Wood County. There was no house. The tall, strong boys set out at once to cut logs and split rails, meanwhile boarding with an old man and his wife who lived nearby. The brothers saw themselves as real pioneers, and they boasted to each other of the increasing firmness of their muscles as the days went along.

Shortly before the Christmas season the old couple with whom the Hogg brothers boarded were invited to a dance by friends who lived in Van Zandt County, just across the Sabine, and it was urged that Jim and John be brought along. The boys, who had declined a similar, earlier invitation, now, at their landlord's entreaty, decided to attend the "shindig." On the evening of the party, just as the old gentleman, his wife, the Hogg boys, and another young man were mounting their horses, heavy rain began to fall. Reaching the Sabine, they left their horses tethered, and "cooned" logs to cross the river. James, who had suffered from malaria and was now thoroughly wet from the rain, felt a chill coming on as they climbed the steep bluff atop which stood the house, the usual double log-cabin structure. The aged hosts greeted them in the center hallway, and the Wood County old couple went into the room at the left. Spying a log fire in the room to the right, Jim hurried in, followed by John and the other guest. There they found themselves confronted by a number of big, rough men, all sporting six-shooters. No girls were present, there was no dancing, no fiddler was to be seen. Suspecting that something was wrong, Jim nevertheless went up close to the fire, for he was shaking with chills. After a few strained moments, the ruffians filed silently out of the room. John and the other young man thought it would be best to get back to the horses. Jim told them to go along, and when he was over his chill he would ask the old couple to leave with him. His own words recount what happened next.

They left, and in a little while as I was standing by the fire, a big fellow with one eye out, came to the door and looked at me in a savage manner,

[24] Conversation with Mrs. J. F. Haines, June, 1946. Many of the volumes are preserved in the family library.

and then went back into the yard . . . I concluded to go into the room where the old folks were. As I had about passed across the hallway and was entering into the other room, the scoundrels who were in the yard shot me, the ball entering my back, and I fell on the floor inside the room where the old folks were. As I fell, my hand struck the side of a bed made of pine boards and nailed up in one corner of the log house. I pulled myself up and got into it. The mattress was made of shucks of seed cotton. The ruffians came to the door, cursing and swearing they would finish me. But the blood was flowing freely from me, and the old folks begged them not to shoot me again as they had already killed me, and they went off muttering oaths.

The ruffians who shot me were the desperadoes . . . whom I had helped to arrest on the occasion that they were going to kill the Sheriff in Quitman. They had planned to get me over into Van Zandt and murder me. All night long I lay in a pool of blood, on that hard mattress, without medical attention, in a half-conscious condition.[25]

That night was full of terrors. In moments of consciousness, Jim wondered why John did not return—was he lying wounded or dead on the river bank? Then in the pitch darkness something crashed down in Jim's face, and he thought wildly that the assassins had returned and were knocking him in the head with a mall. The noise and his groans aroused the old people, who discovered that the assailant had been an old tomcat; trying to stay awake the rest of the night, they passed most of the time by swapping gruesome ghost stories. They said that John had gone to rouse a country doctor miles away, but Jim, having heard them say he was dying, wondered whether he would live until the doctor came.

Just before daybreak he heard a rider approach the yard gate. His spirits rose, but then a harsh voice called the old gentleman out and, cursing, asked if "that Hogg was dead." "No, but he is dying," the old man replied. The assassin said he was glad of it, for he had come to finish the job if Hogg seemed to be reviving; then he rode away.[26]

Not until afternoon did John and the doctor arrive. Having no surgical instruments, the doctor probed the wound with a pine stick; he was unable to remove the lead, which had lodged near the spinal column. Then he dressed the wound as best he could. The Sabine, swollen by the rain of the night before, was over its banks, but James insisted on being

[25] Judge V. B. Harris, "A Historical Sketch of Wood County," pp. 1–12, type-script copy presented to the writer by Lucille Russell of Mineola; also, Colquitt, "James Stephen Hogg," Terrell *Times-Star*, November 4, 1892.

[26] Colquitt, *op. cit.*

taken out of the neighborhood. They made a pine raft, then carried him down to it on the ancient mattress, and laboriously got him back to the house in Wood County.

After two weeks he was still seriously ill. A doctor summoned from Quitman, fifteen miles away, looked at him in alarm, loaded him in a wagon, and took him to the town. For many days he lingered near death, often only half-conscious. Martha Frances Davis came from Gonzales to nurse him, and Dr. McDugald, his brother-in-law, came from Rusk,[27] staying with him until he was well enough to be driven in a buggy back to Cherokee County.

The sensible care James Hogg had always taken of his health and his strong will to live had helped to save his life. And during some of the long, sleepless nights in Quitman a memory of an oft-told story about his father had fortified him. About a year before Jim's birth Joseph Hogg, as a consequence of his efforts to rid Rusk of a group of law-flouting gamblers, had been ambushed and shot by young Rufus Chandler.[28] The wound was a serious one, and the Colonel's fight to live was valiant. Recalling this, the son had determined to win his own fight, especially when it occurred to him that his wound had been, like his father's, incurred as a result of assisting the enforcement of law.

It was good to be back at "Mountain Home," and as soon as Jim could get about he took short walks into the woods, still winter-dormant, to renew his friendship with the birds and animals resident there. The wound was long in healing, however, and sometimes he was discouraged. Certainly nothing in the news from outside or in the events near home was calculated to lift his spirits. In the elections of 1869, held under the auspices of General J. J. Reynolds, the military commander in Texas, Edmund J. Davis, former Unionist and now Radical Republican, who had in 1866 advocated complete disfranchisement of all former Confederates, had become governor by an exceedingly narrow margin over Moderate Republican A. J. Hamilton. Most Texans believed that a

[27] A short time before the shooting, Martha Frances had shown concern about Jim. Writing from Gonzales December 1, 1869, she remarked to Tom and "Sister Anna" that her brothers would find her "more reserved than formerly; I suppose 'the woman' fits me better than 'the girl' of former days." She cautioned Tom that if he ran for office he should not be surprised if the "Rads" won. She seemed inclined to go to Wood County to help James and John get settled, then added, "Unless I change my mind, and James does not get settled, I shall cast myself among you at Mountain Home next Spring." Fam. Let.

[28] Chandler was an orphan youth whom Joseph Hogg brought home after the Mexican War. He had been a protégé of Hogg's, but had fallen into the company of the gamblers whose lawlessness the Colonel was fighting.

recount would have shown a different story, and, daily, there were tokens that Davis ruled the state as a virtual dictator. Letters from Mississippi told that Hogg cousins there were doing far from well; some of the men continued to suffer from war wounds and were expecting forced sale of their lands.[29] At "Mountain Home" the financial picture had not brightened, and it was probable that more land must soon be sold.

When spring finally arrived to touch the dogwood into bloom and to make the woods into a fresh green wonderland, James spent much of his time wandering among the trees; keeping thus to himself, he at least was not worrying his family by letting them see his obvious depression. His health had much improved, but the wound was still enough unhealed to need daily dressing, and he was deeply troubled about the uncertainty of his future (an uncharacteristic mood, due no doubt to his still-weakened physical condition). There came a day when his mood was so black that he scarcely knew where he walked and was blind to the trees and the sun patterns playing through their boughs. Then a sound began to pierce through his enwrapping self-concern. Finally listening, he knew it was a mockingbird's song. He could not discover the singer among the thickly new-leafed boughs, but the song kept pouring out in unstinted sweetness, filling him with a happiness he had not known in months. As he walked toward home, he believed that his gratitude to the bird and the trees that gave it harborage would never leave him.

When he assessed what could be done about his immediate future, it was clear that heavy work was out of the question for some time. Tom Hogg's steady determination to complete his legal studies, despite the scarcity of hours that could be spared from his teaching and the farm management by which he supported the family, had kept the goal of a law career before Jim, too, until recent events had put all such matters out of mind. Now the dream slowly revived, and he began dropping into law offices in Rusk to talk to his father's friends. Judge L. H. Dillard, who had shared Joseph Hogg's sponsorship of education in Rusk and was presently interested in the recent resuscitation of the railroad development which had been in prospect before the war, found Jim Hogg an intelligent visitor and had many conversations with him, applauding and encouraging the ambition to study law.[30] The encouragement was

[29] Thomas J. Hogg to Thomas E. Hogg, dated near Calhoun City, Mississippi, July 8, 1868, Th. El. Hogg Fol.
[30] Hattie J. Roach, *Cherokee County*, pp. 43, 71; St. Clair Reed, *A History of Texas Railroads*, p. 315.

more than verbal; opening his law library freely to the boy, he provided not only books but a quiet place to study. Charles Young, who had been devotedly dressing Jim's wound for him every morning, soon was making his way each day to Dillard's library, where he would find Jim engrossed in one or another of the formidable-looking volumes from the shelves.

Young has recorded that there were mornings when Jim seemed "downhearted." He naturally worried about the ultimate results from his wound, and for about six weeks he seemed quite distressed. During this period of depression he almost made a bad choice of a companion. Prior to Jim's return to Rusk, a blacksmith newly arrived in town had gone to work at Newton's blacksmith shop. He was a fine mechanic and appeared to have a keen mind, at least a glib tongue. After work he would put on a broadcloth suit, box-toed shoes "shined to a finish," and a silk hat, and then, with a gold-headed cane, he would walk around the square. This "Chesterfield in manner and dress" was the talk of the town, but no one seemed to know anything about his background. Somehow the social climber made Jim's acquaintance and tried to work through him to meet people in town. Young believed that the man, who was several years senior to James, was up to no good. He may have been hurt that James did not share his estimate of the dandy right away. It was characteristic of Jim Hogg not to judge a man hastily but to give him a chance to prove his worth. However, it did not take Jim long to break off the acquaintance. Young concluded:

Had it not been for Jim's great natural sense of right from wrong he would have gone to the bad, but with that irresistible force in his nature, even in his boyhood, his determination to do what was right, . . . he cut him off as quickly as he had fallen in with him. I merely refer to this incident to show that Jim Hogg as a boy was keenly alert to withstand corrupt influences and had a mind to think and guide and direct his actions. . . . I met him often afterwards, and it was my privilege to help him all I could in every election in which he engaged for state offices. . . . He was a great boy as he was a great man.[31]

James Hogg's efforts from 1867 to 1870 to become self-supporting had coincided with the depressing period of Congressional-Military Reconstruction in Texas—a circumstance that might understandably have spelled defeat to him, but instead furnished a strong spur to his intelligence and will to succeed. On April 16, 1870, General Reynolds for-

[31] Charles Young to George Bailey, February 4, 1923, Let. Biog. of J. S. Hogg.

mally ended military rule and turned the government of Texas over to civil officers. However, the Radical Republicans had control of both houses of the Texas legislature, and when President Grant, on March 30, had approved an act finally admitting Texans to Congress, the Texas senators to be seated were Morgan C. Hamilton and James W. Flanagan, both of them Republicans and both strong opponents, in 1861, of secession. Therefore James Hogg joined his brother Tom and Whistlin' Jackson in not agreeing with the local Republican paper, the *Cherokee Advertiser,* when it followed the line of the Houston *Union* and announced that "Reconstruction has come to an end at last."[32]

[32] Houston *Union,* January 18, 1870.

CHAPTER III

Small-Town Editor, 1870–1875

WHEN GENERAL REYNOLDS declared Military Reconstruction in Texas at an end in April, 1870, he was aware that the majority of Texans would not be satisfied until they had ousted the distrusted Republican rule of Governor Davis. Even as Reynolds was about to withdraw, the Davis government was continuing to retaliate for certain actions engaged in by some Democrats at the time of the elections of the previous fall, such as the scattered violence in Cherokee County on Election Day. During the spring of 1870 the people in and about Rusk were subject to a rigid investigation being conducted by an agent of the State Police, Lieutenant Thomas Sheriff, concerning the "election outrages." The charges included fraud and intimidation of the freedmen.[1]

The Democrats' fight for majority rule had far to go, facing such hurdles as the subsidy furnished by the Radical Republican government to many local newspapers and the domination of key towns in various counties by Scalawags and Negroes—the towns of Tyler, Longview, and Marshall, near Rusk, for instance, were all thus dominated. Among the Democrats of the area who sought to end this control, there were several who believed that the day could be speeded if a Democrat could own the Rusk *Cherokee Advertiser,* which had been the powerful and consistent mouthpiece of the Radicals. Thomas Hogg, ready to practice law and to enter politics—and not averse to having an outlet for his literary talents—decided to risk some of his scanty capital on the venture, especially since Frank A. Templeton, a friend since army days, agreed to join him in purchasing the paper. Under its new management, the *Advertiser* soon became a thorn in the side of the Davis administration.[2]

Still determined to support himself, the convalescent James began

---

[1] Hattie J. Roach, *Cherokee County,* p. 67.

[2] *Ibid.; Texas Almanac, 1873* (Galveston, Richardson and Company, 1873), pp. 57–58 gives founding dates. Thomas Clark, *The Southern Country Editor* (Indianapolis, Bobbs-Merrill Company, 1948), p. 20, states that the 182 "tattered weeklies" alive in the South in 1865 had become 499 by 1869, and twenty years later there were 1,827 weeklies in twelve states.

once more to think about returning to newspaper work. The duties would not be so strenuous as farming, there would be opportunities to study law, and he would be "in out of the wet" as Dr. McDugald had counseled. Further, Jim had observed that candidates for public office often edited, owned, or had an interest in a paper. Thinking back over the places where he had worked—Cleburne, Palestine, Quitman, Rusk, and Tyler—he decided that Tyler offered the most promise and had the added advantage of being near home. A letter to H. V. Hamilton, editor of the Tyler *Democratic Reporter,* brought him an offer of a job, and, by the summer of 1870, James Stephen Hogg was at work again, making about ten dollars a month, plus board and room.

Fifteen years later Hamilton wrote this description of his nineteen-year-old printer's devil:

He was large of limb and physically well developed, but rather awkward, not very well educated, not particularly handsome, as poor as Job's turkey, and by no means a dude. We liked his looks, nevertheless, and gave him a job. He went to work as though he meant business, and during the two or three years [this must cover the brief period in 1868, and the months in 1870–71] of his stay in our office we never knew him to flinch from any duty assigned him, though he would occasionally say "by gatlings" when called upon to "roll" for an old hand press then in use, or to "pull off" forty or fifty quires of paper in August weather. Jim was then a sober, industrious boy. His moral character was without blemish, and his conduct always that of a gentleman by nature and by habit. His leisure hours (and he had not many) were assiduously devoted to study, and many a time, while he had a home in our family circle, midnight found him bending over his books; and with only a few hours sleep each night, the dawn of day found him again plodding his unaided and slow, but sure way along the paths of knowledge.[3]

James soon found congenial friends in Tyler, partly through the thoughtfulness of his father's former law partner, Stockton P. Donley,[4] and partly on his own. He was especially drawn to seventeen-year-old Horace Chilton, who worked for a rival paper. Horace was the son of Colonel George Chilton, who had been Tom Hogg's commander in the battle of Oak Hill and earlier had been closely associated with Joseph

[3] Tyler *Democrat and Reporter,* August 31, 1886. J. S. Hogg Scrapbook No. 2, p. 79.
[4] Walter P. Webb and H. Bailey Carroll, *Handbook of Texas* (Austin, Texas State Historical Association, 1952), I, 513; Albert Woldert, *A History of Tyler and Smith County, Texas* (San Antonio, Naylor Company, 1948), pp. 66–67, 70–73.

Lewis Hogg in the Secession Convention. In the early days of Reconstruction, Congress had not seen fit to seat Colonel Chilton; upon his return to Texas he found the military rule so odious that he decided to go to Kentucky. There he taught at Lynnland Institute, coming back to Texas to live only after Democratic supremacy was restored in 1874.[5]

Hard times dictated that Horace Chilton should take his meals with his publisher, but he lived at home with his mother and sister. He was ambitious to become a lawyer like his first cousin, keen-minded Sawnie Robertson,[6] a son of Judge John C. Robertson. Sawnie had just completed a course at Judge Oran M. Roberts' law school in Gilmer and was ready to practice. His example was an inspiration to Jim Hogg also. For the many evenings spent in the Chilton home, Jim was forever grateful. He enjoyed the wit of Horace's sister, George-Ella, and the association with the Robertsons and Frank Bowden, Colonel Chilton's brother-in-law, and he tremendously admired Horace's devotion to his mother in her loneliness during the long separation from her husband. The Damon-and-Pythias friendship that was forged between the two boys was to be a dominant link in their lives.[7]

Early in September, James was invited to become a member of the Debating Society and soon afterwards was asked to participate in a public debate. Pleased by the honor of membership, he was also somewhat startled by being asked to take part so soon in public debate with seasoned speakers. He wrote Tom the evening he was notified of the debate that he had even thought of resigning rather than make a poor showing. However, he wanted his brother to know he was not afraid to compete; nevertheless, he hoped that Tom would come to his assistance with a "short speech, just to the point . . . and then by exerting myself to the highest pitch, I can hold a hand with them in the debate." He was to take the negative on the question—"Would a Republican Form of Government Be Better for the United States Than a Limited Monarchy?" The letter (in large, clear, and firm handwriting) continued:

Tom write one this time for me, and I'll make out the next time myself. Be sure to write it in time for me to get it by next mail; the mail starts from Rusk on Thursdays. I would not prepare for this debate, was it not for

[5] *Ibid.*, pp. 38, 67–69; H. B. Marsh interview, April 9, 1935 (typescript), Interv. Fol.; H. M. (Rode) Owens interview, February 16, 1935 (typescript), Interv. Fol.
[6] Webb and Carroll, *op. cit.*, II, 488.
[7] Personal interview with Mrs. George-Ella Henry in Tyler, June, 1946. In a wheelchair, she still had a mental sparkle and a sense of humor. See *Handbook of Texas*, I, 340.

wanting to belong to it [Debating Society] in the future. If I do not stick, then the cry will be, "he's timid, will not do for a lawyer." If I had the time I would not ask this of you, for I feel perfectly competent to debate with that crowd, although it consists of young lawyers and printers. The debating Society and Sunday school are the only institutions that I intend to belong to, while I am a "greenhorn," as you call me. Well, write this for me, and I'll try and cripple some of the "Tylerites." All I want is a showing, and that I have not in this instance, and they know it, and therefore I want to surprise them. Give me something short and a regular "deadener."

My love to all—Goodnight
Your little Bro.
James S. Hogg[8]

Tyler's vigorous Republican and Democratic papers afforded an excellent opportunity for James Hogg to observe how news could be slanted, especially since Horace Chilton was obliged for a time to take employment with Representative S. D. Wood's *National Index,* the Republican paper. Jim had always understood there were two sides to a question, but now he recognized the necessity to ponder the basic human reasons for mixed motives. The clash of quick minds in editorial columns or in practice debate was stimulating to a young man who enjoyed good fellowship and mental exercise—and it was also an assistance toward maturity.

He was very much interested in Tyler's ambitions to become a railroad center. The original plans for the Houston and Great Northern Railroad had been incubated in M. H. Bonner's law office in Rusk, but the chaotic conditions from 1866 to 1870 had delayed investments and building. In December, 1870, the contract was finally let for building the first section northward from the docks on Buffalo Bayou.[9] For many months James watched the chartering game in Austin from his vantage post in the composing room of the *Reporter,* giving especially careful attention to the point at which the Houston and Great Northern and the so-called Southern Pacific (actually the Texas and Pacific) might intersect west of Marshall. Longview, already a terminus, Tyler, and Quitman—all or each might become important as railroad centers.

Horace Chilton and James Hogg had many long conversations about their ambitions, particularly in the light of present events. They agreed that newspaper ownership appeared to be an excellent steppingstone to political activity, and offered, besides, a congenial way of earning

[8] James S. Hogg to Thomas E. Hogg, September 26, 1870, Fam. Let.
[9] St. Clair Reed, *Texas Railroads,* pp. 315 ff.

money for the study of law on the side. A law career was still the important main goal for both boys. Night-long "bull sessions" on what the future has in store are common to most young men in their late teens and early twenties, but to these two in Tyler the talk was not merely the stuff of unfulfilled dreams. Before the year 1871 was out, each of them had started a newspaper of his own, Horace, age eighteen, the tri-weekly *Sun* in Tyler, James, age twenty, the *News* in Longview.

Nothing illustrates more forcibly the alert mind and self-confidence of James Hogg than this decision to establish his own paper in the railhead town of Longview. His direct planning was based partly on the expectation that the movement of the cotton crop to the railhead from September to Christmas would assure cash collections in the initial months, during which time he could build up circulation and gain the confidence of business concerns in the paper as an advertising medium. The prosperous and growing town's establishments included several grocery stores and dry goods emporiums, and there were numerous wool, hide, and cotton buyers—all of these factors seeming to assure eventual and substantial advertising revenue.

The ambitious venture was well threshed over with the rest of the family. Tom's own newspaper venture could use more capital, and he now wanted to move into Rusk and run for justice of the peace; to help finance both newspapers, as well as Tom's move, it was decided to offer a large part of what was left of the family estate at public sale, reserving the house and some surrounding land. To Jim's delight, Mrs. Davis agreed to join him on the *News*. Her duties would include sifting the exchanges and writing some of the editorial matter, while Jim attended to circulation-building and the mechanics of printing.

The first issue of the *News* appeared in October, self-proclaimed as a "Tri-Weekly, Tuesday, Thursday & Saturday."[10] Jim had chosen an office opposite the railroad depot, to be near the source of incoming news. Subscriptions were $5.00 a year, $2.75 for six months, and 50 cents a month. Liberal inducements were offered to interest advertisers in contracting for space on a monthly or yearly basis.

On the first Tuesday in November, as arranged, the public sale of the estate took place in Rusk. Three hundred sixty acres were sold in squares, "not exceeding forty acres each," for a total of $574, at less than $2.00 an acre, a low price but at least better than that in the earlier

[10] The Longview *News* for November 11, 1871, was Vol. I, No. 14. This is the earliest issue available; a copy is in the Hogg Collection.

sale.[11] Money aside, probably no member of the family went through the proceedings without sadness at the thought of parting with this remainder of their once substantial and loved heritage. Nevertheless, for all of them there was a proud later day when the *Texas Almanac* for 1871 included listings of the Longview *News* and the *Cherokee Advertiser* as papers owned by members of the Hogg family.

"James S. Hogg, Publisher" was not content to carry only local advertisements. In Tyler, Jefferson, and Galveston he managed to get contracts from hotels, attorneys, a barber, owners of livery stables, land agents, and commission merchants. His own confidence must have infected these men, for certainly in size the paper was unimpressive, being only seven and three-quarters inches by twelve and one-quarter, with three columns. The venture was profitable from the outset.

Page one of the earliest issue extant, Volume I, No. 14, November 11, 1871, is probably typical, with its one column of ads and two columns of exchanges. The tiny paper carried little foreign news, but the German victory over France was told in terms of corrected estimates of casualties, with the following interesting comment on French patriotism:

Patriotism in young maidens in Metz is tantamount to all the virtues. A young French lady of that city recently refused a Prussian officer's offer of marriage, and the next day received ten applications for her hand among the richest men of the town.[12]

The publisher's devotedly Democratic and anti-Grant-administration policy was apparently demonstrated in every manner possible, to judge from a few samples of items:

J. W. Flanagan, U. S. Senator, returned to Henderson last Tuesday morning, from Austin. Wonder if he is colicked on chicken-pie?

* * * *

The Radicals in Austin tremble in their boots for fear their petty master, E. J. Davis, will be impeached. This fear is excited by the number of Democratic Senators and Legislators who are just taking their seats with that villainous body.

* * * *

[11] Judge Micajah Bonner made application in the July Term, 1871, "to sell the lands of said estate for the payment of the debts thereof"; and stated that the homestead of 200 acres had never been separated from the 530 acres of the Stephen Halbert headright. They proceeded to survey with permission to sell to the highest bidder "for currency." District Court Report Book A (Rusk), November, 1871, gives a report of the sale.   [12] Longview *News*, November 11, 1871.

It is said that the Legislature will not sustain Gov. Davis in his martial law proclamation in Limestone and Freestone counties.[13]

In the issue of December 7, 1871, James Hogg expressed doubt as to the authenticity of a report from Marshall that President Grant had directed Governor Davis to certify men who received majorities in the last election and that he had expressed disapproval of martial law in Limestone County:

If this be so, Grant must be preparing to take a new departure, else why does he assume the role of justice and political honesty.[14]

The Democrats were gradually making some headway in their efforts to return to power in Texas, although the Davis administration frustrated them at nearly every turn. When Moderate Republicans and Democrats, for instance, had joined in a taxpayer's convention in September, 1871, aided by former Republican governors A. J. Hamilton and E. M. Pease, the Radicals retaliated by postponing the regular state elections until November, 1872.[15] Nevertheless, the fact that Thomas Hogg, a Confederate captain and son of a Confederate general, had been elected justice of the peace in Cherokee County was an indication of the new trend. James and Thomas Hogg joined other Democratic papers in pressing all possible embarrassing charges against the Davis administration and fighting the Radicals on any provocation, not unaware that Major Hearsey, Democratic editor of the *East Texas Bulletin*, had been arrested again and fined by the Radical officials in nearby Marshall.[16]

James enjoyed copying a blast of Tom's in the *Advertiser* against Webster Flanagan:

Jerrymander Flanagan, the son of the old man Flanagan, sometimes called in common parlance, Web, who fathered a bill in the Legislature to tear up the Senatorial Districts of Texas, and cobble them together so as to neutralize the power of the white people, and perpetuate Radical infamy, passed through Rusk Wednesday night for his home, covered with glory, such as shineth from a pewter dollar in a mud hole.[17]

---

[13] *Ibid.*
[14] *Ibid.*, December 7, 1871.
[15] Rupert N. Richardson, *Texas*, pp. 282–283; Charles W. Ramsdell, *Reconstruction in Texas*, pp. 298–299.
[16] Longview *News*, December 7, 1871.
[17] Cherokee *Advertiser*, December 7, 1871.

James Hogg's reputation as a courageous and able publisher soon spread through the region. In December, 1871, he was paid a visit by Colonel H. Keys and Dr. B. B. Hart of Quitman, who were on their way to Shreveport. He audaciously published the news they brought:

These gentlemen inform us that a number—some fifteen or twenty—of the most respectable citizens of Quitman and vicinity, have been arrested as ku-klux and carried to Tyler for investigation, on the affidavit of one M. Brock, a well-known scoundrel and scalawag, who has for sometime been trying to perpetuate a difficulty in that county. It is well known that some of the meanest thieves and murderers that ever lived make their homes between the Sabine and Lake Fork rivers in Wood County, but none of the citizens arrested on Brock's affidavit can be accused as being anything but quiet, peaceable men. This is the way with all such arrests; none but the peaceable Democrats are ever disturbed by such villainous scamps as the above named.[18]

Despite all the bitterness over prolonged Reconstruction, the young editor of the *News* advocated a constructive program. He admonished the people of Longview to assist Professor John T. Kennedy from Rusk County in his endeavors to establish a school. "Nothing," he wrote, "will do more to build up Longview and make it a desirable town to live in than good educational facilities."[19] For emphasis he added an item about a teachers' convention in Boston. He believed it significant that Professor Agassiz of Harvard, the famous naturalist, had said that in public education "too much was made of the memory and too little of the mind."[20] Hogg sought ways to assure a substantial growth of Longview. He emphasized that the making of

... a single plow, wagon, scraper, broom, or any other article the increasing population may need, is a great gain for us. Let us encourage those who come among us with a view to manufacturing, it matters not how insignificant the article they propose to manufacture, so it has utility.

This is the age of energy, progress and vigor, and if we will develop our own resources, build up institutions of learning, churches, and manufactories, Longview must continue to grow more rapidly than it has ever done, and will astonish in its strides to greatness, even its best friends.[21]

Before James Hogg was twenty-one he had become a man. He had

[18] Longview *News*, December 7, 1871.
[19] *Ibid.*, December 12, 1871.
[20] *Ibid.*, December 9, 1871.
[21] *Ibid.*, December 15, 1871.

59

matured during the worst of the Reconstruction years, retaining a sense of humor and building a pungent vocabulary that adequately expressed his thoughts.

The November 21 issue of the *News* carried an interesting item, especially significant as an insight into the thinking of the editor on the increasingly important subject of local bounties to railroads. A bill was before the legislature to grant a charter for the Tyler Tap Railroad, a short connecting line to Palestine; Hogg noted that the Tyler *Reporter* declared that Smith County was ready to do anything reasonable to get the line but should be prepared for being left out in the cold. Hogg showed his hand:

Of course, Mr. Reporter, there is no "harm" in securing all the railroads in your power, that's to your interest; but be sure not to get so excited and liberal as the green horn did when he first saw a steamboat, and offer all you are worth to get them.[22]

He went on to express his view that railroads were mechanical things and would be useful or detrimental depending upon the type of men who managed them.

With the *News* prospering, James was quite content in Longview. But certain people in Quitman who had read his editorials on railroads had another idea for him. Wood County residents who opposed a bond subsidy to the Texas and Pacific Railway felt they needed a newspaper to express their views. Two routes had been surveyed along the proposed expansion from Longview to Dallas, and the Texas and Pacific Railroad was stalling on building westward from Longview, hoping to play off the factions and obtain $100,000 from county bonds. It was possible that Smith County might vote a bond issue and swing the line as far south as Tyler, while other counties and towns along the routes to Dallas were also being pressured to make generous grants. Captain W. M. Giles, as spokesman for the group that opposed the bond subsidy, came to Longview offering inducements to Hogg to relocate his paper.

Hogg for some time had been considering enlargement of the *News*, and to this end had looked over the plant of the Marshall *Reporter*, owned by J. M. Kennedy, who had been having difficulty with the federal authorities and had decided to go out of business. After the Quitman invitation Jim bought Kennedy's press and type for about four hundred dollars; the extra equipment would enable him to print a bigger paper, doubling the number of columns from three to six. Then

[22] *Ibid.,* November 21, 1871.

Captain Giles sent his wagon to aid in the move. A "cub" on the *Reporter,* W. A. Adair, helped Jim load the machinery and just after daylight on Christmas morning watched the loaded wagon disappear over the hill as Jim headed for Longview to pick up his personal belongings.[23] Early in 1872 the Quitman *News* was established.

Friends from his former days in Quitman noted that the boy had turned into a man, but found his youthful spirit and fun-loving disposition unchanged. His self-assurance and ease of expression impressed both old and new friends, and his courtesy and personal charm made him a welcome guest in many homes. He said that he intended to make Quitman his home from now on, and to intimates he confided his purpose to continue his study of the law.

James Hogg was in earnest as he set out to combat the forces which wished to saddle the county with a large railroad bond issue. He knew that the Texas and Pacific Company had to build one hundred miles of its line in two years, and that the more direct routes to Dallas ought to bring the railroad across Wood County.[24] Therefore, he argued, the company would not run the risk of losing the charter, bond issue or no, and the people could afford to await developments. The graphic articles in the *News* found a wide reading public, and business enterprises, which expected to have to pay much of the tax burden, joined with the farmers in supporting the stand taken by the new paper. James Hogg was not opposing railroad construction, but he was warning, as he had done earlier in Longview, that railroads could cost a community too much if it was not alert to the dangers of exploitation.

During the debate significant developments took place in Austin and Washington, D.C. The Texas legislature authorized the Texas and Pacific Railroad to purchase the Southern Pacific and Southern Transcontinental companies, but withdrew the ten-thousand-dollar-a-mile subsidy in lieu of land grants. This eliminated potential competition between the parallel lines projected between Texarkana and Dallas. The Grange movement was approaching a peak membership, reflecting the increase of depressed conditions among the farmers, and the Grangers of North Texas did not overlook this flagrant violation of their appeal to maintain competition and to weaken, not encourage, the forces of

[23] George W. Bailey, "James Stephen Hogg" (typescript), p. 60.

[24] *Texas Almanac, 1871* (Galveston, Richardson and Company, 1871), pp. 176–183. Congressman John H. Reagan had shown his interest in protecting stockholders against irresponsible management of the Texas Pacific Railroad project on the eve of secession. See Walter F. McCaleb (ed.), *Memoirs of John H. Reagan,* pp. 78–80.

61

monopoly that did nothing to satisfy their need for better transportation at reasonable rates.

Congress re-entered the picture on May 2, 1872, to name the combined lines the Texas and Pacific Railroad Company. The following clause was calculated to impose restraints upon any hostile state legislature:

The Texas and Pacific Railroad Company shall be and is hereby declared to be a military and post road; and for the purpose of insuring and carrying the mails and troops, munitions of war, supplies and stores of the United States, no act of the Company nor any law of any state shall impede, delay or prevent said Company from performing its obligation to the United States.[25]

The railroad, which had preferred the subsidy of ten thousand dollars per mile to the award of sixteen to twenty sections of land for each mile, protested the legality of the change. Congress provided a way out by permitting the issuance of bonds up to forty thousand dollars per mile, plus a total stock of $50 million. General Grenville M. Dodge was appointed Chief Engineer at twenty thousand dollars per year, and by August 6, 1872, the California and Texas Construction Company was ready to build the line west from Longview.[26]

Due to popular feeling that the railroads were extravagant in their demands and that they had engineered a consolidation through the Davis Republican regime, the bond issue was rejected. Then, to the disappointment of the young editor and his friends north of and in Quitman, it was learned that the Texas and Pacific would not go through the county seat but across the southern part of the county and through Mineola. Nevertheless, both James and the Quitman community prospered during the rest of 1872 and in 1873 until the depression hit.

Editorially, the *News* continued to oppose the Davis regime, applauding meanwhile the efforts of the Liberal Republicans in the North and the union, in Texas, of Moderate Republicans and Democrats that were increasing the hope of an ultimate redemption from corruption, graft, and political demoralization in both North and South. The *News* also made no compromise with local lawlessness, corruption, oppression, or extravagance. Its editor, though busy with these social and political problems, somehow found time also to study law.

[25] The charter is quoted in Reed, *Texas Railroads*, p. 361.
[26] *Ibid.*, pp. 361–362.

One day in 1873 James proudly presented Martha Frances with a new book, *The Fate of Marvin,* by Thomas E. Hogg.[27] This long epic of the Civil War was especially significant in being one of the first stories to treat the conflict with candor and yet make for better feeling between recent foes. Considering the bitterness Thomas had expressed earlier in his poem, "The Soldier's Grave," which dealt with the desecration of their father's grave at Corinth, the book was even more significant—an early landmark along the road to reunion.

During 1873, "Jas. S. Hogg, Proprietor" issued forty-five editions of the weekly *News,* "Devoted to the Interests of Texas."[28] To maintain the editorial standard James had set for himself in the six-column, four-page paper (measuring twenty-five by fifteen inches) demanded long hours of work. Still persisting in his wish to become a lawyer, he studied whenever he could, but progress was slow. However, his good friend and adviser, Captain Giles, frequently spent an evening helping him with his studies, and Martha Frances, as always, urged him not to be discouraged, often reminding him that his father did not complete his legal training until the age of twenty-five.

When Richard Coke of Waco and Richard Hubbard of Tyler campaigned against Governor Davis in the fall of 1873, James Hogg decided to run for justice of the peace in Precinct No. 1. This was an important civil office at the time, because the county justices made up the commissioners' court and the justice for Precinct No. 1 became the chief justice, ex officio; in effect, he was responsible for many duties that now belong to a county judge. Wood County was in debt, the roads were bad, taxes were high, and scrip was discounted almost 75 per cent.[29] Lawlessness was on the increase. The main handicaps James faced were his youth and inexperience, but all who knew him testified to his courage. He pledged to improve the county's finances and the roads, and to try to restore parity of the scrip; he asked for the support of all honest, law-abiding citizens. To the surprise of many who had urged him to stay

[27] Thomas E. Hogg, *The Fate of Marvin* (Houston, E. H. Cushing, 1873). Cf. Thomas N. Page's *Red Rock* (New York, Scribner's, 1898) and "Meh Lady" (1893); Paul Buck's *The Road to Reunion, 1865–1900* (Boston, Little, Brown and Company, 1937).

[28] Quitman *News,* January 10, 1874.

[29] Property valuation in Texas had dropped from $365 million in 1860 to $159 million in 1870, while the taxes doubled from $533,000 to $1,129,577, according to the 1870 Census quoted by *Texas Almanac,* 1873, pp. 55–56; Cotner (ed.), *Addresses of James Hogg,* pp. 64–65.

out of the race, he won on his platform of law and order and honest finances, sharing in the honors of the general election in December in which Richard Coke had won the governorship and which brought about the downfall of the Radicals in Texas.

The Christmas social season in Quitman was an especially happy one, and twenty-two-year-old Editor and Justice-elect James S. Hogg was a welcome guest at many parties. To describe these events in the *News* he used a whole column, so that the worthies might see their names in print and so that he could express adequately his own sincere appreciation for thoroughly enjoyable times in the many homes which had graciously opened their doors to the young people. The column began, "The old and young, gay and grave, threw off all cares for the time, and joined each other in the pleasures and merry-making of the holiday,"[30] and then went on to describe the "pleasures" in detail. On the Thursday before Christmas, Professor Hart's students had given an interesting "exhibition." Miss Mollie Patton entertained with a concert on Friday, followed by a dance. Mr. and Mrs. Good opened their hotel to the young people on Monday, and Captain and Mrs. Trout gave a party "until a reasonably late hour" on Wednesday. Christmas morning the young people "coupled off" by seven o'clock and went "a-calling." Some twenty couples were "on the war path" determined "to war to the bottom of many a glass of eggnog." When a young blade would crook his elbow "a-kim-bo and a lump of blessing swung thereunto," the couple would proceed to visit other friends. The couples gathered at Dr. Patton's at nine, enjoying conversation, music, and eggnog until twelve, when they moved to the house of Captain Giles, where dinner was served—"an extravagant collation." They disbanded for the afternoon to meet again at Dr. Patton's in the evening:

And sure enough they did unite in the handsome and capacious parlor of that good friend of the young folks, and a more brilliant galaxy of beauty was never seen in Quitman. The evening was passed off gaily, and the magnificent supper was enjoyed by every one. Though not in great humor for eating, after the day's "proceedings," the dainty and delicious sweetmeats in great variety that were tempting the company could not be resisted . . . May our young friends, ladies and gentlemen, and the good old folks who joined us in merry-making live long and ever enjoy themselves as we know they did this Christmas, is the wish of the happy writer.[31]

On Sunday the editor had been in his usual place at church; the column

[30] Quitman *News*, January 10, 1874.   [31] *Ibid.*

64

congratulated the Reverend Mr. Pender on his "well-timed and pointed sermons."[32]

With the coming of 1874, James rejoiced to see the friends of his father returning to power. The election had, it is true, been accompanied by fraud and intimidation on both sides, and when Governor Davis refused to relinquish his office rioting broke out. Both sides assembled armed men in Austin, while George Clark, one of Coke's campaign managers, tried to obtain from Governor Davis a promise of peaceful withdrawal. The situation was tense, as President Grant's reply to Davis' appeal for the support of federal troops was awaited. Governor Coke installed himself on the second-floor of the Capitol, while Davis held control of offices on the first floor. On January 17, the arrival of Grant's telegraphed decision not to support Davis with troops marked the end of nine years of Reconstruction.[33] Richard Coke was inaugurated, and before long Oran Milo Roberts left his law school in Gilmer to become chief justice of the Texas Supreme Court. John H. Reagan would take a seat in the U.S. Congress in 1875.

The Democrats' long-sought day of deliverance seemed almost at hand, but problems to be faced did not cease to present themselves. In the late fall of 1873, following the financial panic in New York, the Texas and Pacific had suspended construction on the railway. The first issue of the *News* for 1874 carried local evidence that the country had started on the course of a long depression: a wholesale grocer announced that he gave credit no more, and a large lumber company found it difficult to dispose of surpluses for cash.

In January, 1874, Justice of the Peace Hogg presided over the commissioners' court. His campaign promises were carried out to the best of his ability; rigid economy was practiced, leaks being stopped where funds hitherto had been wasted. Within a short time it became apparent that Wood County bonds might eventually reach par, and by the end of 1874 they were quoted at 50 cents on the dollar. To retire some of the debt and to make tax collection easier, it was ordered that a percentage of old scrip would be received for taxes at par—a shrewd device to further restore confidence in the county's ability to pay. The floating debt was gradually reduced despite the depression; by the end of the second year of James' administration it was paid off, and county scrip was receivable at par. The tax rate was also reduced from 75 cents per one-

[32] *Ibid.*
[33] Grant wired Davis that it would "be prudent as well as right" to accept the popular demand. Quoted in Richardson, *Texas,* p. 284.

hundred-dollar valuation to 25 cents, which was a record few counties could equal.[34] Even with these reductions the roads had been improved, since under the Radicals the road tax was looked upon as a form of oppression, and therefore often resisted.

When it came to dealing with the lawless element Hogg's job was more difficult. A number of influential citizens had grown careless about abiding by local ordinances, especially those statutes they found personally irksome—such as the Sabbath laws. Saloons persisted in keeping open on Sundays. Drunkenness and gambling were common, reaching their peak on Saturday afternoons and nights, with a general fight a frequent climax. Nevertheless, James Hogg let it be known that he played no favorites and that all laws would be enforced until repealed.

Since it was then the rule, rather than the exception, for men of affairs to drink in public and to cultivate the habit of buying a prospective voter a drink, saloons had acquired a special political significance. Jim Hogg was not a total abstainer and did not set himself up as a mentor of personal morals, but he avoided (as he always had) too frequent association with those who made a habit of drinking in public places. The Quitman saloonkeepers were extremely unhappy over the fines imposed for being open on Sunday, and some of his friends thought that young James took his new responsibility too seriously, warning him that he would not go far in politics if he did not change his ways.

However, he did not deviate from what he considered to be his duty. He notified the peace officers in his district that he intended to enforce the law impartially and on all occasions. Certain prominent citizens were surprised and chagrined to be fined for offenses that had been generally overlooked in earlier days. Instead of "a dollar and costs," the fines were graduated with the number of offenses, and more than a few county expenses were paid by this new money coming into the treasury. The process had a personal meaning for Jim Hogg, as well: as able lawyers came to defend some of those fined, he realized how much he needed the license to practice law and especially the knowledge the license would represent.

Meanwhile the *News* had not desisted from the attack on Grantism. On January 10, 1874, the middle of its front page was given over to a story from the Chicago *Times* which decried Grant's latest message urging government aid as impractical and paternalistic and holding up to

---

[34] James S. Hogg, Address at Rusk, Texas, April 19, 1890, quoted in Cotner (ed.), *Addresses of James S. Hogg*, p. 65.

scorn, as fit only for people living in the new German Empire, its recommendations. These included:

1. Postal telegraph
2. Postal saving banks
3. National university
4. Purchase of existing canals
5. Canal in the Rocky Mountains for irrigation
6. Residences in Washington for Cabinet members
7. Residences in Washington built by States for Senators
8. Making greenbacks as good as gold by legislation
9. That the nation divide the bankruptcy of the District of Columbia and pay its debt.
10. To give the Mennonites, a sect of Russia, special land-grant privileges for doing us the favor of coming to the United States.

* * * *

The worst of it all is that Mr. Grant is actually unconscious of the fact that this government is a democracy which has no right to do for the people anything they can do for themselves. . . . The national government shall do nothing which the people as individuals, or the States as units, can do for themselves.[35]

To emphasize this "do for themselves" doctrine, which the Democrats had adopted during the depression, Hogg added an example of self-help from a Georgia report, to the effect that the Grangers would plant only one-third of their crop area in cotton and buy nothing on credit.

The January 10 issue also denounced corruption in Democratic Tammany Hall. It was fitting, Hogg wrote, that William M. Tweed, ex-boss of the New York political ring, should be in prison; however, the editor looked forward to reading Tweed's autobiography, because he expected it to be a startling revelation of hundreds of supposedly "strait-laced proper acting people" in their true light, from which the world at large would obtain a clearer insight into the inner workings of a gigantic political ring.[36]

With all his professional activities, Jim Hogg had little time for personal affairs. Yet he had somehow found time to make trips now and then fourteen miles to the east of Quitman to call on vivacious little Sallie Stinson, who had made a deep impression on him when he first met her in 1869 at Mr. Baggett's school. The visits were given a minimum of encouragement by Sallie's father, Colonel Stinson. In fact, Jim

[35] Quitman *News,* January 10, 1874.   [36] *Ibid.*

may have figured that the infrequency of advertisements in the *News* for the Stinson sawmill near Big Sandy River was due to the Colonel's reluctance to provide Jim with the excuse of coming to the house to collect for the ads. In any case, Stinson had made it clear that he did not want Sallie distracted while she was attending Professor Looney's school in Gilmer.

In the early spring of 1874, James requested Colonel James Stinson's permission to marry his daughter.[37] Stinson was a prosperous, respected, and kindly man. He had enclosed his sawmill machinery, so that his workers were protected from the cold. By virtue of his extensive farm and timber holdings and his interest in scientific farming he was a leader among the Grangers. At times he served as a Methodist preacher. He had nothing against the tall young justice, but he wanted to be sure his daughter would be well provided for; after all, Hogg had only recently entered politics and was not yet prepared to practice law. True, the newspaper had done well, but the Colonel felt it was risky business to start a home during a national depression. He asked James to wait. At this point Sallie entered the room and announced that she loved Jim and wanted to marry him very soon. The Colonel's opposition melted, and it was agreed that the wedding would take place on April 22, 1874.

Sallie and Mrs. Stinson then began busying themselves with the trousseau. Their good neighbors, the Gunstreams, offered the services of their newly acquired sewing machine, the only one in the county. Daily, mother and daughter worked happily at the Gunstreams' house, turning out garments of the high standard Sallie had always set for herself.[38]

April is usually a rainy month along the ridge in North Texas. The April of 1874 was no exception—except in being more rainy than usual. On the twenty-second James made the fourteen miles to the Stinson home with some difficulty, but the Methodist minister who was to officiate bogged down in the mud and water. Word was sent to the Baptist minister, Pressly Davis, who, after fighting his way across the raging, swirling Big Sandy, arrived amidst a new downpour. To this day, the

[37] Sarah Ann Hogg Fol., H.C. In the Genealogy Folder is a letter from Colonel Stinson to his daughter, dated August 27, 1894, in which he states that his great-great-grandfather was an earl, at Donegal, Ireland, until his actions in the Ocenur Insurrection cost him his lands and title. His grandfather, Alexander Johnston, was a brother of Governor Gabriel Johnston of North Carolina. Alexander was a patriot, and changed the name to Johnson. Sarah Ann's grandmother was a daughter of Isaac Moorland of Jasper County, Georgia, and she married a West, who was active in the Georgia Legislature before 1860.

[38] Pictures of Miss Stinson show that she was meticulous about her clothes and other aspects of her appearance.

natives point out "Press Davis Crossing." The ceremony had to wait still longer until Mr. Davis could be dried out, but finally Jim and Sallie were pronounced man and wife. The usual country merrymaking continued well into the night, and then, as it was not safe in the darkness to try to go to Mineola, Gilmer, or Quitman, the entire wedding party spent the night with the Stinsons.[39]

The small four-room house on the Gilmer road into which Mr. and Mrs. James S. Hogg moved may have seemed a little cramped to Sallie, but it was full of happiness, because it was their own.[40] All of Jim's friends were soon Sallie's friends, and the house often rang with the laughter of young couples who drove out to call. The justiceship, the newspaper, and the study of law made a long day for James, but he found time to chop his own wood and cut rails to enclose a large garden. Through the summer months Sallie dried corn and preserved fruits and vegetables for the winter, often going to her old home to take advantage of the better equipment and her mother's help. Mrs. Stinson's advice was wanted on another matter, too, during that summer and fall; Sallie was pregnant, and on January 31, 1875, a son was born to the James S. Hoggs. He was named William Clifford.

To Jim the joyful prospect of becoming a father had been another incentive for hastening the day when he might practice law. He now wanted very much the greater financial security that admittance to the bar ought to provide. Further, although he had been successful as justice of the peace, in many of the cases that came before him he had realized how much he needed the authority and the full knowledge of legal intricacies that completing his studies would afford him.

However, the office itself had been in a sense a legal education, developing to a keen point his sense of justice; it had also brought him admiration from those who noted his determination to see that the law was enforced and that justice was rendered to all who entered his court. A case that illustrated his great desire to make fair decisions—and that also made for him a great many friends among the working people—had to do with the plebeian matter of the size and amount to be paid for digging a ditch. An Irishman named Tom Riley, at a slack time in his regular job as a railroad worker, had dug a ditch for John Baldwin,

[39] The Stinson home was standing in 1947. One wing of the second story was one large room, suitable for entertainments, and for religious or Grange meetings.

[40] This home was moved to the State Park at Quitman. Miss Ima Hogg refurnished the home, and on March 23, 1952, a formal opening was held, at which time she and Railroad Commission Chairman Ernest O. Thompson were the principal speakers.

who later refused to pay him on the grounds that the ditch was not dug according to contract specifications. The case was being tried without a jury, and Justice Hogg was worried by the contradictory testimony. At the noon recess he borrowed a horse, rode out to the ditch to make his own examination, and decided the specifications had been met.[41] Returning to the bench, he promptly rendered a verdict in favor of Riley.

Despite numerous such admired decisions, James Hogg himself had grown increasingly aware of the disadvantage of not being a practicing lawyer. An outstanding example was a case involving a charge of breach of the peace, in which the county attorney failed to appear to prosecute. The defendant, a man of intelligence, had the benefit of an able attorney, L. Z. Wright.[42] Hogg examined and cross-questioned the witnesses in order to bring out the facts for the jury. Convinced of the defendant's guilt, he then consulted privately with friends as to the propriety of his directly addressing the jury; getting a favorable opinion from them, he proceeded to speak to the jury and to strongly rebuke the defendant. Attorney Wright cannily seized the advantage thus open to him: upbraiding Hogg for assuming the role of judge and prosecutor both, he made the justified plea that the court was prejudiced and a fair trial had not been given. The jury forthwith acquitted the defendant.

This was a lesson never to be forgotten. During the first few months of his son's life, James Hogg completed his studies and stood the bar examination. At the spring term of court, 1875, he was admitted to practice.

The past year had been his happiest since his boyhood. Texas, with the departure of the Radical Republicans, had regained majority rule; and Hogg had been able to carry out his campaign promises to improve services and lower taxes, and thus to justify the encouraging trust his community had reposed in him despite his youth. He had forced dispensers of kerosene or whiskey to provide full liquid measure rather than a short quart. Today in Wood County the natives still refer to a standard legal measure as a "Jim Hogg Quart." And he had finally fulfilled the dream of becoming a lawyer. Above all, his marriage had brought him a joyous reciprocal love and companionship and had satisfied two of his deepest needs—a focus for tenderness and, after the years of restless moving about, a home.

[41] Personal interview with Dr. S. Cloud Noble, dentist of Mineola, in June, 1948.
[42] L. Z. Wright was a brother of Dr. Wright, for whom James had labored in 1869 with unsatisfactory financial return.

CHAPTER IV

County and District Attorney, 1876–1886

WHEN THE CONSTITUTIONAL CONVENTION began its deliberations in Austin on September 6, 1875, it became the center of James Hogg's attention, particularly in regard to the policies it would set for the Texas judiciary. John H. Reagan, as chairman of the Judiciary Committee, advocated enlarged jurisdiction of the lower courts, fewer officials, longer terms, and higher salaries, but the strong economy trend of the Convention eventually defeated him on all these points.[1] An "Address" to the people, which was authorized by the Convention and signed by Reagan, attempted to explain the substance of the controversy and admitted that these questions had furnished the delegates with their "most difficult problems." When the Constitution of 1876 (sometimes called "the Granger Constitution," because forty of the ninety Convention delegates had been Grange members) was submitted to the people on February 15, 1876, many of its measures aroused dissatisfaction, but none more so than those dealing with the reorganization of the judiciary.[2] A Court of Appeals of three members had been added, to relieve the burdened State Supreme Court, but many of the other measures reflected the retrenchment mood, that was probably in part due to reaction from the excesses of the Reconstruction period and the distrusted Constitution of 1869. Membership of the Supreme Court was reduced from five to three, the number of district judges from forty to twenty-six, of district attorneys from thirty-eight to ten. The annual salary of a district attorney was cut from twelve hundred dollars to five hundred dollars; county attorneys would be paid on a fee basis. It was hoped that

---

[1] Walter F. McCaleb (ed.), *Memoirs of John H. Reagan*, pp. 241–242.
[2] Ernest W. Winkler (ed.), *Platforms of Political Parties in Texas*, Bulletin of the University of Texas, No. 53 (Austin, University of Texas Press, 1916), p. 169. The official Democratic Party organ, the Austin *Democratic Statesman*, January 5, 1876, maintained that the proposed constitution "was the worst constitution ever submitted to the vote of a free people." See also Seth S. McKay, *Seven Decades of the Texas Constitution of 1876* (Lubbock, Texas Tech Press, 1942), pp. 134 ff.

the reduction of personnel and salaries would cut the expense of the judiciary in half.[3]

For a time James Hogg had pondered the idea of running for attorney of Wood County, but the financial insecurity of the fee system and the additional burdens that would now fall on county attorneys because of the reduction of district attorneyships made the office unappealing. Furthermore, the next legislature, whose duty it was to set the fees and perquisites for county officers, would very likely still be motivated by the Grangers' depression economy program. With a wife and son to support, he decided that he could not tolerate such uncertainty.

He well understood the causes and the need for the retrenchment program the farmers were pushing so staunchly, and his record on the Commissioners' Board testified to his own deep interest in eliminating waste to relieve the taxpayers' load. Nevertheless, he deplored the serious weaknesses of the Constitution's judiciary article and believed that they should be corrected by the legislature, for he was convinced by Reagan and his own experience that the uncertainties of the fee system would deter well-qualified men from becoming public attorneys or justices. He knew that lawyers throughout the state were discouraged and that in some localities the office of county attorney would lack even a single candidate; as for justices, a few words penned in his Criminal Docket Book indicated how he felt the fee system would apply:

To be paid when the State of Texas becomes financially able to stand it and generous enough to award it.[4]

Since some redress of the situation by the next legislature seemed the only solution, Hogg began thinking about entering the 1876 race as a candidate for one of the two legislative seats from the Twenty-second District. If he won, he could help to swell the collective voice of those who wanted changes made in the judiciary article. The financial inducement of the office was small, the Constitutional Convention having reduced the pay of legislators from eight dollars to five dollars a day, but Hogg considered that the campaign itself offered certain intangible benefits, not least among them the opportunity to broaden his acquaintanceship with citizens of the district's counties to the west, Rains, Van Zandt, and Kaufman.

[3] The estimated current expense of $1,600,000 is itemized in Winkler, *Platforms,* pp. 170–171.
[4] Criminal Docket Book, 1873–1876, Justice of the Peace, Precinct No. I, Wood County, February 23, 1876, p. 285. Original in H. C.

When Hogg declared as a candidate he found himself arrayed not only against General John S. Griffith and T. J. Towles of Van Zandt County but also L. Z. Wright of Wood County, the able attorney who had rebuked the young justice for appearing as both judge and prosecutor in a breach-of-the-peace case. Wright's candidacy was apparently a surprise to James Hogg, and not a pleasant one, for the rivalry between the two men had been enhanced by a more recent legal contretemps.

Just prior to his announcement for the legislature, Justice Hogg had heard the case of *The State of Texas* v. *L. Z. Wright* on a charge of "carrying unlawfully a pistol on or about his person."[5] Wright had waived arrest and appeared in court, with two attorneys for his defense. The record reads that the jury heard "the evidence, the law, and the argument of counsel and rendered the following verdict:"[6]—and thereupon the remaining half of the record book page is blank. What happened next is therefore not known, but, whether or not Wright was found guilty and hence obliged to pay the twenty-five-dollar fine customary in Hogg's court (set purposefully high to discourage repetitions of such violations of the law), it can be assumed that Hogg, as always in his determination to maintain law and order in the community, would have made no concession to the defendant's influence and social status, and that a mere appearance before the young justice, whom Wright already considered overzealous, would have been galling in itself.

Wood County's remarkable financial recovery during Hogg's term as justice of the peace furnished a sound basis for his campaign: at the close of his administration the county was entirely out from under the former indebtedness of twenty thousand dollars, scrip was discounted at only 25 cents on the dollar, and the tax levy that fell so heavily on farmers had been reduced from 75 cents per-one-hundred-dollar valuation to 25 cents.[7] It was an excellent record, and one that should appeal especially to the retrenchment mood of Grangers and others. Hogg's friends felt the young man deserved the undivided support of his home county, since its fiscal soundness was now the envy of surrounding counties.

Hogg realized, however, that he must campaign with special diligence in Kaufman County, which had been General Griffith's home for fifteen years before he moved to Terrell in Van Zandt County (pop. 11,620) and from which he had served with distinction in the Tenth Texas Leg-

---

[5] *Ibid.*, p. 179.   [6] *Ibid.*
[7] Dallas *News,* August 19, 1886.

islature. If Hogg could run a close second in populous Kaufman (pop. 13,616) this might offset the divided vote in Griffith's own county. The General accepted the young Justice's invitation to debate land and railroad issues, with the result that many more citizens of the district became aware of James Hogg's ability, zeal, and clear-headedness.

The divided vote in Wood County (pop. 11,000) proved too much of a handicap. General Griffith and Towles won the seats, although James Hogg came within 100 votes of the total needed. The defeat, which was to be the only one of his political career, was explained by Judge V. B. Harris thus: "Our district, at that time, was composed of several counties, and he was not so well acquainted with voters in some of the counties as he was in his own county."[8] Although not mentioned by Judge Harris, the local rivalry between L. Z. Wright and Hogg appears, from other records, actually to have been responsible for the defeat.

James Hogg seemed undaunted, possibly because he had known from the beginning that the chances were slim for a young man, even with so excellent a record as his, to triumph over more seasoned opponents, especially in his maiden political venture outside of his own county. Deciding not to return to newspaper work, he began at once to make plans, in his year-old role as a practicing attorney, for touring the precinct courts and district sessions—ready for clients. He had once written in the Longview *News*, "Hardship is the native soil of manhood and self-reliance. He who cannot abide the storm without flinching lies down by the wayside to be overlooked or forgotten."[9] His intention now was not to lie "down by the wayside" but to proceed with his vigorous enjoyment of life—whether working in his garden, trying a case, studying the deeper intricacies of the law, pondering the meaning of current events, or seeing old friends and making new ones.

Deepest of all was the continuing joy he found in his beloved Sallie and his son Will, for whom he was determined to provide comfort and security. His happiness in his new home was the greater because of his boyhood deprivations, and throughout his life his family was to be the source and focus of his deepest satisfactions. In a letter written to his school friend E. C. Dickinson of Rusk, just three days after the elections, he expressed his proud pleasure in young Will:

[8] V. B. Harris, "James Stephen Hogg" (typescript), H. C. See also Homer L. Kerr, "Migration into Texas, 1861–1880" (Ph.D. thesis, the University of Texas, 1953), Maps 3 and 5, pp. 118–122.
[9] Longview *News*, December 19, 1871.

My boy is walking and prattling, which, you know Ellie, makes me feel proud. Everybody says the little fellow is an improvement on the *old stock!* They allude to his *daddy,* when they make use of such expressions. . . . Let me hear from you soon, in regard to affairs in general—socially, politically, religiously, etc.[10]

The letter went on to discuss the sale of the remaining lands at "Mountain Home," and Dickinson was asked not to forget to "reserve the family grave-yard." Apparently Tom, John, and James had recently decided that it was unlikely any of them would live in Rusk again and therefore they would be unwise to try longer to manage what was left of "Mountain Home" from a distance. James also noted his gratification that Tom, who had moved to Denton County in 1873 and there published the Denton *Monitor,* had been successful in his campaign for the county judgeship. Nowhere in the letter was there a sign that its writer was brooding over his defeat in his own campaign.

Somewhere in the life story of every public figure can be found an event of seeming insignificance that is proved by passing time to have been a piece of great good fortune. For several reasons James Hogg's failure to win a legislative seat in 1876 was such an event. To begin with, the five-dollar-a-day representative's allowance was scarcely a living and certainly enabled a man to save nothing; whereas before long Hogg's determination to put his fledgling wings as a lawyer to good use would improve his financial situation beyond anything he had known since he was a small boy. His persistent travels in his buggy to the courts of the precinct and district began to yield him clients from the first, and soon the calculated regularity of his visits led him to be expected, so that men in need of an attorney would plan ahead to retain him when he arrived.

More important, had his attention been centered during the two years following the election on his duties in the legislature, when a young man is pressured unmercifully by the powerful lobbies, it is possible that his talent for self-education would have had far more restricted scope than was furnished by his itinerant law practice. As a young lawyer he had opportunity for knowing and understanding the problems of the "plain people," who later would be his constituents. With the growth of his practice he was continually adding to his knowledge of both the theory of law and its intricacies when applied to the vagaries of human beings; he was discovering what every man practicing law must discover before he can be truly termed a good lawyer—that justice is not an abstraction,

[10] James S. Hogg to Ellie Dickinson, February 18, 1876. Original in Fam. Let.

but a warm, living ideal that may assume as many protean shapes as the situations in which it is dispensed, and yet must retain its purity and never lose its own essential form. He was also learning about politics lessons quite unknown during the 1876 campaign, and he was constantly extending his circle of friends and acquaintances. Outside events, too, during these two years were taking a turn for the better. The status into which the judiciary had been cast by the "Granger" Constitution was so obviously dismal that Governor Coke and, later, Governor Roberts felt obliged to take various steps to keep the court system from failing completely. As the situation was thus gradually alleviated, the outlook for public attorneys grew brighter; by 1879 a way had been provided to amend the fee system for county attorneys and to restore most of the district offices that had been cut back by the Constitution.

Attorney Hogg's practice kept on growing, and, with more money to spend, he was at last able to further his long-standing and serious desire to build a sound library as a basis for a continuing study of law and public events.[11] It was another piece of good fortune that he had begun his private practice at the time when residents of the northern counties were beginning to reap benefits from the resumption in 1877 of railroad construction, which had swelled depression-starved payrolls and put the sawmills back in business. With the revival of the railroads came an expansion of cotton production, which in its turn increased railroad freight revenue. The lawyers of the northern counties had their share of the returning prosperity, since increased commercial activity usually means an increase in litigation, but in 1877–1878 two other factors were also responsible for the remarkably sharp upturn in court actions.

The railroad era was ushering in technological problems that stimulated all manner of new litigation. For instance, Texas in its 1876 Constitution had followed Pennsylvania's example in declaring railroads to be common carriers and subject to regulation.[12] New legislation had also made it possible for an individual shipper to go to court and collect five hundred dollars for a freight overcharge, and lumbermen and farmers were learning that they could collect damages when railroads

[11] An inventory of his library and office furniture made in 1886 lists value and edition of his books. J. S. Hogg Fol.

[12] The Constitution of Texas, Article X, Section 2. McKay, *The Constitution of 1876*, p. 113; Solon J. Buck, *The Granger Movement* (Cambridge, Harvard University Press, 1913), pp. 200 ff.

failed to furnish a contracted number of cars soon enough to permit products to reach markets before a price drop.[13]

The second potent factor in the increase of court actions was the wave of depression-aggravated lawlessness, which had shown no sign of slackening even with the beginning of the business revival. In Wood County responsible citizens (including many Grangers, among whom was Hogg's father-in-law), thoroughly alarmed, were vociferous in their demand for stricter law enforcement, more determined pursuit of criminals, and greater punishments. As the talk began to center on the fact that a strong man was needed as attorney for the county, Jim Hogg's name was increasingly mentioned; his record, as justice of the peace, for enforcing the law firmly and impartially was still fresh in people's minds.

In 1878, when James Hogg campaigned for the office of county attorney, he was twenty-seven years old, an impressively erect six feet three, and weighed something over two hundred firm and muscular pounds. As he towered on a speaker's platform he was a figure to hold attention even before he opened his mouth; when he started to speak attention deepened, because most of his listeners found that they were believing every word he said, as he paid them the compliment, unusual for the time, of discussing local issues with directness and reasoned logic. The ringing slogan on which he campaigned—"Enforce the Law"— quickly became his established trade mark, but just as characteristic was the quick homespun wit with which he could answer the hecklers who were part and parcel of the rough-and-tumble politics of the era. The Grangers, seeking a better material and moral life for their families, found Jim Hogg to their liking and gave him their support.

Captain Hogg (he had kept up his militia duty) became a delegate to the Democratic State Convention to be held in Austin. He and Colonel Stinson found that most of the Wood County people were inclined to agree with Worthy Master of the Texas Grange, W. W. Lang, that Governor Hubbard and Congressman J. W. Throckmorton, the major contenders for the office of governor, were too close to the railroad interests. The county delegates were instructed for Lang, and a district senatorial convention, which Hogg attended, drafted a resolution denouncing the policy of Hubbard in permitting convicts to work outside prison walls—whether as contract labor working for railroads or other-

---

[13] Texas *Senate Journal, Fifteenth Legislature (1876),* p. 284. This was Senate Bill 103.

wise. Newspaper articles during the summer warned that the so-called Granger cases, including *Munn* v. *Illinois* (1877), and the Texas "Granger" Constitution were forcing railroads to take more interest in state and local politics.

On the train to Austin, Hogg and Stinson discussed the Wood County resolutions urging free and unlimited coinage of silver, an experimental farm for the new Agricultural and Mechanical College, and federal aid for improving Galveston harbor. Jim Hogg was also the center of a group of eager listeners as he related how his brother, Judge Thomas Hogg, along with his brother-in-law, Attorney H. C. Ferguson, and cousins Will Davis and A. E. McMath, had once pressed Sam Bass so closely near Denton that he was forced to run, deserting a hot dinner then in preparation. The gambler and train and bank robber had found the region about Denton and Dallas too hot for him and was now on a long eastern swing via Terrell, heading southwest, but no one dreamed that he would be shot down near Round Rock while the convention was in session.

On July 16, Austin was a crowded town with almost 1,500 delegates trying to squeeze inside the unfinished Millet Opera House. As Hogg broadened his acquaintances, many older Democrats learned that he possessed the earnestness and directness of his father but was possessed of more humor. His short mustache and dark sideburns were in marked contrast to Colonel Stinson's full and greying beard. Horace Chilton and James Hogg stood out among the younger men with old and honorable names, obviously expecting to be ready to fill positions of trust in the future. As a neophyte in state conventions, Hogg was now primarily a keen observer and a voter. The Wood County delegation was a center of attention as one of seven groups instructed to vote for "Granger" Lang. His delegations had a block of 105 votes, while there were some 333 instructed for Throckmorton and 337 for Hubbard, leaving 715 uninstructed. With Hubbard obviously on the defensive, Lang had a chance to gain votes by an appeal to the uninstructed delegates, but he became cautious when threatened with being ousted as a "Granger Party" candidate. Hogg observed that Democrat Lang was bluffed. He noted that Reagan, who was beginning his long fight in Congress for railroad regulation, appealed for unity. After three ballots Lang withdrew, and James Hogg became more active in the caucuses as Wood County votes shifted to Hubbard, of Smith County, rather than to Throckmorton. A deadlock ensued; Judge Thomas Jefferson Devine of San Antonio, who left the Supreme Court in 1875 to promote the extension of the International Railroad to Laredo, was put in nomination.

Hogg would not forget that Hubbard's chances for a second term were hurt by repeated charges of lax law enforcement, too many pardons, and too many convicts working outside of the penitentiary. The convention ran on to Sunday afternoon. Reagan's name was put in nomination, but he withdrew. Grangers did not want Hubbard in Congress, fearing he would not push railroad regulation. Oran M. Roberts was finally named the candidate. The ways of politics are devious, and young Hogg learned to distinguish the broad-gauged men from those who took the course of expediency. He was pleased that friends of his father were back in power in Texas and that Senator Richard Coke and Congressman Reagan were becoming influential in Washington.

On Election Day the residents of Wood County made it clear that they wanted Jim Hogg to be their county attorney. It was not an enviable office; in recent months several men in the course of capturing and prosecuting criminals had lost their lives. Hogg was unafraid, but he soon had reason to be cautious. Before the end of November there was a disastrous fire in the Quitman courthouse; many people believed that one or more of the region's notorious desperadoes, well aware of Hogg's unswerving determination to enforce law, had chosen this method of destroying court records.[14] Not deterred, the new county attorney and County Judge W. J. Jones, working in efficient harmony, were agreed on trying to keep the number of appeals to the minimum possible within the law, as one way of curbing the hitherto largely unhindered wave of law-flouting.

When Oran M. Roberts came to the governor's chair in 1879 he faced the crime problem with a realism that had been lacking in Richard Hubbard. In his message to the legislature, January 1879, Roberts firmly stated that the "amount and character of crime and civil wrong"[15] was entirely unprecedented all over the country. The Sixteenth Legislature responded by the formation and adoption of a new Code of Criminal Procedure. Among other provisions to improve the efficiency of law enforcement, the number of district attorneys was increased to twenty-two and a district attorney was authorized for the Seventh Dis-

---

[14] *Wood County Democrat* (Quitman), December 3, 1942.

[15] Inaugural Address, January 21, 1879. *Journal of the House of Representatives,* Sixteenth Legislature, 1 Session (1879), p. 107. Cf. Gov. Hubbard's January 14 address, *ibid.,* pp. 47–51; Oran M. Roberts, "The Political, Legislative, and Judicial History of Texas, 1845–1895," in Dudley G. Wooten *A Comprehensive History of Texas* (Dallas, W. G. Scarff, 1898), II, 233–238.

trict, which now included the counties of Wood, Gregg, Upshur, Van Zandt, Henderson, and Smith.

County Attorney Hogg noted with interest that certain types of litigation were transferred by the new act from county courts to district courts, and that district attorneys were to be paid more rewarding fees. After some reflection he decided to become a candidate at the next election for attorney of the Seventh District. He could count among his political assets the fact that he had lived in three counties in the district and had influential friends in the other three. He also had by this time no dearth of fortunate political connections, among them District Judge John C. Robertson, the father of his friend Sawnie Robertson, and Governor Roberts, who had been General Hogg's friend.

The Code was to take effect at once, and, since there would be no regular election until the fall of 1880, Governor Roberts named interim district attorneys. For the new Seventh District he chose Democrat Felix J. McCord, from the Republican stronghold of Longview.[16] Mc-Cord was a tall, slender young man, a native of Mississippi, who had worked on farms and in the sawmills of Upshur County from 1869 to 1872, his experience somewhat paralleling Hogg's early days in Wood and Smith counties. He had studied law in the office of Congressman David B. Culberson, father of the future Governor Charles A. Culberson. While a student, McCord met former Tennessean John M. Duncan, who had worked in the Nash Iron Works in Marion County during the Civil War. Later he labored as a brickmason to save money to study law. Between 1877 and 1879, the law firm of McCord and Duncan had built up a busy practice in Longview. James Hogg, both from his own observations and the accounts of others, knew that the interim district attorney was a man of high character and ability. He hoped that Mc-Cord would decide to return to his busy practice in Longview at the end of the interim appointment rather than run for the office in the regular election, for he would obviously be an exceptionally difficult opponent to beat.

Although the Democrats were no longer the "have-not party" in Texas, their statewide success in the 1880 election, especially in regard to local offices, was by no means assured. The Republicans were now more active than in 1878, and in the "black" counties of northeast

---

[16] His daughter, Miss Hallie McCord of Longview, supplied a picture and personal description. John H. Brown, *Indian Wars and Pioneers of Texas* (Austin, L. E. Daniell, c. 1891), pp. 586–587; Webb and Carroll (eds.), *Handbook of Texas*, I, 443.

Texas they had an established record of winning local seats. Further-more, the new Greenback Party was a question mark. The Greenback movement had started in Texas in 1876, when agents of the National Greenbackers Party, capitalizing on the agrarian unrest, stimulated the organization of local clubs. In March, 1878, the first Texas Greenback Convention was held in Austin, and the platform, advocating that green-back money be issued as full legal tender and plumping for general re-trenchment, was attractive enough in the 1878 elections to enable the Party to replace the Republicans as second in power to the Democrats.[17] However, now that improvement in economic conditions was notable enough to be graphically reflected on county tax rolls, it seemed likely that the Greenbacks would have lost much of their strength, but the Democrats were still not discounting the fight that lay ahead. In prep-aration for the struggle, Robert N. Stafford, a relative of Hogg's friend Ellie Dickinson, and J. B. Perry (both Democrats) were encouraged to launch the Quitman *Record*. James Hogg was especially interested in the venture, for he knew that it would assure him favorable publicity in his own campaign.

Felix McCord decided after all to run, and, as the contest for the Democratic nomination narrowed to McCord and Hogg, Smith County became the crucial area, since it was the most populous county in the Seventh District, numbering nearly twenty-two thousand people. Hogg, having learned in the State Convention at Austin the importance of lining up delegates early, showed up at the County Convention at Tyler with a majority of the delegates pledged to him, but the two-thirds rule still held. Most of the older Democratic politicians in Tyler, including W. S. Herndon and James Douglas, and some of the younger leaders, such as Thomas Bonner and the Finley brothers, were for McCord. Nevertheless, Horace Chilton, who had been active in the Smith County precinct meetings, along with bookseller R. B. Long and merchant H. M. Owens, had succeeded in getting a split delegation. Chilton later said:

The most animated political labor which I undertook in 1880 pertained to the nomination of James S. Hogg for District Attorney. The office itself was not so commanding but in its wake came very far-reaching conse-quences. I had first met Hogg in 1870, when he was nearly 20 and I was nearly 17 years of age. We were printers, working on competitive papers in Tyler, but became friends. He had moved. . . . We had not been thrown

[17] Winkler, *Platforms,* p. 180; Rupert N. Richardson, *Texas,* pp. 322 ff.

together frequently, but our acquaintance had been kept up, and when he announced himself a candidate for District Attorney I was among the first to champion his cause. Smith County was pivotal in the district. If Hogg lost it entirely his chances were gone but if he could divide the vote half and half, he would go into the district convention with a majority. It looked at first as if his opponent, Felix J. McCord, would carry Smith County. McCord was a worthy man and some of my best friends were supporting him. But I could not forget the days when Hogg and I were printer boys together and knew that he was as worthy of the distinction sought as any man in the District. I have never put forth more effort in any political contest than I did in this Hogg and McCord contest, and was opposed by such able workers as Webb Finley, afterwards a conspicuous political leader in Texas, and many others of skill and experience. When the Smith County Convention met it decided to divide its vote one-half each between Mc-Cord and Hogg and this insured Hogg's nomination and election.[18]

When the November returns were counted, Hogg had won by a twenty-six hundred majority, carrying his own county almost two to one in a three-cornered fight, and having a three-to-one victory in Van Zandt, Upshur, and Henderson counties. Smith and Gregg counties had given a slight majority to the Republican candidate, E. B. Ragland.[19] The people of the Seventh District in electing James Stephen Hogg to a position in which he could demonstrate his capacity had provided him with a challenge to which he was determined to give his best efforts. Within the next four years the new Seventh District would become distinguished in the judicial annals of Texas.

Reflecting on the problem of travel facilities to the seats of the six counties in the district, Hogg decided that the railroad junction town of Mineola offered the most convenient solution. From this point he could reach Tyler, Longview, Gilmer, and Athens by rail; Quitman would be only twelve miles by buggy or stage, and Canton about the same distance from the train stop at Grand Saline. Thus, although some weekends would necessarily be spent in Canton and Athens, he could be assured of being at home on the majority of Sundays. He found

[18] Horace Chilton to Ima Hogg, May 19, 1921, Interv. Fol.
[19] Official Returns, 1880, Sec. State Elec. Ret.:

County	Hogg	Ragland
Gregg	622	661
Smith	1,880	1,935
Henderson	1,008	333
Upshur	1,099	326
Van Zandt	1,452	599
Wood	1,042	647

a small white house west of town for sale—a large dogwood tree in the back yard being a main attraction—and the family was soon settled in it; his law office was established not far from it, on West Broad at Line Street.[20]

Mineola was a noisy railroad town, its main row of buildings still dominated by the first crudely constructed buildings, "generally made out of rude boxing plank," but with here and there a brick structure. Social life for Jim and Sallie Hogg was pleasant. Among their good friends were grocerman (later deputy sheriff) William (Bill) McDonald and his wife, the former Rhoda Isabel Carter, whom McDonald had met through Jim Hogg. In 1866, McDonald, aged sixteen, had been tried for treason by Union authorities; fortunate in having for his attorney David B. Culberson, he was acquitted. He was to become famous in the 1890's and later for his exploits as a Texas Ranger.[21] An especially meaningful friendship was that formed with Judge C. W. Raines, Princetonian, brilliant historian, and editor and owner of the Mineola *Hawkeye*.[22] Friends were particularly precious to James Hogg this autumn, because of his grief over the loss of his brother Tom. On a business trip to Dallas in connection with a railroad survey, Thomas Hogg had sickened with typhoid fever; he died on September 29, 1880.

One of the first cases the new district attorney brought before Judge Robertson was a carry-over charge in Canton against a doctor and a widow for the alleged poisoning of the deceased husband. The case was already famous beyond the district; during the three terms it had dragged on, Jerome Kearby of Dallas had been brought in as a prosecutor and General C. B. (Buck) Kilgore of Wills Point (soon to be a member of Congress) had taken part as defense counsel. When Hogg took up the prosecution, a new jury was formed from a sixty-man venire, unusual then in North Texas. Kilgore was now aided by new counsel, including W. B. Wynne and J. S. Spinks, men of wide experience; Hogg was assisted by Colonel D. W. Crow. Since charges of sending poison through the mails were involved, postmasters and a

[20] *Wood County Democrat* (Quitman), August 6, 1908 and October 29, 1936. During the Texas Centennial in 1936, Assistant Attorney General H. T. Faulk, Grady Puckett of the Mineola *Monitor*, F. A. Watts of Humble Oil and Refining Company, and Dr. S. Cloud Noble erected a marker at the site of the law office. J. W. McDugald to Ima Hogg, May 6, 1936, Ima Hogg Fol.

[21] Albert B. Paine, *Captain Bill McDonald, Texas Ranger* (New York, J. J. Little & Ives Co., 1909), pp. 31–32, 42; Walter P. Webb, *The Texas Rangers* (Boston, Houghton Mifflin Co., 1935), pp. 444, 558–60.

[22] Walter P. Webb and H. Bailey Carroll (eds.), *Handbook of Texas*, II, 431. Cadwell W. Raines published *Bibliography of Texas* (Austin, Gammel Book

handwriting expert were brought in to testify. Several doctors admitted being confused by the nature of the patient's illness for some time before his death. Hogg built his case on circumstantial evidence and skillful cross-examination, "pressing vigorously every point for the State." After several hours of deliberation the jury brought in a verdict of "murder in the first degree." For the first time in Texas history a woman was given a life sentence in the penitentiary.[23]

The reputation of Van Zandt County as a refuge for notorious bad-men had changed so little since 1869, when Jim Hogg had been shot there, that law-abiding citizens were almost a minority. A recent effort had been made to remedy the situation by improving the caliber of sheriff and clerk; however, as the Canton *Chronicle* had pointed out, the new incumbents "were all right in their respective stations," but needed also was "a hearty cooperation of judge and prosecutor in the fearless discharge of their duties to put Van Zandt in the right attitude before the world."[24] Desperadoes had gone largely unscathed, no matter what their crimes; no white man had ever been sentenced to be hanged in the county until the Hogg-Robertson team changed this dubious distinction by means of the case of Dan White, charged with shooting George Conquest.

The shooting had occurred in February, 1877, after which the grand jury had indicted D. C. White, transient and sometime cotton picker, for an assault on George Conquest with a shotgun charged with gun-powder and leaden bullets, "wilfully, feloniously and with malice afore-thought," shooting him in the back of the head so that he died from the wound.[25] The charge was murder. Conquest, of English extraction, was a peddler with a wagon and two mules, traveling for his health; White had been hired at Shreveport, Louisiana, to drive for him on the trip through Texas. Nothing was done about the indictment for some time. Finally a Van Zandt deputy sheriff, stirred to do his duty, asked good citizen Wentworth Manning for help. After obtaining a requisition from the governor of Texas, which was honored by the governor of

Company, 1896) and *Six Decades of Texas or Memoirs of Francis Richard Lubbock* (Austin, B. C. Jones Company, 1900). Personal interview with Mrs. Lillie (Stinson) Burkett at Winnsboro, Texas, June, 1946.

[23] Dallas *Daily Herald*, November 12, 1881, clipping in J. S. Hogg Scrapbook No. 2, H. C. p. 69; Dallas *News*, November 27, 1881; Minute Book, District Court, Van Zandt County (Texas), Vol. F, November Term, 1881.

[24] N.d., J. S. Hogg Scrapbook No. 2, p. 67.

[25] The *State* v. *D. C. White*, Van Zandt County Case No. 1465, as quoted in Wentworth Manning, *Some History of Van Zandt County* (Des Moines, Homestead Company, 1919), I, 204 ff.

Louisiana, Manning went along to Minden, near Shreveport, to help arrest White; on arrival there the sheriff became so sick from nervousness that Manning, with the aid of a local deputy, had to bring White in. To Jim Hogg, it was obvious that good and fearless citizens like Manning deserved the cooperation of the most vigorous prosecution the district attorney could provide.

When Hogg was ready for the trial on May 6, 1881, he had seen to it that the defendant had counsel and was also ready. The jury found the defendant guilty of murder in the first degree and assessed his punishment as death. The case then went to the Court of Appeals, where the work of the prosecutor and judge was sustained—"no error in the judgment of the court, below." On November 26, 1881, Judge Robertson ordered that the verdict of the court should be carried out: "D. C. White, be, on Friday the 3rd day of February, A.D. 1882, by the sheriff of Van Zandt county, Texas, hanged by the neck until he is dead, dead, dead; and that the same be done according to law in such cases."[26] The word spread quickly over the district that the only white man so far hanged in Van Zandt County after a fair and impartial trial before a judge and jury had been prosecuted by District Attorney James S. Hogg.

The orderly and well-managed work of the Gregg County Clerk of Court, R. B. Levy, was especially pleasing to the District Attorney, and after seventy years these records remain among the most accessible and best preserved in the district. The following simple notations for the February 1881 term tell their own story of Hogg's activities in Longview:

Case No.	Charge	Decision	Penalty	D. A. Fee[27]
354	Murder	Guilty	10 years	$50
355	Murder	Guilty	4 years	$30
356	Theft	Guilty	2 years	$30
359	Theft	Guilty	2 years	$30
360	Burglary	Guilty	2 years	$30

In the spring of 1882, the docket was light and the results as follows:

270	Attempt. Murder	Guilty	5 years	$30
407	Theft (felony)	Guilty	2 years	$30

[26] *Ibid.*, p. 206.
[27] The fees as listed were certified by Judge Robertson, February 12, 1881. Minutes of the District Court, Gregg County (Texas), Book C, p. 83.

In the spring of 1881 the general consensus of newspaper opinion throughout the district was summed up by the Mineola *Hawkeye*:

The exceptionally strict enforcement of the criminal law, as evidenced by the increased number of convictions all over the judicial district, is a matter of congratulation with all law-abiding people.[28]

Other evidence of the esteem for Jim Hogg's vigorous public service was abundant. The foreman of the Henderson County Grand Jury in the April term, 1882, stated:

We are thankful to our able and worthy district attorney Captain Hogg, for his aid and advice, and do not think it out of place to say that to his fearless and able manner of prosecuting is due to a certain extent the decrease of crimes in our county.[29]

The Longview *Democrat* headed a column: "AN UNWITTING COMPLIMENT TO MR. HOGG."

Two colored suffragans were standing at the courthouse door, as the bar moved out to attend Mr. Burke's funeral, the one pointing out the notables to the other. One, with suspicious anxiety, wanted to see "dat man what made so troublesome for folks yer sens he come." His comrade well knew the troublesome man to be Mr. Jas. Hogg, the efficient prosecuting attorney, and he was pointed out to the questioner, with the comment that "he got 'way wid all of dem. I tell you, niggah, he de berry debbil ter git after you, and if he does git after you you wish de debbil had you afo' he gits done wid you." There is more truth than poetry in this, as evil-doers have found.[30]

By 1882 reports of criminals passing through the railroad centers to Huntsville from jails in the Seventh District became a common occurrence. Two comments, the first from the Mineola *Hawkeye,* the second from the Canton *Sentinel,* are typical:

The dockets in this district are being dispatched with unprecedented rapidity, and the penitentiaries are getting an unusual share of convicts from this district.[31]

One of our most substantial merchants said to us last week, "Why, if we don't organize an immigration society here, we won't have enough men to

---

[28] Quoted in undated clipping, J. S. Hogg Scrapbook No. 2, p. 67.
[29] Quoted in Mineola *Hawkeye,* April —, 1882; clipping in J. S. Hogg Scrapbook No. 2, p. 68.
[30] *Ibid.,* p. 69; clipping undated.
[31] *Ibid;* undated clipping from Canton *Texan.*

work the lands that are now open—why, the last one will be sent to the penitentiary. . . . Jim is doing his duty. In the prosecution of criminals he has no equal, . . . if we can keep him as low as his present office, we must never give him up." This cannot last long, such a man will soon fill a place of higher honors.[32]

The Tyler *Courier* and Athens *Narrow Gauge* also joined in the praise. The latter noted how the district attorney had complimented the jurors in announcing that morality was gaining ground in Henderson County; the editor remarked that such recognition of the people's efforts to improve their communities was pleasing and that "his worth has made itself known by his able, fearless, and impartial course."[33] When Hogg had completed his second official round of the Seventh District, an enterprising reporter on the Mineola *Hawkeye* counted up the results: trials 59; convictions 45, aggregating 439½ years in the penitentiary; and out of 9 murder trials there were 7 convictions. The editor of the Longview *Democrat* reprinted the record and concluded:

This is a rare showing for efficiency in prosecution. Can any other district in the state equal it? Lawbreakers must now make up their minds to meet the penalties of the law, while law-abiding citizens have an assurance of protection. We cordially endorse this item from the *Hawkeye*. It is especially noteworthy as a contradiction of the old saying of the prophet "without honor" etc.[34]

The prophecy of the Wills Point *Local Chronicle* that Attorney Hogg would carry every county in the district in 1882 was unduly optimistic. He almost failed of re-election. Horace Chilton was running for a seat in Congress, and Hogg, in his zeal to repay his friend for securing the nomination for him in 1880, incurred the enmity of the Bonner, Herndon, Douglas, and Hubbard faction in Tyler, which was supporting former Governor Richard Hubbard against Chilton in the congressional race. However, by this fight Hogg firmed his alliance with the resurgent forces of the Roberts, Robertson, and Chilton families and organized a staunch personal political following that loyally supported him the rest of his life.

Tyler was at this time the political center of East Texas, supplying three governors in ten years, and the factions there were to be long important in Hogg's political career.[35] The Hubbard-Herndon-Bonner

[32] *Ibid.*   [33] *Ibid.*, p. 70.

[34] Longview *Democrat*, February 24, 1882; clipping in J. S. Hogg Scrapbook No. 2, p. 69.

[35] Richard Hubbard and O. M. Roberts preceded James Hogg.

group had become the postwar Democratic leaders at a time when Colonel George Chilton and O. M. Roberts, having been elected to Congress but denied seats there by the Radicals, were obliged to stay out of politics; both of them left Smith County when military Reconstruction began in 1867. The new leaders were conservatives and "cooperationists," with northern financial connections. Aided by astute railroad attorney Colonel George Clark of Waco, a postwar newcomer from Alabama who had been Richard Coke's campaign manager in 1873 when Reconstruction Governor Davis was defeated, they built a powerful state organization. The presidential victory in 1877 of the Republican Hayes over Tilden, after the disputed 1876 election, dictated Democratic unity for 1878, and the Robertson and Chilton reform-rural forces temporarily backed Governor Hubbard (who had finished Coke's term when Coke went to the U.S. Senate in 1876) for an elected full gubernatorial term. But even then the Tyler *Courier* warned that the party lash was badly worn:

If the Democratic party of this County cannot stand on principle and merit, let it die of its own rottenness as did the Republican party. What we need is a representative Democratic Convention in this County . . . We have had the promise of reform sounded in our ears for about six years now and we, naturally enough, shall expect to witness the beneficial results much more than we have yet done.[36]

When James W. Throckmorton and Hubbard deadlocked the 1878 Convention, the rural forces nominated Roberts. Before leaving office, Hubbard had appointed Micajah Bonner as an associate justice of the Texas Supreme Court; now in 1882 Bonner was retiring, on account of age. Therefore Thomas Bonner and W. S. Herndon, who had benefited from the political advancement of Governor Hubbard and Judge Bonner, were especially anxious at this time to have Hubbard win a seat in Congress, allowing them to continue their political leadership and control of patronage.

James Hogg was to go as a delegate to the State Democratic Convention held in July, 1882, at Galveston, although he almost missed fulfilling his political duty because of a personal and family obligation. The birth of Hogg's second child was imminent, but there was doubt as to the exact date; however, the event took place on the evening of July 10, in

[36] Quoted in the Austin *Democratic Statesman*, May 24, 1878. C. Vann Woodward, in *Origins of the New South* (Baton Rouge, Louisiana State University Press, 1951), p. 21, noted divisions among Texas Democrats.

J. S. HOGG,

District Attorney 7th District Texas.

RESIDENCE.
MINEOLA
Wood Co.

COUNTIES IN 7TH JUDICIAL DISTRICT.

Smith,   Van Zandt,
Gregg,   Henderson,
Upshur,   Wood.

Mineola, July 13, 1882

J. W. Hogg, Esq.
    Decatur, Texas.

Dear John—
    Our Cup of joy is now over flowing!—We have a daughter of as fine proportions and of as angelic mien as ever gracious nature favor a man with, and her name is Ima! Can't you come down to see her?

    She made her debut on last Monday night at 9 oclock. Sallie is doing extremely well, and of course Ima is.— First Saturday or Sunday I shall start of the State Convention at Galveston, as a Delegate from this Co. Would be glad to meet you there. Love to Eva and the babies.

                Your Bro, James

Jim Hogg to His Brother John

plenty of time for the proud father of a daughter to make his other commitment. His only daughter was named Ima, after the heroine of Tom Hogg's book, *The Fate of Marvin.* The letter to John Hogg, reproduced here, shows some of the father's elation.

The delegates had been instructed by Granger-dominated Wood County that, if Governor Roberts could not be nominated for a third term, they must help to keep the South and East Texas alliance together by working for John Ireland of Seguin and by supporting Ireland's profarmer program of protecting the public lands for actual settlers.

The Convention had difficulty getting organized, and Hogg, as a member of the Credentials Committee, learned something of the state's east-west feuds when he crossed swords with one of the most able northwest politicians, Avery L. Matlock of Montague County, a former Tennessean who had come to Texas after his graduation from Cumberland Law School.[37] Matlock strove to increase the number of western delegates by giving unorganized counties in the Panhandle a delegate if they had 150 voters. Hogg, who knew that Governor Roberts had opposed organizing the western counties before they had sufficient population to carry on the normal functions of government, objected to Matlock's proposal. In this he was assisted by George W. O'Brien, a southeast Texas leader from Beaumont, who declared that such action would give double representation, because the unorganized counties were being represented as precincts of organized counties.[38] Hogg headed the group of nine members making a minority report; his group was defeated on the floor. Matlock's performance was to be remembered later by the big ranching interests, some of which were managed from headquarters in Chicago and London. Hogg, the native Texan, and Matlock, representing out-of-state or foreign interests, would tangle again.

When the Convention was at last organized Roberts withdrew his name, and John Ireland, the "Sage of Seguin," was nominated. Known alike to friend or foe as "Honest John" or "Oxcart John," Ireland definitely represented a victory for the farmers and stockmen who wanted the public lands reserved for actual settlers; he favored the termination of the policy of land grants for railroad construction, largely because the available public domain was already overpledged to railroads. On Ireland's plea for party harmony, John D. Templeton, a Roberts-trained lawyer who was a friend of Thomas Hogg, became the nominee for attorney general.

[37] Galveston *Daily News,* July 19 and 20, 1882.
[38] *Ibid.,* July 19, 1882.

90

Chosen to second the nomination for the incumbent Court of Appeals judge, who was from South Texas, James Hogg had his first opportunity to appear as a delegate before the whole Convention; in a clear voice which could be heard by all, he said:

As a private citizen, as a public servant, his [John P. White's] integrity and character are above reproach; and as a jurist his record and his reputation are unsurpassed within this State, and his name is engraved upon the hearts of an appreciative people without reference to sectional lines. Therefore, on behalf of the section that I represent especially, and in behalf of the great commonwealth in general, I respectfully move the renomination to this high trust be tendered the Honorable John P. White by this convention.[39]

Observing the work in the convention of the "youngsters," such as Chilton, Hogg, and Richard Morgan of Dallas, the Galveston *News* had this to say:

Youth, energy, daring and brains of Texas are still loyal to the Democracy. The Republicans have boasted that the young men of the State were disaffected, and determined to throw off their allegiance to the Democratic party. These young men are here to speak for themselves, and not one of them has failed to disappoint the allegation.[40]

District Attorney Hogg had served his apprenticeship. He went home a member of the Democratic State Executive Committee, thus strengthened for the fight in behalf of Chilton and for his own campaign for re-election.

Smith County delegates to the district convention were instructed for Horace Chilton in the race for Congress, and Hogg had been able to line up the Wood County delegation and a majority of the votes in Upshur County for him also, but the pro-Hubbard forces lined up enough votes in other counties to bring about a deadlock. Neither Chilton nor Hubbard could be nominated. After forty ballots Chilton withdrew in favor of James H. Jones, who was acceptable to the Hogg-Chilton reform forces.[41]

When efforts were made to get Hubbard to run as an independent against Jones, he wrote a public letter to Herndon, Bonner, and Douglas thanking them but urging party unity as "paramount to all personal considerations.[42] But the Bonner-Herndon forces did not yield gracefully

[39] *Ibid.*   [40] *Ibid.*, July 20, 1882.
[41] *Ibid.*, August 23, 1882; Dallas *Daily Herald*, August 23, 1882.
[42] Dallas *Daily News*, October 3, 1882.

and vowed to defeat Jim Hogg for his prolonged support of Chilton; Captain Thomas W. Dodd, the one-armed ex-Confederate who was then mayor of Tyler, was induced to enter the race against Hogg.[43] In their intense desire to cut short the political career of James Hogg, the Herndon faction blundered; their animosity forced Hogg to build up a series of new Democratic clubs throughout the Seventh District, which were to furnish him loyal support for over twenty years. He gained even more adherents when people heard that the disgruntled group was supporting an independent Greenbacker for the state Senate rather than Democrat J. C. Buchanan, and also aiding Stillwell Russell for Congress rather than Jones. When the returns were in, Hogg had won his re-election, despite the disgruntled group, and probably in part because of it.[44]

Jim Hogg went back to his job of enforcing the law, and during his second term his fame continued to spread outside of his district. For example, the Greenville *Banner* wrote:

Perhaps the evil-doers don't like Hogg much, but in early times the devils themselves asked permission to go and dwell in the bogs. Things have changed since then. And when evil-doers come to dwell in his range, he does not plunge into the water and drown himself, but faces the devils, and thrusts the worst ones into h—ades, and the remainder into the State penitentiary.[45]

Certain mores developing since Reconstruction days often presented problems to Hogg's determination to see justice done to all men. On one occasion in Tyler he was prosecuting a white man for assault to murder a Negro. The proof was strong and Hogg believed the white man guilty,

---

[43] Albert Woldert, *History of Tyler and Smith County,* p. 300. The editor of the Canton *Texan* (Van Zandt County) called the anti-Hogg crowd "the Burns, Lorance, Bonner, Henderson, Douglas Sorehead Democracy." J. S. Hogg Scrapbook No. 2, p. 69.

[44] The official election returns (Sec. State Elec. Ret.), 1882, are as follows:

County	Dodd	Hogg
Gregg	842	522
Henderson	642	791
Smith	2,412	1,287
Upshur	872	913
Van Zandt	420	1,713
Wood	463	1,528
	5,651	6,754

[45] Quoted in Dallas *Daily Herald,* November 10, 1882. Undated clipping in J. S. Hogg Scrapbook No. 2, pp. 68–69; clipping quoting a Mineola dispatch to Fort Worth *Gazette,* April 26, 1883 (?), describing Hogg's prosecution in an uxoricide case, *ibid.,* p. 70. The *State* v. *Israel Lovelady* (1883).

but the jury acquitted him. Then followed a case of a Negro from Troup charged with assault to murder a white man.

Mr. Hogg had the case *nolle prosequi* on the ground that the jury had turned loose the white man and he would not prosecute the Negro; and his act in doing this caused the Negroes to respect him. It was at that time a display of great courage.[46]

T. N. Jones, a schoolteacher who was present, said Hogg criticized the jury severely. Jones put it this way:

He had been present in the grand jury room, while the cases were being investigated and knew that the case against the white man was much worse than that against the Negro. . . . This was, indeed, a most fearless act and especially with feeling acute in Smith County, because the Negroes, up to that time, had always voted against the Democratic nominees. This act in dismissing the case met the approval of the bulk of the white people.[47]

✓ This moral fearlessness was matched by his physical courage. The old bullet still lodged near his spine in the small of his back gave him pain from time to time. One day during a Tyler session the pain was so intense that at noon, between cases, he called on Dr. John D. Warren and requested that an operation to remove the bullet be performed at once. The doctor urged delay saying that he had no anesthetic, antiseptic, or proper instruments. Hogg said he could stand anything to relieve the pain. Straddling a chair, he told Warren to go to work. As the doctor began to probe, Hogg gripped the back of the chair, urging completion of the operation; when he felt the bullet come out, he requested that the wound be washed with turpentine—some accounts say kerosene. Then he paid the doctor and went back to the court room. Eventually the wound closed, leaving a permanent and dark, deep indentation about the size of a quarter.[48]

When ill health forced Judge Robertson to resign from the district bench in 1884, his appointed successor was Felix McCord. The teamwork of judge and prosecutor that had produced the truly great revolution of law enforcement in the Seventh District was not disturbed by the change. Minor officials continued to feel that they could afford to do their duty because they had support. After a year of working together, McCord and Hogg received deserved praise—even in Tyler, where the

[46] Henry Marsh interview, February 15, 1935, Interv. Fol.
[47] T. N. Jones interview with Miss Hogg, March, 1935, Interv. Fol.
[48] Personal interview with Albert Woldert, M.D., in Tyler, July, 1947; personal interview with Miss Ima Hogg in Austin, March, 1953.

bar was able and very critical. The February, 1884, term had been extraordinarily crowded with civil and criminal cases, but, as an editor noted, Judge McCord and Hogg had tried to keep the convenience of the people in mind. When the jurors had to be held together according to the law, for instance, McCord would hold court at night to speed up the cases so that the men could be back at their work sooner; only a judge and district attorney who worked in harmony and had superior knowledge would agree to keep up such a pace. As to James Hogg, the Tyler *Courier* said:

He needs no comment from us. We think we can say, without disparagement of others, that he is the finest prosecuting officer in Texas. The State is always ready, and woe to the guilty wretch who is subjected to the fiery ordeal of a trial with the mammoth officer of the law to prosecute him. It has been rumored that he contemplates retiring from office at the end of his present term. We hope that this is a mistake, for we should regard it as a public misfortune to lose the services of such a man. We might get a good man to succeed him, but there is not his like in the District or State.[49]

Early in March, 1884, when James Hogg made a special trip to Tyler on personal business, the rumor of retirement from prosecuting duties proved to be founded on fact. After many preliminary talks, he and McCord's former partner in Longview, John M. Duncan, who had been attorney for Gregg County from 1876 to 1878 and a state senator from 1878 to 1882, had agreed to form a partnership. On this March day an office was rented, a commodious suite with a reception room and a private room for each of the partners. Tyler's leading furniture dealer, J. G. Woldert, was commissioned to provide furniture for it, including Axminister carpet for the floor and even curtains for the windows.[50]

Sometime later Hogg bought a small house near the town square. He was fully aware that an office and residence in Tyler would increase his availability for future political advancement, but other factors were also important to his decision in making this move. He was tired of the constant travel a district attorney was subject to and he wished to spend more time at home with his much-loved family. Will, now nine years

[49] Tyler *Courier*, February 11, 1884. Twenty-five out of 26 cases had resulted in convictions.

[50] Tyler *Reporter*, March 8, 1884; J. S. Hogg Pers. Acc. Bk., 1884; undated clipping from the Gilmer *Mirror*, J. S. Hogg Scrapbook No. 2, p. 71. The youngest daughter of the late Judge J. L. Camp, Jr., and her husband, Dr. Seth Shepard McKay, professor of history at Texas Technological College, Lubbock, have answered many questions for the writer.

old, needed a better school than Mineola could provide, and both Jim and Sallie Hogg looked forward to the cultural, and especially the musical, advantages of the larger town. Arrangements were made to move to the new house in the fall of 1884.

Democratic hopes were higher for the 1884 presidential campaign year than at any time since 1860. For a quarter of a century the Republicans had been in power at Washington. In Smith County a combination of white and colored Republicans still made up a majority of the voters. Early in the summer there was a "Hogg-for-Congress" boom, and for a while Jim Hogg considered entering the race. On July 5, however, he thanked Robert Stafford of the Mineola *Monitor* for his efforts and declared that Jones deserved a second term.[51] The congressional race was tempting, but he very much wanted to try his hand at private practice in Tyler.

Following the Democratic convention at Houston, at which Chairman J. M. Claiborne discussed the splintering of the party in the 1882 campaign and pointed out "independent" Democrats who had worked with Greenbackers and Republicans to defeat Democrats,[52] there was evidence of some desire on the part of the formerly warring Democratic factions to cooperate in defeating the Republican presidential nominee, James G. Blaine. In Smith County both local factions cooperated now at least in turning to James Hogg as the man most qualified to speak to Negro audiences and to encourage the colored people to vote for Grover Cleveland. As district attorney, Hogg had earned a reputation of fairness to all men, regardless of race, and the colored people considered him one of their friends. His ability to tell dialect stories and his ease of manner before a colored audience were attained by few white men of the time.

To Democrats the region from Smith County east and north to Red River was a crucial one that embraced a strong Republican vote which might be "redeemed." As ex-Governor Hubbard had said during the National Democratic Convention which nominated Cleveland, the Democrats had been out of power twenty-five years and to win there must be more votes, as well as "harmony."[53] T. N. Jones managed the

---

[51] Mineola *Monitor,* June (n.d.), 1884, and July 5, 1884, J. S. Hogg Scrapbook No. 2, pp. 75–77; Gilmer *Mirror,* July 3, 1884; Houston *Post,* June 28, 1884.

[52] Galveston *News,* August 20, 1884; Winkler, *Platforms,* 221–223.

[53] Copy of speech in J. S. Hogg Scrapbook No. 2, p. 72; Henry Marsh interview, April 9, 1935, Interv. Fol.

Smith County campaign; he hired a band and borrowed from the state a cannon, which was discharged from place to place to notify the people to assemble. John Duncan and Hogg, relatively newcomers to Tyler, worked to bring about a local *modus vivendi* between the Bonner and Chilton factions. When Jim Hogg spoke at Negro rallies, throngs of colored folk gathered despite the efforts of Republican bosses to dissuade them from listening. Friends who heard him at the rallies said he was "in a class all by himself, when speaking to Negroes, causing them to laugh, cry, or shout as the occasion demanded."[54]

On election day many Negroes voted Democratic; Smith County was "redeemed," the Republicans losing their long-time control of it because they had lost Negro votes.[55] Nationally, with Cleveland's triumph, the Democrats returned to power for the first time since Lincoln's election.

The election over, Jim Hogg turned his attention more fully to the affairs of his new home town. One of Tyler's main problems, however, reached beyond the local sphere, since it concerned railroads. Hogg fully recognized the value of railroads to any community, but as always he was concerned about the policies of railroad management and their effect on local communities. Having seen Quitman stranded when the Texas and Pacific bypassed it, he understood what it meant to Tyler not to be on the main line of the International and Great Northern from St. Louis to Laredo. The Tyler Tap Railroad had been chartered in 1871 by citizens of Tyler led by Richard Hubbard and had been built to Big Sandy by 1877, but the meager financial resources of one town placed it at the mercy of Jay Gould and the directors of the Missouri Pacific, which controlled the I.&G.N. Tyler men had also projected a line to St. Louis, the Texas and St. Louis Railway, chartered in 1879, which acquired the Tyler Tap in 1881. Colonel Sam W. Fordyce, who had been made vice-president to give the company the benefit of his experience, became the receiver in 1885, and a reorganization was planned. Then Fordyce, hitherto known for his fights against Gould in construction, operation, and rate policies, began "to smoke the pipe of peace."[56]

[54] Henry Marsh interview, April 9, 1935. Cf. T. N. Jones to Ima Hogg, March 1935, Interv. Fol.

[55] Woldert, *Tyler and Smith County,* p. 38; Henry Marsh interview, April 9, 1945, Interv. Fol.

[56] Quoted in St. Clair Reed, *Texas Railroads,* p. 414; J. S. Hogg to J. P. Douglas, V. P. Horticultural Ass'n., Tyler, July 20, 1888, J. S. Hogg Let. Pr., I, 449–450. Original and typescript in H. C.

In January, 1886, the receivership was terminated and the road was rechartered as the St. Louis, Arkansas, and Texas Railway Company of Texas; in February all old rights and property were sold at foreclosure sale. As a result, the Tyler men lost control, a bondholders' committee, dominated by out-of-state interest, holding everything except the land grant that had been sold previously. Colonel Fordyce created new mortgages and proceeded to buy rails to replace the narrow gauge with a standard gauge, and before long the line could not meet its obligations. Failure to pay Andrew Carnegie led to a "forced sale" to Jay Gould. The lengthening shadows of Erie and Wabash hung over the Southwest.[57]

The Texas Traffic Association was formed, with Jay Gould's blessing, on July 28, 1885, at a meeting in Galveston. Texas farmers were quick to see its implications for them; in Grange and Alliance meetings there were urgent debates on the announcement by the five major lines of their intent "to establish and maintain equitable and uniform rates."[58] The railroads were trying, apparently, to make more money and, perhaps, to pay interest and dividends on inflated stocks and bonds. Gould, at least, would benefit if the stock values went up; he had played that game in the Midwest through the Western Truck Line Association the year before. The farmers observed that profits would not necessarily come from increased efficiency, and pooling had been, not an incentive to railroad expansion, but the opposite, judging from the experience of the defunct Iowa Pool and Western Truck Line Association.[59]

Governor Ireland publicly called the attention of Attorney General John D. Templeton to the Texas Traffic Association and requested an investigation of its relationship to monopoly. Templeton and J. Waldo, commissioner for the Association and formerly general freight agent for the Huntington-controlled Houston and Texas Central, exchanged a

[57] Reed, op. cit., pp. 414–415; Lewis H. Haney in *A Congressional History of Railways in the United States, 1850–1887*, being University of Wisconsin *Bulletin* No. 342 (Madison, 1910), II, 107–113, discusses pooling and stockholder complaints against the Union Pacific. Charles F. Adams, Jr., *Railroads: Their Origin and Problems* (New York, G. P. Putnam's, 1886), pp. 176–188; Robert E. Riegel, *The Story of the Western Railroads* (New York, Macmillan Company, 1926), pp. 274–289; Charles F. and Henry Adams, *Chapters of Erie* (New York, J. R. Osgood and Company, 1886).

[58] Galveston *News*, July 28–29, 1885; Ralph Smith, "The Contributions of the Grangers to Education in Texas," *Southwestern Social Science Quarterly*, XXI (March, 1941), 312–314; Roscoe C. Martin, "The Grange as a Political Factor in Texas," *The Southwestern Social Science Quarterly*, VI (March, 1926), 363–384.

[59] Julius Grodinsky, *The Iowa Pool* (Chicago, University of Chicago Press, 1950), pp. 153–162.

number of letters and held conferences. In September 1885, Templeton wrote Waldo of his concern about the consolidations of Texas lines into one or two systems, but implied that he proposed to do nothing about pooling:

The Legislature has always undertaken to fix maximum rates and if the rates do not exceed those maximum rates, I doubt if there has been any violation of the law by pooling.[60]

Farmers, merchants, lumbermen, and Texas stockholders were not satisfied with Templeton's brand of *laissez faire*. Skill and courage would be needed to battle successfully to uphold the charter requirements against the highly paid and well-trained railroad attorneys when the time came to call the hand on pooling, rebating, taking headquarters or shops outside the state, and failing to keep up the roadbeds and to provide safe and adequate rolling stock. Furthermore, the attorney general would be expected to insist that the International and Great Northern should not be drained of all profits merely to aid Gould's other ventures, and that the line was to be kept in good condition as required by the Texas charter. In East Texas many of the groups to whose livelihood a successfully waged battle was vital were hoping that Jim Hogg would transfer his reputation for unswerving law enforcement to the wider area of the state. Horace Chilton did not hesitate to say that no ordinary lawyer could possibly get the job done, but that a Tyler man was available: his friend Hogg had the trained scent of a prosecutor and the stamina demanded for the battle.[61]

A rapid sequence of events between the fall of 1884 and the summer of 1886 had made James Hogg aware of the possibilities for political advancement. His vigorous campaigning for President Cleveland had been noticed by the Executive Committee of the Democratic Party. In April, 1885, in connection with a vacation trip to the World Exposition at New Orleans, he and Mrs. Hogg joined former Governor Francis Lubbock, who had been an aide to President Jefferson Davis and was now state treasurer, in a visit to Davis in retirement at Biloxi. While there Hogg admired a big rooster, which Davis gave to him and later sent to

[60] Attorney General J. D. Templeton to J. Waldo, Sept. 28, 1885, Att. Gen. File, 1885.

[61] H. Chilton Diar., 1886–1894, p. 173. (Appreciation is expressed to Attorney Chilton O'Brien, Beaumont, for permitting limited use of the manuscript diaries of his grandfather. Arrangements were made by Miss Winnie Allen, University of Texas archivist.)

Tyler. Word soon spread that Hogg had a rooster named "Jefferson Davis." Governor Lubbock was favorably impressed with the Tyler attorney and passed word along in Austin.[62]

Young Allison Mayfield, who had been studying law with Horace Chilton and who later became head of the Railroad Commission, has left a good description of Hogg at this time:

In May 1885 . . . I traveled from Mineola to Quitman in a two-horse drawn, open, two-seated hack. There was one other passenger. He was a large, well dressed man with open pleasing countenance and very blue and observing eyes. He introduced himself as "Mr. Hogg." Conversation revealed that he had been County Attorney in Wood County; District Attorney . . . and was then expecting to be nominated and elected Attorney General of Texas. "Mr. Hogg," as he called himself, was a very large but handsome man, neat in person and dress and to me in every way interesting. He looked to be about thirty-five to forty years of age. I was not long out of school—had read law while teaching—Judge Felix J. McCord appointed Mr. Hogg, Judge Dave Crow, and W. H. Giles a committee to examine me. . . . Mr. Hogg and I returned to Tyler together. He used the opportunity to tell me how to start and how to avoid mistakes in getting started in the practice. He related his own experiences. He said when he started he got a buggy and two mules or ponies (I think he said mules) and, whether he had business or not, he attended each court day all justice and precinct courts of Wood County. The people learned to expect him and he seldom failed to be employed by someone to attend to some legal matter. That is the way he acquired acquaintances and clients. He advised me to do likewise. I have told the lesson to many other young lawyers; those that had the energy to follow it got on to success.[63]

Hogg was taking cases farther and farther away from Tyler—in Greenville and Dallas, and to the northeast as well. His legal reputation was reaching state-wide proportions. Senator Morris Sheppard left this memoir:

My father, John L. Sheppard, was at that time prosecuting attorney for the seven northeast Texas counties. A prominent citizen of one of these counties had been indicted for mishandling of public funds while discharging some public capacity. James S. Hogg, a rising lawyer in a neighboring district had been employed to defend him. It was during the trial of that case, Hogg defending, my father prosecuting, that I first saw Mr. Hogg. Though

[62] Francis R. Lubbock, *Six Decades in Texas* (Austin, B. C. Jones Company, 1900), p. 658.
[63] Allison Mayfield to Ima Hogg, May 23, 1921, Interv. Fol.

a child I felt the thrill of his commanding presence. I shall never forget the scenes of the court room. . . . Great crowds attended and breathlessly observed the proceedings. The opposing lawyers strained every energy for their respective sides. Nothing was overlooked that might give a proper advantage. The outcome was that James Hogg won not only the case but the life-long, personal and political allegiance of my father as well. His manliness and fairness as an adversary as much as his consummate ability as an advocate captivated my father who became one of his chief supporters in all his political campaigns.[64]

The approach of the election of 1886 found most Texans experiencing only a relative and spotty prosperity. The year 1882 marked the completion of the Southern Pacific Railroad from Houston and San Antonio and the Texas and Pacific from Texarkana and Dallas to El Paso. The resultant rush of people to the Great Plains would soon destroy the census conception of a frontier line of settlement, but meanwhile the process of adjustment to the Plains environment would be painful and ruinous to many families. A freezing winter in 1884–1885 followed by years of drought hit the western ranchers hard. Hogg knew that friends of Congressman Reagan and Attorney John Gooch in Palestine, where the International and Great Northern had its original headquarters, as required by the charter, were being joined by Houstonians in demanding that the general offices be returned to Texas from St. Louis. Offices and shops meant increased payrolls, more work, more customers for merchants, and a better living for more people. It was the business of the attorney general to correct these irregularities. With Templeton overworked by land cases in the Panhandle, the railroads found that he had little time, since the resignation of the state engineer for railroads, to investigate or prosecute them. Such were the general conditions in 1886 when James Hogg contemplated the race for the heretofore rather insignificant office of attorney general. The generally accepted unimportance of this position is proved by the startling fact that the official Democratic newspaper at Austin did not publish a single campaign speech of any of the four Democratic candidates seeking the nomination. Nor have any complete speeches, including those of the Republican candidate from Young County, C. N. Johnson, been found in other major daily papers consulted.

While the potentialities of the office of attorney general were attractive to James Hogg, he still had some reservations about seeking nomina-

[64] Morris Sheppard to Ima Hogg, November 4, 1921, Interv. Fol.

tion for it and decided that he needed to be sure that he would not be campaigning against Charles Culberson, son of Congressman Dave Culberson, whose candidacy would mean a divided East Texas vote. Hogg enjoyed his private law practice, both for the variety of the work and for the greater amount of time it allowed him to spend with his family. His income was good, and would undoubtedly be better, surpassing the established salary for attorneys general. This was particularly a point to ponder, because his personal responsibilities had again increased. On October 28, 1885, Sallie had borne a second son, happily greeted by parents and brother and sister and given the name of Michael (Mike).

Soon after the February, 1886, meeting of the Democratic Executive Committee, which included several of Hogg's friends, Hogg, still willing to seek the advice of older leaders, wrote former Governor Roberts. He explained that, although his ambition had been to occupy "a high position as a lawyer" and to have a "select lucrative practice," he now "had flattering prospects of getting the nomination for attorney general."

I wish you to tell me freely and frankly what would be the best for me under the circumstances. I have been practicing law almost exclusively since March 1875, and by it have made more than a living. I am now nearly thirty-five years old; have a wife and three children, a comfortable home, a convenient office and excellent library, a good law practice, agreeable surroundings and am out of debt....

In a spirit of candor, upon a claim of long standing friendship, I seek your suggestions and advice as to what course will be best for me now.[65]

Roberts wrote a lengthy and fatherly reply to Hogg. He pointed out frankly some of the drawbacks to the course generally necessary to attain distinction in public employment, among which was the danger of neglecting the training of children; he indicated also, however, that it was possible through public service to gain support of the great mass of the people.

Really, I have always thought that a man of ordinary judgment knows what he ought to do better than any one else can tell him, though sometimes that fails to be the case. From what I know and have heard of you, I think you can gain distinction in public life, if you have a strong desire to do so, and will use reasonable efforts to do it....

A man to fill the full measure of himself must follow the bent of his aspirations, controlled by his best and most deliberate judgment, and I

[65] J. S. Hogg to O. M. Roberts, March 11, 1886, O. M. Roberts Papers, VI, Pt. 2 (1881–1890), p. 164. Typescript in H. C.

101

might say, candidly impartial judgment as to what he is best capable of doing; for himself and for those dependent upon him.[66]

With this balancing of advice Roberts left Jim Hogg to make the momentous decision which was to hurl him into the maelstrom of extending social, economic, and political forces.

Several factors of the general political situation aided Hogg's candidacy. The Bonner and Herndon groups were sponsoring William J. Swain, former state comptroller, and D. C. Giddings, Brenham banker, for governor.[67] As the other Democrats in Tyler surveyed the field of potential candidates for governor it became obvious that they had no one to propose who would have any prospect of winning against Lawrence S. ("Sul") Ross of Waco, who could count upon considerable soldier and Granger support, having been one of the youngest brigadier generals in the Confederate forces, and having succeeded to the command of General Hogg's old brigade.[68] As sheriff of McLennan County after the war he had organized the Sheriffs' Association, which wielded considerable political power. The Chilton-Roberts-Robertson group were willing to trade with the Ross forces if this would obtain the attorney general nomination for Hogg. Before Hogg formally announced, Charles Culberson, son of Congressman Dave Culberson, withdrew, apparently with a promise of future support from Chilton and Hogg.[69] Then the East Texas delegates began to concentrate on one candidate. The Fort Worth *Gazette* on June 9, 1886, said editorially: "Since the declination of Mr. Charley Culberson, Mr. James Hogg of Tyler has advanced rapidly to the front as the strong man for Attorney General."

Another advantage for Hogg at the convention was the fact that Colonel George Clark was Ross's campaign manager for governor. Clark had managed Coke's campaign and had become by appointment his attorney general. Clark served on the Court of Appeals, 1879–1881, and them became a very successful lawyer in Waco. He was a native of Alabama and was graduated from the University at Tuscaloosa after the Civil War. While an officer in Virginia, he had fought beside Captain

[66] O. M. Roberts to J. S. Hogg, March 14, 1886, J. S. Hogg Let. Rec., I, 21A.
[67] Galveston *News,* August 12, 1886; Webb and Carroll, *Handbook of Texas,* II, 694.
[68] Victory M. Rose, *Ross' Texas Brigade* (Louisville, *Courier Journal,* 1881), pp. 64–66; Senator Richard Wynne (Ft. Worth) to O. M. Roberts, June 4, 1886, in O. M. Roberts Papers, Vol. 6. Wynne opposed Swain and advocated the selection of Ross.
[69] James W. Madden, *Charles Allen Culberson* (Austin, Gammel's Book Store, 1929), pp. 3–5.

James McMath, an uncle of James Hogg, and had been with McMath at his death on the battlefield at Frazier's Farm, June 30, 1862. Clark knew that Hogg had gone to school in Alabama and that he had stayed for a while with Mrs. James McMath.[70] In 1886 Clark and Hogg were friends, and Clark was not averse to trading for votes from the strong Smith County delegation. Dallas County, the most populous in Texas, planned to nominate her county attorney, able but pint-sized Charles Clint. He was a college graduate and a man of considerable courage, which had been demonstrated with some success in his fight against gamblers and low life in Dallas. However, he was younger than Hogg and not particularly impressive in a long cutaway coat which almost hid a stature of five feet two inches. Although there was a difference of only a year in ages, Hogg appeared older than Clint.[71] Hogg had more experience and a wider reputation as a criminal lawyer. The immediacy of his audience-appeal was described by Chilton: "His personal appearance, large of frame and broad of face, was a self-made introduction to every audience, even his very name Jim Hogg—was a reminder to the man who stood on the ground, that he, too, stood on the ground."[72]

Each of the leading contestants, Hogg and Clint, respected the legal record of the other. Delegates saw them meet in the hotel lobby and exchange friendly greetings. This was the first time many of the delegates had seen either candidate, and the friendliness of Hogg and his physical bearing, made even more impressive by contrast with Clint, won many votes from the uninstructed delegates. The lawyers generally supported Hogg, and his friend, M. M. Crane, had made many friends for Hogg at a recent Grand State Farmers' Alliance convention at Cleburne. The farmers looked for a man ready to develop vigorously a larger concept of the office of attorney general. They had resolved just a week before the Democratic convention: "That the statutes of the State of Texas be rigidly enforced by the attorney-general, to compel corporations to pay the taxes due the state and counties."[73] When the first ballot was taken, Hogg led with 294 votes. Clint came next with 178, while District Attorney Walter Acker, from the drought area about Lampasas, received 174. Colonel P. E. Pearson, wounded in the Battle of Franklin, who represented the Gulf region, received only 83 votes.[74] One by one the

[70] George Clark, *A Glance Backward* (Houston, Rein & Sons, 1914), pp. 88–89.
[71] Galveston *News*, August 12, 1886.
[72] Quoted in Cotner (ed.), *op. cit.*, p. 28.
[73] Winkler, *Platforms*, p. 236.
[74] For Pearson see *Southwestern Historical Quarterly*, V (October, 1901), 166;

candidates withdrew. Upon motion by W. L. Crawford of Dallas the vote was made unanimous for Hogg. Despite the poor acoustics of the hall—a skating rink—all could hear the nominee:

I have sought, obtained, and now accept with thanks the high trust. . . . Through the influence of friends, I have been elevated to a point from whose summit I can see the chasm into which I may fall by a misguided step. The official duties I do not underrate, and I will fearlessly, impartially, and earnestly discharge every obligation resting upon me; I shall honestly try, at least, to do my whole duty. . . . My competitors have my respect and many of them my gratitude and friendship for the honorable manner in which they have sought success over me. To all of you and to the people of Texas, I return my grateful thanks, and I pledge you a record at the end of my official term, that you, as Democrats, will not have just cause to complain of.[75]

The Democratic nomination assured election.

Clarence R. Wharton, *History of Fort Bend County, Texas* (San Antonio, Naylor Company, 1939), pp. 190 ff.; Anderson J. Sowell, *History of Fort Bend County* (Houston, W. H. Coyle and Company, 1904), p. 331. For Acker see his *Grand Orator Address* (Houston, Gray, Dillaye and Company, c. 1909), delivered to Grand Royal Arts Chapter of Texas at Waco, 1909.
[75] Galveston *News,* August 13–14, 1886; Winkler, *op. cit.,* pp. 237–242.

CHAPTER V

The Attorney General Goes to Work

BEFORE THE END of December, 1886, James and Sallie Hogg and their children moved to Austin, taking up comfortable temporary quarters in the excellent boardinghouse of Widow Andrews. At the corner of Lavaca and 11th streets, the two-story, Austin-limestone house faced the side yard of the Governor's Mansion. Thus conveniently situated, Hogg was only a short downhill walk from the office building on Congress Avenue then being used as a temporary Capitol. Since 1883 the new Capitol had been in process of construction by the Capitol Syndicate of Chicago, which would receive, as payment from the state, title to the three million acres of land in the Texas Panhandle on which it had established the XIT Ranch. Construction was still somewhat over a year from completion.

Setting about to learn the routine of the office and to become acquainted with its unfinished business, Hogg studied Attorney General John Templeton's biennial report. There seemed to be a good deal of unfinished business, including several problems with state-federal complications. Large among the latter was the long dispute with the United States government over the area occupied by Greer County. The federal position was that the Melish Map of 1818 (attached to the treaty with Spain in 1819), although it erred in showing only a main stream in the upper course of Red River rather than the forks, delineated the area as part of the United States. After the annexation of Texas the state boundary had been further complicated when U. S. Captain Randolph B. Marcy located the hundredth meridian east of the forks. Greer County had been formed by act of the Texas legislature in 1860, but because of the war the organization of a county government had been delayed. In 1886 the settlers had finally named the town of Mangum as the county seat and proceeded to elect county commissioners, to establish schools, and to operate in other ways as a self-governing community.

About the same time President Cleveland began a vigorous championship of federal jurisdiction in the area, which resulted in confusion and

105

many land suits instituted by county residents. A Boundary Commission had met in Galveston and Austin during early 1886, with little tangible result. Templeton had made a recommendation to the legislature that it simplify the whole matter by declaring void all patents to Greer County lands, thus avoiding separate litigation on each patent; he also indicated, however, that any interested party could test the proposed law in the courts.

It was discouraging for the new attorney general to discover how little attention the legislators had seemed to give to many of Templeton's recommendations in matters of proposed legislation. For example, a request made in 1883 for changes in the Penal Code and the Code of Criminal Procedure—involving merely several matters of terminology—had resulted in nothing but two years of inaction, and had to be repeated in 1885.

James Hogg took the customary oath of office on January 18, 1887, surrounded by a small group of friends, his new assistants, and the retiring staff. He had been grateful for Templeton's recommendation that the assistant attorney general should be appointed, if not on the recommendation of the attorney general, at least on the governor's consultation with him. Templeton had pointed out that if the attorney general and the governor happened to be of opposing opinions on certain matters and the assistant was the governor's appointee, the work of the attorney general's office could be hampered. When Governor Ross accepted the recommendation, Hogg named his friend William L. Davidson, of Gonzales, as incumbent. His former law partner, H. B. Marsh, of Tyler, had also been persuaded to become a member of the staff. Some time later, after Ross had readily responded to Hogg's request for legislative approval of an additional lawyer for the understaffed department, Richard H. Harrison, from the governor's own county of McLennan, joined the group, chosen particularly because of his previous noteworthy efforts to protect school and other public lands.

After his swearing-in, the attorney general attended the inauguration of Governor Ross in the Hall of Representatives of the temporary Capitol. The tone of the inaugural address was cautious, as was that of the subsequent First Message to the Twentieth Legislature. In particular, Ross expressed opposition to the idea of a railroad commission, with an evident intention of scotching that often-recurring issue; he also mentioned the recent railroad strike on Gould-operated lines but carefully avoided declaration of any definite policy whatsoever. Since special-interest groups, as well as the rank and file of voting citizens, usually first gauged the policy of a new administration by what was said in these two initial addresses, the railroad interests must have been pleased by what they heard, the average citizen less so. Most were willing for the governor to try to find peaceful solutions to new disagreements between labor and management.

However, the strong distrust of current railroad tactics lately evinced by Texas farmers, especially Alliance men at their Cleburne meeting in 1886, which had helped in the nomination and election of James Hogg as attorney general, was soon re-emphasized. When the legislature balloted to select a successor to U.S. Senator Samuel Maxey, the East Texas farm members threw all their support to Congressman John Reagan, who was elected over former Governor John Ireland and Alexander W. Terrell, state legislator from Austin. The vote was an expression of appreciation for Reagan's conspicuous and unremitting efforts, during his years in Congress, to obtain railroad regulation, which had culminated recently—this February of 1887—in the passage of the federal Interstate Commerce Act, and of confidence in his continuing efforts to advance this policy.

Attorney General Hogg had gladly taken time out of his already crowded schedule to testify to Reagan's qualifications for higher office and was delighted with the final result. Even at the start of his study of railroad practices it was clear to him that activity concerning railroads would be a main order of business for the attorney general's office, and it was heartening to know that there would be support and advice available, if needed, from a wise United States senator, long versed in the subject.

The routine duties of the office were heavy, and Hogg also needed, without delay, to find time to continue his study of railroad practices, to clarify the local implications of the new Interstate Commerce Act, and to prepare the planned suits against Jay Gould's Texas Traffic Association. In late January, almost before he and his staff were oriented, one of the inheritances from his predecessor thrust upon him an immediate duty, which quickly increased the already heavy pressures bearing down upon him. The Texas House decided to honor the request of Judge Frank Willis for an official investigation of Templeton's charge that Willis had been unduly influenced and negligent when presiding, as Judge of the Thirty-first District, over the Panhandle lease cases of January, 1886. An ambitious new attorney general would naturally prefer to select for his first major test case one which he had good prospects of winning. The letter from Representative Kirlicks reproduced

107

here indicates that Hogg did not have freedom of choice in this instance.

The long and involved background of the lease cases included numerous components: clashing personalities and theories, greed and graft, well-meant but possibly misguided legislation, and—most important in the long view—the confusion of motives that always accompanies inevitable social change.

For many years the High Plains of the Panhandle had seemed so vast and their ranchmen occupants so few and far between that the question

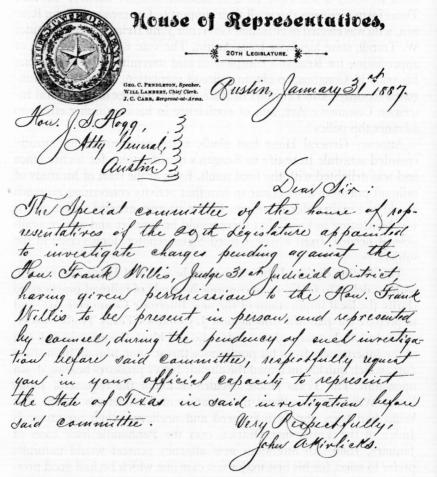

Representative John A. Kirlicks to Attorney General Hogg

108

of tenure had been of little concern to anyone. In the late 1870's, however, it began to be apparent, and first of all to the ranchers themselves, that the hitherto free frontier bounties of grass and water would not much longer be freely and easily available to anyone who chose to claim them. The more aggressive of the ranchers began to fence the ranges they had established by long usage and to buy additional land; and in 1880, partly to improve breeding methods and to rid the region of outlaws, and partly as a means of control and protection against fever-ridden longhorns from the south that streamed across the ranges, the Panhandle Stockmen's Association was formed.

A leading founder of the Association was Charles Goodnight, a first settler in the Panhandle, a veteran plainsman, and one of the state's richest cattlemen. Goodnight's early exploits as an Indian scout and the trails he had carved for cattle drives to New Mexico (risking death innumerable times from Indian attack) were celebrated.[1] In 1876 he moved 1,800 head of Durham cattle from Colorado to Palo Duro Canyon and the next year formed a partnership with a wealthy Scot, John G. Adair, who furnished the money for fencing vast areas of their JA Ranch.

One of the earliest acts of the Panhandle Stockmen's Association was to send a representative to Austin to lobby in 1880 for a lease act, but the bill failed of passage because of the opposition of the free-grass element. In the next few years, however, the cattle industry boomed—and the conviction grew stronger in the older portions of the state that the cowmen were becoming wealthy from the public domain. In April, 1883, the legislature enacted a law providing for competitive leasing of the alternate school sections at not less than four cents an acre; a State Land Board, composed of the governor, the attorney general, the comptroller, the treasurer, and the commissioner of the General Land Office, was set up to administer the law.

Each range had been held for years by the cowmen on terms of mutual understanding and cooperation with each other—whether it was one of the few actually owned or one of the many still a part of the public domain. Thus, when the Land Board asked for bids, the "code of the range" was invoked and no competitive bids were offered, each man merely filing application for his already established range at the mini-

---

[1] J. Evetts Haley, in his *Charles Goodnight* (Norman, University of Oklahoma Press, 1949), presents an interesting and lively version of the case from Goodnight's point of view. See Texas *House Journal* (1887), pp. 501 ff. for Hogg's efforts on behalf of the state to obtain removal of Willis by "address" proceedings.

mum prescribed by the law. The Board then announced that land would not be leased for less than eight cents an acre. Complicating the difficulties was the fact that counties were being created in the Panhandle during the decade 1876–1886, before the population was actually sufficient to sustain the normal functions of local government. Therefore, when Attorney General Templeton attempted to enforce the Land Enclosure Act of 1884, the legal machinery in the counties concerned was primitive and inadequate.

Only 1500 inhabitants lived in all of the twenty-six counties west and north of Childress on Red River. Only three counties in this area had enough inhabitants to qualify legally as a county, and it was said that Hemphill County, with 149 people, may have listed a dog in order to obtain the necessary 150 names on the petition. The legislature had helped to create the situation in which cowboys would sit on juries at trials involving the interests of their employers.

It was inevitable, therefore, that when in December, 1885, Attorney General John D. Templeton attempted to enforce the enclosure law, difficulties in court procedure would result. He served notice upon W. H. Woodman, the district attorney for the Panhandle, that suits must be brought against cowmen in his district for illegal enclosure. The following January, when court convened in the little town of Clarendon, Woodman asked the grand jury, consisting of cowmen drawn the preceding July, for indictments. The grand jury, of which Goodnight was foreman, obligingly found a total of eighty-six truebills against many Panhandle cowmen, including Goodnight and others serving on the jury, on charges of unlawfully fencing public school lands.

The suits were tried, of necessity, before juries made up of cowboys, some of whom were working for the men being tried. The defense attorneys argued that the cattlemen had bid "the legal" four cents an acre for lease, that leases had been awarded by the county surveyor in each case, and that the lessees had tendered payment annually to the Land Board, at the legal rate. Goodnight took a wheelbarrow of money to the Capitol to make payment on some 200,000 acres, but it was refused because Goodnight would pay only at a 4-cent rate rather than the 8-cent rate set by the Land Board. Judge Frank Willis charged the jury that if this defense was found true the verdict should be "not guilty." Acquittals followed, as was expected.

Attorney General Templeton felt that here was a problem of fair judicial procedure and law enforcement. He had gone out personally to investigate, and in his report for 1884–1886 he stated that, in a vast

110

area of Texas, sentiment was hostile to paying for the use of public lands, and that this attitude affected the administration of justice and the enforcement of the laws:

It [this hostile sentiment] goes, doubtless, with the juries into the jury box, and it is present with the grand jurors in their deliberations, and while the judge may preside over the court, this sentiment presides over the judge in at least one district in the State, and that is the district wherein a very large part of the most desirable school land is situated.[2]

In reply to this section of the attorney general's report Judge Willis, after some prodding by Charles Goodnight, wrote a letter to the legislature requesting an investigation of the charges made by Templeton against him. Meanwhile Goodnight was in Austin lobbying for a lease law with low rent provisions. The Panhandle residents were divided in their interests, but Goodnight was shrewd enough to label his fight for the fenced-in cattlemen a fight "for the Panhandle."[3]

The Willis case had more serious implications than may be immediately apparent. For two and one-half years the Dallas *Morning News* had been urging the state to insist upon collection of payments for the use of 20 million acres of school lands. It continued to repeat these demands, and October, 1885, assigned its Austin correspondent, John E. Thornton, to study the land situation in the Panhandle. Through a series of objective reports he made clear the conflict between cattlemen (both "free-grass" and "fenced-in") and farmers, and the need for adjustment to the changing economic patterns of this area.

Since the legislature was bogged down with work, there was no time for formal impeachment proceedings against Judge Willis, and hearings continued through the technical forms of a resolution for address. Hogg's charges were:

1. His [Judge Willis's] actions were collusive, fraudulent and farcical. They were irregular and invalid as to the defendants, but estopped the State.

2. The judge was responsible for them, for he was the supreme power in charge, and as such, if he knew it, he was corrupt; if he did not, he was guilty of criminal negligence. For the former he was impeachable, for a high crime; for the latter he would be guilty of an official misdemeanor.[4]

[2] John D. Templeton, *Report of the Attorney General,* 1884–1886 (Austin, 1886), pp. 19–20.
[3] Haley, *op. cit.,* p. 401.
[4] Austin *Statesman,* February 19, 1887. Cf. Haley, *Goodnight,* p. 397, and "Charges against Judge Willis," Appendix to Texas *Senate Journal* (1887), p. 136.

During the personal examination of the defendant before the House committee of five, Hogg obtained affirmative replies to his questions as to whether Judge Willis knew that members of the grand jury had indicted themselves, that the district attorney and the sheriff were in the employment of the cattle association to which the jurors belonged, that in fifty-four of the fifty-six trials the verdict was "not guilty," and that all these cases were tried without witnesses and without forewarning of the defendants. He obtained an affirmative answer also to his question as to whether Judge Willis had failed to raise objections to these proceedings. The majority vote of the committee was for the resolution that the governor remove Judge Willis from office.

The Judge was granted extra time for his defense before the House. Hogg was convinced that Willis should leave office, and he made an impassioned plea for prosecuting corruption in public office and for strict legal procedures. After depicting blindfolded Justice as "guarding with equal jealousy the respective claims of Texas and of those cattle barons," he declared: "Such is an enviable picture!" Then he exhorted the House to view the situation clearly and realistically:

On the other hand, clear up your visions, lay aside your fancy and meet stern facts face to face. Look at the man playing traitor to the bench, in judicial ermine! See him with the folds from his eyes and the scales of Justice from his hands. Behold him witnessing the test made by the cowman's long arm, rusty steelyards in the hands of "Bonus" Woodman and the defendant's lawyers! View him as he tremblingly crouches upon his seat and watches those liberal lords called up for trial! There are stacked before him those eighty-six monstrous indictments—the five days' work of the self-confessed criminals; to his right sits a jury composed chiefly of their employees; to the left stands the Sheriff in their pay; in front poses that mild-mannered District Attorney on a salary by them, and surrounding him from every source arise the foul fumes of conspiracy, fraud and corruption which every honest man there smells with disgust and shame! And all for justice? God spare the term.[5]

The Willis-Goodnight lobby had been diligent. Many of the large cattle owners came to Austin with their henchmen and filled the hotels and boardinghouses where the members of the legislature lived. Some made it a special point to become acquainted with persons known to be friends of the Attorney General. John Vorhees, a representative from

[5] Quoted from Fort Worth *Gazette,* March 3, 1887, clipping in Hogg Scrapbook No. 5, pp. 15–16; San Antonio *Express,* March 2, 1887; Cotner (ed.), *Addresses of James S. Hogg,* p. 36.

northern Wood County, is a fair example. Just serving his first term, he was inexperienced. He had farmed for Assistant Attorney General Marsh's grandfather in the seventies, and after going to Wood County he had become a friend of James Hogg. Now he made the office of the Attorney General his "holding-out place." Soon after the trial began, Jim (Cyclone) Davis,[6] who edited a paper at Mount Vernon, near Vorhees' home, arrived and, posing as Hogg's friend, was introduced to Marsh. Marsh completed the story:

One morning . . . Vorhees dropped in, and we had not talked long when the conversation led to the Willis case. Vorhees told me he had, the night before, met Willis, and found him to be quite pleasant and he could hardly believe he was as bad a man as Mr. Hogg thought he was. I at once said, John, where did you meet and become acquainted with Willis? To which he answered in effect that Jim Davis had invited him and several other members of the Legislature to be his theatre guests, all of whom were to assemble in the hotel lobby. . . . About the time they had gotten together, Willis passed by, spoke to and shook hands with Davis, and then Davis introduced him to the crowd, and told him they had assembled in a group to go to the show and insisted that Willis should go with him. He at first declined the invitation; but, after being urged by Davis, he consented to go. They spent a very enjoyable evening, and Willis proved to be very pleasant and agreeable. When I explained to him that the meeting was not accidental, but was a well-laid scheme to enable Willis to come in contact with him and the other representatives, his triers, Vorhees at once "saw the light," and lost no time in leading his benighted friends to also see it. . . . While a majority of the Legislature voted for his [Willis's] removal, the powerful and varied influences brought by Willis and his friends on the Legislature, circumvented a vote of two-thirds of the members of each house in favor for removal. The masterly handling of the case caused the people of the State to have that implicit confidence and high respect for your father as a law enforcement officer that the people of this section [East Texas] had for him. Your father left nothing legitimate undone to bring about Willis' conviction.[7]

After an overnight recess the House adopted the resolution, 67–21.

The procedure of an address, not impeachment, was followed also in the Senate. The charges submitted by the House to the Senate were that Judge Willis had organized a grand jury in which nine members

---

[6] W. J. Minton, "A Brief Biographical Sketch," in James H. (Cyclone) Davis, *Memoirs* (Sherman, Courier Press, 1935), pp. 317–324; Webb and Carroll, *Handbook of Texas*, I, 470.

[7] H. B. Marsh to Ima Hogg, April 9, 1935. Interv. Fol.

had an interest in defeating the state out of income from school lands, that the indictments against the foreman, Goodnight, and four other members were made with intention to defraud, that Willis knew the jurors were usually disqualified by previous actions connected with one of the fifty-six cases, that O. H. Nelson was tried and acquitted without notification or being present, and that Willis allowed a district attorney in the pay of Goodnight and others to prosecute.

Frank Willis submitted to the Senate committee his own ably written defense against the five charges, pointing up the problems created in establishing normal functions of government before the population is ready to conduct them properly. Much of the questioning covered by the House was gone over before the Senate committee, which finally adopted the House charges and recommended that Judge Willis be requested to appear in his own defense before the Senate. While smarting under the charges and "invectives" used against him, Judge Willis pleaded for mercy, telling the Senate: "I asked for an investigation. Not for such a one as I got![8]

On April 1 Hogg reviewed for the fourth time the case for the prosecution. After a dramatic defense by Judge Willis the concurrent resolution for removal was lost, 5–22, in spite of Hogg's persistent, vigorous, and skillful efforts. The Attorney General was relieved that this unpleasant duty was over, especially as he had foreseen the possible outcome when the address proceedings became entangled in Goodnight's lobbying tactics to change the land-lease law.

The big freeze and drought, which stimulated the free-grass–enclosure feuds, brought a number of land and lease measures before the House and Senate. While the hearings went on regarding House Bill No. 364, favored by Goodnight and some of his friends who under it would obtain 4-cent instead of 8-cent leases and would have less trouble over enclosures, Representative James N. Browning, from the huge Forty-third District, led the fight for the "free-grazing" men against the men favoring large acreage leasing of the school lands. Browning's bill would abolish leasing, while another bill, proposed by Senator Temple Lea Houston, the brilliant trial lawyer in eccentric

[8] James S. Hogg, "Notes on The State of Texas vs. Frank Willis in Senate," a short manuscript in J. S. Hogg Misc. Fol. Toward the end of the case Willis asked: "If you convict me will you turn your battery on the Attorney General for irregularity . . . ?" Willis claimed he was not treated fairly and, probably knowing George Clark's connections with Ross and Goodnight, saw fit to quote Clark, hoping to gain friends in the Senate.

dress, not unlike that of his father Sam, would make the continuation of unauthorized enclosures a penal offense, subject to fine and imprisonment. These proposals would put teeth into the act of 1883, as Governor Ireland had suggested, and might protect the lands for future homesteaders.

Goodnight was worried over these measures, but seemed to make little headway in furthering the legislation he preferred until Col. William "Buck" Walton of Austin (a former attorney general) suggested that Goodnight secure the services of George Clark of Waco, who had so successfully acted as Governor Ross's campaign manager. Clark came to Austin; Walton explained the situation; and Goodnight asked Clark what his fee would be to lobby against the "free-grass" measures.

"Five thousand dollars!" said Clark.

"If you kill it, I'll pay you your price," replied Goodnight.[9]

Clark went to work at the Capitol and reported that the bill was tabled. We now have Goodnight's version of what happened:

The next day he [Clark] went back and when it [Houston's bill] came up those old East Texas fellows jumped on it and just stomped the hell out of it. Houston looked like lightning had struck him. When Clark came back to the office, I said: "Look here Clark, how did you do it? I've been here two weeks and didn't do a thing." Clark sat down and explained: "I went up to these corncob pipe fellows, from down in East Texas, and referring to the enclosure bill, said, "What are you going to do with Goodnight's bill?" "Goodnight's bill," they would say; "that's not Goodnight's bill. That's Temple Houston's bill. I understand that Houston and Goodnight don't even speak." "Why should they speak? Don't you know Houston is working for Goodnight, and that that old son-of-a-gun wants this law passed because he wants free grass?" "O-o-h-h-h," the old corn-cobber would say, "is that so?" "Of course, it's so! Aren't you a hell of a fine fellow to be up here trying to serve the State!"[10]

Goodnight knew what the enclosure bill meant to men who were enclosing lands, and he got the Texas Live Stock Association to meet in Dallas and foster a ten-year lease system to help promote improvements such as killing prairie dogs, fencing, making tanks, erecting windmills, and, not stated but important to them, keeping out newcomers. Governor Ross had said industry wanted "stability"; so Goodnight argued that their proposals would give stability to the Plains and bring in lease

[9] Haley, *Goodnight*, p. 399. [10] *Ibid.*, p. 400.

money which could be counted on for ten years. Considering the pressures, it is interesting that the measure as passed allowed leases for only five years at 4 cents an acre![11]

"Bullionaire" Goodnight had fought two hard battles and had won just about all he wanted. Five years under new leases would put off another round until a new man was elected attorney general. Hogg had met defeat, was politically dead—or so it seemed to Goodnight. Actually, Hogg had profited from these experiences, which had broadened his vision of the inner workings and relationships between law and politics and social behavior. During the Willis hearings he was convinced, like Templeton, that he was fighting for respect for law and that the Judge deserved to be removed. He had made his pleas for support of the laws he took an oath to enforce. Had he known that George Clark, Governor Ross's own campaign manager, was promised a five-thousand-dollar lobby fee, Hogg's general optimism and faith in leaders of the people might have received a worse jolt. Receiving pay as a lawyer for legal advice was one thing; but lobbying by a corporation attorney who was also the governor's trusted adviser, was, in those days, something else.[12]

The legislature had created the awkward, and ironic, situation in which it was placed by organizing counties before the area was ready, economically or politically, to administer them. And now, with things going in favor of Goodnight—the legislature ready to abolish the Land Board and to cut the lease rates to 4 cents—it would have been even more ironic if the Judge had been humiliated while Goodnight wired Mrs. Adair's agent:

Our lease bill will pass. I have paid for it and should know.[13]

Goodnight would fight Hogg during the remainder of his political career and try to turn other men in the Panhandle against him; with what success would be indicated by later events. Evetts Haley, himself an Adair Ranch man, felt that Hogg did not understand the enclosure–free-grass fight. This is doubtful, for he had already made the acquaintance of John W. "Bet-a-Million" Gates[14] of Braddock Wire Company,

[11] The Act Providing for the Sale and Lease of School and other Public Lands was approved April 1, 1887. Gammel, *Laws of Texas*, IX, 885–886.

[12] Clark does not mention this episode in his brief memoirs, *A Glance Backward* (Houston, Rein & Sons, 1914), pp. 87 ff.

[13] Haley, *Goodnight*, p. 401.

[14] Webb and Carroll, *Handbook of Texas*, I, 675.

116

who was demonstrating the uses of barbed wire. However, this was beside the point. Hogg was doing his duty in law enforcement, and he wanted everyone, public servants and private citizens, to understand that he would continue to do just that until the law was changed. Goodnight so well understood Hogg's responsibility that he did the best thing for himself and those who shared his interests—he got the law changed. Of course, Hogg and the free-grass men of the Plains did not read the telegram disclosing how the Browning and Houston bills had been shelved. Hogg intended to remain the champion of law enforcement, and he intended that if nothing else was gained from the hearings at least all law enforcement agents of the state would be alerted to do what he considered their duty or to expect his public denunciation. Even the powerful Texas Sheriffs' Association was publicly chastized for acting like a political party in subjecting candidates for office to demands calculated to increase the income for sheriffs. (Texas must emerge from a state of rampant lawlessness and lax enforcement in all areas, whether the subject be land leases, Capitol Syndicate land holdings along the New Mexico line, local option liquor laws, or lynching.) After he had seen the legislature fold up under pressure of a small but powerful lobby he understood more fully why the job of enforcing special-interest laws was so unpopular. Did the public believe he had done his whole duty? Only time would tell.

Among the stipulations of the Texas Constitution of 1876 for the duties of the attorney general were the following:

He shall especially inquire into the charter rights of all private corporations, and from time to time in the name of the State take such action in the courts as may be proper and necessary to prevent any private corporation from exercising any power or demanding or collecting any taxes, tolls, freight or wharfage not authorized by law.[15]

Thus Hogg's routine duties included the inspection of many insurance company and railroad charters. In the first obligation he had the cooperation of the commissioner of insurance, who acted as a double check on insurance companies; however, since the position of state engineer for railroads had been eliminated, the burden of any investigation of railroads became largely his sole responsibility.

[15] Constitution of the State of Texas (1876), Article IV, Section 22. See Hogg's Speech at Rusk, April 19, 1890, quoted in Cotner (ed.), *Addresses of James S. Hogg*, p. 66.

James Hogg looked upon a charter of incorporation as a two-way responsibility. The laws of incorporation specified minimum requirements, and those businesses which wished to meet them were free to request and secure permission to carry out the purposes of each charter. On the other hand, the state should protect a legitimate business against concerns which received charters under false pretenses or which operated illegally with or without charters, and thereby created a situation of unfair competition. Specifically, in regard to insurance companies, he understood that the state's responsibility was to strengthen and protect legally operating concerns from the "wildcats" and at the same time to protect the public against any fraudulence whatsoever; in regard to the railroads, the state must require that they perform their charter obligations to the public—by using safe equipment, providing adequate depots, maintaining shops and offices within the state, and abstaining from the consolidation of parallel lines or illegal combinations to fix rates.

In the midst of the Willis case Commissioner of Insurance L. L. Foster requested the Attorney General to make an inspection of the charter, bylaws, and annual statement of the National Mutual Fire Insurance Company of Salina, Kansas, to determine whether the company should be permitted to do business in Texas. The National Mutual was a private corporation organized to secure protection for its members against "loss or damage of property by fire." According to Kansas law, private corporations were of three kinds: 1) religious, 2) charitable or benevolent, and 3) profit-making; furthermore, two general types of insurance were permitted, one a "stock" plan, the other a "mixed" mutual and stock plan. The National Mutual appeared to be of the second type. By Kansas law the company was authorized to take "premium notes," which became liens on the property insured; the liability of the members was fixed, and cash premiums, fees, and premium notes were declared to be the capital of the company. Hogg told Foster that, while the laws of Kansas seemed to fully authorize the company in that state, "protecting its *members in* Kansas, under the cooperative or 'Mutual assessment' plan, there was no reserve fund or capital stock required for the protection of 'outside' parties who may insure this company, especially if they should be non-residents of Kansas."[16]

Hogg emphasized that in Kansas under the stock plan, which this

---

[16] J. S. Hogg to Hon. L. L. Foster, February 26, 1887, Att. Gen. Let. Pr., 38 (typescript), pp. 353–360. Originals in Office of the Attorney General, Capitol Building, Austin.

company did not claim to have, a security capital of $100,000 was required to protect policyholders. In this respect Texas law was similar, but every insurance company was also required to have an actual bona fide capital stock of not less than $100,000, with restrictions upon its investment.[17] Furthermore, purely benevolent societies in Texas had to make an annual report to the state, and failure to do so caused them to be considered profit-making operations. The Attorney General ruled that although "a company may be called a 'mutual aid' or charitable, or benevolent association, if it is in fact conducted for *profit to its officers,* etc., it is an *insurance* company, and subject to the general insurance laws of Texas." He concluded:

It is a well settled principle of law, that no action can be maintained by an officer of a benevolent society against a member for his initiation fees or dues; for the mere moral obligation, though it be strengthened by a written express promise to pay, affords no sufficient consideration in law.

Every safeguard surrounds this company in Kansas for the certain collection of its "premium rates," executed by its home members, and it is therefore run for profit, and is in every respect—in name, in object and in fact—an *insurance* company, and cannot work in Texas under that Article 2971a, which was, without a doubt, created alone for those humane institutions operated for the mutual aid of its lodge members and their dependents in distress and not for the pecuniary benefit of its officers and members.

The "National Mutual" derives its authority from laws unknown to Texas; is an insurance company for business purposes, having in view the profit and advantage to its officers and agents directly and to its members remotely; and although it may incidentally contemplate the promotion of the interests of others in a benevolent way, it cannot be lawfully permitted to operate in this State without strictly complying with the general laws of insurance, and you are so, most respectfully, advised.[18]

Apparently, from available records, the company was not then able or did not see fit to meet the Texas requirements, after this interpretation.

On receiving letters in complaint against companies operating illegally,[19] Hogg would request Commissioner Foster to investigate. A list of "wildcat" or illegally operating companies was drawn up, and the

[17] "Incorporation of Insurance Companies," Title LIII, Chapter I, *Revised Statutes of Texas* (Galveston, 1879), pp. 421 ff.

[18] J. S. Hogg to L. L. Foster, February 26, 1887, Att. Gen. Let. Pr., 38, pp. 353–360.

[19] Allison Mayfield (Sherman, Texas) to J. S. Hogg, August 8, 1887, Att. Gen.

Attorney General sent out the list in his famous "Circular Letter" to district and county attorneys and advised them to do their duty.[20]

However, not all the burden of enforcement was left to the county attorneys. Hogg gave substantial assistance. For example, in the fall of 1887, when a complaint was received, he checked with the commissioner of insurance and found that the so-called Masonic Mutual Benefit Association of Fort Worth had no authority to do business. He then requested his informants to notify County Attorney A. G. McIlwaine of Troup of the facts and promised action; at the same time, he wrote McIlwaine of the case, instructing him to institute prosecution against the agent.[21] On another occasion County Attorney Ben S. Rogers of Brenham was urged to proceed against George P. Banks for writing insurance for the Pierre Insurance Company of Dakota, the German-American Insurance Company of New Orleans, Louisiana, and the Royal Insurance Company of Birmingham, Alabama—all unauthorized companies; furthermore, in the interest of immediate and vigorous prosecution for the offenses, Rogers was told that he could cite certain parties Hogg named as witnesses.[22]

In a case at Abilene against the Guarantee Mutual Accident Association of New York, County Attorney A. P. Hardwicke was told to have policyholders appear before the Justice of the Peace "following the proceedings of *Smith* v. *the State* (18th Court of Appeals)," and to proceed against the agents, Hogg again furnishing their names.[23] This same company was also prosecuted at Waco. In a case at Brenham, Hogg forwarded the state's brief and the Supreme Court decision in the *quo warranto* action of *Texas ex rel.* v. *S. M. Farmer, et al.* from Tarrant County. The information was also to be used against "a similar, but worse, concern," of Paris.[24] The damage from frauds was so great as to

---

Let. Pr., 40, p. 483; J. G. Bonner (Tyler) to Attorney General Hogg, August 18, 1887, Att. Gen. Let. Pr., 40, p. 625.

[20] J. S. Hogg to L. L. Foster, February 26, 1887, Att. Gen. Let. Pr., 40, p. 284.

[21] J. S. Hogg to Messrs. F. R. Gilbert and John O. Collier, October 1, 1887. Att. Gen. Let. Pr., 40, p. 251.

[22] Assistant Attorney General R. H. Harrison to Ben S. Rogers, October 29, 1887, Att. Gen. Let. Pr., 41, pp. 383; 399–400. Cf. J. S. Hogg to L. L. Foster, June 18, 1887, Att. Gen. Let. Pr., 40, pp. 21–22, citing *Revised Statutes of the United States*, Chapter I, Title 23, Section 1851 to uphold his ruling that mere chartering of a company by a territorial government did not bar it from doing business in Texas.

[23] J. S. Hogg to A. P. Hardwicke, December 30, 1887, Att. Gen. Let. Pr., 42, p. 125.

[24] J. S. Hogg to J. H. Lyday, February 20, 1888, Att. Gen. Let. Pr., 42, pp. 562–563.

necessitate immediate action to clear up the nature of these companies or force them out of business.

The Attorney General was also careful to check on new companies moving into Texas. In the fall of 1887 he asked the commissioner of insurance if he had found any other companies unlawfully operating in Texas since the previous report.[25] Working diligently to stamp out the frauds, Hogg was nevertheless courteous to those men who indicated concern about the companies they represented and who announced their intentions to wind up the business if it was found to be illegal.[26]

The insurance world from New York to Kansas was soon aware that Texas laws were strictly enforced, and the word spread that Texas encouraged only legitimate business. However, Hogg was not hostile to out-of-state companies per se. No company which complied with the law need fear his office, although the commissioner of insurance enforced other routine requirements which possibly were irksome to some agents. In 1885 the Fidelity and Casualty Company had received an adverse opinion from Hogg's predecessor, Templeton. Toward the end of Hogg's first term the agents resubmitted the question of lawful admission to do business. The Attorney General told Foster that there was no limit on the number of companies or persons who could engage in the insurance business in Texas, but that articles of incorporation must be in order and that the companies must have not less than $100,000 of capital stock. If the applicants had submitted the necessary papers and had met the "tests of solvency"[27] imposed by the commissioner, only the arbitrary action of withholding a certificate of authority would exclude legal entry. Therefore, if any company, including the Fidelity and Casualty Company, met all the normal legal tests, Hogg advised the commissioner to issue a certificate.

The Circular Letter and subsequent actions were effective; suspect companies either folded up or made changes so as to meet the legal requirements. Only one firm felt aggrieved sufficiently to sue the Attorney General. A. F. Settig and two other officers of the Equitable Relief Society of Houston personally sued Hogg for $10,000 each, alleging the Circular was libelous. Hogg was accustomed to threats of physical danger in retaliation for his wholehearted enforcement of the law, but

[25] J. S. Hogg to L. L. Foster, November 7, 1887, Att. Gen. Let. Pr., 41, p. 454.
[26] J. S. Hogg to J. M. Reagan in reference to the "Fril Assessment Association of Dallas," which was held to be illegal as then operating, October 13, 1887, Att. Gen. Let. Pr., 41, p. 309.
[27] *Revised Statutes* (1879), Articles 2910 and 2911; J. S. Hogg to L. L. Foster, December 31, 1888, Att. Gen. Let. Pr., 45, pp. 626–634.

a legal threat involving financial loss was more difficult to combat. His attorneys, Michael Looscan, M. W. Garnett, and F. Z. Schaefer, filed a demurrer in Harris County District Court. He based his claim of no cause for action on several counts:

1. Plaintiff's petition shows that if any injury was intended or inflicted it was on the reputation of a private corporation, or a society assuming unlawfully to be a corporation.

2. If the officers formed an unlawful association in composition and usurped corporate functions, they neither can in fact or in law be libeled.

3. No reason was given for not bringing suit in name of society which plaintiff represents.

4. Does not show authority to bring suit.

5. Shows no special damage to said corporation and consequently none to himself as a promoter.

6. Fails to show malice.

7. Actually corporation and each member materially benefited from the alleged libel.

8. It sues to recover damages from a public official for the alleged performance of an executive-judicial act in advising and instructing subordinate officials to discharge their duty against violators of the law.

9. It is argumentative and seeks to advertise through this court the wisdom and sagacity of plaintiff and his associate promoters of an insurance company, under the guise of a "Benevolent society."[28]

Finally, if abatement were denied, the Attorney General denied all and singular the allegations of the plaintiff's petition and called for strict proof.

Hogg went down to Houston to defend himself at the March, 1888, term. He acknowledged having questioned the modes and ultimate object of several so-called benevolent societies in the Circular to district and county attorneys, and suggested solemnly that if the societies wanted to make the contents of the Circular public he would not object. Here was a new self-assurance and a new tone for an attorney general. Hogg sought no compromise; the wholehearted enforcement of the law was desired. He declared that he expected results from the Circular, and he wanted it widely known that he hoped to rid Texas of the illegal insurance societies. If necessary, he stated, he would issue another circular in stronger language, as he did not expect to dodge any responsibility of his office.

[28] J. S. Hogg to Major M. Looscan (Houston), March 14, 1888, J. S. Hogg Let. Pr., 1, p. 296.

Attorney H. F. Ring, for the plaintiff, contended that the Circular was not a privileged communication, that it worked personal injury to his client, branding each officer of the society a thief and swindler. He wanted to know if the Attorney General was exalted so high above the people that he could with impunity and with the endorsements of the courts publicly brand private citizens as thieves and not be liable. Ring argued that the Relief Society was legal, stating that the officers served without compensation. Colonel Brady, another lawyer for the plaintiff, put forth as argument that he was defending men who were fighting for a principle of government, insisting that Hogg had in substance argued that the Attorney General's Office could do no wrong. A reporter told of Brady's dramatic appeal:

Kings have been tried for violating the law, but in Texas the Attorney General would have citizens understand that he ranked above the majesty of the law. He . . . arraigned the Attorney General as "the power of the State" in cutting terms of irony.[29]

After Attorney Garnett presented a forceful defense, Judge J. R. Masterson announced that the Court would sustain that part of Hogg's demurrer relative to the liability for damages, but added that he thought the Attorney General would find the Equitable Relief Society "a good legitimate institution."[30] However, available records in the Office of the Commissioner of Insurance do not reveal that the Society either qualified or chose to continue operation.

Hogg had succeeded in ridding the state of many companies which by fraud and misrepresentation were robbing people of all classes. Legitimate companies were encouraged and strengthened, and the commissioner of insurance estimated that the people of Texas were saved at least $250,000 per year between 1887 and 1890. Hogg publicly praised Commissioner Foster:

By the aid of an efficient and faithful Commissioner of Insurance through the courts I effected the extermination of every one of them [the wildcats] within twelve months.[31]

Equally important was the arousing of the public and the legislators to the seriousness and magnitude of insurance rackets. Furthermore,

[29] Houston *Post*, March 26, 1888.
[30] *Ibid.*; Hogg's Speech at Rusk, April 19, 1890.
[31] Quoted from Hogg's Speech at Rusk, April 19, 1890. Between February and July, 1888, Hogg and his staff worked on a list of twenty violators of the law. See Austin *Statesman*, July 12 and 19, 1888.

123

long before Attorney Louis D. Brandeis[32] made a national reputation through the insurance exposures in New England and Charles Evans Hughes[33] won similar fame in New York, Jim Hogg had made Texans conscious of the loss of a vast investment potential, should all premiums flow out of the state. Among the results of this awareness were two later statutes of major importance to Texas. By a law passed in 1893, when Hogg was governor, a gross premium tax of 1¼ per cent was collected by the treasurer of Texas, while counties, cities, and towns were prohibited from levying an occupation tax on insurance companies. Though the Act eliminated a potential source of revenue for the local subdivisions, it paved the way to better regulation and simplified tax records for the state and for the companies. This step was generally agreeable to the companies, as was the practice of offering tax reductions to those companies that would reinvest large percentages of their collections in Texas. Capital was scarce in the Southwest, but Texans took the long look and moved toward more direct action. Secondly, the famous Robertson Insurance Law of 1907, written by Hogg's law partner James H. Robertson of Austin, required that 75 per cent of premiums be reinvested within the state.[34] Passage of the law was followed by the haughty withdrawal of many major and minor national companies. Some years later, however, most of these firms, seeing the fat incomes of the young Texas companies that had grown vigorous as population and wealth had rapidly expanded, returned, paying their fines with interest. Some major companies pouted until after World War II and then decided to pay up in order to share in the expanding insurance business.

The pressure of routine questions and cases on the Attorney General's Office in 1887 may be judged from the fact that from ten to twenty letters, some of a highly technical nature, went out each day. The Willis case had stimulated inquiries from old and new officials in doubt as to proper proceedings and the limits or duties of their offices. For example, the county attorney of Young County wanted to know if the commis-

---

[32] Louis D. Brandeis, *Other People's Money* (New York, Frederick A. Stokes Company, 1913, 1932), pp. 4–5, 51 ff.; Alpheus T. Mason, *Brandeis* (New York, Viking Press, 1946), pp. 154 ff.

[33] C. C. Hyde, "Charles Evans Hughes," *American Secretaries of State,* ed. Samuel F. Bemis (New York, A. A. Knopf, 1929), X, 222; Merlo J. Pusey, *Charles Evans Hughes* (New York, Macmillan Company, 1951), I, 140–169.

[34] Robertson, who in 1895 had resigned his district judgeship (to which Governor Hogg appointed him in 1891) to become Hogg's law partner, later ran for the legislature with the purpose of writing the Act.

sioners' court could not authorize paying county attorneys extra salary in special cases. H. B. Marsh, writing for the office, recognized that the law might work a hardship upon the newly organized and sparsely settled counties, even "in many instances depriving them of the services of efficient officers," but did restrict payments to "fees and perquisites." However, if a doctor was required in a lunacy case, the commissioners might authorize a fee for him.[35] Hundreds of letters went out to sheriffs urging them to be diligent and to help with tax cases. Cattle and hide inspectors, who were especially busy, frequently sought advice, because the farmers and ranchmen in some parts of the state were not taking kindly to inspection.

As Hogg turned to the less routine problems of the railroads, he found their managements equating in at least one way to these farmers and ranchmen—they did not take kindly to inspection either. Not yet ready in March 1887 to begin a frontal attack on the powerful Texas Traffic Association (involving nine railroads), the Attorney General set about with such legal tools as were available to him and began to plug up the holes in the dike of judicial responsibility. He intended that new railroads should have their charters drawn so carefully that at least they would not be able to join their predecessors in flying to federal courts every time they got into trouble from Texas decisions, and he hoped to end the rule of federal receivers.

The Texas Revised Civil Statutes of 1885 had made it the duty of the attorney general to examine the articles of incorporation of proposed railroad companies.[36] During Hogg's first term, twenty-three original charters were certified as drawn in accordance with the law, and ten amended charters were examined and approved.[37] He required that the following clause be inserted in all charters, whether new or just coming up for revision:

[35] H. B. Marsh to T. B. Wadley (Midland), June 22, 1887, Att. Gen. Let. Pr., 40, pp. 40–41; H. B. Marsh to W. J. Croom (Wharton), July 1, 1887, Att. Gen. Let. Pr., 40, p. 146.

[36] Article 1190, effective 1883, covering "foreign as well as domestic corporations," S.B. 254, "An Act requiring the Attorney General to institute legal proceedings against corporations doing business within this State in violation of Section 5 and Section 6, Article X, of The Constitution of Texas," had been approved March 28, 1885. Hans P. N. Gammel (ed.), *Laws of Texas, 1822–1897* (Austin, Gammel Book Company, 1898), IX, 685–686; S.S.B. No. 219, approved, *Ibid.*, 90, provided for institution of suits in Travis County District Court in private or corporation land cases over illegal fencing, etc.

[37] James S. Hogg, *Report of the Attorney General,* 1887–1888 (Austin, 1889),

The corporation hereby created and its successors shall be forever subject to all the changes, rules, and regulations that may be prescribed by the laws of Texas.[38]

Most of the companies, whether old or newly petitioning, complied without delay, understanding that the restriction was due to the high-handed actions of a few corporations and grew out "of an abundance of caution," but some unsuccessfully fought the clause. During his second term Hogg approved forty-three new charters and eleven with amendments. The aggregate of approvals stands as evidence to refute the often-leveled charge that James Hogg was hostile to the main purposes of railroads.

Opponents of Hogg's vigorous policies of law enforcement also claimed that his actions discouraged railroad building. Actually, the major Texas railroads had already been laid out; their continued extension so far in advance of settlement often made paying returns almost impossible, especially at the time when the drought of 1886–1887 discouraged small farm expansion and people were barely "hanging on" in the area west of a line from Austin north to Mineral Wells.[39] Charles Francis Adams, observing the national trend, wrote that the period of railroad expansion was slowing down and that a new era of consolidation was at hand.[40] Nevertheless, charters continued to be sought in Texas—some for building railroads into the West, such as the Fort Worth and Albuquerque or the Waco and Llano projects, and a large number for city transit systems that evidenced the growth of urban centers in Texas. Dallas had a half-dozen chartered companies, Sherman and Denison were connected by an "electric," and Austin had its "Rapid Transit," encouraged by the prospect of a power dam near the city.

In the fall of 1887, Richard V. Evans, general manager of the Texas,

---

p. xvi. The St. Louis, Arkansas, and Texas Railway Company in Texas and the Gulf, Colorado, and Santa Fe twice presented and received amended charters. Attorney General Templeton had approved 24 original charters and 8 amended charters in 1884–1886.

[38] Articles 4090, 4101, and 4102 of the *Revised Civil Statutes*, (Austin, 1889); Gammel, *Laws of Texas,* IX, 1045; J. S. Hogg to E. L. Gregg, April 17, 1889, Att. Gen. Let. Pr., 47, pp. 140–141.

[39] Theodore Fetter, *Southwestern Freight Rates* (Boston, Christopher Publishing House, 1934), pp. 29 ff.

[40] Charles F. Adams, Jr., *Railroads,* p. 197. Reed, *Texas Railroads,* pp. 516–517, and Henry V. Poor, *Manual for Railroads, 1889,* (New York, H. V. and H. W. Poor, 1889), p. vi, show that almost 1,000 miles were built in Texas during 1887, but a long decline set in, which continued until 1901 with slight variations.

Sabine Valley, and Northwestern, complained that the Attorney General had exceeded his powers in rejecting the company's charter. Hogg wrote:

You will recollect that the certificate of this Department was refused and upon the objections being pointed out you removed them by striking out the obnoxious features. . . . If the professional pride of Messrs Sullivan & Cromwell has been wounded by this action it is truly regretful but it could not be avoided. Should your company object to the charter in its present condition and wish to test and submit an amendment incorporating the rejected parts then the certificate will be promptly refused by this Department and those aggrieved lawyers can have an opportunity to right their wrongs.[41]

In order to get on with building the railroad, the company met the conditions without further commotion, and the charter was then approved. Hogg's fair but firm handling of this matter was typical of his approach. The companies that were not bent on evading Texas law found the Attorney General encouraging and cooperative. The Honorable James B. Simpson, an outstanding businessman of Dallas, wrote later in 1887 complaining of the rejection of a charter for the Dallas and New Orleans Railway because fewer than ten incorporators had been named. (Article 4090 of the Revised Statutes clearly required that no less than ten persons were necessary to form a railway corporation.) The Attorney General replied:

Fearing this decision had been first made with reference to your company, and that apparent injustice had been done you (this supposition arising from the tenor of your letter) an examination has been made of all the charters, now on file in the Secretary of State's Office, and which have been approved this year, but without finding one wherein less than ten of the incorporators sign the charter. Of course what can be done by the principal can be done by the Agent on whom has been conferred the proper power, which may relieve you of the necessity of sending your charter back to the Old Country for signatures of the incorporators.[42]

Early in January 1888 the charter was resubmitted and approved. The assistant attorney general told Simpson that it was satisfactory "in every way except the affidavit, which is hardly up to that standard of certainty

[41] J. S. Hogg to Richard V. Evans, October 20, 1887, Att. Gen. Let. Pr., 41, p. 340.

[42] J. S. Hogg to James B. Simpson, January 8, 1888, Att. Gen. Let. Pr., 42, pp. 95–98.

desired, but it is in the language of the law, which of itself will justify the Secretary of State in accepting it."[43] The cooperation evident here does not accord with the picture of Hogg as an irritable dogmatist which was promulgated by some men, among them Abner Taylor, of the Capitol Syndicate, and Charles Goodnight, most of whom wanted to grind axes that Hogg believed needed instead, for the public interest, a slight blunting.

To James Hogg the basic proposition concerning railroads appears to have been simple, though its application might be fraught with complications: the people of Texas needed and wanted railroads, but the need would be truly served only if the lines, whether new or old, observed the charter stipulations, which had been designed in the public interest. Therefore the Attorney General considered that his duty within the limits of his office was twofold. On the one hand he must encourage both new enterprises and those already established; on the other he must assist the people to secure the maximum advantage possible from any new or old franchise and be always alert to charter violations, unwitting or intended.

Encouragement entailed a certain flexibility of viewpoint, especially in regard to new charters. For example, charters were required by law to name the counties through which a proposed line would run. Hogg knew, since final decisions about routes depended on surveys, that obstacles might arise in preliminary planning stages; he often therefore recommended that all possible counties be listed—"a series of counties contiguous to each other" along the projected line, but "do not scatter too much"[44] so that there could be no reasonable objection if the line actually did not go into all the counties. Construction, too, was sometimes avoidably slow in getting started. The Attorney General's Office was always ready to provide information about the leeway for eligibility to receive land grants from the public domain. The law provided that roads chartered before 1885 might have two years in which to begin construction and to equip and put in running order at least ten miles of the proposed line. This would establish eligibility.

Larger problems were presented by the state's need to see to it that established roads kept themselves in a condition of safe operation and furnished the services required by their charters. Early in February, 1887, the citizens of Sabine Pass had petitioned Governor Ross to com-

[43] H. B. Marsh to J. B. Simpson, January 8, 1888, Att. Gen. Let. Pr., 42, p. 220.
[44] J. S. Hogg to Messrs. Whittaker and Bonner (Tyler), June 29, 1889, Att. Gen. Let. Pr., 48, pp. 370–371.

pel repairs and resumption of operation on the Sabine and East Texas Railroad. The region had suffered from a tropical storm the year before, and the thirty-mile lumber and passenger line between Beaumont and Sabine Pass, actually a part of the Southern Pacific System, was not operating. Legally it was competitive but a feeder, and operated under a separate Texas charter. Mill owners and merchants of the region were distressed for lack of transportation, and many lumbermen would soon be out of work. The Attorney General, who was in the midst of the Willis trial, had received some information from citizens of Beaumont, and he informed the governor that he was gathering evidence and would proceed to give the matter "due and full attention as soon as the other pressing business before me will permit."[45]

As soon as the Willis trial was over and the insurance cases were under way, Hogg brought suit against this section of the C. P. Huntington railroad domain in District Court of Jefferson County. By *quo warranto* proceedings, he expected to force the company either to repair and operate the Sabine and East Texas Railroad or to forfeit its charter. Efforts were made by the company to obtain a continuance, but Hogg told its chief attorney, Colonel E. P. Hill, who was also a vice-president of the Southern Pacific System, that the state wished to dispose of the case at Beaumont.[46] Though the case concerned a small line, the principle involved was very important, especially at the outset of a new administration and at a time when Jay Gould was being charged with draining capital and rolling stock from Texas roads and with failure to make much-needed repairs.[47] The Sabine and East Texas was decaying and not in use; therefore the case would serve as a precedent without risking an estoppel. Hogg was ready for the test.

In June the Galveston *News* reported that the Attorney General was in Beaumont to bring about a forfeiture of charter, an unusual proceeding.[48] For the new Attorney General to venture so far from Austin and for such a purpose was news. Since the company knew very well that it had a good franchise in a rich lumber area and did not wish to lose its

---

[45] J. S. Hogg to His Excellency, L. S. Ross, Governor, February 11, 1887, Att. Gen. Let. Pr., 38, p. 216. The Willis case was taking all of his time.

[46] J. S. Hogg to Judge E. P. Hill, June 2, 1887, Att. Gen. Let. Pr., 39, p. 566. He quoted the act of 1885 "requiring the Attorney General to institute legal proceedings," etc. Gammel, *Laws,* IX, 685–686.

[47] Cf. Robert E. Riegel, *Story of the Western Railroads,* pp. 174–177; Vincent V. Masterson, *The Katy Railroad* (Norman, University of Oklahoma Press, 1952), pp. 222–225; map, p. 235.

[48] Galveston *News,* June 7, 1887.

charter, its lawyers were prepared to promise restoration of the tracks and trains and resumption of operations as soon as possible. Hogg agreed to a continuance on the basis of an affidavit by the defendant that the road would be rebuilt and in operation by the next term of court.

To prepare himself for a possible future argument about the status of repair if the case should eventually have to be fought out, Hogg then made an inspection trip down the line of the road to Sabine Pass. The see-for-himself procedure had worked well in the case of the Irishman's ditch in Wood County. Once again it was a felicitous method; everyone was now convinced that he meant business, and the prospect of renewed transportation in the region brought smiles to the faces of lumber workers, mill owners, and merchants along the route.[49]

With the coming of summer the Attorney General had at last a certain breathing space—but not much. In spite of the fact that from the day of his swearing-in events had been piling in on him without surcease, his energy had carried him triumphantly through the months, in large part because of his deep interest in what he was doing, his remarkable powers of concentration when a job was to be organized and then performed, and his equally remarkable ability to relax, particularly in the evenings at home with his family and on Sunday. The increase in weight that had begun when, as district attorney, he had to spend long sedentary hours at his desk (contrary to his former invariable habits of exercise and performance of routine physical activities enjoyable to him—such as wood chopping and fence building) had continued in Austin. Now weighing over 250 pounds, he was definitely a fat man. Yet his energy appeared no whit diminished, and the breadth and height of his great frame carried the pounds well, so that in any gathering he was an even more commanding figure than formerly.

The pressure in his office abating somewhat, Hogg was forced by public opinion to turn his attention to another matter. The temperance movement in Texas had been growing throughout the winter and spring months into an ever more thorny issue for political leaders. To avoid confusion at the regular 1886 election, the State Democratic Convention had agreed that a prohibition amendment would be submitted to the voters in a special election on August 4, 1887. Jim Hogg would have preferred to stay out of the increasingly bitter controversy, because of the strict attention he needed to give to his pressing official duties, but George Clark, manager of the antiprohibition forces, besought him to

[49] J. S. Hogg, *Report of the Attorney General,* 1887–1888, p. iii.

answer some of the outstanding speakers of the prohibition camp. In fact, all officials in high public office were forced to state their position. Therefore, in early summer Hogg spoke at Tyler, and on July 26 at Fort Worth to a rally that drew about fifteen thousand people. The two speeches were elaborations of a letter written in May to W. W. Douglas of Winnsboro and later widely circulated.

Hogg believed firmly in personal temperance. He still observed his father's rule of not drinking in saloons, as had been his practice at least as far back as his days as justice of the peace in Quitman. Hogg enjoyed having beer and wine at home, and he never presumed to criticize the habits of his friends and acquaintances, although in at least one instance he helped to raise a fund to assist a friend win a fight against alcoholism. The letter to Douglas put forth his reasoning on the matter, which added up to a philosophical pattern somewhat unusual for the day. At many times during his career Hogg's opponents accused him of opportunism (a vague tag that is eminently useful when critics have run out of other specifics); however, this charge is the most easily refuted of all the many made against him, for in his letters and other papers is found solid evidence both of the reasoning that underlay his every action, whether personal or official, and of the philosophy which invested the acts with a significance far beyond their immediate political setting. The "prohibition letter" is a prime example of this fact, as the following excerpts demonstrate:

Replying to your inquiry by letter of the 11th instant, I beg to say that it is true that I am opposed to the adoption of the proposed amendments to our constitution on the subject of prohibition. . . . If you were to ask me if I am opposed to temperance and sobriety, then I should cheerfully tell you no, and that I yet practice what I preach in this respect.

Aside from the great fundamental principles involved which touch the very heart of a freeman's government, I should oppose the proposed measure on the grounds of its utter impracticability and of the prolific evils that would certainly flow from its adoption. The objects of its advocates are commendable, in so far as they intend to abate intemperance. . . . Such results are not possible, however, from prohibition or any species of coercion. Morality, sobriety and religion spring from a different source than brute force or the lash of law. Men cannot be made moral, forced into temperance or whipped into religion. The way to happiness and to heaven is pointed out by our Savior, whose great influence has been most felt from his humility, meekness, kindness, forbearance, precept and example. . . .

By the powers of "moral suasion" in the church and around the family

131

hearthstone, and in the school room, followed up by worthy examples by those who lead the way in society and business—especially of those who assume the role of moral reformers—temperance and sobriety will prevail, for by these methods men's pride and honor can be cultivated and aroused to the elevated standard of honesty and truth in all things.

In revolt at dictation and coercion in private affairs men become combative when there is hope in open resistance, but so soon as this feeling is gone they sneak next in the hiding places of cowards, criminals and outlaws, to evade what they conceive and contend to be oppression. In such refuges tricks are conjured, and deception and hypocrisy are practiced, and perjury is bred, nurtured and emulated.

The proposed amendment does not prohibit the *importation* of liquors, but it does intend to prevent the *sale* of them except for *medicinal, scientific, mechanical* and *sacramental* purposes. Therefore anyone can get the liquid who may order it by the pint, quart, gallon, keg, barrel or cargo, which he can give away or drink at will. . . . and it is possible—*barely possible*—that if the amendment is carried the saloons will close up, and as an expedient if closely pressed, be transformed into drugstores; or will only keep liquors for "sick people," "scientific gentlemen" and those engaged in the "mechanics." . . .

If the war is really on the evil influence of the Saloons, as some avow, then it can be made more successfully in the legislature than by the present methods. Remove the screens so that all drinkers can be seen; abolish the vulgar pictures which arouse the evil passions; drive out the enchanting music which draws the crowds, and clear away the gaming tables that afford sport, recreation and amusement for the patrons. A step further, on this line, if necessary close them up at night, or not permit lights to be used in the saloons from sun-down until sun-up, so that he who goes there after night will do so alone for a drink and must grope in the darkness to slake his thirst. Supplement this by heavy bonds and high license; exclude the sale of liquor from every other place and there will be some chance at least of confining a great evil under the surveillance of law where it can be made to defray a large share of the tax, as it does now, and to carry all the odium which the rules of society and the temperance people can place upon it. . . .

Hogg then offered very practical legislative methods which could lessen the "evil influence" of saloons and insure obedience to law by saloon operators. Returning to the proposed amendment, he pointed out more of the unfortunate effects he believed it would have:

If, for no stronger reasons, this amendment ought to be defeated upon the grounds that it would scatter the traffic and use of intoxicants and force them into low dives and high places alike, without the attendance of law or the burdens of taxation, where in the former they would be productive of the most hideous and corrupting forms of crime, and in the latter they would play the part of "keen-cut" reapers of the fairest flowers of our land. . . .

Yes, my friend, I am opposed to and shall vote against the so-called prohibition amendment, for what I believe to be the welfare of morality, the protection of virtue, the promotion of honesty and the perpetuity of good government. With great respect and sincere friendship,

Your Ob't. Sev't.,
J. S. Hogg[50]

The Prohibition Amendment was defeated and did not come up again during the nineteenth century. Hogg was never the idol of the liquor interests, and local dealers were restless because of his efforts at strict law enforcement. His concern over the spread of drinking among women was distorted by some of his Tyler temperance neighbors, who opposed him politically, into "rumors" that he had "insulted" the ladies of Tyler. Hogg was irritated by these slanders and expressed his appreciation to friends who set the record straight.

During the months since coming to Austin, the Hogg family had been enjoying the many advantages of the capital city, although the Attorney General's strenuous duties kept him, in unhappily great degree, from sharing many of the family's pleasures. After a short time at the Widow Andrews' establishment, they had moved to the good-sized, two-story house that, true to his home-owning pattern, Hogg purchased on Fourteenth Street. Here once more Sallie Hogg had plied her skill in making a home, although by early summer she was in very delicate health. Another baby was due in August; while none of her pregnancies had been easy, for she had never been robust, this time the difficulties were much greater. The weeks of late July and early August were anxious ones for James Hogg. When the baby, another son, arrived on August 20, Sallie was extremely ill and continued so for some time afterward. The baby, named for Captain Thomas E. Hogg, was soon found to be "pining"; with his mother unable to nurse him, no other food would agree with him. Dr. Swearingen finally recommended a wet nurse, and before long Tom was plump and rosy-cheeked. Mrs. Hogg, however, though recovering from the serious stages of her illness, from that time never regained the even minimum stage of good health she had known before.

Official duties in the Attorney General's Office resumed their pressure before the end of summer. Among the problems demanding attention

[50] Cotner (ed.), *Addresses of James S. Hogg,* pp. 40–46.

133

was the controversy over acceptance of the new Capitol.[51] That such a problem existed had become apparent in May, when the roof of the magnificent new building leaked during the dedication ceremonies. In this problem, as in all others, Hogg's objective was to work out a solution for the welfare of the people of Texas, in keeping with the law —in this case fulfillment of the contract; yet in solving it he was charged, by his political enemies, with demagoguery, and accused of using the Capitol issue for political gain.

Abner Taylor, the contractor in charge of construction, was a business associate of Charles and John Farwell, Chicago financiers who organized the Capitol Syndicate at Chicago and with other stockholders formed the Capitol Freehold Land and Investment Company, a London syndicate which was to help finance the building of the Capitol. The Capitol Syndicate was to be given, instead of money, title to over three million acres which became the famous fenced XIT Ranch in the Panhandle.

The year 1887 had been a bad one for the XIT: taxes had increased; capital outlay had been great; the drought continued; and income resulting from small sales on a slow market had been unsatisfactory. The growing sentiment against alien ownership in Texas was another worry. All over the Great Plains Scotch and English investors had large ranch holdings. The Farmers' Alliances were complaining that these holdings should be broken up for native frontiersmen. The Texas Capitol contract called for American ownership of the XIT lands, but lack of cash funds had caused the Chicago interests to sell stock in England. Losses from the freeze of 1884–1885 and the prolonged drought, in addition to the poor results from attempts to produce beet sugar, made foreign stockholders uneasy. So in December the impatient stockholders, meeting in London, requested Taylor to obtain title to the XIT lands immediately in order that a division into English and American companies could be made if financial or legal pressures dictated such a move.

All during construction Taylor had made requests to change the specifications of the contract, but these requests began to come more frequently after the December stockholders' meeting in London, just about the time Hogg assumed his duties as attorney general. Hogg consistently fought against any changes in the contract, maintaining that

[51] R. C. Cotner, "Attorney General J. S. Hogg and the Acceptance of the State Capitol: A Reappraisal," *West Texas Historical Association Yearbook*, XXV (October, 1949), 50–75. See J. Evetts Haley, *The XIT Ranch of Texas* (Norman, University of Oklahoma Press, 1953), pp. 49 ff.

the architects knew what they were doing and that sticking with the specifications was the safest way to insure to the people of Texas the best possible Capitol.

Early in 1888 Taylor proposed using another kind of roof rather than the copper roof called for in the specifications, arguing that the copper roof would not hold up in the variable Texas climate. Hogg sought technical advice from an experienced Swedish craftsman and from the Harry Brothers of Dallas, who assured him that a copper roof could be put on effectively if the contractor used small, rather than large, sheets, thus making adequate provision for expansion and contraction. Hogg insisted that the contract be carried out, and a copper roof went on.

About a week before the formal dedication, Hogg moved into his new office. It was a proud day for him. Ever grateful to his sister, Fannie, who had encouraged him to become a lawyer like his father, he sat down to write the first letter to her:

As a native I was the first State officer to christen the Greatest Edifice of this proud Commonwealth, and of course feel gratified enough over it. . . . Every convenience is at my command, and the good will of the Senate, House of Representatives, the Governor and every member of the whole administration seems to surround and certainly cheer me. Not a jar, not a jealousy, not a spite nor a misunderstanding exists between two of the executive officers, but each with the other is upon the most brotherly, friendly terms. . . . Up to this time our Department has lost but one case, and that will be won we believe in the Supreme Court where it is now on appeal by the State. This "luck" continued for eight more months will certainly be quite enough to retire on. At least I hope so.[52]

Then, on dedication day, May 16, 1888, the roof leaked.

The Capitol was tendered to the Capitol Receiving Board for acceptance near the end of August, 1888. During the spring and summer other state offices had moved into completed areas of the building, all in strict accordance with the terms of the contract. This situation had given Hogg full opportunity to observe and to receive reports of other structural defects. The roof had not yet been repaired. So on August 31 the Attorney General wrote to the Capitol Receiving Board to remonstrate against acceptance as inflicting great loss on the people of Texas. The Board chose to reply in a hot letter informing the Attorney General that his officious opinion was "altogether unsolicited." He offered to protest

[52] J. S. Hogg to Mrs. Martha Frances Davis, May 11, 1888, J. S. Hogg Let. Pr., 1, pp. 352–354.

as a private citizen, but reminded the members that in case of litigation his office would receive heavy additional work and to prevent this unnecessary extra load he had offered "precautionary advice." The situation cooled fast, and before long the Receiving Board sought his advice. Furthermore, he offered to go before the old Capitol Board and make official complaints to that body prior to the acceptance of the new Capitol by the Receiving Board.

The Austin *Statesman,* by editorial, on September 8, pointed out that after the Receiving Board looked over the Capitol and decided it had no authority to enforce corrections of defects it rejected the building.

On September 10, at a called meeting of the original Capitol Board, Hogg, as a member of the Board, presented his recommendations as to procedures to be followed in getting the desirable adjustments.

The Attorney General realized that the only hope of securing the best possible Capitol was to have the specifications met while the state still had bargaining power—before final title to the remaining thousands of XIT acres was relinquished to the Syndicate upon acceptance of the Capitol. He was interested, also, in protecting his office from the additional work which would certainly result after occupancy of the building if he was negligent in holding Taylor to his contract. He knew, too, that suits instituted later to collect damages over a leaking roof and other defects would probably be carried to the highest federal courts by the Syndicate, which was well connected politically in Washington. It was much better to secure adjustments while Texas still had title to some of the land. The Knights of Labor had boycotted and instituted suits against the contractor because granite cutters had been brought in from Scotland contrary to the federal Contract Labor Law. Hogg did not believe the Capitol should be accepted until all outstanding claims were settled.

Taylor, of course, was having difficulty in explaining to stockholders the expenditure of extra time and money in repairing a roof which he had not built properly at first on a building from which he had been absent too much during construction. He had to have a scapegoat, and Hogg was made to serve the need. Taylor did not explain another basic reason for not liking the Attorney General. For a year Hogg had upheld state and county efforts to collect taxes on lands already granted to the Syndicate. Fearful of more taxes, Taylor cautioned Matlock not to stimulate interest in the organization of counties. Taylor told the stockholders that Hogg was a political demagogue, who was making political capital out of the Capitol, pretending that the building was faulty so that he could pose as the protector of the people's interests and thus procure votes in the upcoming November elections.

In making these charges Taylor considerably weakened his case by overlooking the fact that Hogg, in the summer primaries, had already been chosen the Democratic nominee for attorney general, and thus by September was certain of election—there was no need for any such drastic device to get votes. However, the stockholders, not too sympathetic with Hogg politically, were credulous, and the charges have found acceptance even among current writers.[53]

Hogg's insistence on strict enforcement of the laws and on contracts finally got for the people of Texas a better Capitol and made possible the avoidance of otherwise inevitable lawsuits. This experience with Taylor developed in Hogg an even deeper concern over alien ownership of land in Texas, monopolies, and the failure of corporations to sell granted lands to bona fide settlers within the time limits stipulated in contracts and grants to railways. Hogg was also learning that an old political opponent, Avery L. Matlock, was busy in the employment of Abner Taylor and the Farwells. Taylor gave Matlock a position as supervisor of the legal and political department of XIT Ranch, saying:

You are to do all you can to have men elected to office who are not unfriendly to our interests, and to be in Austin for legislative sessions.[54]

His instructions advised also:

We don't want Hartley or any organized county in which we have interests organized. You are to do everything possible to keep any people from going in with the railroad and laying out a townsite in Hartley County away from our land. We want to control the selling of any lots in any townsite. There are many places we would not want to build up towns and bring in settlers for the reason that they would be organizing the counties and laying additional taxes upon us. They would be demanding roads and running them through our pastures to the detriment of our cattle interests.[55]

By 1890 Matlock, Taylor, and Goodnight were out to defeat Jim Hogg for any public office and would even join another "rugged in-

[53] Lewis Nordyke, *Cattle Empire* (New York, William Morrow and Company, 1949), pp. 188 ff.; J. E. Haley, *Charles Goodnight*, pp. 396 ff. But see Ruth Allen, "The Capitol Boycott: A Study in Peaceful Labor Tactics, 1885–1889," in her *Chapters in the History of Organized Labor in Texas* (University of Texas Publication No. 4143, November 15, 1941), pp. 45–88; Frederick W. Rathjen, "The Texas State House," *Southwestern Historical Quarterly*, LX (April, 1957), 454–462.

[54] Nordyke, *op. cit.*, p. 173.   [55] *Ibid.*, p. 171.

dividualist," Jay Gould—who had developed an interest in the Fort Worth and Denver Railway, which ran through Goodnight and XIT shipping points.

Meanwhile old railroad problems were demanding attention. When Hogg inquired into the state of affairs on the Sabine and East Texas line he found that the promised rebuilding had progressed very little, partly because of an outbreak of malarial and other fevers in the region. The people of the Sabine Pass area began to question the company's good faith. However, in October, after the hurricane season, J. F. Lanier, who had been secured to assist with the case, reported that the company promised to have crews busy within ten days. He was instructed to keep posted on developments and told that, if the terms of the agreement were not kept, suit would be instituted to "the fullest extent."[56]

The agreement had called for reopening of the line by the beginning of the federal court term at Galveston in November. When Hogg arrived in Galveston he learned that the road was not making progress according to agreement. First calling upon M. F. Mott, one of the company's local attorneys for an explanation, he then wrote to Colonel Hill in Houston. Hill soon telegraphed a report of progress. Hogg sent word back that he would go to Beaumont "to investigate in person." Advisers Cheatham and Lanier were requested to learn the date on which the company now would promise to have the road completed: "If it is not likely to be done before the adjournment of the present Court then my desire is to press the case. . . . Please write fully what amount and character of work has been done."[57]

While awaiting the report, Hogg wrote Hill that there was public apprehension about the delay, but that Hill's letter had led him to believe the alarm was unfounded.

But still I must in some way gratify the public immediately interested. To this end I have asked the case postponed until the next Monday, at which time, unless we otherwise agree between now and then, it will be necessary for you to meet me at Beaumont if possible. If you are not misled yourself as to the progress and good faith of the company's work, which can only be known by a personal visit over the road, then the probability is that the State will not feel called upon to do more than give reasonable time

[56] J. S. Hogg to J. F. Lanier (Beaumont), October 13, 1887, Att. Gen. Let. Pr., 41, p. 308.

[57] J. S. Hogg to Messrs. E. A. Cheatham and J. F. Lanier, November 21, 1887, Att. Gen. Let. Pr., 41, pp. 515, 536–537.

for the work's completion. It has been truly regretful to me that the work was not finished by the meeting of the Court, but this cannot now be well helped, and only can be avenged by aggressive proceedings which I do trust will not become necessary.

Nothing interfering, I will leave here for Beaumont Sunday night, so as to meet you at Court next Monday.[58]

Hill replied that Cheatham and some other citizens had expressed satisfaction with the progress made in repairing the road. Hogg thereupon wrote Cheatham on November 26:

My purpose is to have that road reconstructed without fail or undue delay. If yourself, and Mr. Lanier, who is with us in the case, think this result will be well accomplished by a continuance as by pressing a forfeiture, then, acting upon your judgment, consent to a continuance until next term. Should the present efforts of the Company be for effect, and to "get time," without intending to equip the road, etc., then I wish to cooperate with you in pressing the case to its speedy termination.

In the event a conclusion is reached by Mr. Lanier and yourself that a continuance, under the circumstances, is advisable and best for the public, please, on receipt of this telegraph me: "Will Continue" and to Col. Hill, at Houston: "Will continue by consent," which will save each of us the expense of going to Beaumont next Monday. On the other hand say "Come on."[59]

On the same day Hogg told Hill that if he received a telegram from Cheatham "to agree to it, authorize the order to that effect entered, and you need not go to that Court on next Monday." Hogg concluded:

Now, my dear sir, the State has been indulgent to this extent, I trust properly so, and I wish to urge upon you to keep an eye on the progress of the road until its early completion, so that the public can have no just cause of complaint.[60]

The continuance was granted. But when the spring court term in Galveston was approaching, some of the terms of the agreement had still not been fulfilled. Hogg personally notified Hill of reports of "refusal" to erect a depot of any sort at Sabine Pass. Graciously stating that

[58] J. S. Hogg to E. P. Hill, November 24, 1887, Att. Gen. Let. Pr., 41, pp. 578–579.
[59] J. S. Hogg to E. A. Cheatham, November 26, 1887, Att. Gen. Let. Pr., 41, pp. 590–591.
[60] J. S. Hogg to E. P. Hill, November 26, 1887, Att. Gen. Let. Pr., 41, p. 589.

he thought Hill had never had the matter called to his attention, he expressed his belief that the company would act "in good faith." In a few days he was able to report to the citizens of Sabine Pass that Hill assured him that a suitable depot would be built immediately.[61]

By the time the Attorney General's biennial report was written, the work was completed and the railroad in operation again. The report could proudly list the case of *Texas ex rel.* v. *The Sabine and East Texas Railway Company* as the first accomplishment in the fight to make the railroads live up to their charters and obey the laws of Texas.

Under the proceedings so instituted the company repaired the roadbed, rebuilt depots, began and yet continues the daily operation of its trains over the whole line. The purposes of the action having been thus accomplished, it has been dismissed.[62]

James Hogg had succeeded in getting a railroad rebuilt with a minimum of legal expense to the state and had established a useful precedent. His fairness had gained him an influential new friend: from then on Hill was convinced that Jim Hogg was a trustworthy public servant and not an enemy of the railroads.

The problems inherent in absentee ownership of railroads had been harassing Texas state officials for many years. Railway financing had swiftly become a tremendous business that involved the resources of great banking houses in Boston, St. Louis, San Francisco, and New York. One of James Hogg's outstanding tussles with the difficulties posed by out-of-state ownership began in January, 1888, when complaints reached him about the condition of the Texas Trunk Railroad, originally chartered by leading citizens of Dallas as the Dallas, Palestine, and Southeast Railroad.

Dallas aspired to be the railroad hub of the Southwest. Paradoxically, the Panic of 1873 had brought good fortune to the town. During the five years after 1873, as railroad building slowed and sometimes ceased, Dallas was the western terminus of the Texas and Pacific, which had brought its first train there just before the depression hit. In 1870, before the coming of the railroads, the population of Dallas had been one thousand; by 1880 Dallas could boast of over ten thousand. To assure the building materials made necessary by this rapid growth, much lumber must be transported from the piney woods, and the argu-

---

[61] J. S. Hogg to Messrs. A. N. Perkins and J. F. Gilliland (Sabine Pass), March 31, 1888, Att. Gen. Let. Pr., 43, p. 173.

[62] J. S. Hogg, *Report of the Attorney General,* 1887–1888, p. iii.

ment ran that more railroads would bring rates down through competition. Dallas citizens were also concerned because the I.&G.N. was developing the more thickly settled East Texas region and business was beginning to go into Texarkana and northward or to Houston and overseas via Galveston. In August, 1878, progressive Dallasites, including Alex Sanger, a leading dress and drygoods merchant, W. H. Gaston, outstanding realtor who in time came to handle accounts for Hogg in his own real estate ventures, and Jules E. Schneider, the banker, chartered the Dallas, Palestine, and Southeast Railroad. In 1879, it was rechartered as the Texas Trunk, a line reaching Beaumont near the Gulf.

By 1883 the line was fifty-one miles long and had reached Cedar, in the midst of a rich blackland agricultural area—making it sufficiently interesting to attract an out-of-state buyer, who was thought to be friendly to the Huntington interests. The plague of absenteeism began: during the fifteen years before officially passing into the hands of the Southern Pacific in 1897 the road changed receivers seven times, the record for Texas.

Dallas's rapid growth was continuing through the 1880's, and it was vital that all supply lines should be maintained in excellent condition. Merchants of Dallas were indignant about the deterioration of the Texas Trunk's roadbed after the out-of-state purchase. After receiving several letters of complaint the Attorney General informed an old friend in January, 1888:

I addressed a communication to the County Attorney there [Kaufman] to look into and officially report to this Department the condition of the T.T.R.R. No doubt it, as most other roads in Texas, is in a fearful condition. To rectify all such outrages is one of the purposes of your humble servant; but he is forced to take hold of them *one at a time.* A full redemption of 30 miles of one *wholly abandoned road,* a general row on hand with another now, is part of the work done here so far. Others will follow.[63]

In late January the agents for the Trunk promised the Attorney General to make some repairs as soon as weather permitted. Hogg told Kaufman County Attorney Lee Stroud that the promise would suffice, *"for the present,"* and instructed him further:

The purpose of the State is to *compel* railroads to do their duty towards the public. This *fully* done no trouble need be apprehended by them. Other-

[63] Jim Hogg to J. S. Woods (Kaufman), January 11, 1888, Pers. Let. Pr., I, p. 205.

wise they may abide the consequences of a relentless fight, in which the "sun-light of Justice" will expose their wrongs. Keep an eye on the road, and give the company a reasonable time in which to repair it in *safe, decent* condition in respect to road-bed, rolling stock, depot buildings, &c., as may be in demand by the general public.

Within a *reasonable time,* making of course due allowance for the bad condition of the weather, if the company shall have failed to do what is necessary and right in the premises, please report the facts here, together [with] the names of witnesses who will support them, and the proper proceedings will be instituted.[64]

In November, while attending to a tax case at Dallas against Abner Taylor of the XIT ranch on lands received for building the Capitol, Hogg went to Kaufman to see for himself what progress had been made. Before leaving for Austin, he requested M. H. Gossett to keep him informed. In reply to a consequent letter from Gossett he asked him to obtain the names of the officers of the road at Dallas and Kaufman, and to report on details of general conditions, "including the company's insolvency and financial mismanagement that can be clearly proved on a trial of the case. It is impossible yet to determine at what time or whether action by the State will be brought."[65]

In March 1889, Hogg asked Colonel R. F. Slaughter, the new county attorney at Kaufman, for an official report on action taken since November toward putting the road in good condition. The Attorney General considered that the company had by now been given ample time to overcome charges of "misuser, nonuser, and abuse of the corporate franchise, gross violation of corporate duties to the public, insolvency," and neglect of roadbed and track to the extent that they had become dangerous to life and property carried over them. Finally, in late March, Hogg entered *quo warranto* proceedings in the District Court of Dallas County to force forfeiture of charter, "to withdraw its corporate franchise, and to have a receiver appointed to wind up its affairs."[66]

At a preliminary hearing the court appointed John H. Traylor receiver, effective September 25, 1889, to take charge of the property of the company pending the suit. When the company's counsel sought to

---

[64] J. S. Hogg to Lee Stroud, January 25, 1888, Att. Gen. Let. Pr., 42, pp. 348–349.

[65] J. S. Hogg to M. H. Gossett, November 16, 1888, Att. Gen. Let. Pr., 45, p. 243. The letter of November 8 from Gossett is not available.

[66] J. S. Hogg, *Report of the Attorney General, 1888–1890* (Austin, 1891), pp. 5–6. J. S. Hogg to Col. R. F. Slaughter (County Attorney, Kaufman), March 20, 1889 *(confidential)*, Att. Gen. Let. Pr., 46, p. 549.

end the receivership, the motion was overruled. Two days after the receivership became effective, A. T. Watts of Dallas wrote Hogg that Henry Kneeland of New York, the apparent owner, had requested that Watts ascertain what assurances or bond would be required to repair "this Trunk in order that this company could take possession & go ahead."[67]

On September 20, H. G. (Brock) Robertson of Dallas, who was now looking after the state's interest in the case, reported that Traylor wanted to get his inventory in shape and then take steps to raise money to put the road in better condition. He continued:

Your information does not half tell the tale. It is practically without rolling stock. The engines are all out of repair, and two out of the three worthless, the other in bad condition. Box cars belonging to this Company and other Companies are lying scattered along the track upside down with no machinery to lift them on the track. The Road bed is if possible in a more deplorable condition. The grading itself, the Road bed proper is wasting and sinking so that the track is uneven, unstable and dangerous. The wooden ties are rotten and the iron rails broken, rusted & badly out of repair. This and passenger coaches unfit for decent or safe travel, is the condition Traylor found the property of the Company in. As to the finances, there was no money on hand and up to last night the Company had taken in $3.50. According to the Superintendent (Donahoe) the expenses exceed the receipts about $1000 possibly per month. . . . The facts therefore will fully justify you in the action you have taken. . . . The fact that a certain individual owns all the stock and is virtually the owner of the Company, and that he is wealthy does not affect the question of the Company's solvency. It is rather an aggravation of the condition of affairs. The fact is that Kneeland of New York bought this Road in much better condition than it is now and organized the present Company simply to keep life in the charter for his future use in manipulation and speculation. He placed a lot of incompetent men in charge of it to run it and calls on them for just as little money as possible and the thing has been running down ever since he got control of it.[68]

He outlined two alternate lines of procedure: if Kneeland made a hostile fight, then insist upon forfeiture; if he came forth as suppliant and advanced money to repair the road, then ask that Traylor be retained

[67] A. T. Watts to J. S. Hogg, September 27, 1889, J. S. Hogg Let. Rec. (typescript), II, 48.
[68] H. G. Robertson to J. S. Hogg, September 29, 1889, J. S. Hogg Let. Rec., II, pp. 49–54.

to see that the work was done properly during suspense-of-forfeiture proceedings.

Just two days later, on October 1, Robertson wrote that Judge R. E. Burke, instead of waiting until November, had set early October for hearing the defendant's motion to vacate order of receivership, and Receiver Traylor could not have his data ready. When the matter came before Judge Anson Rainey on change of venue to District Court of Ellis County, the motion to vacate having been renewed, it was granted upon the company's paying all costs up to that date. Kneeland's attorney signified a desire to put the road in order and without the expense of a receiver. This having been granted, the possibility of suit continued.

When writing to thank Traylor for his efforts, though brief, to improve the road through legal action, Hogg commented on Judge Rainey's decree:

In holding the proceeding legal a high compliment was done Judge Burke; in declaring it improvident Judge Rainey exercised a discretion and taste on which no question of law can arise. Perhaps the future management of the road will so far respect public interests as to fully justify this able judge's action. The past could not. Judge Rainey has my confidence as an upright judge, though I feel confident his action can hardly prove beneficial to the road or the public.[69]

Writing to Robertson in December 1889, Hogg expressed his disgust more freely, in a wryly joking vein:

I note your remarks by recent favor with much interest. As Gov. Lubbock (an old clerk) asked on reading of that decision: "What does *improvident* mean, in law, anyhow?" Well Judge Burke was sustained on the legal phases of the case and that is at least consoling; and Col. Traylor has a record as a railway manager that, as turnip raisers would say, "trumps the world!" He's a good one certain. As for yourself, I indulge the hope that no material injury has resulted, and that your compensation has not been inadequate. When the case is tried I expect to be on hand to its finish. In the meantime I shall watch the road's rapid improvement with unusual interest. Continuing to witness the destruction of law and the wreck of the Constitution under the crushing reed of Corporate power, I shall hold my temper, and at each opportunity gasp in amazement over the antics of Courts.[70]

[69] J. S. Hogg to John H. Traylor, November 27, 1889, Att. Gen. Let. Pr., 47, pp. 155–156.
[70] J. S. Hogg to H. G. Robertson, December 12, 1889, J. S. Hogg Let. Pr., 4, pp. 187–188.

By mid-February, Aldredge and Fitzhugh, attorneys for the Trunk Road, were pressing for a continuance of the case pending at Waxahachie. Because Judge Rainey's decision on the receivership had not forced the Kneeland interests to say unequivocally that they intended to fix up the road and pay all expenses, Robertson counseled forcing trial. The case, originally scheduled for March 3, 1890, was set up to March 17 by Judge Rainey; Robertson urged careful preparation, for he "determined to win it." It became known that a list of improvements carried out since regaining possession had been filed by the defendant to answer the writ of the state. Robertson told Hogg:

Possibly the best thing for you to do is to write a letter to Messrs. Watts & Aldredge or Fitzhugh & Wozencraft in a plain stiff business way stating the terms clearly on which you will discontinue the case. Don't neglect this business and be caught with your unmentionables down on the 17th of March. I believe when they see you are in dead earnest and will forfeit the charter unless the conditions described are complied with they will come to their milk.[71]

In the face of the insistent demand for more roads forfeiture of a railroad charter appears to have been a more severe penalty than any Texas judge at the time was ready to hand out. "Improvident" continued to have a shaky legal history. True, the defendants were able to report progress; the case was continued. At the end of his term the Attorney General reported:

The case is still pending. . . . In the meantime the company has, as this department is advised by its counsel, gone to work and expended large sums in repairing its road bed, depots, etc., and restoring the same to that state of safety and usefulness contemplated and required by the charter and the laws of the State.[72]

Nevertheless, Hogg was still wary, for he had learned many things in the past three years about stock manipulators. He also believed that Judge Rainey's decree had left the matter so open that it would be only a matter of time before the suit for forfeiture of title would have to be pressed, and he was proved right in 1891—by which time the Southern Pacific system was openly showing its interest in the Texas Trunk—when Hogg's successor found it necessary to carry on the case.

The railroad companies had found Attorney Hogg persistent in car-

[71] H. G. Robertson to J. S. Hogg, March 4, 1890, J. S. Hogg Let. Rec., III, pp. 186–187; Reed, *Texas Railroads*, p. 232.
[72] J. S. Hogg, *Report of the Attorney General, 1888–1890*, p. 6.

rying out his duty to enforce the laws of Texas, but most of them knew that he had been fair to them. Jim Hogg himself knew that he had sometimes wrestled in vain, or with little immediate result, as in the Texas Trunk case. He had witnessed the young giant of corporate power growing swiftly to alarming maturity and power, and he realized that the battle joined in these past few years would achieve far more resounding crescendos. It would become increasingly difficult for him to "hold his temper," and to merely "gasp in amazement over the antics of the Courts."

CHAPTER VI

The Fight for Fair Competition and Fair Valuation

DURING THE 1880's "young business giants" other than the railroads were also flexing their increasingly powerful corporate muscles. Manufacturers, on the upswing after the long depression, pursued the heady prospect of national market control through great sales campaigns aimed at both acquiring nationwide distribution for their products and besting their larger competitors and the small local operators. The steady sharpening of competitive practice since the end of the Civil War had reached a symbolic culmination in the establishment in 1879 of a new type of large industrial combination, the Standard Oil Trust. The philosophy of the new order was, in essence, "consolidate or fail," rather than "competition is the life of trade." The result of the trend toward consolidation was politically apparent in the rise of the antimonopoly parties.

The several suits launched in 1887 by out-of-state manufacturers to test the right of the State of Texas to collect an occupation tax from their agents or salesmen were symptomatic of the new trend of business and industry that would harass the regulatory efforts of the states for many years. The Texas occupation tax had originated in a comprehensive license and registration law of May, 1882, which listed specific levies for professions and occupations. Lawyers and dentists, for instance, paid a tax of $5 a year, doctors $40; patent medicine salesmen paid $175; other salesmen (except for certain ones exempt, such as those selling religious books) were subject to a tax of $35, payable in advance, "from any commercial traveler, drummer, salesman, or solicitor of trade, by sample or otherwise."[1] The system had at least one advantage for those thus licensed: they were protected by law from paying any city, town, or county occupation tax.

The corporations based their sortie against the Texas law, as they had against similar laws in other states, on the clause in the United States Constitution that gave Congress the power to "regulate Com-

[1] Hans Gammel (ed.), *Laws of Texas*, IX, 278–283, quotes the law of May 4, 1882.

147

merce . . . among the several States."[2] Before the mid-1880's the commerce clause had not been often invoked "as a means for limiting state powers or as an affirmative instrument for promoting commerce between the states,"[3] but now in the midst of the strenuous and quickening race for nationwide distribution of products corporation lawyers were beginning to use it frequently.

Because the corporate actions resulted in a serious defeat for Texas and Attorney General Hogg, and because one of the suits was the occasion for Hogg's first appearance before the United States Supreme Court, two of the "drummer cases" will be examined here in some detail. Drummers Robert C. Stockton and W. G. Asher, Jr., had been given jail sentences in Smith and Harris counties, respectively, for refusing to pay when found guilty of evasion of the occupation tax. When the salesmen asked their employers to pay the tax for them, the companies, having won similar cases in Louisiana and Tennessee,[4] confidently initiated litigation; corporation counsel in both suits instituted habeas corpus proceedings under the commerce clause, claiming the Texas statute unlawful in restraint of interstate trade. Attorney General Hogg, in preparing to defend the state, considered that two fundamental issues were involved: the extent to which limitations could be placed upon the power of states to tax, and the validity of the new interpretation of the commerce clause.

When the Stockton case reached the United States District Court at Galveston on appeal in November, Jim Hogg was pitted against his friend and former partner, John M. Duncan, who had been employed to direct the corporate assault. Duncan rested most of his argument on *Robbins* v. *Shelby County* (Tenn.) *Tax District*. However, as Hogg pointed out, there was an important difference between the Tennessee law and the Texas law: the former imposed no tax upon firms residing or having their supply depots within the taxing district, while the latter was state-wide, applying to resident and nonresident alike and therefore according equal treatment to all. In the Robbins case the U.S. Supreme Court had held that a tax could not be imposed upon drummers representing foreign or outside firms, because interstate commerce could not be taxed by state or local governments. Duncan also made use

[2] Article I, Section 8, The Constitution of the United States.

[3] Felix Frankfurter, *The Commerce Clause* (Chapel Hill, University of North Carolina Press, 1937), pp. 7, 84 ff.

[4] *Robbins* v. *Shelby County* (Tennessee) *Tax District*, 120 U.S. 489 (1886); *Simmons Hardware Company* (St. Louis) v. *McGuire, Sheriff* (La.), 2 *Southern Reporter* 592.

148

of a recent Louisiana case, *Simmons Hardware Co.* (St. Louis) v. *McGuire, Sheriff* (La.), upholding the paramount authority of the United States Supreme Court and the Robbins decision.[5]

Although Hogg recognized the supremacy of the United States Supreme Court, he maintained that the Robbins decision was open to criticism, especially since Chief Justice M. R. Waite and Justices Stephen Field and Horace Gray had dissented. He believed that the Chief Justice had held that a drummer who sold goods from samples was not engaged in interstate commerce but was actually a peddler and thus subject to an occupation tax. Hogg argued also that Congress had never taken the new position of the Supreme Court, and he maintained that "if the Robbins case were not challenged, then the rights of the State would be further interfered with and infringed. There is something lurking there which needs exposing."[6] He called the Robbins case "a weapon to wreck the sovereign rights of the State, to attack its revenues and to that extent would injure its credit."[7]

Contending that the thirty-five-dollar tax was not excessive, Hogg was reported to have said that it added only "about 25 cents to each county in the State when divided between them. Why, your drummers dig up 25 cents worth of dirt every time they cross the street; they tread heavier than ordinary people."[8] He argued that Stockton—who had said that he could vote at Fort Worth, that he had been in Texas fourteen months, and that he had signed a contract with his company to stay another year—was therefore considered a resident citizen and subject to the same taxes as other Texas drummers, since he had claimed no home outside of Texas.

The Galveston *Daily News* reported that the Attorney General departed from his "able" argument "to denunciate Drummers as a class who wanted the best of everything in hotel rooms and meals and yet paid no taxes,"[9] denounced Stockton, president of a Fort Worth drummers' association, "for having defied and irritated the State authorities into arresting him," and concluded "with an eloquent peroration on the

[5] Galveston *Daily News,* November 19, 1887. The Simmons Hardware Company case had been settled in the Supreme Court of Louisiana, June 20, 1887.

[6] Austin *Daily Statesman,* November 19, 1887; J. S. Hogg Scrapbook No. 5, pp. 93–94.

[7] Fort Worth *Gazette* (n.d.), clipping in J. S. Hogg Scrapbook No. 5, pp. 93–94.

[8] Austin *Daily Statesman,* November 19, 1887. On October 29, a Traveling Men's Association had voted to reimburse all expenses of this test case.

[9] The quotations in this paragraph are all from the Galveston *Daily News,* November 20, 1887.

harmony existing between the federal and state courts, delicately complimenting the court on its well-known freedom from all partisan bias." (To properly savor the irony of Hogg's conclusion it is necessary to recall that the overtones of Reconstruction persisted and that Republicans still dominated the federal courts despite Cleveland's 1884 victory.) For an entire afternoon Hogg had held the attention of a number of bar members who were in attendance; according to the *News*, "it was generally conceded that he made a masterly effort and did himself and the State great credit." The Attorney General then left for Austin, leaving John Duncan to conduct his plea for the petitioner without interruption.

The Court held against the state and ordered the applicant discharged on the basis of the Robbins case, declaring that the Texas law as applied to nonresident houses and drummers was in conflict with the commerce clause. Texas appealed to the United States Supreme Court. The case was pending when James Hogg went to Washington to argue the Asher case before the high tribunal in November, 1888.

Drummer W. G. Asher represented an office-supply manufacturer in New Orleans. In 1887 he had been convicted before a justice of the peace in Harris County for failure to pay the annual Texas occupation tax of thirty-five dollars. He sued out a writ of habeas corpus in the Court of Appeals, contending that the law under which he was fined conflicted with the United States Constitution in the matter of the commerce clause and was invalid. After a hearing, the Court upheld the Texas tax as collectible on all concerns whether resident or nonresident. When remanded to the sheriff, Asher prosecuted the case by writ of error to the United States Supreme Court. The writ was served in August, 1887, and Hogg called upon Assistant Attorney General W. L. Davidson to furnish a brief they had discussed earlier: "Get it up in your most approved style—'to the point impressively.' When you have it done come up [from Georgetown] and we'll review it together and have it printed here."[10]

Asher's company engaged Abel Crook of New York City as counsel. By letter to Attorney Crook in late November, Hogg agreed to January or February, 1888, but "not earlier than the middle of January, as I wish to meet you in oral argument . . . before the Supreme Court."[11]

[10] J. S. Hogg to Assistant Attorney General W. L. Davidson, August 29, 1887, Att. Gen. Let. Pr., 40, p. 695. Davidson made his home in Georgetown while not actually practicing before the perambulatory Supreme Court.

[11] J. S. Hogg to the Honorable Abel Crook, November 22, 1887, Att. Gen. Let. Pr., 41, p. 561.

Hogg was prepared to point out the serious implications of the case for state taxing powers and its possible bearing upon further centralization of powers. As he told Abel Crook in December, "I wish to argue that case, without regard to technicalities, but upon the important questions directly involved in it."[12] Knowing that the state would face damage suits if county officers continued to enforce fines or imprisonment on drummers following the Stockton decision, Hogg was anxious to set out for Washington. In the midst of making arrangements to leave on February 1, he received a "courteous favor" from Crook requesting a delay. Hogg agreed to wait until Crook had a date set for a hearing later on in February or in April; he could not come in March because of "press of business."[13] (The pressing business would be the initial proceedings against the powerful Texas Traffic Association.) Meanwhile, Hogg procured his license to practice before the Supreme Court.

Finally the motion was filed, and the case was set for October 11, 1888. In September, T. M. Miller, attorney general for Mississippi, who had been sent a copy of the Texas brief for comment and advice, wrote to Hogg: "When do you expect a decision in the Asher Case? I was much interested in the argument for the State of Texas and thought it entirely sound."[14] Hogg was encouraged by Miller's interest, but his reply showed the realism of his thinking: "Texas will be there to press the case, but the possibility of getting the Court to overrule the Robbins case is very slim indeed."[15]

When Hogg arrived in Washington, excitement over the coming national elections, and especially the Cleveland-Harrison presidential campaign, was mounting. Texas Congressman Roger Q. Mills greeted Hogg with gratitude. Up for re-election, Mills had been so busy trying to obtain passage of the Democratic tariff bill which bore his name that he had been unable to carry on a campaign in Texas; Hogg, at his own expense, had gone into Mills' district to speak in his behalf.

The summary of the Asher case in *United States Reports* is terse. In the statement of facts, Hogg agreed that William G. Asher was not a resident of Texas but a citizen of Louisiana and resident of New Orleans, and that he traveled for Charles G. Schulse of New Orleans, maker of rubber stamps and stencils. Asher had not taken out a license

---

[12] Hogg to Crook, December 27, 1887, J. S. Hogg Let. Pr., 1, p. 195.
[13] Hogg to Crook, January 31, 1888, J. S. Hogg Let. Pr., 1, p. 251.
[14] T. M. Miller to J. S. Hogg, September 12, 1888, referred to in J. S. Hogg to Γ. M. Miller, September 21, 1888, J. S. Hogg Let. Pr., 2, p. 80.
[15] J. S. Hogg to T. M. Miller, September 21, 1888, J. S. Hogg Let. Pr., 2, p. 80.

required under Article 110, Chapter 5, Title 4 of the Penal Code of the State of Texas and was arrested and fined in Harris County.

Citing *Robbins* v. *Shelby County* (Tenn.) *Tax District,* Hogg pointed out that the Tennessee tax was collected from those drummers "not having a regular licensed house of business in the taxing district";[16] Drummer Robbins was from Ohio, representing an Ohio firm. Hogg then emphasized that the Texas law treated residents and nonresidents alike, which the Tennessee law discussed in the Robbins case did not. Two weeks later Justice Bradley delivered the opinion. He brushed aside Hogg's contention that the Robbins and Asher cases were different, but he did discuss what Texas had "strenuously contended," that the Robbins decision was "contrary to sound principles of constitutional construction and in conflict with well-adjudicated cases formerly decided by this court and not overruled." Then the Justice bluntly said:

Even if it were true that the decision referred to was not in harmony with some of the previous decisions, we had supposed that a later decision in conflict with prior ones had the effect to overrule them, whether mentioned and commented on or not.[17]

He would not discuss again the principles which he held were clearly set forth in the Robbins case, but cited a more recent case, *Deloup* v. *Port of Mobile,*[18] relating to a general license tax on telegraph companies and decided by unanimous concurrence. Asher was ordered discharged from imprisonment.

Hogg was disappointed but not surprised at the decision. He and Davidson had done their best to block federal encroachment on the state taxing power, but the tide of the prevailing doctrine of strong national government ran forcibly against them. He also knew that the character of the Supreme Court's conservatives had been changing since the 1870's, and he would have agreed with an evaluation of this change as stated in a book published in 1948:

The conservatives of the seventies had been concerned with the protection of the old established state-federal relations, against upheavals of the Civil War and the onslaught of Radical reconstructionism. The conservatism of

---

[16] Quoted from *Report of the Attorney General,* 1886–1888, p. iv. For the Tennessee case see 120 U.S. 489 (1886).

[17] *Asher v. Texas* was argued October 11–12, 1888, and decided on October 29, 1888. 128 U.S. 781 (1888).

[18] 127 U.S. 640.

the new judges, on the other hand, was concerned primarily with protecting the property rights and vested interests of big business and with the defense of the prevailing economic and social order against agrarian and dissident reformers.[19]

The decision had cooled for several weeks, the elections were over, and Governor Ross and Hogg had been re-elected when the Attorney General wrote his biennial report for 1887–1888. Therefore, his discussion of the drummer cases should be thought of, not as part of a campaign document, but as a candid report of stewardship and intention. If a Texas law was held to be unconstitutional, he was obliged to tell the legislature in order that the law might be repealed or modified. At the same time, he did not subscribe to the infallibility of the United States Supreme Court even though recognizing its authority.

To this high authority of course all other courts and officers must yield. By its decision, however, the Texas law imposing taxes upon her citizens who pursue similar occupations, though not denied to be valid as to them, certainly is a discrimination in favor of the non-residents. In truth it seems to place a premium upon non-citizenship. Section I of Article 4 of the Federal Constitution provides that the citizens of each State shall be entitled to all the privileges and immunities of the citizens of the several States, and Section I of the fourteenth amendment to it among other things declares that no State shall deny to any person within its jurisdiction the equal protection of the laws. This strange anomaly into which the "drummer tax law" is placed by this decision forcing it into violation of the two provisions last quoted by declaring it in conflict with another section of the Federal Constitution is at least worthy of the serious consideration of the Executive and Legislative Departments of the State.[20]

Having lost the case, the Attorney General recommended to Governor Ross the payment of the fees due, but, as he stated to Abel Crook "it may be possible that the Legislature which meets here the second week in January will have to act upon it."[21] In 1889 the legislature rewrote in great detail the occupation tax law.[22] Texas had lost a tax case, and out-of-state corporate interests had won an advantage for their brand of "free competition."

---

[19] Quoted from Alfred H. Kelly and Winfred A. Harbison, *The American Constitution* (New York, W. W. Norton, 1948), pp. 514–515.

[20] Hogg, *Report of the Attorney General*, 1887–1888, p. v.

[21] J. S. Hogg to Abel Crook, December 28, 1888, Att. Gen. Let. Pr., 45, p. 665.

[22] Gammel, *Laws of Texas*, IX, 1052–1057.

The power of the out-of-state companies was being enhanced by the new trust structure of business organization, created by John D. Rockefeller's attorneys for Standard Oil.[23] The railroads were achieving similar results by means of pools and traffic associations. Attorney General Hogg had not been satisfied with his predecessor's view that, since the Texas Traffic Association had not exceeded the legislative maximum in fixing rates, intervention therefore was not needed, but he had been unable in 1887 to initiate a frontal attack on the Traffic Association, because the gathering of evidence on its dealings had been delayed by such matters as the Willis hearing, the insurance cases, the prohibition campaign, and the proceedings against the Sabine and East Texas Railroad. In late February, 1888, however, when he was working on the suit against the Association, he revealed to his good friend, Judge C. W. Raines, now of Quitman, his long-range strategy:

In the midst of a continuous, hard, and even unpleasant contest to uphold the law and make it supreme and impartial to all classes and subjects of the Government, I am today much gratified on receipt of your very complimentary letter of yesterday endorsing my course.

My friends abroad have but a slight conception of the difficult work that I have had on hand since I came here. That I have accomplished some good which will bear fruits, rich, for my native State, at sometime in the future, I am fully confident. That I shall rectify many wrongs now infesting the Country *I know,* for if I cannot *beat them down,* outright, I shall force them to wilt, wither, and *dry up* in the burning sunlight of justice while they are *lying on* and *wearing me out.*[24]

Despite alleged efforts on the part of the Association to meet the regulations of the Interstate Commerce Act on the long- and short-haul clause, and "rates so as to conform thereto," public suspicion of the actions of the Association had become more pronounced following a secret meeting of its officials in New York on September 16, 1887. A report of the meeting issued to the press stated that "the Association was remodeled and reorganized."[25] Meanwhile, the Attorney General had obtained a copy of the Association's basic agreement of 1885. His case, however, was so prepared that the details of organization would not be a major concern because Article X, Section 5, of the Texas Constitution

[23] Ralph W. and Muriel E. Hidy, *Pioneering in Big Business, 1882–1911: History of Standard Oil Company* (New Jersey) (New York, Harper & Brothers, 1955), pp. 44–45.

[24] Hogg to Raines, February 23, 1888, J. S. Hogg Let. Pr., 1, pp. 269–270.

[25] Galveston *Daily News,* September 18, 1887.

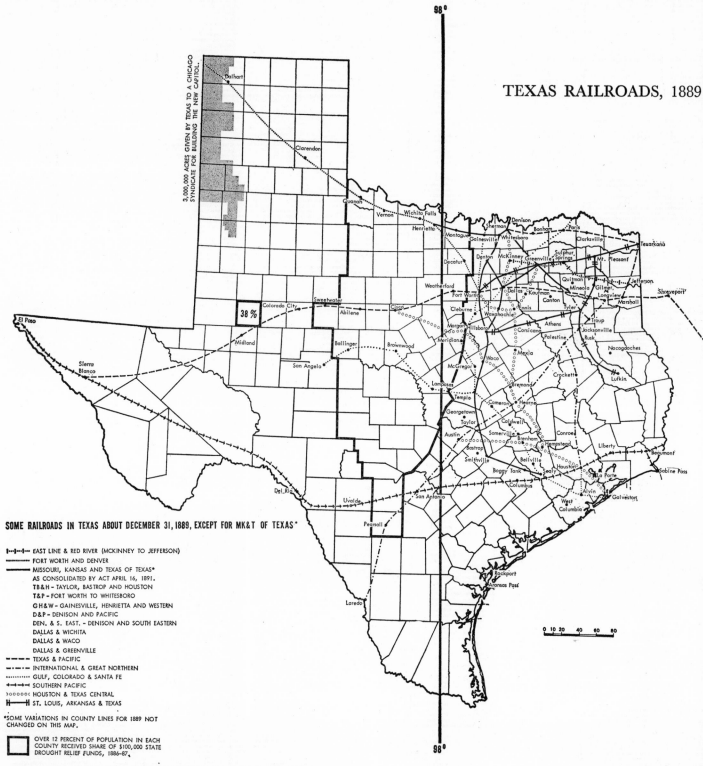

TEXAS RAILROADS, 1889

3,000,000 ACRES GIVEN BY TEXAS TO A CHICAGO
SYNDICATE FOR BUILDING THE NEW CAPITOL.

38 %

SOME RAILROADS IN TEXAS ABOUT DECEMBER 31, 1889, EXCEPT FOR MK&T OF TEXAS*

⊢•⊢•⊢•⊢•⊢	EAST LINE & RED RIVER (MCKINNEY TO JEFFERSON)
•••••••••••	FORT WORTH AND DENVER
▬▬▬▬	MISSOURI, KANSAS AND TEXAS OF TEXAS*
	AS CONSOLIDATED BY ACT APRIL 16, 1891.
	TB&H - TAYLOR, BASTROP AND HOUSTON
	T&P - FORT WORTH TO WHITESBORO
	G H&W - GAINESVILLE, HENRIETTA AND WESTERN
	D&P - DENISON AND PACIFIC
	DEN. & S. EAST. - DENISON AND SOUTH EASTERN
	DALLAS & WICHITA
	DALLAS & WACO
	DALLAS & GREENVILLE
▬ ▬ ▬	TEXAS & PACIFIC
▬·▬·▬·	INTERNATIONAL & GREAT NORTHERN
•••••••••	GULF, COLORADO & SANTA FE
⊹⊹⊹⊹⊹	SOUTHERN PACIFIC
∘∘∘∘∘∘∘∘	HOUSTON & TEXAS CENTRAL
H▬▬▬H	ST. LOUIS, ARKANSAS & TEXAS

*SOME VARIATIONS IN COUNTY LINES FOR 1889 NOT
CHANGED ON THIS MAP.

☐ OVER 12 PERCENT OF POPULATION IN EACH
COUNTY RECEIVED SHARE OF $100,000 STATE
DROUGHT RELIEF FUNDS, 1886-87.

BASED ON HOUSTON AND TEXAS CENTRAL RAILWAY MAP OF TEXAS BY RAND, MCNALLY & CO., CHICAGO, C. 1888.
ARCHIVES COLL. U. T. AND JOSEPH D. SAYERS, RAILROAD CONSOLIDATIONS IN TEXAS, 1889-1903, pp. 10 ff.

0 10 20   40   60   80

was so strictly written that degree of control was not a deciding factor. The provision under which Hogg sued read:

No railroad or managers of any railroad or corporation shall consolidate the stock, property or franchise of such corporation with, or lease or purchase the works or franchises of, or in any way control any railroad corporation owning or having under its control a parallel or competing line; nor shall any officer of such railroad corporation act as an officer of any other railroad corporation owning or having the control of a parallel or competing line.

In Travis County District Court the Attorney General charged the nine trunk-line members of the Association with 1) creating a monopoly and pool of railway rates, 2) preventing or lessening competition, 3) being a hazard to free competition in rate-making, and 4) operating in a manner contrary to their charters and to the public interest as set forth in Article X, Section 5, of the Texas Constitution.[26] Hogg maintained that some of the parties to the Association agreement were parallel and competing lines and that the Association formed by them was thus prohibited by the Texas Constitution. He held that consolidation had occurred in 1886 (before Hogg took office) when the Santa Fe took over the Gulf, Colorado, and Santa Fe, a Texas-chartered company,[27] which was a parallel and competing line to the Houston and Texas Central, and that rate competition between the lines was ended by the Traffic Association. In effect, a monopoly had been established contrary to the Texas Constitution, and rate-making was no longer subject to competitive procedures.

In April, 1888, Hogg won the initial battle with the Association in the case of *The State of Texas* v. *Gulf, Colorado, and Santa Fe Railway Company et al.*[28] Judge John C. Townes wrote the opinion granting a permanent injunction restraining the nine trunk lines and eight connecting lines forming the Association from continuing the Traffic Association or carrying on its functions. Because of the excellent legal reputation of Judge Townes (later Dean of the Law School of the University of Texas) the decision was most encouraging to Hogg. The Association, acting upon the advice of the Houston law firm of Baker, Botts, and

[26] St. Clair Reed, *Texas Railroads*, p. 556. Reed has his reference to the Constitution of Texas confused on p. 557.

[27] See Reed, *op. cit.*, pp. 288 ff.; Lawrence L. Waters, *Steel Rails to Santa Fe* (Lawrence, University of Kansas Press, 1950), pp. 828 ff., 94–97.

[28] 72 Texas 404; Richard C. Overton, *Gulf to Rockies* (Austin, University of Texas Press, 1953), map, pp. 164–165.

Baker and Judge J. W. Terry, counsels for the Santa Fe, sought the protection of the Supreme Court of Texas under the federal commerce clause, having in mind postponement of dissolution, or possibly a final stand before the United States Supreme Court.

Baker, Botts, and Baker and J. W. Terry for the appellants listed what they termed seven major errors of the lower court and requested reversal. Because the listing gives an insight into railroad practices, it is stated below in some detail. Attention is called to Sections 4 and 5, which clearly indicate the new era of legal confusion introduced by the Interstate Commerce Act:

1. It was charged that Article X, Section 5, of the Texas Constitution applied only to parallel or competing lines, but the state had made no effort to prove the defendant's lines parallel or competing.

2. The district court was declared in error in holding that the articles of association made each of the members a manager or gave control over other lines. Maintaining that the "voluntary" nature of the Association left each member free to act itself, it was denied that the executive committee in effect had powers of an interlocking directorate.

3. The Court was declared in error for holding the Association violated any section of the Constitution of Texas.

4. "The Court erred in enjoining the Association from acting upon matters of interstate traffic under the articles of association when the proof showed that by far the largest part of its legitimate business" was connected with interstate traffic. It was declared to be outside the province of the state government and, instead, a matter of "the exclusive control of Congress." This position was supported by eight citations, including the Wabash case of 1886.

5. Congress had established the Interstate Commerce Commission to regulate commerce among the states and the federal government had exclusive jurisdiction. Therefore, Texas had "no jurisdiction" to determine legality of actions of the Texas Traffic Association relating to interstate commerce.

6. It was maintained that the objects of the Association—1) to adjust differences between the parties, 2) to facilitate business, 3) to establish uniform classifications, and 4) to meet to discuss rates—were "beyond question reasonable and proper, and the Court erred in enjoining the continuance of the Association in toto or the formation of any similar organization."

7. Finally, they contended that any injunction should cover only the twenty-day notice clause, necessary before any change of rates should

have been covered by the injunction, if any injunction at all was granted.[29]

The five most material points insisted on by Attorney General Hogg for the state were as follows:

1. The Texas Traffic Association was prohibited by law for two reasons: 1) It combined and controlled parallel and competing lines of railway, and 2) the officers of it and the railway members composing it were also officers and agents of parallel and competing lines.

2. The Association was not authorized by law nor by the charters of the railways composing it and was therefore illegal.

3. The Association was a pool of railway rates, was in restraint of trade, prevented competition, and was contrary to public policy. Hogg maintained that "any association whose purpose was to prevent, restrict, or lessen competition, was a menace to commercial freedom, violated public policy, and should be restrained." He then cited several references to monopolies tending to show that competition was "encouraged as the life of trade," while combinations in restraint of trade were illegal.

4. While admitting the areas of congressional power to regulate commerce, the Attorney General declared that railway charters were contracts between the corporations and the state and any violations of the terms were matters that the "State can restrain and prevent." Furthermore, the laws of Texas required him to take action, by quo warranto or other proceedings, and Texas law demanded that charters be strictly construed.

5. The Association in all its parts was tainted with illicit purposes to "pool" rates, to consolidate franchises, and to combine against competition. The Court's construction of the "Articles of Agreement," that it was in all its parts unlawful, was correct.[30]

Associate Justice Reuben Gaines, who wrote the Texas Supreme Court decision, upheld the state's contention "that the parties to the agreement were parallel and competing lines" and as such were prohibited by Section 5 of Article X of the Constitution from joining or creating a combination to carry out the illegal purposes named in Item 5 above. He referred to the petition in which the lines were frequently called the "main trunk lines and leading railways of Texas" which "so traverse the State as to touch and penetrate her commercial centres and become and are lawful competitors for the country's traffic concentrated

---

[29] Summarized or quoted from the case, 72 Texas 404 ff.
[30] *Ibid.*

in the cities."[31] Gaines accepted Hogg's contention that the case was submitted to the court for final disposition upon the petition, the answers, and the supporting affidavits, and the Gulf, Colorado, and Santa Fe and the Fort Worth and Denver City railways admitted all allegations of the petition not specifically denied; the St. Louis, Arkansas, and Texas also accepted the answer of the Santa Fe, and not one of them denied that they "were parallel to or a competitor for traffic with any other." These were matters of common knowledge, and Gaines defended Judge Townes' use of "logical facilities" and his "own sources of knowledge," adding for emphasis: "A Court is bound to take judicial knowledge of the leading geographical features of the land, the minuteness of the knowledge so expected being in inverse proportion to the distance."[32]

Judge Gaines also accepted the state's argument that the Houston and Texas Central and the Gulf, Colorado, and Santa Fe touched at Dallas and Houston and ran "during a considerable portion of their lines practically parallel to each other, and that they must necessarily compete for traffic lying between them." He upheld the lower court's finding that just these two defendants having been shown to be competitors with each other for traffic was sufficient evidence upon which to take action.[33]

The Attorney General had proved to the satisfaction of the Court that a prime object of the Association was "to fix rates of transportation so as to prevent competition among the several parties to the contract," and Judge Gaines held that if the Constitution prohibited "any" company from making such an agreement it prohibited competing lines from so "fettering" themselves. Therefore, the manner and extent of the control were in this case immaterial. The language of the Constitution was declared to clearly evince that control "in any manner and to any extent" was intended to be prohibited, provided it was calculated to enable "one railroad by means of a contract or agreement for an interference in the other's affairs to keep down competition between them." Gaines upheld Hogg's contention that the Traffic Association's executive committee became in effect the managers of the other companies.

Hogg had argued, not that the Traffic Association was charging rates over the legislative ceiling, but that it was doing an illegal thing in entering into and carrying out the terms of an agreement which had as a

[31] *Ibid.*

[32] *Ibid.;* Francis Wharton, *A Commentary on the Law of Evidence in Civil Issues* (Philadelphia, Kay and Brother, 1879), Section 339.

[33] 72 Texas 404.

major purpose the restraint of competition, contrary to law and public policy. The Judge sustained the state's contention that the Wabash case was irrelevant in this instance because it dealt with interstate commerce, whereas the Gulf, Colorado, and Santa Fe and the Houston and Texas Central were Texas-chartered companies and, having made a contract with the state, were subject to the jurisdiction of Texas. The Association was declared to be "clearly illegal as to some of the parties to it,"[34] meaning the Texas-chartered railways.

The Texas Supreme Court upheld the judgment of the lower court on December 21, 1888. The lawyers for the Association immediately sought ways to obtain a rehearing, but were refused. The Association could either disband, appeal to the United States Supreme Court, or try an expedient pointed out in the opinion itself in the following words:

We are inclined to the opinion that if none of the corporations composing the Association owed their existence to our laws that the State would have no power to prohibit or interfere with a contract of this character in so far as it regulated charges upon freight carried to and from or between this and other States.[35]

James Hogg was well aware that the railroads were not done with the fight. Gould and Huntington obviously had not given up their efforts to control the Texas railway network. The actual scope of their "secret agreement" and other "gentlemen's agreements" was unknown to him, but there was constant and ample evidence of their unremitting purpose. Following the Association's defeat in the Gulf, Colorado, and Santa Fe case, two subterfuge "International" associations were formed, one at New Orleans and another at Chicago, purporting to have little to do directly with Texas. In a speech at Rusk in the spring of 1890, Hogg announced that he had "succeeded in dissolving" these "by the power and effect of the decree in the first instance"—but he may have implied too much. He mentioned, too, that by the action he had made more political enemies.[36] Railway lobbies in Texas and throughout the country were progressively more skillful in refining their techniques, and

---

[34] *Ibid.*

[35] *Ibid.*; see Law of April 4, 1887, on railroad consolidations in Gammel, *op. cit.*, IX, 935–936. Overton, *op. cit.*, pp. 224–226, shows the Fort Worth and Denver a member in the Trans-Missouri Freight Association.

[36] J. S. Hogg's speech at Rusk, April 19, 1890, in Cotner (ed.), *Addresses of James Hogg,* p. 66; Charles S. Potts, *Railroad Transportation in Texas* (Bulletin of the University of Texas No. 119, Austin, 1909), pp. 79–83. Texas Traffic Association records cease in May, 1888, but see International Association Circular 100 (1888), quoted by Theodore A. Fetter, *Southwestern Freight Rates,* n. 26, p. 27.

the well-paid counsel for the railroads were highly inventive in finding means of evading the already weakened bite of the federal Interstate Commerce Act. Hogg knew that if the states were to continue to do battle, on anything like equal terms, to protect their citizens against the rapidly burgeoning monopolies created by the railroads and by other market-cornering "big business," there was drastic need for stronger legal weapons. In 1889, first Kansas, then Texas, forged such weapons —in the shape of antitrust acts; in 1890 the Sherman Antitrust Act was enacted, and by 1893, fourteen other states would have followed suit.

The idea of antitrust legislation was not new in Texas. The Constitution of 1845 had adopted the common-law doctrine that monopolies were contrary to the genius of free government and should never be allowed, but its framers had made no provision that would assist future lawmakers in grappling with the astounding surge of consolidation and incorporation that occurred from 1870 on. Certain provisions of the 1876 "Granger" Constitution, such as the Article on which the Traffic Association suit was based, were attempts at restraint of combinations. Popular pressure for stronger legislation against trusts had been mounting, especially since 1885, when the Gould-blessed Traffic Association was formed. The Texas Grange and the Farmers' Alliance had protested the Association from the beginning. And under the alert leadership of magnetic, Wisconsin-born Charles W. Macune, the Farmers' Alliance had continued to wage a vigorous fight against any combination in restraint of trade which threatened the welfare of farmers—such as the jute and bagging trust, that was attempting to corner the market in sale and purchase of bagging for grain and cotton.[37] By 1886 the Alliance was projecting a system of joint-stock stores and cooperatives and had grown to include nearly three thousand lodges in eighty-four counties—a strong political voice not to be ignored. In the next few years its consolidation with other farm groups of both Texas and other Southern states to form the Southern Alliance, with Macune as executive secretary, created an agrarian power to be reckoned with. In March, 1889, Macune, who had been editor of the *Southern Mercury,* the Texas Alliance newspaper in Dallas, went to Washington, D.C., as the editor of the newly established *National Economist,* official journal of the South-

---

[37] John D. Hicks, *The Populist Revolt* (Minneapolis, University of Minnesota Press, 1931), pp. 130 ff.; C. W. Macune, "The Farmers' Alliance," pp. 41–59, typescript, 1920, Archives Collection, the University of Texas.

ern Alliance, continuing his battle against monopolies. For several years this paper exerted enormous influence in farm circles.

In August, 1888, the Texas Alliance had recommended a railroad commission and the passage of "a law prohibiting the formation of trusts and combinations by speculators to secure control of the necessaries of life for the purpose of forcing up prices on consumers, imposing heavy penalties."[38] The Grangers went along with these recommendations, particularly because they did not wish provisions of the 1876 "Granger" Constitution to be thwarted by new types of trusts at a time when Attorney General Hogg was making the state's case stick against the Traffic Association. In the 1888 election campaign, the so-called Non-Partisan Party, one of the forerunners of the Populist Party, nominated Evans Jones, outstanding Alliance leader from drought-stricken Erath County, for governor. This party was made up of the farmers' groups that had successfully sponsored agrarian county tickets in 1886 and of some Knights of Labor. Their platform opposed monopolies and trusts and advocated free and unlimited coinage of silver and government-owned-and-controlled communication and transportation systems, "as is the United States post office."[39]

While the Democratic Party's combination of the conservative Ross and the crusading Hogg had no difficulty in being re-elected, the Non-Partisan platform demanded attention, for it represented the disillusionment of increasing numbers both of the settlers who had risked the Great Plains environment and of the established farmers whose livelihoods in the fertile woodlands were now threatened by persistently unfavorable economic conditions. Members of the Alliance and the Grange expected action, and some were no longer moderate. As a result, many middle-of-the-road Democratic representatives, at last responsive to the ground swell of public opinion, went to the Texas legislature in January, 1889, intent upon the passage of a railroad commission law and an antitrust law—both to regulate "big business."

The United States Congress had been working on antitrust legislation for a year. In January, 1888, Representative William Stone of Kentucky had introduced a bill on the subject. Texas' interest in federal trust legislation was manifested not much later by no less than three bills: Representatives David Culberson and Jo Abbott each initiated a bill in

---

[38] Winkler, *Platforms*, p. 271.
[39] *Ibid.*, pp. 260–261; Jeremiah Jenks, *The Trust Problem* (New York, Doubleday, Page, and Company, 1920), pp. 244–245.

the House, and in the Senate John H. Reagan introduced a short, three-section bill on August 14, the same day that Senator John Sherman, of Ohio, introduced his bill. In September, Senator Shelby Cullom, of Illinois, with whom Reagan had debated the final form of the Interstate Commerce Act, introduced his bill on trusts.[40]

Action on these measures had been delayed by the confusion over the fight on the Mills tariff bill and by the presidential election of 1888, in which Benjamin Harrison defeated President Cleveland. The issue had appeared in the 1888 national party platforms. The Republicans asserted their "opposition to all combinations of capital, organized in trusts or otherwise, to control arbitrarily the condition of trade," and sought legislation to prevent all schemes to oppress the people by "undue charges on their supplies"; the Democrats declared that the principles of democracy were betrayed by trusts and combinations calculated to "rob" the people and "unduly enrich" the few because "natural competition" had been destroyed.[41] Texas Democrats, in endorsing this platform, further resolved: "That the next [Texas] legislature shall pass laws defining trusts, pools, and all illegal combinations in restraint of trade, and imposing severe penalties in regard thereto."[42] The delegates also commended Senators Reagan and Coke for exposing the beef combine.

As the legislature assembled in Austin in January, 1889, the state-wide ferment for trust legislation had been further stimulated by the Texas Supreme Court's late December affirmation of Hogg's victory over the Traffic Association. Governor Ross in his inaugural address (the first such address to be delivered in the impressive new Capitol, which had been opened officially the preceding May) still opposed a railroad commission law but made clear his recognition of the need to curb monopolies; he attributed the growth of the monied combinations to the fact that the liability of corporations was limited and asked whether it would not be wise to curtail a corporation's privileges.[43]

---

[40] Shelby S. Cullom, *Fifty Years of Public Service: Personal Recollections* (Chicago, A. C. McClurg and Company, 1911), Chap. 16; *Congressional Record*, 50 Cong., 1 Sess., pp. 8239, 8596.

[41] Section of the Democratic platform, "Taxation"; the Republican statement in section on "Foreign Contract Labor."

[42] Winkler, *op. cit.*, p. 267. At the Chicago Conference on Trusts in 1899 Dudley Wooten spoke on the part the "individualistic spirit" of Texans had in the promulgation of the Texas antitrust law. Cf. Civic Federation of Chicago, *Chicago Conference on Trusts, 1899* (Chicago, 1900), p. 52; Henry Nash Smith, *Virgin Land* (Cambridge, Harvard University Press, 1950), pp. 193, 248–249, where he adds the idea of the "independent yeoman" to the "myths" of the West.

[43] Texas *House Journal* (1889), p. 89.

At the time Ross spoke, three antitrust bills had already been introduced in the House; later, Representative W. R. Hamby, a director of the Austin *Statesman,* introduced a fourth.[44] Members of the Judiciary Committee made it their first concern to consolidate these proposals aimed "to promote free competition." The substitute bill passed the House in February with only one dissenting vote,[45] but passage in the Senate was delayed until March, largely because of the fight over the railroad commission bills. After the vigorous railway lobby, ably led by George Clark of Waco, had manipulated, as usual, the defeat of the railroad commission bills, the Senate on March 22 passed the antitrust bill, with a last-minute amendment to Section 6 through the insertion of "knowingly acted," relating to persons subject to punishment.[46] The House was reluctant to accept this change, but the wording finally became "knowingly carry out any of the stipulations, purposes, prices, rates, or orders," and was approved March 30, 1889.

While these measures were being debated, the Attorney General had not been an unconcerned observer. Alvin C. Owsley of Denton, who was chairman of the special subcommittee charged with writing the composite bill, gives credit to Hogg for his part in the preparation of the law:

James S. Hogg was then Attorney General and I consulted with him about the matter and we together drew the substitute bill which was reported to the general committee and afterward the House, and became the anti-trust law of 1889. Attorney General Hogg and I consulted together several times and worked on the bill several nights, and my recollection is that Hon. L. L. Foster, who afterward became Railroad Commissioner [by appointment from Hogg] consulted with us and worked with us two or three nights. Foster was at the time Commissioner of Agriculture, Insurance, Statistics, and History. We had the Reagan bill, which had been introduced in Congress, and took it as a copy. Otherwise the law was peculiarly a Texas product, and, while it may not have been generally known, its leading ideas were those of Attorney General Hogg. We discussed all

[44] Albert Stephenson of Weatherford introduced the first bill on January 11, 1889. None was introduced in the Senate; House Bills 9, 117, 130, 192, 313. Hamby's bill excepted associations of laboring men. Texas *House Journal* (1889), pp. 157, 1139. Hamby's action is noteworthy, as the paper employed many skilled workers. He was a friend of Hogg's, becoming one of his campaign managers in 1892.

[45] February 14, 1889, Texas *House Journal* (1889), p. 412.

[46] Texas *Senate Journal* (1889), p. 581, March 21, 1889. In the Senate the Chairman of the Committee on the Substitute was W. H. Pope, who worked to block the railroad commission measure.

163

kinds of trusts that were in any way calculated to affect commodities, transportation, and insurance.

My recollection now is that after the substitute bill had been reported to the House serious objection was made to it on the ground that it might prevent the Farmers' Alliance and other bodies of farmers, as well as stock raisers, from acting together to procure a fair price for their products, and that to meet the objection I offered an amendment on the floor of the House, which was adopted, providing that the law should not apply to agricultural products and livestock in the hands of the producer or raiser.[47]

The Texas Antitrust Act was four times the length of the Reagan bill, an evidence of the special efforts made to cover as many contingencies as possible. For example, Hogg was not content with Reagan's definition of a trust as a combination of "capital or skill by two or more persons for the following purposes"; the Texas passage read, "capital, skill, or acts by two or more persons, firms, corporations, or associations of persons, or of either two or more of them for either, any, or all of the following purposes." The first two purposes, dealing with restriction of trade and limiting, reducing, or increasing production or prices, were practically the same in both bills, but Reagan's simple statement of the third purpose—"prevention of competition"—became in the Texas law: "Third—To prevent competition in manufacture, making, transportation, sale, or purchase of merchandise, produce or commodities."[48] Owsley was correct in saying that farmers and cattlemen were concerned about the interpretation of this section, and he joined with Representative Albert Stephenson to provide Section 13, which read: "The provisions of this act shall not apply to agricultural products or livestock while in the hands of the producer or raiser." In this matter the Texans were more forthright than the federal makers of the Sherman Antitrust Act of 1890, for it would not be until the passage of the Clayton Act of 1914 (sometimes called the Magna Charta of Labor) that agricultural and labor groups were protected as originally intended by the early proponents of national antitrust legislation.[49]

One of Hogg's contributions was the omission of the word "mo-

---

[47] Quoted in Tom Finty, Jr., *Anti-Trust Legislation in Texas* (Dallas, A. H. Belo Company, 1916), p. 16; Texas *House Journal* (1889), February 6, 1889, pp. 319–320.

[48] Representative Albert Stephenson, who had introduced one of the antitrust bills, was alert to the transportation features. See Texas *House Journal* (1889), pp. 319–320.

[49] Ernest von Halle, *Trusts* (New York, Macmillan Company, 1896), p. 122, confusing several points, including the time sequence, declared: "The Populists

nopoly." Reagan's fourth purpose referred to the creation of monopoly, but the Attorney General realized the difficulty of proving monopoly, which was outlawed already by the Texas Constitution. Nevertheless, he did not hesitate to reflect the cattleman's and the cotton grower's concern over price-fixing by adding a fifth purpose, not appearing in Reagan's bill:

To make or enter into, or execute or carry out any contract, obligation, or agreement of any kind or description by which they shall agree in any manner to keep the price of such article, commodity, or transportation, at a fixed or graduated figure, or by which they shall in any manner establish or settle the price of any article or commodity or transportation between them or themselves and others to preclude a free and unrestricted competition among themselves or others in the sale or transportation of any such article or commodity, or by which they shall agree to pool, combine, or unite any interest they may have in connection with the sale or transportation of any such article or commodity that its price might in any manner be affected.[50]

It was generally understood both in and outside of Texas that the new law on trusts constituted a "dragnet of great sweep and close mesh,"[51] and there were many indications that it was influencing thought and activity far beyond the borders of the state. In February, while the measure was being written, Governor Ross had received word from Governor Lyman Humphrey of Kansas that the Kansas legislature had called for a convention of states at St. Louis on April 12 and 13, 1889, to investigate the beef combine. On the second day of the conference, one of the Minnesota delegates, E. M. Pope, chairman of the Committee on Needed Legislation, proposed that all nine states represented adopt an "Act to define trusts, and to provide for penalties and punishments of corporations, persons, firms, and associations of persons connected with them, and to promote free competition in the State of ———." The proposal carried, and the Texas delegates were able to take home the proud report that the Texas law had been adopted almost in its entirety; one section only, which related to a specific earlier Texas statute, was

detest every sort of capitalistic organization. They deemed it fit, in the Texas anti-trust law, whilest forbidding combinations in manufactured goods, to exempt agricultural products in the hands of the farmers from this restriction."

[50] Section I, Part Fifth, of the Texas law on trusts, Gammel, *Laws,* IX, 1169–1170; Cotner (ed.), *Addresses of James Hogg,* p. 59.

[51] Finty, *op. cit.,* p. 48. An excellent study of the various features of state anti-trust laws is by former Commissioner of Corporations Joseph E. Davies, *Trust Laws and Unfair Competition* (Washington, Government Printing Office, 1916), pp. 142–230.

omitted, and to another section was added a clause against the price-fixing of beef and pork, a point on which the cattlemen and farmers were especially concerned.[52]

In the spring of 1890, Senator Reagan offered parts of the Texas law in his substitute for the Sherman Antitrust Bill, but the substitution was not accepted. The final federal bill, drafted by the Senate Judiciary Committee and passed on July 2, 1890, as the Sherman Antitrust Act, had several critical weaknesses, among them its obscure and ambiguous phrasing and failure to clearly define such words as "trust" and "restraint"—and, most notoriously, its lack of specific exemptions for labor and farm organizations.[53] It has been customary to interpret farmer reaction to the high McKinley Tariff Act of 1890 as a major factor in the defeat of the Republicans in 1892; however, farmer and labor reaction to the ambiguous Sherman Antitrust Act also contributed largely to the general revolt, as well as to the formation of the Populist (People's) Party, which had up its sleeve the threat of a spreading campaign for government ownership and management, if regulation was not to be honestly tested by the old, established parties.

The widespread speculation in Texas newspapers during the spring and summer of 1889 concerning the Attorney General's political future was only one sign of the acclaim for his contributions to the trust law and his successful fight against the Traffic Association. James Hogg had no time to pause for basking in the warmth of this appreciation, but the comments from friends both in and out of Texas undoubtedly gave him pleasure and encouragement as he quietly proceeded with plans for the railroad and land battles ahead. At the beginning of court action in the spring of 1889 against the Missouri, Kansas, and Texas Railway as part of his strategy in his efforts to free the International and Great Northern from Jay Gould's control, he received a particularly heartening letter from Senator Reagan:

Thank God that Texas has a brave, honest & earnest and able man for her Attorney General who can not be influenced by favor or fear in the

[52] *Convention of States with Reference to Beef and Pork Combines . . . held at St. Louis, Mo., April 12–13, 1889* (Topeka, 1889), pp. 16–18.

[53] Senator Zebulon Vance of North Carolina said in the debate on the Sherman bill: "My opinion is that we never shall get a bill for the suppression of trusts and combinations . . . as long as we consign all of our bandlings to the fostering care of the Judiciary Committee." Quoted in Marion M. Miller (ed.), *Great Debates in American History* (New York, Current Literature Publishing Company, 1913), XI, 66.

discharge of the high trust conferred on him by the good people of a great State.

At a time when public demoralization is so prevalent that railroad corporations notoriously control state legislatures and courts, and exercise undue influence in the congress of the United States; and when they impudently and audaciously violate and defy constitutions and laws and plunder the public with impunity, it is most gratifying to see that there is one high public functionary who has the ability and courage to call some of them to the bar of justice to answer the offended law, and for their outrages on the rights of the people.[54]

A letter from an Ohio friend, George Rice of Marietta, probably constituted an excellent epitome of the public's appreciation of Hogg's efforts. Rice, owner of the Ohio Oil Works, had been among those to call Hogg's attention to the powerful force of the business trust as employed by Rockefeller against smaller competitors such as Rice himself.

I thank you sincerely for favors extended—and will highly appreciate the copy of investigation that broke up the Texas Traffic Association. In this connection would say that they have lately continued the fashion of overweighting my cars going to Texas, and that inquiry developed the fact that J. Waldo as head of "*International* Bureau and weighing Association" was responsible. Headquarters, Houston. I am just advised that May 1 this was discontinued. It may be your trust law made them conclude such operations in your state unsafe. I hope so, and that they will not arise in any new form. You deserve great honor and credit for having so successfully freed your state from the evils of monopoly. In the name of all the independent refiners of oil, I thank you, and trust you may reach all the political honors to which you may aspire, and be everlastingly successful.

Yours truly
George Rice[55]

---

[54] Senator John H. Reagan to J. S. Hogg, April 6, 1889, J. S. Hogg Let. Rec., I, 137.

[55] George Rice to J. S. Hogg, Attorney General, May 7, 1889, J. S. Hogg Let. Rec., I, 197.

CHAPTER VII

The Railways Openly Enter Politics:
The Hogg-Hall Controversy

THE POPULAR DEMAND for more effective railway regulation in Texas
had grown with each session of the legislature after 1876. Failure to
satisfy this demand had led during the summer of 1888 to conventions
of farmers, laborers, and stockraisers, the so-called Nonpartisans, held
at Waco and Dallas, and to a meeting of Union Laborites at Fort Worth.
These forerunners of the Populists called for government ownership of
railroads and telegraphs.[1] This socialistic program was advocated by the
radicals, among whom were some hard-working farmers made desperate
by the drought and high costs for feed or by the long price decline of
cotton. Therefore, the legislature of 1889 became a crucial one. While
farmers and stockmen were in the majority, they were, almost without
exception, without legislative experience. Many of the lawyer-members
had been in the legislature before. George Clark, campaign manager for
two governors, again came down from Waco, this time to be the organizing genius for the railway lobby. He benefited from the able leadership and earnest speeches of Senator H. D. McDonald of Paris, who
developed ambitions to become governor, and Senator G. B. Gerald of
Clark's home county, since both of these senators worked to check any
bolt for a railroad commission.[2]

The commission bills of Cone Johnson and R. T. Milner, from East
Texas, and Thomas J. Brown, of North Texas, designed in part to head
off demands for government ownership, were defeated by the Senate.
The devotees of Gould and Huntington were jubilant, until a vote was
obtained for submitting a constitutional amendment to the people to
settle the issue which had baffled their representatives for fourteen years.
If the amendment should carry, Article X, Section 2, of the Constitu-

[1] Ernest W. Winkler, *Platforms of Political Parties in Texas*, pp. 256–257, 261.
[2] Texas *Senate Journal* (1889), p. 321. Senator McDonald made his forceful
anti-commission speech February 25, 1889, arguing that the legislature could not
delegate its powers and citing *Willis* v. *Owen* 43 Texas 59. In the 1920–29 era
McDonald was president of the Southern Pacific, Texas and Louisiana branches.

168

tion, which provided for legislative regulation, would be amended to read:

and to the further accomplishment of these objects and purposes, [the legislature] may provide and establish all requisite means and agencies invested with such powers as may be deemed adequate and advisable.[3]

By this action, which would make a railroad commission legal, the Twenty-first Legislature provided the major issue of the political campaign of 1890. The railroads squared off for the fight. The big city dailies, such as the San Antonio *Express,* the Houston *Daily Post,* the Galveston *Daily News,* and the Dallas *Morning News* immediately lined up against the commission amendment. Would any candidate for governor be so audacious as to wholeheartedly support the amendment and to advocate a plenary commission as the plan to carry the will of the majority into effect after the amendment was adopted?

There is no known evidence that Attorney General James Hogg became even an armchair advocate of a railroad commission before 1889. For three years with the Ross administration he had worked diligently to enforce existing laws, and by his actions he had succeeded in forcing the International and Great Northern to return to Palestine, Texas, the offices and shops which Jay Gould had moved out of Texas. The Texas and New Orleans had returned offices and shops from New Orleans to Houston. Hogg had instituted suits and issued many notifications which led to the restoration of safer conditions of travel over run-down lines. He had caused depots and tracks to be repaired or to be rebuilt. During 1888–1890 he pressed land suits against the major systems and set about to block Jay Gould from saddling unwarranted stock and bond issues on the I.& G.N. through his control of the Missouri Pacific and Missouri, Kansas, and Texas lines. In an effort to defeat the amendment, George Clark, the leader of the anti-commission forces, was to say that Hogg's vigorous prosecution of railway cases through the courts demonstrated that a railroad commission was not necessary.[4] While the legislature was in session in 1889, Hogg had been more concerned with the passage of an antitrust law than with the commission bills. However, he was aware that railroad cases were taking a disproportionate amount of the time of his office. Since the legislature had concluded that no machinery existed to handle day-by-day railroad questions, such as rate charges, and since the Attorney General had learned that numerous minor issues

[3] H. P. Gammel, *Laws of Texas,* IX, 1199.
[4] Quoted in the Galveston *News,* April 30, 1890.

prevented the most effective attention to major legal matters, a commission experiment was worth serious consideration.[5]

Soon after the legislature adjourned, enterprising reporters began to try to smoke out Hogg's intentions. As early as May, 1889, the editor of the St. Louis *Republic* indicated that he expected James Hogg would be a candidate for governor of Texas in 1890.[6] The Houston *Post* set the political pot boiling by reporting "a rumor" to the effect that Jay Gould, Tom Bonner, W. S. Herndon, and James Hogg were working together. Gould was to gain control of the I.& G.N. and Hogg was to be made governor. "What Does It Mean?" asked the *Post*,[7] a query which reflected the suspicions of the Huntington Railroad interests. Hogg followed the advice of Horace Chilton to ignore the article, but Tom Bonner and W. S. Herndon rushed into print to defend themselves against any charge that they were subservient to Gould or that Hogg's action in bringing suit against Gould, seeking to revoke the charter of the I.& G.N., was other than correct.[8] The *Post's* articles seemed to have the effect of uniting for Hogg, with few exceptions, the Democratic factions in Tyler.[9]

By the middle of 1889, sentiment was widespread that Attorney General Hogg was the man best qualified to become the next governor and to put a commission plan into operation. However, when he discussed these matters with a few close friends, including Horace Chilton, Sawnie Robertson, A. W. Terrell, Jot Gunter, and Web Finley, Chairman of the State Executive Committee of the Democratic Party, Hogg expressed an intent to give special attention to the pending Gould cases and to some land cases involving Huntington and Gould interests. There was too much to do to think of campaigning.

Meanwhile members of the Grange, the Farmers' Alliance, and labor organizations were outspoken in hailing him as their choice for the exec-

---

[5] R. C. Cotner (ed.), *Addresses of James S. Hogg*, pp. 74 ff.

[6] Dallas *News*, editorial, May 17, 1889; Galveston *News*, May 20, 1889.

[7] Houston *Post*, May 22, 1889.

[8] W. S. Herndon to J. S. Hogg, May 25, 1889 (confidential), J. S. Hogg Let. Rec., I, 258–259; Tom Bonner to J. S. Hogg, May 25, 1889, J. S. Hogg, Let. Rec., I, 254–255. Bonner wanted letters placed in the Austin *Statesman* and the Fort Worth *Gazette*: "It will clear up some false positions now taken by the Press. At all events it will place General Hogg precisely where he ought to stand before the public, and also places the I.&G.N. on the true basis." The above is Bonner quoting Herndon. See also Horace Chilton to Dear J, May 25, 1889, J. S. Hogg Let. Rec., I, 256; Julius Grodinsky, *Jay Gould, His Business Career, 1867–1892* (Philadelphia, University of Pennsylvania Press, 1957), pp. 541 ff.

[9] Bonner to Hogg, June 3, 1889, J. S. Hogg Let. Rec., I, 281–282.

utive office in 1890, and friends increasingly urged that he run as the champion of the proposed constitutional amendment that would settle the question of the legality of a railroad commission with plenary powers to fix and enforce freight and passenger rates.[10] Yet Hogg did not desire another public office. Despite charges by his political enemies, among them Abner Taylor, Charles Goodnight, and Land Commissioner Hall, that he was playing up the railroad and land cases solely with an eye to the governor's chair,[11] the evidence is ample that he wished and intended at the end of his second term as attorney general to return to Tyler to rebuild his private law practice. There were many ties waiting him in Tyler: he had not sold his home; he had left behind, when he sublet his office, his personal library and his safe; and in 1889 construction had begun on a two-story building, just off Tyler Square, in which he planned to open a new office, using the rest of the space as rental property. The modest properties he had acquired in Dallas and Greenville needed his attention; the new fruit and nursery enterprises that had developed near Tyler aroused his eager interest, and he had been buying fruit and shade trees to be planted about his house. The years in Austin had been exhausting ones, even to a man of his abundant energy, and had allowed him little time to spend with his family. Furthermore, Sallie Hogg had been recently suffering from severe headaches that the doctors could not explain, and it seemed probable that the quieter life in Tyler would be a help to her.

Opposing his strong urges to return to private life were the constant exhortations of friends to continue the fight, so that as governor he might put the railroad commission plan into action. Hogg agreed that a commission was essential to effective regulation of the railroads in the public interest, particularly in the face of the skillful manipulations of George Clark, the chief lobbyist for nearly all the Texas roads, but his own suggested candidate for governor was his good friend Sawnie Robertson, who had recently resumed his law practice in Dallas after a year on the Texas Supreme Court bench.

[10] John Kennedy, W. H. Bailey, Proprietor Houston *Daily Herald*, and Mrs. J. V. Haxthanson, Proprietress *Texas Deutsche Zeitung*, to J. S. Hogg, July 20, 1889, J. S. Hogg Let. Rec., I, 372–374; Sawnie Robertson to J. S. Hogg, July 5, 1889, J. S. Hogg Let. Rec., I, 344–345. In Horace Chilton to J. S. Hogg, July 7, 1889, J. S. Hogg Let. Rec., I, 347, Hogg is advised to say it is "too early" rather than to decline to run. Chilton intended to keep Hogg available.

[11] Quoted in Lewis Nordyke, *Cattle Empire* (New York, W. Morrow, 1949), p. 190; J. Evetts Haley, *The XIT Ranch*, pp. 84, 216; Haley, *Charles Goodnight*, p. 401; Dallas *Morning News*, editorial, May 17, 1889; Galveston *Daily News*, May 20, 1889.

In the summer of 1889 Robertson was carrying on a prolonged and courageous debate with George Clark, through the columns of the Dallas *Morning News,* over the issue of regulation by commission. Among Clark's attempts to blacken both Hogg and Robertson politically were his taunts that they were friends of the Knights of Labor (who in 1886 had fought Jay Gould from Fort Worth and Marshall to Chicago). Sawnie Robertson had learned his political lessons well at the feet of his father, Harvard-trained Judge John C. Robertson—with whom Hogg had made his great law enforcement record as district attorney—and as a law student at the school of the staunch states'-righter and former governor, O. M. Roberts. Sawnie was determined, he had told Hogg, that Clark would not make another governor who would oppose a state railroad commission without giving the people an opportunity to hear the other side. He wanted to make it clear that Clark's presentation of the issue in a recent newspaper interview was of vast importance to the present and future of Texas.

Clark had charged that the reform politicians were enemies of private enterprise and encouraged labor's "anarchists and communists."[12] He had accused Robertson of embracing "esthetic communism" and urged his friends to get him out of his "benighted condition" before he started around the country lecturing on the "single land tax" advocated by Henry George. Robertson replied that Clark was too able a lawyer not to know that, according to the Texas constitution, railroads were public carriers and subject to government regulation as stipulated in their charters.

To understand the references to communism it is necessary to recall that the Gould crowd had turned off many a harsh word directed against their railroad methods by having the newspapers report the "communist" activities of the Knights of Labor in 1886. Here was a new political weapon. Furthermore, after the trials and execution of some of the "anarchists" in Chicago following the Haymarket Riot, fear of Marxian communism and Russian anarchism spread over this land. It was the railroad corporation lobbyists and some politicians who first raised the smoke-screen of "Communism" in a Texas election. Robertson, as a loyal and progressive Texan, resented Clark's unfair characterization, and replied that he had known for some time that the railroad lobby had adopted in Texas the practice of impairing the influence of

---

[12] Dallas *Morning News,* July 14, 24, and 28, 1889; Galveston *Daily News,* July 25, 1889; Richard H. Harrison to George Clark, July 15, 1889, J. S. Hogg, Let. Pr., 3, pp. 493–500.

those who favored railroad regulation by industriously circulating that they were erratic cranks.

In conferences with a group of close friends, including Robertson, Horace Chilton, A. W. Terrell, Jot Gunter, and Web Finley, Hogg advocated Robertson's candidacy, and tried to make it clear that he [Hogg] would be engrossed for many months to come with the pending Gould cases and the land suits that involved both Gould and Huntington. But the group would not let the matter of Hogg's candidacy rest, and neither would the newspapers.

The Houston *Post,* as the Huntington mouthpiece, hoped with fervor that Hogg would not enter the race. Two other Houston papers, the *Daily Herald* and the *Texas Deutsche Zeitung,* expressed gratitude for Hogg's part in effecting the return of the shops and offices of the Texas and New Orleans Railroad to the city. The owners of these papers and John Kennedy, a Houston real-estate broker, in midsummer sent Hogg a paperweight made of grapeshot from the battlefield of San Jacinto as "a continual reminder of the public trust which has descended from the fathers of Texas to you."[13] The New Braunfels *Zeitung* praised his work; when a friend sent Hogg a translation of one of the articles, Hogg thanked him and then said he was honestly "very tired of public life," adding that other fields were easier, "less responsible, more lucrative, and, possibly, more honorable."[14]

Time and again corporate interests showed their fear of Hogg's possible candidacy by seeking to embarrass or compromise him either directly or through his friends. When the alternate section school lands case was appealed by the Galveston, Houston, and San Antonio Railroad, Sawnie Robertson was asked by interested parties opposed to the state to be one of their counsel. Robertson wanted Hogg to know just where he stood:

I have been applied to by a party representing a number of persons largely interested in the case adversely to the State to know what my fee would be to brief and represent oral argument on the side of the appellee. The appellee itself I suppose is already ably and sufficiently represented— but I am asked to fix fee that would satisfy me to brief and argue the case against you . . .

I wish for fear of embarassment [sic] in the future to commit myself now in advance of all complications for you for Governor "first, last and all the

---

[13] J. S. Hogg Let. Rec., I, 372–374.

[14] J. S. Hogg to S. D. Blake (Dallas), July 30, 1889, J. S. Hogg, Let. Pr., 3, pp. 52–54; Winkler, *op. cit.,* pp. 275–276.

time"—in spite of this land Suit and the manifesto to the Sheriffs, I think the era calls for you for that place.[15]

During the next seven months, Robertson and his cousin Horace Chilton, along with Web Finley and various labor, lawyer, journalist, and Grange and Alliance leaders, tried repeatedly to elicit Hogg's promise to run. He was equally persistent in his refusals; not playing coy, he simply did not wish to remain in public office. Meanwhile, the commission debate grew warmer, especially when United States Senator Richard Coke declared his stand for a plenary commission. Coke, who knew his Waco fellow citizen George Clark well (Clark had been his secretary of state briefly, and then his attorney general), privately warned Hogg:

Recent indications prove conclusively to my mind that henceforth the railroad people are to be openly and publicly, instead of being secretly as heretofore, in politics in Texas. The disguise is being thrown off, and they mean *business*. Texas must dominate and control the railroads, or the railroads will dominate and control Texas, as they do now some of the other great States in the Union. I have no fear of the result of the contest, but they will be found stronger than many suppose.

Yr. Friend, Richd Coke[16]

One definite indication of the railroaders' more aggressive policy was their reaction to the Freight Rate Conference held in Dallas early in July, 1889. The conference, called through the efforts of the Dallas Merchants Exchange and various legislators, notable among them Representative T. J. Brown of Sherman, aired grievances against "the railroad combination" that set rates detrimental to Texas industries and lumber and agriculture operations. It was well attended by manufacturers, jobbers, and legislators, but railway officials were mostly conspicuous by their absence. Brown was made permanent chairman. The meeting voted to create a Committee of Thirty-One, which was to request a conference before August 15 with the railway traffic managers in which all parties might endeavor to reach an agreement on "just and reasonable rates." Such a conference could possibly have resulted in a compromise amenable to all. However, George Clark apparently coun-

[15] Sawnie Robertson to J. S. Hogg, July 5, 1889, J. S. Hogg Let. Rec., I, 344–345. The reference to the complaints of the sheriffs over fees will be discussed in the chapter on the election of 1890. Horace Chilton on July 7 advised Hogg to say it was "too early" to decide.

[16] Richard Coke to J. S. Hogg, August 15, 1889, J. S. Hogg Let. Rec., I, 443. See Galveston *News*, August 15, 1889, for evidence of the broadening debate; also Waxahachie *Enterprise*, August 9, 1889.

seled "no compromise" (perhaps in light of the fact that the meeting had also resolved to urge the people to vote for a commission amendment); in any case, railway representatives did not meet with the new Committee, giving as their interesting reason that they were afraid of violating the new trust law.

By mid-August many great and near-great had entered the commission debate. The Galveston *News* and the Dallas *News* as a public service published speeches, week after week, on both sides of the issue. When James Hogg learned of the explanation offered by the railroad representatives for not meeting with the Committee of Thirty-One he warned that this was merely another of their subterfuges and pointed out that here were strong indications of a "secret 'understanding' or combination between the railway companies of this State, or with others outside it, to maintain rates, or rates established by agreement."[17] He then called upon persons with material facts bearing on such an "understanding" to report them, so that offenders might be brought before the bar of justice.

While Hogg was endeavoring to squeeze "the wind and water" out of railway securities, he recognized that fair valuation might be a function which could be taken over by a railroad commission, but he knew that the land suits must continue to be a proper function of his office, working, he had hoped, in conjunction with the land commissioner. While preparing for the hearing of the school lands or Val Verde case before the Supreme Court, Hogg had requested Land Commissioner Hall to furnish his office data on those lines which had received lands for "sidings and switches" in addition to the lands for the main track. Hogg and Hall had crossed on the issue of acceptance of the Capitol in 1888 when it seemed that Hall was ready to give the balance of the 3 million acres to Abner Taylor and the XIT Ranch stockholders without the final checkup insisted upon by the chief legal officer.[18] Relations between the men were strained further over a land patent requested by W. S. Herndon of Tyler. Hall had turned him down, but when Herndon forced Hall to seek legal advice, the Attorney General's Office told Hall that legally Herndon was entitled to the land. Unexplained delays in furnishing information requested by the Attorney General in July, 1889,

[17] J. S. Hogg to S. D. Blake (Dallas), July 30, 1889, Let. Pr., 3, pp. 52–54; Winkler, *op. cit.*, pp. 275–276.

[18] J. S. Hogg to Governor L. S. Ross, September 10, 1889, Att. Gen. Let. Pr., 49, pp. 465–466; R. C. Cotner, "Attorney General J. S. Hogg and the Acceptance of the State Capitol: A Reappraisal," *West Texas Historical Association Yearbook*, XXV (October, 1949), 50–75.

at a time when Hogg felt that early action was essential, added to the tenseness of the situation.

The Houston and Texas Central Railroad (Huntington-controlled) had opened the rich, black, waxy prairies of Central Texas to world commerce, but, in 1885, the Houston and Texas Central and the Waco and Northwestern went into the hands of federal receivers, much to the disgust of the richest woman in America, Mrs. Hettie Green, who claimed that Huntington and his Southern Pacific System were to blame for the failure to keep the lines in good condition.[19] The people of Waco had put up $100,000 in bonds to help build the Waco and Northwestern, and they insisted on separate receivers. Subsequently, many people complained when the H. & T.C. began to dispose of the Waco and Northwestern lands. In the fall of 1888 the "Western Division," or the line northwest of Hempstead, was purchased by Frederick P. Olcott, President of the Central Trust Company of New York, acting as purchasing trustee for the Southern Pacific. Huntington had thus been able to obtain a line competing with Gould's Missouri, Kansas, and Texas and proceeded on August 1, 1889, under the laws of Texas to reorganize his line to Denison as the Houston and Texas Central Railroad Company. Like the Galveston, Houston, and San Antonio, the H. & T.C. was a Texas-chartered company, but in effect both roads were parts of the Southern Pacific System, which, strange to relate, operated under a charter granted by the State of Kentucky. When the H. & T.C. signed the "respect-for-Texas-law clause" and signified that it did not belong to a pool or trust, Hogg had no apparent legal grounds upon which to deny a recharter.[20]

However, Hogg was watching various practices of the H. & T. C. He had been informed of the alienation of over one hundred sections of land in Hardeman County in the northwest at three and one-half cents per acre, which the informant thought to have been fraudulent.[21] A fourteen or twenty-one-year time limit had been set on grants to railways for alienation to settlers and, under the pressure from the Grange and Alliance to get lands into the hands of actual settlers, sales would normally be encouraged. However, there was a question as to the ability of the H. & T. C. to give title to lands granted to the Waco and Northwestern

---

[19] St. Clair Reed, *Texas Railroads*, p. 220. Cf. Stuart Daggert, *Chapters on the History of the Southern Pacific* (New York, Ronald Press, 1922), pp. 348–369.

[20] Reed, *op. cit.*, p. 221.

[21] Reference in H. B. Marsh to M. M. Hawkins (County Attorney), October 6, 1888, Att. Gen. Let. Pr., 44, p. 660.

or claimed by it. Hogg had been warned that if action was not taken soon it would be too late to regain lands for nonalienation. Party planks of 1888 on alienation were being taken seriously by the railroads, but they tried to force the Attorney General to delay suits by charging that he was beclouding land titles. Instead, Hogg urged G. W. Walters of Vernon to check affidavits of General G. M. Dodge, builder of the T. & P. and the Forth Worth and Denver, and five witnesses to see whether bona fide citizens occupied the "more than 20 business and residence houses" said to be in the town of Harrold on the Fort Worth and Denver, which had been laid off under an Act of April 1, 1887, granting railways lands for town sites.[22] Aware that Receiver Charles Dillingham was frantically selling lands and giving quitclaim deeds,[23] Hogg always advised real-estate dealers and individual purchasers to insist upon warranty deeds.

When Hogg had not received by September, 1889, the "sidings and switches" information he sought from Commissioner Hall, he recommended to the governor and to Hall that no more patents be issued to the H. & T. C., which had recently placed all of its lands on the market. He held that the assignment of the Waco and Northwestern claims to the H. & T. C. was illegal and unauthorized and that the Waco and Northwestern had actually never earned the lands in question. Sixteen sections for each mile of "sidings and switches" amounting to about a million improperly acquired acres were involved in the H. & T. C. allotments. Later, Hall declared that if Hogg had reported to him a failure to obtain the information sought he would have supplied it. As it was, he asked a clerk, who said that he had misplaced the letter, to go to Hogg and apologize for his negligence.[24]

Hall was not encouraged to aid the Attorney General by a report concerning remarks of former Governor Richard Hubbard, of Tyler, which

[22] R. H. Harrison to G. W. Walters, February 15, 1889, Att. Gen. Let. Pr., 46, pp. 254–256; Gammel, *Laws of Texas*, IX, 884. Special Ranger Bill McDonald at Clarendon was congratulated for his work protecting timber on the school lands from illegal cutting. Hogg to McDonald, July 22, 1889, Att. Gen. Let. Pr., 48, pp. 673–674. See also Reed, *op. cit.*, pp. 393–397.

[23] W. J. Jones to J. S. Hogg, July 5, 1889, J. S. Hogg Let. Rec., I, 343; Reed, *op. cit.*, pp. 174 ff.; Richard C. Overton, *Gulf to Rockies: The History of the Fort Worth and Denver-Colorado and Southern Railway 1861–1898, pp. 160–190;* W. R. McMath to J. S. Hogg, November 5, 1889, J. S. Hogg Let. Rec., II, 125–126. This letter is a complaint against high legal costs to protect land titles in Texas.

[24] J. S. Hogg to Governor L. S. Ross, September 10, 1889, Att. Gen. Let. Pr., 49, pp. 465–466; J. S. Hogg to the Honorable R. M. Hall, September 10, 1889, Att. Gen. Let. Pr., pp. 463–464; Hall to Hogg, October 19, 1889, J. S. Hogg Let. Rec., II, 91–93.

first appeared in the New York *Herald*. It was reported that Hubbard, while in the East on railroad business, had drawn a "harsh but correct" picture of Hogg trying to bind the H. & T. C. "forever by obnoxious laws which may be repealed at the very next session of the legislature."[25] Thus the Texas law on trusts and the land recovery suits received additional national publicity, and Hogg came to be known in the East as a vigorous law enforcement officer. However, one *Herald* reporter admitted that Hogg had not opposed the new charter of incorporation for the H. & T. C. but merely insisted that this and all such certifications must embrace a clause declaring the corporation "shall forever be subject to such rules and regulations as may be prescribed by the laws of Texas, and that it will not become a member of or be in any way controlled by a pool or trust."[26] Meanwhile, Hogg asked his friend Hyde Jennings, in Fort Worth, to keep him informed of developments, since the state might wish to intervene in the case of *H. & T. C.* v. *Knott et al* at Cleburne, as that case involved the right of the H. & T. C. to control the Waco and Northwestern.[27]

Until October 12 the feud over land patent policy and land recovery suits had remained largely within the executive branch of the government, but an alert reporter for the Dallas *News*, John E. Thornton, got Hall to release his retort to the Attorney General through the newspapers, even prior to the receipt of the letter by the Attorney General. This action was hardly good manners and was not an astute political move for Hall to make, now that he was ambitious to be governor. The *News* headlined the letter:

SOME LAW GOSPEL

LAND COMMISSIONER HALL DROPS A LOADED BOMB
OVER IN THE JUDICIAL DEPARTMENT

In his letter Hall saw fit to defend innocent purchasers and maintained that Texas must uphold her agents. He stated that Hogg's letter to him and to the governor had implied that he had issued patents to the H. & T. C. without legal sanction. Hall went back to a law of 1854 for authority to give land for sidings and turnouts and, in so doing, invited a blistering lecture on the law in this matter from the Attorney General.

[25] Galveston *News*, August 3, 1889.
[26] Quoted in Galveston *News*, August 3, 1889.
[27] J. S. Hogg to Hyde Jennings (Fort Worth), September 18 and October 3, 1889, J. S. Hogg Let. Pr., 4, pp. 65, 83. The city of Waco employed George Clark to defend its interest.

Hall then threatened to resume issuing patents unless a suit was filed "within thirty days."[28]

Attorney W. T. Levy, who had moved from Longview to Childress, observed the reaction in the northwest to the *News* article and warned Hogg that the people in the H. & T. C. country were really alarmed over land titles. Furthermore, the land speculators and railroad agents were stirring up the people to call upon him. Levy spoke frankly, reporting that Hogg was called a "demagogue" and was charged with attacking railroads to make himself governor. Furthermore, Hogg was charged with opposition to the settling of the Panhandle and with instituting the suits for the purpose of retarding immigration. Levy continued:

Yesterday—Genl. Mgr. Meeks of the Ft. W[orth] and D[enver] C[ity] R.R. passed up the road—telegraphing ahead for the citizens of the various towns to meet him at the depot—*if they had any greviences against the road*. No one here seemed to have any "grevience" . . . and only two men met him at the depot. The cat was out of the bag in a few minutes however —Meeks wanted a mass meeting of citizens to petition you to push the suit against the H.& T.C. R.R. to a speedy conclusion and to go to Austin for that purpose—the R.R.s giving every person wishing to go *free* transportation. Of course this mode of procedure took well—and now every town along the Ft.W. and D.C. R.R. is aroused—mass meetings will be held— committees appointed—and then you will be bored to death for a few days. Being in a situation to understand such things you probably see Meeks' innocent (?) object. The corporations hate you and seeing your increasing popularity they have commenced their war already. They are indeed in the saddle and from now on it might be well for you to look to your line of battle. . . .[29]

General Manager Meeks had a difficult assignment. The Fort Worth and Denver had recently been completed in the midst of falling beef prices, and months of prolonged drought lay ahead. Cotton was not yet planted in large enough amounts in this area to supplement the easily damaged wheat crops. The Forth Worth and Denver used the H. & T. C. tracks to ship to the Gulf and any losses of revenue from delayed land sales could affect adversely the favorable rate structure. Furthermore, these two lines were members of the Texas Traffic Association,

[28] Austin *Statesman*, October 12, 1889; Dallas *News*, October 8, 1889; W. D. Bell, Proprietor, Tyler *Weekly Courier*, to J. S. Hogg, October 7, 1889, J. S. Hogg Let. Rec., II, 63–64, asking for open letters, etc.

[29] W. T. Levy to J. S. Hogg, October 12, 1889, J. S. Hogg Let. Rec., II, 70– 72; the Austin *Statesman*, October 12, 1889, quoted R. G. Horr of Michigan as saying to Texas: "Raise more Hogg and less Gehenna."

which Hogg was striving to break up through court action. The probability that valuations of railway properties would soon be fixed by a commission for rate and tax purposes was in itself enough to create hostility to potential candidates who sponsored the commission amendment. While the Fort Worth and Denver was fighting for its life, Jay Gould watched its weakening condition and planned to bring it under the control of the Union Pacific. Professor Overton has traced the steps of this consolidation, which was completed between November, 1889, and February 20, 1890.[30]

The railways were determined to check the land suits. At 3 P.M. on October 18, about 225 "fine looking, sensible men" from the northwest, but all wrought up over the prospect that the Attorney General might be "stopping settlement in their country," filed into Hogg's office. Efforts had been made to round up all possible chairs and the reporter for the *Statesman* said that the men were received "with that hospitality for which Mr. Hogg is distinguished."[31] Hogg welcomed them and told them that his official records were open and that he was glad to answer their questions.

It had been arranged that James N. Browning, long a member of the legislature, representing a huge district containing about seventy western counties, would be spokesmen for the delegation. He presented resolutions which expressed uncertainty over titles and voiced resentment at any discouragement to settlement at a time when Oklahoma was being flooded with "Sooners" and "Boomers." Browning avowed that any harm to the Panhandle would also hurt Texas as a whole. He sought a promise from the Attorney General to protect innocent purchasers and suggested that this protection should take the form of a postponement of suits until the people could petition the legislature for redress. While this virtually repeated the language of the land commissioner's public letter, the spokesman wanted it understood that the northwesterners were not entering into any discussion over the difference of opinion between Hogg and Hall. Browning believed that if the principles involved in the suits were valid, then much damage would also be done to titles by quitclaim deeds in East Texas. By way of summary, he said that since Templeton had waited and Hogg had not acted for over two years, it would not

[30] Overton, *op. cit.*, pp. 242–257.

[31] Austin *Statesman*, October 19, 1889; Dallas *News*, October 19, 1889. Hogg's letter to Land Commissioner Hall, dated October 14, was published in the *News* on the 18th. Meanwhile an editorial in the Austin *Statesman*, October 15, tried to drive a wedge between Alexander W. Terrell, who had long exposed the ruthless power of some corporations, and Hogg.

hurt to delay until the next session of the legislature. The *Statesman* reported Browning as saying:

We are not here to intimidate you for you are not of the material to be intimidated. We believe you are just, and hope, when all the facts are laid before you, we will have that consideration from you that we demand.[32]

It was hard to answer men who had pioneered, had fought Indians and outlaws (Hogg knew that his brothers John and Tom had done just that), had checked wire-cutting, had survived drought, and now were facing uncertainties over titles. But Hogg was frank. He was glad they had come. He believed that they were honest men and meant well, although some of them were being misled about the law. Briefed in advance concerning the delegation, he said: "Some of you probably came hoping to do some good; others to see the Capitol; some out of curiosity, and some to get a free ride on the railroad."[33] But he added that he could not delay suits because of their requests. The law did not permit it, and he was awaiting from the land commissioner information upon which he intended to base the suits.

When Hogg mentioned the quitclaim deeds as evidence of sharp practice from the railroads, there were interruptions and questions about East Texas titles, indicating that the delegates, too, had been briefed. This did not upset Hogg, but he insisted that he was trying to protect their interests and the interests of those immigrants they wanted to settle in their country. One reporter said that Hogg drew pictures of the Panhandle "under a Damascus blade" and "resting on a slumbering volcano," which provoked "a broad grin on the part of his hearers." Hogg wanted the men to understand that he was not their foe, but that the great Panhandle was in the grip of the railroad and land corporations and he was trying to create every possible homestead out of the public domain. This part of his talk was "vociferously applauded."[34] It now came out that there had been a division in sentiment among the delegates from the start. Some were opposed to the land sale and rate policies of the H. & T. C. Railroad; they wanted regulation. This element was strengthened by the Attorney General's speech and his gracious reception of the delegation. Actually, he had made new friends among the Panhandle men.

---

[32] Dallas *News,* October 19, 1889.

[33] As reported in the Austin *Statesman,* October 19, 1889; Dallas *News,* October 19, 1889.

[34] *Ibid.;* N. W. Finley (Chairman, State Democratic Executive Committee) to

When some of the delegates stayed over to see Governor Ross, they found him opposed to a special session of the legislature and disposed to await the final decisions of the courts. He regretted the differences of opinion among his official family but, having a high regard for the sincerity of Hall and Hogg, he intended to see what he could do to adjust matters between them. One reporter quoted Ross as saying: "As to the Attorney General, though he may be what we call bull-headed, yet he recognizes that he is a servant of the people."[35] Hall received the depleted delegation with enthusiasm and spoke of his gratitude for their "assurances of personal regard." In contrast with Ross's assurances that innocent purchasers would not suffer, Hall declared:

I have always thought and do still, that the welfare of the people and the good of Texas were proper objects for the care and consideration of her state officers. To this end I have labored. . . . For this same thing, however, I have as you are aware, been rebuked with sarcasm, almost bitterness. . . . Upon the objects of your visit here, gentlemen, my ideas are better expressed in my letter to the Attorney General, to which you have alluded. . . . If all the departments of our state government—executive, judicial and legislative—cannot cooperate for your protection and safety there should be some change in its form and relations. None but the innocent can suffer now.[36]

Hogg was appreciative of the fact that the Fort Worth *Gazette* had printed his replies to Hall in full and ordered copies for distribution. Considerate of the problems of an editor, Hogg wrote Colonel W. L. Malone:

By your impartiality as a journalist you have been perhaps too partial to me. The very fact that you give both sides in the Hall-Hogg controversy implies the espousal of my cause—in the estimation of that class of journals who have never been able to see in me a single element of merit. I trust you will not go so far as to injure the 'Gazette' financially. I fear you may have done this already. It seems that the prosperity of our great daily journals depends on their consistent opposition to the enforcement of law, and to that class of officials who move at the call of duty rather than splutter under the impulse of sentiment. I desire to see you and your paper flourish and

J. S. Hogg, October 19, 1889, J. S. Hogg Let. Rec., II, 86–87. Finley declared he was prepared to support Hogg for governor.

[35] Austin *Statesman*, October 19, 1889. See also Gerald Langford, *Alias O. Henry: A Biography of William Sidney Porter* (New York, the Macmillan Company, 1957), pp., 50, 61, 68 ff.

[36] *Ibid.*; Richard M. Hall, *Report of the Commissioner of the General Land Office, . . . 1890* (Austin, State Printing Office, 1891), pp. 7–9.

for this reason beg to suggest that it may be best for you to "set the back-hand back." In time principle will win but it rarely ever does so without having its way marked by the wrecks of its most faithful advocates. Men can afford downfalls—institutions cannot. There is hope for the rise of the former—none for the latter.

My purpose is not to advise the course of your paper, but only to ad-monish you not to do anything out of personal friendship for me that may possibly weaken its usefulness, or impair its stability as a financial concern.

At anytime I can be of service to the "Gazette" its editor, or its force unto the "devil" himself, I shall feel happy to know it.

Your Friend

Personal Jim Hogg[37]

Hogg's warning to Malone was timely. Commenting upon the friendly attitude of the *Gazette* toward Hogg, the editor of the Austin *Statesman* gave Lieutenant Governor Wheeler, known as a "western" man, his cue to enter the governor's race: "Gov. Wheeler is for hog and hominy; the *Fort Worth Gazette* is for Hogg and hominy. Next !"[38]

At this point the corporate interests, having by now acquired a healthy respect for the Attorney General's endeavors at the "bar of justice," ap-parently decided some way must be found to relegate Hogg to a seat on the side lines. The announcement of a "reliable" politician's intention to run for governor might at least take the spotlight off the Attorney General. About this time sixty-five-year-old former Governor and Con-gressman James W. Throckmorton, who was known to be smarting from his failure to obtain the gubernatorial nomination in 1878 at the time the agrarians strengthened their hold on the Texas Democratic Party, decided to enter the race. How much the railway interests had to do with his decision directly is not known, but Throckmorton himself declared he would run as a friend of the business interests, although favoring a limited form of railroad regulation. Sawnie Robertson's speeches, after the former governor's announcement, were well calculated to etch on the minds of Texans a picture of Throckmorton as the close friend of railways—an impression that Throckmorton's later able biographer, Dean Claude Elliott, did not dispel.[39]

Still James Hogg would not accede to his friends' pleading. In the

[37] J. S. Hogg to Editor W. L. Malone, November 13, 1889, J. S. Hogg Let. Pr., 4, pp. 130–134; Hogg to Malone, October 26, 1889, J. S. Hogg Let. Pr., 4, pp. 112–114.

[38] Austin *Statesman*, December 22, 1889.

[39] Claude Elliott, *Leathercoat: The Life of James W. Throckmorton* (San Antonio, Standard Printing Company, 1938), pp. 286–288.

midst of the "sidings and switches" land cases and the controversy involving the propriety of Land Commissioner Hall's threat to continue patenting lands to the H. & T. C. Railroad when the Attorney General was testing in the courts the railroad's claims to the land,[40] he confided to Horace Chilton that his work was so heavy and important that he could not spare time for callers and communications on the political outlook.

Of all others you know my feelings on the subject best. The encouragement I have received lately is simply astonishing; but withal I am sick of public life and feel like "kicking out." Keep down ill-tempered expressions at home until I see you.[41]

Neither at a September meeting with Duncan, Finley, and Chilton in Tyler nor at a conference with George Smith, Jot Gunter, and Sawnie Robertson at the time of the October Dallas Fair did Hogg consent to run. A week before Christmas, 1889, he wrote confidentially to Sawnie's brother.

Confidential   December 18th [18]89
H. G. Robertson, Esq.,
Dallas, Texas
Dear Brock—

I feel proud of and must thank you for your favor of the 14th, and especially that portion of it wherein you urge me to run for Governor. For many months I have been receiving letters of similar import from all parts of Texas. The implied endorsement of my official course, as Attorney General, contained in such solicitations on the part of all classes and especially of the legal fraternity, is certainly a high compliment which I deeply appreciate. At no time have I aspired to be Governor. I have, though, always yearned to do my duty in this office regardless of consequences. That I have done this my own conscience is the best judge, and the people now generally seem not to doubt it.

To be Governor is another thing. In the first place I have never and do not want that position. In the second place I cannot see how I could make the race for it or even accept it if nominated and elected without causing more or less failure in this Department, thereby violating my obligations to the public. The work here is important, and as every lawyer knows, cannot be performed decently in an indifferent way. Earnest, assiduous and undis-

[40] Austin *Daily Statesman*, October 19, 1889; Dallas *Morning News*, October 19, 1889; Richard M. Hall, *Report of the Commissioner of the General Land Office, State of Texas, for the Fiscal Year Ending August 31, 1890* (Austin, 1891), pp. 7–9.
[41] Hogg to Chilton, October 3, 1889, J. S. Hogg Let. Pr., 4, pp. 84–85.

turbed thought and study of legal questions must be given to it, or the State's interests would necessarily suffer. This cannot be done in a political campaign as every one ought to know. And thirdly, while my modesty has never been regarded as oppressive, I have a sensitive aversion for conspicuous places that magnify my threads of poverty. The honest truth is I am too poor to hold such an office.

I fully appreciate what you say as to the necessity of a leader who will not deceive the masses after his election on the great issues on which the weal or woe of our State will soon turn; but I have no idea that I can under any circumstances undertake the task. Any vigorous, faithful, able, fearless "Offspring of Peace" who shall declare himself for Governor in the next Campaign, and who will pledge himself to favor and if elected to carry unto successful operation a Railway Commission; a law prohibiting land corporations in the future and placing a short tenure for the existence of those now in the State; and an appropriation out of which to impeach federal judges when they violate their oaths of office and obligations to respect the laws of Texas, can get my support in no uncertain way. On these points badly stated I am "well set" and hope to join yourself and others in finding a man who will champion and carry them into successful execution. . . .

Your Friend,
J. S. Hogg[42]

The fact that by February 1, 1890, neither an outright anti-commission nor a plenary-commission man had announced did not keep the political ball from spinning. The antis seemed to hope that Throckmorton would win the Democratic nomination as the champion of a moderate or limited commission program. The editor of the Galveston *News* declared: "Attorney General Hogg, it may be said, could hardly, if he desired, change the plot of the play at this late date."[43] The antis, in an attempt to drive a wedge between the Attorney General and other state officials, stimulated an announcement that Hogg's election would end the careers of Treasurer Wortham, Comptroller McCall, and Land Commissioner Hall. State Senator R. S. Kimbrough, owner of the *Mesquiter* (Dallas County), general merchant, and cotton buyer, not content with Hogg's idea that Sawnie Robertson should run, wrote Hogg: "I have thought and think yet, that it is your duty to the people to make the race for governor."[44] The pressures on Hogg were increasing.

---

[42] J. S. Hogg Let. Pr., 4, pp. 199–205.
[43] Galveston *Daily News,* editorial, February 3, 1890.
[44] Kimbrough to Hogg, February 2, 1890, J. S. Hogg Let. Rec., III, 74; Richard M. Hall, *op. cit.,* pp. 7–9.

Around February 10, Hogg traveled to Dallas for a prolonged session with Sawnie Robertson, Jot Gunter, and others, and here the Alphonse-Gaston debate between Robertson and Hogg came to a head. Hogg argued that Robertson had an excellent reputation among the lawyers, partly because of his father, Judge John Robertson, but largely because of his own record on the State Supreme Court and his courageous challenge to—and besting of—Clark in the newspaper debate, which had also spread his name around the state. Their friend Web Finley of Tyler, as State Democratic Executive Committee chairman, would look after Sawnie's interests well. Winding up his argument, Hogg promised to make some speeches for Sawnie when work permitted, and then he stressed again his desire to return to private practice in Tyler to build up financial reserves needed for his family.

On the other side, Robertson argued that Hogg was the better known of the two and that his lawyer friends, many business and professional men, members of the Farmers Alliance and the Grange, and railroad workers were urging him to run. Furthermore, Hogg's record of law enforcement was now so well known over the country that his election would serve notice to all persons, corporate or otherwise, that Texas intended to enforce its laws; few men challenged his honesty or doubted his courageous character. Robertson insisted that, of the two of them, Hogg was much the more forceful stump speaker, and he reminded him of the loyal friends all over the state who were ready to form Hogg Clubs and to assist campaign manager Horace Chilton in raising funds.

Hogg listened, but still maintained that he could not leave his work to campaign until after the court sessions in April, when the railroad "sidings and switches" test case would come up—which might be too late to begin a campaign. When the others asserted that they would speak for him and carry on the organizational work until the latter part of April, the many months of persistence of these loyal friends was about to bear fruit. After one further talk with Horace Chilton and Web Finley at Tyler, Hogg agreed to make the race.[45]

It was clear to all the Tyler group that Jay Gould would be searching for ways to break Hogg's influence. In the major legal battles with Gould in recent months the Attorney General had a record of two wins and one loss. He was making progress in efforts to separate the East Line

---

[45] J. S. Hogg to Sawnie Robertson, February 17, 1890, J. S. Hogg Let. Pr., 5, pp. 1–2; Galveston *News*, February 12, 1890; Fort Worth *Gazette*, February 12, 1890. R. S. Kimbrough to J. S. Hogg, February 12, 1890, urged use of Dallas *Times Herald*.

Railroad from the Missouri, Kansas, and Texas and had won the initial battle on the stock and bond cases involving the Missouri, Kansas, and Texas and the International and Great Northern. Even the decision of the Supreme Court in December, 1889, denying his efforts to bring about forfeiture of charter for the International, because of failure to abide by it, and to restore to the state the right to tax the line prior to the expiration of the twenty-five-year exemption as provided in the charter, had results that were beneficial to Texas, among them the receivership that was necessary to straighten out the confusion.[46] While Tom Bonner and J. M. Eddy represented Tyler's and Gould's interests in the new receivership, Hogg had a hand in getting Tom Campbell, one of his former schoolmates at Rusk, appointed to the important office of Master of Chancery. The cases then came before Judge Felix McCord, a prospect entirely unpleasing to Gould. Before the Texans were done there would be few secrets about the I. & G. N.

Meanwhile, Hogg was pressing the land recovery suits and trying to obtain state control of the receivership of the East Line, at a time when the strategy of both Huntington and Gould was to obtain a federal receiver whenever possible and thus take control out of the hands of a Texas official. As the Attorney General began his preparations for the April court session, his political opponents were busy "shelling the woods" for delegates to the county conventions. His supporters were also busy. Influential Alf H. H. Tolar of Abilene, who was writing a series of articles on the land question for publication in the *Southern Mercury*, warned Hogg that farmers would find it difficult to go to San Antonio for the Democratic Convention and therefore urged diligence in order to *"block the game of the trixsters"* at the primaries throughout the state.[47] He also reported that, although the Panhandle newspapers were

---

[46] 75 Texas 357; J. S. Hogg, *Report of the Attorney General*, 1888–1890, p. 4; Reed, *Texas Railroads*, p. 326; R. E. Riegel, "The Missouri Pacific, 1879–1900," *Missouri Historical Review*, XVIII (1923–1924), 173–196; W. Q. Gresham, "The Wabash Railway Receivership," *American Law Review*, XXI (1887), 104–126. See Julius Grodinsky, *Jay Gould, His Business Career, 1867–1892* (Philadelphia, University of Pennsylvania Press, 1957), p. 553, n. 22, in which the author indicates the reluctance of Gould's lawyers to be forced to accept a state receivership, when they had frequently sought federal receiverships to foster Gould's interests. Grodinsky's study would have profited from a more thorough investigation of Charles T. Bonner's and H. M. Whitaker's business and social relations with the Attorney General. Cf. *Jay Gould*, pp. 543 ff., with related notes, and p. 282 of this study.

[47] Tolar to Hogg, n.d., 1890, J. S. Hogg Let. Rec., IV, 460. Three of Tolar's articles on "Our Public Lands" appeared in the *Southern Mercury*, (April 10, 17, and 24, 1890).

booming Lieutenant Governor Wheeler, the farmers of that section were in a majority and would support Hogg.

Hogg planned to advocate a school term of six months (the current average was less than four months) and more financial aid for the University and its branches. He discussed school affairs with State Superintendent O. H. Cooper, and before long Cooper's series of twelve articles on schools began appearing in the *Southern Mercury*.[48] These and the many other articles on railroad issues, public lands, and public regulation coming out in the Dallas *Morning News,* the Alliance *Southern Mercury,* and Granger Shaw's *Texas Farmer* were eagerly read and debated by city dwellers and farmers. The many years of work for adult education on the part of the Farmers' Alliance and the Grangers were bearing fruit: the people of Texas were very well informed about the great issues of the day.

Jay Gould was also well informed. He was a shrewd fighter, and the issue for him was clear: the Attorney General of Texas had challenged his way of doing business in the Southwest. Controlling a popular vote might not be as simple as controlling a legislature, but Gould calculated the stakes and decided to visit Texas to see what he could do about keeping Jim Hogg out of the governor's chair.

[48] *Southern Mercury* (Dallas), February 13–June 12, 1890. See also Ina Hollis, "Oscar H. Cooper," Master's thesis, (the University of Texas, 1925).

CHAPTER VIII

"Hogg and Commission"—the Election of 1890

LONG BEFORE ACTIVE CAMPAIGNING began it was clear that the main issue of the 1890 election would be the proposed constitutional amendment to make legal a state railroad commission. To the Gould-Huntington "go easy on the railroads" group, any one of the five other Democratic candidates who eventually entered the race for the gubernatorial nomination was more acceptable than James Hogg. But, despite the group's efforts to build up a strong opposition to Hogg and to the commission, only Lieutenant Governor Thomas Benton Wheeler campaigned until defeated in the State Democratic Convention. Although George Clark never became a candidate, his resourceful leadership of the anti-commission forces was an important factor at all stages of the campaign.

Wheeler was ten years senior to Hogg. He had served in the Confederate Army and had been mayor of Austin from 1872 to 1877. In 1873–1874, during the Coke-Davis controversy, he was importantly instrumental in preventing serious rioting. Prior to returning to Austin as lieutenant governor in 1887, he had been district judge in the Breckenridge region for six years. He was a striking figure, tall and slender, with the goatee and handle-bar mustache that constituted the fashionable symbol of a Southern colonel. Hoping for popular support, he advocated a commission, but, since he also hoped to obtain railroad assistance in building up his properties at Aransas Pass, he made it clear that he opposed Hogg's stand for a plenary commission. Candidate James Throckmorton, U.S. congressman and former governor—popularly known as Old Leathercoat—also favored limited regulation of railroads. He was forced by ill health to withdraw from the race before the convention assembled, but if either he or Wheeler had won the Democratic nomination, the railroad magnates and land development interests would have been happier, or so they thought.

The young Texas reform Democrats of 1890 understood clearly that they faced strong opposition from the corporation-Confederate colonel combination which had recently been controlling Democratic politics in

189

Texas, as well as throughout the Solid South. Although Jim Hogg, Sawnie Robertson, and Horace Chilton were sons of Confederate officers and a part of the conservative tradition by nurture and by personal experience with Reconstruction tactics, they believed that the railroads under Gould and Huntington had gone too far in demanding (and often receiving) subservience from legislators and political leaders. They also believed that the old Texas tradition of independence of spirit had been endangered and should be given new strength and restored as the basis of political action. Long associated with the agrarian wing of the Democratic Party, they were responsive to the protests of the Grangers and the Alliance, but their own protests were shaped for action in the essentially conservative mold, avoiding the extremism of the Populists. When Hogg parted company with the Old Guard leadership of Governor Ross and George Clark, it was still as a conservative—but a conservative who had the rare trait of being able not only to heed and evaluate the public will but also to furnish stable direction to reform. As champion of the commission amendment, James Stephen Hogg had finally emerged clearly to the public view for what he was—a reform leader, a progressive conservative.

The quiet letter-writing campaign used by Hogg's friends from early February to mid-April, 1890, put opposition leaders and newspapers at an exasperating disadvantage. Without any speeches from Hogg himself to dissect, his opponents could not tear down his position. However, opposition newspapers did not hesitate to attack his record and his personality, by improvisation or otherwise. When the evangelist Sam Jones said from a pulpit in Tyler that "a four-legged hog never uses profane language," Dallas *News* editorials, for example, surmised that the reference was to the prohibition campaign of 1887, during which Hogg had been accused of using profane language, and pressed the implication that he was therefore not dignified enough to be considered for governor.

Until mid-April no outright anti-commission candidate had declared, but when it became apparent that Throckmorton's health would probably not sustain him in what promised to be a bitter and prolonged campaign, H. D. McDonald, state senator from Lamar County, one of the most vigorous and consistent opponents of railroad regulation during the legislative debates of 1889, entered the race. Described by a political observer as young, ambitious, fine-looking, and good in debating, McDonald had a noteworthy record in the Senate and a reputation for sincerity and fair play. After the anti-commission candidate's opening

190

campaign speech, Hogg wrote former Lieutenant Governor Barnett Gibbs of Dallas:

I am proud of McDonald's speech. He is a fine fellow anyway but his blow at the "Warwicks" by favoring *Regulation by law* is terrible to them, and stamps him well as a fair man. The principle admitted, the method ought not to give excuse for trouble.[1]

To comprehend the total image of the ferment of commission sentiment and activity—both pro and anti—it must be remembered that many other groups besides the farmers had reason to be vitally concerned about railroad regulation. In John D. Hicks' definitive and excellent book, *The Populist Revolt*,[2] the elements of agrarian discontent and the demands of farmers for regulation were so forcefully detailed that subsequent writers and theorists on the period have sometimes underplayed the other elements involved. In Texas, for instance, merchants, shippers, and lumbermen, beleagured by what they deemed rate discrimination and long- and short-haul irregularity, were vociferous about the need for regulation. Nevertheless, it is true that Texas (like most of the states outside the Eastern Seaboard) was dominated by farmer-stockmen interests, as evidenced by the fact that since 1873 no man had been elected governor who failed to receive their support.

A proposed constitutional amendment that would permit counties to increase taxes 15 per cent for road-building was also a campaign issue, but distinctly secondary in interest to the commission. When the Dallas Board of Trade called for an April meeting of county judges and county commissioners on the road amendment, the Dallas County Alliance was alarmed, thinking this might be an attempt to sidetrack interest from the

[1] J. S. Hogg to Barnett Gibbs, April 16, 1890, J. S. Hogg Let. Pr., 5, p. 226. By editorial the Galveston *News*, April 15, 1890, praised McDonald's anti-commission position, saying that it was strengthened by the Minnesota rate cases. See also an anti-commission speech by Judge A. T. Watts of Dallas in the same issue.

[2] *The Populist Revolt* has several pages on the work of C. W. Macune and the Texas Alliance. Professor Hicks recognized the value of the *Southern Mercury*, Alliance paper published at Dallas, but he failed to note that this paper was aware of the important actions taken by Dallas merchants through their Board of Trade to force rates down. The *Southern Mercury* for August 22, 1889, reported the issuance of a Freight Committee Circular and a conference with railway officials which failed to satisfy Dallas merchants, retail and wholesale, and shippers. Sawnie Robertson and other Dallas lawyers were close to these interests. Dallas was a growing market for Gould's McAlister, Oklahoma, coal, and he saw fit to visit Dallas to offset the pro-commission sentiment. Basic reasons for commissions are clearly stated in Frederick Merk, *Economic History of Wisconsin During the Civil War Decade* (Publications of the State Historical Society of Wisconsin, Studies, Madison, 1916), pp. 334–343.

commission amendment or to sponsor some special bond scheme. Delegates from twenty-five counties responded to a call from the Alliance to meet on April 12. By the time the delegates assembled they were pleased to be able to commend the judges and commissioners for not having endorsed any bond scheme or taken any action calculated to create political strife and thus divert attention from the railroad commission issue. The Alliance meeting 1) resolved for uniform textbooks at low cost (but did not specify state printing); 2) opposed paternalism and condemned class legislation; 3) advocated the commission as the way to secure justice; 4) opposed "unjust tariff restrictions"; 5) demanded a more flexible financial system and specified abolition of the national banking system; 6) proposed that "pooling and dealing in futures" be made a felony; 7) favored free coinage of silver; 8) advocated direct election of senators.[3] The "Demands" were conservative when compared with Alliance actions in some other states,[4] and leaders among the young Democrats read them very carefully.

The Texas Alliance delegates had met with the express intent of keeping the commission the foremost campaign issue, and Attorney General Hogg was impressed by the firm but moderate views expressed. The mild tone, in contrast to the radical "Demands" of the Southern Alliance and Knights of Labor meeting in St. Louis, December, 1889, was due to the Democratic Party farmer element in the Alliance that wished to solve the problems of railway abuse short of experimenting with government ownership and was against a third party. In 1886 the Texas Alliance members, in their meeting at Cleburne, had envisioned the work that a vigorous attorney general could accomplish in their behalf; James Hogg had not disappointed them. Now they awaited Hogg's first official

---

[3] Ernest W. Winkler, *Platforms of Political Parties in Texas*, pp. 281–284.

[4] For the "Demands" of the Southern Alliance and the Knights of Labor in St. Louis see Resolution 9 on government ownership of railways, quoted in *Political Science Quarterly*, VI (January, 1891), 293–294; Albert D. Kirwin, *Revolt of the Rednecks: Mississippi Politics, 1876–1925* (Lexington, University of Kentucky Press, 1951), pp. 64 ff.; *ibid.*, pp. 86–92 (which shows that the racial and election issues confused Mississippi's agrarians); Francis Simkins, *Pitchfork Ben Tillman* (Baton Rouge, Louisiana State University Press, 1944), pp. 153 ff.; C. Vann Woodward, *Tom Watson* (New York, 1938), pp. 136–166. Alex M. Arnett, *The Populist Movement in Georgia*, Vol. CIV, No. L, in Columbia University *Studies in History, Economics, and Public Law* (New York, Columbia University Press, 1922), p. 116, describes one of the greatest Alliance victories: "In six out of ten Congressional districts, the 'Bourbons' lost their seats. . . . The Alliance controlled the state convention, chose the governor, wrote the platform, named three-fourths of the senators and four-fifths of the representatives."

campaign speech as a candidate for governor, having made clear what they wanted.

While Hogg was studying the Alliance Demands and working on his speech, Jay Gould, with his attractive daughter Helen and a retinue of several friends and railroad officials, arrived in Dallas on his private train. Hogg was not surprised. To newspaper reporters Gould announced that he was touring Texas "for his health," but he took time also to briefly intimate that the unsettled condition of political affairs in Texas would make "capital cautious."[5] As Gould interviewed and entertained and otherwise tried to bolster the drooping spirits of his business associates, the Missouri Pacific declared that it was prepared to meet all rate cuts and that all previous "gentlemen's agreements" were off.

Hogg's campaign-launching speech was scheduled for Rusk on April 19. On the morning of that day approximately 3,000 people were assembling in or still traveling toward Rusk. As the train bringing Hogg and many of his old friends (with whom he had enjoyed talking during the journey) pulled into the station, the Campbell Guards from Longview were shouting a welcome and the Jacksonville and Tyler brass bands in full regalia were playing at the top of their form. After greeting the welcomers, Hogg went to the home of his boyhood friend Ellie Dickinson, whose mother had given him an autographed Bible in the trying days of 1861. Here he rested and thought quietly about the message he was to deliver. Meanwhile the members of his audience ate their lunches near a spring in the shady grove where the meeting would be held, then hastened to find vantage points for listening.

At one o'clock the crowd had grown so large that those on its outer edges, including the men and boys who had climbed tall trees, had to strain to catch the remarks of introductory speakers. But Jim Hogg's strong, clear voice carried to the most distant as he began with a brief summary of his record and a declaration that all candidates should state their positions on the new issues well prior to the convention, since nomination on the Democratic ticket "was tantamount to election." Then he went straight to the heart of the main issue:

I am in favor of the State regulating and controlling the rates of railway traffic having origin and destination within her limits to the end that justice may be done the public. As an instrument for this purpose, if I am

[5] Dallas *Morning News*, April 15, 1890; Galveston *News*, April 20, 1890.

elected Governor and the constitutional amendment is adopted, I shall do my part in having an effective railway commission created and clothed with all the power necessary to make, establish, and maintain, under rules prescribed by law, reasonable rates of charges for the transportation of passengers and freight.[6]

Well aware of the powerful corporate and political influence which opposed him, Hogg restated his faith in the democratic processes: "Let facts be stated, truths told, the law explained, a decent campaign made, and a correct verdict will be rendered." By simple illustrations he pointed to what he considered to be the real issues and dangers in the light of what he foresaw as the "corporate era" of the twentieth century, the transition to which he purposed to ameliorate by more carefully worded charters and by agencies of government powerful enough to cope with corporate institutions:

Realizing the prerogatives, immunities, exemptions, growing wealth and independence they are beginning to enjoy by their licensed oppression and defiance of justice, a large class of men are fast casting their lot with them. Within a few years, unless something is done, most of the wealth and talent of our country will be on one side, while arrayed upon the other will be the great mass of people, composing the bone and sinew of this government. The picture is not overdrawn. We are fast drifting into that situation. When that day comes it will strain the patriotism of the remainder of the people who are left upon one side, and the ability, talents, and capital of those who are on the other, to keep down the mob, to restrain the commune, and to suppress the anarchist. The commune threatens us but it is the legitimate child and offspring of the cormorant.[7]

He made it plain that Gould by his stigmatizing of the Western Union and railroad strikers of 1886 as anarchists and communists had not created friends for his brand of "free enterprise," but rather had caused the rise of searching questions about certain captains of industry:

The issue so sharply drawn in the present campaign is, shall corporate power or the State control? The fight is on and the issue is unmistakably presented. Its disguise by either side will be reprehensible.[8]

He declared his belief that three trusted citizens serving as a railroad commission would serve with propriety and would respect the proper

[6] "The Rusk Speech," quoted in Robert C. Cotner (ed.), *Addresses of James S. Hogg*, p. 74. Personal interviews with Judges James and B. B. Perkins and Mrs. Bessie Dickinson Wrightman at Rusk, June, 1947.

[7] Cotner, *op. cit.*, pp. 81–82.   [8] *Ibid.*, p. 82.

interests of railroads as well as those of farmers, manufacturers, and men engaged in commercial activities of all types—in short, the public.

When I speak of the public I mean to include every person or corporation within the State, together with the railways themselves. Justice to the public means justice to all under the law; the prosperity of the public means the prosperity of every individual and institution composing it.[9]

Here was Hogg's reply to Jay Gould's remark that "the attitude of the Attorney General of the State is such as to cause some fright among capitalists."[10]

The audience listened intently as he detailed some of the freight rate inconsistencies and illogicalities that meant hardship to Texas shippers and buyers. In Georgia, which had a commission system, lumber was hauled one hundred miles for fourteen dollars a carload; in Texas on Gould's Texas and Pacific line the cost per one hundred miles was eighty dollars. A carload of cattle traveling forty miles between two Texas points might entail a forty-dollar hauling charge, although the total cost for shipping a carload via those forty miles and all the rest of the way to St. Louis, about one thousand miles, might be only seventy-two dollars. Texas ice factories paid eighty dollars for shipping a carload of ice two hundred miles within the state, while St. Louis competitors sent a carload one thousand miles for sixty dollars. A Texas wagon manufacturer was closing his factory down, because wagons coming from Illinois could reach a point in Texas forty miles from him for a charge that was less than his own for a short haul over those same forty miles. Hogg declared:

I can go on with these instances without limit, and only state facts sadly familiar to you all. Now the only question is, what shall be done about it? Justice answers that it is the State's duty, in obedience to Democratic principles, to check its corporate creatures and give the shippers equal rights with them in the race for life. After many years of trial by thirty of the States only one of them has abandoned the commission.[11]

Passing to other issues, he first took up education. In 1890 the public school program was limited to a term not exceeding, at best, four months. Hogg pledged to do all within his power to provide a six-months school term, then the goal of most states, and committed himself to "the principle and policy of the proper and just maintenance" of the

[9] *Ibid.*, pp. 85–86.
[10] Fort Worth *Gazette*, April 12, 1890; Galveston *News*, April 12, 1890.
[11] "The Rusk Speech" quoted in Cotner, *op. cit.*, p. 93.

State University and the Agricultural and Mechanical College.[12] In promising enforcement of the clauses of the Texas Constitution which held that perpetuities and monopolies were contrary to the genius of a free government and should never be allowed, he was hitting at the great corporate landholdings, many of them controlled by foreign syndicates. In Jeffersonian vein he spoke to whites and blacks alike:

The greater the number of homes the larger the number of patriots. Deprive our people of lands and they become tenants subject to the will of those who own their homes. In time they grow poor, diseased, degenerate, and servile.[13]

He made it clear that corporations would have time to dispose of their lands and that manufacturing and transport corporations could have lands necessary for their operation, but *land corporations* were to come to an end.

In concluding, he expressed his conviction that "fealty to the law" provided the only basis for prosperity:

Neither sentiment, personal taste nor political principles control my conviction in this respect. When laws are passed they should be enforced, for they are but the commands of the people to their officers. Idle and obnoxious ones should be repealed, but none of them can be disregarded except at the expense of official integrity. A people who would encourage and not condemn the crime of official delinquency have but to wait to glean oppression's harvest. . . . Texas wants capital but craves not a dollar that would defy her laws in one instance and invoke them in another. She welcomes immigrants but on condition that they obey her laws. On high principles of equality and justice to all under the law, before the law, let her proclaim to and assure civilization that life, liberty and property are guaranteed safety within every section of her dominion, and there can be no restraint or influence that will check the great influx of honest brawn, brains and capital. Let the world know that in Texas the

"Sovereign law, the State's collected will,
  O'er thrones and globe elate
  Sits empress—crowning good, repressing ill,"

and copious showers of prosperity will pour in on us from every land and every clime.[14]

Hogg had spoken for nearly three hours, but the attention of his audience had not wavered. The address was hailed generally by the newspapers as "a masterpiece," "well-received." Even the Gould-

---

[12] *Ibid.,* pp. 95–96.　　　　[13] *Ibid.,* p. 97.　　　　[14] *Ibid.,* p. 99.

196

favoring Dallas *News* declared that for "Hogg's line of argument" it was a "masterpiece" and evidenced skilled preparation. The printed version of the speech, as published by the press of Granger Shaw's *Texas Farmer,* ran to forty pages, thirty of them concerned with the railroads and the potential benefits of a commission. Hogg had now made it clear publicly that he believed in regulation as the way to check the corporate power that had debauched legislatures, influenced judicial decisions, and threatened to remold the whole system of state and federal relations. His further argument that the state railway commission, if properly constituted, might be able to complement the work of the Interstate Commerce Commission openly challenged George Clark's evaluation of the Interstate Commerce Act.

On April 28 George Clark publicly parted political company with Hogg. Choosing to ignore Hogg's proposal of a three-man commission operating under law, which would be created only after the passage of the amendment, Clark said:

I had hoped all along that my friend Hogg would conclude to advocate a government of law, for he has done more than any other man to demonstrate the power of the law over railroads when administered through the courts. But it seems that he has concluded to take an opposite view of his duty, and no one will accord him greater sincerity in his position than I do. I have always admired the man, and have watched his advancement with more than a friendly interest, because, among other things, his near kinsman and the man for whom he is named, fell by my side on one of the bloodiest fields of old Virginia. I part company with him on the railroad amendment with sincere regret and with no diminution of my personal regard for the man. . . . If the argument is weak it is the fault of the cause and not of the advocate.[15]

When Clark later declared that he was not a candidate for office, the distressed editor of the Galveston *News* called upon him to organize clubs to "keep alive the Democratic faith" by working to defeat Hogg "the tyrant" and the new "Lucifer" in the Texas railroad Eden.[16] (In late summer Barney Gibbs reported a brief encounter with the railroad lawyer in St. Louis, during which Clark had said that if Jim Hogg were elected and the commission adopted Clark expected to make one hundred thousand dollars in fees, fighting the commission in the courts.[17])

[15] Galveston *News,* April 30, 1890; *ibid.,* editorial, April 24, 1890.
[16] *Ibid.,* editorial, May 1, 1890.
[17] Barney Gibbs to "Dear Jim," August 2, 1890, J. S. Hogg Let. Rec., VII, 242–243.

Granger Shaw's *Texas Farmer* press was kept busy printing the Rusk speech in lots of one hundred and five hundred for distribution in areas where the local Throckmorton-McDonald papers had ignored the content of the speech. Newspaperman O. B. Colquitt, later governor, also turned out hundreds of copies on his Terrell *Star-Times* press.

On April 26 Hogg spoke at Houston, giving special attention to Jay Gould. He was quoted at length in the Alliance *Southern Mercury* and even in the Huntington-dominated Houston *Post:*

It is said than when he [Gould] appears at the great financial center on Wall Street millionaires tremble as innocent sparrows in an open field when a hungry hawk swoops down upon them. He kindly visited Abilene, El Paso, Laredo, San Antonio, Austin, Dallas. . . . Perhaps he winked at or smiled at Houston. In most of the cities and towns he planned great railway schemes, talked of building union depots, paving streets, constructing packing and refrigerating works and of generally investing his money. The railways he has laid out to build in Texas within the last few weeks would make many of our towns look like railroad centers—*on paper.*[18]

Hogg prophesied that one day a telegram would be sent reporting that "capital was timid" and the boom would be turned off. Quoting from an Associated Press dispatch that said a group of "honest" capitalists in the East had met to try to work out a plan for a "fair deal" on railroad bonds, he continued:

Honest capital, like an honest man, fears not the laws nor the tribunals of justice. But sneaking, dishonest capital is like villains everywhere, for it hates law except when made or executed to further its nefarious ends. Honest capital seeks honest security, and there is no honesty in watered stocks or inflated bonds. Capitalists are not usually fools, and when they see a state with less than eight thousand miles of railroad bearing $452,000,000 in bonds and stocks, they know rascality and not honesty has held sway in the work. . . .

How can honest capital compete with such rascally tricks? It will not submit to such wrongs. Enforce the laws, show no quarter to any man who will practice frauds on the people by inflated, fictitious securities.[19]

At the end of April, Hogg's office assistant, John Craddock, reported to campaign manager Horace Chilton:

To me the outlook, on the whole, appears more hopeful. . . . Beauregard Bryan writes . . . that since General Hogg's visit [to South Texas] there are

[18] Houston *Post*, April 27, 1890, quoted in Cotner, *op. cit.,* pp. 100–101.
[19] *Ibid.*

many of those who were non-committal supporting him, and he himself, who heretofore has been a Throckmorton man, is for the General straight out.[20]

Hogg was strengthened in Central Texas by the support of George Jester, cotton buyer and banker of Corsicana, who would take a Senate seat in the next legislature; the railroad forces meanwhile lost ground in the cattle country of western Central Texas when the Vest Committee of Congress announced on May 1, 1890, the existence of a beef trust dominated by packing and railroad interests. The timing could not have been more fortunate for Hogg—he was scheduled to speak in Alliance territory, at Brownwood, Coleman, and San Angelo, on May 1–3.

The potential winners among the Democratic candidates were working in remarkable harmony. There was a close and trusting friendship between Hogg and Grange leader and former Speaker of the House George C. Pendleton, of Bell County, candidate for lieutenant governor. Representative W. L. McGaughey, wealthy Granbury farmer and Alliance member and candidate for commissioner of the General Land Office, had known Jim Hogg since 1869; he offered to go with him into West Texas, where Wheeler was strongest, and requested permission to say a few words from the speaking platforms. "I will do you good," he wrote. He promised that the farmers would turn out for county conventions.[21] William B. Wortham, former merchant at Sulphur Springs who had Francis R. Lubbock's blessing to succeed him as state treasurer, often spoke from the platform with Hogg. Seldom had such harmony prevailed among fellow candidates, and seldom had a young aspirant (Hogg was thirty-nine) to the governor's chair possessed such a wealth of influential friends among the elder leaders and the winners-to-be. The young Democrats rallied at the call of Sawnie Robertson, Horace Chilton, and Jot Gunter; young City Attorney Allison Mayfield of Sherman, for instance, sent in a petition signed by many prominent citizens of Sherman, assuring Hogg of a large audience even in this Throckmorton region.

Jim Hogg's ability to draw out the friendship and trust of all manner of men was not only one of his greatest political assets but also a measure of the man. Professional men, politicians, farmers, laborers, both young and old, were represented among the thousands in his audiences who,

[20] John Craddock to H. Chilton, April 29, 1890. J. S. Hogg Let. Pr., 5, p. 380.
[21] W. L. McGaughey to J. S. Hogg, April 24, 1890, J. S. Hogg Let. Rec., IV, 224.

once hearing him speak, seldom thereafter doubted his sincerity. The city dailies, voicing the extreme opposition's stand, made much use of such value-loaded words as "rabble," "disgruntled," "ignorant," "radicals" in describing Hogg's following. Hundreds of letters received by Hogg attested to the accuracy of one of these labels: there were indeed many "disgruntled," among the bankers, editors, merchants, substantial farmers, teachers, and lawyers who believed that Texas had been endangered both by the corporate interests and by the lack of the firm law enforcement which Hogg had long demonstrated he believed in and was extraordinarily capable of carrying out. His interest in all the matters that would make a better Texas and protect and strengthen its citizens brought him the staunch support of such men, for example, as State Superintendent of Public Instruction Oscar H. Cooper and Leslie Waggener, chairman of the University faculty. Waggener, to be the University's first president in 1895, wrote in behalf of the faculty and regents:

So far as I know you are the first prominent Statesman of Texas, who, in a campaign speech, has had the boldness to speak an earnest word in behalf of the State University; and, if you are elected Governor, you will be the first one who had committed himself beforehand to the adequate and proper maintenance of this institution, since its organization.[22]

As might have been expected, every complexion of school scheme was presented to the candidates for endorsement. Throckmorton made a serious blunder in his school platform; speaking at Bellville on May 7, he advocated not only uniform textbooks but books published by a state-owned press. Soon after the speech, Percy Pennybacker, school superintendent at Tyler, Tom Bonner, and the president of D. C. Heath Publishing Company wrote a joint request to James Hogg that he not speak on the book subject until they had a chance to talk to him.[23] They need not have worried, because Hogg had no intention of putting Texas in the business of publishing textbooks. There was a certain irony in the fact that, whereas Hogg was often accused of playing to the "common people," Throckmorton, the reported favorite of the corporations, had been the one to espouse, in his effort to gain Alliance votes, what was essentially a socialistic scheme. The repercussions from his unfortunate

[22] Leslie Waggener to J. S. Hogg, April 17, 1890, J. S. Hogg Let. Rec., IV, 270. Superintendent Cooper had an excellent series of a dozen articles on the educational problems of Texas in the *Southern Mercury*, January–March, 1890.

[23] Percy V. Pennybacker to J. S. Hogg, March 24, 1890, J. S. Hogg Let. Rec., III, 307–308.

step may have speeded his decision to retire from the race because of failing health. In any case, soon after the Bellville speech, Throckmorton did abandon his candidacy.

A fatal blow was dealt the anti-commission ticket when McDonald withdrew from the race late in May, after he witnessed the landslide swing to Hogg in North Texas following Throckmorton's retirement. Representative Tom Brown of Grayson came out for Hogg, as did W. T. Gass, editor of the *Farmers' Review* at Bonham, Ben Haynes, chairman of the Fannin County Democratic Committee, Attorney Hiram M. Garwood of Bastrop, and Dr. Richard Swearingen of Austin, former State Health Officer.

While the Clark Business Clubs were deciding what action to take next, Land Commissioner Richard M. Hall entered the race, advocating, like Wheeler, a limited commission. Hall expected strong Panhandle support, as promised by state Senator Avery Matlock, who spoke for Republican Abner Taylor of the XIT Ranch, but his candidacy only tended to split the small western vote Wheeler had counted on. Being more anti-Hogg than pro-railroad, Hall never had the support of the Clark forces, which were looking for a stronger, all-out anti-commission man. As early as May 20, the Waco *Day* had editorialized to Wheeler and Hall that they might as well "blow in their dogs," meaning that they were not acceptable to the Clark contingent.[24]

George Clark, on the verge of admitting that the popular demand for Hogg could not be diverted, decided to support one more candidate; if the candidate showed little promise, then efforts should be concentrated upon the defeat of the commission amendment rather than Hogg. Meetings were called in Waco and Dallas. Prominent among those who gathered at one or the other meeting were men who had not obtained what they wanted from the Attorney General's Office. Leon Blum, of Galveston, large-scale land operator, railroad stockholder, and wholesaler, had several axes to grind against Hogg. (On one occasion, just before the Attorney General was to make a land case ruling, Blum had sent him a gold fountain pen, which may have been an innocent appreciation for Hogg's earlier referral of land buyers to Blum. In any case, the ruling was not favorable to Blum's contention.) F. M. Maddox of Austin, vice-president of the Day Land and Cattle Company, had been taken to court by the Attorney General. Representing the Sheriff's Association, which was not yet reconciled to Hogg's blunt

[24] Waco *Day*, May 20, 1890.

treatment, was Sheriff J. N. DeWare of Marion County. Tax Collector Charles Gillespie of Dallas also attended. Hall went to the Dallas meeting but apparently was never taken into the inner circle.[25] South Texas was pleased to furnish Clark's final candidate, one-legged, able, fifty-five-year-old Judge Gustave Cook of Houston. The draft of Judge Cook, a Confederate colonel and an anti-prohibitionist, was Clark's final effort to line up the old soldier and anti-prohibition vote.

The young Democratic leaders, who were working for a better Texas and a new South, had no use for "bloody shirt" waving; many of the older veterans, among them Frank Lubbock and A. W. Terrell, also resented Clark's action. The following query to Hogg is evidence of the effort made to take the old soldier vote away from him:

Did you or did you not use the language in your speech at Ennis Tex., "That you had no tears to shed over the graves of our ex-confederate dead." We get it from the Dallas *News* that you used said language on that occasion. Our County Convention comes in about two weeks—we would like to know as to the truthfuless of the above as soon as possible so that our County papers can give it publicity before the convention meets.[26]

Hogg denied using the words attributed to him. Anyone knowing his regard for his father and for others of the "Cherokee Boys" who died at Corinth in that cruel May of 1862, could have told the opposition that the story would not wash. True, Hogg's speeches had never dwelt upon battlefield exploits; this new generation coming to power in Texas had their attention on the road to reunion, not on the licking of old wounds.

A story from the Dallas session for Cook drifted back to Austin. State Health Officer Dr. Robert Rutherford, who was anti-Hogg and knew that he would not be retained should Hogg be elected, was reported to have burst out over the selection of Cook: "You fellows have now played hell. You have elected the anarchist [Hogg] by naming a man who can't carry a one of the precincts in Harris County."[27] However, Hogg knew that both as a veteran and as a man of proved capability Judge Cook might be hard to beat; he had substantial financial backing, was a good lawyer, and had served fourteen years as a district court judge. Hogg had worked side by side with Cook in the anti-prohibition

[25] John Craddock to Beauregard Bryan, June 6, 1890, Let. Pr., 6, p. 459.
[26] Attorney D. H. Cabeen (Cooper, Texas) to J. S. Hogg, July 7, 1890, J. S. Hogg Let. Rec., VII, 41.
[27] John Craddock to Tom M. Campbell, June 5, 1890, Let. Pr., 6, p. 460.

campaign of 1887 and had respect for him. Consistent with Hogg's instructions not to debate personalities, John Craddock, who ably handled most of the campaign mail, wrote party worker Sam Ashe of Houston:

> I regret very much to see the announcement of Judge Gustave Cook of your city for Governor. He is a gentleman for whose ability I have a very high regard. . . . We are glad to note the work you and other friends are doing in Harris, and believe you have adopted the proper policy in calling the county convention early.[28]

To assist the Hogg campaign workers in Houston and in the southern counties generally, copies of speeches by former Lieutenant Governor Gibbs, Senator Cone Johnson, Senator Kimbrough, Judge Terrell, and others were rushed to Captain Joseph C. Hutcheson, former U. S. Congressman, for distribution. The Houston *Zeitung* was useful in reaching the German vote, and a working-man's attorney, H. B. Ring, talked with labor groups. William Malone, editor of the Fort Worth *Gazette*, blasted away at the action of "the coterie of railroad lawyers" who had brought Judge Cook into the race, declaring that although they could not beat Hogg they would attempt to deadlock the convention.[29] Meanwhile, the Alliance's *Southern Mercury*, now edited by Hogg's friend Sam Dixon, week after week published sections of the Trammel report of the work of the Georgia Railroad Commission as an assist to "Hogg and Commission." Sam Dixon was a graduate of Baylor University and had published an excellent history of Texas literature. Editor Dixon rendered Hogg's cause great assistance, and the way his friends accomplished his appointment was one of the major strategy victories of the campaign. The more important Granger and Alliance papers championed "Hogg and Commission."

Cook's backers, who seemed to have plenty of money to spend, early in June distributed one hundred thousand copies of a booklet prepared by the Austin correspondent for the San Antonio *Express*, J. J. Lane, which dealt with the need for more railroads and more traffic, the costs of construction, and so on. It pictured Hogg as deterring railway expansion, and it reiterated Gould's warning against making investors "coy."[30]

[28] John Craddock to S. S. Ashe, June 2, 1890, Let. Pr., 6, pp. 473–474.
[29] Fort Worth *Gazette*, June 3, 1890.
[30] Craddock believed that John Thornton of the Galveston *News* was the real author, with Lane's name just to "daddy" the booklet. Craddock to Barney Gibbs, June 6, 1890, Let. Pr., 6, pp. 473–474.

Cook set a policy of "no instructions" for delegates in county conventions, hoping this would check a pledged vote for Hogg.

Cook, knowing that his late announcement as a candidate was a severe handicap, set out at once to try for that all-important factor—the farmer's vote. He opened his campaign in the rich blackland region with a speech at Kyle, in Hays County. He argued against any of the functions of the traditionally "separate" three branches of government being placed in the hands of a commission. He declared, without qualification, that Texas was building more railroads than Georgia or Mississippi, both of which had commissions, then seemed to contradict himself by saying that would-be West Texas settlers were being frightened away by restrictions on railroad building that would curtail transportation in the western part of the state.

Discussing the speech, the Galveston *News* emphasized that Cook was a candidate by "solicitation" and that he did not feel justified in "rehearsing the service" he had done the state. Cook was quoted as saying of Hogg:

I can only imagine how exuberant must be the joy one feels when he can recite . . . a series of victories over "the world, the flesh and the devil" and part and smack his lips over what appears to him to be an easier task than falling off a log, viz: running the state government of Texas. . . . For me the exercise of the mighty powers intrusted to my keeping by the people carries with it such a sense of responsibility to myself, my country and my God that I tremble at the contemplation.[31]

The self-portrait of a "trembling" candidate was hardly what the farmers sought in their search for sincere and heroic leadership. Nor had the audience, cut by rain to 300 from an expected 1,500, been happy over his conclusion that the people must beware of the "clamor of communistic and agrarian rapacity." The speech actually confirmed the view of many farmers that Hogg was their man: not only did Hogg trust them, but he was a Jacksonian to the extent that he did not believe government had become too complicated for an honest and able citizen to make it function in the interest of the people.

The Dallas *News* hammered on the Clark-Cook theme that the rail-

[31] Galveston *News*, June 8, 1890. J. S. Hogg to S. S. Ashe, June 9, 1890, Let. Pr., 6, pp. 394–395, gave the local Houston men virtually a free hand to adjust their campaign as they saw fit; since Hogg had his "suspicions" that "the men who procured him [Cook] to run have not done so out of love for him but from antipathy to myself, I shall leave my friends there to take such course as they please and I shall stand by them."

road commission and "every such measure points to the final conversion of government into an engine of communism."[32] In spite of the many times Hogg and Robertson had pointed out that the Texas constitution held the railroads to be public highways and carriers, and that therefore the issue was not the right of regulation, but rather which agency—the legislature, the office of the attorney general, or a commission—could do the job best, the opposition persisted in spreading the anarchist label. Adjutant General Wilburn H. King (who had mishandled a difficult racial situation in Fort Bend County and knew that Hogg would not keep him in office if elected governor[33]) joined other men in bolting the Hopkins County Convention at Sulphur Springs. A leader of the Hogg forces reported: "We as well as yourself are denounced as Knights of Labor—communists and the like. They do not do this to our faces, but to our backs. The commission fight comes next."[34]

Hogg was the first candidate for the governorship of Texas to face this brand of vilification based on terms that had more European connotation than American. The theme of nihilism had also been skillfully employed by Jay Gould and his ilk against the increasingly articulate leaders of the farm and labor organizations, and the rank-and-file Texas members of these organizations knew the absurdity of such labels; consequently Hogg suffered little from the charges. However, as Hogg later pointed out to the editor of the Dallas *News,* the purveyors of phrases had probably contributed much to the popular notion among Easterners that Texas was a wild, lawless, and dangerous land.[35] In general and despite labels, the people knew they had in Hogg a sympathetic and vigorous champion.

Hogg had surmised in his April speech at Houston that railroad building programs would be halted during the campaign. The day after

---

[32] Galveston *News,* editorial, June 8, 1890. Speaking of "a widespread communistic propaganda," the editor said: "By the almost criminal negligence or indifference of statesmen and politicians who should have stood up reasonably and effectually as beacons and bulwarks of a true conservatism, the propaganda was allowed to go on with its work. The result is that multitudes in Texas and throughout the country have been wrought up to sentimental exasperation against all forms of aggregated capital and all instances of great amassments of private wealth."

[33] Clarence R. Wharton, *History of Fort Bend County,* pp. 203 ff.; Houston *Post,* September 8, 1888.

[34] B. W. Foster to J. S. Hogg, July 27, 1890, J. S. Hogg Let. Rec., VII, 208; Theodore Kurzman (ed. San Antonio *News*), July 21, 1890, J. S. Hogg Let. Rec., VII, 165.

[35] J. S. Hogg to Col. F. Doremus (personal), August 6, 1890, Let. Pr., 7, pp. 451–452; Doremus to Hogg, April 28, 1890, J. S. Hogg Let. Rec., IV, 274–275.

Cook opened his campaign the M. K. & T. began laying off engineers between Henrietta and Seymour, Major Wathen's survey office was moved from Dallas to Denison, and construction to Waco was canceled. With the calling off of paper plans to build 300 miles of track costing $3 million (ten thousand dollars per mile), Hogg's prophecy was more than fulfilled.[36] The Dallas *News,* which carried Cook's Waco address, also published a letter from President Enos of the Katy Railroad to the Cameron Lumber Company of Waco, which stated that there would be no more construction in Texas until the commission question was settled. If the railroads wanted to use economic pressure as a weapon, Hogg also could exert pressure. The attorney general's office had recently received for examination a group of charters designed to permit changes in the lines from Hearne to Brenham and from Denison to Sherman; they were sent back for correction—as well as for addition of the now customary clause declaring that the corporation would agree to abide by the constitution and laws of Texas.[37]

In spite of the increasingly bitter infighting, the Hogg forces began to believe they might be able to capture the nomination on the first ballot. However, they also realized that if Wheeler won in the west and picked up scattered delegations over the state, if Hall won even a few votes in the middle regions near his home in Williamson County, and if Cook carried much of South Texas, there was a chance that Hogg would be blocked from obtaining the two-thirds vote required for nomination. The Hogg clubs therefore increased their efforts to offset the new "Business" clubs manipulated by Clark, which were also going into high gear. One Cook-supporting effort backfired helpfully for the Hogg forces— the reprinting of a letter written in 1886 by Cook condemning the Knights of Labor, which angered railroad workers and laborers in general. The Galveston *News* and the Dallas *News* stepped up their emphasis on the theme that Hogg followers were "Union-Laborites, Anarchists, and Communists," but Hogg wrote Tom Nash of Garland that the Dallas *News* could keep up "these charges as much as it likes. The more it makes them, the stronger and more active it will make our friends."[38]

More serious and more difficult to combat, because they were in the American idiom and close to home, were the charges of "Tillmanism."

[36] Galveston *News,* June 10, 1890.

[37] J. S. Hogg to Hyde Jennings, January 22, 1890, J. S. Hogg Let. Pr., 4, p. 265; J. S. Hogg, *Report of the Attorney General of the State of Texas, 1889–1890,* pp. 16–17.

[38] J. S. Hogg to T. F. Nash, June 12, 1890, J. S. Hogg Let. Pr., 7, p. 35.

It was probably inevitable that the fiery name and tactics of "
Ben Tillman, who was jousting wildly with the Bourbon
South Carolina, should be dragged into the Texas fight w
parison that would discredit Jim Hogg was needed.[39] The
coupling strategy succeeded to an extent sufficient to keep Hogg supporters, especially the older leaders and professional men, busy counteracting the rumors and insinuations thus initiated. Echoes of the effects
of the charge exist even today, being found, for instance, in such an
estimable book as Arthur M. Schlesinger's *The Rise of Modern America,*
which is used as a college text. After a discussion of Alliance influence
on the established parties, Schlesinger wrote:

> In various parts of the South, men "fresh from the soil," like Ben Till-
> man in South Carolina and Jim Hogg in Texas, sprang into prominence.
> Inflaming the rural masses against the well-to-do and the towns, they cap-
> tured the Democratic party in their states.[40]

Actually, despite a common concern with the welfare of the people in
the face of hostile economic forces, two men could scarcely have differed
from each other more than did Tillman and Hogg. Tillman—intense,
vitriolic, and given to coarse, vituperative speech—after sporadic efforts
to solve the farmers' problems through agricultural education, had
jumped onto politics as the rampart from which to wage the class war-
fare he deemed urgent; Hogg had become a reformer by thoughtfully
progressive steps that were always tempered by his essentially conservative background and his loyalty to law and order—seldom losing his
sense of humor. Tillman was intent on overturning South Carolina's
reigning "Bourbon dynasty" and putting control of the Democratic
party into the hands of the "hitherto inarticulate whites" of the "back
country"[41]; Hogg, departing from the traditions of the Texas Democratic Party only where they did not uphold his conception of the inter-
relation of government by law and the needs of the people, neither desired nor attempted to disrupt the Party but molded it to reflect the will
of the "vital center,"[42] and thus to gather strength to itself. Tillman was
a farmer and an Alliance member; Hogg, though reared on a prosper-

[39] Francis Simkins, *Ben Tillman* (Baton Rouge, Louisiana State University
Press, 1944), pp. 156, 203.
[40] Arthur M. Schlesinger, *The Rise of Modern America* (New York, Macmillan
Company, 1951), p. 148.
[41] Hicks, *The Populist Revolt,* pp. 143 ff.
[42] For this political concept see Arthur M. Schlesinger, Jr., *The Vital Center*
(Boston, Houghton Mifflin Company, 1949).

ous plantation that he had seen fade away during Reconstruction, was definitely not "fresh from the soil"; he had moved to town and dealt in city properties. His agrarian ideas, despite the fact that he understood the significance of the powerful Texas Farmers' Alliance, were closer to those of the Grangers. He did not condemn wealth in general or the wealthly, but only individuals who, like Jay Gould, for their own aggrandizement used tactics oppressive and unfair to any of the public, whether farmers or citymen, rich or poor.

Further, it is erroneous to maintain that the Alliance through Hogg, or Hogg through the Alliance, "captured the Democratic party" in Texas. The Democrats had studied Alliance "Demands" since 1886, but, as mentioned earlier, these had never reached the extremism of demands emanating from such organizations in other states. As for Jim Hogg, members of both the Alliance and the Grange had long seen in him the honesty, forcefulness, and intelligence that was needed to champion the farmer's cause, not through revolution but through a forthright application of law. Even the ultimate firebrands among Alliance membership had no reason to suppose that Hogg would depart from the Democratic Party but learned that he would try to make it a progressive party of reform. When he entered the race for governor, the Granger and Alliance papers supported him because he was the only candidate who championed a plenary commission and who asserted that he would use it in the public interest. The events leading up to the campaign of 1890 and of the campaign itself make it clear that if any "capturing" was done, it was the record of Jim Hogg that captivated the farmers and their editors.

With Hogg leading the Democrats, most of the farmers saw no reason to bolt or revolt. This was his great service to his party in 1890. His personality and record delayed the advent of a third party, kept an Alliance man from entering the governor's race on the Democratic ticket, and directed the Democrats toward a progressive reform program which gave it a defendable record in 1892. Some reactionary Democrats wanted to make membership in the Alliance a bar to participation in the Democratic Party, but Hogg warned against thus driving Alliance men into third-partyism. Those members of the Alliance who advocated a separate party were quarreling with Macune's leadership in 1890,[43] but they were obliged to move slowly because the majority, still staunch

[43] C. W. Macune, "The Farmers Alliance in Texas," typescript, Archives, the University of Texas Library; Martin, *The People's Party in Texas*, pp. 35–37.

Democrats, believed that Hogg was their best chance to obtain regulation of the railroads.

Toward the end of June the Clark forces made one final effort to ruin Jim Hogg before the people, making use of an old enmity that had started in 1887–1888 when Hogg locked horns with Abner Taylor over details in the construction of the new Capitol.[44] (See Chapter V for a detailed account of the Capitol troubles.)

The state had originally agreed to furnish convict labor for quarrying the native granite to be used and building the needed rail facilities between the quarries and Austin, but organized labor groups at once bitterly opposed this use of convict workers and declared a boycott against the job. Abner Taylor aroused labor antagonism further by importing granite-construction workers in 1885 from Scotland; when the Scots arrived in New York they were met by union labor representatives and a United States marshal, because the importation was held to be a violation of the Alien Contract Labor Law of 1865. A few of the Scots withdrew, but some sixty of them went on to Austin, where charges were finally filed against the Syndicate in the Federal District Court, with a resulting fine imposed on the Syndicate. Taylor chose to believe that Attorney General Hogg could have alleviated the Syndicate's difficulties in this respect but instead had "coddled" the Knights of Labor in a vote-getting manner. Further difficulties for the project arose when the native limestone was discovered to be unsuitable; a long argument, in the course of which Taylor besought release from the contract, followed. As a final fillip, when the building was at last opened officially to the public on May 16, 1888, the roof was found to be leaky—and the dedication officials and visitors were well dampened when a spring rain chose that day to visit Austin. Abner Taylor and Hogg again met head-on, with Hogg and the Texas Capitol Board insisting that repairs must be made before the contract would be considered fulfilled. Taylor was a great deal less than happy, being harried by drought, falling prices for beef, and the British investors, who began to see their investment going up in steam from the boiling cauldon of troubles; from then on he made the most of every possible opportunity to castigate Jim Hogg.

Taylor's henchman Avery Matlock was the instrument used in the June, 1890, effort to confound Hogg's campaign. Being determined that

[44] Lewis Nordyke, *Cattle Empire*, p. 173; Robert C. Cotner, "The Acceptance of the Capitol: A Reappraisal," *West Texas Historical Association Year Book*, XXV (October, 1949), 50–75.

Hogg must be stopped, Senator Matlock was only too glad to continue his own east-west feud with him, which had begun in 1882 during District Attorney Hogg's successful debut as a convention delegate in Galveston. After Throckmorton dropped out of the race in May, Matlock traveled with Wheeler for a time and helped to spread the story that Hogg was playing up to the Alliance groups and the Knights of Labor, knowing that this would please Taylor, who had charged that Hogg was doing just that in 1888 instead of helping him get out of putting a proper copper roof on the Capitol. Now Matlock began paying friendly visits to Richard Hall's campaign headquarters, in the course of which he spread a new story concerning the period of delay in acceptance of the Capitol. It was insinuated that Hogg had approached Taylor and his associates with a suggestion: if they would buy timber lands in Wood County belonging to Colonel Stinson (Hogg's father-in-law) for the sum of fifty thousand dollars, he would not press the technicalities of the Capitol contract. Matlock further claimed that Hogg let up on his pressure for repairs to the new building while he thought the Chicago men would make a deal, but, when he found that they would not be *"bribed,"* had renewed his attacks with a vengeance.[45]

The known facts about the incident are these: Colonel Stinson, who had been wanting for some time to plan for his retirement, and Hogg had been looking for a buyer for the valuable timber holdings. At the same time, agents of some of the Chicago group were in East Texas looking at timber lands, with an announced purpose of building a railroad to the Panhandle to carry timber to the XIT and to bring back cattle. The Taylor group had actually dangled an offer before Hogg and Stinson, possibly hoping thereby to get the Attorney General involved or to feel a "sense of obligation" resulting from a favor. Matlock's account quoted a Mr. Bell, representing Taylor, to the effect that the group did not want the land but "thinking this a way to end trouble practically agreed to buy the land for Bell's brother."[46] In any case, no sale resulted.

The Dallas *Times-Herald* carried this statement from Hogg:

The insinuation by Matlock that I ever acted dishonorably or dishonestly or ever attempted blackmail in my life is false. If he or others know any-

[45] Nordyke, *op. cit.,* pp. 173, 190; Fort Worth *Gazette,* June 23, 1890. J. S. Hogg to T. S. Reese (Hempstead), June 19, 1890, J. S. Hogg Let. Pr., 7, p. 128, shows that Hogg was trying to avoid discussing any "side shows" such as the "blackmailing scheme."

[46] Nordyke, *op. cit.,* p. 214; Galveston *News,* June 29, 1890.

thing that reflects upon my official or personal integrity they owe it to me and above all to the people of Texas to make it public at once, so that it can be fully investigated, and, if true, that Texas may be spared the humiliation of instructing her delegates to vote for the nomination of a corrupt man for governor.[47]

The story had circulated rapidly in West Texas, where the Syndicate men were well known. Even before Hogg had made his public statement in the *Times-Herald*, a reaction had been registered. When the Hardeman County convention met at Quanah, it resolved:

Whereas, the "capitol syndicate" have attempted to blacken the name of James S. Hogg, an honest, patriotic and fearless officer of the State of Texas, and now the choice of the people for governor; and

Whereas, we . . . believe the statements made by the capitol syndicate to be malicious and false and intended to injure an officer. . . .

Therefore be it resolved, . . . the delegates . . . be instructed to cast the vote of Hardeman county, first, last and all the time, for James S. Hogg for governor . . . and to take with them their winter clothes and, if necessary, stay until November 7 to secure his nomination.[48]

There were other quick and angry reactions among Hogg supporters. Many men volunteered to make public addresses. J. B. Simpson of Dallas, who had been active in the Freight Rate Convention of 1889, championed Hogg's cause in a debate with Colonel W. F. Hughes at Hutchins; Lieutenant Governor Barney Gibbs of Dallas spoke for Hogg at Waxahachie; Jot Gunter went over to Fort Worth to speak before the Cattlemen's Convention on freight rates and "Hogg and Commission."

At the end of June, Hogg had 222 votes out of 258 delegates already chosen and on July 2 carried Judge Cook's own Harris County delegates. (It should be noted that Cook when speaking in Dallas on June 27 did not mention the Matlock charge.) By mid-July it was evident that most of the delegates between Midland and Amarillo would be for Hogg, and by August it was clear that he would carry the Convention.[49] The campaign, however, was taking its toll of him. On July 9 he asked

[47] Dallas *Times-Herald,* June 26, 1890; Galveston *News,* June 29, 1890.

[48] W. J. McDonald, Hogg's friend of Mineola days, was chairman. Fort Worth *Gazette,* June 23, 1890; also copy in Hogg Scrapbook No. 3, pp. 32–33. Hogg appreciated the assistance of William A. Stinchcomb and his San Antonio *Times* for combating the *Express*. Stinchcomb to Hogg, July 23, 1890, J. S. Hogg Let. Rec., VII, 190; Hogg to Stinchcomb, July 24, 1890, J. S. Hogg Let. Pr., 7, p. 414.

[49] J. C. Hutcheson to J. S. Hogg, July 1, 1890, J. S. Hogg Let. Rec., VII, 5–6; Sawnie Robertson to J. S. Hogg, July 9, 1890, *ibid.,* VII, 74; R. H. Harrison, Secre-

a friend to speak for him at Abilene, writing: "I am bilious, fatigued, fat, and to some extent collapsed. . . . In haste and hard at work."[50] Nevertheless, the fascination of politics and a rousing contest had laid firm hold on him, strengthening even more the original incentive of his conviction that reforms were needed if the people of Texas were to make the most of their heritage. A letter from his sister Martha Frances Davis in mid-July, apparently consequent to a report of Hogg's activities from her son Will, reflected the feelings of those closest to the candidate:

William says you are a goner into politics—that it is too fascinating for a man to pull out easily. He says you'll be in Congress next, because you are a born politician. *I* believe that the tide is in and swishing for captains whose crafts are filled with the rare cargo of sterling integrity. . . .[51]

There were a few crises still ahead. In late July the policy-making men among the Democrats were taking alarm at the increasing insistence of the Farmers' Alliance that some mention of their "subtreasury plan" ought to be included in the Democratic platform.

Proposed by the redoubtable C. W. Macune during the proceedings of the St. Louis meeting of the Southern Alliance in December, 1889, the subtreasury plan had been included in the "Demands," along with proposals for government ownership of railroads and telegraph facilities. Macune had long opposed using the Alliance for political ends, but he had finally concluded that the government must help the farmer and the farmer must see that government did so; the plan was his suggested panacea. After the meeting Macune, other editors of Alliance papers, and numerous touring lecturers set about popularizing the scheme, which was an astounding one for the time.

It called for abolishing the system of using selected banks as United States depositories and for establishing a subtreasury in every county of each of the states that offered for sale during any year farm products valued at a half million dollars. Each subtreasury would have in connection with it warehouses or elevators where farmers could store their crops; certificates of deposit would entitle a farmer to an advance through the subtreasury up to "eighty per cent of the local current value of the products deposited."[52] Instead of the 10 to 12 per cent interest

---

tary Hogg Democratic Club, to George W. McKnight, Secretary Hogg and Commission Club, Cameron, June 20, 1890, Let. Pr., 7, p. 153. On Saturday, July 5, Hogg spoke at San Antonio.

[50] J. S. Hogg to G. W. Smith, of Colorado, Let. Pr., 7, p. 314, July 9, 1890.

[51] Fam. Let.

[52] Macune, "The Farmers Alliance in Texas," pp. 47 ff.; Robert L. Hunt, *Farmer*

being demanded on farm loans by bankers and insurance companies, the government rate of interest on the advance would be 1 per cent, with a slight charge being made for handling and storage. Farm products could be stored for a year, during which time the farmer could sell his certificates whenever the current price for the product suited him, receiving from the buyer the difference between the amount advanced by the government and the selling price agreed on. Prices could be presumed to be better under this system than when every farmer who did not have storage space or could not afford to risk high interest rates on a subsistence loan was forced to sell just after cotton-picking or harvest time. The buyer of the certificates could claim the product at the warehouse by paying the sum advanced plus interest.

News of the plan spread rapidly and far. Alliance members of Congress, immediately after the St. Louis meeting, began proposing bills to implement the plan, and all congressmen in Washington from farm states were soon deluged by ardent petitions and memorials. It took a little time for natural opponents of the plan to realize what was going on, but before long debates could be heard and read on every hand, and the weapon of ridicule was turned on both the Alliance and the plan. Today, price support by government loan is an accepted part of the American economy; in 1890 the subtreasury plan was "radical"—enchantingly so to its supporters, outrageously so to its opponents.

Texas Democrats traditionally shied away from any plan of government ownership or support. During the early part of the 1890 campaign, most Alliance members had not been vociferous about the subtreasury plan, to the relief of the young Democrats in the Hogg camp, who most definitely did not want to contend with this issue. Hogg himself, who had been an advocate of free and unlimited coinage of silver since the 1878 Bland-Allison silver law, opposed the national banking system as it was operated in 1890. It is probable that the subtreasury plan interested him, therefore, but his legal mind noted its pitfalls. In any case, he was willing to listen to his lawyer and banker friends, who heartily disapproved the plan.

At the end of July, Robertson, Gunter, A. M. Carter, and Dick Wynne met in Austin for a pre-Convention conference with Hogg. Agreeing with former Democratic State Chairman Joseph C. Hutcheson that the resolutions had better be worked up ahead of the rough-

---

Movements in the Southwest, 1873–1925 (College Station, A&M Press, c. 1935), pp. 36–40; cf. Daniel M. Robinson, *Bob Taylor and the Agrarian Revolt in Tennessee* (Chapel Hill, University of North Carolina Press, 1935), pp. 146–147.

and-tumble scramble of the Convention, they purposed to head off the subtreasury and government ownership proposals.[53] Their own reform program must not get out of hand. Since they had already agreed to a platform plank opposing the abuse of federal power by federal receivers, consistency at least indicated that they should not sponsor new and very radical programs which would further concentrate power in Washington. However, they were Jacksonian to the extent of supporting a request for federal aid for Galveston Harbor, holding that it had long been a bipartisan and constitutional practice for the United States to spend money on harbors and internal improvements, but that they were prepared to voice opposition to the federal elections bill and to the Blair bill providing federal aid to education. They also looked on the proposed railroad commission as an agency well qualified to keep an eye on the Interstate Commerce Commission, as well as to supplement it in areas to which its authority did not extend.

When the State Democratic Convention assembled at San Antonio on August 12, Hogg's friends had the proceedings under control. The critical San Antonio *Express* commented upon "the absence of those distinguished and patriotic leaders whose counsels had so often prevailed with the Democracy. . . . New men were there; new plans were proposed."[54] Only Lieutenant Governor Wheeler was fighting Hogg to the finish—Governor Throckmorton, Senator McDonald, Land Commissioner Hall, and Judge Cook had all dropped out of the race.

The platform did not mention the subtreasury plan but did offer half a loaf to the Alliance by opposing the national banking system. It also, however, centered a direct blow on that section of the St. Louis "Demands" of the Southern Alliance and the Knights of Labor that sought to experiment with nationalization or socialism; to these would-be experimenters, the Democrats replied in the language of the Texas Alliance meeting at Dallas:

We oppose paternalism in all its forms, and acting upon this principle

[53] A. M. Carter to J. S. Hogg, July 30, 1890, J. S. Hogg Let. Rec., VII, 230; Norman G. Kittrell to J. S. Hogg, July 21, 1890, J. S. Hogg Let. Rec., VII, 161–164; Kittrell, "James S. Hogg," *Texas Leaders I Have Known* (Houston, Dealy-Adey-Elgin Company, 1921), pp. 100–106. The Austin *Statesman*, July 23, 1890, warned that the Democratic Party in Texas "would be more homogeneous, would be better officered and more effectively governed were not its majority so ponderous." Editor Sam Dixon in the *Southern Mercury*, November 6, 1890, suggested that the Alliance not make the subtreasury a political issue but give time for the Democrats to reconsider their anti-subtreasury stand.

[54] San Antonio *Express*, August 13, 1890; Winkler, *Platforms*, pp. 286–290.

we oppose the ownership by the government of the railways and telegraph lines of the State, as destructible to the rights and liberties of the people and tending to establishment of despotic government.[55]

Here was Hogg's reply to the charge made by the "double-ended-whizzer"—the Dallas *News* and the Galveston *News*—that Hogg's election would start the state on the road to communism or anarchy.

Plank 6 of the platform called for support of the commission amendment, and the next three planks emphasized other issues on which Hogg had based his campaign. Plank 7 declared that the constitutional provision on perpetuities and monopolies should be enforced and necessary enabling legislation passed; Plank 8 advocated a six-months' school term and proper endowment of the University, its branches, and other public educational institutions; Plank 9 called for state support for a Confederate home. Plank 10 endorsed a bill—which had been passed by the last legislature but which Governor Ross had refused to sign— favoring separate coaches for white and black passengers on the railways. Hogg accepted this reluctantly, deeply regretful that such a measure had become necessary in Texas, but admitted that extremists, both white and black, had brought matters to the place where legislation of some sort was required.

When the time came for nominations for governor the names of Hogg and Wheeler were presented. Horace Chilton, who had managed Hogg's campaign devotedly, arose to proclaim how the people had sustained Hogg in his great fight in behalf of law enforcement:

They have pierced motives with that unerring judgment which belongs to great masses of men. They have reached conclusions with the force of an inspiration. They have seized him—not he, them. They have laid their hands upon him in affection and confidence. They have sworn him to their cause. Thanks to their efforts the false badges of "business danger," terrorized capital," and "railroad confiscation" have been thrown to the ground as fast as his defamers have picked them from the mud and sought to fasten them upon the banner which he holds. . . . [After the election] his will be the arduous task to clear away obstacles and make the great reform. . . .

From this day forth let all Democrats turn their backs upon that sham picture which paints him as a dark destroyer and uplifted sword, cutting the threads of our industrial progress. Let us look at him as he is—as the man who sees in that star, which represents our glorious state, not only the

[55] Winkler, *op. cit.*, pp. 283, 288; cf. *National Economist* (Washington, D.C.), December 21, 1889.

symbol of territorial greatness and material wealth, but of sovereignty and public justice—as the man who would make every one of the five points of that star as sharp as spikes and as terrible as dynamite to those who would trample upon it, but arms of welcome and support to those who cross our borders and ask no privilege but the protection of our equal laws.

Enough. I present him to you, a native Texan, a fearless officer, a true democrat, strong in body and in mind, him I nominate for governor, James S. Hogg.[56]

William S. Fly, of Gonzales, seconded, saying: "It is time for the young Democracy to assert its power and nominate a native-born Texan for governor."

When the count was taken Senator Matlock had departed for the Panhandle and thus even the lone vote of Dallam County went to Hogg. Wheeler had 18 3/4 votes, Hogg 836 1/3; the vote was then made unanimous. In a brief acceptance speech Hogg thanked his friends and commended the straightforward platform: "The policy to which it commits the party cannot fail, when fully accomplished, to make Texas the home of prosperity, where every legitimate calling, trade, avocation and institution will move in harmony."[57]

The Austin *Statesman,* the official Democratic organ, had opposed Hogg but now announced:

The *Statesman* is of and for that party and gracefully falls into line. . . . Mr. Hogg certainly has the courage of his convictions, and he may be expected to stand squarely upon the platform, to the making of which he by his campaign so liberally contributed.[58]

The Houston *Post,* as a Democratic paper, fell in step with Hogg, although still opposed to the commission amendment. The San Antonio *Express* chose to continue the battle by running an annoying caricature of Hogg.[59]

Hogg had hoped that the Galveston *News* and the Dallas *News* might see fit to make some concession or correction, not so much because of the

---

[56] Galveston *News,* August 13, 1890.
[57] Cotner (ed.), *Addresses of James S. Hogg,* pp. 105–106.
[58] Austin *Statesman,* August 14, 1890.
[59] W. A. Stinchcomb, manager for the San Antonio *Times,* to J. S. Hogg, August 14, 1890 (confidential), J. S. Hogg Let. Rec., VII, 279: "I would like to call your attention to the caricature in the Express of this morning. Don't you think it a shame that a Texas paper should furnish the Northern Republican journals with such disgraceful material? Not only politically do these things injure Texas, but they do more to interfere with immigration than anything else. I call upon the Convention to rebuke the Express, and hope it will do so."

abuse toward him as because their editorials had given Texas so much bad publicity. Just before the Convention he had sent the following letter:

Aug. 6, 1890
Personal
Col. Doremus,
Ed. "News," Dallas, Texas.
Dear Sir—
On careful reflection and mature deliberation I have concluded to ask that you release me from the promise to submit to an interview by the "News" after the State Convention. When you requested and I consented to it the moving cause was the statement by yourself that the impression had gone abroad that my sentiments and course, if I should be elected Governor, would be unfriendly to non-resident capitalists and their honest transactions in this State. The purpose of the interview was to remove that impression. At the time you spoke of it I was somewhat at a loss to know why I should be so misunderstood. Since then leisure has permitted me to more carefully look over your paper in which I am constrained to believe I have discovered the cause. Its leading editorials often insinuate or charge that the doctrines that I advocate are "communistic" and propose confiscation. I regret that any paper having the good of Texas at heart, would sound such false alarms, and must abide its pleasure in correcting them.
Yours Truly,
J. S. Hogg[60]

Interestingly enough, on the eve of the election in November, both papers announced that the future of Texas was bright and the state was a safe place to make investments regardless of which party won.[61]

The Republican Convention, meeting in September, selected Webster Flanagan of Henderson, associated with the Waters-Pierce Oil Company of St. Louis, to carry the banner of national banks, opposition to "class legislation," and opposition to a railroad commission, although favoring stricter railroad regulation by legislation and judicial enforcement.[62] The anti-commission plant was practically identical with the position espoused by Democrat George Clark.

Hogg's supporters, though assured, as Democrats, of winning the

---

[60] Let. Pr., 7, pp. 451–452.
[61] Dallas *Morning News,* November 4, 1890.
[62] Winkler, *op. cit.,* p. 291, Plank 6. Flanagan declared the commission "paternalistic" and declared he would lead "a mob" against any who would try to divide the State of Texas. See Dallas *Morning News,* November 1, 1890, for his last speech at Dallas.

election, were still concerned with the necessity for a pro-commission legislature. After the Convention, Hogg made several speeches for the commission and road amendments, including a notable one at Sulphur Springs in which he urged the people to send legislators to Austin pledged to carry out the instructions of their constituents. The Alliance's *Southern Mercury* repeatedly stressed the need to "sow down" the legislature with commission men. In July a *Mercury* editorial asked, "Has the man who asks your vote to help elect him governor or to the legislature ever done anything heretofore to regulate and control railroads?" On October 30 the slogan was "Put none but Commission men on guard."[63]

Hogg's political relationship with Flanagan, whom he had known for many years, was a model of decorum, and the campaign was straightforwardly Democrat versus Republican. The Negroes were learning that the Democrats now had more local patronage to offer than the Republicans, although Negro Republican Boss N. Wright Cuney as Collector of the Port of Galveston continued to control federal patronage. Hogg could expect a relatively large vote from the colored people. His Negro lieutenant to get out the vote in East Texas was John Anderson, a trustee of the Negro Baptist Church at Tyler. While an attorney in Tyler, Hogg had successfully protected the properties of the congregation of this church during a suit initiated by the town. Anderson, a schoolteacher, was later rewarded by an appointment to the staff of the state normal school at Prairie View.

In 1890 the Republican Party in Texas was predominantly a colored man's party, with Cuney's forces being their strongest in the "German" counties of South Texas and in the "black belts" of East and South Texas. The party was actually on the eve of a black-white feud, as the white Republicans increasingly refused to accept Cuney's "dictation." National Republican Headquarters had chosen to work through Cuney rather than through Andrew Jackson Houston, son of Sam Houston; although this decision no doubt assured most of the Negro vote, it ruined the Republicans' chances (slim at best) of seriously threatening the hold of the Democrats on the Solid Southwest.

When the November 4 vote was counted the Republicans had carried only eleven counties, three of them in the Mexican border region where the party pronouncement that it knew no class restrictions had made friends among the Latin-Americans. Democratic strength in Texas was

---

[63] *Southern Mercury* (Dallas), July 17, 1890; *ibid.,* October 30, 1890.

further illustrated by the fact that Land Commissioner McGaughey was the only outright Alliance man elected (contrasting with South Carolina and Georgia where Alliance men captured governorships).

The official count reported was: [64]

Democrat—Hogg	262,452
Republican—Flanagan	77,742
Prohibition—Heath	2,463
Pro-commission amendment	181,954
Anti-commission amendment	73,106

Following election day Webster Flanagan addressed the incoming governor with customary East Texas familiarity as "My Dear Jeems," pledging his support as "a good citizen" to help make Texas in fact "the Empire State."[65]

The majority in favor of the amendment was impressive. However, there were many rank-and-file Democrats and Republicans who did not accept the stand of their respective parties on the commission. It remained to be seen whether the incoming legislature would accept the popular referendum.

[64] Rec. Sec. State; Winkler, *op. cit.*, p. 292.

[65] The Webster Flanagan letter is reprinted in Cotner (ed.), *Addresses and State Papers*, p. 107.

CHAPTER IX

The Lawmakers and the Commission

AT NOON of January 20, 1891, when the state officers and other dignitaries filed into the House chamber of the Capitol, the balcony had been overfilled for hours and people were even crowding the wide window sills. Despite a morning rain the plain people had come early to witness the inauguration of James Stephen Hogg, who symbolized their victory. Mrs. Hogg, Will, and Ima sat proudly among the guests of honor; Mike and Tom were considered too young to grace the occasion. Chief Justice of the Supreme Court John W. Stayton administered the oath of office and Hogg replied: "I do solemnly swear it." After retiring Governor Ross had introduced the new governor to the audience, Hogg turned to him and said, "Governor Ross, I honor and respect you. I hope I will be able to emulate your example."

His voice was firm as he began his inaugural address by saying that he was aware the people expected "much of this administration"; he promised that they would not be disappointed.

This government was instituted for the safety and happiness of the people, and the object of all laws should be to accomplish those ends. The splendid body of Senators and Representatives now in session, with those objects alone in view, will receive my hearty and earnest assistance in accomplishing the work that lies before them.[1]

Declaring that he wanted the people's representatives to know that he would take pride in being accessible, he pledged, "I join in a common work for the good of a proud and confiding constituency, whose pride centers in the glory, the honor, and the advancement of a great State."

During the long applause at the end of his speech and on through the

[1] Austin *Daily Statesman,* January 21, 1891; Texas *House Journal* (1891), p. 96. The Dallas *Morning News,* January 21, 1891, estimated 3,000 persons present. The legislature later voted to publish and distribute 9,000 copies of the inaugural address: 5,000 in English, 2,000 in German, 1,000 in Spanish, and 1,000 in Czech. This distribution is an interesting comment on the linguistic character of the Texas citizenry at that time.

congratulations and the festivities of the day and the evening's inaugural ball, the new governor may well at times have wondered how much travail lay between his midday promise to the people and its fulfillment. Fundamentally a realist, he was well aware that the "splendid body of Senators and Representatives now in session" might fall, as other Texas legislatures had done, under the spell of railroad and allied interests and fail to pass railroad commission legislation. Ten years had gone by since Judge James Q. Chenoweth, of Bonham, while chairman of the House Committee on Internal Improvements, had fought for a commission on railroads and telegraphs. His plan provided for an appointive, three-man commission to hold power for terms of two years, but after Jay Gould in 1881 began the first tour of inspection of his properties in Texas, stressing the "*one peril*—injudicious interferences by Congresses and State Legislatures with Business,"[2] that measure was defeated. Again in 1883, Chenoweth, Representative L. L. Foster (later appointed by Governor Ross as commissioner of insurance, statistics, and history and retained in that position by Hogg), and Senator A. W. Terrell of Austin had worked for a commission. This effort also failed; so it had been in each succeeding legislature.

The contest over the House speakership was indicative of the fact that Hogg might not have a large, well-organized majority for administration measures. Robert T. Milner, the progressive reform editor of the Henderson *Times,* barely won (53–50) over the West Texas candidate, James N. Browning, who had been leader of the Fort Worth and Denver City Railroad area delegation that went to Austin to protest Attorney General Hogg's preparation of suits to recover the "sidings and switches" lands from the railroads. Browning and Milner were symbols of the East-West rivalry which would become more influential in Texas politics. And although Hogg had the backing of a fresh state-wide mandate from the people in the vote for the commission amendment and in the fact that the election had retired many members of the Twenty-first Legislature—only 22 of the 106 House members having been returned[3] —the railroad lobbyists were not averse to capitalizing on or stirring up all the confusion they could, recognizing that this was a showdown fight. Of the newly elected House members, 36 had previous legislative experience; thus, 58 of the 106 members were experienced lawmakers and 48 were inexperienced. The first-termers would be subjected to the

[2] Charles S. Potts, *Railroad Transportation in Texas,* pp. 117–118; Galveston *News,* February 20, 1881.
[3] Texas *House Journal* (1891), p. 2.

same lobby blandishments that had worked so well on their predecessors. Furthermore, the Twenty-second's membership included several of the able "railroad lieutenants" and anti-Hogg leaders, among them Clark's ally George Gerald, of Waco; there were also others, among them Senator Cone Johnson of Tyler, who seemed blinded to the exigencies of the situation by their own overweening ambition.[4]

It is rare that the public shows much interest in a chief executive's message to the legislative body, more often than not read by a clerk, but before 11:00 A.M. of January 21, despite the late hours of the inauguration ball, people again crowded the galleries and hundreds more were admitted to the Senate and House floors through the courtesy of members. It was well known that the new governor would not deliver his message in person, but many desired to learn as early as possible of his reform program. Besides sight-seers and well-wishers, many of them from out of town and staying over after the inauguration ceremonies, the crowd included men who came to gauge the message and the legislature's reaction to it—distinguished attorneys who looked after the interests of corporate businesses, representatives of the Farmers' Alliance and the Knights of Labor, and a large number of the nonprofessional politicians who had worked to elect Hogg.

As always when James Hogg wrote or spoke, the vigor of clear intention—something more than the undaunted spirit of youth—pervaded his words. About 11:30 A.M. the clerks of the House and Senate began the reading of the message, which required over an hour. Governor Hogg began by paying tribute to "the valor, patriotism, and wisdom of our fathers" to whom "we are indebted . . . for the heritage of civil rights,"[5] and most of the listeners knew that he had not written hollow oratory but was expressing sincere devotion to the men, including his own father, who had set the early pattern of Texas tradition. He then called upon the legislators to return to the democratic principles of the "consent of the governed":[6]

With what degree of perfection and satisfaction this voluntary task will be

[4] T. N. Jones to Ima Hogg, 1935, Interv. Fol.; Martin M. Crane, "Recollections of the Establishment of the Texas Railroad Commission," *Southwestern Historical Quarterly*, L (April, 1947), 478–486.
[5] Governor James S. Hogg, "Message to the Twenty-second Legislature, January 21, 1891," Texas *House Journal* (1891), p. 103. The complete text of the Message may also be found in Cotner (ed.), *Addresses of James S. Hogg*, pp. 109–140.
[6] Texas *House Journal* (1891), p. 103.

performed depends much upon the harmony among the public servants in their work and the zeal and alacrity with which they yield obedience to the sovereign will.

At the threshold the question arises, what do the people want?[7]

He pointed out that the constitution placed the highest obligation upon the lawmakers and that it had been recently amended to provide for railroad regulation by a commission. He stressed that the platform of the dominant political party should be carried into effect; party pledges should never be slighted when no fundamental law would be violated by giving them effect. Therefore, he reminded the Democratic members that they and he were committed to the enactment of laws in the following order:

1. Creating and providing for the successful operation of a railway commission.

2. Prohibiting corporate monopolies and perpetuities as to land and titles thereto.

3. To provide for the support and maintenance of public free schools for six months of each year.

4. To provide for the proper endowment and maintenance for the University and its branches and other educational institutions.

5. Establishing and supporting a home for the disabled Confederate soldiers.

6. Requiring railways in the State to provide separate coaches for their white and black passengers.[8]

Turning to the details of the first-named enactment, Hogg "with great respect" begged to suggest that the commission to be created should be composed of three members, to be appointed by the governor, with the advice and consent of the Senate, and be entrusted with "all the power necessary to make, establish and maintain, for the government of railway companies, reasonable rates of charges and rules for the handling and transportation of passengers and freight . . . having origin and destination within this State." He called for (1) a definition of the common carriers involved, including express companies; (2) provision for adequate reports from the railways; (3) authority for the commission to inspect books and call witnesses in making investigations; (4) power to prohibit and punish rebating, discriminations, and extortion by carriers; (5) the establishment of penalties for failure to obey the

[7] *Ibid.*   [8] *Ibid.*, pp. 104–106.

commission's orders on rates adopted; (6) such other powers as would be needed to carry out "its laudable purpose—to give freedom to commerce, security to the railroads, and protection to the public."[9]

Each of the recommendations was taken up in detail, and Hogg emphasized the warning that the commission law must be worded with great care, to avoid frequent challenges in the courts. Furthermore, the law should protect citizens from contests with the carriers involving the validity of any rate or rule prescribed by the commissioners; such cases should be between the commission and the railway companies. However, shippers should be given classifications and rate schedules so that they would know their rights and what damages they might recover if it became necessary for them to go into court. Finally, so that the commissioners would be removed from the temptation to use their powers for political ends, he argued that they should not be engaged in "any commercial, agricultural, mining, or other avocation" while in office or hold railway stocks or bonds. They should be ineligible for other public office until two years after ceasing to be commissioners. They should be paid well, the salaries to be "commensurate with the services demanded and the responsibilities imposed." Seldom has a chief executive been more explicit in the specifications for effective legislation.

After taking up each of the five other legislative commitments, Hogg dealt with other phases of his reform program. He questioned the practice of working convicts on the railways or on private farms; imprisonment at hard labor was required by law, but this did not mean that favored groups should be permitted to lease convicts to work on jobs needed by men trying to earn a living for their families. If ample buildings were not provided to house convicts and if the policy of working the convicts elsewhere was to be adopted or continued, then the law or language of "judgments and sentences" should be changed. He favored all efforts toward rehabilitation, but he doubted whether reformation could be accomplished by corporate or private groups whose main interest was in the exploitation of the convict as low-price labor; he doubted especially whether the convicts' morale was helped when they were publicly paraded on the highways surrounded by armed guards.

The State can not, should not, expect to make a profit out of convict labor. To reform the offender by humane, legal punishment administered under rules of law without hope of pecuniary gain, so that he may be returned to

[9] *Ibid.*, pp. 111–112.

224

civilization and liberty a better man, comports more with her sovereign dignity and sublime sense of justice.[10]

The Governor wanted the prisons to become self-sustaining, if "reasonable" methods could bring about such results. He believed that the inmates should learn trades as well as farming, so that all might have a means of making a living when freedom came. He suggested that convicts produce the clothing, furniture, and implements needed to supply public institutions and that consideration possibly be given to the manufacture of articles similar to those produced and sold by "trusts" and "combines" in violation of Texas laws. He recommended expanding the penitentiary farms, to produce much of the food required for patients and prisoners in all state institutions. This would also have the virtue of permitting the men to be out of doors part of the time.

He advocated a change in the confusing charter law for both indigenous and outside corporations operating in the state. He was also anxious that the wild and reckless issues of municipal, county, and railway bonds be checked, and to that end recommended a system of registration and supervision, which, while not guaranteeing dividends or the end of failures, was calculated to protect the taxpayer from higher interest rates, which were bound to follow if cities and counties became indebted beyond their ability to pay. Despite its worthy intent, the plan also gave George Clark an opportunity to charge Hogg with being a "centralist," concentrating authority in Austin.

Suffrage was a touchy subject in 1891. During 1890 the Republicans in Congress had tried to pass a federal election law or "Force" bill, hoping thereby to regain the Negro vote in the South or, failing to enforce the voting rights of the Fifteenth Amendment, to succeed in cutting the Southern Democratic representation in Congress. Hogg bluntly declared that the ballot box in Texas had not long been viewed with the "suspicion of fraud around it," but his next statement was hardly the whole truth: "Of late years the influx of population from other sections may have brought among us some who do not appreciate the untrammeled, free exercise of the sacred franchise or the hallowed precincts of the voting place." Without doubt he referred to the carpetbaggery of Reconstruction and those out-of-state organizers who attempted to line up racial block votes, but he knew as well as any other politician in Texas that the Democrats had taken a lesson from the Republicans and

[10] *Ibid.*, p. 114.

were using parallel tactics, to their advantage, in some of the "Negro" and "Mexican" counties. Hogg told the legislature that, while complaints had been few, it was well "to guard the ballot by stronger laws for future use."[11] This, we can be sure, was his way of warning Congress to leave the election laws to the states. (Texas was one of the few Southern states without a poll tax, and Hogg hoped it would continue so. The tax was imposed, however, in 1902.)

Former Texas governors had soft-pedaled assertions concerning state-federal relations, partly because efforts were being made to collect from the United States something over a million dollars due Texas as expenses for putting down Mexican border and Indian raids.[12] Hogg and Sawnie Robertson believed the time was ripe for a clarification of state-federal jurisdictions. The aggressive, highhanded actions of United States marshals and federal receivers had stirred the ire of many men besides those of the states'-rights school. The Dallas County Democratic Convention in 1890, under Robertson's guidance, had protested the ease with which national corporate interests had been able to use federal receivers. The receivership cases involving certain railroads, including the East Line and Red River, the Houston and Texas Central, and the International and Great Northern, were still not settled. Hogg declared:

In her independent autonomy, Texas should be sovereign and free in the management of her own domestic affairs. Cordially and with pride she claims and feels an interest in the Federal Union as one of its important members. In all the powers delegated to it, she cheerfully joins, to the end that the general government may be honored and respected within its legitimate sphere. In the administration of her own affairs she expects and demands recognition and respect.[13]

Hogg charged that deputy marshals and special detectives, in association with informers and secret detectives, had spread fear and caused many Texans to feel that the national government had become "an institution of oppression instead of one for the performance of its functions under the Constitution." He said that favoritism and nepotism had been practiced, no doubt referring to a recent congressional investigation of federal Judge Andrew P. McCormick of Dallas, involving an appointment of his son.[14] Pointing out that nonresident receivers operated more

---

[11] *Ibid.*

[12] Edmund T. Miller, *A Financial History of Texas* (Bulletin of the University of Texas, No. 37, Austin, 1916), pp. 161–162.

[13] "Message, January 21, 1891," Texas *House Journal* (1891), p. 114.

[14] *Ibid.;* Dallas *Morning News,* September 10, 1891.

than one Texas railway under the orders of federal judges in other states, he asserted that decisions of Texas courts were often "held for naught," and that several railroads, without foreclosure proceedings, had been permitted to increase their incumbrances, to the detriment of the public and of lawful creditors. He strengthened his argument by quoting from Justice Miller of the United States Supreme Court:

If these receivers had been appointed to sell the roads, collect the means of the companies, and pay their debts, it might have been well enough. But this was hardly ever done. It is never done now. It is not the purpose for which a receiver is appointed. He generally takes the property out of the hands of its owner, operates the road in his own way, with an occasional suggestion from the court, which he recognizes as a sort of partner in the business; sometime, though very rarely, pays some money on the debts of the corporation, but quite as often adds to them, and injures prior creditors by creating a new and superior lien on the property pledged to them.[15]

Hogg recognized some notable "honorable exceptions" to the misconduct and declared that they were well known to the public and "fully appreciated." However, because abuses were so frequent, he asked the legislature to make an appropriation to aid Texas in assisting citizens in their cases involving marshals and receivers when the rights of a "sovereign state" were infringed.

Finally, the Governor turned to his favorite subject, law enforcement. He wanted the chapter of the Penal Code dealing with "Manslaughter" reworked so that the wording of the judge's charge to the jury would be simplified and therefore be less confusing and less likely to result in a retrial or mistrial or freedom for the guilty. There should no longer be any reason to hear the comment that thieves were more often and more harshly punished in Texas than murderers. After a technical discussion, which merits restudy even today (particularly since the legislature did not effect the whole clarification he sought) Hogg laid down four principles:

1. That the law of murder be changed so that when a person of sound mind and discretion unlawfully and with malice aforethought kills a human being in this State, he shall be guilty of, and on conviction punished for, the first and second degree of that offense, according to the facts developed in the trial.

2. Qualify the law of self-defense so that when a person takes the life of another and relies on the "appearance of danger" for protection, the jury,

[15] "Message, January 21, 1891," Texas *House Journal* (1891), p. 115.

227

not the defendant, must determine from all the evidence whether the "appearances" were sufficient to justify a prudent man in believing the "danger" in fact existed at the time the killing occurred.

3. Make every slayer who provokes the attack which results in the homicide, or who voluntarily engages in the combat, knowing that it would or might result in death or serious bodily injury to his adversary or himself, guilty of murder in the first or second degree, according to the facts of the case.

4. Repeal the chapter of the Penal Code relating to "manslaughter," and remove that word from every other section of the statute that contains it.[16]

He believed that the right of self-defense would not be interfered with by these principles, nor would any protection surrounding the citizen in his rights be weakened, but that the "mesh-work of technicalities," the "loop-holes," and other "complicated impediments" in the pathway of justice must be removed; otherwise, murderers would continue to "tread with shameless indifference over the lifeless forms of their innocent victims."[17]

Praising the message of outgoing Governor Ross, Hogg emphasized that the departmental reports were worthy of study. He then briefly called attention to the road amendment, which required implementation, to the need for reapportionment (the 1890 census having revealed that Texas was entitled to additional seats in Congress), to benefits that would ensue from a lower legal interest rate, to the justice of a revision of tax laws in the interest of equalizing burdens of government, and to the necessity of providing for the retirement of the public debt (from Reconstruction days) soon coming due. He expressed both his confidence in the "unselfish patriotism" of the lawmakers and the hope that the "arduous" tasks would be performed "in harmony for the good of Texas" so that, on returning home, each might be "entitled to and receive the plaudits of the people whose hearts ever pulse with deep affection for their faithful servants."[18]

The new governor had laid down a clear and uncomplicated pattern for needed basic reforms. He was optimistic, but he was also, as always, a realist; he must have been aware that it would take many more than two or four years to achieve even some of the progressive program. It is not outside of the bounds of possibility that, as he returned to the Mansion on the evening of January 21, he found a wry symbolism there.

The Governor's Mansion had been built in 1855 and, as designed by Abner Cook, was a noble house. The Hoggs had moved to the Mansion

---

[16] *Ibid.*, p. 117.   [17] *Ibid.*   [18] *Ibid.*

with high expectations of enjoying a spacious, hospitable home, and were in no way prepared for the interior they saw for the first time as tenants, and not as guests. The Rosses had of course removed their personal possessions, with their ameliorating effect, although the basic furniture went with the house. In short, the residence of the state's highest official was in dire disrepair, and, apparently, earlier efforts to have something effective done about it since Governor Roberts lived there had been vain. Governor Hogg felt that something better was due, not to him personally, but to any Texas governor as the state's chief executive. He also was very proud of Mrs. Hogg's fastidiousness and grace as a homemaker, and he encouraged her desire for improvements. Setting to work immediately with her usual skill in achieving an exquisite result at a minimum cost, Sallie Hogg soon had carpenters and painters at work, coping with the worst of the disrepair. She chose fresh new lace curtains for the impressive long windows, and the most badly worn carpets were also gradually replaced. For the parlors and the library, some simple and comfortable rattan furniture, much in fashion then, was purchased to take the place of the shabbiest old pieces. The one, and inadequate, bathroom was modernized. All of this was paid for personally by James Hogg, but he was later reimbursed by the legislature, which should have seen to it that the Mansion, as part of the state's valuable property, was in fit condition for both officials and public to enjoy. Because of the heavy cost of heating the high-ceilinged rooms, Hogg suggested that it might be economical to build a more modern structure; however, the depression of 1893 ended talk of a new Mansion, and the old one still stands.

By January 21, when Hogg's message was read, several commission bills had already been introduced and referred to the House and Senate committees on internal improvements. Since the railroad lobby was already in evidence, Hogg was willing to take the risk of again being called a "demagogue," as long as he could let the friends of a plenary commission know that he stood with them to carry out the purposes for which they had been elected. He fully recognized the constitutional limitations surrounding his office, and knew how much he must count upon able lieutenants to carry on at their posts in House and Senate. He knew particularly the importance of having as speaker of the House a commission man and one who shared his ideas and had confidence in him.

Robert Milner, the same age as Hogg, had long been a champion of progressive reforms. As owner-editor of the Henderson *Times* he fought

229

the crop-lien system, which had settled down heavily on the postwar South; to break the chains of this new slavery he had advocated diversification of crops. Like Hogg, he had been willing to hear the side of the Knights of Labor during the strikes against the Gould railroads. As a freshman legislator in 1887 he had stood with Hogg in opposition to the prohibition amendment. He had also voted that year to promote John Reagan to the United States Senate, having been especially impressed with Reagan's words on railroad rates as the elder statesman looked at the unfinished Capitol:

It seems that the biggest fool in the land need only to open his eyes to see the pernicious effects on the general prosperity of the country growing out of the fraud and corruption of the mighty corporations. . . . For instance: the dome of the new capitol is being built in Belgium. It will cost more, I am reliably informed, to ship the dome from Galveston to Austin, than it will from Belgium, many thousands of miles distant, to Galveston.[19]

Milner had further endeared himself to the young reform Democrats by defeating Republican candidate Webster Flanagan for a seat in the House in 1888. On May 5, 1888, his "Editor's Letter," regularly sent home to his paper in East Texas, thus described James Hogg:

The Attorney General hangs his coat upon a peg, places his huge corporal avoirdupois in a big chair and works like a Trojan, and all violators of the law, whether they be railroad magnates or cattle kings, know that he means business.[20]

Hogg knew, however, that he dared not rely alone on the younger men. He needed the support of experienced legislators, especially those who had long standing as champions of antimonopoly. Alexander W. Terrell had been ahead of his time when in 1883 he advocated in the Texas Senate the moderate, Massachusetts fact-finding type of railroad commission. Out of office for two years, he had been convinced by Hogg in 1890 that he should run for a House seat and carry on the commission fight. As a resident of Austin since 1852, except for a brief period at the close of the Civil War, he had known most of the men closely identified with Texas legislative history.

Terrell, at sixty-three, was an imposing figure at any gathering, well over six feet tall with a heavy shock of white hair and a white "handlebar" mustache. Born in Virginia in 1827, he graduated from the Uni-

[19] Rosalind Langston, "The Life of Colonel R. T. Milner," *Southwestern Historical Quarterly,* XLIV (April, 1941), 438–439.
[20] *Ibid.,* p. 445.

versity of Missouri and practiced law in St. Joseph before coming to Austin. From 1857 to 1862 he was a judge of the Second District. Entering the Confederate Army in 1863, in the closing days of the Confederacy he had been made a brigadier general. He later served in the legislature in both Senate and House and played a prominent part in establishing the University of Texas; he was also co-author of the law which gave Texas its new Capitol. He was widely known for his championship of justice for the rural masses against the tyranny of the railroad corporations and other monopolies; his ideas on this subject, as set forth in a famous speech at his alma mater in 1885, were widely circulated in a reprint titled "The Cormorant and the Commune."[21]

Hogg and Terrell had become friends in 1887, and Hogg spent many hours listening to the older man expound his economic and political theories and experience. Governor Ross and Terrell became estranged in 1888, but Hogg continued to value Terrell's advice and his encouragement of Hogg's efforts to enforce the law. Disappointed in his hope of being sent to the United States Senate in 1887, Terrell continued to speak at farmer rallies, asking for regulation of railroads and for laws to check monopoly, and was thus anathema to the railroad leaders. The Galveston *News* had frankly urged the vigorous Attorney General to stick with the Clark-Ross school, rather than with Terrell. During the 1890 campaign the opposition made efforts to depict Hogg as a reflection of Terrell, although it was well known that Chilton, Robertson, and Hogg were more or less on their own as part of the "Young Texan Democratic" school, which, while making no abrupt break with the past, confidently looked ahead to a better Southwest. However, Terrell was their battle-tested regiment in reserve, and when the battle got too hot for some of the youngsters Hogg did not hesitate to send him into the midst of the fray. Hogg had foreseen the need for his experienced leadership and in June had urged Terrell to enter the race for a seat in the legislature.

Another experienced tower of strength for the commission forces was Thomas Jefferson Brown of Grayson County. He had introduced a strong commission bill in the House in 1889 and, exerting his skill as a parliamentarian and masterful debater, had secured its passage—only to see the railway lobby kill it in the Senate. The lobby then withdrew

[21] The Speeches Folder of the Terrell Papers contains a printed copy of "The Cormorant and the Commune and Labor," dated Austin, April 8, 1886. See also Professor Charles Chamberlain, "Alexander W. Terrell," Ph.D. dissertation (the University of Texas, 1957), pp. 269–274, 336 ff.

from the Senate, permitting the Lane-Field freight-rate bill to pass, and next showed its strength in the House by dividing friends of a commission to secure the defeat of the freight bill there.[22] Early in the campaign of 1890, Brown had taken the time to write twelve articles for the *Southern Mercury* on "Railroad Regulation."

The articles evidenced considerable knowledge of the development of commission plans in other parts of the United States. Brown emphasized that Tennessee was the only state to give up a commission, and that was because the badly devised law had thrown the commissioners into politics and control by the railroads.[23] Having made a careful study of Poor's *Railroad Manual* and the railroad reports turned in to the Texas Comptroller, he was able to show the discrepancies between tax valuations averaging $8,351 per mile for 1888 and efforts to collect rates to pay interest on stock and bonds valuations of $40,000 to $60,000 per mile.[24] In his Article 5, Brown detailed how the powerful railway lobby had worked to defeat the commission and freight bills in 1889, concluding:

This is a dangerous power to be exercised by corporations and a pernicious influence in the policies of the state. Their continuance means the domination of the railroads as in Pennsylvania and other states, of one of which it is said that its legislature has taken no action on the subject of railroads except to pass resolutions thanking the railroads for the passes furnished its members.[25]

Since Brown had at first supported Throckmorton before coming over to Hogg's camp, it was good generalship on Hogg's part to put him in the forefront of battle. Soon after the election Hogg requested that he draw up a commission bill which they would go over together prior to the meeting of the legislature. Brown understood the value of compromise on sectional interests and the importance of the competitive water and rail rates. Therefore, although from North Texas, he emphasized in both his writings and speeches the necessity of making Galveston a deep-water port.[26]

Senator Martin M. Crane was another trusted legislative lieutenant. Born in West Virginia in 1855, he was orphaned at an early age. In

[22] Statement by Brown in the *Southern Mercury* (Dallas), February 13, 1890; Texas *Senate Journal* (1889), p. 165.

[23] Article 2, *Southern Mercury* (Dallas), February 20, 1890.

[24] Article 3, *Ibid.*, February 27, 1890.

[25] Article 5, *Ibid.*, March 6, 1890.

[26] F. A. Battery Company, staff, *Biographical Souvenir of the State of Texas* (Chicago, F. A. Battery Company, 1889), p. 119; *Southern Mercury* (Dallas), March 13, 1890; Winkler, *Platforms,* pp. 275, 280.

1870 he settled at Cleburne and was practicing law there by 1878. He became attorney for Johnson County in 1879, then served in the Texas House from 1884 to 1886. In 1886 he had worked diligently for Hogg's election as attorney general. Now he became a sort of watchdog in the Senate for the interests of the plenary commission, although introducing no bill of his own. He was soon alarmed to find that Cone Johnson of Tyler, on whose Senate Internal Improvements Committee he served, and young Hiram M. Garwood of Bastrop did not seem to be working for the administration plan and he so reported to Hogg.[27]

Hogg found a staunch supporter from the blackland country in George Jester, successful banker and planter at Corsicana. Born in Illinois in 1846, Jester had moved with his family to Texas sometime before the Civil War. He later served under General John Hood in the Confederate Army. A teamster, buying hides on the side, for a time after the war, he finally launched into a new business, as the result of noting that the cotton factors were concentrated in the port cities; he was sure there would be an advantage to both farmers and spinners in furnishing graded cotton direct from the farmers to spinners in the East. When he made trips East to expound his point, he necessarily became an assiduous student of freight rates. His plan prospered; in 1881 he was president of Jester Brothers Bank, which became a national bank in 1889. He was well aware of the injustices of railroad rates and how the railroads had fought the teamsters.[28]

The anti-commission forces continued to picture Hogg's advisers and followers as deluded at best—dreamers or members of the disappointed and misguided poor—and at worst as dangerous radicals. Actually, most of the Governor's supporters were men of substance who had built themselves up from modest beginnings; several of them had the advantages of college or law-school training. An outstanding characteristic of Hogg as a political leader was this ability to attract able men. However, it is also true that, as railroad practices became so notoriously oppressive, men of every walk of life who had any regard for justice were almost obliged to stand up to be counted in the efforts to bring about some degree of regulation. Hogg and his friends were not radicals, nor was regulation by commission any longer in the experimental stage. Now that commission

[27] Martin M. Crane to Ima Hogg, March 18, 1935, Interv. Fol.; Dallas *Morning News,* August 4, 1943; Walter P. Webb and H. Bailey Carroll, *Handbook of Texas,* I, 431.

[28] Lewis E. Daniell, *Personnel of the Texas Government* (San Antonio, Maverick Printing House, 1892), pp. 232–237. Jester, whose son Beauford was to be governor in 1947, became lieutenant governor in 1895.

advocates had a leader in the Governor, they rallied around to create a regulatory body strong enough to do the job.

Recognizing that the Governor meant business, the railway lobby determined to concentrate on beating him on the issue of appointment versus election. Hogg wanted to avoid Tennessee's mistake of letting the commission get into election politics before it could prove its value; the railway leaders preferred an elected commission, which they might be able to control. Pressures from many areas had been growing, even prior to the assembling of the legislature. Various groups had tried to get a commitment from Hogg that he would appoint a railroad man and a farmer on the commission, but he had turned them aside by saying that it would not be appropriate to make commitments ahead of the passage of the law.[29]

Five commission bills were eventually introduced in the Twenty-second Legislature—two in the Senate, by Cone Johnson and Hiram Garwood, and three in the House, by Thomas J. Brown of Sherman, J. M. Melson, a recent University graduate, and David Derden of Waco. By late January a subcommittee of the Senate Committee on Internal Improvements composed of Johnson, Garwood, and C. L. Potter of Gainesville had worked the Johnson and Garwood bills into the Senate substitute bill.[30] As Martin Crane had warned, Johnson had shifted his support from the appointive commission plan to the elective plan.

During the Twenty-first Legislature, Johnson had presented and vigorously defended a strong, appointive commission bill in the lobby-ridden Senate. When Senator H. D. McDonald became the visible leader of the anti-commission forces in 1889, no one had made a more impressive speech against his position than Cone Johnson; during the campaign, when McDonald briefly entered the race for governor, the address had been widely reprinted with telling effect. Johnson had given much time to the study of regulation, and Hogg had hoped that he would come to an early agreement with Brown, who was his opposite number as chairman of the House Internal Improvement Committee. The fact that Johnson was close to W. S. Herndon and others in Tyler

[29] See draft of a commission law by James B. Simpson of Dallas in the Galveston *News*, December 25, 1890. It called for an appointive commission of three—one was to be a lawyer; one was to have railroad experience; the qualifications of the third were not given.

[30] Texas *House Journal* (1891), pp. 17–21; Texas *Senate Journal* (1891), pp. 32, 314–315. See also Texas *Senate Journal* (1889), pp. 425–432, for Johnson's

who had considerable railway business may have influenced his switch to the elective commission plan. However, one observer explained Johnson's defection thus:

Soon after the legislature convened a lot of people convinced Cone Johnson that he could be elected governor, and Johnson commenced to fight Governor Hogg. He and Garwood were in the Senate and there wasn't anything to it except a lot of folks wanted to raise a controversy and Johnson had no better sense than to believe they really intended to run him and talked him into it, and he fought Hogg during the entire session of the Senate of 1891 and until [Johnson] went out of office in 1893.[31]

In later years, when the Railroad Commission had become a success and Garwood was famous as a member of the firm of Baker, Botts, and Garwood of Houston, Garwood declared that Hogg had been right to insist on an appointive commission, making it possible for the body to start off free from an initial political fight. However, in 1891 this was not his position, and, while friends of Johnson and Garwood always have maintained that these two men were hard workers for a commission, it should be recorded that they opposed the crux of Hogg's plan and felt that the Governor was unreasonably stubborn on the issue of an appointive commission.[32] Hiram Garwood had been practicing law for about five years when he entered the Texas Senate at the age of twenty-six. Having read law in the office of Congressman Joseph D. Sayers, who came out in favor of a commission during the 1890 campaign, Garwood turned to Sayers for advice on the regulation issue. Sayers, in turn, appealed to William M. Morrison of Illinois, chairman of the newly created U.S. Interstate Commerce Commission. It appears that Morrison agreed to draft two bills on the condition that their authorship should not be disclosed. One bill provided that the commission's rates should be absolute, a point of questioned constitutionality at the time; the other measure declared that rates should be considered "reasonable" until declared otherwise by the courts. This latter position was in line

bill in that session; Mizell F. Kennedy, "A Study of James Stephen Hogg, Attorney General and Governor," Master's thesis (the University of Texas, 1919), pp. 127–130.

[31] T. N. Jones to Ima Hogg, June 29, 1935, Interv. Fol.

[32] Charles S. Potts, *Railroad Transportation in Texas*, pp. 123–126, makes no mention of the Johnson-Garwood tactics. Cf. Robert L. Batts, "Hiram Morgan Garwood Memorial Address, July 3, 1930" before State Bar Association in Baker, Botts, Andrews, and Wharton, *Hiram Morgan Garwood* (Houston, [n. pub.] 1930), pp. 11, 22, 43–48.

with Hogg's position from the start and therefore he did not object to this feature of Garwood's moderate bill.[33]

Tom Brown, according to plan, had introduced an administration bill in the House; it emerged from committee almost intact, and then Brown and Johnson began their meetings to harmonize the House and Senate substitutes. As they worked day after day, it became apparent that Johnson was now convinced that the conservative Senate would not accept the appointive feature and that the plenary features must be watered down. At this stage Senator Crane, observing that Garwood and Johnson were drawing closer together and that Brown was not making headway, proposed that a special committee be appointed from each house to see if a bill could be written. The proposal was accepted, but Crane became even more suspicious when Johnson left him off the special committee.[34]

One morning, when the committee had been at work for almost three weeks, Crane, leaving his boardinghouse for the Capitol, met Judge Eldred J. Simkins, a member of the University Board of Regents and Senator from the Corsicana district, who was on the committee. The following conversation ensued:

"Well, Senator, how are you getting along with your railroad bill?"
Simkins: "Not at all. I haven't been there for two weeks. Have you seen what they propose to report?"
Crane: "Yes, and I am going to fight them on the floor of the Senate."
Simkins: "You will not get anywhere because Governor Hogg has endorsed it." [How he got this impression is not clear.]
Crane: "I do not care—that is not the kind our plan calls for."[35]

When they had reached the corridors of the Capitol they met Governor Hogg, who turned to Crane and said in a tone indicating his dissatisfaction:

"Have you seen the commission bill—how do you like it?"
Crane: "Not at all, I could drive a coach and four through it. I have just been told that you have endorsed that measure."
Hogg: "From this time on, by Gatlins, I am going to take stock in it myself."[36]

---

[33] Garwood's Commission bill was introduced January 16. Texas *Senate Journal* (1891), p. 32; Martin M. Crane to Ima Hogg, March 18, 1935, Interv. Fol.
[34] J. S. Hogg to T. J. Brown (Sherman), December 2, 1890, J. S. Hogg Let. Pr., 7, p. 872; Martin M. Crane to Ima Hogg, March 18, 1935, Interv. Fol.
[35] *Ibid.*
[36] *Ibid.* See also *Proceedings of the Twenty-fourth Annual Session of the Texas*

Hogg likened the situation in the legislature to a wagon which had lost its coupling pin and was trying to go in all directions at once. He knew that the corporate interests had filled the Austin hotels with their representatives and, having pooled their grievances by conferences and agreements, now presented an almost solid front in opposition to the Hogg measures. The very fact that the people had spoken so forcefully at the polls for the amendment seemed to bind corporate interests closer together, and the numbers, influence, and pertinacity of the lobby were the talk of the town. On hand were the general solicitors for the great railway systems, the general attorneys for local lines—usually very able men—the railroads' local attorneys, traffic experts, prominent politicians, and other men of influence. All of these consulted endlessly with their old friends in the legislature and began to reach out to the newcomers. Even friends of the administration were not neglected, and some of these accepted the lobby's attentions, believing themselves immune to being influenced. The farmers were especially naïve in this respect, not being accustomed to look for covert motives in those who generously dispensed hospitality. Before long the Governor was appalled at the forces arrayed against him. For six weeks the special committee simply bogged down.[37]

The lobby was continually alert. When a home-town friend of a legislator came to Austin, the lobby saw to it that he called on his representative and put in a word for the railways—such as "don't be too hard on them," "we need them," "Hogg is bitter," "Hogg is a demagogue," "he wants too much power," or "make the commission elective."[38] An Austin caterer was very busy at various hotels serving famous feasts, morning, noon, and far into the night. Rare wines and stronger drinks were served freely. The young men, the farmers, and the small-town lawyers among the legislators had never been able to afford such delicacies as shad roe, Potomac shad, extra choice sirloins, porterhouse steaks, and English mutton chops that were offered them so graciously. Many were impressed. Should Austin seem monotonous, the lawmakers would be invited to make a week-end trip. Frequently these trips were in the form of grand excursions to the coast, arranged especially for members of the legislature and many correspondents, such a junket as

---

Bar Association (Sherman) (Austin, 1905), pp. 79–80; frontispiece is portrait of Garwood.

[37] Terrell Papers, No. 20; H. B. Marsh to Ima Hogg, April 9, 1935, Interv. Fol., pp. 32–35; Texas *House Journal* (1891), pp. 10–17, 323, 466.

[38] George W. Bailey, "At Grips with the Lobby," typescript, George W. Bailey Notes, pp. 3–6. Dallas *Morning News,* March 11, 20, 1891.

that Judge William Atwell, then editor of *The Texas University,* a student magazine, has described in his autobiography.[39]

A somewhat more sophisticated form of persuasion was carried on in the lobby of the Driskill Hotel. Here lawmakers could meet influential Texans, stately in Prince Albert coats, gleaming white shirt bosoms, and well-tailored trousers, their longish locks—barbered in the fashionable "statesman's cut"—topped off by broad-brimmed black Stetson hats. Daughters and wives of men of note were often agreeably in evidence also. These men and women for various business or social reasons were not averse to discussing political problems in such a way as to hint that the Governor was "just too radical."[40] Many of them had come to believe Gould's insistence that Hogg's work while he was attorney general had kept out capital and they now felt the Governor must be further retarding the development of Texas.

In an old limestone hotel on Congress Avenue, where the rooms were named for the States of the Union, lawmakers were offered diversion in card games and the hosts saw to it that the "old darkies" kept the sideboards filled with food and drink. The games often lasted until morning; back at his desk in the Capitol later, an unsophisticated solon might boast about how much he had won the night before, not understanding that it was part of the bigger game for the hosts to be good losers.

Friends of the Governor kept him informed of what was going on; sifting the information, he learned who were the men that he could depend upon. Frequently, when legislators came to see him on business, he put them on guard against the lobby's tactics, particularly warning the more inexperienced men. But in committee and later on the floor of both House and Senate, certain lawyer members continued to offer plausible amendments designed to extract the teeth of the commission measure. Hogg watched developments closely, gauging each committeeman's fidelity to the cause. He was determined that the Democratic lawmakers should not default upon their obligation to write a strong commission law, and he was convinced that the appointive feature was essential to the measure's strength. Any measure lacking this provision would receive his veto. He was ready, if necessary, to go to the people again and ask them to instruct their representatives prior to a call for a special session. There was some encouragement in the warnings about the tough fight issued by Alliance and Granger leaders to their constitu-

---

[39] William H. Atwell, *Autobiography* (Dallas, Warlick Law Printing Company, 1935), pp. 7–8.

[40] Bailey, *op. cit.,* pp. 7–8.

ents and in the resolutions that began to come in from local Alliances to strengthen the backbones of their representatives. The *Southern Mercury* kept faithfully to the theme first expressed on November 6, 1890: "Let your representatives and senators go to Austin with a clear conception of what you sent them for." As long as the people were informed and vigilant, Hogg would not despair.[41] In fact it was encouraging to find Representative J. N. Browning from the Panhandle speaking for the appointive plan and telling his colleagues to expect a veto if any other plan was written into the bill. Hogg was not surprised to find Representative George B. Gerald from Waco fighting his measure because of an alliance with George Clark and their open opposition to a commission law as an unconstitutional delegation of legislative powers.

Out of the Governor's chance encounter with Crane and Simkins in the Capitol corridors in mid-February came an agreement that the two Senators would meet with him and go over the bill to bring it into line with the platform pledge. Similar meetings were arranged with Representatives Brown and Terrell. For several nights lights burned late, sometimes in the Executive Office, sometimes in the Mansion. It was obvious to agents of the opposition and to newspapermen that something special was going on.

When Terrell, Brown, Crane, Simkins, and Hogg were ready, a night caucus was arranged of those members they deemed reliable. The draft bill was read. After a few minor changes were suggested, it was agreed that Terrell would introduce the bill as a substitute for all pending bills. Brown, who was an excellent parliamentarian, was to open the debate and Terrell was to close. On February 25 they were ready to act. The Terrell substitute was proposed in the House, and the opposition was surprised to find that Brown, who had been known to be working with Johnson on coordinating pending Senate and House bills that had just passed second reading, moved that two hundred copies of the substitute be printed.[42]

On March 2 the copies reached the House, and, a majority having

---

[41] Hoover Alliance Resolutions, March 27, 1891, expressing thanks to "Brother Joseph Frances, Hon. Ed Rogan and Senator Clemons for their firm front displayed in this question despite the machinations of the most powerful anti-administration railroad lobby ever seen at Austin, who have sprung this issue (elective vs appointive commission) as a last resort in their endeavor to counteract the people's expressed will, and fight the battle of the last campaign over again." In J. S. Hogg Scrapbook 3, p. 50.

[42] Texas *House Journal* (1891), pp. 466–467; Alexander W. Terrell Papers, No. 20.

been pledged to vote for the measure, the Terrell substitute was adopted on the question of the engrossment of the bill and then the House adjourned for the usual holiday observance of Texas Independence Day.[43] When consideration was resumed on March 4 the opposition had rallied. Walter Gresham of Galveston, director and attorney for the Gulf, Colorado, and Sante Fe Railroad and vigorous worker for making Galveston a deepwater port, moved an amendment to strike out a part of Section 6, which provided that "no mandamus injunction or other restraining order should issue against any action of the Commission before a final determination of the issue in the trial."[44] Friends of the bill voted down the amendment, 65 to 30. The vote was indicative of the majority in favor of the administration bill; nevertheless Representative John J. King of Bowie County, serving his first term at twenty-seven years of age, then submitted a new proposal to make the commission elective. Hogg had told more than one group that if the people and the legislature wanted to make the commission elective later on that was their right, but that he intended to carry out his campaign pledge of championing an appointive commission initially in the interest of getting it off to a good start without delay. The opposition's cry had been that Hogg merely wanted power for power's sake. Therefore, the vote on King's proposal concerned the chief disputed and vital commission issue; his measure lost 27 for to 49 against.[45] Granting that the men who championed the elective feature were sincere, it is still of interest that King later became a vice-president and director of the Texarkana and Fort Smith Railway and the Port Arthur Canal and Dock Company, while Garwood became a director of the Texas and New Orleans Railway and general attorney for the Southern Pacific lines in Texas.[46]

Some of the statements made by the voters on King's bill were significant.[47] R. B. Hood of Parker put into the record: "I vote aye because in my opinion to do otherwise is a virtual acknowledgment that the ballot box is a failure." Edgar Rogan of Lockhart declared the majority was carrying out the popular will, and he voted to take the commission

---

[43] Texas *House Journal* (1891), p. 467; Martin M. Crane, "The Railroad Commission," Dallas *Morning News*, February 20, 1938.

[44] Texas *House Journal* (1891), p. 477.

[45] *Ibid.*, p. 478. One of King's constituents wrote Hogg: "I am satisfied our young man at Austin, now serving his first term, has fallen among the Philistines."

[46] Webb and Carroll (eds.), *Handbook of Texas*, I, 959, 674; Dallas *Morning News*, February 7, 1940; Claude Elliott, "Building the Southern Pacific Railroad," Master's thesis (the University of Texas, 1928), p. 125.

[47] For the statements that follow, see Texas *House Journal* (1891), pp. 478–479.

out of politics, maintaining that if parties or interests nominated candidates for a commission the people would not have a widely representative group of men to choose among, whereas for an appointed commission the governor could look over the whole state for qualified men who would fearlessly and wholeheartedly carry out the purposes of the law. Furthermore, Rogan believed it would be difficult to make an elective commission responsible, whereas the Terrell bill placed the responsibility clearly upon the governor and the Senate, and this would "compel exercise of great wisdom and judgment in the selection." In opposition, Alexander Breitz declared that the measure was a step toward centralization of power and "contrary to the genius of our free institutions." James Moody voted for the appointive commission with the understanding that any subsequent legislature wanting to change to an elective commission would be free to do so.

A study from a geographical standpoint of the vote for the elective feature indicates that it was not sectional. Miles Crowley of Galveston, the only "labor" representative, was joined in the vote for the elective feature by the representatives from Laredo, Brownsville, Houston, Beaumont, and Waco, and several from the gate cities of the Red River counties in North Texas. Some of these men felt that the railroads were the life-blood of their town and they therefore would not antagonize the executives; others were reflecting a certain degree of popular interest in making the commission elective. It is notable that no representative from the Dallas-Fort Worth area, where Hogg's friends, Sawnie Robertson, Jot Gunter, Judge Kimbrough, Dick Wynne, and A. M. Carter, had been working, voted for the elective commission. Thus it cannot be said that the support for the elective plan came entirely from the cities or that living in a railroad town kept a representative from voting for the appointive plan. No definite occupational pattern emerged either; among farmers, lawyers, editors, and teachers there was support for both sides of the issue.

Representative Walter Gresham, financier and railroad man, typified the few men with railroad interests who did not fight the basic principle of regulation by commission. Such men were rare; much more prevalent was Jay Gould's attitude, which was made even more clear when he forced Charles Francis Adams, who was an active advocate of state and national regulatory bodies, from the presidency of the Union Pacific in 1890.[48] Gresham had been involved in the fights among the different

[48] Charles F. Adams, *Autobiography* (Boston, Houghton Mifflin Company, 1916), p 198.

roads coming into Houston and Galveston; he knew that pools, traffic associations, and secret agreements had not ended the rebating, discriminations between persons and places, and extortion by and among railroads—all practices which hurt transportation profits at the same time that they created bad feeling among the shippers and the general public. Therefore, Gresham found it logical to work for fixed rates and published schedules that all the lines would be obliged to obey and, in this new experiment, he was willing to let the government be the policeman for these enterprises that did not trust each other.

Gresham won a practical concession by an amendment which covered an exception to the general long- and short-haul clause:

Provided, that upon application to the Commission any railroad may in special cases, to prevent manifest injury, be authorized by the Commission to charge less for longer than for shorter distances for transporting persons and property, and the Commission shall from time to time prescribe the extent to which such designated railroad may be relieved from the operations of this provision *Provided,* that no manifest injustices shall be imposed upon any citizen at intermediate points.[49]

There is no available information to show whether or not Hogg opposed this addition. Gresham understood, as other railroad men claimed not to, that Hogg was not an enemy of business per se, and knew that his own great interest in the development of deepwater ports on the Gulf was shared by the Governor. Both men saw this latter development as a way to help Texas to prosperity.

The next hurdle was the Senate. No one knew whether the upper house, which had blocked so many commission bills in the past, would consent to the Terrell substitute. Trouble loomed when amendments came thick and fast from the senators. Finally, as a gesture to the opponents of a strong commission and in the interest of harmony, friends of the Governor proposed that the commission should become elective after 1894. When, on March 17, the vote was taken on this proposal, proponents of the appointive commission had mustered 10 votes, the opposition 14, with 7 members not voting.[50] The vote was again without sectional significance, but its strategic bearing was clear. Cone Johnson

49 Texas Railroad Commission Law, Section 13(c). Daniell, *op. cit.* p. 237, gives a sketch of Gresham with picture.

50 Senator R. S. Kimbrough (Mesquite) made the proposal; Texas *Senate Journal* (1891), pp. 318, 422. A. R. Starr of Marshall declared the Senate had gone back on the platform and "some pretty little tombstones [were] being prepared." J. S. Hogg Let. Rec., IX, 215, dated March 13, 1891.

of Tyler came out boldly against; Crane and Simkins voted for, while Frank Lubbock of Houston, A. M. Carter of Fort Worth, and W. H. Pope of Marshall did not vote. The Governor's friends had also wished to change Section I to include "that no commissioner shall be eligible to any other State office for two years after the expiration of his term of office as commissioner provided that nothing herein shall prevent the re-election of a commissioner." This final effort to keep the commission out of politics failed, and Judge Terrell later declared the omission of the change was a great weakness.[51] During the campaign Hogg had championed a two-year gap in officeholding;[52] blocked in the Senate, he was now obliged to wait for the House to act.

Brown called a pro-commission caucus. Acting upon its advice, he moved that the House not accept the Senate amendments to the Terrell bill and requested a free conference committee. Speaker Milner appointed Terrell, Brown, Rogan, Cochran of Dallas, and King to represent the House.[53] From the Senate side Lieutenant Governor Pendleton chose George Tyler of Belton, Crane, Jim Clark of Clarksville, and William L. Crawford of Dallas.[54] Possible provisions that would restrict the commission appointments to one term or declare that all subsequent commissioners must be elected were not agreed upon, but the new committee did add a provision that a commissioner could not hold any other state or federal office while serving or engage in "any occupation or business inconsistent with his duties."[55] (Stipulated previously had been an oath that a commissioner was not to be connected with a railroad company and must not own stock, mortgages, or receive earnings from a railroad.[56]) The Terrell substitute at last came through with little amendment, and was approved on April 3. It passed in the House by 92 yeas to 5 nays, 9 not voting; in the Senate by 26 yeas to no nays, 5 not voting.[57]

The Railroad Commission had become a fact, and for the time being there was little the opposition forces could do about it. George Clark quickly determined that the best way to weaken the Commission was to go to the polls in 1892 with the elective issue; in the meantime he en-

---

[51] Texas *House Journal* (1891), pp. 663, 670; Terrell Papers, No. 20, written in 1911, concluded: "We failed and now behold the result!"

[52] "Message, January 21, 1891," quoted in Cotner (ed.), *op. cit.*, pp. 114–115.

[53] Texas *House Journal* (1891), p. 670.

[54] Martin M. Crane to Ima Hogg, March 18, 1935, Interv. Fol.

[55] Added to Section 1 (b).   [56] Section 1 (d).

[57] The opponents could now claim they had voted for the popular Commission law.

couraged anyone who could stir up trouble for the Governor to do so. In the closing days of the session Cone Johnson, Hiram Garwood, George Gerald, and others put through a motion calling for a legislative investigation of the I. & G.N. receivership to take place during the period between sessions.[58] They hoped to embarrass Governor Hogg because of his friends at Tyler.

Final passage of the commission measure had come so late in the session that Hogg did not attempt to send up any names of persons to fill the three new posts. After adjournment, regardless of pending investigations and continued criticism of the stringency of the Commission Law, he set about making selections for the appointive positions. First, he invited United States Senator John H. Reagan (then seventy-three years old) to visit Austin before returning to Washington. After welcoming his guest to the Mansion the Governor handed the Senator a copy of the new law. As Hogg told the episode a few years later, Reagan read carefully, then expressed surprise:

Reagan: How was it that such a law as this got through? It is the best commission law I ever saw.

Hogg: It is the best law that has been passed in Texas in many a day and in habilitating the commission I am going to reach up and get the curtains of heaven to clothe it in, even if I have to pull somebody out of the United States Senate. The people expect great things of the commission and you are the man to take hold of it and make it what the people intended it to be.

Reagan (seemingly dumbfounded): There is plenty of good material in the State for the duties of the commission and I am interested in important legislation [in Congress], which the country demands.

Hogg: There is plenty of good material, but plenty of good men are not well known, and they would not be in the office long before they would be charged with having been bought up by the railroads. I want a man at the head of the commission that everybody knows to be clean and honest, and by Gatlins, I would take the dust from the window sills of the skies to polish up the commission. It must be above reproach.[59]

Hogg continued to plead his case for Texas before his guest. Would not the new work be of greater material benefit to the people than his staying on in the Senate? Finally, Hogg promised not to press the matter,

[58] St. Clair Reed, *Texas Railroads,* p. 326; Texas *Senate Journal* (1891), pp. 545 ff., 628; Texas *House Journal* (1891), p. 768.

[59] After the Railroad Commission law had been sustained by the Supreme Court in 1894, Hogg told the story. See J. S. Hogg Scrapbook 3, pp. 64–65.

but asked Reagan to think it over carefully and to give his answer as soon as possible.

Late in April, Reagan agreed to accept the appointment.[60] The news was received with rejoicing by those who wanted a strong commission and with great distaste by the railroad forces. Newspaper comment reflected the divergent views. Papers that had long fought Reagan, such as the Galveston *News* and the Dallas *News,* renewed their attacks. Those favorable to the Governor were perhaps overlyrical. The following excerpt from the Corsicana *Daily Light* is typical; however, granting a certain prejudice in the editorial writer, it is not difficult to understand the triumphant spirit of men who had waited fifteen years for victory on the commission issue:

Every successive act of Gov. Hogg seems to send him up higher and higher in the estimation of all intelligent and honest people who are capable of discerning the right in the public acts of men. In the appointment of Hon. John H. Reagan as railroad commissioner, he has simply accomplished a feat. Had he searched the state over he could not have found a better man for the place. . . . He [Reagan] has ever been ready at the call of his country and the people. He has fought monopoly. . . . He has always been a Democrat among democrats, fought the isms, and stood by the conviction of a skillful judgment and a pure conscience.

Gov. Hogg is paying but little attention to the slander mills, but is doing his level best to make Texas the best governor she ever had, not simply for his own aggrandizement, but for the good of the people of Texas. As governor of Texas he is not called upon to appoint any to office simply because he is an alliance man, a commercial man, or a railroad man, but he is called upon to put the man in office who will best fill that office.[61]

Although Hogg intended to fight back at the continuing attacks of the opposition on his own account, he also hoped to protect Reagan from unnecessary abuse. A San Antonio *Express* reporter later related that the Governor told him he ought to give some thought to Reagan's record and suggested that he visit Reagan. Reminding the reporter that the Senator had been the associate of leading men over the past fifty years, Hogg said he considered him "the repository of invaluable historical reminiscences, the most clear-sighted and far-seeing statesman the South has ever produced."

He will tell you more in two hours than you'll find in the histories. He is a

[60] Walter F. McCaleb (ed.), *Memoirs of John H. Reagan,* pp. 294 ff.
[61] Corsicana *Daily Light,* April 27, 1891.

wonderful and great man, and whenever you correspondents see fit to differ with him you ought to do it in a fair way. I understand that you are not responsible for the dirt your papers throw at him. . . . So far as I am concerned, I don't care what you say about me, for I'll be foot-loose again soon and I've got a hatful of bricks for you, but I do think that Judge Reagan's age and the many valuable services he has rendered the people entitle him to kinder consideration from you newspaper fellows.[62]

Simultaneously with Reagan's appointment, Hogg announced the appointment of Horace Chilton to the vacated U.S. Senate seat. And in May, as the other two members of the three-man Commission, the Governor selected L. L. Foster and William P. McLean.

Foster as commissioner of insurance, statistics, and history, to which post he had been appointed by Governor Ross in 1887 and reappointed by Hogg in early 1891, had accumulated a large store of factual knowledge about railroad affairs, which Hogg considered, together with his known patience and technical skill in dealing with masses of facts, would make him invaluable to the new body. He had served in the House, beginning in 1880, for four terms, becoming speaker in 1884, and his acquaintanceship was wide. Clark's railroad lobby made a determined effort to block Foster's appointment by advocating an amendment to the Commission Law that would have made him ineligible, and he was also charged with having openly lobbied for the administration bill as an agent of the Governor. In the subsequent showdown fight over the charges Senate members were asked by friends of the Governor to name even one man among them with whom Foster had, as alleged, discussed the commission bill, either in or out of the Capitol. No Senator was able to do so, and one more of Clark's intended blows against the Commission was averted.[63]

McLean had been a Texan since 1839, when at the age of three he had come from Mississippi with his mother. His law training was received at the University of North Carolina, and in 1861 he was elected to the Texas House, later resigning to join the Confederate Army. He served as a representative in the Forty-third Congress, and in 1875 he was a member of the Texas Constitutional Convention. Becoming a

[62] San Antonio *Express*, n. d., J. S. Hogg Scrapbook 3, p. 48.
[63] H. B. Marsh to Ima Hogg, February 15, 1935, Interv. Fol.; Martin M. Crane to Ima Hogg, March 18, 1935, Interv. Fol. Walter L. Malone, of the Fort Worth *Gazette,* may have been offered a place on the Commission. We know he had declined the office of secretary of state.

district judge in 1884, he gained an outstanding reputation for his judicial attainments. He had known Jim Hogg a long time and at the beginning of the 1890 campaign strongly supported "Hogg and Commission." However, after his brother-in-law, Land Commissioner Richard Hall, came out against Hogg, McLean wrote a frank letter to Hogg saying that he had decided the only way he could resolve this embarrassment was to remain quiet for a while.[64] Hogg's regard for the Judge was in no way altered by this, and he believed that McLean's legal qualifications would bring to the Commission the balance necessary to guarantee its strength.

The Texas Railroad Commission held its first meeting in June, 1891, and at once began to gather data, study tariffs, and hold hearings that involved shippers, agents of commercial bodies, and railway representatives. Each step, however, was taken with deliberation, because the commissioners were fully aware that preparations were being made by the opposition to test their actions in the federal courts. The resulting slow pace was criticized, but the commissioners, knowing that criticism from many sides was inevitable in this initial period of the controversial body's existence, were not deterred from proceeding with the caution they deemed necessary to make their actions stand up in court.

That much of the criticism came from Farmers' Alliance sources surprised many people. However, a split in the Texas Alliance had been widening for some time. During the 1890 campaign James Hogg had successfully convinced a majority of Grange and Alliance men that their best interests lay in helping him and the "young" Texas Democrats bring about the reforms called for in the state Party platform, but when the platform failed to advocate the subtreasury plan, the more radical Alliance men were highly dissatisfied. It was largely these men who went to the national meeting at Ocala, Florida, in December, 1890, and joined the vote favoring the creation of a new national party based on Populist doctrine, despite Dr. Macune's efforts to keep the Alliance from becoming a political party. Senator Reagan had foreseen that the Texas delegates might be outvoted, and warned against attendance. Naturally, the Populist element therefore did not welcome Reagan's appointment to the Commission. Hogg was adamant. The Commission was not to become impotent by catering to Alliance and railroad agents, who

[64] William P. McLean to J. S. Hogg, August 8, 1890, J. S. Hogg Let. Rec., XI, 266–267; *Biographical Directory of the American Congress, 1774–1927* (Washington, Government Printing Office, 1928), p. 1546.

would then hold the power of blocking the action proposed in the public interest.

The Populist ferment throughout the country was the direct outcome of bitterness among farmers who believed—and with justification—that the two major political parties had virtually ignored their worsening plight. The McKinley Tariff of 1890 had brought no relief to the producers of the great staples, with the exception of the sugar growers, and, with the increasing concentration of both Republicans and Democrats on matters affecting industrial, financial, and transport interests, it is easy to understand the farmers' belief that they were being sold down the river. As mentioned earlier, James Hogg had done in general a unique job in holding most of his farm supporters with this conservative-reform line, but in 1891, during the commission bill debate, Harry Tracy, a leader of the Alliance committee that kept an eye on legislation, feuded with Alliance men in the legislature who were Hogg's friends and who also were determined to keep the Alliance per se out of politics. At this time also the pro-Hogg Alliance men had issued what came to be called the "Austin Manifesto," denouncing the organization's legislative committee as the agency that was trying to push the Alliance into politics.[65]

Furthermore, early in the session a group of Alliance men had come to the Governor with a virtual demand that he promise to put a farmer on the commission, naming S. D. A. Duncan, president and business manager of an Alliance commercial agency in Dallas, as the man satisfactory to them.[66] Hogg had reacted almost as electrically as he would have done had a delegation from the railways asked him to appoint George Clark. He told the group flatly that he would have none of their proposal, since he intended to pick commissioners who, not beholden to any special-interest group, would have a sense of responsibility to all factions and all Texans. The disaffected Alliance radicals used his answer as a further argument for the need of a third party in Texas. It remained true, however, that the great majority of farmers in both Grange and Alliance believed emphatically that their clubs should not

[65] Dallas *Morning News,* May 31, 1891; Dublin *Progress,* March 28 and April 11, 1891; Roscoe C. Martin, *The People's Party in Texas* (the University of Texas, Bulletin No. 3308, Austin, 1933), pp. 36 ff. On January 29, 1891, the *Southern Mercury* quoted from several Alliance papers showing opposition to a third-party movement.

[66] The Alliance was divided. Alliance President Evans Jones and Thomas L. Nugent sponsored A. L. Murphy, of Erath County. See Erath County Scrapbook, Arch. Un. Tex. Lib.

248

become political organs, in spite of the few politically ambitious Alliance members who were ready to subvert the original by-laws to accomplish their own ends.[67]

Shortly after the passage of the commission bill, the new editors of the *Southern Mercury*, Milton Park and Harry Tracy, brought the split far into the open, by charging that the Alliance Democrats had surrendered to the "bossism of Hogg" on the appointive issue as the price for a commission.[68] The division in the ranks of the Alliance was meat and drink to George Clark's hopes to defeat Hogg's renomination in 1892. Before long Clark was making speeches to the farmers, calculated to win interest among the leading Alliance men, although he was still the bellwether of the reactionary Democrats.

Hogg's political future was in the hands of those Democrats who were willing to await the accomplishments of the Commission and to study thoughtfully the effects of the other reform legislation enacted by the regular and special sessions of 1891 and 1892. Many Texans would not forget that Hogg had recognized the plight of farmers producing cotton and wheat and cattle on the inland prairies without benefit of navigable streams by which to reach profitable markets, at a time when the railroads were charging whatever freight rates they pleased. James Hogg had become the standard-bearer in the fight to make the railroads give service for a reasonable compensation that would still permit every sound institution to prosper reasonably. In retrospect, Martin Crane called the commission program of Governor Hogg "the foundation of the future prosperity of Texas,"[69] but in 1891 there was no assurance that the Commission would survive new political and legal attacks in 1892.

[67] J. S. Hogg to Dr. J. D. Fields, March 14, 1892, J. S. Hogg Let. Pr., 9, pp. 612–616. The Anti-Tracy and Anti-subtreasury Alliancemen called a meeting at Fort Worth beginning July 10, 1891. Dallas *Morning News,* July 11–12, 1891. See Harry Tracy, "The Sub-Treasury Plan" in James H. (Cyclone) Davis, *A Political Revolution* (Dallas, Advance Publishing Company, 1894), Appendix, pp. 292–399.

[68] *Southern Mercury,* editorial, April 9, 1891. When the Alliance split, Sam Dixon sensed he would be *persona non grata* and went to Austin for the legislative session, becoming chief clerk of the House.

[69] Martin M. Crane to Ima Hogg, March 15, 1935, Interv. Fol.

CHAPTER X

The Rise of the Populists

THE PERIOD from March, 1891, to the summer of 1892 in Texas was characterized politically by the splintering of both the reactionary and the progressive forces within the Democratic Party and by the division of the Republicans into "Regulars" and "Lily Whites." Another major development was the split in the Texas Farmers' Alliance, when its more radical element wished to transform it from an educational and economic group into the main support of the local People's (Populist) Party. The advent of the national People's Party, organized formally at St. Louis on February 22, 1892, coincided with factors creating a world-wide depression, and its platform of government intervention attracted many thousands from both major parties in many states, especially in the Northwest and in the South. In Texas the Democratic Party stood to lose heavily with the growth of a third party. Governor Hogg was well aware of the responsibilities incumbent upon him as a party leader to maintain the dominance of the Democrats.

The Democratic reactionaries led by George Clark evidenced during the legislative session of 1891 that they were prepared to enter into strange alliances to check "Hoggism"—their brand name for the new leadership and the progressive program. Since practically all Democratic members of the Farmers' Alliance had voted for Hogg and a strong railroad commission in 1890, the Clark forces were all the more delighted when early in the 1891 legislative session the *Southern Mercury*, edited by pro-third-party Milton Park and Harry Tracy, rather than by Hogg's friend, Sam Dixon, brought the divergent points of view within the Alliance into the open by championing the elective plan for the commission. Clark kept himself well informed about the growing dissatisfaction of some of the more radical Alliance men with Hogg and the Texas Democrats for being "too conservative" on such issues as the subtreasury plan, the legal rate of interest, and free textbooks. Thus informed, the Clark forces could join with the disaffected Alliance leaders in subtle criticism of the Governor, pointing, for instance, to his part in securing a new law that strengthened the superintendent of public instruction in his authority over county school superintendents, certification, and approval of contracts as evidence of Hogg's lust for power and desire to centralize authority in Austin.[1]

Not a few of the frustrations Hogg suffered during the 1891 session of the legislature were the direct or indirect result of the strange temporary fraternizing between Clark men, Cuney Republicans, and Alliance men. In the Senate the farmers, through suspicion, and the railroad lobby, by design, blocked the railroad stock and bond bill, by which the Governor had hoped to increase available school funds through lending permanent school funds to railroads for expansion and for new competitive lines after their securities had passed rigid tests to be administered by the Railroad Commission. Hogg also failed in his efforts to redistrict the state and to obtain a better mechanic's lien law and supplementary legislation strengthening the Antitrust Act of 1889; further, a bill to define perpetuities and to outlaw land corporations failed. He did obtain an alien land law, but, because of a strange omission in the caption, a suit to test its constitutionality was started immediately. In a sense the reform program had bogged down; nevertheless, Hogg could point with justifiable pride to having fulfilled almost all of the platform commitments, although the Jester public school fund amendment, the interest rate amendment, and an amendment increasing the number of courts awaited confirmation by the people at a special election in August. Progress was being made in improving the civil and criminal codes, the management of the prisons, and the general tone of law enforcement.[2]

There were not many days, however, when the Governor was not the target for a barrage of criticism from one quarter or another. The appointment of Horace Chilton of Tyler to take John H. Reagan's seat in the United States Senate came increasingly under fire, and the *Southern Mercury*, the Galveston *News*, and the Dallas *News* constantly carped at the appointive feature of the Railroad Commission. Even the Grange paper, *Texas Farmer*, which during the debates on the Commis-

---

[1] *Southern Mercury* (Dallas), March 3 and 10, 1891; Dallas *Morning News*, March 5, 1891, editorial, "Regulation within Bounds of Reason and Equity." Cf. George Clark's speech at Denton, December 19, 1891, and another at Austin, May 16, 1892. See also Frederick Eby, *The Development of Education in Texas* (New York, Macmillan Company, 1925), pp. 199–202. The St. Louis *Globe-Democrat*, May 12, 1891, denied that book companies opposed the uniform textbook bill.

[2] The laws enacted in the 1891 session of the Texas legislature printed to 355 pages, indicating a normal production. See Hans Gammel, *Laws of Texas*, X; Albert B. Paine, *Captain Bill McDonald, Texas Ranger*, pp. 139 ff., 154–164.

sion had staunchly defended the appointive plan, was critical through-out much of 1891. Editor Shaw seemingly had expected more from the administration, perhaps a place on the Commission, and he also fretted because the Alliance had claimed, and from the daily press had received, far more than its share of the credit for putting Hogg into office.[3] Texas Alliance leaders, including Harry Tracy, R. L. Sledge, and President Evans Jones, along with Macune from his *National Economist* editorial desk in Washington, D.C., were not loath to express publicly their unhappiness at the Democrats' refusal to sponsor in Congress the new subtreasury plan for the storage and financing of grain and cotton surpluses. However, Macune cautioned patience, apparently expecting that enough pressure would be built up to force adoption by the time another election came around.

Since 1889, Macune had been busily engaged in building up the Farmers' and Laborers' Union of America, which included elements of the Louisiana Farmers' Union, Farmers' Clubs of North Carolina, and other groups.[4] The Arkansas Wheel came in by February 1891. It is doubtful whether Macune foresaw that the relatively nonpartisan pro-gram of the Texas Alliance might be overwhelmed by the new labor and farmer elements who were desperately seeking for some economic im-provement through political action. The radical elements were strength-ened by notable political victories in the Dakotas and Kansas in 1890 and by the election of Alliance men as governors of South Carolina, Georgia, and Tennessee.[5] An effort to take the Texas Alliance into politics in 1888 had been kept down by such leaders as Macune, Judge Thomas Lewis Nugent, Dr. J. D. Fields of Manor, and Evans Jones of Erath County. Nugent, however, had more recently been gravitating toward the third-party movement.

At the nationwide meeting of Alliance men in Ocala, Florida, in

---

[3] *Texas Farmer* (Dallas), March 28, 1891; November 24, 1892.

[4] Carl C. Taylor, *The Farmers' Movement, 1620–1920* (New York, 1953), pp. 209–214, 260–276; Ralph A. Smith, " 'Macunism' or the Farmers of Texas in Business," *Journel of Southern History*, XIII (May, 1947), 231–244; A. J. Rose (Worthy Master, Texas State Grange) to John Trimble, September 17, 1890, A. J. Rose Papers.

[5] John D. Hicks, *The Populist Revolt*, pp. 153–185; William A. Peffer, "The Farmers' Defensive Movement," *Forum*, VIII (December, 1889), 464–473. The governors were "Pitchfork" Ben Tillman of South Carolina, William J. Northen of Georgia, and John P. Buchanan of Tennessee. See Francis Simkins, *Ben Tillman*, pp. 152–169; C. Vann Woodward, *Tom Watson*, Chap. X. Cf. William B. Hesseltine, *The South in American History* (New York, Prentice-Hall, 1943), pp. 574–575.

December 1890, Macune opposed the formation of a third party,[6] but it was clear that forces were at work in the West, the South, and even in Texas to try political action. Impetus was given to this point of view by the meeting of Midwest Alliances at Omaha, Nebraska, in January, 1891, where the delegates voted for 1) direct election of the President, Vice-President, and senators, 2) foreclosure of government mortgages on railroads as a way to obtain government ownership, 3) the right of landowners to borrow money at the same interest rate as obtained by banks, and 4) a declaration that the Alliance "shall take no part as partisans in a political struggle by affiliating with Republicans or Democrats." By implication many assumed that this meant that they should form a party of their own, although a clear-cut decision was to be delayed until the meeting of the Confederation of Industrial Organizations called for St. Louis in February, 1892.[7]

Known friends of the cattlemen and farmers, such as Senator Vest of Missouri and Senator Reagan of Texas, were seriously alarmed at the prospect of a third party. Reagan wanted Hogg to supply the names of delegates to the Ocala meeting in order that he might write each of them a personal letter urging them not to attend, pointing out how the Democratic Alliance men would be outnumbered or outmanuevered. If they persisted in attending, then he wished to warn them to take no step which "would prevent the members of the Alliance from cooperating with the Democracy in the future." Reagan told Hogg:

The Sub-Treasury bill is the dangerous question. . . . They ought to throw Macune and his set overboard. If he is not being paid to try to break up the Democratic party he is doing that work as effectively as if he was; and for the good of the country he ought to be squelched."[8]

Macune had obviously failed to convince Texas Democratic leaders of his party loyalty, while advocating a novel economic remedy. It is now clear that Reagan had just cause to be alarmed. The end result seemed to vindicate his evaluation of the trend, but the regular poli-

[6] *Southern Mercury* (Dallas), December 9, 1890; Woodward, *Origins of the New South*, p. 236; St. Louis *Republic*, December 5, 1890, in A. J. Rose Papers, Scrapbook I. Annie L. Diggs, "The Farmer's Alliance and some of Its Leaders," *Arena*, XXIX (April, 1892), 598–600, describes Macune's qualities of leadership, his frankness, and diligence.

[7] Hicks, *op. cit.*, pp. 210–211; New York *Times*, December 5, 1890. A list of organizations may be seen in *National Economist*, December 19, 1891, p. 213, or Carl C. Taylor, *The Farmers' Movement*, p. 295.

[8] John H. Reagan to J. S. Hogg, November 16, 1890, J. S. Hogg Let. Rec., VIII, 241–242.

ticians were hasty in their appraisal of Macune and his deep concern for the welfare of the farmers.

If Southern Alliance men held back from starting a third party, in part because of the Negro voters, other regions were not reluctant.

Hogg's first open break with the Alliance leaders had come during
✦ the debates over the elective and appointive features of the commission bill. By March 2, 1891, the lines of division were closely drawn.[9] Alliance President Evans Jones subscribed to the appointive plan, but under the leadership of Harry Tracy the Alliance lobby, called a "legislative" or "steering" committee and originally supposed to aid Alliance members in writing measures affecting the welfare of the organization, was geared to fight for the elective plan. Some of the other Alliance leaders may have acted in good faith, believing that the people should be permitted to elect the commissioners, but Tracy was thought to have made a deal with Clark.[10] The editor of the *Daily News* in Waco, Clark's home town, declared the Alliance would probably split on "the rock of the subtreasury issue," and reminded Alliance members that the people had voted for the appointive plan when they adopted the commission amendment.[11] At this point several pro-Hogg Alliance members of the legislature defied the steering committee, and Benjamin Rogers, a farmer-legislator from Palestine and a champion of the appointive feature, carried his personal defiance to the point of blows with Harry Tracy, who, although not a member of the House, was active on the floor.

The strained relations between the two Alliance factions were definitely severed by the Austin Manifesto, signed by eight Alliance legislators on March 6, during the legislative debate on the commission bill. The Manifesto maintained that the legislative committee of the Alliance was "torturing" principles of the organization into a political platform and urging the subtreasury plan in such a way as would necessitate a third party, and that the Alliance could purify "the leading party, if purity was needed." A reporter indicated that several more Alliance men were in agreement with the Manifesto but, as they were "more timid members" of the legislature, had refused to sign.[12]

[9] Texas *House Journal* (1891), pp. 466–481; Dallas *Morning News*, March, 3–8, 1891; Austin *Daily Statesman*, editorial, March 19, 1891, asked the "elective brethren" to explain all the commotion when the people understood they had voted for an appointive plan.
[10] Brock Robertson interview in Dallas *Morning News*, April 25, 1891.
[11] Waco *Daily News*, March 3, 1891.
[12] *Ibid.*, March 7, 1891; Dallas *Morning News*, March 6, 1891, in reply to

Dallas *News* reporters rushed to get a statement on the Manifesto from Macune, who had just arrived in Dallas from Washington. He claimed that he had not been keeping up closely with Texas politics, but that he favored Alliance discipline. He thought the few men who wrote the protest "just didn't know what they were doing. . . . The Steering Committee represents all Texas." When asked about the third-party movement, he replied:

As to whether the movement inaugurated in Kansas and the Dakotas will spread beyond those states and sweep the rank and file of the Alliance elsewhere depends altogether on how the people are treated by the Democratic Party. Personally, I am opposed to the third party in the Alliance and always will be, and I have exerted my prestige in order to save it from such a course.[13]

Macune also said he believed the majority of Alliance members in Texas were opposed to the third-party movement, although he confirmed that there was a faction of politicians within the order who sought to dominate it "in the interests of the corporations and monopolies." He expected war with that faction, because the Alliance "must ever compose the rank and file of the Democratic Party."[14] Apparently in an effort to prevent an irreconcilable break with the Democratic administration of Texas, Macune was both warning Alliance members not to follow the railroad lobby in fighting the appointive commission and suggesting that they await developments.[15] Governor Hogg should have thanked him for his stand, but there is no available evidence that he did.

Dr. Roscoe Martin, authority on the Populists in Texas, in his discussion of the conflict, maintained that the Alliance split in March, 1891, "on the rock personified by Governor Hogg" and concluded that neither faction in the Alliance proposed a compromise, both proceeding "full tilt toward a point where a legal divorce could be obtained."[16] However, a sequence not mentioned by Martin occurred. The Terrell substitute bill with the appointive feature had come up on March 2. On March 4, after the legislators returned from the holiday recess, Hogg

---

Brown's charges against "bought and hired newspapers," quoted the Waco *Day* as praising Representative Gerald for declaring that reputable papers in Texas were not bought by the railroads. See also Roscoe C. Martin, *The People's Party in Texas* (the University of Texas Bulletin No. 3308, Austin, 1933) pp. 36–37.

[13] Dallas *Morning News,* March 8, 1891.
[14] *Ibid.*
[15] Dallas *Morning News,* April 12, 14, 1891.
[16] Martin, *op. cit.,* p. 37.

had sent in a special message on redistricting so as to reflect the new census figures. This would give the western part of the state, where the Alliance was strongest, more representation in Congress. The Governor pointed out that, if the legislature could not get around to voting the commission bill and other bills pending, redistricting might be delayed. His gesture was by no means "a deal"—redistricting was needed—but it was certainly a means of applying pressure, as was the ensuingly called Democratic caucus, which obliged members in both Senate and House to stand up and be counted on the appointive commission plan.[17] But Hogg knew that Harry Tracy, "Stump" Ashby, and W. R. Lamb had full intentions of trying to see to it that all Alliance men in the legislature should vote the views of the Alliance steering committee in favoring the elective plan and thereby a third party, and the matter had gone beyond the point where compromise was possible, since Tracy from the beginning had intended none and the loyal-Democrat Alliance members had none to offer in view of the fact that they were simply following the original laws of their own organization in not favoring a third party. Considered in this light, the split had less to do with Hogg, than with the unwillingness of the Democratic Party to capitulate to the Populist leaders. Hogg tried to be patient, and did refrain from openly calling Tracy's group a third party at this time, because he agreed with Macune's statement that the majority of Alliance men were Democrats and would go on being so, but he tried to lend what encouragement he could to those Alliance elements who wished to steer clear of the third-party heresy.

Developments in other parts of the nation also had some bearing on the roots of the crisis in Texas. Hicks, in discussing the Populist revolt, has pointed out that Macune's success at Ocala in December, 1890, in getting postponement on a final vote to join the third-party movement had annoyed the radicals from Kansas and Nebraska. Soon after returning home they began to draft delegates for a meeting at Cincinnati in May, 1891, from such groups as the Independent Party, the People's Party, the Union Labor Party, Union and Confederate veteran groups, the Farmers' Alliance—Northern and Southern—the Farmers' Mutual Benefit Association, the Knights of Labor, the Colored Farmers' Alli-

---

[17] Texas *House Journal* (1891), pp. 468–469, 482–488; *Texas Farmer* (Dallas) March 28, 1891; Austin *Daily Statesman,* March 2–9, 1891; Waco *Daily News,* March 3, 7, 1891, Gov. Let. Pr., I, 428, typescript, original in Arch. State Lib. An editorial (Sen. W. B. Page, ed.), in the Crockett *Courier,* March 24, 1891, speaks of the House under the administration "dictatorship."

ance, and other groups which had signified their acceptance of the St. Louis Demands of 1889.[18] Strength is added to Congressman John Davis' statement that the call was drawn up by the Vincent brothers of Winfield, Kansas, the editors of the radical *American Non-Conformist,* by the fact that one of their associate editors, M. W. Wilkins, came to the Texas Alliance meeting held at Waco, April 21–23, 1891, and worked to line up delegates for the meeting at Cincinnati.[19] Wilkins emphasized that the Kansas Alliance had killed Senator John J. Ingalls politically with the victory of the farm editor, William A. Peffer, and implied that some able Texas editor should join the "rolling revolution spreading over the nation" and try his hand at retiring Congressman Roger Q. Mills, who was against free silver.[20] Meanwhile in Atlanta, Georgia, Southern Alliance leader Colonel L. F. Livingston was saying that the call of Kansas Alliance President Frank McGrath to join the third-party movement at Cincinnati would not be heeded by Southern Alliance men.[21]

Governor Hogg by then had already appointed two members of the Railroad Commission, neither of whom was an Alliance man, when the radicals at the Waco convention passed a resolution which had the effect of testing Hogg's subserviency to or independence of the Alliance. After voting to oppose the investment of school money in railroad bonds, as advocated by Hogg, the delegates made their demand (discussed on pp. 258 ff.) that the Governor appoint S. D. A. Duncan, manager of the Alliance cooperative interests at Dallas, to the remaining unfilled place on

---

[18] Hicks, *op. cit.* p. 209; Raymond C. Miller, "The Background of Populism in Kansas," *Mississippi Valley Historical Review,* XI (March, 1925), 469–489; Alex M. Arnett, *The Populist Movement in Georgia,* p. 119; Woodward, *Tom Watson,* p. 163.

[19] New York *Times,* December 5, 25, 1890, and May 18, 1891; Waco *Daily News,* April 22, 1891.

[20] Dallas *Morning News,* April 22, 23, 1891. Riots in Jewell County, Kansas, were discussed in the *News,* May 29, 1891. Cf. William E. Connelley, (ed.), *History of Kansas State and People* (Chicago, American Historical Society, Inc., 1928), II, 1164 ff. U.S. Bureau of the Census, *Report on Farms and Homes: Eleventh Census: 1890* (Washington, Government Printing Office, 1896), pp. 246, 258, 278, shows that just one-half of Kansas and Nebraska farms were mortgaged, but the record did not include tenant farms. Texas was relatively well off with less than 6 per cent encumbered, but half the farms were rented, whereas in Kansas 38 per cent were rented. See also, William A. Peffer, *The Farmers' Side* (New York, D. Appleton and Company, 1891). William E. Connelley, *The Life of Preston B. Plumb 1837–1891* (Chicago, Brown and Howell Company, 1913), pp. 421 ff., discusses briefly the Republican fight against the Alliance in 1891 in Kansas.

[21] Quoted in Waco *Daily News,* April 21, 1891.

the Commission.[22] Unless this was intended as an ultimatum, nothing could have shown more eloquently how these Alliance leaders had misjudged Jim Hogg, Democrat. Chief Clerk Sam Dixon, the former editor of the *Southern Mercury,* Land Commissioner McGaughey, and other Alliance friends of the administration had tried to sidetrack the resolution but had failed. The resolution and an indirect test vote for adherence to the third party, which failed by only two votes (85 to 83), indicated that the Populists had almost taken over. The "soreheads" who had been sat upon by the close vote on the third party then proceeded to hold a separate meeting at the City Hall, under the leadership of labor leader W. R. Lamb of Montague County, J. J. (Jake) and Lee Rhodes, W. E. (Bill) Farmer, and H. S. R. (Stump) Ashby, former Methodist circuit rider. Before the meeting adjourned a state branch of the National Citizens Alliance had been created, with Bill Farmer as president, Lamb as secretary-treasurer, and Ashby on the executive committee, all of whom were now ready to advance the cause of Populism.[23]

Pro-Hogg editors, understanding that the banner of the new enemy had been raised over Texas, sounded the alarm. J. R. Bennett, editor of the Waco *News,* insisted that the farmers who composed the warp and woof of the Alliance were "not really third party advocates," and that it was clearly the duty of the Democratic Party to throw aside "all tendencies to affiliation with these wild and dangerous new party moves and to unite for the advancement of their own, the party of the people.[24]

The following resolution arrived in Austin a few days after the Waco meeting:

To his Excellency, Governor James S. Hogg, we of the Farmers' Alliance of the State of Texas in conference assembled demand of you the appointment of a true and tried Alliance man as one of the railroad commissioners and we do hereby recommend S. D. A. Duncan as a competent and reliable person for said position.[25]

---

[22] Duncan had followed Macune at the Dallas Exchange. It was observed that Robert B. Parrott, district general manager for the Provident Savings Life Assurance Company, trustee of the University of the South, president of the Waco Board of Trade, and Clark supporter, arranged a carriage drive about the city and a banquet for the Alliance delegates. Waco *Daily News,* April 25, 1891. Charles Stewart to J. S. Hogg, November 28, 1890, Gov. Let. Rec., III, 444–445, shows early interest in Duncan.

[23] Dallas *Morning News,* April 24, 1891.

[24] Waco *Daily News,* editorial, April 25, 1891.

[25] Austin *Daily Statesman,* April 25–26, 1891.

Hogg showed the letter to the Capitol reporter for the Austin *Statesman,* who relayed the Governor's comment thus: "Shall I appoint Mr. Duncan? Well, as to that I will say this much: I have appointed Senator Reagan in lieu of Mr. Duncan."[26] Bennett wrote in the Waco *News* that the Alliance "exhibited a monumental mass of cheek . . . after denouncing the governor and the appointive feature. To have been consistent the Alliance should have demanded of the governor the *election* of Duncan."[27] The Alliance leaders had chosen the wrong tactics and misjudged their man when they addressed a "demand" to His Excellency, Governor James S. Hogg, especially if they really wanted him to consider their choice; if, however, they wanted to know whether they "ran" the Governor, they did not have long to wait for their answer.

Soon after the adjournment of the Waco meeting Judge Norman Kittrell wrote to congratulate Hogg for appointing Senator Reagan as chairman of the Commission and L. L. Foster as a member. Hogg replied: "The people need not feel any uneasiness about my obeying the demands of any man or set of men outside of the organized Democratic party. It is always a pleasure to have suggestions from any citizen, but *demands* are just a little too much."[28] To Representative R. S. Kimbrough of Dallas, Hogg wrote: "I am not obeying *demands* these days, except when they come through the formal method of Democratic platforms."[29] The Governor then proceeded to appoint Judge William P. McLean as the third commissioner. So that a member of the Commission might profit from the experience of the Georgia commissioners in railroad regulation, it was arranged for Foster to visit Commissioner L. N. Trammel in Atlanta. By June, Reagan, Foster, and McLean were hard at work with hearings, gathering testimony, and weighing the merits of different principles used in rate-making.[30]

The disaffected radical Alliance leaders, like Tracy and Park, used Hogg's rejection of Duncan as a further argument proving the need for a third party in Texas. It remained a fact, however, that the majority of farmers, in both Grange and Alliance, believed emphatically that

---

[26] *Ibid.*

[27] Waco *Daily News,* editorial, April 27, 1891.

[28] Hogg to Kittrell, April 30, 1891, Gov. Let. Pr., New Series, 1, p. 300. H. C.; Norman S. Kittrell to Hogg, April 27, 1891, J. S. Hogg Let. Rec., X, 240–241.

[29] Hogg to Kimbrough, April 30, 1891, Gov. Let. Pr., 1, p. 301.

[30] Hogg to Trammell, May 9, 1891, J. S. Hogg Let. Wr., II, 120; Austin *Daily Statesman,* editorial, May 26, 1891. Foster attended the Southern Baptist Convention while in Atlanta. Texas Railroad Commission, *First Annual Report* (Austin, 1892), pp. iii–iv, viii–xxiv; John H. Reagan to J. S. Hogg, May 15, 1891, J. S. Hogg Let. Rec., X, 441–442.

their clubs should not become political organs, in spite of the few politically ambitious men who, stimulated by developments in the Northwest, were ready to subvert the original by-laws to accomplish their own ends.

As radicals in the Alliance began to put more pressure on the politicians to take a stand on the subtreasury and money issues and continued to push the formation of a new party, the Texas Democrats were compelled to face an important question. In the bitter mood brought on by drought, depression, and the long decline in farm prices, would large numbers of Alliance members in Texas and the South in general decide that the Democratic Party had failed them?[31]

Governor Hogg sincerely believed that the Democratic Party under his leadership was "a people's party" and not the party of any special interest. He had more than once said that as governor of a growing state he was proud to lead the "Conservative Democratic Party" in a state reform program, using the term "Conservative" in the Texas sense of a contrast to the "Radical" Republican Party. In 1892 the term took on a new meaning, standing for opposition to the socialistic tendency of the radical Alliance and labor leaders dominating the Populists. Professor Chester Destler in a recent article on western radicalism declared, "It would be a mistake to conclude that it [the Populist Party] was socialistic either in purpose or spirit."[32] However, even granting that the majority of Populists hoped merely to strengthen "competitive capitalism and save small enterprise," their platform advocacy of government ownership did not entitle Populists to be free of the adjective. Furthermore, a close study of areas of Populist voting and the Texas leadership in the 1890's indicates an easy transition for many voters and leaders to the Socialist Party after 1900; the Rhodes brothers, for instance, both ran for governor as Socialists, and the son of E. O. Meitzin (a one-time

[31] By 1878 cotton production over the South had equaled the yield of 1860, and in the next twenty years the crop doubled. In Texas the yield of 805,000 bales in 1879 had almost doubled the 1859 figure of 431,000, and in 1889 Texas produced 1,471,000 bales. The price of 11 cents a pound in 1890 began to fall off rapidly, reaching 7½ to 7 cents in the fall of 1892. *Texas Almanac and Industrial Guide, 1952–1953* (Dallas, 1952), p. 190.

[32] Chester M. Destler, "Western Radicalism, 1865–1901," *Mississippi Valley Historical Review*, XXXI (December, 1944), 356 ff. Herman C. Nixon, "The Cleavage within the Farmers' Alliance Movement," *ibid.*, XV (June, 1928), 22–23, shows the distrusts existing between Northwest, Middle West, South, and Southwest, with the Dallas *News* concerned over "Hogs in Politics" and the Iowa *Homestead* conjuring up a vision of an Alliance-controlled "gigantic cotton trust."

Populist candidate for state comptroller) ran as a Socialist Party candidate for governor in 1914.[33]

As Governor Hogg and his political advisers viewed the situation early in the summer of 1891, they understood that the administration was attacked on several flanks. Republican opposition might be dismissed temporarily as traditional and not serious, although complacency about it could be dangerous in the present shifting political climate, especially as developments, including party splitting, were evaluated by astute N. Wright Cuney. The Farmers' Alliance constituted a serious problem in its issuance of demands upon both major parties; if its members voted as a bloc they could control many county primaries in a state predominantly rural. Meanwhile, the Clark forces, still licking their wounds over the commission battle, pushed the I.& G.N. investigations by the special committee of the legislature through which they hoped to embarrass the administration.[34] Also, since they attributed Hogg's success in no small part to Alliance support, they were ready to welcome the advent of a new party, believing it would drain away Hogg support in the primaries and help them to victory in 1892. But Clark, Gerald, Johnson, Garwood, Herndon, and Bonner did not consider carefully what a dangerous game they were encouraging. At the Cincinnati meeting in May the Populists had declared for an alien land law, an eight-hour day, a graduated income tax, and "the most rigid, honest, and just national control and supervision of the means of public communication and transportation, also insisting that if abuses were not eliminated in public communication and transportation government ownership should follow.[35] Conservatives should have moved to strengthen Hogg's position in the "vital center" rather than undermine their foremost defense line.

A decision of great moment confronted the Democratic leadership in Texas. Would they stand by and see the groups of organized labor and farmers drift along into Populism, would they compromise on the subtreasury, or would they call on all Democrats regardless of economic classification to stand by the Party and work to bring about the reforms —short of government ownership—which the majority wanted? Action

---

[33] Martin, *op. cit.,* p. 79 and n. 28; Dallas *Morning News,* July 5, 1900.
[34] Texas *House Journal* (1891), pp. 768, 859, 873; Joint Committee of Twenty-second Legislature To Investigate the Receivership of the I.& G.N.R.R., *The I.&G.N. Inquiry* (Austin, 1892), I, 1–256; II, 1–168.
[35] Hicks, *op. cit.,* pp. 211–218.

of some sort was clearly necessary before the Populists convened at St. Louis in February, 1892, else it might be too late to save the Democratic Party in Texas, and perhaps in the South. Southern Alliance President Leonidas Polk of North Carolina released through the pages of his *Progressive Farmer* this statement:

The new party has adopted the Alliance demands into its platform. Does anyone suppose intelligent Alliance-men will vote against a party that adopts those demands, and in favor of a party that not only fails to adopt, but even resists those demands?[36]

Governor Hogg and the Texas Democrats made their decision. They would make a determined effort to hold in the Democratic fold the Alliance men now wavering, but not yet committed to the third party. Thus they might keep the Populists weak in the Southwest. Congressman Dave Culberson, father of Attorney General Charles Culberson, was among those who began speaking throughout the state, trying to combat the third-party movement and emphasizing the need to elect Democrats who would work to repeal the McKinley Tariff as one way to reduce the cost of living. Culberson favored increasing the circulating medium. Maintaining that only the Democratic Party could break the control of money by Wall Street, he gave full support to free and unlimited coinage of silver, but he staunchly declared that the subtreasury plan was class legislation and he would have no part of it. At the end of May he debated with Harry Tracy in Bonham, in the midst of the great farm region north of Dallas.[37]

Macune had said earlier that the Alliance had three alternatives—to start the third party, to fight within the old parties, or to capture the Democratic Party. The reality of these propositions was not lost on the pro-administration Alliance members of the legislature who were being singled out for defeat by the Tracy group; and there is no doubt that Governor Hogg welcomed the determination of the Tracy opponents to call a meeting of Alliance men who were against the subtreasury plan and government ownership, and for the original nonpartisan principles of the Alliance.

The call for the Alliance meeting, scheduled for July 10 at Fort Worth, declared that the "Tracy type of bossism" must go. When Lamb and Sam Evans of the Fort Worth Alliance and other subtreasury ad-

---

[36] *Progressive Farmer* (Raleigh, N. C.), June 3, 1891, quoted in Hicks, *op. cit.*, p. 217.
[37] Dallas *Morning News*, May 30–31, 1891.

vocates tried to establish a right to seats, they were reminded of the instructions in the call and told that they did not qualify. Lamb then declared, "If this is an Alliance meeting, I have a right to be here; if it is restricted to men opposed to the subtreasury idea, then I am ineligible."[38] Lamb and his followers left the hall. The lines of battle began clarifying when B. J. Kendrick, from George Clark's home county, and friendly to Hogg, was chosen president of the meeting and an ardent admirer of Governor Hogg, young William H. D. Murray (later known as "Alfalfa Bill," governor of Oklahoma), became secretary.[39]

The anti-subtreasury leaders had invited as a speaker the only man of the twenty-four on the Alliance Executive Committee to defy Macune's plan at Ocala, W. S. Hall of Missouri. His speech made clear his belief that the Alliance was doing all right until it went into politics, via the St. Louis and Ocala demands, and began advocating class legislation and government ownership of railroads and communications. W. L. McAlester of Mississippi spoke along the same lines and stressed especially the need to rescue the order from the hands of "mercenary impostors." Alliance member and Texas Land Commissioner McGaughey spoke at a night session. After reviewing the work of the Hogg administration and explaining Hogg's plan to lend school funds to build more railroads, he went on to advocate tariff for revenue only, free silver, and more federal treasury notes. There was undoubtedly justification for the Dallas *News* report that the Commissioner seemed to be giving "more a political Democratic speech than a non-political Alliance speech."[40]

Several speakers objected to having to accept all of the Ocala demands in order to be in good standing with the Tracy group and to avoid being threatened by the *Southern Mercury* with expulsion from the Alliance. The sentiment to stay with the basic principles of the order was general; there was also a trend toward supporting the Hogg administration, but the way was left open for members who wished to support the nominees of their respective parties. Members of the legislature present included F. M. Sellers from Limestone County, in which the fight with the Populists and the Clark-Cuney combination would be tough and where the Democrats needed all of the aid that could be

[38] Dallas *Morning News*, July 11, 1891.

[39] Gordon Hines, *Alfalfa Bill, An Intimate Biography* [*William Murray*] (Oklahoma City, Oklahoma Press, 1932), pp. 271 ff.; Edwin C. McReynolds, *Oklahoma* (Norman, University of Oklahoma Press, 1954), pp. 359 ff. Kendrick may have been born in Cherokee County, where Hogg was born.

[40] Dallas *Morning News*, July 11, 1891.

mustered.[41] Benjamin Rogers, who had had "forcible contact" with Tracy, was there, along with Reed M. Weisinger of Victoria, J. L. Goodman of Robertson, Dan McCunningham of Williamson, and Will Sargeant of Stonewall—all friends of the Governor. A set of resolutions opposed the subtreasury plan and land-loan schemes and denounced public servants who went off after the Populists, aided Republicans in fastening the protective tariff on the people, or joined with railroad combines. Tracy was condemned along with the other men who were trying to make the Alliance a political party. A newspaper, *The Farmers' World,* would be started with Sam Dixon in the editor's chair.[42] As might have been expected, Tracy characterized the meeting as a "caucus of recalcitrant members" acting without authority.

Events moved rapidly. W. R. Lamb[43] and the other founders of the National Citizens Alliance were able to round up forty to fifty delegates to constitute themselves the First State-wide Convention of the People's Party of Texas on August 17, 1891, at Dallas, convening while the annual meeting of the Alliance was also in session at Dallas.[44] Lamb acted as temporary chairman until Stump Ashby became permanent chairman. The secretary was Thomas Gaines of Comanche, another of the Alliance leaders and third-partyites who came from the drought-stricken, financially depressed western counties. During much of the ferment about the third party it was evident that drought and depression had stirred people to extreme action that probably would not have occurred to them had they lived in the more prosperous eastern part of the state.

The preamble to the Texas Populist platform pledged to enact radical reforms of the abuses of power by men elevated to positions in the national and state governments. The Democrats and Republicans were accused of assisting the "banks and sharks of Wall Street and Lombard

[41] In the 1892 election returns from Limestone, Hogg received 1,819 votes, or 43.8 per cent, while Nugent got 1,205 or 28.6 per cent, and Clark 1,075, or 25.4 per cent.

[42] Dallas *Morning News,* July 12, 1891; Austin *Daily Statesman,* July 12, 1891; J. S. Hogg to A. W. Cunningham, March 1, 1892, J. S. Hogg Let. Pr., 9, p. 551; personal interview with L. W. Kemp, April, 1954.

[43] Lamb was a leader of the Texas Federation of Labor. He had attended the Cincinnati Convention in May, where he was made a member of the National Executive Committee of the Populist party.

[44] Ernest Winkler, *Platforms,* pp. 293–297; Dallas *Morning News,* August 18–19, 1891; Ralph Smith, "The Farmers' Alliance in Texas, 1875–1900," *Southwestern Historical Quarterly,* XLVIII (January, 1945), 346–369. The Austin *Evening News,* August 20, 1891, quoted Ben Terrell as saying that if the Democrats would meet farmer demands, "they would all be first class Democrats."

Street in controlling the volume of money." The old party leaders in Congress were charged with refusing to accommodate farm producers with warehouses, although warehouses had been built for "the importer's merchandise and the whiskey man's spirits." Appeal was made to Alliance members to forsake the ties which had "so long deceivingly held them to this unreciprocated allegiance" with the Democrats and to come out in favor of a party pledged to the subtreasury plan and to the platform of the People's Party of Texas, which 1) called for the crystallization of the political reform forces into the People's Party; and 2) endorsed the St. Louis (1889), Ocala (1890), and Omaha (1891) Demands. Specifically added for Texas were these further Demands:

1. Recovery of all public lands possible for actual settlers; no alien ownership of land allowed in Texas and the present law should not be repealed.

2. Tax wild or unimproved lands as improved lands "of the same quality in the same county or district."

3. Six months effective free school system, in which the "nature and effects of alcohol on the human system shall be taught."

4. Adoption of a uniform series of textbooks for Texas published at state expense and furnished the children free.

5. Amendent to the constitution to permit lending of the permanent school funds to the people on land security.

6. An eight-hour day.

7. More equitable and just lien law to protect laborers, mechanics, and material men.

8. Convict labor to cease to compete with citizen labor; and convicts be given intellectual and moral instruction, and any surplus earnings above expenses of their keeping should go to their families.

9. Enforcement of the local option law where legally adopted.

10. Railroads to pay their workers "monthly in the lawful money of the country," and if discharged, paid at once at the nearest station.

11. Fair elections and honest count, under either the Australian or similar system of voting.[45]

The seventeen-member State Executive Committee, with Stump Ashby as chairman, included no more than four East Texans and no one from the area south of Seguin. This was a western-dominated group, reflecting the economic desperation caused by drought and falling prices for cattle and wool, and by high transportation costs—these men voiced their dependence on government for assistance. Realizing the strength

[45] Winkler, *op. cit.*, pp. 295–297.

of the appeal, the editor of the Fort Worth *Gazette* called on the Alliance loyal-Democrats to make known their resistance to the Populists: "Rally round the flag, boys, and be Democrats in profession and practice."[46] Pro-Clark papers, however, among them the Austin *Capitolian*, objected to even this mild crack of the Party whip and urged "the gang of Balmecedaites [to] call off their bloodhounds. . . . Soon or late, the time will come when the reign of King James I will end and his blind followers may stand in need of clemency."[47]

The reform Democrats' war on the People's Party continued. As the Populists were making plans to convene their national Convention, Hogg's good friend Web Finley, chairman of the Democratic Executive Committee, issued an open letter "To the Democracy of Texas," in which the Party whip was applied sharply. There was no mistaking Finley's warning, as he defined the status of those Alliance men who accepted the subtreasury scheme and planned to attend the Convention. Since in its 1890 platform the Texas Democratic Party had clearly ruled out the subtreasury scheme, and whereas Alliance men were pledged (in thirteen states) to support that scheme, they were pledged, in effect, to attempt to capture the Democratic Party and to compel it to adopt a policy which had been specifically rejected. Finley made use of the following Democratic plank: "We oppose the collection and distribution, by the Federal government, of any money in aid of the educational system of the several States, or any of them; or in any way of advancement, or loan to any citizens or class, upon any sort of security, whether government or commercial bonds, farm or other products."[48]

Finley declared the Alliance was in fact a political party, and therefore "its members should not be allowed to participate in Democratic primaries."[49] Governor Hogg wrote to Finley:

In the haste and pressure of my official duties I have neglected to congratulate you on your splendid letter to the Democracy of Texas. As you are being "fired into" about it I halt long enough to do so. The position that no

[46] Quoted in Austin *Evening News*, September 2, 1891.

[47] Quoted in Austin *Evening News*, September 17, 1891. The reference is to President Balmeceda of Chile, who had fled a few days before to the Argentine legation for safety; on September 19, two days after this item appeared, he shot himself. See A. Whitney Griswold, *Farming and Democracy* (New York, Harcourt Brace, c. 1948), p. 146.

[48] Quoted from Winkler, *op. cit.*, p. 288, being part of Item 3 of the platform of 1890.

[49] Dallas *Morning News*, October 25, 1891. For Democratic protests see *ibid.*, November 1 and 7, 1891; Martin, *op. cit.*, pp. 40 ff. See also Smith, "The Farmer Alliance in Texas," *op. cit.*, pp. 366 ff. John B. Long to A. J. Rose, June 19, 1893,

man has the right to participate in Democratic primaries who owes fealty to another political party will be sustained because of its justice and soundness. All true party men can afford to make the fight on this line. Democrats should settle their differences in the party in good faith, and it is timely for the Chairman to say so at any time, or any occasion and as often as he pleases.[50]

Democrat George Clark complained bitterly of Finley's action, making an obvious bid for Alliance votes by means of the complaint, even if this meant implied approval of Populist demands.[51] The Republicans, however, were more fastidious. Over a month before Finley's ouster notice, the leading Negro Texas Republican, Wright Cuney, had warned that when "secret societies" attempted to shape public policy they became "dangerous and inimical to the public welfare and democratic institutions." Cuney thought that patriotic citizens should "keep them as far removed as possible from public matters and impress continually upon their leaders that their duties are benevolent and not political, *as they would create factions* which would be injurious to the public good."[52] While not as pointed as Finley's "ukase," the meaning was clear. The Republican Party would relish fighting a divided Democratic Party, but no third-party entry would be welcome which would take Negro voters away from the Republicans.

In an effort to drive the wedge still deeper between the Alliance and the Hogg Democrats, the Dallas *News* on December 19 reprinted a long letter from Alliance President Evans Jones to the *Southern Mercury* in which he endeavored to picture the Alliance as being "in politics" but not being a "political party." Evans admitted that from the beginning

---

A. J. Rose Papers, refers to Evans' joining the Grange, May 37, 1893. Cf. C. Vann Woodward, *Watson*, pp. 163, 190 ff.

[50] J. S. Hogg to Web Finley, October 31, 1891, J. S. Hogg Let. Pr., 9, pp. 7–8. Senator Chilton had spoken in Austin, October 16, opposing the subtreasury plan but strongly endorsing silver. The Alliance *Echo* (Mexia, Texas) was quoted: "Never before . . . has there been such an onslaught on an organization as is now being made on the Alliance. Almost the entire press outside of the reform press are making a relentless fight against it, both Democratic and Republican. Nearly all the leading politicians on both sides are fighting us." See also Austin *Evening News*, November 3, 1891, warning the Alliance not to become a third party, and claiming that Kansas membership dropped from 140,000 to 60,000 after the state organization entered politics.

[51] Austin *Evening News*, November 10, 1891, suggested Clark reread Ocala demands; Austin *Evening News*, November 28, 1891.

[52] Author's italics. Probably appeared in the San Antonio *Light*, but here quoted from Maud Cuney Hare, *Norris Wright Cuney* (New York, Crisis Publishing Company, 1913), p. 139.

the order had set up certain goals or platforms which, by pressure of one sort or another, they had expected to force the major parties to adopt. However, he emphasized that the Alliance stopped short of being a separate political party.[53]

On the day the letter was published and just after Hogg had met defeat before the Supreme Court (because of a faulty caption) in his efforts to enforce the new Alien Land Law, George Clark made an important address at Denton. Once more he made a play for Alliance votes, this time by pointing out how he and some Alliance members had worked together at the last legislative session for the elective commission plan. The lengths to which Clark was prepared to go in his efforts to defeat James Hogg by attracting the unhappy farmers to his own banner were disclosed when he boldly announced that "most of the Ocala demands were first-class democracy."[54] As part of his caustic attack on the Governor's leadership, he derided the appointment of Chilton to the U.S. Senate. Roger Q. Mills had recently been defeated for the speakership of the United States House of Representatives; Clark now called for a special session of the legislature, expressing the hope that Mills would be selected for Chilton's seat. When he concluded by attacking the appointive Railroad Commission as a "constitutional monstrosity" it was clear that Clark was in the 1892 race for the governorship.

Welcoming the prospect of a strong Democrat to contest Hogg's candidacy, the editor of the Dallas *News* opened the year 1892 with a tirade against the renomination of Jim Hogg and predicted, "Unless all signs fail, there is going to be a thundering campaign in Texas this year, a war to the knife, and the knife to the hilt, is only a mild way to express it."[55]

Since the Clark followers planned a strategy meeting for February 2, Hogg and a group of friends met in Tyler at the end of January. Judge R. W. Hudson and Hogg's close friend, Lafayette Camp, came all the way from Southwest Texas, Robert Stafford was there from Mineola, and Sawnie Robertson came from Dallas—all wanting to make sure that Hogg would pledge the Democratic Executive Committee to seek renomination. They also wished to discuss with Finley the effects on Alliance Democrats of his late autumn strictures concerning the Democratic primaries. Apparently not even Hogg's closest friends were entirely sure that he would wish to run again, especially since the Commission was now established and working; it was more certain now than

[53] Dallas *Morning News,* December 19, 1891.
[54] *Ibid.,* December 20, 1891. [55] *Ibid.,* January 1, 1892.

ever that, did he return to private practice, he could make much more money than his executive salary furnished. However, Robertson and some of the others who knew him best must have known that Jim Hogg would not quit under fire; the Populist threat to the Democrats, George Clark's almost-avowed candidacy, and the fact that the Commission was certain to be given a court test through the efforts of its opponents were all challenges that a fighter such as Hogg would scarcely turn his back on.

As Robertson arrived at the station to return to Dallas after the meeting he was of course pursued by reporters. His remarks to them seem to have been issued practically on the run to catch his train. He was a man of reserve always, so that the reporters did not glean much, and later on in Dallas he refrained from adding any further comment to what he had said in Tyler. The gist of his words promised that Hogg was not quitting and would make it very interesting for those who had misrepresented and "slandered" him. Stressing that the Governor had been faithful to the Party platform, Roberton said the Democrats would make a strong canvass—since Hogg's defeat would be a "triumph for the enemies of Texas." His parting remark just before the train pulled out was, "He will make the race and be re-elected."[56]

The editors of the *Southern Mercury* interpreted the Tyler meeting as a gesture to extend "the olive branch to the Alliance" but maintained that it was now "too late." The precision with which the third-party movement progressed indicated careful planning. On February 10 the subtreasury Alliance men met in Dallas; calling themselves "Jeffersonian Democrats," they approved a platform varying only slightly from the one just adopted by the avowed Populist group at Fort Worth.[57] Harry Tracy was chairman of the Committee on Resolutions and on the Executive Committee. Finley was accused of branding the Jeffersonians with the name of "Skunk Democrats." The name stuck, actually to the benefit of the splinter group which could thus claim persecution by the regular Democrats. When George Clark later opened some of his campaign speeches by addressing the assembled farmers as "Fellow Skunks," there was usually cheering and laughter.[58]

At the same time that the Jeffersonians met, disgruntled Editor Shaw

[56] Dallas *Morning News,* February 1, 1892.
[57] Winkler, *Platforms,* pp. 300–301; Dallas *Morning News,* February 11, 1892; Martin, *op. cit.,* p. 42, n. 45.
[58] Dallas *Morning News,* February 29, 1892; Austin *Evening News,* March 4, 7, April 4 (Rusk speech), 1892; Dallas *Daily Times Herald,* March 3, 1892; Austin *Daily Statesman,* May 17, 1892.

and Barney Gibbs joined a small group in Fort Worth, who went on record as favoring "some good business man" for governor. Names mentioned included well-known men—William D. Cleveland of Houston, James Moroney of Dallas, George Sealy of Galveston, and E. Rotan of Waco, but if these were ever approached they either declined or hedged on acceptance, for nothing came of the effort. Gibbs and Shaw later returned to Hogg's camp, although Gibbs, in 1896, was a Populist leader.

No one watched these developments with a keener interest than the Republican Party boss, Wright Cuney, known popularly as "the Yellow Rose." Born in Waller County of parents who were slaves of the James Bowie family, Cuney had received a good education. He had settled in Galveston in 1859, read law, and later virtually controlled the stevedoring business. A man of substance and power, with the manners of a gentleman, he had a standing among the white businessmen of his city which was rare. Whenever Cuney gave out a public interview, it was news.

In an interview given on February 12 he was farsighted enough to hold out an inducement to the anti-Hogg faction to break with the Governor. As reported by the Galveston *News* and the Dallas *News* on February 13, his remarks were timely and significant. When asked if he anticipated a Democratic bolt, Cuney replied, "If the opponents of Governor Hogg have the courage of their convictions, and if they are not afraid of the old slogans of Democracy—Edmund J. Davis and Negro domination—there will be a bolt." Then came the question: "In the event of a bolt how would the Republicans vote?" Cuney replied: "In the event of a bolt, I should, in the interest of my state, use my influence to have my party abstain from putting candidates in the field, and would stump the state to secure the election of the reform candidate."[59] "Reform candidate" meant Clark, not Hogg; "reform," to the "Party of big business" and to the railroads, meant freedom from Hoggism, freedom from strict railroad regulation, freedom from the Governor's plans to re-enact the Alien Land Law, to pass a sort of "securities act" in the form of a stock and bond law, and to plug up gaps in the Texas Antitrust Law to make it more effective.

It was not a secret that, after Clark had criticized Finley's October ruling for ousting the subtreasury Alliance men from the primaries, Harry Tracy and George Clark had been in conversation about their

[59] Galveston *Daily News,* February 13, 1892.

270

possible cooperation. Tracy found Clark adamant on the money issue and the subtreasury plan, but there was complete agreement that Hogg must go. Therefore, Tracy and the Jeffersonian Democrats had not closed the door to joining a combination against Hogg, and George Clark expected a great and decisive rallying to his banner whenever he chose to announce his candidacy.

On February 13, the day that Cuney's statement appeared in the papers, George Clark announced through the Dallas *News* that he was a candidate for governor. The timing seemed too good to be accidental. When asked about issues Clark promptly replied that there were "plenty, but the Railroad Commission was not one of them"; the people by voting the amendment had determined upon that method of regulation, and he "knew of no one who wished to question their decision." However, saying that he thought some aspects of the law were subject to discussion and revision, he specified the power of the governor to make the appointments and the provision which he interpreted as virtually stopping "the railroads from going to court to protect their property." If elected, he promised to submit revision along lines that would sustain "well-established principles of civil liberty," and he said he wanted public office to be "considered a public trust rather than a public snap." He called for treatment of "our neighbors [the Alliance Democrats] as we would they should do unto us."[60]

On February 18, 1892, Governor Hogg issued a proclamation to convene the legislature in special session commencing on March 14.[61] Many individuals and organizations had for some time been sending in requests for a special session, and the administration itself was more than anxious to better the legislative record by proceeding with measures left incomplete or neglected in 1891, because of the long fight over the commission bill. The March 14 date was a strategic one, focusing attention on the reform program of the Democratic leadership shortly after the return of the Populists from the St. Louis meeting, yet allowing plenty of time for action prior to the national and state campaigns of all parties.

Late in February delegates from the third-party movements and Alliances throughout the country proceeded to the long-planned St. Louis meeting. An old Texas Democrat and Alliance lecturer, Ben Terrell,

[60] *Ibid.;* Buckley B. Paddock, *A History of Central and Western Texas* (Chicago, Lewis Publishing Company, 1911), II, 799–800, says Clark espoused a "liberal attitude toward capital."

[61] Dallas *Morning News,* announcement and editorial, February 18, 1892. Hogg's message to the legislature, March 14, 1892, Section 9, dealt with trusts and conspiracies against trade.

271

president of the Confederation of Industrial Organizations (which had Macune support), was one of the candidates for permanent chairman. Apparently, he still hoped to obtain "reform through Democratic channels," but the "basic principle" men from the South were outnumbered by the radicals from over the nation, the convention being composed of twenty-two different groups or orders, ranging from the Woman's Christian Temperance Union to the Knights of Labor.[62] Georgia's large anti-third-party delegation was not allowed to be seated, and when Leonidas Polk of North Carolina, president of the Southern Alliance, was selected over Terrell to be the permanent chairman, the trend into the third party was clearly indicated.

Labor leaders and strong anti-railroad delegations from the Northwest wrote into the platform an endorsement of government ownership of railroads and communications. Many of the Southern delegates regarded such policies as essentially paternalistic and socialistic and links in the chain of centralization, but northern delegates got their way on both the subtreasury plan—"or some better system"—and on the ownership plank.[63]

When Ignatius Donnelly of Minnesota, who had been in the forefront of the agrarian movement since the 1870's, read the Preamble of the platform, it was not merely his famous dramatic delivery or even the fact that he himself was a symbol of the long road that had been traveled to reach this occasion that sent a unifying current through the crowd. To some of the leaders the "People's Party of the U.S.A.," now formally organized, may have represented a way to personal power, but to the rank and file it was a crusade for a "new day," the terms of which were set as Donnelly spoke:

The conditions which surround us best justify our cooperation. We meet in the midst of a nation brought to the verge of moral, political, and material ruin. Corruption dominates the ballot box, the legislatures, the Congress, and touches even the ermine of the bench. The people are demoralized. Many of the States have been compelled to isolate the voters at the polling places in order to prevent universal intimidation or bribery. The newspapers are subsidized or muzzled; public opinion silenced; business pros-

[62] Hicks, *op. cit.*, p. 226; *National Economist*, March 5 and 12, 1892. Fred E. Haynes, *Third Party Movement since the Civil War, with Special Reference to Iowa* (Iowa City, State Historical Society, 1916), pp. 249–250, describes the Populist Party organization.

[63] *Southern Mercury*, February 25, 1892; St. Louis *Republic*, February 24, 1892; *National Economist*, March 5, 12, 1892. Photostats from files of the Library of Congress.

trated; our homes covered with mortgages; labor impoverished; and the land concentrated in the hands of the capitalists. . . . From the same prolific womb of governmental injustice we breed the two great classes—tramps and millionaires. . . . Silver has been demonetized. . . . A vast conspiracy against mankind had been organized on two continents, and it is rapidly taking possession of the world. If not met and overthrown at once, it forebodes terrible social convulsions, the dislocation of civilization, or the establishment of an absolute despotism.[64]

The Texas Populists returned home vibrantly conscious of their role as crusaders, full of that fire which can sometimes burn away the most formidable and deep-rooted obstacles.

[64] Most easily accessible in Hicks, *Populist Revolt*, pp. 336–344. Cf. William E. Connelley, *Ingalls of Kansas* (Topeka, the Author, 1909), pp. 142–197, in which the author declared the Populist uprising "was begotten of oppression and born of an appeal for justice," while the leaders proclaimed "preposterous remedies for a sick nation."

CHAPTER XI

Hogg Stays on the Middle Road: the Campaign of 1892

THE WEATHER was still cold in the North Texas town of Weatherford when George Clark began there on February 27, 1892, his month-long speaking tour of the region. But temperature mattered little to this most alert, able, and ambitious critic of Governor Hogg, since he knew that by opening his campaign at that time he would have a clear field for several weeks—while the Governor was kept in Austin by the special session.

There were at least two factors that made Weatherford a strategic point at which to start building his political organization: it was the heart of a region well populated by Alliance-Populist men, whose favor Clark had been openly courting, and it was the town in which he had settled as a fledgling lawyer after having served from his native Alabama in the Confederate Army with the high rank of lieutenant colonel. The Confederate gray hat was and would remain one of his campaign symbols, a particularly useful one at a time when James Hogg was making efforts to heal the old but still painful wounds of sectionalism.[1]

Characteristically, Clark began his address with a story of a battle

[1] Governor Hogg had invited Republican President Benjamin Harrison to visit Texas in the spring of 1891 and had traveled with him during his trip through the state. He was now working through Guy M. Bryan in an effort to interest Rutherford B. Hayes, a director of the Slater Fund, in studying educational needs in Texas. Ernest W. Winkler (ed.), "The Bryan-Hayes Correspondence," *Southwestern Historical Quarterly*, XXV (October, 1921), 93–120 and later issues; Robert C. Cotner and Watt Marchman (eds.), "Some Additional Bryan-Hayes Correspondence," *Ohio Archeological and Historical Quarterly*, LXIII (October, 1954), 349–377. In discussing the need for a home for veterans, Hogg had advocated opening it to all Texas veterans of whatever war or side. It was in part from this that the story that Chilton "was not embarrassed by a Confederate record" got started, and Clark made the most of complaints from those who thought that the home should be for Confederates only. Cf. full-page statement by Hogg's friends in *Texas Farmer*, June 4, 1892. Hogg had engaged the painter, William H. Huddle, to paint a portrait of his father. From then on General J. L. Hogg in Confederate uniform looked reprovingly at any visitor to the Mansion who might have questioned the loyalty of his son, a product of the Old South and a builder of the New.

in which there had been a great loss of life and of which it had later been said, "Someone had blundered." He then drew a parallel between the havoc of battle and the terrible economic plight of Texas, placing the blame for the adverse conditions on the "blundering" of Governor Hogg, despite the fact that even Jay Gould had recognized the depression as world-wide, and the further fact that Texas was actually better off than many other states. Had the Governor looked after the people's interests in a constitutional manner he was of course entitled to renomination, Clark admitted, then declared Hogg could be proved "unfaithful," having administered public affairs for the interest of "himself and his friends" with the result that there were "hopeless hearts and ruined homes and a general prostration of material and commercial advancement."[2] He advised the people to demand an immediate change. Clark's slogan became "Turn Texas Loose."

He maintained that the "Hogg Laws" had driven investment capital from Texas and that the long political war on the railroads and other corporations had cost Texas millions in additional interest payments. Anticipating possible criticism of his status as a railroad attorney and lobbyist, he said:

I am not here for the purpose of defending railroads, for they have abler men than myself employed for that purpose. I have no connection with them and no special interest in them except in so far as their interest may comport with the interest of the people of Texas. Recent lessons in government have taught us that these interests are reciprocal and interdependent, and that a blow aimed at one will necessarily recoil on the other. Texas cannot destroy her railroads without bringing ruin upon her people, no more than she could destroy her people without injury to her railroads. We are all in the same boat and must float or sink together.[3]

He admitted that other states had railroad commissions and alien land laws but claimed they were unlike the Hogg laws. Announcing that he was willing to risk his reputation as a lawyer on the statement that the Railroad Commission Law would not stand up "one hour" before the Supreme Court of Texas, he cited Section 6, in which was provided the basis for handling complaints of the railroads in the courts, as delusive

[2] Clark's speech at Weatherford, February 27, 1892. Quoted in Dallas *Morning News*, February 28, 1892; Austin *Evening News*, February 29, 1892.

[3] *Ibid.* The railroad-dominated Denison *Herald* declared: "Yes, Texas wants more railroads, less commission, more George Clarks and less Jim Hoggs." Quoted in Austin *Evening News,* March 4, 1892.

and fraudulent, "ingeniously framed to cut the railroads off from their constitutional rights."[4]

Carefully avoiding mention of the legislators who helped frame the commission bill, Clark objected to the great power of appointment concentrated in the governor's hands:

What use has the governor made of the Commission? Why, his very first step in the organization was to pervert it for the benefit of himself and his friends. Who thought of Horace Chilton as United States senator before the appointment by Gov. Hogg? . . . By some hocus pocus not yet intelligible to observant minds a distinguished citizen [Reagan] of the state who had been honored with this high and dignified office, stepped down and out and took a much humbler position and the governor appointed his friend even before the vacancy had actually occurred in law and before the people of Texas were aware that a vacancy existed.

After taking exception to Hogg's insistence that the Commission was an issue of campaign, Clark concluded:

I may be an old fogey, but this I can not help, for I still believe with the old fathers, notwithstanding the opposite tendency of the times, that the best government for the interest of the people is the least government.[5]

Within the next few days, the Austin *Evening News,* Dallas *Morning News,* Waco *Day,* and San Antonio *Express* had lined up on the Clark side, and all of them featured former Governor Ross's announcement, from his presidential office at the Agricultural and Mechanical College, that he would heartily support his Waco neighbor. Former Governor Richard Hubbard of Tyler, who was close to President Cleveland and Eastern financial interests, also announced for Clark. However, the gathering "Klark Klan," as the *Texas Farmer* later described them,[6] was greatly surprised at the failure of the Houston *Post,* which was closely affiliated with the Southern Pacific, to support the "railroad lawyer." The *Post* made it clear that it believed Texas should be "turned loose" from the "calamity howlers" (its name for the Clark forces), who, if this first sample of the Clark campaign tactics was a criterion, would surely hurt Texas credit and capital investment more than Hogg was doing. The editor hoped that another Democrat would enter the race who could pull the warring factions together and give Texas peace— in the midst of the Populist storm it was not political wisdom to widen

[4] A suit was being prepared, when Clark spoke, to test the Act.
[5] Clark's Weatherford speech.
[6] *Texas Farmer* (Dallas), August 27, 1892.

the breach in the Party—and bluntly declared that Clark could not be elected.[7] A few days later the Democratic mayor of Galveston, Roger L. Fulton, voiced the same conclusion. The reasons for the *Post's* distaste for Clark probably included his closeness to Jay Gould, which could have been a source of uneasiness to C. P. Huntington and his agents. In 1892 the *Post* was closely related to Southern Pacific interests.

The split over leadership in the Texas Republican Party also began to loom large at this time. On March 8, less than a week before the special session was due to convene, the Republicans gathered in Austin for a showdown fight. The "Black-and-Tan" element attending far outnumbered the leadership of the white faction, an indication that many white Republicans had become Democrats or now considered the fight within the party hopeless and had given up.[8] While most of the delegates selected to attend the Republican National Convention were white men, including Webster Flanagan and Austin Postmaster Jacob C. DeGress, there was no doubt that the Collector of Customs at Galveston, Wright Cuney, still held the strings of federal patronage and had the Austin meeting tightly in his grasp. When he spoke the atmosphere in the meeting room reflected his every mood, and when the votes were taken his majorities rolled in. When disgruntled white men accused Cuney, De-Gress, chairman of the Republican State Executive Committee, and J. B. Rector, former chairman, of running the Party for patronage and not for the good of Texas, adding that they were driving the better element out of the Party, Cuney gave them a tongue-lashing and once more the Negro vote overwhelmed them. A platform was adopted that endorsed President Harrison for renomination and expressed appreciation for his interest in a deepwater harbor on the Texas Gulf Coast and in reciprocal trade relations with Central and South America. A number of the followers of Sam Houston's son, Andrew Jackson Houston, then held a caucus and discussed plans for independent action.[9]

When the Republican Leagues met at Dallas on April 12 the followers of Houston and a number of other dissatisfied white men con-

[7] Houston *Post*, February 28; March 1, 1892. For "Turn Texas Loose" cartoon and poem see Grady S. St. Clair, "The Hogg-Clark Campaign," Master's thesis (University of Texas, 1927), p. 104.

[8] Dallas *Morning News*, February 28, 1892; J. S. Hogg to N. W. Finley, March 5, 1892, J. S. Hogg Let. Pr., 9, pp. 567–568. Cf. Seth S. McKay, *Texas Politics, 1906–1944* (Lubbock, Texas Tech Press, 1952), pp. 9–20. See also Maude Cuney Hare, *Norris Wright Cuney*, pp. 92 ff., for beginnings of the "Lily White" movement in Fort Bend and Wharton counties.

[9] Austin *Daily Statesman*, March 9–11, 1892; Ernest Winkler, *Platforms*, pp. 301–302; Hare, *Cuney*, pp. 144–150.

stituted themselves into a Republican State Convention, the first held in Texas without a single colored delegate. The "Lily-Whites," as Cuney contemptuously referred to them, nominated a separate state ticket with Houston for governor. An address was issued to Republicans throughout the state, giving the reasons for the white party and maintaining that the leaders "were free of all hope of political reward." The Cuney crowd at Austin was termed "an unorganized mob," and support was asked for the new departure, which was aimed at rebuilding Republicanism in Texas and giving the Party a basis of "intelligence and respectability." The new splinter party agreed to support 1) the protective tariff, 2) the development of home industries, and 3) efforts to obtain "fair international reciprocity" in world markets for farm products. The current effort in Congress to revive a federal election bill was declared unnecessary and impolitic, and the hope was expressed that the proposal would be dropped. This numerically small group of Republicans chose to be called "Reform Republicans," in contrast to Cuney's "Regulars."[10]

Cuney kept national headquarters informed of developments, and the Harrison administration continued to dispense patronage through him. Flanagan, who had been defeated by Hogg in 1890, agreed with Cuney that the "Regular" Republicans should await developments, possibly not run a candidate for governor, and not call a convention until after the Democrats had selected their nominee.

Cuney was engaged in a political maneuver which would entitle him to be ranked among the greatest political leaders in Texas.[11] The Republicans could not win an election alone, but they might ally with the Populists or with the Clark Democrats in an attempt to defeat Hogg. The Populists apparently made no overtures, counting upon the Negro Alliances to get out the Negro Populist vote.[12] Therefore Cuney, who in any case opposed the subtreasury and government ownership schemes of the Populists, boldly made a bid for an alliance with the Clark forces and encouraged them to plan on a bolt.

When the special session got down to business on March 14, all eyes were turned toward Austin and every bill was evaluated in terms of its worth in the political campaign ahead. The Governor's proclamation calling the session had listed sixteen topics to be considered within the

---

[10] Winkler, *op. cit.*, pp. 302–305; Hare, *Cuney*, pp. 150–153.

[11] See Maude Cuney Hare, *Cuney*, pp. 154–155, for Edwin Markham's statement that Cuney's work as head of the Republican Party in Texas was part of the great experiment of self-government.

[12] Roscoe Martin, *The People's Party in Texas*, p. 95.

thirty-day period. Of these there were two which his enemies hoped would cause him embarrassment:

8. To receive and act on the report of the committee appointed to investigate the case of Jay Gould v. the International and Great Northern Railroad, under a concurrent resolution passed at the general session by the Twenty-second Legislature. . . .

15. To elect a United States Senator.[13]

The Governor's message on March 14 began by complimenting the legislators on the important work accomplished at the first session and listing the outstanding laws passed. Then in summary he said:

As a whole, your labors have proved vastly beneficial, and will continue to grow in importance and material advantage to the public as long as free institutions last. . . . Except for the financial stringency, beginning in Europe year before last and recoiling on all the States of this Union last and this year, caused by reckless speculation, departure from conservative methods of business, and the maintenance of laws by foreign countries and by the Federal government discriminating in favor of special interests against the welfare of the masses everywhere, added to the low price of cotton prevailing in all the Southern States, Texas would to-day be enjoying an era of prosperity never before experienced by her people.[14]

He then discussed twenty subjects to be considered by the special session, among which were reapportionment, allocation of the Permanent School Fund, "an enforceable" local option law, a corporate bond and stock law, a livestock quarantine, strengthening of the antitrust law, provision to receive the refund on the federal direct tax of 1861, a mechanic's lien law, reconsideration of the uniform textbook bill (the enacting clause had been omitted), re-enactment of alien land legislation, action on perpetuities and land corporations, and payment of maturing bonds issued in 1871.

Hogg was well aware when he called the special session that Topic 15 in his Proclamation, "To elect a United States Senator," would provoke

[13] "Proclamation of February 18, 1892, Convening the Twenty-second Legislature in Extra Session," Texas *House Journal, Extra Session,* (1892), pp. 1–2. Robert Cotner (ed.), *Addresses of James Hogg,* pp. 158, 184. Attention was given to getting the Governor's message to the country newspapers via the plate method, using the American Press Association at Dallas. John W. Spivey to Wheeler and Rhodes (Galveston), March 10, 1892, J. S. Hogg Let. Pr., 9, p. 603.

[14] Texas *House Journal* (1892), p. 17; Cotner (ed.), *op. cit.,* p. 160. At this time Hogg was forced to depend upon friends to answer Clark. For A. W. Terrell's speech at Georgetown, March 19, and results, see Chamberlain, "Alexander Watkins Terrell," pp. 354 ff.; Austin *Statesman,* March 20, 1892.

a battle which he would probably lose. The opposition to his 1891 appointment of Horace Chilton to replace Reagan in the Senate had increased rather than abated. Chilton had been seated and had made a good first impression upon his congressional colleagues by a speech on tariff policies, but since then nothing spectacular had occurred that would give him an opportunity to display his ability.

The Clark faction and the Dallas *News* made the most of the situation that had complicated the issue in regard to Chilton. After the Democratic victories of 1890, Texans had expected that Congressman Roger Q. Mills, because of his efforts in behalf of tariff reduction, would be elected Speaker of the House (where he had represented Texas since 1873), but he was defeated by Charles F. Crisp of Georgia. Riding the wave of sympathy for Mills, the Clarkites attempted to turn the masses against Hogg by saying that he should have elevated Mills to the Senate in the spring of 1891, thus saving Mills from the humiliation he was to face later: Crisp had not even done Mills the honor of returning him to the chairmanship of the Ways and Means Committee, where he could carry on the tariff fight.[15] The Clarkites failed to indicate that Hogg was in no way responsible for this turn of events.

A mass meeting had been held at Waco on January 16, 1892, for the purpose of instructing local members of the Texas legislature to support Mills. Not unexpectedly George Clark presented the resolutions and spoke in high praise of Mills. Fiery Representative Gerald bluntly declared that if he were instructed to vote for Chilton he would resign his seat. The meeting was given wide publicity. The Galveston *News* correspondent added interest to his report of it by telling that he had interviewed over fifty farmers, "nine out of ten" of whom said that they had voted for Hogg in 1890 but now were "all strongly for Mills and against Hogg." Several days later the Dallas *News* ran a tabulation of how al-

---

[15] Austin *Daily News,* December 10, 1891, reported the defeat of "anti–free-silver Mills" and the Dallas City Council resolving for Mills for the Senate. The chairmanship of the Ways and Means Committee went to William M. Springer of Illinois, whose son in Dallas aided the Anti-Chilton campaign by joining the "Mills-for-Senate" group. See Woodward, *Tom Watson,* pp. 186–193; Myrtle Roberts, "Roger Quarles Mills," Master's thesis (the University of Texas, 1928), pp. 91–101; Hamlin Garland, "The Alliance Wedge in Congress," *Arena,* XXVIII (March, 1892), 447–457. Ida M. Tarbell, *The Tariff in Our Time* (New York, Macmillan Company, 1911), p. 211, gives an interesting sidelight on Mills' relations with Speaker Crisp. The Alliance *National Economist,* April 2, 1892, pp. 31–38, accused Clark of doing work for Wall Street and not really wanting the governorship. Dallas *Morning News,* May 15, 1892, reviewed the first chapter of Mills' projected book on protection and plutocracy.

most every man in the legislature would vote on Dave Culberson, Chilton, and Mills, making clear that Mills was the choice of the majority. An attending comment intimated that Hogg might put pressure on the legislator to select Chilton.[16]

As the special session progressed through its first week the newspaper battle went on. Eloquent tributes to Mills appeared, usually including a chastisement of Hogg, the "power conscious boss in Austin," who wished "to humiliate Mills further by forcing Chilton on the legislature the way he had [forced] the Commission." In the midst of the clamor there was one striking indication of Chilton's abilities. Colonel William Greene Sterett, correspondent for the Dallas *News* and one of the ablest journalists Texas has ever sent to Washington, chose to risk the wrath of his paper's known opposition to Hogg by writing:

There was a great cry in Texas that Chilton had been selected because he was a personal friend of the governor, and this cry had sufficient volume to reach the outside. It was said on the other side that the governor of Texas did not make this appointment entirely because of his friendship for Chilton, but that the appointment came first from the worth of the appointee, which is not denied by his enemies, and from the fact that an entirely new element in the State—the young men—were in the saddle and intended to take charge of the affairs of that commonwealth for a while. It is the habit of men to conceal all that they know that is good of those whom they oppose, and exaggerate the virtues of those whom they politically favor. It is fair to Senator Chilton to state that he has made a most favorable impression since he has been here, not only on the public, but on his associates. He has not been obtrusive, for that is not his nature, but when occasion has arisen for him to express himself in the senate, he has done it in such a manly and clear way as to provoke the warmest praise. I am aware that this may not be palatable to many who oppose him, now that the campaign is on in Texas, but it is the truth that he has made a most enviable record for himself, as a strong man in intellect, a wise man in speech, an honest man in his opinions, and a gentleman in his deportment.[17]

The senatorial election was set for a week after the opening of the Texas legislative session. Congressman Dave Culberson was the first to

[16] Dallas *Morning News*, January 17, 1892; the voting tabulation was reprinted in the Austin *Daily Statesman*, March 15–21, 1892. It was standard practice to "sample opinion" in the days before the "scientific polls." It was a human failing, however, to sometimes omit the opinions of those not coinciding with the political bias of the journals they represented.

[17] Dallas *Morning News*, January 24, 1892; Ted Dealey, *Colonel Bill* [William Sterett] (Dallas, Dallas *News*, 1939), p. 26. For a caustic article on Chilton and the "Tyler Gang" see Austin *Evening News*, editorial, April 4, 1892.

withdraw from the contest. Then, on the morning the vote would be taken, Senator John Kearby reported that Horace Chilton did not wish his name presented.[18] Chilton, understanding the great issues that would be at stake in the November election of 1892, had decided not to risk giving aid and comfort to Clark's reactionary forces by prolonging the present contest. Chilton's abnegation proved more than helpful to his friend Jim Hogg; from the moment Mills was chosen senator, the forces of reform rallied and drew closer to the Governor.

George Clark continued his speaking tour, apparently expecting the state senators to block more of the Hogg program than they were able to do. However, he did find satisfaction in the failure of various proposals, including 1) the municipal and railroad stock and bond bills, 2) the amendment to the antitrust law, 3) the textbook law, and 4) the Governor's special plea for a law defining perpetuities and ending corporate land ownership. Clark spent considerable time belittling Hogg's knowledge of business, thus making himself more popular in the several cities whose charters Hogg had vetoed,[19] and encouraging the image many city dwellers had of Jim Hogg as a rustic from the "Piney Woods" of East Texas.

At the time the legislature was considering the majority report on the International and Great Northern investigation, which upheld the Governor despite Clark's efforts to turn it against him,[20] another able Democrat entered the gubernatorial race—Roger L. Fulton, who had been Mayor of Galveston since his election in 1877, when he had defeated Wright Cuney and at the same time learned to recognize his abilities. Fulton said that "other things being equal he would have voted for Hogg for a second term according to custom," but, on the other hand, he did not think there was an abler man than George Clark. He quoted Hogg as saying that Clark was a smart man, "yes, too smart." Fulton,

---

[18] Texas *Senate Journal, Extra Session* (1892), pp. 44–53; Texas *House Journal, Extra Session* (1892), pp. 61–63, 94; Austin *Daily Statesman*, March 22, 1892. The *National Economist*, March 19, 1892, declared Texas farmers would not swallow Mills and Clark.

[19] Texas *House Journal* (1891), pp. 633, 767; Gammel, *Laws of Texas*, X, 229 ff.; W. H. Bailey, editor, Houston *Daily Herald*, to Hogg, April 3, 1891, J. S. Hogg Let. Rec., X, 11–12.

[20] Joint Committee of the Texas Legislature, *The I.&G.N. Inquiry*, II, 119 ff.; Hogg to Colonel Thos. B. Greenwood, March 26, 1892, J. S. Hogg Let. Pr., 10, p. 31. Hogg was concerned over the effects of Clark's speeches during the session; he asked Jot Gunter to confer and invited Thomas Franklin of San Antonio to go east along the I.& G.N. route and meet Clark in debate. Hogg to Franklin, March 21, 1892.

rejecting his opponents' estimates of each other, believed both were men of ability and integrity, who represented different philosophies of government. He regretted that their friends would carry on a campaign of vilification, making conservative expression next to impossible; "win or crush" seemed to be their tactics, and the resulting publicity would hurt Texas. Change, he argued, should not be brought about by the "wild war whoop of 'Turn Texas Loose' " or by those who wished to "tie up the 'calamity howlers.' " Fulton urged a more rational approach: "Give Texas a rest. Let us have peace."[21]

Hogg's most serious charge against Clark was substantiated by Fulton's statement that Clark was known as the representative of the railroad interests and as preferring no railroad commission at all. However, Fulton also complained that Hogg stuck stubbornly to the appointive commission, when "two-thirds" of the Democrats wanted an elective commission. As for Clark, Fulton thought he would "regret not considering more maturely" Fulton's advice not to run, given on the basis that the railroad attorney was not the "most popular candidate" who could have been selected to oppose Hogg.

Throughout the month of the session the Governor and the legislature worked diligently, but not always in agreement. Arrangements were made to receive from the United States the direct tax money which had been collected under the act of 1861; redistricting was accomplished; a mechanic's lien law was passed; and arrangements were made to pay off the state's bonded debt contracted in 1871. The alien land law was re-enacted, but the stock and bond bill was defeated. Especially gratifying to Hogg was the way the House answered when the Senate passed a resolution favoring an elective commission; the House fired it back, stating that the Senate was out of order in bringing up a subject not covered in the Governor's call.[22]

On the whole, Hogg could take at least some satisfaction in the accomplishments of the session. It was probable, too, that the defeat of some of the administration's programs would insure re-election of those legislators who had been pledged to the reform program by their constituents in 1890. The pro-Hogg papers had not let their readers forget who of the opposition had been responsible for the failure of various measures.

Of all the pro-Hogg papers, the *Texas Farmer* (whose editor had re-

[21] Houston *Post*, March 22, 1892; Galveston *Daily News*, June 29, 1896.
[22] Texas *House Journal, Extra Session* (1892), pp. 262–263. Dan McCunningham introduced the House substitute.

joined the Hogg camp) carried the sharpest sting. The conservative Grangers who made up the bulk of its subscribers were frequently the most intelligent and progressive men in their respective farm communities. The Grangers' able Worthy Master A. J. Rose of Salado was a staunch champion of the Governor and had tried to line up support for Chilton.[23] When illness dictated that Rose give up his high office, John B. Long of Rusk, for many years a friend of the Hogg family, became Worthy Master. Long and Rose and Granger Secretary Buchanan worked throughout the campaign to get out the vote for Hogg; in return the Hogg forces aided Long in his successful race for a seat in Congress. This phase of the 1892 campaign has usually been overlooked, but there can be no doubt of the importance of active "old Grangers" in checking the inroads of the Alliance-Populists.[24]

On April 21, San Jacinto Day, Hogg made his opening campaign speech at Wills Point in Van Zandt County, the county that had done so much to speed him on a successful political career by its votes that assured his election in 1880 as district attorney. Over 5,000 people assembled to hear him. He knew hundreds of them by name, and as he came to the platform that cool pleasant morning in the great grove south of the T. & P. railroad tracks, he knew he was among friends. Men and women from every walk of life were there, representing nearly every county of East Texas. A great variety of banners and campaign decorations floated in the air or waved from hats and coat lapels, some of the legends a little crude in their humor but all attesting a confidence in Jim Hogg and cordiality toward him. Several volunteer bands, some in uniform and some not, vied with each other in stimulating the bubbling

[23] Chilton thanked him by letter, April 6, 1892, A. J. Rose Papers, Fol. XI. Archibald J. Rose, *Annual Address to the Texas State Grange*, McGregor, Texas, August 13, 1889 (Galveston, Clark and Courts, 1889), p. 11, defined a Granger's place in politics.

[24] John B. Long to A. J. Rose, November 28, 1892, A. J. Rose Papers, Fol. XI. See R. B. Long to Hogg, April 27, 1891, J. S. Hogg Let. Rec., X, 242. Roscoe C. Martin, "The Grange as a Political Factor in Texas," *Southwestern Political and Science Quarterly*, VI (March, 1926), 376, 382–383, credits the Grange with influencing legislation 1872–1892, but seems to judge effectiveness primarily in terms of the number of organized Granges, and implies that it had little effect in the election of 1892. This appears to overlook the influence of the Grange educational programs for twenty years and activities of such men as Lieutenant Governor Pendleton, Long, Rose, and "Farmer" Shaw. See also printed "Minutes of Annual Meeting of Board of Directors of Texas Cooperative Association, July 26, 1892," bound with other annual minutes as *The Texas Cooperative Association 1880–1895*, pp. 39–40, A. J. Rose Papers.

enthusiasm of the crowd.[25] All of this was deeply gratifying to the Governor, who, though by nature seldom a prey to discouragement, had sometimes in the past year wondered if the people were as unhappy with his administration as most of the city papers, the Alliance leaders, and George Clark had claimed they were.

The huge audience listened intently for nearly three hours. After a careful review of his work as attorney general, Hogg went into the details of his record of the past fifteen months as governor, particularly examining the complaints and charges of the opposition. Then he pledged support for five major policies which he believed necessary to round out the reform program:

1. I shall obey the Constitution, adhere to carrying out the instructions of the people expressed through their platform, and see that the laws are faithfully executed.

2. I shall stand by and support the Commission as it now stands.

3. I shall favor a law that will restrict and effectually prohibit the issuance of watered stocks and bonds by railroad companies.

4. I shall favor a law that will prevent the useless and extravagant issuance of bonds by cities, towns, and counties in this State, restricting them within constitutional limitations to actual public necessities.

5. I shall favor a law that will define perpetuities, and prohibit the further operation of land corporations in the State, requiring those now holding title to or possession of lands to dispose of the same within such reasonable time as may not impair vested rights.[26]

He explained carefully why he believed that, for the public good, corporations must be authorized by the state government. Making a play

[25] Personal interview in 1947 with Dr. James Noble of Mineola, who played in one of the bands; Fort Worth *Gazette,* April 22, 1892; Dallas *Morning News,* April 22, 1892; Cotner (ed.), *Addresses of James Hogg,* pp. 186–187. By now the *Gazette* was no longer a Hogg paper, but followed the advice of the St. Louis *Republic* to pick a western man—Congressman Samuel W. T. Lanham of Weatherford, representing ninety-eight western counties of the "Jumbo" District. He did not campaign.

[26] For his elaboration of these points see Cotner, *op. cit.,* pp. 222–232. Hogg to Sawnie Robertson, February 10, 1892, Let. Pr., 9, pp. 347–354, declared that if the extra session did not give him the stock and bond law, he would make it an issue on the campaign. He told Robertson he would "gracefully yield" on the appointive commission if people "in their sovereign capacity" wanted the elective plan. Hogg constantly sought new information. A letter to the editor of the *Iowa State Register* (Des Moines) expressed desire for a copy of Governor Campbell's speech relative to railroad bond issues, J. S. Hogg Let. Pr., 9, p. 654, dated March 7, 1892; Texas *House Journal, Extra Session* (1892), pp. 123, 280–281.

BOOMS.

No. 1.—Clark's boom as he blew it up at Weatherford.

No. 2.—Condition of the boom when Clark's friends called him in to repair damages by the Waco convention.

The Clark Boom. Texas Farmer, May 7, 1892.

on Clark's campaign slogan, he declared that they could not be "turned loose" from the law because what they wanted was "freedom, not law; monopoly, not regulation:"

In efforts to overthrow the people's will, corporate agents and newspapers have gone beyond the limits of the State and misrepresented and wilfully maligned the honor and integrity of the masses, calling Texans repudiators, anarchists! It is confidently trusted that at no time may the intelligence, stability or patriotism of the people be shaken or swayed by such unholy methods. . . . Texas is capable and will manage her own affairs, with justice to her own citizens and fairness and liberality towards persons of other countries, in the full assurance that time will correct wrong impressions, allay ill feelings, and demonstrate to the world that the interest of the masses is consistent with universal prosperity, only to be destroyed when sound principles of government are subverted or changed to gratify the avarice and whims of despoilers of private rights and enemies to public justice.[27]

In conclusion, he expressed his faith in the voters to give "freedom to the masses now and forever from corporate power. The people will rule Texas. Enforce the law."

George Clark, after his many speeches in North Texas in March, had been busy throughout the state during April. Now the two chief Democratic contenders agreed to urgings that they meet in joint debate at the towns of Cameron and Cleburne, in the heart of the central blackland country. Each man had devoted followers in the region, and on May 3 a great crowd gathered at Cameron, coming by train and wagon, or on horseback. Clark's Waco friends attended in large numbers, arriving with Clark on the morning train. When Hogg called upon the older man at his hotel, it was agreed that Clark would speak first and for an hour, and have a concluding rebuttal.

As the two men mounted the platform, the contrast in their size reminded many of the Lincoln-Douglas debates. Clark, while not as stocky as Douglas, was a short man and had often been called the "Little Giant." Hogg's avoirdupois was a far cry from the lean, lank figure of Lincoln, but his six feet three inches of height gave him a towering

[27] Cotner, *op. cit.*, pp. 231–232. Hogg discussed rapid rate changes decreed from St. Louis, Chicago, or New York. For a discussion of "reasonable rates" and figures on earnings see Reed, *Texas Railroads*, pp. 608–640; Theodore Fetter, *Southwestern Freight Rates*, pp. 47–75. The Texas Railroad Commission, *Annual Report, 1894* (Austin, 1895), p. 4, discusses return to common point system. Cotner (ed.), *op. cit.*, pp. 276, 285–289 (speech at Dallas, October 1, 1892); Overton, *Gulf to Rockies*, pp. 285–294.

spacial advantage over his opponent.[28] Clark opened the debate with the charge that Hogg was "the representative of a government of centralism at the capital." To support his contention, he cited Hogg's championship of an appointive commission and his interference with local self-government through his vetoes of city charters.

Most of Clark's hour was spent discussing Hogg's cases while he was attorney general. He said that the law of 1891 that had permitted the incorporation of the M. K. & T. of Texas was evidence that Hogg favored all and any railroad consolidations. He predicted that the state would not recover the 1,254,000 acres under the precedent of the "sidings and switches" suit, as Hogg claimed. (Time would prove Clark wrong.) Pointing out that the Governor had advocated lending the Permanent School Fund to railroads and opposed lending them direct to farmers on land securities, Clark asserted that he himself was for lending the school funds to farmers and for increasing the circulating medium beyond the Alliance demand for fifty dollars per capita. Because the suits brought by Hogg were "unsettling land titles," Clark declared he would not have brought such suits. Finally, he was convinced that the policies of the administration had done much to make the depression worse and to prevent capital from coming to Texas.

Clark was a thoroughly polished and knowing speaker, but, since his voice was not too well adapted to large crowds and outdoor speaking, the audience missed some of his words. However, the applause indicated that his friends were still convinced that he had the sharpest mind in Texas, a judgment with which Jim Hogg might have somewhat wryly agreed.

Thomas S. Henderson of Cameron, a fine orator and a man who wholeheartedly enjoyed political battles, then introduced the Governor, whereupon Hogg's friends responded as if they intended to down the memory of any and all past demonstrations. When Hogg could finally be heard he expressed his appreciation for the applause—"as evidence of your indorsement of me"—suggesting, however, that his supporters should not allow themselves to "become excited" but, rather, conserve

---

[28] Buckley B. Paddock, the Mayor of Fort Worth, builder of a railroad, and president of the Chamber of Commerce—and the man who helped turn the *Gazette* into a pro-Clark paper—said of the Cameron debaters: "The contrast in the physique of the two rivals was an amazing incident of the campaign, Judge Clark being only half the size of his competitor, but his superior as a scholar and as a polished speaker." Dallas *Morning News,* May 4, 1892. The Austin *Evening News,* May 4, 1892, declared Clark commanded confidence abroad and at home and would end "the war" on outside capital.

A VERY LITTLE GIANT
ON A VERY RICKETY PLATFORM.

GOULD TOUCHES THE BUTTON, GEORGIE TRIES HARD TO DO THE REST.

Texas Farmer, *October 22, 1892*

their energies for the contest ahead. "Don't fall into any passion or permit your reason to be obscured, because when men lose their reason it is time for patriots to think." Then, moving into the debate, he said:

The question is, what is the issue? What is it, Judge Clark? I haven't heard you say. [Applause] I have listened patiently to the eloquent gentleman, and the question remains unanswered. What plank is he running on? What issue is it he wants to be elected on? [Cries—That's right] Is he running on my record as Attorney General? [Applause] Judge Clark takes up and devotes the first hour to a discussion of the cases brought by me during the four years I was Attorney General. Does he discuss any other question except the investment of the school fund? . . . Now after discussing these cases did he make you any promises of what he would do if he was elected Governor? [Cries—No, No] We will part company right here. I propose to call your attention to some few things that I propose to do if I am elected your Governor.[29]

At that point a voice called out, "You never will be, though." Hogg whipped back, "You wait till I get through and see." Amid mounting confusion created by partisans of each side, Hogg said he would tell "a different tale" from the one Clark had told about the railroad cases, as "he has run along touching only some of the high places. I am not going to abuse anybody. I have no malice in me at all."

A young man perched in a tree roared "Hurrah for Clark!" to which Hogg responded firmly: "Young man, keep quiet. I shall extend to this audience all the politeness due to ladies and gentlemen. I presume you are honest and fair people and I did not expect to deal with badgers."

These remarks brought more applause, and then for a time the crowd was more orderly, friends and enemies alike responding to the commanding poise in Jim Hogg that was virtually his trademark. A friend recalling in later years her memories of the Governor remarked, "He was not afraid of anything. . . . Sometimes tall, big men have nothing to back up their size with. But Governor Hogg had a commanding presence and plenty of intellect and character with it."[30]

When Hogg mentioned that George Clark had been the attorney general when the certificates were issued to railroads for lands for sidings as well as for the main tracks, Clark arose to say that he had issued them, not under the act of 1876, but under an act of 1854, "which authorized them." Hogg resumed, "The act of 1854 did not authorize a grant of lands for sidings. The road was not entitled to sixteen sections until it

[29] Cotner, *op. cit.*, p. 233.
[30] Typescript of interview with Mrs. E. C. Dickinson, June 3, 1935, Interv. Fol.

had built the necessary turn-outs. . . . Are the people prepared to put a man in the Governor's office who thus let people unlawfully hold lands?" He reminded the crowd that the men who had fought the Commission were the ones now fighting the proposed school fund investment plan.

Turning toward Clark, Hogg asked him if he had voted for the constitutional amendment providing for the Commission. When Clark answered "No," there was applause and the confusion mounted again. Hogg stayed on the offensive: "Why, he says he is a Democrat and the Democratic platform declared for the Commission amendment. He said he voted against it. [Applause] He violated the Democratic platform. You know he hated it."[31]

As the end of his stipulated hour drew near, the Governor promised that he would stand by his record and the Democratic platform, and once more urged his listeners to maintain their voting rights. The applause as he finished resounded throughout the grove for a long time. When finally the audience seemed to have worn itself out, the Little Giant stepped forward for his rebuttal. At once the triumphant Hogg adherents chose to renew the confusion; in vain, Clark appealed for a hearing. It was not until Jim Hogg, broadly smiling, raised his big hand that the bedlam began to fade enough for even the Governor's far-carrying voice to be heard as he asked them to be quiet and listen to Judge Clark's concluding words. After a final "Hurrah for Hogg!" they gave attention. But something seemed to have happened to Clark during the verbal battle; according to Thomas Henderson, "he labored hard to cover his retreat."[32]

On the following day the debaters met again, at Cleburne. Amidst the early shouting and stamping of feet a part of the grandstand fell down, injuring a few people. Governor Hogg's presence of mind and strong voice helped greatly to restore order and calm, and then he went ahead with his address. Thomas Henderson's account of the result of the two contests undoubtedly represents a degree of hindsight:

The battle was decisive. Up to this time Hogg was comparatively new to Texas public life. Democracy had looked to the grim old veterans who had won their spurs following the white plume of Lee on the bloody fields of Virginia and who bore the scars of the great struggle they waged to drive the carpetbaggers from the State. Governor Hogg had a splendid record, but it was a young man's record. His followers were much like the Israelites

[31] Cotner, *op. cit.*, pp. 236–239.
[32] Statement by Thomas S. Henderson, of Cameron.

HOW WE ARE RIDDEN.

A sell-out press rides the people.
Clark rides a sell-out press and the people.
The whole business is straddled by Gould and "sich."

Texas Farmer, *May 7, 1892*

at the Valley of Elah, when David went forth as their champion to meet the giant; they hoped for him, but they feared for him. When he struck a mighty blow and they heard the giant's armor rattle, they raised a shout of victory. A new leader had come and from that hour Jim Hogg rode the Texas sky in unrivaled splendor. . . . They [Hogg and Clark] met the next day in debate at Cleburne. The meeting was merely perfunctory, for the debate had ended and the verdict had been given at Cameron. A new day had dawned for Democracy. . . . New issues had arisen and a new leader had been found.[33]

The contestants continued their separate campaigns, each fully recognizing the abilities and purpose of the other. Long after the contests at Cameron and Cleburne, Clark wrote: "Hogg had the power of dominating his followers that I had never seen excelled in any public man, and his influence was dominant and controlling in every measure."[34] This was praise enough from George Clark.

Meanwhile the Populists, with considerable dexterity, were holding out promises to several segments of society. Following the People's Party Convention at Dallas in June, the Democratic and Grange papers chided the leaders for "a lack of steadfastness in the cause of the doctrine of Populism."[35] The Convention's statement of principles was a skillful catch-all, demonstrating among other things that the Texas Populists were less radical in June, 1892, than they had been in August, 1891. Instead of pressing their earlier suggestion of a Gulf to Red River

[33] *Ibid.*

[34] George Clark, *A Glance Backward* (Houston, Rein and Sons, c. 1915), p. 88. For the debate at Cleburne see Waco *Daily News,* May 5, 1892; Dallas *Morning News,* May 5, 1892; Austin *Evening News,* May 5, 1892. The last two blamed Hogg followers for the "disgraceful scenes." "It was the first outbreak of the kind ever witnessed in Texas, being the result of an appeal to ignorance, and prejudice." "Anarchy, even if led by Mr. Hogg, cannot, must not, prevail in this State. Texans to your posts. Remember the Alamo! Remember Goliad!" No credit was given the Governor for helping to keep order when a portion of the grandstand fell down just as he arose to speak.

[35] For replies see *National Economist,* September 17, 1892, quoting *The Truth* (San Antonio) and items on Senators Coke and Mills. The Houston *Post* was so alarmed at the potential Populist victory due to the divided ranks of the Democracy that the paper called upon Clark and Hogg to withdraw. Quoted in editorial, Austin *Evening News,* June 1, 1892. Carl C. Taylor, *The Farmer's Movement, 1620–1920,* pp. 28 ff., p. 287, n. 14; C. Vann Woodward, *Origins of the New South,* pp. 252 ff.; *Southern Mercury,* VIII (April 23, 1892), 88–89; *ibid.,* VIII (Sept. 17, 1892), 4; Albert D. Kirwan, *Revolt of the Rednecks: Mississippi Politics, 1876–1925,* pp. 92–96, especially references to John Sharp Williams' correspondence with President-elect Cleveland, n. 5 and n. 13. See also, W. Scott Morgan, *History of the Wheel and Alliance and the Impending Revolution* (Hardy, Arkansas, Morgan, 1889), p. 774.

government-owned railroad that would be built with convict labor to create competitive rates and to serve as a "yardstick," they favored giving a trial to an elective commission, although they added: "We regard government ownership as the ultimate solution." Instead of free textbooks, the Populists proposed that the state publish the books and "furnish them to the children in the schools at cost." Like Hogg, they advocated an efficient mechanic's lien law, but also wanted it to protect "material men." Also like Hogg, they advocated an end of land corporations and no further grants to aliens. Reflecting the depression and the tax burden, they wished to limit county salaries to a maximum of two thousand dollars and demanded no county debts over five thousand dollars without popular consent. Labor's strong influence was shown in a plank for an eight-hour day and one calling for a board of arbitration to adjust all differences between corporations and employees. Another plank declared that national bankers and anyone connected with railroads or with telephone or telegraph companies, including their lawyers, could not be eligible for a legislative or judicial office for a period of two years after they had severed their business connections.[36]

It was proper that the People's Party should select its nominee for governor from the region of Texas that had produced the revolt. The man chosen had been a staunch supporter of Governor Hogg in 1890 and a former judge, a man of high integrity who had written and spoken about Alliance philosophy and demands, a man with a mission, Thomas Lewis Nugent of Erath and Tarrant counties. Nugent, born in Louisiana in 1841, was ten years older than Hogg. He had moved to Texas in 1862, the year after his graduation from Centenary College, and then volunteered as a private in the Confederate Army. After the war he taught school in Austin and began studying for the Methodist ministry, later changing to law. He was a delegate from Erath County to the Texas Constitutional Convention in 1875, and four years later Governor Roberts appointed him district judge, to which office he was twice re-elected. Ill health caused him to resign the judgeship in 1888, and he removed briefly to El Paso. In 1891 he opened a law office in Fort Worth.[37]

[36] To compare platforms see Winkler, *op. cit.*, pp. 293–297, 314–316. Of interest was Dohoney's plan to attempt a speed-up of prohibition by leaving all chartering and taxing of liquor interests to the states. This was tabled.

[37] Martin, *op. cit.*, pp. 114 ff. "Farmer" Shaw described Judge Nugent as "the slick lawyer nominee" who had told the People's Party Convention that "he favored the Railroad Commission as a temporary expedient only." Nugent was still working for government ownership. *Texas Farmer*, July 2, 1892. For his speech at the People's Party Convention see Dallas *Morning News*, June 24, 1892.

JOSEPH LEWIS HOGG

LUCANDA MCMATH HOGG

MARTHA FRANCES HOGG DAVIS   THOMAS E. HOGG

JOHN W. HOGG   JULIA HOGG McDUGALD FERGUSON

Jim and Sallie Hogg's First Home, Quitman, Texas

WILL HOGG

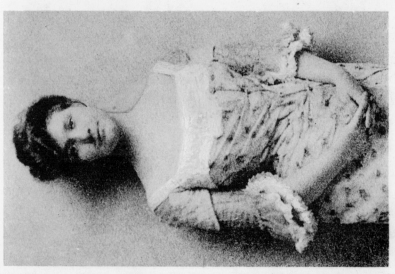

IMA HOGG

MIKE, IMA, *and* TOM

GEORGE W. CLARK

GUSTAVE COOK

THOMAS L. NUGENT

N. WRIGHT CUNEY

JAMES STEPHEN HOGG, 1893

JAMES S. HOGG, JOHN H. REAGAN, JOSEPH D. SAYERS, *and* THOMAS S. SMITH

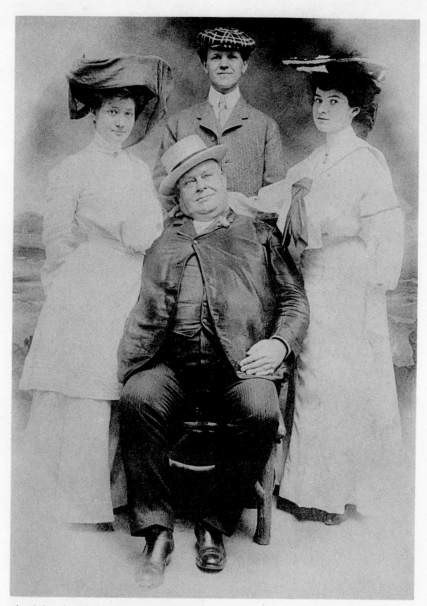

At Atlantic City: J. S. HOGG *with* IMA, BAYLESS LEE, *and* ROWENA LEE

JOHN NANCE GARNER

MARTIN M. CRANE

JOSEPH W. BAILEY

WILLIAM R. HAMBY

CHARLES A. CULBERSON

HORACE CHILTON

THOMAS M. CAMPBELL

SAWNIE ROBERTSON

West Columbia Oil Boom

LEROY G. DENMAN

JAMES H. ROBERTSON

RICHARD H. HARRISON

WALTER B. SHARP

WILL *and* MIKE *with* RAYMOND DICKSON

JAMES STEPHEN HOGG, *London, 1902*

Varner Plantation

Nugent was ever a student, delving into the classics. Of "meditative nature and sober mien," he continually sought an answer to man's problems in the Scriptures and in the philosophers of various eras, finally becoming a disciple of Emanuel Swedenborg. Political enemies charged that he was irreligious, but anyone who knew him could attest his kindly and pious nature, his Christlike practices.[38] Hogg might berate the principles of Populism, but not the man who led the party; always respecting Nugent's sincerity and frankness, Hogg never meted out to him the rough treatment sometimes accorded Clark and Cuney. Nugent had seen the suffering of his farm neighbors on the dry plains during the drought and depression.[39] His sympathy for the unfortunate and his long residence in Erath County, where the Alliance was strong and a spirit of independence in politics had wrested local control from the Democrats, were among the factors that turned him to Populism and the Populists to him. The Prohibitionists rallied to him as well as to Marion Martin,[40] who had been their leader in 1888 and who now accepted the second place on the Populist ticket.

Increasingly Democrats turned to State Senator Martin McNulty Crane of Cleburne as their choice to become lieutenant governor. He was popular with Alliance men and would help to stop the exodus from the Democratic to the Populist Party. His hard work for the commission law made him entirely acceptable to Hogg. The rapid growth of the Populists so alarmed the policy makers of the Houston *Post* that the editor called upon Hogg and Clark to withdraw in order that Democrats could concentrate on one man and avoid a shattered party. On June 1, 1892, the Austin *Evening News* quoted the request of the *Post* editorially. Mayor Fulton did withdraw, but neither Houston, Nugent, Clark, nor Hogg would give up the race.

One of Hogg's staunch supporters was "Farmer" Shaw of Dallas, whose paper carried the best pro-Hogg cartoons and the most biting sarcasm relative to Clark's inconsistencies. The farmers and those city folk who read the *Texas Farmer* were reminded week after week that

---

[38] Catharine Nugent, *The Life and Work of Thomas L. Nugent* (Stephenville, C. Nugent, 1896), pp. 57 ff., 297–316; Wayne Alvord, "T. L. Nugent, Texas Populist," *Southwestern Historical Quarterly*, LVII (July, 1953), 65–81. Alvord says there was little evidence "that Nugent was aware that elsewhere contemporaries were attempting to socialize Christianity."

[39] Walter P. Webb, *The Great Plains* (Boston, Ginn and Company, c. 1931), pp. vi, 507.

[40] Martin was from Navarro County, which the Populists carried in 1892. He had polled 98,477 votes in 1888.

Clark had opposed the commission amendment and the railroad commission law, even forming an alliance with Populist Harry Tracy in an effort to block Hogg's program in 1891. The issue of July 2, 1892, leveled one of its milder broadsides against Clark, making reference to his former role as a governor-maker:

HOW BIG IS WARWICK CLARK, PAPA?

Why he 'twas that fought commission,
And then to Austin went,
And with his own volition
A note to Tracy sent,
Asked him to come at once,
With "true" and "loyal" band,
To whip the legislature
On the "Appointive" plan.

During May, June, and July the Democratic precinct and county conventions were held according to the rules laid down by the county committees. Some of the Clark areas instructed early, and Clark had a majority of the instructed delegates until late in May, when the Hogg forces forged ahead.[41] Partisan rancor and bitterness increased. Even children wore campaign buttons, organized Hogg or Clark clubs, and frequently separated along partisan lines at school and at play. A story is told that a man who had business connections with a Gould railroad came home one afternoon to find his son astride a fence cheering a Hogg parade; the lad was promptly taken into the house and spanked.[42]

Minority groups in the precincts tended increasingly to set up bolting delegations during July, with rival county conventions resulting. Clark's lieutenants, realizing that they probably could not nominate Clark, began to aim at controlling a third of the delegates so as to block Hogg. There is no doubt that Hogg had considerable advantage in his control of the Party machinery, and, as the subsequent vote of the people would show, Clark was no match for him in popularity with the white masses. In the early summer, however, Clark was picking up some of both the

[41] *Texas Farmer* (Dallas), May 28 and June 4, 1892, issued a tabulation of the instructed county votes. By June 25 the count was estimated at 715 for Hogg and 230 for Clark. Secretary Spivey's count was more conservative, June 7 showing Hogg 162 and Clark 101; by June 25 he expected Hogg to have about 700 of the 950 votes. The Austin *Evening News*, May 23, 1892, declared Clark had 162 votes and Hogg 114.

[42] Personal interview with Dr. Seymour Connor, March 15, 1954.

German Republican and the anti-Prohibition vote in southern and western counties; Hogg's friends then busily passed the word that the Governor was part German and, though practicing temperance, was not a prohibitionist.[43]

On July 8 the Governor ended his campaign speeches with an appearance at Marlin, in the heart of the Clark country. The campaign so far, in an exceptionally hot summer, had been strenuous, and even Hogg, whose excellent health and well-meted energy usually seemed to be proof against all strains, needed a rest, not least because of the burden of sorrow he had carried since the death of his dear friend Sawnie Robertson on June 21. On a campaign tour Hogg allowed himself no quarter. He might be forced to endure long waits for trains to make connections. He might be seen sleeping in a station, or, if the weather was exceedingly hot, on a shaded loading platform. On returning to Austin he would acknowledge exhaustion briefly to his family. If the homecoming occurred on a weekend, he would usually stay in bed for part of an ensuing day; since he could direct his great power of concentration on rest, when it was needed, as strongly as he directed it otherwise on work, the short interval of relaxation would almost always bring immediate repair. In the 1890's the regular hours of work, even for a governor, extended from the beginning of daylight to dusk. Hogg was normally at his desk at the Capitol at a very early hour. He went home for the customary midday dinner, after which, no matter how pressing affairs might be, he would take a fifteen-minute rest. Sometimes during these rests, he would hold a closed pocket knife in his hand, so that if he dozed the falling of the knife hitting the floor would waken him. He had thoroughly relaxed and was ready to return to work during a busy afternoon and, frequently, evening.[44]

On July 12 Hogg indicated to a friend in San Marcos that "the outlook was all right" for controlling the Democratic convention in August (the trend seemed to be a two-thirds vote for Hogg) but that he did not

[43] The German-American Association Convention met at Houston on May 30, 1892. The chairman of the Committee on Resolutions was J. Schutze, who owned a famous Austin beer garden. In May, Houston and Harris County were flooded with a fictitious circular supposedly coming from the "State Prohibition Committee," Austin, dated May 16, 1892, saying Hogg should be supported as he would favor re-submission of the prohibition amendment: "Go to work for Hogg and prohibition, but let your work be secret and thorough [signed] State Evangelist." Hamby to Wheeler and Rhodes (Galveston) to Hogg May 23, 1892, J. S. Hogg Let. Pr., 10, pp. 395–396, warned it was a "premeditated falsehood."

[44] Ima Hogg, "Life in the Governor's Mansion, 1891–1895," typescript, H.C.

expect Clark and Cuney to give up—the opposition would continue to fight "until November."[45] General William R. Hamby, chairman of the Austin Hogg and Commission Club, was diligently running the campaign for the Governor, ably supported by E. M. House, who planned on a wider scale, while Horace Chilton worked hard in East Texas. Letters went out urging the presence of full delegations at the convention. Both the Clark and the Hogg forces planned to send to Houston every man they could muster. By the end of July the county meetings had spawned a great number of contesting delegations, and when a county was lost to one side, usually the Clark side, the losers attached themselves to other delegations where their friends had won.[46] The Houston Convention promised to be an exciting experience, unique in the annals of Texas politics.

Troubled over the effect the contesting delegations might have on the Party, and still saddened by the fact that Sawnie Robertson was no longer one of his political mentors, Hogg wrote on August 6 a very personal letter to Web Finley:

Since closing my campaign I have been feeling too sluggish and unwell to do more than helplessly struggle with the accumulated work on my groaning desk. Now the Convention is about at hand. I would like to see you here before it meets. If you cannot come down get Chilton, Marsh and our other friends to join you and meet me at Houston by the 14th. My two-thirds have been complete and safe for sometime, but we must preserve the party.[47]

The Democratic Convention was scheduled to convene in the huge "car stable" or "car shed" in Houston on Tuesday, August 16. Gover-

[45] J. S. Hogg to L. H. Brown, July 12, 1892, J. S. Hogg Let. Pr., 10, p. 603; Hogg to M. M. Crane, August 5, 1892, J. S. Hogg Let. Pr., 10, p. 720. Hogg to Jot Gunter (Dallas), July 14, 1892, J. S. Hogg Let. Pr., 10, p. 616, indicates that Hogg realized he ran weakest in the cities, but he wanted friends in all precincts to get out the vote.

[46] Personal interview with Judge S. J. Isaacks of El Paso while he was serving in the Texas legislature, 1953; Houston *Post*, August 15–19, 1892; Austin *Daily Statesman*, January 24, 1915; W. R. Hamby to Sawnie Robertson, March 4, 1892, J. S. Hogg Let. Pr., 9, p. 564.

[47] J. S. Hogg to N. W. Finley, August 6, 1892, J. S. Hogg Let. Pr., 10, p. 765; Finley to Hogg August 10, 1892, J. S. Hogg Let. Rec., XIX, 151. Finley wrote: "I believe there is but one safe course to pursue, and that is to carry out the will of the people, by nominating you Governor of the State, and in doing so, to do that which is right, just and according to Democratic usage, in the matter of settling all contesting delegations."

nor Hogg, General Hamby, E. M. House, Adjutant General W. H. Mabry, Horace Chilton, and Web Finley arrived in Houston early. Hogg set up headquarters at the Capitol Hotel, Clark at the Hutchins House. As the delegations began to pour into the sweltering city, the excitement and tenseness were almost palpable. Many of the groups were twice their normal size, having split their votes in order to seat more delegates who might be useful on voice votes. More than a few men had come armed, determined that their opponents would not "steal" the Convention. Both Hogg and Clark looked at the seething situation warily, and their lieutenants were briefed to advise restraint.

At the Clark caucus on Monday morning State Senator Jonathan Lane presided, and it was planned to put him in nomination for temporary chairman of the Convention. If it became apparent that a strategy move to obtain a viva-voce vote—in which they hoped to mask their numerical weakness by means of the voices of the padded delegations—could not be won, the Clark followers would then try to stampede the Convention by rushing Lane to the platform. Lacking success in this, they would bolt, although they hoped to effect the bolt by the reverse strategy of filling the available seats so completely that the Hogg forces might decide to meet elsewhere and thus could be declared by Clark the "bolters." When Clark appeared at the caucus, rebel yells rent the air and the old Confederate gray hat was much in evidence. Clark announced:

Whatever course you may adopt, whatever path you may tread, I am ready to go with you, in the rear or in the front. . . . And if you see fit to entrust to me the pure white flag of Democracy, I pledge you that I will plant it on the pinnacle of your capitol or I will perish.[48]

When the Governor's caucus got under way at the Opera House in the evening it was clear that he had the delegates to control the convention. Venerable Francis R. Lubbock, one of the organizers of the Texas Democratic Party and a former governor, spoke in Hogg's behalf and let it be known that, despite his service as aide-de-camp to Jefferson Davis in 1864, he did not approve of Clark's efforts to use the Confederate gray hat to confuse basic issues in any neo-Bourbon fashion. During the caucus speeches Hogg remained in his room, talking with the trusted

[48] Galveston *Daily News*, August 16, 1892; Austin *Daily Statesman*, August 16, 1892; Clark, *A Glance Backward*, pp. 90–91.

leaders who would carry on his fight on the Convention floor. Ranger Captain Bill McDonald reported the rumors of the plan to pack the convention with Clark men—an easy trick, since one side of the car shed was not walled; he then hastily collected a crew of men, and during the night they fenced in the open side, leaving a "little wicket-gate" for official admission.

On Tuesday morning the men of the padded delegations, arriving early to make their scheduled rush and pack the floor, found themselves confronting a barrier, with Hogg men standing ready to defend it. Those on the outside were entirely frustrated—aside from calling names and throwing such objects as umbrellas, old shoes, even handbags, there was nothing to do about the situation.[49] After considerable delay the regular delegates for both sides who were wearing official badges were admitted to their places in the hall.

The predicted bolt by the Clark forces over organization was not long in coming. On the second morning most of the bolters went directly to Turner Hall, according to plan, where Clark's name was put in nomination, and where he was drafted to head the new party—"Jefferson Democrats." Some of the bolters, however, had stayed at the car shed to vote instructions and act as observers; they championed the Democratic presidential nominee, Grover Cleveland, and the gold standard program. Hogg wished the Texas Democrats' platform to challenge the double talk of the national platform by boldly declaring for free and unlimited coinage of silver. The silver plank won in committee, 14 to 12; the Clark remnant fought it on the floor, unsuccessfully. As a compromise in the interests of party unity, Hogg made no objection to a plank on an elective commission, provided that the Texas Constitution was amended in such a way as to assure election of only one commissioner every two years, each to serve a six-year term. Clark and Tracy, individually, claimed the credit for forcing the Governor to yield on this point; Hogg was secure, however, in the knowledge that the railroads could not immediately gain control of the Commission, and he hoped that in the meantime the railroad men would come to see that they benefited from the Commission.

Other platform provisions called for 1) a stock and bond law to the end that railways would be "constructed upon commercial principles and not as gambling devices"; 2) a municipal and county bond law to

[49] Albert Paine, *Captain Bill McDonald*, pp. 151–153; Houston *Daily Post,* August 15–17, 1892; Galveston *Daily News,* August 16, 1892.

"preserve the public faith" and "to insure a lower rate of interest";
3) a law defining perpetuities and prohibiting land corporations; 4)
legislative assistance to indigent ex-Confederate soldiers; 5) a promise
to effectively carry out the six-month public school program and to
assure proper endowment of the higher institutions of learning; and 6)
a better mechanics' lien law. The platform also declared the welfare of
laboring people to be a concern of the party, protested the leasing out
of convicts, pledged to continue efforts to regain land illegally obtained
by railroads, and denounced as false the party's alleged opposition to immigration, legitimate corporate enterprises, and the investment of foreign capital in Texas. Another plank was calculated to answer the
Populists and Clark's "calamity howlers."

We are opposed to communism in any and all forms and pledge ourselves
to the just and equitable protection of the interests of both capital and
labor. We deny that it is the purpose or policy of the Democratic Party of
Texas to make unnecessary war upon railroad companies and incorporated
capital, or to deprive them of equal and exact justice before the law. We
believe the railroads are entitled to just compensation for all services rendered, and that they should not be hampered by unnecessary and vexatious
legislation.[50]

The real strength of the Hogg middle-of-the-road program was apparent in the vote by which the majority report was adopted, 693–168.
The minority report was filed by Dudley Wooten, E. P. Hamblen, and
D. C. Giddings. The money issue was prominent in it, making clear the
opposition to Hogg's free-silver advocacy.[51] On the vote for governor,
Hogg received 697, Clark 168, Lanham 5½. Clark later said that he
was not consulted about going to Turner Hall and "felt that this was a
mistake."[52] However, his earlier speech at the Monday caucus presented
contrary evidence.

When Hogg came to the platform to accept the renomination he
wore a large yellow rose in the left lapel of his neat black suit. His speech
was conciliatory, as was proper after the bitterness of the campaign. Yet
what he said about malice was more than political expediency; to those

---

[50] Winkler, *Platforms,* p. 320. The Dallas *Morning News,* August 21, 1892,
intended to be uncomplimentary by speaking of the "Hogg-Reagan Platform."
[51] Winkler, *op. cit.,* pp. 318–322.
[52] Clark, *op. cit.,* pp. 90–91. For Judge R. E. Beckham's statement on the bolt
see Dallas *Morning News,* August 21, 1892.

among his listeners who knew him best, it was the true expression of the man's philosophy and hope—notwithstanding the fact that when fighting was required he was a champion.

The Democrats of Texas have spoken as they did two years ago, and gratefully, I again bow to their will. With me, the verdict of a Democratic convention, on any issue of which it claims jurisdiction, is supreme and final until such time as the organized Democracy may change it. We all can not have our way, but at times must be with the minority and submit to the stronger side, for in our party, as well as in the government, the majority must rule. Not since the first blow was struck for civil liberty and popular rights, have any people or party been in full accord on a single measure or question. To settle political differences, public contests and conventions have become expedient, the ends of which generally witness the weak yielding to the strong, the few to the many. The Democracy of Texas has never escaped this condition or denied its benefits. . . .

Either on men or measures, we have often had differences, at times unreasonably bitter. . . . It is not well for differences in principle to become dogmatic or extreme, for the like tends to destroy a cause and belittle its advocates. Discussion of public questions with modest deference to the opinions of all leads to public enlightenment and to the establishment of sound principles through the action of the majority, for human good. Personal malice in political action is an element of vice and weakness, the presence of which from the hearts of patriots should be removed to make way for the higher attributes of moderation, charity and compassion, whose mission has never [been] less in view than peace.

My disposition has not been, is not now, and shall never be, to inject personalities into politics nor to join in ostracism of those who may differ with me. . . . If we have family rows, we take our licks back, and with vehemence lay them on to the Republicans and *others* when they enter the household to widen the breach. We simply tell them it is our fight, and that we will quit in time to give them the severest drubbing they ever got, and we always keep our word. . . .[53]

Four days after the rival conventions nominated Hogg and Clark the political battle was intensified by a court decision which sent the spirits of the Clark group vaulting from weariness into the realms of ecstasy. Federal Judge Andrew P. McCormick in Dallas granted a sweeping injunction restraining 1) the railways from putting into or continuing in effect the tariffs or orders of the Texas Railway Commission, 2) the

[53] This quotation is from the typescript notes in J. S. Hogg Misc.; also Dallas *Morning News,* August 19, 1892.

302

commissioners from undertaking to enforce compliance or to certify them to the attorney general in actions to recover penalties, and 3) the attorney general from in anywise seeking to prosecute the railroads or to recover penalties from them. In other words, practically every important function of the Commission was suspended. The court claimed action on constitutional grounds, but since Judge McCormick went out of his way to quote some of the Governor's caustic opinions on federal receivers and federal courts and in other ways indicated somewhat unjudicial personal interest in the current political campaign, something more than the Texas Constitution seemed to be at stake. Many of Hogg's rank-and-file followers who did not know the law or the frailties of judges were depressed.[54]

Hardly had the Clark group begun to rejoice, when on August 23, Senator Mills made a speech at Comanche, in the midst of the Alliance stronghold, in which, to Clark's chagrin, he not only challenged the Populists but recognized the Governor, M. M. Crane, nominee for lieutenant governor, and Charles Culberson, nominee for attorney general, as the official nominees of the Democratic Party. His full statement brought home to many wavering Democrats the importance of accepting the majority decision; many men who would not heed Hogg's early appeal to stay with the party now listened to Mills. Despite his high personal regard for Clark, the Senator, who would have to stand for election to a full term in 1893, recognized that the "Regular" Democrats would no doubt control the next legislature. Two days after the speech the editor of the Dallas *Morning News*, obviously distressed, declared that "Lion Mills" was "tamed" and had joined "the love feast of demagogues."[55]

---

[54] *Mortgage Trustees* [Mercantile Trust Company and Farmers Loan and Trust] *of the Texas and Pacific, the St. Louis and Southwestern, the Tyler Southwestern, the International and Great Northern, and the Gulf, Colorado and Santa Fe v. Texas Railroad Commission and C. A. Culberson, Attorney General* (51 Federal Reporter 529). The decision was quoted in full in the Dallas *Morning News*, August 23, 1892. As early as June 25 the *Texas Farmer* had said that Clark knew the Judge's decision. For sketch on Judge McCormick see Webb and Carroll (eds.), *Handbook of Texas*, II, 184; Andrew McCormick, *Scotch-Irish in Ireland and America*. (New Orleans, n. pub., 1897). In February, Congressman John Bankhead of Alabama had introduced a resolution to investigate complaints from Graham, Texas, concerning the appointment by McCormick of his son, "barely 21," to be a railroad receiver. The Fifty-first Congress subsequently passed an act to prevent judges of the United States courts from appointing their relatives to places in the courts over which they presided. Austin *Evening News*, February 19 and March 10, 1892.

[55] Dallas *Morning News*, August 24, 25, 1892.

Texas Farmer

PUBLISHED BY TEXAS FARMER PUB. CO. }

DEVOTED TO AGRICULTURAL INTERESTS OF TEXAS AND THE SOUTHWEST.

{ SUBSCRIPTION: 1 YEAR, $1; 6 MONTHS, 50c

VOL. XIII.   DALLAS, TEXAS, SATURDAY, AUGUST 27, 1892.   NO. 15.

KALI KLARK'S KLAN.

KALAMITY KLOSES OVER THE KICKERS.

Thuggery Transferred to Texas.

HISTORY OF THE HOUSTON DEMOCRATIC CONVENTION.

Incidental Reference to Turner Hall Political Excrement.

Pressure upon these columns last week by Grange proceedings and other agricultural matter made it impossible to include a report of the Democratic Convention among its news items.

Our readers are now so familiar with the news features of that remarkable occurrence that TEXAS FARMER will only touch upon such features as may have bearing upon the campaign before us.

For reference both tickets are here given:

The Democratic Ticket.

For Governor—James S. Hogg, of Smith.
For Lieutenant-Governor—M. M. Crane, of Johnson.
For Attorney-General—Charles A. Culberson, of Dallas.
For Treasurer—William B. Wortham, of Hopkins.
For Comptroller—John D. McCall, of Travis.
For Land Commissioner—W. L. McGaughey, of Hood.
For Superintendent of Public Instruction—J. M. Carlisle, of Tarrant.
For Judges of Criminal Court of Appeals—W. L. Davidson, of Fort Bend; R. J. Simkins, of Navarro.

Opposed to this is a ticket nominated by a mob organized by George Clark for the express purpose of attempting to ruin a party which the people would not permit himself and other corporation politicians to rule:

The Bolteratt Ticket.

For Governor—George Clark, of McLennan.
For Lieutenant-Governor—C. M. Rogers, of Travis.
For Attorney-General—E. A. McDowell, of Coryell.
For State Treasurer—T. J. Goree, of Cherokee.

For Comptroller—C. B. Gillespie, of Dallas.*
For Land Commissioner—W. C. Walsh, of Travis.
For Superintendent of Public Instruction—Jacob Bickler, of Galveston.
For Judges of Criminal Court of Appeals—W. D. Wood, of Hays; R. H. Phelps, of Fayette.

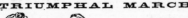

Committee, the then only representative of Texas organized Democracy.

Chairman Finley rapped the delegates to order, delivered a ringing Democratic speech, and declared the first business to be the selection of a temporary Chairman.

Tom Brown, leader of the Hogg side, named Hon. John L. Shepherd, of Camp County. A. L. Matlock, chief thug under Kali Klark, the new divinity which essays to preside over political death in Texas, named Jonathan Lane, "Johnnie" being the most brazen and experienced Bolteratt Kali Klark could suggest.*

The roll of counties was demanded.

Thug Matlock moved that the vote be taken *viva voce*. Tom Brown made the point of order that the convention must be governed by the rule that no *viva voce* vote can be taken where there are

TRIUMPHAL MARCH!

KALI KLARK AND HIS KLAN.

How the Mob Managed Their Bolt.

In the course of this review the testimony of Boltercrats themselves will be given to prove that the bolt was predetermined by all Clark's leading supporters under certain contingencies, while the evidence is plain that George Clark had a secret understanding with a chosen few, more revolutionary and anarchic than the others, that if no pretext for a bolt was furnished, they would make one.

To give readers a correct idea we will begin with the convention when the hall had been turned over to the Executive

*"Mr. Gillespie "declines with thanks."

two candidates before the body. Chairman Finley sustained the point of order. Matlock appealed from the ruling of the chair, and Finley refused to entertain the appeal.

*NOTE—Kali was the goddess served by a sect of enthusiasts in India called Thugs. Her chief demand was human sacrifices which her votaries strangled. She presided over impure love, sensual indulgences, and death. The analogy between Kali and her thugs and Clark and his Mobocrats is this: Kali presides over impurity, sensuality and death in love and religion; Clark has set himself up as the divinity presiding over impurity, over-indulgence and death in politics. Kali's thugs strangled human beings as a sacrifice to their goddess; Clark's thugs are attempting to strangle Democracy and all that is pure in politics at the command of their Apollo-shaped divinity. The weakness and effeminacy of their methods would not warrant comparison with those of a masculine god.

If TEXAS FARMER understands the parliamentary point involved, Thug Matlock's appeal was absurd and Finley's ruling was correct. There was no organized body of Democracy to appeal to except the Executive Committee, and the appeal being against a rule made by that committee was clearly out of order. It has been contended that Finley committed a technical error in not entertaining Matlock's motions and declaring them lost. By so doing Finley would have fallen into the strangling trap set by Kali and watched by his thugs, and they would have captured temporary organization by strangling the voice of delegates through the medium of organized thuggery brought to Houston for that express purpose.

This will be plain to any one who will for a moment consider the parliamentary point involved. Kali Klark and his thugs wanted to apply the rule applicable to mass-meetings. Had this been a mass-meeting and not an organized Democratic Convention, the people present would have had the right to choose their own methods for temporary organization.

Finley, on the contrary, held that this was a convention of Democrats, represented in its organized capacity only by the Executive Committee, which organization the Democracy at San Antonio had entrusted to them for safe keeping until it should again regularly organize as a convention which could legally resume control of the organization.

Can any sane man for a moment dispute this—to say nothing of the lack of reason and common sense in Matlock's position? To have followed Kali Klark's and Thug Matlock's demands would have been to turn Democracy over to a mass-meeting composed of all colors, creeds, conditions and shades of politics. Following the rule made by the Executive Committee kept Democracy under organized control of its own members according to a just and legal basis of representation.

The criminal absurdity of Kali and his thugs could have been no more repugnant to common sense had Matlock offered something like the following:

Whereas, More than two-thirds of the

(Continued on fourth page.)

Kali Klark and His Klan, Texas Farmer, *August 27, 1892.*

A glance at the newspaper situation seems in order. Editor W. L. Malone of the Fort Worth *Gazette* had been such a source of strength for Hogg since attorney general days that it was natural that efforts would be made to change the policy of his paper. More than once Hogg had thanked him and had even warned him not to jeopardize his future on Hogg's account. Malone was a reformer at heart; he loved fair play and stood for what was fine in independent journalism. But now his rectitude was to be sharply tested.

With the completion of the Fort Worth and Denver Railroad, Fort Worth became more and more a railroad and meat-processing center. The new Mayor Buckley B. Paddock was a lawyer, historian, railroad promoter, and banker and joined with others in putting the necessary pressures on the owners of the *Gazette* to change its political policy to one of support for Clark. The San Antonio *Express* and Dallas *Morning News* continued to oppose Hogg and to support Clark. The Dallas *Times Herald,* friendly to Hogg since its founding in 1888, began, as the campaign grew hotter, to feel pressure to change its policy. The publisher, C. E. Gilbert, stubbornly resisted. The business interests supporting Clark then began to cut advertising and soon the subscribers and revenues fell to distressingly low figures until the paper was forced to reorganize to survive. Most of the smaller town papers still gave Hogg support and he had one pleasant surprise in Houston. The Houston *Post,* prior to the convention at the "car-shed," had opposed both Clark and Hogg, but in August a decision had to be made. Most of the policy makers were opposed to helping Hogg's campaign, but E. P. Hill, attorney for the Southern Pacific and vice-president of the *Post,* recalled how Attorney General Hogg had worked candidly with him on the problem of rebuilding the Sabine Pass line. He was convinced that Hogg's advocacy of the Railroad Commission had not been made in a vindictive spirit but stemmed from his basic interest in the public welfare and from a belief that the railroads actually would be benefited by cooperating with the Commission. Hogg should be given a chance to prove himself, and as the regularly selected nominee of the Democratic Party he ought to be supported as the best hope of blocking the Populists. At great risk to his own business future, Hill argued his point, and won. The Houston *Post* became a much needed ally of Jim Hogg.

When the Republicans met at Fort Worth on September 13, with "Save the State" as their slogan, many of their leaders had decided to support Clark, although some of the delegates wanted a state ticket and others would "Turn Texas Loose" by instructing for no particular candidate. Cuney's address to the delegates endorsed Clark, an action which Cuney later explained in a public letter: his party "had an undisputed power as a balance but absolutely no power as a prime factor," having never polled more than the 77,742 votes given Flanagan in 1890. Cuney explained further that Clark's views were close to Republican principles and were needed to overcome the business stagnation created by "the Hogg Hurricane." Cuney also gave his reasons for opposing the Populists:

I objected to Mr. Nugent because he is in line with Mr. Hogg; but a few steps removed toward socialism and communism—for instance, the Government ownership of railroads and the subtreasury. His principles seek to undermine our whole system of business, which has existed for years, and under which our country has become great and strong, and made itself the foremost among the nations of the world. . . .

The Republican party is not a cast iron institution, it is reasonable, flexible, liberal and patriotic, and has given an example of wisdom and devotion to Texas in this matter of which every Republican has cause to feel proud.

The Republican party has clothed itself with a new dignity which should be worn by every member of it with pride and pleasure. At a single stride you have gone to the very front of the procession with a compact organization of one hundred thousand votes; you have subordinated all personal ambition and, prompted by patriotism alone, have laid your offering at the feet of Texas, that she might live.[56]

Although James Hogg tried to keep away from political vilification, some of his supporters did not. Angered at Clark's alliance with Republicans, Senator Coke called for defeat of the "Three C's—Clark, Cuney and the Coons."[57] Tempers grew short during August and September, difficult months for carrying on political campaigns under a Texas sun. Much of the work was confined to letters, interviews, and published statements, but now and then friends of the major opponents debated. Among the young men who entered the lists to do battle for Hogg was "Alfalfa Bill" Murray. His strong voice had enabled him to become permanent secretary of the "Car Shed Convention." He had won his political spurs by out-talking Harry Tracy at Birdston schoolhouse and by

[56] Quoted in Hare, *Cuney,* pp. 158–162; New York *Tribune,* September 14, 1892; Dallas *Morning News,* September 14, 1892.
[57] Quoted in Cotner (ed.), *op. cit.,* p. 186, n. 2.

working as an associate editor with Sam Dixon on *The Farmer's World* and as a reporter of the special session for the Fort Worth *Gazette*. A story is told that, after the Convention, Murray went to visit some of his relatives, at whose home he caught a severe cold. Collinsville merchant J. L. Harbison came racing to the house, tied a foam-flecked horse at the gate, and called out that Murray was needed in town to make a speech:

"I'm sick. I wouldn't make a speech for any man alive," declared Murray.

"It's a durned Populist—Bob Bell. He's running against Joe Bailey," the crestfallen Harbison said, gloomily.

"A Populist, huh?" Murray exclaimed, fire glinting in his eyes. "I'm well: Get my clothes!"[58]

In Austin, E. M. House worked with General Hamby's committee constantly to perfect a large, loyal, and effective organization to get out the vote. This was House's great contribution to Hogg's campaign. While much of the planning continued to be done in Austin, Hogg's cause had been further and materially strengthened when Waller S. Baker, the experienced chairman of the Democratic Executive Committee for McLennan County (Clark's own), agreed to manage the last part of the campaign. This choice was made in the Houston Convention and graphically indicated that Clark would not control the "Regular" organization. Baker received valuable assistance from Richard Harrison, who had served with Hogg as assistant attorney general. The wealthy planter, General Felix Robertson of Waco, continued as Clark's manager.[59]

Having waited for cooler weather, Hogg finally invaded Dallas with a carefully prepared speech on October 1. In 1892, Dallas was a recognized financial, industrial, and distribution center with over fifty thousand population. Clark had considerable Democratic and Republican support in the city from both natives and Yankees, and Hogg knew that his own chances to carry Dallas had slumped with the death of his firm supporter Sawnie Robertson in June. As he began his speech he was fully conscious of the fact that he was standing in a Gould stronghold.

Fellow Citizens: When, as a candidate for Governor, I opened my campaign two years ago, I did not mistake the condition of the political path-

[58] Gordon Hines, *Alfalfa Bill*, pp. 80–81.
[59] Webb and Carroll (eds.), *Handbook of Texas*, II, 487.

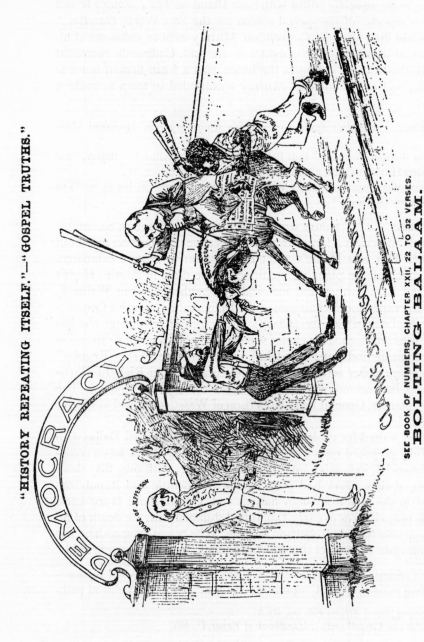

"HISTORY REPEATING ITSELF."—"GOSPEL TRUTHS."

BOLTING BALAAM.

SEE BOOK OF NUMBERS, CHAPTER XXII, 22 TO 32 VERSES.

And the "Spirit of Jefferson" stood in the way for an adversary against him. Now he was riding upon his ass, and his two servants were with him.

And the "Spirit of Jefferson" said unto him, Wherefore hast thou smitten thine ass these three times? Behold, I went out to withstand thee, because thy way is perverse before me.

way before me. Standing before a vast assemblage on my native heath in Cherokee County, I then told them that I was not unmindful of the formidable corporate and political influence that I had to combat, but that I had faith that the power of plain truth would carry conviction against the turbulent stream of prejudice, over artful sophistries, and establish sound doctrines in the minds and hearts of a just, patriotic people. From that time until this I have had no peace save in conscience, but have been under fire in a relentless, unceasing fight. Faint hearts may quail in the contest, but there are enough men amongst us used to hardships whose nerve and patriotism will never falter in the support of principle for the good of Texas.[60]

The speech is forty pages long in print, but it should be read in its entirety by anyone interested in understanding the great fight Hogg waged against a combination of formidable foes which attacked from both the Right and the Left.

Hogg maintained that he had fulfilled the 1890 platform pledges and the big issue remained: "Shall the corporations or the state control?" He bluntly and specifically took Judge McCormick to task for making a "personal and political" decision about the Railroad Commission.

There is yet hope in the land; and if the people will stand by their rights, Texas will see the day when in her sovereign power even the political element of the Federal judiciary will be scourged back for the sake of the rights and liberties of the masses.

The decision may not, will not stand, for there is a higher court not so deeply tinctured with political prejudices that will have it finally to settle. Pending this temporary injunction, the people are from necessity compelled to pay extortionate, extravagant rates.[61]

---

[60] Dallas *Morning News*, October 2, 1892; Houston *Daily Post*, October, n.d., 1892, No. 2838, Special Edition. Dean E. M. Potter, Tyler Junior College, to R. Cotner, September 22, 1951, quoting Miss Lucia Douglas, a history teacher in Tyler, who reported there was some opposition to Hogg for "speaking in the Western manner"; S. A. Lindsey to R. C. Cotner, June 1, 1949, indicated how confusing it was to young voters to see local Democrats in Smith County supporting the Clark-Cuney combination when they had been taught "To never vote for no Republican for nothing at no time never."

[61] Cotner (ed.), *op. cit.*, pp. 280–281; middling cotton on September 30 sold at Dallas for 6¾ cents; at Galveston for 7½ cents and at New Orleans for 7 7/16 cents. Reed says the Commission lowered rates 70 to 65 per cent per cwt., or 25 cents per bale, and not 46 cents as Hogg claimed. However, Hogg's total estimate of saving one million dollars is also used in the first Commission *Report*. See St. Clair Reed, *Texas Railroads*, p. 595. On October 12, Finley told the Penitentiary Board that McCormick's decision had made it impossible to buy Texas-milled flour and he had to get it from outside mills. J. W. Spivey to J. S. Hogg, October 13, 1892, J. S. Hogg Let. Rec., XXI, 165.

Attorney General Culberson was pushing the case as rapidly as possible to the Supreme Court of the United States. If the law should be found to be defective in any of its sections, Hogg promised to ask the legislature to make the necessary revisions, but meanwhile he wanted all to know the goal of his administration:

We intend to have a commission to fix and maintain rates, and the railway companies had just as well submit to it. I say Texas will have it! She will regulate the railroads and not be regulated by them.[62]

During most of the campaign Hogg had seen fit to say little about the Populists, believing that many of the former Democrats among them would return to the fold when they saw the danger of a Clark-Cuney victory. At Dallas he referred to Populists as "ex-Democrats, poisoned from disappointed ambition, mad with the world in general, chimerical in political convictions, shifting in party name, . . . [who] can not stay . . . with any party long." He pointed out that Nugent had withdrawn his early support of Clark after Clark's Weatherford speech.

"Nugent is for government ownership of the railroads; Clark is for turning them loose. I want neither, but advocate their just control and regulation through the Commission."[63] In those two plain sentences Hogg had stated the basic seriousness of the 1892 battle, as well as the essence of the progressive conservatism that made him the strong leader of the "Vital Center." The Dallas speech turned many among his audience into Hogg adherents, especially some of the former "Yankees"—newcomers to the city—who liked what they saw and heard of this vigorous man in his fight "for principle for the good of Texas." Hogg was encouraged when W. L. Moody, Galveston banker and a director of the Gulf, Colorado, and Santa Fe, after reading the Dallas speech, asked for one hundred copies for distribution to bankers and financiers in the East.

It is probable that at this point in the campaign James Hogg's opinion

---

[62] Cotner (ed.), *op. cit.*, pp. 281–282.
[63] Dallas *Morning News*, October 2, 1892; Moody to Hogg, October 3, 1892, J. S. Hogg Let. Rec., XXI, p. 16. For Nugent's speech at Stephenville, June 11, see Dallas *Morning News*, June 13, 1892; for his Austin address see Austin *Daily Statesman*, August 19, 1892. Clark's crowds fell off in size after the convention; about 200 people heard him at Hillsboro, October 3, and in the afternoon, T. S. Johnson, chairman of the County Central Democratic Committee, organized a Hogg Club of 435 members. Johnson to Hogg, October 4, 1892, J. S. Hogg Let. Rec., XXI, 30–33; B. W. Brown (Abilene) to J. S. Hogg, October 18, 1892; *ibid.*, p. 222.

of George Clark, especially for personal reasons, was at its lowest. The usual course of a Democratic campaign in Texas was that of 1890—wherein most of the rugged work was done prior to the state convention, and a nomination was tantamount to election. The bolt of the Clarkites had changed all that. Instead of having time during the late summer and early fall to spend with his family, sharing with them the leisure pursuits he enjoyed—reading, music, his pets, and explorations into nature—Hogg was caught up in a fight to the finish. However, a good honest fight, with the issues drawn clearly, was something that Jim Hogg was never afraid of and never dodged. But this fight was being battled out on grounds that often resembled quicksands, and it was difficult to tell whether any of the hard work had found the bedrock it needed as a base for effective results. The Republicans were split. Hogg could not imagine Clark's distress in being forced to depend upon Cuney and his Republican following for the most of his votes. This fact deterred many Democrats from voting for him. At times the Populists appeared to be growing rapidly. On these shifting sands Hogg fought for re-election.

The Governor continued to be a masterful campaigner, enduring with good grace and joviality such routine difficulties as bad train connections, layoffs at a deserted junction at midnight, arrivals at a destination in unholy early morning hours, rain-drenchings as all hands labored to extricate a carriage stuck in the mud—and always the uncertain cuisine of country hotels, as well as the dangers from overeating at the homes of his generous hosts.

When a trip promised to be not too grueling, he took great pleasure in having one of the family as a traveling companion. Sallie Hogg's frailness made it impossible for her to accompany him. Other strong deterrents were reluctance to leave the younger children home alone and the fact that her indignation at the slurs and barbs aimed at her "Mr. Hogg," which was stirred deeply just by seeing them in print, would probably have risen to fiery and unpredictable heights had she heard hecklers in action. Earlier, Will had often traveled with his father. This year, when Will was a busy student, Ima, ten years old in July, was sometimes his companion. As the Governor conversed with men in hotel lobbies, he would often take his daughter on his knee; her presence seemed to symbolize the at-homeness in the world that was characteristic of Hogg. Sometimes Ima visited children in the homes of the Governor's friends. In general, Mrs. Hogg and the children usually spent at least part of the summers at Colonel Stinson's home in Speer. An ex-

311

cerpt from a letter of Hogg's written during a lonely weekend is engaging testimony to his feeling in their absence: "Have a nice time and enjoy yourselves. . . . I'll be there I hope by watermelon time. Then we will all go fishing and have a big frolic. Around the house here from morning 'till night there's not a sound of a rat, cat, or cricket. The cow, parrots, the dogs, all are gone. I am like a ghost in a two-story barn *deserted.*"[64]

Many counties were still being hotly contested throughout October, especially those with "mixed" populations—Negroes, Latin Americans, Germans, Czechs, and the older English-speaking settlers. Just after the Dallas speech W. M. Stone, chairman of the Burleson County Democratic Executive Committee, pointed out to the Governor the serious situation in his own county; of its 3,000 votes, which he said included those of "600 foreigners," 900 Negroes, and "the balance Americans," he estimated that Nugent would get only 200, but that all of the "foreign" vote would go to Clark. He felt that Hogg must arrange to speak in the county to hold the Negro votes he had and to correct recent vilifications.[65] Stone underestimated the work of the Populists, including the powerful organizational and oratorical abilities of mulatto John B. Rayner, the former schoolteacher, deputy sheriff, and minister, who lived in the neighboring county of Robertson and had recently left the Republican party to affiliate with a party claiming to represent the whole people. Hogg eventually led in the county with 41.7 per cent of the votes; Nugent received 31 per cent.[66] Obviously, Hogg drew votes among the Germans and Negroes, and Clark did not capture all of the "Old Soldier" and Republican votes.

The population of nearby Washington County was over 25 per cent German and over 50 per cent Negro. When Hogg spoke at Brenham in June, it was estimated that his audience consisted of 1,300 persons, including 600 colored. When asked about law enforcement, he said:

Now, I have gone this far, when mobs have become too strong in this State for the local officers to cope with them, I have quelled them by the strong

[64] Ima Hogg, *op. cit.;* Fam. Let.
[65] W. M. Stone to J. S. Hogg, October 6, 1892, J. S. Hogg Let. Rec., XXI, 64–65.
[66] M. J. Moore to J. S. Hogg, October 7, 1892, *ibid.,* XXI, 75–76, predicted the correct order of votes, Hogg, Nugent, Clark, but Hogg cut down the estimate for Nugent from 1,700 to 862. Clark received 745 and Hogg received 1,154. Returns of the Election of 1892 in Texas *House Journal* (1893), p. 52; Martin, *People's Party in Texas,* pp. 120–129, gives an excellent description of Rayner.

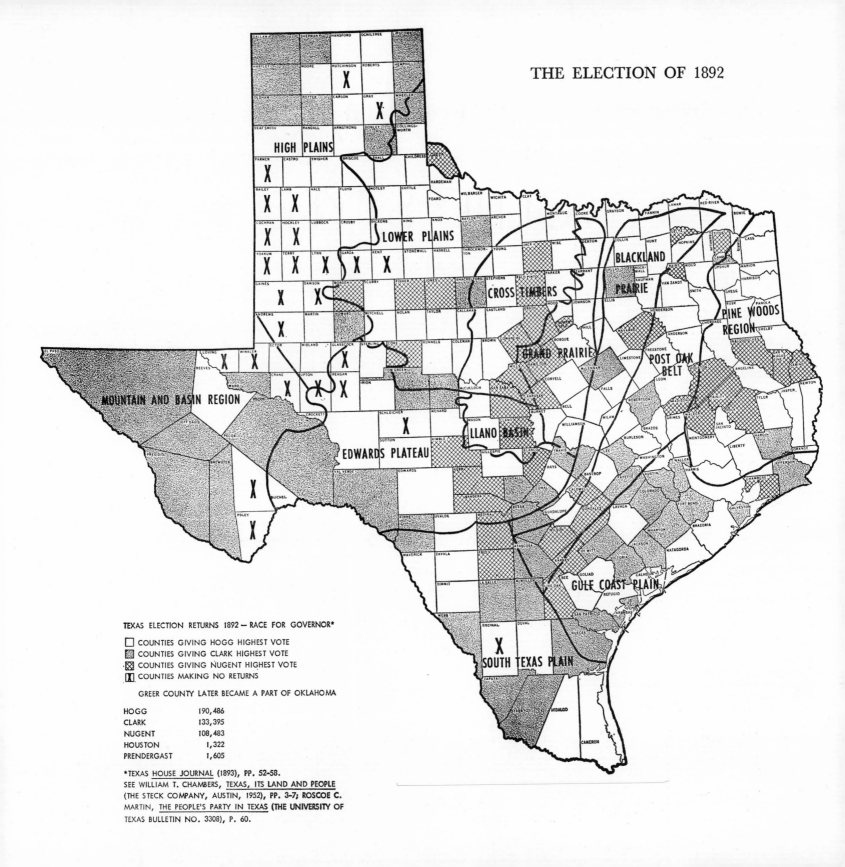

THE ELECTION OF 1892

HIGH PLAINS

LOWER PLAINS

BLACKLAND
PRAIRIE

CROSS TIMBERS

PINE WOODS
REGION

GRAND PRAIRIE

POST OAK
BELT

MOUNTAIN AND BASIN REGION

LLANO BASIN

EDWARDS PLATEAU

GULF COAST PLAIN

SOUTH TEXAS PLAIN

TEXAS ELECTION RETURNS 1892 — RACE FOR GOVERNOR*

☐ COUNTIES GIVING HOGG HIGHEST VOTE
▨ COUNTIES GIVING CLARK HIGHEST VOTE
▧ COUNTIES GIVING NUGENT HIGHEST VOTE
▦ COUNTIES MAKING NO RETURNS

GREER COUNTY LATER BECAME A PART OF OKLAHOMA

HOGG	190,486
CLARK	133,395
NUGENT	108,483
HOUSTON	1,322
PRENDERGAST	1,605

*TEXAS HOUSE JOURNAL (1893), PP. 52-58.
SEE WILLIAM T. CHAMBERS, TEXAS, ITS LAND AND PEOPLE
(THE STECK COMPANY, AUSTIN, 1952), PP. 3-7; ROSCOE C.
MARTIN, THE PEOPLE'S PARTY IN TEXAS (THE UNIVERSITY OF
TEXAS BULLETIN NO. 3308), P. 60.

arm of the law without conferring with anybody. I have suppressed more than one mob too. Did you ever hear of an influential and wealthy man being killed by a mob? Let a humble negro or a poor white man commit some crime and a gang of enterprising and wild and wooly fellows will swing him to a tree without a trial.[67]

The Austin *News* editor, after quoting this much of the speech, accused the Governor of "pandering to the negroes." Had the editor cared to refresh his memory he could have found this theme of abhorrence of mob violence throughout Hogg's addresses and writings, as part of his fundamental concern with and insistence on law enforcement and justice for all manner of men. And had he recalled Hogg's decisive actions as governor to check the growing menace of lynching he would have been forced to recognize Hogg's basic fairness to all people. In any case, Hogg had the support also of Brenham's most distinguished citizens, including Beauregard Bryan, and he won the county with 52 per cent of the votes. Clark received 45 per cent, and Nugent was almost cut out with only 2 per cent, the vote indicating a general Populist weakness in areas with heavy concentration of Negro voting. The Negro Hogg Club later celebrated victory with a grand barbecue.

There were few "breathing" periods for any of the candidates or their adherents right up to election day. When the ballots were counted James Hogg had won by a substantial plurality, receiving 190,486 votes, only 7,000 less than in 1890. Clark and Nugent together polled just over 55 per cent of the total with 133,395, and 108,483 respectively.[68] Hogg received 43.7 per cent of all votes, showing that the Prohibitionists and Houston Republicans had received about 1 per cent. Hogg ran well all over the state, seldom being the low man in any county (as shown by the accompanying map). His greatest strength was in the populous eastern and northern areas of Texas, and he shared honors with Clark and Nugent in the central portion. Clark carried the counties in the

---

[67] Austin *Evening News*, June 12, 1892. There was a vigorous Colored Hogg Club in Brenham. A handbill announcing their "victory" barbecue in November is preserved in the Hogg Collection.

[68] Original Returns of the Election, 1892, Rec. Sec. State; Texas *House Journal* (1893), pp. 52–58. Houston polled only 1,322 and Prendergast 1,605. Co-author of the railroad commission law, Martin M. Crane, became lieutenant governor. His work had helped to hold down the Nugent vote on the western edge of 'the blackland region. Noblin, *Leonidas La Fayette Polk, Agrarian Crusader* (Chapel Hill, University of North Carolina Press, 1949), p. 294, omits Texas from list of Southern states with "impressive" Populist votes.

Sing a song of 'lection;
  "To beat Hogg" is the cry,
And Cuney's flock of blackbirds
  Were baked into a pie.

And when the pie was opened,
  Cuney began to sing;
And little Georgie really thought
  His little self Our King!

But all true Democrats now know
  This pair of schemers sly;
And, on the 8th of November,
  Will knock both into "pi."

Clark and the Blackbirds. Texas Farmer, *October 29, 1892.*

Panhandle that were controlled by the XIT Ranch and Goodnight interests, but elsewhere the farmers and ranchers made Hogg first choice.

Nugent did not run well among the individualists on the High Plains. He picked up some counties on the edge of the South Plains and off the railroad, running best from Frio and Live Oak in the south to Palo Pinto and Jack Counties in the north—the heart of the drought area. In general the Populists made little appeal to the Negroes and practically none to the Mexicans.[69] A careful study of the local box returns made by Professor Roscoe Martin supports his conclusion that "the Populist party in Texas depended primarily upon the allegiance of the native white citizens and that its success was greatest where it found a population free from the complications induced by various racial groups."[70] A further refinement of the Populist sources of voters indicated that "cross timber" or poor agricultural lands often contributed a high percentage of Populists. Taken another way, a survey of estimated value per acre of farm products also indicated that the Democrats won more frequently in the higher-income counties, and this is borne out in reverse by the Populist victories in the heart of East Texas.

In general, it is safe to say that Nugent picked up some of the former Hogg votes of 1890 in the Alliance stronghold from Lampasas to Jack counties, but Hogg usually ran ahead of Clark. The old Greenbackers, Prohibitionists, other chronic reformers, and some new voters joined the Alliance men to account for the Populist vote of 108,000. Whether the People's Party would hold together through another election remained to be tested.

Assuming that Cuney could deliver 85,000 votes (he claimed 100,-000), Clark had picked up over 50,000 votes among irregularly voting Democrats and new voters. Some of his vote, as well as Hogg's, must be accounted for by the intensity of the campaign, which brought out new voters. His failure as a "people's man" was largely due to his inability to disassociate himself both from his corporate connections and from his reputation for opposing the Commission, as well as to his support for "Gold Bugs."

A passage in Clark's *A Glance Backward* deals with the background of Mills' contest for the U.S. Senatorship after his humiliating defeat for the speakership of the U.S. House of Representatives. Clark wrote that Mills had wired him to come to Corsicana. Meeting at the Commer-

---

[69] Martin, *op. cit.*, pp. 96–97.
[70] Martin, *op. cit.*, p. 90. See also his county maps, facing pp. 73, 76, 78 ff.

cial Hotel, they discussed the situation until late at night, and Mills confided that he would not be elected unless "he could get some friend to make the canvass for governor and thus greatly aid him." Clark and Mills saw eye to eye against the tariff and free silver. Since Chilton had clearly stated his free silver position in a speech at Austin on October 16, 1891, there was real interest in the Mills-Chilton contest among Eastern financial circles and in the Alliance headquarters in Washington. Clark's position takes on more meaning if his Texas campaign of 1892 is considered as a part of Cleveland's national anti-silver campaign; Hogg was known to have been for David B. Hill of Tammany Hall rather than Cleveland prior to the National Democratic Convention, and his evaluation of the former President's true stand on the money question was proved correct when the Sherman Silver Purchase Act was repealed in 1893. Clark wrote further:

Mills urged me to make the race [for governor against Hogg]. I suggested several different individuals who could make the race better, stating my affairs were not in good condition and required my personal attention for my professional duties. He was positively insistent, and finally I agreed to make the race, chiefly for his benefit.[71]

Clark became and remained the state leader of the gold standard in Texas, and the campaign of 1892 was in one sense only a skirmish in the prolonged battle of the standards, which would reach a climax in 1896. Senator Mills, however, realized the danger of a split Democratic Party and would not campaign for Clark when he failed to receive the regular nomination.

One other aspect of the campaign deserves attention, namely the role of the Grange. The depression had dealt harshly with the cooperatives, and the organized Granges continued to decline in numbers.[72] However, many of the young men who had been educated in the Grange program

[71] Clark, *op. cit.*, p. 90; *National Economist*, March 2, 1892. Chilton spoke in Austin, October 16, 1891.
[72] Available figures show:

	Grange Members	Lodges
Dec. 1888	6,664	158
Dec. 1891	——	76
Dec. 1893	1,473	27

Proceedings of the Texas State Grange, 1889 (Galveston, 1889), pp. 11–12; A. W. Buchanan to A. J. Rose, January 23, 1891, A. J. Rose Papers. See J. B. Long to A. J. Rose, June 19, 1893, for rejoicing over Evans Jones' entry into the Grange membership, May 27.

of the 1870's were prominent local leaders in 1890–1892; these old "conservative and thinking" Grangers worked for Hogg, because they believed he spoke their language. In localities where Granges had faded out and Alliances arisen, the old Grangers still exercised a conservatism of thought and by their determined democracy, in a philosophical rather than a party sense, helped to hold in check the "revolutionary and communistic tendencies of the less informed."[73] Shaw, in summarizing the situation in his *Texas Farmer*, probably came as near to the truth as his prejudiced pen would allow:

It was at this point that George Clark, his politicians, and that element of commerce which endorses the undemocratic idea that combinations of commerce and capital should have a monopoly of class legislation—it was here they made their greatest mistake in calculating the probabilities of the campaign just closed. They foolishly imagined that in robbing the reform movement of the Alliance strength, together with that of its organ, the *Mercury,* they had taken from Mr. Hogg all the strength of the previous campaign. They did not understand that the conservatism of the Grange had all left the Alliance—the last coming away when the Grand State Alliance was organized. They had not analyzed the movement as had the conservative and thinking elements among the farmers, and hence had not learned that, with some rare and honorable exceptions, only the revolutionary and unthinking farmers were left with the *Mercury* gang of place-hunting frauds and trade-making corruptionists. Hence when the "forks of the creek" rolled up their multiplied thousands of voters who could not be influenced by brass bands nor boodle, but whose votes were exponents of conservative thought and investigation, Clark and his gang were dumb with surprise.[74]

The Texas Grangers won several seats in Congress, while no Texas Populist was successful. More important for Hogg, several of his Alliance enemies in the Texas legislature were defeated, and he could look forward to the passage of more of the reform program in 1893.

Actually, Shaw's rhetorical flourish was partially inaccurate: Clark

[73]*Texas Farmer,* Shaw's editorial, November 26, 1892. Great assistance in evaluating personalities in the election was obtained by the author from personal conversations with Sterling Fulmore, a neighbor, 1948–1952; with former President of the University of Texas A. J. Battle, who first came to Austin in 1893; and with C. V. Terrell, former railroad commissioner and neighbor of John Hogg at Decatur.

[74] *Texas Farmer,* Shaw's editorial, November 26, 1892.

was not surprised. He later recorded that he thought the bolt a mistake, but he did go along with it then and was also a party to the deal with Cuney to work together to defeat Hogg. He might have gained more votes had he continued to deal with Tracy, but it must have been apparent that even the "unthinking" farmers described by Shaw were not likely to accept Clark's leadership. Considering the economic issues and philosophies of business, Clark and the "Regular" Republicans were good company, but on issues such as the tariff and regulation of interstate commerce, more government in business or less, they had little in common. The real ties were the gold standard and the aim to defeat Hogg, who stood for free silver, state-federal regulation of railroads, bond issues, and law enforcement, including enforcement of the antitrust law, which might catch up the oil interests of Rockefeller any day.

The campaign of 1892 alerted the young Democratic leaders and the old "Regulars"—Reagan, Coke, and Mills—to the necessity for a complete reorganization of the Party machinery. It was fortunate for the Party that Hogg had understood the nature of the crisis in time to make use of the volunteered assistance of such a man as the political prodigy Edward Mandell House—banker, plantation owner, cotton grower, cotton buyer, and student of economics and politics. (The title of Colonel, by which he was invariably known in later life, was conferred on him when Hogg, over the protests of House, commissioned him on the governor's staff. In time his uniform became the prized possession of his coachman.) Years later, after House had become an adviser of Woodrow Wilson and a world figure, he described his part in the 1892 campaign:

When I found that the railroads and the entire corporate interests of Texas were combining to defeat Hogg, I enlisted actively in his behalf. Although he had known me but a short time, we had many times discussed political ways and means, and he asked me and the then State Health Officer (Dr. Swearingen) to take charge of his campaign. Later the burden of it fell on me. We selected a committee and got my good friend, General W. R. Hamby, to act as chairman. That campaign was a battle royal. We had no money, and every daily paper in Texas was against us. Hogg's opponent was Judge George Clark of Waco. When the Clarkites found we had sufficient votes to nominate Hogg, they bolted the convention and nominated Clark. The Republicans endorsed him and we had another hard fight at the election, but Hogg won by a decisive majority [sic]. It was a bitter fight and the wounds lasted many years. It was the first firm stand [sic] the people of any American State had taken against the privileged classes, and it attracted attention throughout the Union.[75]

The decisive political battle won, Governor Hogg and Attorney General Culberson turned their attention to the judicial battle being waged over the Railroad Commission before the United States Supreme Court and to the reform legislation to be presented to the next legislature.

[75] "Memorandum of a Conference between Edward M. House, George Bailey, and A. J. Rosenthal, Jr., New York, November 7, 1922," Let. Biog. J. S. Hogg.

CHAPTER XII

Progressivism, Texas Style

THE DEMOCRATIC VICTORY of James Stephen Hogg and the reform forces in the fiercely contested Texas election of 1892 marked the rise to power of a new generation of progressive young men and their older advisers as the champions of constructive change. Within them the flame of humanitarianism would not be quenched by either the past and its bitter memories of reconstruction or the future and its inducements of financial power in the service of the corporate philosophy of *laissez faire*. In the opening chapter of Arthur Link's *Woodrow Wilson and the Progressive Era* the Progressive Movement is described as "the natural consummation of historical processes long in the making," for which the election of 1912 marked "the culmination of more than twenty years of popular revolt against a state of affairs that seemed to guarantee political and economic control to the privileged few in city, state, and nation."[1] One of the strong roots of this twentieth-century development was the Texas progressivism of the 1890's, which constituted the training ground of Edward M. House and the Texas members of Wilson's Cabinet, Postmaster General Albert S. Burleson, Secretary of Agriculture David F. Houston (formerly president of Texas Agricultural and Mechanical College), and Attorney General Thomas Watt Gregory (who in 1916 declined the offer of the chief justiceship of the United States Supreme Court).[2]

Texas was not, of course, unique in being a prologue and a training

[1] Arthur Link, *Woodrow Wilson and the Progressive Era* (New York, Harper & Brothers, 1954), p. 1.

[2] *Ibid.*, pp. 25–30. Link had to be brief. For a more satisfactory appraisal of Burleson as the effective political adviser who used the patronage to assist in passing the great progressive measures, see Richard M. Howard, "The Work of Albert Sidney Burleson as Postmaster General," Master's thesis (the University of Texas, 1938), pp. 5, 38–42; Ray Stannard Baker, *Woodrow Wilson: Life and Letters* (Garden City, Doubleday, Page and Company, 1931), IV, 44–49, 415–418; John W. Payne," David F. Houston: A Biography," Ph.D. dissertation (the University of Texas, 1954), pp. 23–26, 41 ff.; Charles Seymour (ed.), *The Intimate Papers of Colonel House* (Boston, Houghton Mifflin Company, 1926), pp. 28–31;

and proving ground for the movement; other states were also deeply involved in these processes during the 1890's. But the issues of the political tug of war of two-ends-against-the-middle were possibly as clearly cut in the Lone Star State as elsewhere. The huge extent of Texas, hinting of unlimited and as yet largely unplumbed resources, was a lure to settlers and exploiters alike, so various and so determined in quest of their own kind of profit as to make it nearly inevitable that the problem of haves and have-nots common to rapidly developing pioneer areas would show here in exaggerated form. And James Hogg's reputation for vigorous decisiveness (or, as his enemies with some justification called it, stubbornness) in guarding the public welfare through law, which had been more widely established when the young attorney general showed the wildcat insurance companies and the pre-empting railroads that he meant business, was bound to make him and his supporters the focus of sharp-drawn controversy. (Jim Hogg may never have read G. K. Chesterton's comment, "I believe in getting into hot water; I think it keeps you clean," but the practice of this idea was natural to him.) At the same time his adherence to the middle way produced a three-way battle, which pointed up the whole span of issues in a manner impossible for the two-way, radical-conservative battles more usual elsewhere.

In the Texas tug of war the reactionary Democrat George Clark and the Republican Wright Cuney represented two faces of one extreme, with their political defense of the current corporate *laissez-faire* philosophy as an ideological justification of the current exploitive and competitive system. Clark, along with Samuel Dodd, attorney for Standard Oil, would continue to defend that philosophy through the courts until after 1900. At the other extreme were the Populists, with their demands for government ownership and management—demands born of the economic distress of farmers trying to adjust to new machines and often to a drier climate and of laborers snared in the gears of a rapidly changing society wherein law had not yet caught up with newly engendered injustices and needs. Holding the "Vital Center" were the young Democrats, Brock Robertson, Richard Wynne, Horace Chilton, and Jot Gunter, and the older Democrats, John Reagan, Richard Coke, and Alexander Terrell, who had pledged to make their party the instrument of a reform that would by means of legal measures, approved by the

David F. Houston, *Eight Years with Wilson's Cabinet* (New York, Doubleday, Page and Company, 1926), I, 202–208.

people themselves, protect the public from predatory onslaughts of special interests, yet leave the way open to individual initiative and fair competition benefiting all, rather than a self-privileged few.

How much of Texas progressivism would not have flowered except for the accident of James Stephen Hogg's presence in that time and at that place, one cannot say, nor whether some other man would have better headed the movement. From an examination of the records of what did happen it becomes evident that Jim Hogg was peculiarly the leader to fit the occasion. Many of those who were his sponsors and lieutenants were as able intellectually, and had as deep humanitarian concern; some of them had benefited from advanced formal educational opportunities that circumstances had denied him. But none of them had the precise combination of ability, convictions, physical and moral stamina, compelling presence, frankness, good humor, and sometimes, brooding thoughtfulness that they themselves recognized as so helpful to their cause. The leader in this fight must be proof against the excessively vicious charges of an opposition having so much to lose, and he must be unquestionably accepted as honest by an electorate having so much to win.

Hogg was not fundamentally a political or social theorist, but he could and did think reflectively about the practical issues at hand, and he read the theories of others, usually measuring them by his own guiding principle of the efficacy of law in achieving justice for all men. He read widely in the biographies of effective men of past ages and the writings of such American social philosophers as Henry George and Edward Bellamy. Nevertheless, his own experiences of economic and other adversities, his careful study of the writings of Grange and Alliance men, his appreciation of the qualities and achievements of men such as Senators Richard Coke and John Reagan and the outstanding anti-monopolist Alexander Terrell, were probably among the more important factors that led him to join the ranks of those seeking to combat constructively the power of corporate wealth and the economic ills of the period. He welcomed viewpoints developed outside the Southwest and read the *North American Review* published at Boston, along with New York and St. Louis papers.

He found continuous inspiration, information, and support in the older and younger men of the Party. He and other young reformers early learned, both from their own initial experiences and from the seasoned advice of the older men, that success in reform did not come for the single reason that reformers were men of good will. There must be political know-how; the people must be fairly well informed and well agreed upon what they wanted; furthermore, they must be ready to reject the old regime and to support a reform leadership. Public opinion was clarified between 1887 and 1892 regarding policies of government ownership, government regulation, and *laissez-faire* competition.

For example, not long after Hogg received Reagan's promise to head the Texas Railroad Commission, he received a letter from James M. Pierce, president of the important farm paper, the *Iowa Homestead*. The letter read as follows:

Mr. Reagan's name has in this part of the country been synonymous with an earnest effort to secure a just and equitable control of railroads engaged in interstate commerce, not perhaps so much on account of his immediate connection with the Interstate Commerce law as it finally passed, but because for many years he was the advocate, and during most of the time, the sole champion of such enactments as would afford any control or regulation whatever.[3]

In 1892, through the leadership of Governor Hogg and Reagan, chairman of the Platform Committee, the Democratic Party squarely opposed government ownership of railways, telephones, and telegraphs* as advocated by the Populists. Texas Democrats pushed for a strong state banking system to combat the weaknesses charged against the national banking system; they sought effective regulations of railroads by the national and state commissions; and they urged the enforcement of the national and state antitrust laws. Hogg maintained that the Texas and Sherman acts were aimed at combinations of business rather than against farmer and labor groups who had legally organized for some purpose such as forming an incorporated cooperative cheese-making plant or cotton warehouse.

Texas was fortunate in having several influential newspapers, whose editors, although usually opposing corporate regulation in any form and championing *laissez faire,* were not blind to the justified grievances of the people and at times even advocated specific reforms. The Dallas *News* during the 1880's had pioneered a series of articles about the failure of the Goodnight group of ranchers to pay the state for grass leases; another series discussed illegal enclosures. The *News* also joined Colonel Robert Milner's Henderson *Times* and Frank Holland's *Texas Farm and Ranch* magazine in advocating crop diversification. The Robertson-

[3] James M. Pierce to J. S. Hogg, May 11, 1891. Original was forwarded to John H. Reagan, May 14, 1891. J. H. Reagan Papers, Fol. 1891–1894.

Clark debate during the 1890 campaign was one of many such controversies brought to public attention in print. The Alliance and Grange papers steadily carried well-written, informative articles on money, bimetallism, Cleveland's pro-gold stand, cooperatives, scientific farming, land reform, dress reform, woman's suffrage, schools and textbooks, the secret ballot, and prison reform. And even when the Galveston *News* and the Dallas *News*, among others, briskly and often vituperatively fought Hogg's alien land laws and his efforts to regain the sidings and switches lands from the railroads, there was information value to the public in the resulting controversy. In other words, newspaper articles and debates furnished the public with information and opinion which, whether biased or not, helped to create a climate of inquiry and opinion in which the people could be ready to express themselves in support of the opposing philosophies of government—reform or status quo.

Underlying the numerous plans for combating the ills of an agrarian society and the problems arising from the new industrialism were certain facts peculiar to the Southwest. The Southeast blamed many of its troubles on the destruction of property during the Civil War, the migration of old settlers, the large numbers of uneducated Negroes, and the wearing out of old farms; but Texans could not really blame any of these factors for their own unrest. In Texas, for instance, the percentage of colored population declined between 1880 and 1900 from 24.7 to 20.4 per cent, although the absolute number increased from 393,000 to 620,000. Texas had its educational problems, but was trying to solve them. The Blair Bill, providing federal aid to education, was debated hotly in Texas; Democrats were usually opposed, Republicans and Populists tended to support the bill.[4] This threat of federal aid undoubtedly stimulated greater efforts to combat illiteracy by state action, and Hogg always argued that it was the duty of Texans to provide the best education for all children, whether white or colored, and to pay for it. Political education of Negro adults had been advanced by the vigorous efforts of the various parties to obtain their votes in 1892, and the Negro political leaders had status, being spurned only by the "Reform" Republicans. The first generation of free-born Negroes thus had a fair amount of political sophistication and, like most of the other small farmers in Texas suffering agrarian ills, sought political and economic

[4] *Congressional Record,* 48 Cong., 1 Sess., XV, 36, 758, 5,398. See Daniel M. Robinson, *Bob Taylor and the Agrarian Revolt in Tennessee* (Chapel Hill, University of North Carolina Press, 1935), pp. 73–89; Eugene C. Barker, *Texas History* (Dallas, Southwest Press, 1929), pp. 532–534.

changes. As the rest of the South, including part of East Texas, struggled with small worn-out acreages, cotton production in Texas expanded—and further contributed to the lowering of the price of the cash crop all over the South. Settlers poured into Texas, particularly farmers; the population doubled from 1880 to 1900, going from 1½ million to just over 3 million. In 1890 it had reached 2,235,000, of which over 84 per cent was rural.[5]

Unrest among farmers and stockmen in Texas was due to several factors, including the scarcity of good land, dependence upon cotton, and the inadequate transportation and banking systems. By the end of the 1870's almost all of the central blacklands and tree-covered regions along Red River in the northwest and the bottom lands along the rivers that skirted the Edwards Plateau and bubbled out of its base had been taken up. The expanding sheep herds had covered the Edwards Plateau and moved up to the plains near Abilene and Haskell, only to be forced back to the cooler Plateau by drought and depression in the early 1890's. The adjustment of crops and animals to their proper geographic regions had not occurred by 1893, and this contributed to the economic uncertainties and the cultural lag along the frontiers. The decade of the 1880's witnessed the attempts of large numbers of families to farm and ranch in the counties west of the line of 98 degrees, where after 1883 they ran into periods of prolonged drought.

The lack of diversification of occupation as disclosed by the population census—over 64 per cent were in agriculture in 1890—meant that there was little opportunity for two-thirds of the people to escape falling prices for farm and ranch products, since opportunities to shift into industry were still scarce. Cotton production in 1887 was approximately 1.6 million bales and brought $88 million, or less than 7 cents a pound. When more men and women and children produced 400,000 more bales to bring the total to 2 million in 1890, they received $20 million less for their labors.[6] The editors of farm papers and of Democratic city papers stimulated the farmers to action by reminding them that the McKinley Tariff Act did not aid them and actually increased their cost of living, while the railroads and shipping interests continued to receive a larger proportion of the total price cotton brought at New York or Liverpool.

The financial facilities for handling grain and cotton were far from

[5] United States Bureau of the Census, *Compendium of the Eleventh Census, 1890* (Washington, Government Printing Office, 1892–1894), III, 432.
[6] Rupert N. Richardson, *Texas,* p. 352.

adequate in Texas. Prohibited by the Constitution of 1876 from chartering state banks, Texas had struggled along with some private banking houses and thirteen national banks in 1880, handling deposits of only $2 million. By 1890 there were 189 national banks, handling deposits of over $30 million. The large number made Texas unique in the South. Nevertheless, vast areas were still not served adequately; crop loans were so high that it is not surprising that Alliance leader Macune became the champion of the subtreasury plan of low-interest, government-backed loans to farmers. The fact that the Grange and Alliance cooperatives had nearly all folded up by 1893 was another reason for the farmers' interest in the Populist program as stimulated by the *Texas Weekly Advance* and the *Southern Mercury*. The value of farm lands and buildings had increased from $170 million in 1870 to $400 million in 1890, but, as much of this was financed on credit, the high interest rates of 8 to 12 per cent on mortgages were pointing the way to economic ruin. A true evidence of agrarian depression was the decline in the percentage of farm owners from 62.4 to 58.1 between 1880 and 1890.[7]

Railroad indebtedness was being felt as an especially heavy burden: Texans were paying for mileage which had jumped from 3,244 miles in 1880 to 8,710 miles in 1890, but only 1,157 miles were added in the next decade. Much of the mileage crossed Texas to link up California, Colorado, and Kansas with New Orleans and Galveston and often ran through sparsely settled areas. While the railroads speeded up the inland shift to cotton after 1870 by providing transport that was less costly for the farmer than driving his teams to rivers that led to the Gulf ports, the change from a practically self-sufficient economy contributed to the problems of economic and social adjustment. Meanwhile, stockholders wanted interest and dividends, which only a return of prosperity and added tonnage could make possible—short exorbitant rates. Here was a problem which needed attention. The Texas Railroad Commission was just beginning to issue new schedules when Judge McCormick issued the injunction against it.

With these problems in mind when the Twenty-third Legislature assembled in January, 1893, Governor Hogg was ready to press for more of the reform program. The people had given him a continued mandate for the progressive blueprint laid down in the Democratic platform. The

---

[7] Bureau of the Census, *Eleventh Census: Report of Farms and Homes*, p. 439. The number of farms mortgaged in Texas rose from 7,221 in 1890 to 38,408 in 1900. See John S. Spratt, *The Road to Spindletop: Economic Changes in Texas, 1875–1901* (Dallas, Southern Methodist University Press, 1955), pp. 58–60, 292.

reform Democrats appeared to have a clear majority, to Hogg's keen satisfaction, but he did not underestimate the power of the lobbies. In his message of January 12 he bluntly reminded the majority of its pledge of obedience to the provisions of the Democratic platform, including:

1. A pledge to support the Texas railroad commission law as it was—an appointive commission—"unless the constitution shall be so changed as to permit the election of one of the commissioners every two years and making their tenure of office six years."

2. An agreement to submit to the people an amendment providing for the chartering of state banks.

3. A law that would successfully prevent the issuance of fictitious and watered stocks and bonds by railway companies.

4. A law that would prevent the useless and extravagant issuance of bonds by cities, towns, and counties so as to preserve the public faith, to insure a lower interest rate, etc.

5. A law to define perpetuities and prohibit the further operation of land corporations in this state.

6. An amendment to provide for indigent ex-Confederate soldiers.

7. Legislation to assure a full six months' school term and proper endowment and maintenance for the University and other public educational institutions.

8. A better lien law to protect material, men, artisans, mechanics, and laborers.

9. Opposition to hiring out or leasing of penal convicts to corporations and to individuals.

10. A pledge of opposition to communism in any and all forms and of support by Democrats for "just and equitable protection of the interests of both capital and labor."[8]

The Governor's wishes were followed regarding the railroad commission law; an amendment that provided for staggered, six-year terms for elective commissioners would be voted on at the regular election in the fall of 1894. A proposal to submit an amendment relative to the chartering of banks by the state did reach a vote in the House but was defeated. (Not until 1905 was a similar amendment submitted to the people and adopted.) The efforts to amend the constitution to provide adequate support for indigent ex-Confederate veterans became involved in tactics to force Hogg to accept the sugar bounty provided by the McKinley Tariff, when a measure was introduced to authorize the use of the

[8] Ernest Winkler, *Platforms of Political Parties in Texas,* pp. 318–320.

2-cent-per-pound bounty for benefit of a Confederate home. Hogg vetoed it, as he had vetoed a similar measure two years before; therefore an amendment providing for the adequate support of veterans was not submitted to the people, but the legislature did vote a moderate appropriation. The Governor thus lost out on two-thirds of the amendments,[9] but he could be reasonably content for the time being, having won on the most important—the Commission measure—and expecting to increase his percentage on routine legislation.

Hogg had placed high on the list of affairs requiring legislation the subject of railroad stocks and bonds, pointing out the ineffectiveness of legislation passed earlier in an attempt to put in operation the constitutional provision that corporations were not to issue stocks and bonds "except for money paid, labor done, or property actually received."[10] Under the old law only the corporate officers and directors were held accountable, and they were simply made liable to the stockholders and creditors for the full par value. Even this meager protection did not apply to illegal stock or indebtedness, and the Governor declared that the public was altogether unprotected from these abuses.

He was convinced that the task of the Railroad Commission could never be fully accomplished if the courts held that "reasonable returns" upon the investment included any amount of watered securities. The Governor quoted figures showing 170,600 miles of railway in operation in the United States on January 1, 1891, carrying liabilities of over $10,765,000,000. He declared that the lines collected $1,130,000,000[11] from traffic receipts, which permitted, after deductions for operating expenses and rentals, a $90,000,000-payment in dividends—but most Texas roads were not paying any dividends.

Admitting that Texas could not run the railroad business of other states, Hogg argued that it could set an example. He pointed out that the 9,000 miles of railways in Texas were rendered for tax purposes as being worth $67,000,000. Nevertheless, under oath the railroads listed stocks and bonds valued at $465,000,000—more than the valuation of

[9] *General Laws of Texas, 1893* (Austin, 1893), p. 220; Texas *House Journal* (1893), pp. 140, 346, 714. Section XXX, Article 16, of the Texas constitution, providing for the election of railroad commissioners in staggered terms as Hogg recommended, was adopted by popular referendum November 6, 1894. For veto messages, see Cotner, *Addresses of James S. Hogg*, pp. 142–144 and 348–353 and Chap. XII.

[10] *Revised Statutes of Texas* (Galveston, 1895), Article 4410 (4154), p. 761. For State Democratic Platform, 1892, Section 14, see Winkler, *op. cit.*, p. 319.

[11] Poor, *Manual of Railroads for 1891*, p. ii, shows $1,138,024,459 "total traffic revenue," with total mileage for December 31, 1891, listed as 170,601 miles.

all rural land in Texas. He proposed that a law be passed reminding the railroads that their charters permitted only "reasonable charges for their service," which meant that after paying expenses for legitimate performance of their functions as common carriers, they should be permitted "to pay a reasonable return on the capital invested in them."[12] The meaning of capital was to be so defined as to virtually eliminate fictitious stocks and bonds. Not willing to wait for the slow-moving Interstate Commerce Commission to collect enough information to provide national data which would someday be valuable in rate-fixing, Hogg recommended using the sworn statements supplied by the railroads to the comptroller as one way to point out the great discrepancies in the costs and operating expenses of the various lines doing business in Texas.[13]

To build up pressure for passage, the Governor called attention to the fact that the practices of railways trying to keep up stock and bond payments on watered securities included laying off of crews, reducing wages, curtailing services, and increasing traffic rates. When federal receiverships were established the state was usually unable to appear in such cases or to raise its voice in court against the fraud of establishing the amount of the fictitious indebtedness by a court judgment. Hogg declared that the legislature must provide a remedy for the protection of the public and for the bona fide investor. Referring to the unsettled Railroad Commission test case, he said:

Its momentous importance certainly can not be denied now by any intelligent man, since the foreign bondholders, through a Federal court, have obtained a temporary injunction suspending the rates fixed by the Railway Commission, upon the complaint, among other things, that they were not high enough, after paying the expenses of the roads, to meet the interest upon their bonds, many millions of which, with the light of truth shed upon them, would appear to be the depraved offspring of corporate abuse in violation of the express provisions of the State Constitution. By that action the point is sharply, boldly made, that the traffic rates of this country must be maintained to pay interest on all the railway bonds. It is material to the public, therefore, that none but honest bonds, issued in pursuance and within the limits of the Constitution directly, shall be permitted.[14]

Specific remedies proposed included:

[12] Message to the legislature, January 12, 1893, quoted in Cotner, *Addresses of James S. Hogg*, p. 293; Texas *House Journal, Extra Session* (1892), p. 123.
[13] Cotner, *op. cit.*, p. 293, n. 4.
[14] *Ibid.*, p. 295.

1. The Railroad Commission was to be granted authority to report under oath the fair valuation of the railroads of Texas.

2. Railroad bonds and stocks were to be authorized only at the railway's general office in Texas and for limited amounts and purposes mentioned in the Constitution.

3. The Commission must have certified their amount and purposes as legal and their registration by the Secretary of State prior to sale.

4. The Railway Commission was to be authorized to receive and check expenditures of construction and improvement companies to determine that their charges were fair and reasonable before any bonds or stocks over an amount prescribed by the law could be authorized.

5. A time limit was to be placed upon properties in the hands of receivers under foreclosure proceedings; the property was to be sold to satisfy debts and new purchasers were to obtain the property free of incumbrances.

6. Failure to abide by law, "by issuing, hypothecating, or selling fictitious bonds or stocks, or otherwise encumbering" the property would cause a railroad to lose its charter.

7. Every director, stockholder, and officer agreeing to an illegal act should be declared guilty of a penal offense.

8. It became the duty of the State, as plaintiff or intervenor, acting through the Attorney General, or such attorney as the Governor might especially employ, to enter any court having jurisdiction of the case and to contest the validity of such stocks or bonds, and to enforce the laws with respect to them.[15]

Governor Hogg wanted action. He reminded the members that the House at the special session of 1892 had passed a similar bill 62 to 34, but 2 members had refused to vote, 10 were absent, and 19 excused; the Senate had rejected the measure. Again he warned of the strength of the railway lobbyists, and assured the legislators that it was a specious plea that passage would deter capital from investing in Texas. Hogg argued that the proposed law would encourage investment of "honest capital in railway improvement, protect commerce from unjust burdens, guard the people from bankruptcy and servility, and add strength and respectability to the independent autonomy of the State government, which must in time command the approval of all impartial, circumspect men."[16]

The law which was approved April 8, 1893, was not as restrictive as the Governor had recommended it to be. Section 2 permitted the Com-

[15] *Ibid.*, pp. 295–296.
[16] *Ibid.*, p. 297; Texas *House Journal* (1892), p. 175; Texas *House Journal* (1893), p. 17.

mission "in case of an emergency, or conclusive proof . . . that public interests or the preservation of the property demanded it" to authorize bonds and stock in the aggregate not more than 50 per cent over the value of the property. This provision permitted some flexibility, and whether it would be abused depended upon the commissioners. A railway company was to be notified by a registered letter when a report of valuation was ready for filing with the secretary of state; the company then had forty days in which to make objections. Hogg obtained one of his essential recommendations when the law declared that all sales of railroad property were to have the effect of discharging the property from liability in the hands of purchasers for claims for damages, unsecured debts, or junior mortgages, and it became illegal to issue new stock in lieu of the old. Purchasers were always to take over "clear of incumbrances," thus being able to issue stocks and bonds under the limitations prescribed.

Section 6 gave the Commission power to check all new issues prior to formal release, and, when satisfied of the good faith of the company and the amount of the issue, the Commission was to have them registered. A majority of a board of directors was required to meet at the company's principal office in Texas and certify the names and amounts of stockholders. The issues were limited to not more than the value of the property, except as provided in the emergency clause, and a limitation of thirty years for maturity was placed upon the issues. False statements or other illegal action taken by a president, director, secretary, or other official might draw confinement at hard labor for two to fifteen years and liability for damages. The state was protected from being bound to pay any obligation, debt, or claim executed or assumed under this law. Finally, an elaborate set of rules and regulations controlled the Commission in the approval of railroad stocks and bonds.[17]

Such was the law giving additional powers to a Commission which might be declared unconstitutional as a result of the pending *Reagan* v. *Farmers Loan and Trust Company* case, but the Governor had faith in his previous handiwork. The decision of the U. S. Supreme Court in 1894 declaring the Texas Railroad Commission constitutional proved the validity of Hogg's faith. Although forced by the same decision to rework the actual rate structures, because some rates were held unreasonable, the Railroad Commission was now armed with sufficient power

---

[17] *General Laws of the Twenty-third Legislature* (Austin, 1893), pp. 54–55. Charles A. Culberson, *Report of the Attorney General . . . 1893–1894* (Austin, 1895), pp. 18–21, lists railroad issues examined. 154 U.S. 362 (1894).

to fix rates, in time, on fair valuation and to check the most obnoxious practices leading to stock manipulations. The emergency clause was subject to possible abuse, and the long life of old stocks and bonds would delay the best efforts of the Commission.

Writing in 1907, an economist at the University of Texas, Edmund T. Miller, pointed out the wide margin between the actual value of the old roads, not so easy to determine as in the case of new lines, and the amount of stocks and bonds outstanding on the old lines.[18] In 1901 the legislature had amended the law to provide that overcapitalized roads might build extensions and issue new securities in an amount equal to "the reasonable value" of such extensions, whereas up to then no new issues had been allowed unless the old lines and the new raised the total valuation above the book value of outstanding securities.[19] A second amendment, added in 1907, permitted, under certain conditions, excessively capitalized roads to issue securities for the purchase of necessary rolling stock.[20] Professors Charles Potts and E. T. Miller thought the stock regulations strict and the amendments necessary, but they pointed out that the Commission left ways to reward the better-managed corporations and that all were permitted reasonable estimates on the cost of their services.

In the fourteen years prior to the Panic of 1907 the outstanding stocks and bonds on Texas railroads steadily declined in the average capitalization per mile, whereas in the nation as a whole railroad stocks and bonds continued to increase in the average capitalization per mile, Hogg had reversed a trend which in 1893 was adding $30 million a year to Texas railway indebtedness. Instead of stocks and bonds of $373 million in 1894 for 9,000 miles, there were only $404 million (including $16 million unauthorized certificates of indebtedness issued by the Gulf, Colorado, and Santa Fe) for 12,600 miles in 1907. While mileage increased 42 per cent, the indebtedness increased only 11 per cent.[21]

While studying the securities of public carriers, the Governor had

[18] Edmund T. Miller, "The Texas Stock and Bond Law and Its Administration," *Quarterly Journal of Economics,* XXII (November, 1907), 109–119.
[19] Charles Potts, *Railroad Transportation in Texas,* pp. 197 ff.; see also Hogg's address to the Texas legislature, February 5, 1901, quoted in Cotner, *op. cit.,* pp. 483–495; *General Laws of the Twenty-seventh Legislature, Regular Session* (Austin, 1901), p. 257.
[20] *General Laws of the Thirtieth Legislature, Regular Session* (Austin, 1907), p. 297.
[21] Texas Railroad Commission, *Report for 1893* (Austin, 1894), p. 19; Potts, *op. cit.,* pp. 148–149; cf. Joseph D. Sayers, *Railroad Consolidations in Texas* (Austin, 1904), p. 80.

332

also given attention to the question of county and municipal securities. As a fledgling newspaper publisher in the 1870's Hogg had followed with interest the scandals of the New York City Tweed Ring. Other eastern city hall gangs were lately enriching themselves and their allies by fat public works contracts. To finance these gigantic undertakings, the bond issue, which gave the immediate benefits to the people and delayed payment to the second and third generation, was a ready tool of the honest and unscrupulous alike. Street-paving, water and sewerage mains, electric lights, electric streetcars, and gas plants promised huge profits to holders of a special franchise or bonuses to the bond brokers. For the past ten years western cities had been invaded by the virus of eastern expansion and modernity, every city wanting to be a second Philadelphia or New York, at least in area. Texas was not immune to the virus; during the first legislative session in 1891 a rash of requests had broken out for approval of new city charters broad enough to permit almost any kind of improvement, expansion, or bond scheme. Governor Hogg, sincerely believing that the public should be as much protected from unnecessary or fraudulent civic debts as from railroad tariffs calculated to pay off watered bonds, had vetoed several new charters. His popularity was scarcely enhanced thereby, especially in the cities where the daily papers supported the measures, although there was division in Houston and Dallas.

When Austin came up in March, 1891, with a request for a new charter and authority to greatly extend the boundaries, Hogg, after receiving a strong letter against the measure from Professor Oran M. Roberts of the University law faculty and after discussion with other citizens, wrote a resounding veto. For his pains he was called paternalistic and the opponent of progress, and one editor questioned whether the Governor or a city council best knew the interests of the public.[22] Hogg, however, was armed with Roberts' charge that a small group of town boosters and self-beneficiaries wanted the people to bond themselves to provide an ample and cheap water supply to tempt industry to locate in Austin. The Governor had pointed out that the title of the bill did not make it clear that the act would validate water works bonds already issued by the Austin Council. Austin embraced four square

---

[22] *Letter of Governor O. M. Roberts to Governor Hogg in Protest against the New Charter*, March 2, 1891 (Austin, 1891), pamphlet, Univ. Tex. Lib. The original MS is preserved in the O. M. Roberts Papers, Fol. XV. Austin *Daily Statesman*, March 29–30, 1891; Dallas *Morning News*, March 29, 1891; Veto Message of March 28, 1891, quoted in Cotner, *op. cit.*, pp. 145 ff.

miles of territory, and the new charter provided for inclusion of four times that area without any immediate prospect of great expansion. Furthermore, the plan was "irregular . . . devoid of all symmetry in shape and apparent fairness in lines." A dam had been built about two miles up the Colorado, and from that point the city wanted to take in along the "river's meanders" ten varas (c. 28 ft.) from the margin of the high-water mark on both sides as far as the water was backed up by the dam, perhaps twenty-five miles in dry seasons and thirty-five in the rainy periods.

The Governor expressed alarm that the city was to have tax and policy powers over this vast area, while a Board of Water and Light Commissioners, which was to be delegated "many unusual and peculiar powers," would look after the protection, support, and maintenance of the water and light works. This, in Hogg's view, set up two governments, which was not legal. Furthermore, an equalization board was given final authority in the matter of fixing taxes as high as $2.50 per $100 valuation. The city could foreclose a lien on property to collect taxes due, apparently ignoring the homestead law; the bill gave the Council power to buy and use property beyond the city limits, so that taxes could in theory be levied to pay for property anywhere in the state. The Council could define a nuisance within 3,000 feet outside of the city limits, and there was even authority to punish any person who put any filthy substance in the river "above the dam." The imperialism of the city was real; Hogg believed county government still had appropriate functions to fulfill.

The Governor objected that the 157 sections of the measure covered practically all "powers known to the extravagant demands of modern municipalities." He questioned the policy of making broad, general grants of power to cities but did not indulge himself with a discussion of those points, declaring:

A municipal corporation is intended as an agent of the state, to adapt local government to the wants and necessities of a limited locality inhabited by the people within its boundaries. It is one of the convenient methods by which good gvernment is intended to be maintained in the interest of the masses. When such purposes fail, necessities for municipal government cease to exist.[23]

Reminding the city dwellers that they would soon be paying the 32½-

[23] Cotner, *op. cit.*, p. 147; cf. James Bryce, *The American Commonwealth* (New York, Macmillan Company, 1951), pp. 642–648, 656 ff.

334

cent state tax, a 50-cent county tax, and a $2.50 city tax, he frankly called this an extravagance of the times and urged the legislature to reconsider this aspect, since tax measures were primarily a concern of the legislative body. He emphasized other reasons sufficient in themselves to have caused him to write the veto, namely the large area, the extraordinary powers, and the questionable propriety of the executive and legislative branches settling a matter raised by the earlier bond issue election in Austin, May 5, 1890. This, he said, was a matter for the courts:

If the municipal officers assumed to issue those bonds under the power of taxation under such circumstances as did not constitutionally justify the exercise of that power, the legislative act validating the bonds could not make them valid. There are purposes for which a city cannot issue such bonds, even with legislative consent; and when they are issued, the legislative has no power to validate them. . . . As a rule validating acts are mischievous, and I cannot understand any special reason for the legislative attempt to fix such an enormous debt upon the people of the Capital city, even though they should request it. It seems that these bonds were issued for the purpose of erecting a dam across the Colorado river, ostensibly to supply the city with water and light for public and private use. No doubt it is a commendable enterprise, but it should be kept within legitimate bounds. If the bonds are valid, no one can complain. If otherwise, it would be wrong for this legislature to embarrass the people by trying to make them so.[24]

Hogg objected to granting to the new Water Board powers he believed were assigned by the Texas Constitution only to city governments. Furthermore, while state law stipulated two-year terms for all but those whose terms were fixed by the Constitution, the new proposal called for three-year terms for six commissioners. He believed that if the Board was permitted to "stand in the full exercise of its powers, the city of Austin may expect, under her double form of government, to become burdened with officers and expenses beyond endurance."[25] Finally, he concluded that it was a "dangerous policy" to vest any municipal government with such extraordinary powers as proposed. Hogg demanded that all persons interested in modernization of city government, even under the banner of progress, should carefully consider the expense and legality of all measures.

[24] Cotner, op. cit., p. 148.
[25] Texas House Journal (1891), pp. 764–767. Incidentally, Edward Bellamy of Boston wrote for a copy of the veto message; a copy was sent to him April 23, 1891.

The reasoning in this veto of 1891 and the import of the stock-and-bond program were clearly in the Governor's mind when he voiced to the legislature of 1893 his recommendations on county and municipal indebtedness as commanded by the Democratic platform. By way of introduction he said:

This State had not escaped the mania prevalent throughout the United States for loading posterity with debts they do not owe by the issuance of interest-bearing bonds to gratify the extravagance of the present generation. At best, public bonds, as a rule, are not unmixed with evil. County and municipal bonds generally bear an interest of from six to eight per cent, and are payable sometimes beyond the life of the generation executing them, for the construction of roads, streets, and public buildings, which, in the nature of things, will have washed away [this happened to the Austin city dam], grown into disuse, or collapsed into decay long before the debts are due.[26]

He admitted that there were rare occasions of public necessity which required long-term bond issues, but, without any reference to his part in the framing of the document, he reminded the legislature of the section in the platform of 1892 that read:

15. We demand the passage of a law that will prevent the useless and extravagant issuance of bonds by cities, towns, and counties in the State, confining them within constitutional limitations to actual public necessities, so as to preserve the public faith, to insure a lower rate of interest, and to protect the present and future generations from burdens that should never be imposed by such methods.[27]

He pointed to expenditures for county courthouses and jails so lavish that in some of the populous counties the bonded indebtedness for courthouses alone was over thirty dollars per capita.[28]

James Hogg, the progressive conservative, was concerned about the mounting costs of city government, sometimes incurring tax rates three or four times that of a county. He believed it was time to call a halt to "protect the people from oppressive taxation." Aware that there was new interest in public water systems to supplant the customary individual water supply, and that the city dweller was apparently willing to

[26] Quoted in Cotner, *op. cit.*, p. 297.
[27] Winkler, *Platforms*, p. 319; Houston *Post*, August 17–18, 1892.
[28] Examples of the Gothic-Mediterranean mixtures for county courthouses and jails may be seen in Dallas, Hillsboro, Waco, and Waxahachie. Built substantially of red or cream stone, these buildings reflect a sturdy past and a faith in the future, while sometimes they also show skills of the old-time stone mason.

pay for more and better services, including schools, Hogg still emphasized the need for economical government. He believed people should understand that they obligated every bit of city property to pay the bonds.

He therefore recommended, first, as a way to check extravagance, repeal of an act of 1889 permitting the funding of floating indebtedness; second, before any county or municipal bonds could be issued the governmental units should submit their needs to the attorney general, who should determine necessity and validity and then certify if approved; third, bonds should be registered by the comptroller along with the certificate of the attorney general; fourth, make it a criminal offense for any person or official to have any part in any sale of fraudulent or fictitious bonds.[29] In this way the Governor expected to protect the public credit of Texas, guarantee the safety of the investment, promote a reduction of the interest rate, check extravagance, and protect posterity from heavy public burdens.

Here was something new—a Governor wanting to guarantee the securities of the subdivisions of government against fraudulent issue and virtually promising no repudiation. Here was a golden field for the conservative investment banker, but Hogg's concern was for the people who paid the interest.

The county and municipal bond law was passed in April, 1893.[30] It required that bond issues must be accompanied with provisions to collect taxes annually in sufficient amount to pay interest and to establish a sinking fund. The interest rate was limited to 6 per cent, a rate for which Hogg had been working since 1890, and bonds were not to be sold at less than par and accumulated interest, "exclusive of commissions." The examination and registration features were also adopted. These restrictions, combined with restraint imposed by the attorney general, enabled the government subdivisions to find purchasers for their bond issues; the state government itself often invested money from the Permanent School Fund in these bonds as permitted by law. Thus, indirectly, the measure was a protection to this important source of revenue for the public schools, because the law declared that the "only defense which can be offered against the validity of said bonds shall be

[29] Cotner, *op. cit.*, pp. 299–300. The fourth item was long, involving the actions to be taken by the attorney general to make bonds valid. On June 22, 1953, the Austin *Statesman* reported that the attorney general had refused an increased bond issue for a certain county.

[30] Approved April 29, 1893, quoted, *ibid.*, Appendix E, pp. 561–563.

337

for forgery or fraud," with the exception of bonds issued over the constitutional limit or contrary to its provisions. The penalty for a city or county official making false statements to increase bond issues could be imprisonment from one to five years.

The third major progressive law enacted by the legislature in 1893 grew out of the Governor's efforts to supplement the Alien Land Act of 1892 by defining and outlawing perpetuities and setting limitations upon corporate land holding, to the end that the now fast-diminishing public domain might be protected for the individual settler. Hogg himself believed fervently that every family should own a home, and throughout both his boyhood and his later public life he had been exposed to episodes that highlighted the importance of the homestead to men and their families. He knew that his father had written into the Constitution of 1845 those clauses which protect homesteads. As an East Texan, Hogg had more than once been accused of not understanding the needs of West Texas, with its sweep of vast far-stretching lands lacking trees and water, and it is undoubtedly true that at the beginning of his first term as attorney general—his first public office that necessitated a state-wide point of view—his thinking was largely conditioned by his upbringing in the prosperous and often lush farm country east of a line from Austin to Cleburne and Fort Worth. But he had been obliged early to become involved in the problems of western lands and leases; he studied diligently and learned quickly through various cases inherited from his predecessor, John Templeton. These included the dispute over the 1,500,000 acres of Greer County lands— whether they belonged to Texas or to the Indian Territory—which had not been settled by a Joint Texas and United States Commission of 1886–1887 and in 1892 was still not settled; Hogg had been continuously in litigation before the U. S. Supreme Court on the subject. And his first major endeavor as attorney general had been the Charles Goodnight-Judge Willis affair of the Panhandle lease and enclosure cases; further, the problem of western lands had been part of his fight with Abner Taylor of the XIT Ranch over the completion of the new Capitol. Then came the numerous land suits.

Whatever the rights of the Panhandle cases (as noted earlier, Hogg believed that Templeton had stirred up a hornets' nest), as far as they applied to Goodnight, the fight was symptomatic of the changing situation of the frontier, where once land had seemed so unending and inexhaustible that few cared when one man, or a group of men, preempted hundreds of thousands of acres. But the rush of 250,000 home-

338

steaders into Oklahoma within a year after its opening to settlement in 1889 had been additional evidence of the great pressure for homesteads suitable for farming and a warning signal (ignored by most people) that land famine was imminent in the "limitless" West.[31] These were matters that James Hogg had watched and pondered on. He felt an increasing and troubled concern that the frontier might be entirely vanished before the leaders of Texas could grapple with the problem of securing what was left of the public domain to the people.

During the twelve years following 1882, when the last land grants were made to Texas railroads, Hogg had heard the increasing volume of complaints of settlers in both east and west that land corporations and the railways seemed to own all of the desirable land. As early as 1884, Texas Greenbackers, Republicans, and Democrats were agreed that corporate landholding for speculative purposes was detrimental to the public welfare. In 1886 the Texas Farmers' Alliance joined in the outcry against private and corporate holdings of large bodies of land for speculative purposes, but advocated no measures to force the break-up of the large estates other than taxation of all corporate and railway lands at the normal rates charged settlers on 160 acres or less.[32] Since 1887 Hogg had been working on judgments against the railroads for recovery of lands illegally granted for mileage in sidings and switches.

Now in his 1893 message he told the legislature that "there is a land famine in most of the old world and in many sections of the new. In the natural drift of affairs it may reach Texas in the next generation." The statement is an interesting example of Hogg's foresight. He, of course, was witnessing the forces which historian Walter P. Webb would discuss in the 1950's—forces which had caused Webb's own parents to brave the Plains. When Webb worked out ratios between population, land, and wealth and compared sixteenth-century Europe with the almost frontierless twentieth-century world in evolving his "Boom Theory," he declared that the boom based on land was over by the 1930's.[33]

[31] Edwin C. McReynolds, *Oklahoma*, pp. 293–297.

[32] Winkler, *Platforms*, p. 235. For the first platform of the People's Party in Texas, drafted August 17–18, 1891, see Winkler, *op. cit.*, pp. 293–297. Cf. *Report of the General Land Office, 1928–1930* (Austin, 1930), pp. 4–5, showing tables of land distribution and railway holdings; Roscoe Martin, *People's Party in Texas*, pp. 47 ff.

[33] Walter P. Webb, *The Great Frontier* (Boston, Houghton Mifflin Company, 1953), pp. 13–28; Governor Hogg's message of January 12, 1893, quoted in Cotner, *op. cit.*, pp. 302 ff.; see also Webb's *More Water for Texas* (Austin, University of Texas Press, 1954) and V. Webster Johnson and Raleigh Barlow, *Land Problems and Policies* (New York, McGraw-Hill, 1954), pp. 166–194.

The Census of 1890 had been of great interest to Hogg, and he had asked the legislature in 1891 to use it in making a much needed redistribution of the increased number of allotted seats in Congress.[34] A brilliant young historian at the University of Wisconsin, Frederick Jackson Turner, was also interested in the 1890 Census during his exploration of the "significance of the frontier."[35] Turner and Hogg were like lonely watchers at the northern and southern edges of the Great Plains, who saw pass before their eyes the people and land corporations which destroyed two frontiers. Turner's mind encompassed a wider range in time and space, but Hogg had a close-range vantage point for observation of the special conditions operating on the Texas frontier, as he saw barbed-wire barriers thrown around millions of acres by cattlemen and foreign corporations—barriers that sent the on-rushing land seekers swirling in circles, frantically looking for places to homestead, with or without water and trees. Texas distributed her own public lands, and Hogg had frequent occasion to study the Land Office records. He was sufficiently impressed with the population movement to the High Plains to make an effort to obtain votes in West Texas in 1886 and 1890.

Hogg's pondering of the land problem was evident in his Dallas speech of October, 1892, when he spoke of Europe's and especially Ireland's land famine.[36] When in his 1893 message he warned the legislature of diminishing land he was well armed with settlement statistics from annual reports from railways and the official reports of the Texas land commissioner.[37]

When known that there is now in nine of the old States only seven acres

[34] Message of March 3, 1891, Gov. Let. Pr., 1, p. 428; Texas *House Journal* (1891), pp. 468–469.

[35] Frederick J. Turner, "The Significance of the Frontier in American History," American Historical Association, *Annual Report, 1893* (Washington, 1894), pp. 199–227; Everett E. Edwards (comp.), *The Early Writings of Frederick Jackson Turner* (Madison, University of Wisconsin Press, 1938), pp. 185–229. Personal interviews with Dr. Fulmer Mood, who is writing a biography of Turner, May and July, 1954.

[36] In the speech at Dallas, October 1, 1892, after citing conditions in Ireland, Scotland, England, France, and New York City (13,000 real estate owners in a population of 2 million), he declared: "Land monopoly means pauperism and distress of the masses. It destroys patriotism; breeds communism. No government ever survived long in happiness or peace that permits its existence." He quoted Nehemiah 5:1–5. See also James S. Hogg's speech, "Home", typescript, J. S. Hogg Misc.

[37] Texas Railroad Commission, *First Annual Report, 1892*, pp. 162–340; James S. Hogg, *Report of the Attorney General of Texas for 1889–1890*, pp. 4–5; Richard M. Hall, *Report of the Commissioner of the Land Office for 1888–1890*, pp. 6–9.

per capita; that in nine of the others there are only twenty acres per capita; that in twelve others, compartively new States, there are only twenty-two acres per capita; that in nine strictly Southern States there are only thirty-five acres per capita, and that in the whole United States, including the Territories, there are only thirty-seven acres per capita of the whole population, and that about one-tenth of these lands are possessed by land corporations, there is at least some excuse for thoughtful people to be agitated at this time over the land problem.

While the whole area of Texas amounts to about seventy-four acres per capita of her population, she is confronted with the most serious condition of corporate ownership of about one-fourth of it all. Statistics show that in the United States from 1870 to 1880 the cultivatable lands in staple crops increased 66 per cent; while from 1880 to 1890 the increase thereof was only 26 per cent. The evident cause of this is the growing scarcity of agricultural lands throughout the government [sic]. The bread-producing land of the world is fast becoming exhausted while the bread-consuming people are increasing. . . . The land problem, after all, underlies the bread problem. It is the duty of the government to understand this and to act wisely for the good of posterity. This can best be done by restrictive laws, making corporate land monopoly impossible for the future. While the American people have escaped the evil of land monopoly under the laws of primogeniture of the old world, they may yet find themselves involved in a more serious condition—that of land monopoly from titles in perpetuity caused by corporate ownership.[38]

Hogg was interested in breaking up the large corporate holdings which tended to create islands of sparsely settled areas to the great benefit of the few rather than the many, especially when he considered how these holders broke both the fact and the spirit of the law. He wanted a law declaring that no rural land corporation would be chartered in the future. Further corporate acquisition of titles or interest in land for speculative, agricultural, or grazing purposes should be prohibited, and corporations holding agricultural and grazing lands should be given a time limit in which to wind up their affairs and to leave the state. The XIT Ranch was not specifically mentioned, but since it was one of the largest and best-known land and cattle corporations controlled by outsiders and had so far failed to sell off its lands as the charter that granted the lands to the Chicago syndicate for building the Capitol required, most of the Governor's listeners could supply the name. They could also assume that the attack was not wholly unrelated to the fact that a fre-

[38] Message of January 12, 1893, quoted in Cotner, *op. cit.,* pp. 302–303. Hogg saw the great grain and cotton surpluses as temporary conditions.

quent adviser for the Ranch, Senator Matlock, who had fought Hogg in every political campaign, tried to please the now-prominent Republicans, Congressman Abner Taylor (XIT manager) and United States Senator C. B. Farwell of Illinois, both members of the syndicate.[39]

Farmers and small ranchers stood to gain if a law prohibiting corporate holdings could be passed and enforced. To avoid stirring up too much opposition—with the foreign corporation and railway landholdings primarily in mind—Hogg sought to obtain a law which would still permit "all manufacturing, transportation, and other corporations whose purpose may not be the ownership of lands, to possess, use and retain as much real estate as may be proper for corporate necessities." An exception would also be made for corporations building and improving harbors, homes, and additions to towns and cities; the proposed law would not affect "the wholesome laws" already regulating irrigation and mining companies or corporations engaged in redeeming swamp or overflowed lands.

The Perpetuities and Corporation Land Law, passed on March 24, 1893, granted all private corporations "whose main purpose or business is the acquisition or ownership by purchase, lease, or otherwise of lands in this State" fifteen years to make "an actual bona fide sale of all lands or interest . . . and . . . by proper deed to convey in good faith all their right and title." Other corporations authorized under Chapter 101, Article 566, of the Acts of 1891 were restrained to such lands as were "necessary to carry on their business" and any lands over that were to be disposed of in fifteen years.[40] As Hogg candidly told the Boston Chamber of Commerce in June, 1894, "The aim of the movement is to prevent the further investment by land corporations in agricultural and grazing lands and all other lands for speculative purposes."[41] In the age of the rise of the city, it is significant that one of the most promising areas of speculation was specifically excepted by these words: "Provided, that nothing in this law shall be construed to prohibit the lease, purchase, sale or subdivision of lands within incorporated towns, cities, or villages,

---

[39] Cotner, op. cit., pp. 272, 302. The Tascosa Pioneer, May 12, 1888, declared: "A whole half-dozen . . . blarsted Britishers . . . have . . . been looking over the Panhandle with a view to purchasing the rest of it." Quoted in Haley, The XIT Ranch, p. 211. See also pp. 203 ff., 216–221.

[40] Gammel, Laws of Texas, X, pp. 466–467; Cotner, op. cit., Appendix C, pp. 552–553. Pennsylvania was beginning efforts to separate railroads from coal lands not essential to direct operation of the railroads.

[41] Cotner, op. cit., pp. 305, 371.

and the suburbs of such towns, cities, and villages, within two miles from the limits of said incorporations in any directon."[42] Knowingly or unknowingly a new area of land speculation was pointed out, and it did not take long for developers to learn of the benefits.

Despite efforts to enforce the new law, many of the corporations in existence did not dispose of their lands in the stipulated fifteen years. Throughout later years numerous special-purpose features were added to the law, and Professor Rupert Richardson was correct when he wrote: "The law was easily contravened and failed to accomplish its purpose. Large landholdings are common in parts of Texas."[43]

Section 22 of the Democratic platform of 1892 had commended the state officials for their efforts to recover all lands possible under the "sidings and switches" cases. A pledge had been made that innocent purchasers for value from railroads—"actual settlers"—should have their titles validated in so far as the state might claim the lands. The Governor expressed his opinion that legislation was unnecessary at the 1893 session, especially as such a law might tend to complicate the rights of the state "without giving any material benefit to actual settlers or innocent purchasers," but he announced that his administration would continue to withhold patents on land held by certification until after the suits were disposed of in the courts.[44] The only law advisable for the present, he declared, was one which would authorize the attorney general and the land commissioner "to accept for the State such portion of the remaining land held by the several railway companies or their corporate assigns as shall amount to the quantity of land that the records show was originally obtained unlawfully by the company desiring the settlement."[45]

At this point, railroad interests, clever lawyers, and certain persons worrying about their land titles were able to pressure for a bill "to validate certain titles to lands located by virtue of certificates to railroad companies, and now owned by purchasers in actual good faith, for

[42] Section 4. Speaking in Boston, Massachusetts, Hogg declared land corporations had acquired about 40 million acres of land in Texas and 400 million over the nation, but he pointed out that corporations engaged in leasing, buying, and selling subdivisions within incorporated towns or cities were not included in the act.

[43] Richardson, *Texas*, p. 360; *Vernon's Civil Statutes of Texas* (Kansas City, Vernon Law Book Company, 1947), I, 343 ff., for Article 166, and III, 383 for Article 1362.

[44] Message of January 12, 1893, quoted in Cotner, *op. cit.*, p. 313.

[45] *Ibid.*, p. 314.

value, . . . and actual settlers, or belonging to the public free school, the University and asylum funds."[46] Hogg promptly sent in a veto, objecting to the "sweeping terms" that had the effect of "wiping out the claims of the State of Texas to all of the lands illegally or fraudulently obtained from her by railroad companies." He felt that it meant virtual donation of several millions of dollars to railroads, while current cases involved a million and a quarter acres. Listen to the man frequently accused of being a demagogue:

If there are any actual settlers in good faith on any of these lands, they can bide their time until the State settles with the railroad companies and their corporate assigns. If their impatience should lead them to want the State to make the sacrifice demanded of her by this law, then I submit that in their blindness they should receive light by disappointment. In this day and time the State can not be so generous as to make the appropriation of several million dollars' worth of land to any individual or corporation. The number of acres occupied by actual settlers, whose interests it has always been the policy of the State to protect, is very small compared with the amount illegally held by railroad companies and their allies. But a short time ago the Attorney General recovered from the assignee of a railway company, who most probably held the property in trust for the corporation, over a hundred and seventy thousand acres of very valuable land without depriving a single actual settler of any rights whatever.[47]

Hogg told the legislators that the measure on his desk went beyond the platform pledges; it did not stop at statements protecting actual settlers, but swept aside the state's claims to any of the lands, although the people had urged the completion of the land suits for recovery. Hogg was attacked for his position on this, especially since it was frequently misrepresented by Populists, Republicans, and lawyers of the railroads adversely affected as being against the interests of the public, but he held firm. Attorney General Culberson continued to prosecute successfully the land recovery suits.

In discussing economical but adequately financed government, the Governor laid down certain rules, a kind of ten commandments on

---

[46] Texas *Senate Journal,* March 29, 1893, p. 454, shows the bill passed 15 to 13, with 3 absent.

[47] Veto message of May 20, 1893, Texas *Senate Journal* (1893), pp. 90–91, 132. Hogg also pointed out that many of the railroad surveys were not carefully made, with the result that many of the county boundaries were inaccurate. This situation necessitated great expense to the state in running further surveys so as to avoid litigation and debate over school lands. Cf. Charles A. Culberson, *Report of the Attorney General . . . 1893–1894* (Austin, 1895), pp. 7–8.

taxation. All states were beginning to feel the squeeze between the higher tax rates of municipalities and the higher federal taxes:

1. Fix the minimum value of lands, below which the assessor shall not accept it for taxation.
2. Prohibit county assessors from accepting urban property at less than the value rendered to the city assessor for municipal purposes.
3. Direct that the assessor shall not accept any property at less than the amount for which it stands mortgaged.
4. Tax insurance companies on the amount of business done annually.
5. Increase the permit tax on all foreign corporations doing business in the State. Let it be made an annual tax on the franchise.
6. Impose an annual occupation tax upon all persons who sell or offer for sale pistols, bowie knives, dirks, and daggers.
7. Place a tax upon all persons engaged in the manufacture or sale of all classes of cigarettes and the material used therefor.
8. Levy a tax on every telephone used, to be paid annually by the company owning or controlling them.
9. Impose an occupation tax on each sleeping, palace or dining-room car company, and on all companies leasing or renting cars to railway companies for any purposes whatever; or better still, adopt the Pennsylvania law on this subject. Make the right of the companies to do business in this State depend on payment of the tax.
10. Tax rectifiers and brewers.[48]

Hogg clearly intended to "level up" property values, to more nearly equalize the tax burden, and to collect "just dues" from "the many who are now escaping taxation." He declared that if his suggestions were enacted into law he did not see any need to increase the low ad valorem rate to finance the progessive program—in fact he was proud of the rate reductions from 20 to 15 cents per $100 valuation.[49] He had seen the need to shift some of the burdens of supporting state government from the backs of the farmers and other landowners and to require corporations to pay on fairer valuations. However, the legislature did not share his foresight in this and gave little attention to the suggestions. Taxation practices, nevertheless, of a later time have attested to the merit and appeal of Hogg's "ten commandments," although the first three items are seldom followed in practice.

The next several sections of the message had to do with those social

[48] Message of January 12, 1893, quoted in Cotner, *op. cit.*, pp. 320–321.
[49] Message of January 12, 1893, in Texas *House Journal* (1893), p. 28; Texas *House Journal* (1895), Appendix A, pp. 7 ff.

problems which are the burden of all governments. In an executive's approach to them can be read a great deal of his character and the degree of his willingness to accept the responsibility of his office. These problems are useful to demagogues, who may exploit them for personal gain, especially when they present them with impassioned flourish and fanfare; these problems are equally useful to those who wish to make a treasury surplus a talking point in a future election, since the inmates of state institutions, when money has been saved on their care, are usually not able to talk back through a ballot. The manner in which James Hogg handled these problems before the 1893 legislature perhaps constituted one of the best possible refutations of the charge made by Hogg's enemies that he was "power-mad"; it was also an affirmation of his desire to act on the words with which he had opened his message: "The prime object of a constitutional form of government is the perfection of human happiness. To obtain this remote though coveted end, laws . . . have always been and must ever be necessary."

In seeking new sources of income for the state, some of the legislators had been eying the legal lotteries that flourished in neighboring Louisiana and Mexico. To the lottery leeches the relative prosperity of Texans was highly attractive, and, since the forays across the state lines were not few, it might seem logical to consider legalizing the traffic for the sake of revenue. The Governor reminded the legislators and the law enforcement agencies that the Texas constitution forbade lotteries and the sale of lottery tickets, and that any express company or corporation transporting tickets, documents, etc. of any lottery company was subject to fine and loss of charter, if domestic, or loss of right to do business in Texas, if out-of-state.[50] His discussion of "these instruments of public debauchery" was brief, but its import was a matter of deep personal conviction. Hogg hated gambling in all its forms, having seen its disastrous consequences not only for the rough frontiersmen, for whom it was often the only recreation of status among his peers, but also for educated men—among them several of his friends. At the same time, he never criticized a friend or acquaintance for legal gaming, since it was part of his creed that men were entitled to be masters of their own consciences. Thus, when he was a member of a traveling group, for instance, the other men felt no constraint to abjure their usual card games played for stakes; they accepted his "eccentricity" as he accepted theirs. The Governor himself enjoyed playing the popular six-handed euchre with

[50] Texas *House Journal* (1893), p. 29.

346

his family and neighbors at the Mansion of an evening and did well at it, but stakes were forbidden. Lotteries were another matter, however. Being run for the profit of their shrewd and parasitic operators, they must be considered traps for the unwary and inexperienced—those for whom the loss of even the little spent on a lottery ticket was misfortune.

Whenever the Governor discussed the institutions that harbored the insane, the delinquent, the orphaned, he showed that he had still not lost the urge to know the essence of a problem at first hand, the same impulse to find the facts which had sent the young justice of the peace out to see for himself whether a ditch had been dug well or ill. It was his custom to pay frequent visits to such institutions, where he would talk to the managers, doctors, and inmates with the expressed hope both of discovering how the custodial or remedial jobs done there could be bettered and of learning more about the underlying problems that made the institutions necessary. He considered it a large part of the responsibility of his office (and tried to make the legislators see it as theirs also) to seek understanding of these matters, for he had come to view them as social ills, well in advance of the time when they would be generally recognized as such. The presence in the Governor's personal library of Henry Maudsley's book *Responsibility in Mental Disease* (1878), given him by his friend W. L. Crawford of Dallas, was evidence of his personal interest in these social issues. The problem of habitual drunkenness had become of particular interest to him, as he pondered its possible relations to other social problems. He had long ago reasoned that prohibition was not the answer, as his famous 1887 letter to W. W. Douglas explained: "Men cannot be made moral, forced into temperance, or whipped into religion." His own temperance was graceful; he did not drink in public places and had no hesitation in refusing invitations to do so, but, as with gambling, he did not impose his personal strictures on his friends who wished to do otherwise.

The result of his thinking on the drinking problem became apparent when, in the section of his message on charities, he detailed the condition of the various existing institutions and then went on to say:

It would seem that in respect to habitual drunkards . . . the State has been more or less negligent. The time has arrived when it would appear expedient and proper for the Legislature to establish and have maintained an inebriate asylum for the cure of drunkenness and reform of inebriates, authorized by the Constitution.[51]

[51] *Ibid.*, p. 30.

He proposed financing the new asylum from the following sources—some of which obviously indicated the areas of American life he considered linked with the problem:

1. From the surplus department fees.
2. By collecting a special asylum tax, as high as may be necessary, from the liquor dealers.
3. By an increased tax on every pool table, and every pool seller at horse and other races.
4. By appropriating one-half of all the fines collected from vagrants of every character, gamblers, prostitutes, and gambling houses by State, county, city, and town governments, requiring from those several authorities a prompt report and remittance from that source.
5. By charging reasonable expenses to all patients who may be able to pay.
6. By authorizing to be kept a well-bound book as a roll of charity contributions, in which shall be registered for public inspection the name and address of each philanthropist, and the sum or thing contributed to the institution.[52]

Hogg expressed faith that the experiment would free other institutions of caring for this increasing category of patients so that needed space would be available for other kinds of cases, that it would remove the alcoholics from scenes which might further upset their mental balance, and there was good reason to expect a high rate of cure. The legislature and, most emphatically, the sources singled out for taxation did not share his faith. The proposal was radical for its day—and for many future days: on June 12, 1954, it was still necessary for Judge J. E. Hickman of the Texas Supreme Court, speaking in Austin, to express the hope that Texans would soon pass a frequently introduced bill to make the distillery business pay for rehabilitation of alcoholics.

A long-time source of complaint against past and present administrations had been the slowness in processing applications from penitentiary inmates for pardons. The Governor frankly admitted that the delays and method were "detrimental to public interest."[53] The constitution of Texas placed the pardon and parole power solely in the executive's hands. If any kind of proper investigation of the merits of the petitions was made, a formidable backlog was bound to result. Within the two preceding years 2,179 of the some 3,800 total inmates of prisons and the reformatory had filed for pardon or commutation; Hogg had

[52] Texas *House Journal* (1893), p. 30; Cotner, *op. cit.,* pp. 324–325.
[53] Texas *House Journal* (1893), pp. 30–31.

managed to dispose of 625 cases—leaving 1,554 still to be handled. This delay was manifestly unfair to the prisoners and practically invalidated the whole pardon system. Hogg knew that other states were experimenting with pardon boards, and he had written to a half-dozen governors in both the South and the North for advice and information. Believing that some remedy was a necessity, he recommended to the legislature that it create by law a board of pardon advisers to be composed of two reputable men appointed by the governor. Either at stated times or on call from the governor they would investigate and report on the applications. The governor would, however, retain full power to grant or refuse the action recommended. Certainly in this suggestion Hogg would be susceptible to the charge of increasing boards and bureaus, but he was looking for a practical and immediate solution that would not violate the constitutional stipulation. Why he did not recommend an amendment in the matter is not clear, although it is possible that, believing so firmly that the ultimate responsibility should remain with the executive, he felt an amendment might provide some future governor with an excuse to evade the responsibility. (In 1936 a clarifying amendment did authorize a Board of Pardons and Paroles.)

The appropriation voted for the Board of Prison Advisers was small. If it had been the intent of the lawmakers to plan the Board's failure in advance by making the positions on it unattractive to the sort of able men the Governor had in mind (as with the Railroad Commission, he wanted the public to have confidence in the new Board because they respected its appointees), they had reckoned without his resourcefulness. Realizing that the low income would certainly not attract superior men on a full-time basis, especially if they were not already residents of Austin, Hogg decided a part-time basis was his best hope.[54] Former Governor Francis Lubbock and Judge L. D. Brooks, both of whom lived in Austin, accepted Hogg's requests that they serve on the Board, working on a part-time schedule as applications required.

James Hogg was never hesitant in stating the philosophy of government by which he functioned. In the conclusion to the long, but clearly and imaginatively programed 1893 message, he once more set forth with great succinctness the essence of his own and the Party's middle-ground position on reform and law enforcement.

When economically administered, that government is best which neither

[54] J. S. Hogg to Richard Coke, May 22, 1893, Gov. Let. Pr., 11, p. 389; Hogg to Horace Chilton, April 25, 1893, *ibid.*, p. 305.

overrides nor recedes from the full performance of its constitutional obligation to the citizen. The paramount governmental duty is to obey and enforce the law.

Invoking Divine blessing on your labors, in the full confidence that a
spirit of conservatism will attend your deliberations, and that the people's
demands in all respects will be obeyed, each member of your honorable
bodies is hereby extended the freedom of the executive office at all times,
and my services are at your command, to aid in the important work lying
before you.[55]

On May 9, 1893, speaking to the hard-working legislators just before
their adjournment, Hogg was able to congratulate them upon some 150
laws and resolutions, "none of which were vicious." He had already approved 80 laws, permitted 19 to become law without his signature,
vetoed 7, of which one had been passed over his veto.

The overridden veto concerned the establishment of an extra court
for McLennan County. Beginning in his first term, Hogg had consistently urged the necessity of revamping the judicial districts, wishing
to cut down the number of districts to save what he called needless expense; he pointed out that increased case loads in some areas caused
district attorneys and judges to be greatly overworked, while in others
the year's work was so slight that it was often attended to in four to six
months. Rather than numerous regrouping measures, he had made it
clear that he desired a comprehensive law. When R. H. Rogers, McLennan County representative, successfully sponsored a bill to give his
county an extra court, the Governor saw fit to veto the measure on the
grounds that it increased rather than decreased the number of courts
and therefore increased the cost of the judicial branch. He was emphatic
that that veto stemmed largely from his unwillingness to be a party to
piecemeal increases, when he believed that a serious over-all redistricting
was necessary to balance out the case loads. That McLennan was the
home county of George Clark may or may not have had something to do
with the overriding of the veto; in any case, lawyers generally, especially
in the midst of hard times, were not kindly disposed to a cut in the number of districts. The vote to override was 72 to 20, with 10 absent and 24
excused.[56] The districts remained an unscientific patchwork; some
progress had been made, however, toward recodifying civil and criminal
procedure.

The legislature had completed the major work called for in the Demo-

[55] Cotner, op. cit., pp. 329–330.
[56] Texas House Journal (1893), pp. 465–466.

cratic platform, and the session had been in general unusually harmonious, especially in view of the bitterness of the campaign preceding it. The Governor hoped the members were fully conscious of his appreciation of their work. In concluding, he referred to the new laws on railroad stocks and bonds, county and municipal bonds, and perpetuities and corporation lands:

No State in the Union has better laws than these, and the people of Texas will in due time appreciate them and hold their senators and representatives in grateful remembrance for their passage. Cheap money will work its way into railroad construction and into necessary improvements, for it will feel safe and secure from the hand of fraud. . . . As a Texan I am proud of these laws, and beg now, while holding the last official position to which pride, ambition, or desire can lead me, to sincerely thank you for them.[57]

The last sentence was linked so casually with the rest of the conclusion that it was several moments before the audience recognized its full import. Many doubted their hearing. Many more, either at once or on later reflection, doubted the truth of the announcement. In any case, this was something that would set the newspapers buzzing, and each legislator knew that he must have a record of Jim Hogg's exact words to satisfy the curiosity of the people at home. However, it would be many months before the majority of politicians would be convinced that Hogg, as usual, meant what he said.

The legislature had completed the major legislation called for by the Democratic platform, and in a situation unlike that of 1891, Hogg foresaw no need to call an extra session. He hoped that the legislators would go home conscious of his appreciation of their work and the unusual harmony of the session.

The Governor knew that men did not live by bread alone. He regretted the fact that the Constitution contained no provision which would permit appropriations for financing Texas exhibits at the World's Columbian Exposition at Chicago. However, he was pleased to appoint as commissioners men and women who were willing to serve at their own expense. As Governor, he invited public-spirited citizens to make the contributions necessary for a worthy presentation of the growth and

[57] *Ibid.*, p. 1212, dated May 9, 1893; Roberts, "Texas, 1845–1895," in Wooten, *A Comprehensive History of Texas,* p. 311; Reed, *Texas Railroads,* pp. 620 ff.; Louis J. Wortham, *A History of Texas* (Fort Worth, Wortham-Molyneaux, 1924), V, 103, declared that time had proved that the Railroad Commission and the stock and bond law were beneficial to the railroads and had served to place them on "a sounder financial basis."

prospects of Texas. He had asked the legislature to authorize the commissioner of insurance, statistics, and history to send exhibits, relics, and other articles of interest which would entail no expense to the state, concluding:

The importance of this enterprise should not be underestimated by the people nor their representatives; for, in the great struggle for the promotion, enlightenment and success of progress and happiness among the masses, no State possessed of grand and varied resources can afford to fail in having proper representation at this exposition, participated in and supported by the people of the United States and of the civilized world.[58]

Almost a decade earlier Hogg had attended an exposition at New Orleans, and he recognized the value gained by people in seeing the improvements being made in agriculture, industry, commerce, and the arts. Progressive citizens would be encouraged to try new crops and improved farm machinery, and perhaps someone would get an idea which would lead to a helpful invention. The Governor recognized that Texas had reached a stage of development where more time and money could and should be spent on cultivating the arts, as he was attempting to do in preserving the historic paintings of Henry A. McArdle and William H. Huddle. He was encouraging Hally Bryan, a descendant of the Austin family, in her efforts to do effective work through the newly formed Daughters of the Republic of Texas.[59] As a result of Hogg's enthusiastic efforts, Texas used the exposition at Chicago as an opportunity to emphasize the value of its natural resources, the great possibilities in the state for manufacturing, and its political experiments in progressive state government, which included (1) the railroad stock and bond law, (2) the alien land law, (3) the corporation land law to end perpetuities, (4) the county and municipal bond law, and (5) the railroad commission law.

When these laws should be in effective operation for the welfare of all Texans, Hogg would be ready to leave public life.

[58] Message of January 12, 1893, quoted in Cotner, op. cit., pp. 327–328.
[59] Webb and Carroll, Handbook of Texas, I, 466–467; Mary Ann Jones Harvey, "Hally Bryan Perry," a Plan II tutorial paper, (the University of Texas, 1957).

CHAPTER XIII

State and Federal Relations

THE EBB AND FLOW of state-federal relations has ever been a fascinating part of the history of the American federal union. James Hogg became governor of Texas just at the time when one of the bulwarks of the federal nature of the government had been severely strained by the congressional debates over the proposed federal elections bill—or "Force" bill, as it was called in the South. It provided for federal supervision of national elections within the several states as a protection to Negro voters, and carried a threat to cut representation of states which discriminated against the Negro at the ballot box. The Texas Democratic platform of 1890 opposed the bill, which had passed the Republican-controlled House of Representatives on July 2, 1890.[1]

It was not well known to outsiders, however, that Texas had done much better than some other Southern states in honoring the Negro's right to vote. At a time when Mississippi's new constitution and subsequent laws were setting a pattern of subtle and effective elimination of the colored vote (which Professor Van Woodward has unfortunately referred to as "the American Way"[2]), it should be noted that Governor Hogg did not agree with the new pattern. In 1884 he had actively sought the colored vote in Smith County for the Democratic Party. Aside from the admitted political expediency of having the Negro vote, he sincerely believed that the political interests of the colored people, whether wage earners or farmers, usually parallelled those of the whites. When some politicians throughout the South were calling for further Negro disfranchisement and Tom Watson was leading his bitter fight in Georgia to make the Democratic party a "white man's" party, Hogg counseled against such action. In fact, it was because of the progressive political atmosphere engendered by him in this respect that his leading

[1] Senate Bill 2, December 4, 1889 in *Congressional Record*, 51 Cong., 1 Sess., pp. 96 ff.; Oran M. Roberts, "Texas, 1845–1895," in Dudley G. Wooten, *Comprehensive History of Texas*, II, 302–304.

[2] C. Vann Woodward, *Origins of the New South, 1877–1913*, pp. 321–349, especially p. 343; Valdimer O. Key, Jr., *Southern Politics in State and Nation* (New York, A. A. Knopf, 1949), pp. 533–535.

Democratic opponent, George Clark, and all candidates except Andrew Jackson Houston, could afford to openly seek the Negro vote in 1892.

To all political parties in other states, Texas was something of an object lesson in the state and national campaign of 1892 because of the large percentage of Negroes who turned out to vote for Regular Democrats Hogg and Cleveland, for George Clark, the candidate of the Regular Republicans and Bolter Democrats, or for the Populist T. L. Nugent. Texas Negroes in general understood that all major candidates welcomed their votes, and they felt little hesitancy in voting, being unhampered by poll-tax laws.[3]

Even the "Reform" ("Lily-White") Republican convention in Dallas in 1892 wrote into its platform a measure condemning the election bill:

That we condemn the Federal election bill as an unnecessary and impolitic measure, and express the hope that the National Republican party will make no further insistence upon its adoption.[4]

Hogg, recognizing that the bill was part of the Republican plan to regain control of the Congress by dominating the Negro vote in the South, believed that the best antidote to the plan would be a resounding defeat for the Republicans at the polls in 1892. It seemed to him that the flurry over the bill on the part of the outgoing Republican Congress in early 1891 was an indication of the desperation of the Republican leaders, as they sensed that their long period of dominance of national politics was at an end.[5] He hoped that with the defeat of the Republicans the rapid trend toward centralization of governmental powers would be checked; eventually he was to learn that continuing centralization of power at Washington was not due to the Republicans alone.

James Hogg, Democrat, also recognized the McKinley Tariff as another part of the Republicans' desperate effort to cling to dominance of Congress, although, ironically, it was this tariff that was most generally blamed for costing them control of the House in the 1890 fall elections. The protection benefits of the Tariff Act were heavily weighted to the advantage of manufacturers, but a few Republican leaders had recognized that the farmer deserved benefits too. The principle of protection was written into the farm sections of the act, and a few crops were given special treatment as a sort of test run. Sugar was the main

[3] Texas adopted the poll tax in 1902.

[4] Ernest Winkler, *Platforms of Political Parties in Texas*, p. 305.

[5] On February 3, 1891, Hogg wired Senators Coke and Reagan: "We all join in extending congratulations to the patriot Senators who saved the Union from the humiliation and disgrace of the Force Bill." Gov. Let. Pr., 1, p. 171.

southern crop so favored. Feeling that they were on profitable grounds here, because Louisiana growers, regardless of party affiliation, had sought protection from foreign sugar since before the Civil War, the Republicans decided to do something special to call attention to the generosity of the Republican Party. An outright bounty of two cents was granted on every pound of sugar produced.

The state of Texas had a two-thousand-acre plantation in the Gulf coast region which was used for the employment of prison labor in producing sugar. The legislature of 1891 passed a bill providing that Texas should comply with the complicated federal regulations regarding acreage and reports and thereby obtain the bounty. In a vigorous veto message in March, 1891, the Governor took high ground and prophesied that if the measure were allowed to stand unchallenged every farm group would organize a lobby for a bounty and that Congress, through the taxing power, would "end the last vestige of State sovereignty." He highlighted a picture of the government (by which he meant, of course, the Republican Party) picking out the well-to-do for special favors at the cost of "impoverishment of the masses," toleration of which "by a free people finds support only in their ignorance."[6]

He continued by warning that federal bounties might seem "tempting fruit"; however, to accept the conditions of the federal law involved a maze of complications. The superintendent of the penitentiaries would be required to file notice with the commissioner of internal revenue of the United States 1) to name the place of production and manufacture of sugar, 2) to give a description of machinery and methods used in manufacture, 3) to estimate annual production, 4) to apply for a license to produce sugar, 5) to execute a good and sufficient bond as provided by the laws of the United States, 6) to apply for the bounty, and 7) to accept, and receipt for, the bounty. The Governor could not give his consent to acceptance of the bounty by Texas. "To do so," he emphasized, "would commit her to an iniquitous precedent based on the policy of favoritism to the few at the expense of the many, which in time must lead to the government's destruction unless changed."

Those parts of the McKinley Tariff which attempted to require licenses and to tell people what they could grow in the name of reducing the revenue and equalizing the duties Hogg believed to be clearly unconstitutional, and he trusted a "circumspect court" to so declare.

[6] The Sugar Bounty Veto Message is quoted in Cotner (ed.), *Addresses of James S. Hogg*, pp. 142–144; Texas *Senate Journal* (1891), pp. 450–451; Texas *House Journal* (1891), p. 556.

Meanwhile, the State of Texas dared not yield to any supervision of *her affairs* by any officer not subordinate to her own laws.

To do so in one instance would lead to another, and finally to supervision by the Federal government over the cotton patches, wheat fields, stock ranches, lumber yards and factories within her limits. Precedents by government usurpations become stronger than law. . . . There can be no more reason to support a bounty on sugar than on cotton, grain, tobacco or stock. Two cents a pound offered by the government is but the beginning. Let it stand and there must be a premium also on every article produced within the United States. With the premium goes the license; and coupled onto the license follows Federal supervision. So will end the last vestige of State sovereignty. For my part I shall protest and begin to strike now while the precedent is new. For no sum can the State afford to sacrifice principle nor to imperil her sovereign rights. At least, our form of government is fast changing, not by the exercise of the inherent and inalienable right of the people in their sovereign capacity, but by the abuse of the taxing power on the part of Congress.[7]

The Dallas *News,* after reflecting upon its own editorial policy of seeking the bounty to support the proposed Confederate home, in one of its rare complimentary moods admitted its error and praised Governor Hogg for upholding sound Democratic doctrine.[8]

During the campaign of 1892 there had been occasional sniping at the Governor over his refusal to accept the bounty. On January 20, 1893, Representative J. M. Kirk of Lavaca County introduced another measure calculated to enable the Texas prison system to collect the sugar bounty for the benefit of the Confederate home; despite the Governor's well-known opposition, the bill passed both houses. In his lengthy veto Hogg expanded the reasons given in 1891. Repeating his objections on constitutional grounds, he also said that a state debased "her dignity" and would "appear before civilization as a humiliated suckling holding on to the breast of the Federal government," while accepting the bounty. The law was "subversive of the powers of government" and "paternalistic in the extreme," and he also regarded its benefits as misplaced:

I cannot understand how it is to the "general welfare" of the several States, or of the United States, or of the people of the United States, for Texas to be given a bounty . . . for raising sugar. . . . There is as much authority for Congress to give bounty on chickens as on sugar. If the purpose is to promote the general welfare, it would appear that articles of necessity,

[7] Cotner, *op. cit.,* pp. 143–144.
[8] Dallas *Morning News,* March 22, 1891.

such as bread, meat and clothing, would be the first on which a bounty should be given. This would reach and help the wheat and corn raiser, the herdsman and the cotton planter, and give cheap food and raiment to the millions.[9]

This was in the midst of the great depression of 1893. Hogg would never know the lengths to which the Democrats of 1933 would expand the bounty system, but he understood the logical outcome of the initiation of such a program. Granting that the policy would put money into the hands of the great army of producers, he said, in irony: "It would add the finishing touch to the ideal government of those who regard the 'bounty system' as the catholicon of all economic ills."

He believed that economic theory and practices were being mixed up. The state's farm was not as extensive or well-managed as many private sugar plantations nearby; yet it had just made a net profit of $61,976 on two thousand acres of sugar and cotton. Sugar planters generally, he maintained, were wealthy and did not need the bounty. The rule of charity declared that alms should go to the needy, but the burden of federal taxation was resting more heavily on the people because of the expansion of governmental functions, many of which he felt were not legitimate. With bonds and licenses would come rules and inspections and law enforcement agents and additional expenses. Infractions of the law would bring fine and imprisonment through federal courts.

We all know what this means. Spies, informers and irresponsible deputy marshals would swagger and lurk around the farm worse than the locusts of Egypt. Nothing would please them better than to "rope" the State of Texas into the "National Court," where they could magnify the power of the Federal judge at the expense of her independence and integrity. . . . The State of Texas now, and so long as I am Governor, shall treat this sugar bounty with derisive contempt.[10]

In 1891 Governor Hogg was not disturbed by critics who chose to ridicule him for rejecting the federal sugar bounty at a time when he had invited a Republican President, Benjamin Harrison, to visit Texas to study harbor improvements requiring large federal funds. Hogg had become interested in the Gulf ports when, as attorney general, he was trying to break up the Texas Traffic Association. He had in mind the

---

[9] The Second Sugar Bounty Veto was addressed to "the Public," as the legislature had adjourned. Cotner, *op. cit.*, p. 350.

[10] *Ibid.*, p. 353; Texas *House Journal* (1893), pp. 100, 192, 1201.

possibility of connecting the ports with the hinterland by competing lines, hoping that lower water transportation costs from the Gulf coast to the East coast, or from the Gulf coast direct to Europe, would free Texas from Gould's monopoly of transportation to the East via St. Louis and New Orleans. Furthermore, Texas could build up her own packing plants and by using the new refrigerated cars and ships could increase the income of Texas ranchers and stockmen. The long downgrade from Denver or Kansas City, as well as the cheaper water rates overseas, dictated that cattle and grain should one day go in larger and larger quantities from the West to the Gulf ports. Others who wished to speed up the completion of a deep-water harbor at Galveston included Governor John Evans of Colorado and the Fort Worth and Denver Railroad.[11]

Hogg knew that Galveston's interest in a deep-water port had been supported by his friend Guy M. Bryan, a descendant of the famous Austin family. Army engineers had made surveys, but action was slow. Various conferences had been held at Kansas City and Denver in the interest of developing Galveston. On February 5, 1891, a Western Congress was convened at Galveston by Senator H. A. W. Tabor, president of the Denver, Colorado, Chamber of Commerce. Delegates were invited from as far away as Arizona, Montana, and the Dakotas. Walter Gresham of Galveston, an official of the Gulf, Colorado, and Santa Fe line and a member of the Texas House of Representatives, was also keenly interested.[12]

This project was one of the many ties linking up West and Southwest, and Hogg was ready to do what he could to have Texas ports improved. Following his election in 1890, but while he was still attorney general, he made a trip to Washington in connection with the Greer County case. Arrangements were made for him to meet President Harrison. Hogg found Harrison personally charming and unassuming, and he invited him to visit Texas at any time convenient to him. When it became known in the spring of 1891 that the President expected soon to make a western tour, Governor Hogg wired that he hoped Harrison would visit Galveston, promising a "cordial reception and kind treatment."[13]

[11] Overton, *Gulf to Rockies,* pp. 225, n. 33, 237.

[12] Austin *Daily Statesman,* January 29, 1891; Galveston *Daily News,* February 6–12, 1891; Walter P. Webb and H. Bailey Carroll (eds.), *Handbook of Texas,* I, 735.

[13] Telegram, Governor J. S. Hogg to President Benjamin Harrison, April 3, 1891, Let. Wr. Sup.

Governor Hogg and Senator Reagan joined the presidential train at Palestine at 7 A.M. on the morning of April 18. Despite a drizzle, a good crowd had assembled at the depot. At the Governor's request, Harrison made a brief talk from the train.[14] Few older people in that area had ever believed that they would live to see the day when a Republican President would be welcomed in Texas. The knowledge that one of their honored native sons not only had invited him but also saw fit to ride the train with him to Houston and Galveston and then to San Antonio was a startling jolt, which helped many Texans, eventually, to think less of the past and more of the future.

All over Texas the papers carried the story of the great parade and cheering crowds of whites and Negroes in Galveston. Hogg had been a little uneasy about Harrison's reception in Galveston—where political feelings ran high and Wright Cuney reigned over the Customs House by virtue of his appointment by Harrison—but he was gratified to be able later to congratulate the people on their excellent behavior. Citizens had arranged a boat trip on the *Lampasas* for the presidential party, which included Cabinet members Postmaster General John A. Wanamaker and Secretary of Agriculture Jeremiah Rusk. In the Hogg Collection is the photograph taken on deck, which preserves the flavor of dress and tonsorial fashions of the 1890's, and especially the contrast in size of the two leading figures, who seem to be standing in that ease which stems from good nature. When talking with President Harrison Hogg did not hesitate to urge 1) the improvement of the federal judiciary in the South, 2) the need for adequate patrol of the Mexican border, and 3) the importance of congressional appropriations for Galveston harbor. In the evening, after a banquet at the Beach Hotel, President Harrison addressed the people and indicated his interest in their material progress and the harbor project.[15]

One incident of the President's trip directly involved the theory of state-federal rights and responsibilities. Learning that President Harrison was going through El Paso, President Porfirio Diaz of Mexico

[14] Charles Hedges (ed.), *Speeches of Benjamin Harrison* (New York, United States Book Company, 1892), pp. 319–320. Rev. E. F. Fales and Mrs. Fales welcomed her distinguished brother, Postmaster John A. Wanamaker. See also telegram, J. S. Hogg to Mayor George Wright, April 17, 1891, Let. Wr. Sup.

[15] Hedges, *op. cit.*, pp. 324–328. Harrison defended putting sugar, tea, coffee, and hides on the free list in an effort to stimulate South and Central American trade and expressed his belief that the Gulf ports would benefit therefrom. He expressed hope for the early completion of the "Nicaragua Canal." J. S. Hogg to T. U. Lubbock, April 23, 1891, Gov. Let. Pr., 9, p. 208; Austin *Daily Statesman*, April 19–20, 1891.

wished to do him honor by sending the Governor of Chihuahua with a staff and a battery bearing firearms to El Paso to pay respects. As Harrison's train was leaving Palestine, a telegram from the acting Secretary of War was handed to Governor Hogg asking his consent to the Mexicans' request to enter the state bearing arms. The story was magnified in some quarters into a debate between Hogg and Harrison over who had authority to permit the Mexican delegation to enter El Paso. Actually, the two men joked about it and the Austin paper accurately reported a "good-natured discussion," adding: "The Republican president yielded to the states' rights argument and Hogg sent the telegram granting permission."[16]

The important thing is that more cordial relations between Mexico and Texas and the United States were cemented on April 21, San Jacinto Day—(*mirabile dictu*)—when Colonel Ricardo Villanueva, representing President Diaz, extended a gracious welcome and congratulated Harrison as "the first president visiting the border." Harrison expressed regret that he could not leave the country without prearranged permission from Congress. (Mrs. Harrison and others later visited Juarez, Mexico.) He stressed his appreciation of the Mexican Government's part in making his trip a memorable one by providing this opportunity to cement relations personally:

I look forward to a great development. We have passed that era in our history when we were unpleasant neighbors. We have come to a time when we cease to covet their possessions but only covet their friendship [great applause].[17]

Hogg read Harrison's remarks with satisfaction, and hoped that Texans and Mexicans would take them to heart as he and several Mexican state governors worked to improve border relations. The vexatious border situation had been a troublesome problem for which Hogg continually sought solutions. Technically, the matter was the direct concern of the U. S. State Department, but the problems that grew out of the thousand-mile boundary, not yet fully charted, often called for local action. The meanderings of the Rio Grande were also an incitement to

[16] Austin *Daily Statesman,* editorial, April 24, 1891; R. B. Levy, the Governor's secretary, to William F. Whalon, April 20, 1891, J. S. Hogg Gov. Let. Wr., I, 237.
[17] Hedges (ed.), *op. cit.,* pp. 334–335; El Paso *Times,* April 22, 1891. After congratulating El Pasoans on their progress, Harrison said, "You cannot attract foreign capital or increase friendship unless you have a reputation for social order." In San Antonio, the President had referred to an uncle who had fought for Texas independence.

boundary disputes.[18] The United States garrisons were insufficient to keep down border raids, prevent illegal entries, or enforce customs regulations. Further, the presence of the garrisons necessitated various arrangements for their forts and encampments, often productive of legal battles, as in the arguments over the support of schools at Fort Bliss near El Paso.

Smallpox and yellow fever were other distressing diseases that crossed the border. Vaccination was now more popularly accepted in the United States, and Texas had made progress in controlling smallpox, but the disease was still often tragically prevalent in the southwestern part of the state, frequently being brought in from Mexico. Also serious was the menace of yellow fever; at times Texas was compelled to quarantine ships from certain Mexican ports or forbid entirely their entering Texas ports. Dr. Richard Swearingen, whom Hogg had appointed as state public health officer, was nationally famous for his work on yellow fever. He and the Governor cooperated with the State Department in arranging a meeting with Mexican officials to plan for mutual control and elimination of the dread disease. Significant experiments in the Brownsville area antedated the Walter Reed work in Cuba.[19]

There were also vexing questions about the shipment of Mexican cattle into Texas. For many years Texas cattle moving northward had been found often to be carrying the tick that transmitted the devastating splenetic fever, called "Texas fever." The responsibility for the ticks could not be pinned on Mexico alone, but admission of cattle from that country and the well-nigh impossible task of preventing tick infestation across the border contributed largely to the problem. When the states to the north began to pass laws against Texas cattle Hogg became the more interested in the Gulf ports as outlets. Shipping cattle by water would avoid unpleasantness with other states. However, Hogg was also aware of the dangers of the disease, and concerned about them. He set up machinery for strict enforcement of Texas quarantine laws and co-operated fully with federal authorities. In 1893 he supported the legisla-

[18] Gladys Gregory, "El Chamizal, A Boundary Problem between the United States and Mexico," Ph.D. dissertation (the University of Texas, 1937); Webb and Carroll (eds.), *Handbook of Texas*, I, 328; John H. Reagan, "Transporting Merchandise in the Free Zone of Mexico," a speech in the U. S. Senate, July 1, 1890, *Congressional Record*, 51 Cong., 1 Sess., pp. 6838–6842.

[19] George P. Garrison, "Richard Montgomery Swearingen," *Quarterly of the Texas State Historical Association*, VIII (January, 1905), 225–231; R. B. Levy to Secretary of Agriculture J. Sterling Morton, October 13, 1894, Gov. Let. Pr., 6, p. 461. Hogg appointed Dr. J. J. Hill of Hillsboro to attend the Pan-American Medical Convention in August, 1893.

tive establishment of the Texas Livestock Sanitary Commission and appointed able men as commissioners to make the new body as effective as possible in carrying out the provisions of the law. Commissioner Robert Justus Kleberg, whose son developed the famous Santa Gertrudis cattle on the King Ranch, began at once to work with men from the U. S. Department of Agriculture. The renowned Dr. Theobald Smith and others conducted their tests among his cattle, and these experiments eventually led to the discovery that the tick carried the fever and that it could be controlled.[20]

Vexatious as were the problems of disease control along the border, they were in essence simpler than the problem of controlling human beings. Mexicans fleeing from the vengeance of Diaz's troops frequently crossed the border as refugees, becoming international nuisances to both Texas and the United States; there was also considerable border traffic of American and Mexican criminals in flight. Old feuds and plots often found their consummation "across the border"; the following letter from lawyers in Laredo to Governor Hogg is self-explanatory:

This will be hand[ed] you by Messrs R. L. Boltran and T. D. Martinez, who go to Austin to see you in regard to the killing of General Martinez in this city on the 3rd day of February 1891. Mr. Boltran has been here for some time endeavoring to fix the crime on some one and Mr. Martinez is a brother-in-law of the deceased. Any favors shown these gentlemen will be highly appreciated by me.[21]

Another problem of law enforcement in border towns is indicated in a letter recommending Captain G. B. Broadwater for the position of district attorney in the proposed new district that would include Laredo:

He is a fair lawyer, perfectly fearless in the discharge of what he believes to be his duty, is a steady consistent advocate of morality and obedience-to-law, and would do his best to elevate the standard of that country, including the counteracting of the potent political rings there which without any political *principles* at all maintain their power by pandering to vice and to anti-American Mexican prejudice. Broadwater speaks Spanish, understands Mexican nature and customs thoroughly, and at the last election

[20] Thomas R. Havins, "Texas Fever," *Southwestern Historical Quarterly*, LII (October, 1948), 147–162; Preamble for Proclamation of Extra Session, February 18, 1892; Chicago *Herald*, June 17, 1894; Fred Shannon, *The Farmer's Last Frontier*, pp. 240–242. The other two commissioners on the first Livestock Sanitary Commission were T. R. Martin of Midland and W. J. Moore of Galveston.

[21] Marshall Hicks to J. S. Hogg, May 9, 1891, J. S. Hogg Gov. Let. Rec., XIII, p. 82.

carried more Mexican votes than any reform-democrat in the field except Louis Ortiz (for county clerk—a Mexican native of Laredo); and this larger Mexican vote for him caused him to be the only one of the reform-democrat, American idea, anti-gambling ticket who was elected.[22]

Texans had been uneasy over the border situation since annexation and seemed never satisfied with the amount of protection rendered by federal troops. In 1891 the two houses of the Texas legislature adopted a resolution requesting an increase in the garrisons at posts on the Rio Grande.[23] Hogg kept the able but few Texas Rangers operating from Brownsville to El Paso, and Texas often found that it was bearing a large share of the expense of guarding the border, including the job of catching cattle thieves, who worked out of Indian Territory, New Mexico Territory, or Old Mexico. Rangers Captain Bill McDonald and Frank Jones and El Paso City Marshal Jeff Milton, "good men with guns," tracked the most dangerous of outlaws from border to border. Texas officials were always willing to cooperate in extradition cases, but it was not easy to get along with the Diaz government when the wanted persons included robbers, killers, and revolutionists.[24] Diaz and his friends in office received considerably less than wholehearted support from large numbers of intelligent and able Mexicans; men motivated variously by love of freedom, personal bitterness, or threats of persecution often baited the government—all too frequently from the Texas side of the Rio Grande when the situation became too precarious for them in Mexico.

The great semi-desert-like region between San Antonio and Chihuahua worked economic hardship on its inhabitants, especially the Indians. Early in 1891 Indian and Mexican raiding parties were particularly harassing along the Texas border. General D. S. Stanley, U.S.A., from his headquarters at San Antonio, where he was studying the Texas request for more troops, attributed the increase in raids in part to the

[22] G. J. Buck (Waco and Laredo) to J. S. Hogg, March 17, 1891, *ibid.*, XI, 44–45.

[23] Texas *House Journal* (1891), p. 572; Secretary of War Redfield Proctor to His Excellency, The Governor of Texas, March 30, 1891, J. S. Hogg Gov. Let. Rec., XI, 236.

[24] Walter P. Webb, *The Texas Rangers* (Boston, Houghton Mifflin Company, 1935), pp. 441 ff.; J. Evetts Haley, *Jeff Milton* (Norman, University of Oklahoma Press, 1948), pp. 209 ff. Hogg appointed a number of extradition agents. Mexican forces helped to chase train robbers, and Hogg returned a woman who had escaped from a Mexican jail. Austin *Daily Statesman*, March 18, 1891; *ibid.*, April 3, 1891; R. B. Levy to J. S. Hogg, care of Dr. J. W. Gion, Aransas Pass, August 15 and 16, 1891, J. S. Hogg Gov. Let. Wr., IV, 100–102.

U.S. Army's order—part of an economy effort—that troops should be concentrated in the few big forts at El Paso, Eagle Pass, Laredo, and Brownsville.[25]

One of the many rebellions against the heavy hand of Diaz was launched by the newspaper editor Catarino E. Garza, who had fled Mexico, settled on a ranch in Texas, and then proceeded to buy up horses and ammunition for a venture which he hoped would spread immediately from Sonora to Tamaulipas. In the fall of 1891, Garza proclaimed rebellion on the bank of the Rio Grande "in the State of Tamaulipas" and announced an organization, backed by several generals, dedicated to the overthrow of the Dictator and to upholding the Constitution of 1857. He promised to restore civil power, freedom of the press, and safety of person. Proclaiming the principle of *"No Reelección,"* the leader of the rebellion demanded that Diaz be treated as a traitor because he had endangered the integrity of the nation by considering the sale of Baja California, "creating the suspicion that another Santa Anna was in power."[26]

Here was additional proof that the request of Texas for more troops along the border had been a reasonable one, but now Texas officials and the United States government were taken to task by Mexico for permitting a rebellion to be launched from Texas. The situation was tense, especially since only a few days before Garza's proclamation Governor Hogg had written President Diaz requesting him personally to intercede to spare the life of an American, J. W. Clayton, languishing in a Mexican prison.[27] In an effort to do what was proper about the Mexican protests, Rangers, federal troops, and the United States marshal got busy trying to get at the facts. Reports from American army captains indicated that the Mexican population and many Anglo-Americans living in Texas sympathized with Garza. When hard-pressed, Garza's bands had a trick of separating, many of the men fleeing individually to Texas and mingling with the population in such a way as to make it almost impossible for American troops to prove association, despite the most extensive and careful investigations.

Governor Hogg was working closely with the harassed General Stanley. Stanley had pleaded for more men, and some cavalry had been

[25] Austin *Daily Statesman,* April 3, 1891.

[26] Gabriel Saldívar, *Documento de la rebelión de Catarino E. Garza en la frontera de Tamaulipas y sur de Texas, 1891–1892* (Mexico, D. F., 6th Mexican Congress of History, 1943), pp. 13–16.

[27] J. S. Hogg to President Porfirio Diaz, August 31, 1891, J. S. Hogg Gov. Let. Wr., IV, 225–226.

sent from Kansas; Garza was still uncatchable as he slipped back and forth across the river. Hogg informed Stanley in February, 1892, that Adjutant General Mabry, acting under the Governor's directions, had offered a state reward for Garza. If the reward did not prove effective within a reasonable time and the federal government failed to aid Stanley, Hogg would place the amount at Stanley's disposal; he also invited the General to visit him "to the end that concert of action and harmony may prevail in relieving the frontier of *the pestilence*."[28]

In regard to border incidents in general, Mexico continued to accuse the United States of not using enough troops and proposed using small detachments of Mexican and American troops to guard alternate fords along the river in an effort to cover more territory. When Secretary of State James G. Blaine reported 1,800 American troops along the border, Mexico replied that it was using 1,884.[29] Actually neither country was using enough to control the situation. There is a familiar modern ring to Major General Schofield's report which attributed the failure to put an end to raids to the fact that troops had been allotted "in proportion to the service required as the aggregate strength of the Army will permit." He went on to say that bandits stole cattle and horses as far away as the famous horse-breeding grounds of El Randado (in what is now Jim Hogg County). Schofield declared that apprehension should be largely the duty of Texans and United States marshals, the United States Army to act only as an auxiliary posse. Murder, cattle theft, etc., were offenses under Texas state laws, and the troops did not have any right to chase Mexicans across the border in such instances.[30] Once more federal-state relationship problems caused correspondence. Various branches of the federal government, including the Army, tried to pass the buck, usually in the name of inadequate appropriations or lack of jurisdiction rather than poor distribution and something less than optimum use of men available.

[28] J. S. Hogg to General S. D. Stanley, February 13, 1892, J. S. Hogg Gov. Let. Pr., 9, pp. 371–372. J. S. Hogg to Col. Frank Grice (San Antonio), February 12, 1892, *ibid.*, 9, p. 374, indicated Hogg was planning to issue a proclamation in Spanish regarding the reward for Garza's capture. See General W. H. Mabry, *Report of the Adjutant General of Texas* (Austin, 1892), pp. 10–12.

[29] Secretary of Foreign Relations to Ambassador Cayetano Romero, December 31, 1892, in *Papers Relating to the Foreign Relations of the United States for 1893* (Washington, Government Printing Office, 1894), pp. 424 ff., 431–433.

[30] "Report of the Secretary of War for 1893," *Executive Documents of the House of Representatives*, 23 Cong., 2 Sess., pp. 141–142; Gabriel Saldívar, *Historia compendiada de Tamaulipas* (Mexico, D. F., Editorial Beatriz de Silva, 1945), p. 201.

The Governor of Texas felt better after many of the bandit leaders were taken prisoner, some by Mexican troops and some by American troops and Rangers. The Secretary of War reported in 1893 that the Army's success was due in part to using as scouts native Texans, who often operated in areas dense with chaparral and cactus. Further, Garza, as a result of the combined efforts of Mexican, United States, and Texas troops, was forced to take cover, although he reappeared in 1895.[31] However, temporary agreements to extend international comity to the task of chasing raiders (the comity already existed regarding Indians) often led to difficulties when someone was ambushed or killed through mistaken identity. Hogg realized that the uncertain boundary line, especially in the Chamisal tract near El Paso, would continue to furnish areas of dispute and havens for bad characters. A boundary commission had begun to work under the treaty of 1889, but the work went slowly. It was not completed until long after Hogg went out of office.

Hogg had made real progress in creating better relations with the state and federal officials of Mexico, both through the working agreements established between Texas and Mexican extradition agents and through his realistic approach to handling the problem of contagious diseases. Although differences between Mexican and American court procedures and treatment of accused or imprisoned persons long remained sources of confusion and bitterness, the better-neighbor policy had made progress, as was evidenced in 1900 when Galveston suffered its great flood: Diaz sent $30,000 for the relief of the suffering city.[32]

The federal judiciary, the branch of the federal government which James Hogg had come to know best while attorney general, received some of his most outspoken chastisements. In his first message as governor, he spoke of the pride Texans had in the federal Union and said that he wanted people to honor and respect all government—but he also pointed out that there was a legitimate sphere for the "general

[31] J. S. Spivey to Secretary of State W. Q. Gresham, January 3, 1895, Gov. Let. Pr., 6, p. 642; Report of Brigadier General Frank Wheaton, Headquarters, Department of Texas, "Report of the Secretary of War, 1894," *Executive Documents of the House of Representatives*, 23 Cong., 3 Sess., pp. 144–147.

[32] Pauline S. Relyea, "Diplomatic Relations between the United States and Mexico under Porfirio Diaz, 1876–1910," *Smith College Studies in History*, X, No. 1 (Northampton, October, 1924), pp. 69 ff.; J. S. Hogg to Governor of Nuevo Leon, March 10, 1893, Gov. Let. Pr., 2, p. 639; J. S. Hogg to Lauro Carillo, Governor of Chihuahua, September 18, 1891, J. S. Hogg Gov. Let. Wr., V, 155–157, 258.

government," and Texas "demanded recognition and respect" in areas where she had jurisdiction:

For many years past the people have been terrorized by the judicial arm of that government, not for offenses they have committed, but because they dread the menace of arbitrary power that so often threatens their liberties. Removed so far from the seat of the government, it is difficult for the highest officers and courts to fully understand the frequent outrages inflicted upon the innocent people of this State by inferior officers and the subordinate Federal judiciary. Deputy marshals, special detectives, and other officers asserting authority . . . have unnecessarily disturbed the tranquility of the people . . . and . . . caused many of them to believe our Federal government an institution of oppression instead of one for the performance of its functions under the Constitution.[33]

Among his instances were these: people had been taken from their homes on charges punishable only in state courts; ignorant people had been duped into committing crimes and had then been arrested; state officers had been indicted in a federal court for "obstructing the United States mail," when they acted within state law to seize personal property or arrest some conductor in charge of a train or other individual carrier of mail. Federal marshals or judges at times had released citizens who were being held under orders or warrant of state courts. Hogg also complained that the management of some railroads by nonresident receivers was prolonged far beyond the term prescribed by Texas laws, under orders of federal judges operating from other states:

With respect to such property the decrees and opinions of the State's highest courts are held for naught and in contempt, to the injury of the citizen and humiliation of the people. Several of these roads, without foreclosure proceedings, have been permitted to increase their incumbrances, to the detriment of the public and lawful creditors, without check or hinderance; and from all appearances to an ordinary citizen or impartial observer, as he learns of the exorbitant fees and salaries paid to useless officers in the apparent indulgence of favoritism and nepotism, the connection of these judges and officers with the receiverships and roads would demand investigation.[34]

In taking testimony for the defense of the Railroad Commission case before the Supreme Court, Hogg had learned of the experiences Joseph

[33] Message of January 21, 1891, Texas *House Journal* (1891), pp. 114–115; Cotner, *op. cit.*, pp. 134–135.
[34] *Ibid.*, p. 135.

Nalle of Austin and Ennis, who was owner of cotton-compress operations in Ennis, had had with agents of the Houston and Texas Central Railway. He had urged Nalle to testify. On the basis of testimony given in five cases in the United States Circuit Court at Austin, Hogg saw fit to lay before the legislature in March, 1893, a special message on federal court receiverships. He reminded the legislature that he had warned of these situations in 1891, but no investigations had been authorized at the time; now he had found a way to give them details from sworn testimony regarding Receiver Charles Dillingham. Hogg pointed out how Dillingham had become interested in building up his personal holdings in Ennis and, over the protests of the people of Corsicana, moved the railway machine shops to Ennis. When the people of Corsicana, who had given private subscriptions and a bonus on condition that the shops be permanently placed in their town, tried to stop the "high-handed" action by going before a federal circuit judge for a restraining injunction, they were rebuffed.

In another case the receiver swore that he had "disposed" of his interest in the Ennis compress stock. However, according to Nalle's testimony, he then forced his way back in and finally forced Nalle to turn all the stock over to him by means of threats and intimidations to withhold freight facilities, to undercut prices, etc. Nalle was faced with competition from railway-controlled compresses which had the advantages of rebates and special handling. The Governor told the legislature that the record from 1885 showed that "25 per cent of the compress charges collected by the Houston and Texas Central Railway from cotton producers had gone corruptly into the private purses of its receiver and managing officials, and not into the railway treasury."[35] He pressed the point that the receiver and managing officials engaged in these activities held their positions under and by virtue of the authority of the federal courts. Furthermore, due notice had been given to the federal judges several months back, but they failed to remove the offenders.

Nalle's testimony was clear and voluminous and merited careful consideration by the legislature. Before the receiver was appointed, producers paid 50 cents for compressing; afterward, the same compress operators "were coerced" into charging an additional 15 cents per bale as a payment "for the private pockets of the receiver and general freight

---

[35] Special Message on Federal Receiverships, March 8, 1893, quoted in *ibid.*, pp. 336–337; Ouida Ferguson Nalle, *The Fergusons of Texas* (San Antonio, Naylor Company, 1946), p. 147.

368

agent under him." Nalle even had to sell them a half interest in his compresses "at a price less than half its value, arbitrarily fixed by themselves." Private shippers were compelled to use compresses, not of their own choice, but those named by railroad officials; this often entailed longer hauls to reach the designated compress and the shipper paid the extra freight. Finally, the Nalle business was sold to these "federal officers" at about one-third of face value; later the face value doubled, and they paid themselves high dividends. When the facts were filed on affidavit in November, 1892, before United States Circuit Court Judge Don A. Pardee, at New Orleans, Nalle declared that Pardee assured him "that he would have nothing to do with the case" and would transfer it to another court.

Tiring of the situation, Nalle wrote in June direct to C. P. Huntington, admitting that under pressure he had paid tribute to "your receiver" Dillingham and "your freight agent, Daniel Ripley." In one season, 1886–1887, he paid the two men $11,425, being 15 cents on 76,167 bales processed at Waco and Ennis. Huntington asked for more information, but indicated that he was not ready to go into the case just then; he wanted Nalle not to discuss it until further notice. In November, 1892, Nalle notified Huntington that he had been summoned on behalf of the state before the United States Circuit Court to testify in the injunction suit restraining the Texas Railroad Commission. He informed Huntington that he knew that the information previously sent him had not been kept as confidential, because it had been promptly communicated to officers of the Southern Pacific and Texas Central railroads at Houston. Huntington, who had not written Nalle since the June exchange, now replied, stating that he had hoped more information would "exonerate" the parties "as a man's reputation is a thing that should be dealt with very carefully."[36]

All of this testimony Hogg turned in with his message, then made the following recommendations:

1. Charters of all railroad companies and other corporations remaining in the hands of receivers over three years would be forfeited and recharters would be issued only after paying heavy penalties to the State.

2. All railroad officials and traffic agents should be deemed public officials and should be prohibited under appropriate penalties from using properties for personal business.

[36] Nalle's testimony is printed in Cadwell W. Raines (ed.), *Speeches of James Stephen Hogg*, pp. 262 ff. Texas *House Journal* (1893), pp. 574–582.

3. Special appropriations should be made to pay for necessary investigations and prosecutions of federal officials "when they violate State laws or wilfully infringe on State's rights."[37]

He also urged that resolutions be adopted instructing Texas senators and representatives to support 1) a resolution in the Congress calling for an investigation of all railroads in federal receivership in the state, especially the Houston and Texas Central; 2) a bill limiting the jurisdiction of the subordinate federal judges in general and to define "citizens," so that corporations created by the state shall not be subject to the jurisdiction of the federal courts; 3) an amendment to the Constitution making United States judges "appointive for a limited period of years, and renewable by the President and Senate"; 4) "a law abolishing the office of one or both of the circuit judges for this district as being a useless expense to the government." He concluded:

Though the crafty hand of the Federal judge has swung the pendulum of public opinion too far from the line of States' rights for the public good, the alarm has at last been touched and public attention aroused. . . . A change must come. The pendulum must be restored to its equilibrium. Through the Congress of the United States must the work be done.[38]

The special message marked a peak in that phase of state-federal relations which involved vindictive and personal acts. It was clear that Hogg had Republican Judge A. P. McCormick in mind in his remarks about federal judges, although he knew that it would be well-nigh impossible to prove that McCormick had "willfully infringed on States' rights" in issuing the injunction against the Railroad Commission at the precise time in the 1892 election campaign when it would do the most harm to the Democrats. Nevertheless, the malpractices on the part of the H.& T.C. agents needed to be brought into the open. Hogg was on sound ground in pointing out to stockholders that they, as well as Mr. Nalle, were the losers when agents did not turn in all revenues to the company. Even Huntington admitted that he was concerned about this, although he was reluctant to take Nalle's complaints seriously. Before long, however, Dillingham resigned,[39] but there was no federal investigation and efforts to restrict the jurisdiction of federal courts received scant attention.

[37] Message of March 8, 1893, Texas *House Journal* (1891), p. 569.
[38] *Ibid.*, pp. 574–576; Cotner, *op. cit.*, p. 345.
[39] Cotner, *op. cit.*, pp. 338, 341, 366.

370

It was also clear that any recommendation to define "citizens" or "persons" in such a way as to remove state-chartered corporations from federal courts would run into precedent after precedent under the commerce and due-process clauses of the United States Constitution. Supposing a new definition was adopted and held constitutional, it was not a real remedy, since interstate business might then incorporate in the District of Columbia, but certainly not in Texas. A proposal to appoint judges for limited terms, subject to renewal by the President with consent of the Senate, would not necessarily soften a trait such as ambition but could possibly lead to periodic investigation of propriety of conduct and decisions, and possibly thus encourage filing of complaints with more expectation of remedy and make it easier to obtain retirement of the mentally incapacitated.

The Governor's most revolutionary proposal was his advocacy of making railroad officials and traffic agents public officials, legally prohibited from using the semipublic properties they managed for personal gain. This was in truth scarcely a proper remedy, especially since it was based upon the false assumption that public officials were all honest or could be removed or punished more easily than could agents of a corporation. Furthermore, to acquaint the stockholders with the problem would usually bring a change of agents, if not dismissal. Hogg was so anxious to be rid of the H.& T.C. agents who had dealt him trouble in the past campaign that he seemed to overlook Cuney's claim that Hogg and Nugent were not far apart in their attitude toward public control or ownership of railroads. If machinery was established for declaring railroad officials and traffic agents public officials—an arrangement hardly acceptable to private holders of stocks and bonds—it would result in a strange economic institution that charged public officials to make money for the stockholders.

A logical outcome from the efforts of such officials to be good business men, or to overcome the effects of a depression which caused declining income, could be frequent suits by stockholders to force the state to contribute the deficit between actual and the legally determined "reasonable" returns. The Governor's recommendation was threatening and certainly impractical in a predominantly private-enterprise era, aside from the probability that mere reclassification of a company managerial position to one of "public official" would not cure dishonesty but could introduce new elements of tyranny.

As far as is known, Congress did not lay a restraining hand upon

Judge McCormick. Hogg's faith in the integrity of the U.S. Supreme Court increased with time, however, although the uncertainty from April, 1892, to May, 1894, over the final outcome of the Railroad Commission case was galling. Hogg was very proud of the Railroad Commission law he had helped to frame. It was significant that the first suit against the Commission had been brought by Gould interests involving a road in the hands of a Texas-appointed receiver, Hogg's boyhood friend Thomas M. Campbell. The suit had been filed in April, 1892, by the Farmers' Loan and Trust Company of Baltimore, Maryland, in the Circuit Court of the United States at Dallas against the railroad commissioners, Attorney General Culberson, the International and Great Northern Railway Company, and Receiver Campbell. Farmers' Loan and Trust, which held certain bonds of the I.& G.N. amounting to about $15 million, filed as representative of the railroad. The suit sought to restrain the commissioners from enforcing the rate schedules on the grounds that the schedules were so low that operating expenses, interest on the bonds, etc., would not be met, making the rates confiscatory. The constitutionality of the law creating the Commission was also questioned. Before long the Texas and Pacific, the St. Louis Southwestern, the Tyler Southeastern, and the Gulf, Colorado, and Santa Fe lines had entered similar suits.[40]

Hogg believed that Judge McCormick, who would hear the case against the Texas Railroad Commission, should have suggested that the complainants go first into the state courts as the law intended. Instead of challenging specific rates, the railroad attorneys argued that the over-all effects were "confiscatory." In his campaign speech on October 1, 1892, at Dallas, Hogg had charged:

That there was a conspiracy between the railway defendants and the foreign bond holders in the action appears conclusive to the mind of any candid, impartial observer. The case involved the very point on which I warned the people two years ago from stump to stump. . . . I advised restrictive legislation in each of my messages to the general and special sessions. It is this: After the issuance of those factitious bonds they are floated abroad and find their way into the hands of foreign purchasers. They bear interest payable semi-annually. The roads and their earnings are mortgaged to meet the interest and pay the principal. These people holding such bonds came into court and contended that they had the right to collect from the traffic of the country rates high enough to meet their demands. The court, without going into the question as to whether these bonds were

[40] Railroad Commission of Texas, *First Annual Report, 1892,* p. xiv.

legal or not, sustained the claim of the owners, and now the people are called on to pay them.[41]

Hogg explained to the city audience that farmers, while receiving less for their work as cotton producers, were expected, along with the shippers, to keep up the profits for the bond holders by paying the old rates, which would bring in another million dollars a season on cotton alone.

Despite the fact that the Commission had permitted rates higher than the average per ton-mile rate throughout the nation, during the early period of the injunction the railroads increased rates further, a tactic not improving their public relations with Texas shippers. The following was typical of letters received by the Governor:

I offered the railroad agent here two cars of coal for——[distance less than fifty miles] at the commission rate of 60 cents per ton and he refused it, saying that the commission rates were withdrawn. The next day I did the same thing and was offered a rate of $2 per ton for this short distance, which is simply prohibitive, and we can not afford to pay the price. Unless something is done we must close down.[42]

It might have been expected that any tampering by the Commission with rates made by the railroads would encourage delaying tactics in the courts. Take cotton alone; if an additional $2 million could be collected by means of delaying action for just two seasons, the roads could afford the high cost of the ablest legal talent. Actually, total income to the railroads grew during 1891 in the precise period during which Commission rates were in effect and rebating and discriminations were restrained. Nevertheless, because of their long experience with the "common-point" system and the short-haul rates, the lines were disgruntled at the Commission for attempting any other plan. It upset their systems of bookkeeping, lessened potential returns, and made it easier for Texas to check on railroad business. The Commission had defended the shift to mileage rates as follows:

This . . . is the only equitable and just principle on which freight charges can be based, and while, owing to conditions for which the Commission is in no way responsible, it has not in all cases been adopted, it has been applied in every instance where the Commission could apply it without a too violent disturbance of business and trade relations built up under different

[41] Dallas *Morning News,* October 2, 1892. Hogg had tried to protect the I.& G.N. from paying for $15 millions of "watered stock" in 1890.
[42] Railroad Commission of Texas, *Fourth Annual Report, 1895,* pp. 17–23; Overton, *op. cit.,* pp. 276 ff., 280–288.

conditions. The difference between the blanket or common point system and the mileage system can be briefly stated in a different way, as follows: The effect of the blanket or common point system is the obliteration of distance as a measure of levying freight charges, and the placing of manufacturers and producers in any given market at the same rate per one hundred pounds on their goods and wares, without reference to the distance from the point of origin to the market. The mileage system, on the other hand, has for its object the fixing of a rate of charges based on the distance an article may be transported and the cost of the services performed, and the giving to each manufacturer or producer the advantage to which his proximity to the market entitled him.[43]

The Commission never made the complete shift to mileage rates and later returned to the "common-point" system, but the early use of mileage rates was in itself enough to bring about the railroad suits. Furthermore, it was obvious that the new rates were calculated to expand Texas industries.[44]

About the time the stock and bond measure for which Hogg had pressed the 1893 legislature appeared certain to pass, Judge McCormick, on March 23, 1893, overruled the demurrers to the temporary injunction against the Commission and made it perpetual. He declared that:

1. The I& GN should not charge the rates established by the Texas Commission;
2. The Commission or Attorney General should not start suits for recovery;
3. The Commission to issue no further orders as the law creating it was unconstitutional;
4. The rates charged were unreasonable, unfair, etc.[45]

Attorney General Culberson and the Commission appealed, stating that 1) in effect the suit was against the state without its consent, and 2) the attorney general of Texas was forbidden to do what Texas law required him to do.

Hogg had taken great care in the wording of the commission law, and he felt sure that the U.S. Supreme Court would uphold it in principle, as it had the Georgia law. Therefore, after consultation with the Governor, Culberson and the commissioners decided to abandon their plan to

---

[43] Railroad Commission of Texas, *First Annual Report, 1892*, pp. ix–x.
[44] Railroad Commission of Texas, *Fourth Annual Report, 1895*, pp. 15–16.
[45] 154 U. S. 370–378; Railroad Commission of Texas, *Second Annual Report, 1893*, p. 5; Charles Potts, *Railroad Transportation in Texas*, pp. 132–134.

contest both questions—1) reasonableness of the rates and 2) the constitutionality of the law—and to concentrate on the latter. Basically, the second issue had to be clarified to avoid further delays. The International and Great Northern case was chosen as the test case, and the well-known *Reagan v. Farmers' Loan and Trust Company* was the result.

The Commission had been effectively handicapped for almost two years by the suits in federal courts. Meanwhile old rates were restored and local industries again felt the pressure of out-of-state competition. The general rate war in 1893, inaugurated by interstate lines, was possibly connected with the scramble to rearrange the Gould holdings following his death in 1892 and also reflected the interest of Rockefeller and Morgan in railways and steamship lines. The commissioners in their annual report for 1893 pointed out that this war "resulted in the promulgation of rates on some articles beside which those adopted by the Commission, and pronounced by the railroads confiscatory and ruinous, would be excessively high." Furthermore, the rates were lacking "in the quality of uniformity and stability, so necessary to promote the industrial and commercial interest of the country, and have not benefited either the railroads or the people."[46]

Enemies of the Commission had been prone to complain of John H. Reagan as an old man who had been too long in Washington, but they said little or nothing about the able technical staff built up by the Commission, made possible because Governor Hogg had worked to obtain the appropriations required. The secretary, J. J. Arthur, had served as rate clerk for the International and Great Northern for several years. John T. Estill and A. H. Willie, Jr., son of a chief justice of the Texas Supreme Court, were clerks at $1,500 per year. In 1892, E. D. True, H. G. Askew, and H. L. Ziegler were added as "expert clerks." All of these men had been trained in the traffic departments of Texas railroads, and the railroad historian, S. G. Reed, has attested to their ability and to their high standing with railroad men.[47]

In order to rush the case to the Supreme Court, Texas had "admitted the demurrer on the rates."[48] This may have been a mistake; when the opinion written by Justice David J. Brewer was handed down May 26, 1894, it was apparent that Brewer had concluded that this action, "not done thoughtlessly," tended to imply that the commissioners admitted

---

[46] Railroad Commission of Texas, *Second Annual Report, 1893,* pp. 5–6.
[47] *Texas Railroads,* pp. 585–586.
[48] Railroad Commission of Texas, *Second Annual Report, 1893,* p. 21.

the rates were unreasonable. He was impressed by the I.& G.N. exhibits (see below) and rendered his decision without reference to any effects of the depression.

Earnings

1889	surplus	$858,000
1890	surplus	498,177
1891	surplus	555,091
1892	deficit (3 mo.)	69,898

Per-Ton-Mile Revenue

1883		2.03 cents
1884		1.90
1885		1.71
1886		1.65
1887		1.38
1888		1.33
1889		1.44
1890		1.38
1891	(for nine months)	1.30[49]

The Railroad Commission pointed out that per-ton-mile charges in Texas were still higher than in many states, and that, despite the lower cotton rates set by the Commission for the fall of 1891, the railroad had earned more in 1891 than in 1890. The Commission estimated valuation at $15,000 per mile, while Brewer accepted the railroad's figures of over $50,000 paid out and a replacement value of $30,000 per mile. Brewer apparently was not interested in why or how the $15 million of bonds were attached to the road, but he was impressed by the fact that no dividends were being paid and that the stockholders had even paid an assessment, accepting 12 per cent certificates. Attorney General Culberson might have made a more favorable impression if he had submitted more statistical tables for the years involved, rather than the prolonged arguments over McCormick's "disregard" for the state's rights.

Brewer declared that he did not hold that a railroad had to be guaranteed a profit every year; however, he would not pass upon particular rates but held that the rates complained of in the aggregate had the effect of being and were "unreasonable."[50] He forbade the Commission

49 154 U. S. 362 (1894).
50 154 U. S. 362; Railroad Commission of Texas, *Fourth Annual Report, 1895*, pp. 5–19.

to enforce them. Finally, he declared the Texas law establishing the Commission valid.

After some revision of rates, the Commission was ready to embark on a mission of greater usefulness. Overton and Reed have pointed out complaints against the short-haul rates.[51] The *Annual Report* of the Texas Railroad Commission for 1893 indicated some upward adjustments for short hauls; however, the over-all rate structure was downward. The source of increasing income for Texas roads was due largely to increasing traffic. Gross freight for the year ending June 30, 1894, was 13,285,477 tons, while for the year ending June 30, 1895, the tonnage was 15,591,262, an increase of 17.36 per cent. Passenger traffic went up from 6,229,150 to 6,537,250 or 4.95 per cent. This improvement changed the gross receipts by an increase of $1,856,067, while net earnings were more spectacular: $10,522,875 for 1895 as against the $7,188,295 of 1894, a gain of $3,334,580, or 46 per cent. There was a further cut in the cotton rates, but the huge 1895 shipment of 3,300,000 bales more than made up for it. A study of the ratio of net earnings to known indebtedness showed a rise from 1.90 per cent to 2.76 per cent.

The railroads had been trying to make management more efficient; this effort, coupled with increasing tonnage and reasonable rates, might make realizable Brewer's hope that the Texas railways could pay both their dividends and their debts. The Commission also thanked the Southwestern Freight Rate Association for making some reductions in 1895 for carload lots on "a considerable number of commodities," but urged continued study and further reductions, or the Commission would undertake further adjustments in this area.[52] It was obvious that the railroads and the Commission were learning to work together.

The Supreme Court decision on the Railroad Commission was no doubt the most far-reaching development in regard to state-federal relations during Governor Hogg's terms of office. However, a few impromptu remarks to the Texas State Volunteer Guard on a hot July day in 1894 managed to catapult him and another aspect of state-federal relationships into the national limelight in a way that would stamp the episode on the public mind for a good many years.

Hogg always enjoyed the Guard encampments and considered dress reviews there among the more pleasant of his duties as governor—except for the seasonally intense heat, which made the tail-coat suit and the

---

[51] Overton, *op. cit.*, pp. 312 ff., 336; Reed, *Texas Railroads*, pp. 577 ff.
[52] Railroad Commission of Texas, *Fourth Annual Report, 1895*, pp. 4, 15.

top hat required by the occasion resemble medieval instruments of torture. This July he had just returned from the long tour of eastern and northern cities, made at the request of and in the company of a group of men representing business and railroad interests who had wished him to explain his reform program to the wider area of businessmen. (See Chapter XIV.) On the trip he had been highly disturbed by the many evidences of labor unrest and the bitterness between labor and corporate management. There had been recent rioting and dynamiting in Cincinnati. And the prolonged strike at Pullman, Illinois, had developed into a national tie-up when Eugene Debs and the American Railway Union voted a sympathy strike, refusing to handle Pullman cars; the facilities of twenty-five states were by that time involved, but Chicago was the main storm center.[53]

A few days before the review at the encampment, President Cleveland, without a request for aid from Governor Altgeld, had sent federal troops into Chicago with the stated purpose of providing safe conduct for the United States mails.[54] This was an unprecedented action in peacetime, especially without a request from state officials for such assistance and in the face of Altgeld's immediate protest. Many state governors joined the chorus of telegraphed approval for Cleveland's actions, but Hogg had quietly refrained from doing so because his sympathies lay with Altgeld, who was upholding the principle of due regard for states' rights. Hogg also recognized the right of labor to organize, in which view he was again ahead of his time. However, he refused to condone violence in strikes, as he made clear later that year in a speech reviewing his administration.

On the last day of the encampment, July 18, General L. M. Oppenheimer and a group of other officers went to the Governor's tent and summoned him out. Then the General presented him with a watch, saying that it was a token of affection all officers and men of the Guard felt for their commander in chief. The watch was no ordinary instrument that could have been purchased in any store but had been especially designed by G. A. Bahn of Austin; the hour symbols were letters—

[53] Ray Ginger, *Altgeld's America, 1892–1905* (New York, Funk & Wagnalls Company, 1958), pp. 157 ff.

[54] Allan Nevins, *Grover Cleveland* (New York, Dodd, Mead and Company, 1933), pp. 611–628; Henry Barnard, *Eagle Forgotten, Life of John Peter Altgeld* (New York, Bobbs-Merrill Company, c. 1938), pp. 280 ff., 312. Edward O. Browne, *Altgeld of Illinois* (New York, B. W. Huebsch, Inc., 1924) quotes Cleveland-Altgeld letters.

GOVERNORHOGG; on the heavy gold case an enamel letter at each of the points of a raised star spelled TEXAS.

Hogg was genuinely surprised and deeply pleased. Despite his staunchness and ability as a political figher, he preferred the gentler tactics of kindness. Furthermore, it was especially gratifying to have such a token from this group of men whose company he so much enjoyed. He responded quickly with a few words of appreciation and then launched into an extemporaneous talk about the matter uppermost in his mind at that time. He told of the unrest and civic commotion he had seen and heard of on his recent tour and warned the men of the Guard that they, too, might sometime have to be called out to quell such disorders. Graphically, as always, he made it clear that he believed the governor with their support could handle any strike or riot occurring in Texas, and he indicated his regret that a leader of the Democratic Party had seen fit to send federal troops into Illinois without the request of the governor of that state.

Exactly what words were used in the fairly brief and completely extemporaneous talk will never be known. However, a reporter present wrote in longhand from memory some hours later an account of it, which was seized on eagerly by the Dallas *News,* Galveston *News,* and the San Antonio *Express.* The following is a sample from the printed version of what became known as the "liver and lights" speech:

I do not know how soon it will come or how it will end, but this strike is but the preliminary of terrible times in this country. The conflict is bound to come, and unless a change is made those fourteen-story buildings in Chicago will be bespattered with blood, brains, hair, hides, liver and lights, and the horrors of the French revolution will be repeated two fold.

You all know that a few days ago Federal troops were ordered into Illinois without being called for by the governor of that State. This is the first time that this has been done since 1860, and I regard it as a fatal blow to state rights. It's awful to contemplate, and is the precursor of dire calamity. As soon as I returned home from my northern trip I wired to headquarters that I would not tolerate the calling out of Federal troops in this State until I had been first consulted. In times of trouble I mean to try the power of the civil authorities first, and until they fail the military power shall not be called on in Texas. Whenever they try it I'll be there to stop them, and, by gatlins, I'll stick to my ground.

I see before me now some of the generals who will be called upon to lead the hosts, whose business it will be to defend the stars and stripes when the troubles come, not here, but further north and east, and I have faith in your nerve and patriotism, but when the row comes and if disintegration should come I am in favor of Texas standing on the constitution of 1836 and going it alone as a republic again. I am for Texas first, the United States second, and civilization at large next.

The press dispatches tell us this morning that a distinguished jurist has signified his approval of that construction of the constitution which sees no harm in the hurling of federal troops across states without regard to the wishes of the civil authorities. Let me tell you that this kind of constitutional construction is the digging of the mine which will hoist this government off its base, and though the order to invade Illinois was given by a Democratic president, who is the chief of the party to which I belong, my spirit revolts at it. My heart sickens at the thought of the consequences.[55]

Other newspapers picked up the story, with "staff correspondents" and "specials" elaborating certain phrases. Letters of both protest and commendation poured in. General Oppenheimer announced that the Governor had been incorrectly quoted and unfairly represented. When the reporter was identified as George Bailey, who had also traveled with the eastern tour party, his friends tried to stem the mounting criticism of him by interviewing men of the Guard in Fort Worth. They declared that several guardsmen said they were shocked by the Governor's remarks.[56] However, it was not made clear whether the shock was supposed to stem from the wording, from the imagined threat of "secession," or from the realization that they might actually have to quell riots and keep order in a situation charged with dynamite.

The papers printed statements from various governors upholding Cleveland's action, as well as quotes from New York and other papers to the effect that states' rights was not an issue, to highlight their accusations that Hogg had made "incendiary and seditious" remarks and "an unspeakably shocking address," and that he had acted with "boorishness of manner" and "with truculence of speech." The first editorial of the Dallas *News* on July 21 began:

In a public career of phenomenal tumultousness the governor of Texas early acquired and easily maintained a rare eminence of repute for being nothing if not sensational.

He was put in the category of Governor Davis H. Waite of Colorado, who had been credited with a speech about "blood to the bridle bits" growing out of labor troubles in the Cripple Creek area. The editor

[55] Dallas *Morning News*, Galveston *Daily News*, San Antonio *Express*, July 20, 1894.

[56] *Ibid.*, July 21–August 2, 1894.

went on to say that by comparison Debs appeared "moderate and scholarly." Continuing a discussion of Hogg's speech, he wrote:

It is a document that sweats with violent suggestiveness of treasonable conspiracy. At a time when all right-thinking people realize that everything possible should be said to allay bitter feeling and to make for peace; ... this exquisite personification of unfitness in the gubernatorial office chooses to improve the occasion to the utmost in essay or to stir up strife ... to incite sedition, etc.[57]

Brief editorial comments from day to day kept the excitement stirring:

If Gov. Hogg, Gov. Waite, Gov. Altgeld and others of their stripe will enforce the laws of their states they need not fear any invasion by the federal authorities.

* * * *

Governor Hogg seems to have lost all hope of hopping into President Cleveland's shoes, so he is inclined to cut Texas off and run a republic of his own.

* * * *

Think of the governor of the state at this time pouring rot of this kind into the ears of the young men of Texas: Maybe, however, Gov. Hogg expects the [national] ticket to be Altgeld and Hogg.[58]

Hogg's friends all had comment and advice. Judge William S. Simkins of Dallas advised Hogg to let the matter drop. Senator Coke suggested that he prepare a speech and find an occasion during the State Democratic Convention, soon to convene at Dallas, to expose the "infamous perpetrators of the outrage." Judge Nugent, who was running again as the Populist candidate for governor, was reportedly endorsing the sentiments in the published reports. The widow of Jefferson Davis wrote: "I cannot express fitly my admiration of the manner in which you have guarded the honor of your State in forbidding foreign troops to be sent into it except upon your application for them."[59] There were innumerable versions of the "address" in circulation, a situation that especially worried the Governor.

After the newspaper tirade had continued for several days, Hogg

---

[57] Dallas *Morning News*, editorial, July 21, 1894. Supporting Hogg were Houston *Trade Review*, July 21, 1894, and Fort Worth *Gazette*, July 24, 1894.

[58] Dallas *Morning News*, July 21–August 2, 1894.

[59] Richard Coke to Governor Hogg, July 24 and 29, 1894, J. S. Hogg Let. Rec., XXXI, 351–352, 382–385. Commissioner of Insurance John E. Hollingsworth wrote he was leaving for a trip to New York and Philadelphia and he would check reports. Varina Jefferson Davis (Narragansett Pier, R. I.) to J. S. Hogg, July 20, 1894, *ibid.*, pp. 287–288.

sent for George Bailey and asked him to explain how he could have sent in such a story. Bailey apparently was almost as surprised at the glaring headlines and caustic editorials as the Governor himself; certainly he had not expected to cause such a tempest. He said he understood that the speech was impromptu, but the graphic pictures of things to come made irresistibly "good copy." He admitted that he had not taken stenographic notes and had written the account from memory some hours later. Hogg reminded him that the reporter for the Austin *Statesman* had asked for a copy of the speech, and when told that it was not a planned speech had merely mentioned briefly the gift of the watch and that the Governor had made a statement in appreciation.[60]

For some time prior to the incident the Dallas *News* and San Antonio *Express* had been sniping at the Governor's friendliness toward labor and toward the unemployed who "bummed" rides on railroads during the depression as they looked for work. It was to be expected that Bailey would make the most of the story, since for several years he had been writing reports about Jim Hogg that increased the heat supplying the "hot water" that was always bubbling up around Hogg's activities. Bailey had been pro-Clark in 1892,[61] and the *News* was strong for Cleveland and the gold standard. Hogg gave the reporters from city papers an opening in suggesting that civil unrest in the great industrial centers could ever disrupt the nation, and, without a careful statement of metaphorical intention, any reference to Texas going it alone on the basis of the constitution of the Republic was bound to incite Hogg's political opponents. Hogg was always outspoken and often given to bluntly picturesque terms. It seems clear that in his alarm about the unrest he had sensed on the tour (and feeling he spoke to trusted friends who had just evidenced their affection for him) he wanted to make the warning very strong that failure to correct abuses could lead to anarchy—and that human beings might be dynamited against the walls of the tall buildings in the cities.

It is interesting to recall, as a sidelight on the incident, that one newspaper featuring it to the hilt was *The Rolling Stone,* the humorous weekly edited in Austin by William Sydney Porter, later better known as O. Henry.[62] The journalistic venture, which was among the first of

[60] Austin *Daily Statesman,* July 19–20, 1894.
[61] George Bailey to Erwin J. Clark (Waco), June 17, 1922. Let. Biog. J. S. Hogg, p. 5.
[62] A photostatic copy of the complete file of *The Rolling Stone* is in the library of the University of Texas.

Porter's literary career, lasted from April, 1894, to April, 1895; during that time one of its favorite topics was the career of James Stephen Hogg. With quips and occasional cartoons Porter kept up a running barrage of satire, finding plenty of acceptable ammunition in Hogg's picturesque and graphic turns of speech. The northern tour furnished a new setting, and *The Rolling Stone* made the most of it in retelling the stuff of the Governor's speeches. In the issue of July 7, 1894, when it had been announced that the tour was nearly at an end, Porter commented: "Hogg is coming back. The interregnum didn't last long enough to do poor old Texas any good." But it was with the encampment speech that Porter really had the chance to pull out all the stops of satire, and he even kept up his sniping (which was often too exaggerated to be amusing) for several issues after the later San Antonio speech. Hogg never took occasion to answer any of Porter's criticism. How much of the young journalist's criticism was based on conviction and how much on his awareness that Hogg was lifesaving "good copy" for a newspaper struggling to build up circulation, is not known. The fact, however, that Porter lived when he first came to Texas with Richard Hall and later worked as draftsman with Hall in the Land Commission Office may have had something to do with the criticism. Hall's defeat in the governor's race in 1890 caused Porter to resign his appointment in the Land Office and to seek employment in a bank.

The incident, for all its furore, might be held just another of those tempests of controversy which James Hogg had an undeniable gift for stirring up, as is not infrequently true of men of action. There were several factors in it, however, that raised it to importance. It showed, in the first place, a trait in which Hogg resembled Jefferson: he felt uneasiness about the landless proletariat concentrated in the cities, where now the situation was even worse because of the increasing numbers of immigrants who could not read the English language and knew little or nothing of American institutions. The abuses he had dealt with in his reform program had been visited on people who had the balancing advantages of breathing space around them and, to at least some degree, connections with the traditions of their land. It is interesting to speculate what form his deeply basic humanitarianism would have taken had he been early an inhabitant of one of the teeming northern cities.

Second, the intransigence of such newspapers as the Dallas *News* toward Hogg and what he stood for was demonstrated to be unmodified. A distinguished member of the staff of the *News* has stated that with these tirades following the speech, *"The News* shattered the last vestige

383

of its truce with Hogg"—a truce that had developed from Hogg's stance as a bastion against the Populist threat—when it finally declared that the sooner "this State rids itself of this costly incubus, the better for both its credit and its peace."[63] One must remember that this was on the eve of the State Democratic Convention to be held in Dallas, a city whose industrial and financial interests did not want the Hogg-Reagan pro-silver wing of the Party to triumph. Bailey therefore cannot be blamed for the paper's policy decision to give the "widest and fullest circulation" to Hogg's "unspeakably shocking address,"[64] which must have seemed also an unspeakably timely and welcome gift to the opposition.

As for George Bailey, nearly thirty years later, when doing some writing for Will Hogg, he skillfully detailed the event without mentioning his own participation, although the Governor's children (one of whom, Ima, had gone to the encampment with her father) had always known the identity of the "famous" reporter of 1894:

> The sensational interpretations of the address before the soldiers faded away when the truth about the Governor's utterances became known. Even the suggestion that Texas might fall back upon the Constitution of 1836 and resume her status as an independent republic, if the Union should disintegrate, was robbed of all its terrors when considered with the context of his argument. It may be remarked that even so staunch a Union man as Sam Houston had suggested the possibility of such an outcome. . . . All the unfriendly impressions made by the garbled reports of the "livers and lights" speech vanished, and the result of the episode was a material enhancement of his fame. . . . No stenographic report of it was made, however, and the long-hand report, written from memory some hours after its deliverance, by the correspondent of the San Antonio *Express,* presented several of the more or less lurid sentences, without paying much attention to the real argument of the speech.[65]

But the third factor raising the incident to importance could not have been foreseen by the *News:* Governor Hogg on August 1, in vindication of himself, made one of the strongest, most carefully planned, and most thoughtful speeches of his career.

Hogg decided not to wait until Convention time to clarify his position, and friends arranged for a public meeting in San Antonio. The Grand

---

[63] Sam Acheson, *35,000 Days in Texas: A History of the Dallas News,* (New York, Macmillan Company, 1935), pp. 174–175.

[64] *Ibid.,* p. 174.

[65] George Bailey, "The Liver and Lights Speech," typescript, George Bailey Notes, H. C.

Opera House was jammed with people on August 1, 1894, hours before Senator P. J. Lewis rose to introduce the Governor.

Hogg began by expressing his pleasure in addressing "an audience of independent sovereigns" to whose wisdom, patriotism, and "pure sense of right, any cause or issue may always be submitted in the well-founded hope that integrity, not duplicity, that probity, not baseness, that rectitude, not chicanery, will stand forth in companionship with justice to see that the essence of truth is received to the dismay of sensational fabricationists."[66] He then declared that serious charges had been levied against him—reflecting upon the loyalty and fidelity of Texans to the "Stars and Stripes and to the Federal Union." He knew that he had been a storm center for seven years, because men had purposely "darkened" his motives, but now he stood charged with "menacing the Union and sowing seeds of rebellion."

He told of receiving the watch and of making a few spontaneous remarks in appreciation, and then of his desire to speak to his friends at the encampment about the object and purposes of military forces, both because of the Illinois strike difficulties and because hardly a week before the end of the encampment he himself had been urged to send military forces into several Texas counties where a railroad strike situation existed. Refusing to be stampeded, he had wired the sheriffs to do their duty and to keep him posted. He had also urged labor leaders and railroad management to be discreet. Without calling George Bailey by name, he declared that the reporter responsible for the news stories admitted that he took no notes and only "took down" the speech several hours afterward from "memory." Although the reporter denied any intention to misquote or misrepresent, Hogg asserted flatly that he had done so.

After emphasizing the two points he had sought to stress at the encampment, namely 1) that at all times except in war, or when martial law was declared, the military was subordinate to civil authority, and 2) that in the event of insurrections within or invasion from without, or in any kind of war, it was the military's duty to stand by the Union and lead the Stars and Stripes to victory, Hogg launched into a lengthy discussion of the difference between Hamilton's conception of a strong and centralized government and Jefferson's notion of a federal and general government of limited powers and his belief in the people's capacity for self-government. T. B. Macaulay and Herbert Spencer were instanced

[66] Dallas *Morning News,* August 2, 1894; Cotner, *op. cit.,* p. 379; W. H. Brocker to J. S. Hogg, July 24, 1894, J. S. Hogg Let. Rec., XXXI, 354.

THE FATE OF SLANDERERS.

Texas Farmer, August 4, 1894

as among those who had prophesied that our Jeffersonian system of government would fail. Hogg said he had never joined these exponents of failure, but that he was not blind to unhealthy conditions which should be remedied by " 'ballots, not bayonets.' "

As calm returned after the Altgeld-Cleveland debate, Hogg believed it was proper for every "patriot to reflect on and seriously examine into the President's action." He was aware that the great mass of people had called Cleveland's course one of "heroic action," that the martial-law measure had strong popular support, and that a "great Republican constitutional lawyer," Judge Thomas M. Cooley, had congratulated the President in an open letter. Agreeing ironically with Judge Cooley that the President had placed "a construction on the Constitution by the use of federal troops" rather than act in obedience to constitutional demand, Hogg maintained that the people should understand the full import of the action and "if they deliberately indorsed it their condemnation of any future President who may follow it at will must come too late." He believed that Altgeld was right and that the President had acted without authority:

If he acted without authority, where does the precedent point to: Logically to the President of the United States rising above the Constitution and doing as he pleases so long as the army will obey him—the substitution of a military government for the Republic. Are the people prepared to bow to the change? Will they agree to it? If so, what will become of their ballot boxes and liberties? Pause and think! It is now time for cool reflection. Don't go wild and commit a serious mistake because a Democratic President, whom we have always loved and honored, did this. You know that if a Republican President had committed this deed, the last one of you would be screaming and howling and bellowing like lost cattle in a storm. . . . As it is, Republicans are smiling and Democrats are blindly swallowing the "heroic dose." Let me tell you, the day for weeping lies yonder not far in the future, hovering over the great quagmire of despair, if this precedent is to stand. Governments are changed while the people are lulled to sleep by the balm of enthusiasm over "heroic deeds," or are blinded by passions of rage. At times all republics must pass through the throes of distress. During the paroxysms of the malady, dictators rise and, under the pretext of necessity, prescribe rules and maxims and set precedents against the Constitution, paving the way to absolute authority of a central power. Thus new conditions are fastened upon the people, and their government becomes changed to the destruction of their rights and liberties.[67]

[67] Cotner, *op. cit.*, pp. 378–383.

Hogg quickly added that no one thought Cleveland was trying to seize power for power's sake, but other presidents would be elected and the precedent should not go unchallenged. He recalled that Cleveland had been elected upon a platform containing this statement:

We solemnly declare that the need of a return to the fundamental principles of a free, popular government, based on home rule and individual liberty, was never more urgent than now, when the tendency to centralize all power at the Federal capital has become a menace to the reserved rights of the States, that strikes at the very roots of government under the Constitution as framed by the fathers of the Republic.[68]

It was not enough, Hogg continued, to speak of the Chicago situation as a riot or emergency. Reconstruction Governor Edmund J. Davis of Texas had asked President Grant to send troops to Texas in an "emergency" in 1873–1874 and Grant had refused. Under the emergency pleas, President Hayes was importuned to send an army into Louisiana, and he declined. President Harrison heard "bloodcurdling sounds of alarm" and calls to send military forces into the South, and he declined. Hogg drove home his point: "Each time, with this one exception, they refused. By this course civil authorities were left to enforce the laws, and they succeeded, thus demonstrating the people's capacity for local self-government."[69]

Hogg was opposed to the dependence of local authorities upon federal troops for suppression of riots and mobs to the point where the people were taught "dependence in a central authority," maintaining that "the pusillanimous doctrine of paternalism now so strong in the land" would grow until Hamilton's idea of centralism would be "completely accomplished." "Does it not seem strange that a Democratic President shall be the first to act under them [war statutes], and then in one of the strongest states in the North? So far as I am concerned, I seriously dissent from the action, and as a free American citizen, with the fear of God only in my eyes, I solemnly protest against it."[70]

Furthermore, Hogg denied the legality of the sweeping injunction against Debs, the Railway Union, and "all other persons combining and conspiring with them . . . from interfering with . . . the railroads in Chicago," of which there were twenty-three. He did not think the United

---

[68] National Democratic Platform, 1892, Kirk H. Porter, *National Party Platforms* (New York, Macmillan Company, 1924), p. 159.
[69] Cotner, *op. cit.*, p. 386.   [70] *Ibid.*, pp. 388–389.

States marshal had received writs under it or tried to execute them, before the wires were made hot by the railroad representatives and the "so-called" district attorney calling for federal troops. The haste with which the marshal found that he could not execute the "process" of the court was only equaled by the facility with which the President dispatched troops into Chicago. Without studying the "decree" entered in the federal court, men had supported the President's action in their zeal to silence what they called "bloody-handed anarchists." Hogg yielded to no one in his opposition to anarchy, and added, "Surely it is not inconsistent to be for the Constitution and against anarchy."[71] He argued that the brave men of Illinois would have suppressed the "insurrection" or enforced the "judicial process" if asked or given time to do so. Instead, an injunction was issued by a federal court one day and an order for United States troops was obtained the very next day.

Speaking about the resolution of the houses of Congress endorsing the action of the Executive, the Governor declared that it was done in the midst of excitement. He reminded his audience that this same Congress, a few months before, at public expense had sent a committee to investigate the conduct of two federal judges in another celebrated injunction, which, in effect, prohibited employees of a railroad in the hands of a receiver from quitting work. Hogg declared the precedent as compared to the President's action "was but a shadow of a fly's wing compared to the black cloud behind the cyclone." The Chicago injunction was too sweeping, not only including Debs and the American Railroad Union, but "all other persons whomsoever." Not only was it intended to protect the mails and trains from violence, but enjoined everyone "from compelling or inducing by threats, persuasion or violence, any of the employees of such roads to leave the service of such roads . . . or preventing any person from entering the service of such roads"—and, like Judge McCormick's injunction restraining the Texas Railroad Commission, it was made perpetual. Hogg doubted whether Congress realized the import either of the injunction or of its enforcement by federal troops.

Finally, he called attention to actions of federal judges from Tennessee to California in which men were being put in jail under the same or similar injunctions, without jury trial. A judge in California simply had the United States marshal, backed by federal soldiers, bring the

[71] *Ibid.*, p. 391.

men before him, and it was left with his "august majesty" to release them or consign them to jail for contempt as long as he chose—and they were sent to jail for seven months! Hogg insisted:

In all respects this omnibus injunction is a new thing in the land—another precedent! It is said to be necessary to protect the United States mails. A violation of it insures imprisonment for "contempt," while the punishment for "knowingly and willfully obstructing or retarding the mails" as proscribed by the United States statutes is by fine of not more than $100—R.S. 3995. Imprisonment for contempt; fine for obstructing the mails, a clear substitution of court-made law for Congress-made law. This of itself is a high-handed outrage.[72]

Hogg maintained that the third article of the Constitution guaranteed jury trial except in impeachment cases. He quoted the Bill of Rights: "In all criminal proceedings, the accused shall enjoy the right of a speedy public trial by an impartial jury," no person "shall be compelled in any criminal case to witness against himself," and "unusual punishments" shall not be inflicted. Hogg declared that each of the guarantees had been "violated by this new, ubiquitous, judicial ukase."

Turning then to an echo of his own fight for stricter regulation of corporations and the issuance of their stocks and bonds, Hogg described the growth of the Pullman Car Company, first telling his audience now to look to the other side—"labor has received its share of abuse"—and let their "sense of humanitarianism speak." When times grew bad, as during the depression, the company had continued to pay expenses of operation, salaries to officers, interest on bonds and dividends on preferred stock. He charged the management with "skinning the flea for its tallow" by reducing labor forces and cutting wages and raising rents. Then when labor, with hope crushed out, revolted, and the excitement spread, the manipulators fled "to seaside resorts or to 'Hingland' to complacently watch results."[73] Injunctions and troops followed, used in such a way as to aid the corporations, while labor felt that the government had ceased to be its friend.

For warning the country that there were "breakers ahead," Hogg said he was "called a pessimist—a crank." He wanted the people to know that on his Eastern business tour he found that the honest invest-

---

[72] *Ibid.*, p. 394; see *In Re Debs* (158 U. S. 564) 1895.

[73] Andrew Carnegie had been in Scotland ("Hingland") when the Homestead Strike of 1892 began. For Labor's efforts to restrict use of injunctions see Foster R. Dulles, *Labor in America* (New York, Thomas Y. Crowell Company, 1949), pp. 181, 198, 263.

ment men of New York and Boston and Philadelphia were deeply interested in the new Texas laws which regulated the issuance of public securities. "So far as Texas is concerned, she takes care that the proud aegis of law stands with equal justice over capital and labor."

Forty years after the Altgeld-Cleveland tussle over the nature of the federal system, two distinguished historians, Samuel E. Morison and Henry S. Commager, wrote that President Cleveland's action in sending regulars into Chicago on the Fourth of July had an effect "like that of sending British regulars to Boston in 1768."[74] Hogg's warning was widely published, and numerous copies of the full text were sent outside of the state upon requests for them. Governor Altgeld wrote:

I cannot refrain from complimenting you upon the masterly manner in which you treated the question involved. Not even an enemy can read that speech without being deeply impressed with the ability and earnest conviction of the author. It has made a strong impression in this section of the country. The country in the end must sustain this position or else free institutions are at an end.[75]

Having entered the debate over the nature of the powers of the federal executive, Hogg wanted all to know that Texans and their Governor would stand by the Stars and Stripes, and that they were "ever proud to see constitutional liberty awarded and sacredly maintained to all classes without discrimination, and every servant of the people, from constable to President, stand by and jealously uphold the Constitution!"[76]

[74] Samuel E. Morison and Henry S. Commager, *Growth of the American Republic* (New York, Macmillan Company, 1937), II, 162.
[75] John P. Altgeld to J. S. Hogg, August 16, 1894, J. S. Hogg Let. Rec., XXXII, 109.
[76] Cotner, *op. cit.,* p. 400.

CHAPTER XIV

Protecting the Progressive Gains

DESPITE THE DIVISION in the Texas Democratic Party, the defection of the Populists, and the unrest and uncertainty which accompany a depression, Governor Hogg had been able in 1893 to complete a major portion of the legislation necessary to put into effect his progressive reform program. The real test of whether he was a statesman and not just a lucky politician would be his ability to consolidate the gains, bring unity to the party, and assure the operation of the new laws long enough to prove their practicality. One indirect weakness in his administration that he was unable to remedy to his satisfaction—and which showed him the necessity of compromise with his Democratic opposition in order to hold the advance skirmish line—was the matter of federal patronage. The Clark Democrats were the gold standard minority in Texas, and the leaders therefore often obtained appointments from President Cleveland. It also frequently happened that an able man was recommended by both wings of the party, with the result that his appointment could not be claimed as a straight-out victory for the Hogg administration. The governor did assist Alexander W. Terrell to obtain the post of American Minister to Turkey, but in so doing deprived himself of a staunch supporter and astute adviser.[1]

The patronage situation was further complicated because Cleveland tended to listen to the Texas junior senator, Roger Q. Mills, rather than to venerable and independent Richard Coke. Coke had let Hogg know in the fall of 1893 that he wanted the pro-silver Governor to succeed him when he retired from the United States Senate in 1895,[2] and Hogg's friends in Texas began urging him to seek the place Coke would vacate in order to carry on the fight for free and unlimited coinage of silver at the ratio of 16 to 1, hoping to offset the tendency of Mills to go

[1] J. S. Hogg to A. W. Terrell, April 28, 1893, Gov. Let. Pr., 11, p. 322; Dallas *Morning News*, September 10, 1912; Webb and Carroll (eds.), *Handbook of Texas*, II, 725.
[2] Richard Coke to J. S. Hogg, November 25, 1893, J. S. Hogg Let. Rec., XXIX, 222–223; Anna Hooker, "Richard Coke," *Handbook of Texas*, I, 370.

392

along with Cleveland and the "gold-bugs."[3] (Almost no one—whether friend or foe—believed that Hogg really meant to return to private law practice.) Governor Hogg was determined to return Horace Chilton to the Senate, and believed that Senator Mills and his friends could hardly afford to start a fight against Chilton's election after his tactful withdrawal in 1892.

The years 1893 and 1894 witnessed the continued growth of Populism in Texas and in the nation. Until May, 1894, the very eve of the 1894 primaries, it was not known whether the Texas Railroad Commission would be permitted to continue functioning in the interest of protecting the public against the high and fluctuating rate system being used by the railways, and the long uncertainty about the Commission made a good talking point for the Texas Populists in their advocacy of public ownership.[4] The advent of John D. Rockefeller and J. Pierpont Morgan as interested stockholders and directors of western railroads did not decrease Populist interest in government ownership.[5]

Gradually the reactionary Clark Democrats realized that their salvation lay, not in undermining Hogg's progressive leadership (although they had not given up the idea), but in making sure that a united Democracy was victorious over the Populists in 1894. Hogg, equally alarmed by the recent Populist strides, was ready to extend the olive branch to any Democrats temporarily renegade to Clark or Nugent. While the depression was relatively less severe in Texas than in some other parts of the nation, Texas farmers were far from satisfied with 5 to 7 cents for a pound of cotton, the high price of articles they had to buy, and the costs of transportation. In the spring of 1893 sheepmen got perhaps a dollar a head for sheep and 7 cents a pound for wool.[6] The economic distress of farmers and ranchers was increased acutely in some

[3] "Roger Q. Mills," James L. Harrison (comp.), *Biographical Directory of the American Congress, 1774–1949* (Washington, Government Printing Office, 1950), pp. 1568–1569. Paxton Hibben in *The Peerless Leader: William Jennings Bryan* (New York, Farrar and Rinehart, 1929), pp. 154–155, charged that President Cleveland had a part in ending Bryan's congressional career.

[4] *Reagan* v. *Farmers Loan and Trust Company* was settled in May, 1894; Roscoe Martin, *People's Party in Texas*, pp. 71, 114–118.

[5] Compare the People's Party platform adopted at Omaha, July 4, 1892, and Texas People's Party platform of June 21, 1894, sections 5 and 6, quoted in Ernest Winkler, *Platforms*, p. 333. Catharine Nugent, *Nugent*, pp. 203–204.

[6] Winifred Kupper (ed.), *Texas Sheepman, The Reminiscences of Robert T. Maudslay* (Austin, University of Texas Press, 1951), p. 72. Texas middling cotton was selling in New York for 7 13/16 cents on January 1, 1894, and for 5 11/16 cents on November 29, 1894. See New York *Daily Tribune*, January 1 and November 29, 1894.

areas by the prolonged drought; more and more of these men were leaving the Democratic Party to seek relief in the program of the Populists. All signs indicated that the People's Party of radical protests and plans, which had become the second party in Texas in 1892, would be a great threat in 1894, especially with Nugent as its standard bearer.

Early in January, 1894, two former governors, O. M. Roberts and John Ireland, publicly warned the split Democratic Party of the Populist danger and called upon the factions to unite. Ireland proposed that the rival chairmen, Waller Baker and A. L. Matlock, resign to make way for a unity meeting to check the threat of a Populist-Republican combination.[7] George Clark then spoke for the minority. He stated that the issue between the factions was not one of personalities—Hogg or Clark —but of differences in basic principles. However, he believed that Democrats might come together on the national Democratic platform of 1892, which both factions had endorsed.[8]

Late in January, at the invitation of a large group of prominent men that included both Hogg supporters and Clark supporters, Hogg went to Dallas and offered peace terms, made more palatable by his announcement that he did not seek any public office.[9] He said little about national issues, but he let it be understood that he did not intend to compromise on any plan that undermined his reform legislation. The visit was successful to the extent that the basis was laid for a harmony meeting of the factions a few weeks later. Even the Dallas *News* was willing to declare a temporary truce; Hogg visited the *News* offices and talked with the staff. Seeing the new Mergenthaler typesetting machines, he sat down at the keyboard and "touched off the inevitable SHRDLU," which reminded him of a dream he had had when he was a printer's devil—that some day a machine would be invented which would knock him out of his job! "By gatlins, it was like a nightmare to me and made me perfectly miserable!"[10] Then he likened the harmony of men and machines in the plant to a smoothly functioning Democracy.

[7] Austin *Daily Statesman,* January 3 and 10, 1894. The *Statesman* wanted former Governor Ross to run again, reflecting its pro-Clark stand but also its awareness of the need for Democratic unity. On January 22 the editor mentioned Ireland as a candidate for the U.S. Senate, hoping to head off Hogg or Chilton.

[8] *Ibid.,* January 11, 1894. See also report of Hogg's address to the cattlemen in which he stressed the importance of improving Galveston harbor, building meat-packing and refrigeration plants, and making use of overseas shipments as a way to break the railroad's high rates.

[9] Austin *Daily Statesman,* January 29, 1894.

[10] Sam Acheson, *35,000 Days in Texas,* p. 172. For Clark's views on Hogg's Dal-

Clark and Hogg began working through Waller Baker in Waco to reunite the party, with Matlock offering suggestions. Agreement seemed urgent, for on February 15 the Texas Alliance Executive Committee announced that an all-out campaign to organize every precinct for a Populist victory had begun.[11]

Negotiations at this stage were not easy for the Governor, and for the first time in his career he virtually ignored a piece of John Reagan's advice—to let the Clark forces alone. Hogg believed at the time that Culberson could win the nomination for governor and would be safe on the reform program and on the silver issue, but he also thought that Culberson might need the 40,000 to 50,000 Democratic votes Clark had drawn off, especially if the Populists and Republicans should combine. The degree of Reagan's fears of the Clark group in the guise of gift-bearing Greeks was revealed in a letter he sent to Senator Coke after Waller Baker had been in Austin trying to obtain a go-ahead signal from Hogg and the other leaders of the pro-silver, reform wing. After a "full private conference" with Baker, Reagan was convinced that Matlock would not dissolve Clark's executive committee unless the Clark forces obtained what they wanted—endorsement of the Democratic national platform of 1892, endorsement of Cleveland's pro-gold administration, and an agreement to refer national questions to the President and to Congress and leave questions of state policy to the state Democratic Convention. Reagan wrote:

If this plan should be agreed to it would be an abandonment by the state committee of the position of the state democratic convention on the questions of coinage and finance. It would be going back on most of our members in Congress. It would be a defiance to the will and a disregard of the interests of the people of Texas. It would be to align the democracy of Texas with the fifty democratic members of the House of Representatives [mostly Eastern men] who voted recently against the bill for the coinage of silver in the Treasury and with their Republican allies, 79 in number, and against the 141 democrats [Southern and Western men] who voted for the measure along with 19 Republicans and 8 Populists.[12]

Reagan believed Cleveland's policies were making the depression worse.

---

las speech see Dallas *Morning News* and Austin *Daily Statesman,* February 2, 1894.

[11] For Chairman Baker's views see Austin *Daily Statesman,* February 16, 1894.

[12] John H. Reagan to Richard Coke, March 8, 1894, J. H. Reagan Papers, Fol. 1890–1894.

Bankruptcies over the nation had increased 271 per cent over 1892, and one-sixth of the total railroad mileage of the country was in the hands of receivers. He told Coke that the recent sale of $50 million of United States bonds was calculated to benefit the speculators in gold and the national banks. To endorse the Cleveland administration would, Reagan was positive, drive many more Democrats into the Populist ranks. The "Matlock plan" was declared to be a specimen of Clark's shrewdness, and Reagan hoped Coke would warn Baker, whom he considered "woefully overreached by their [Clark's and Matlock's] cunning and duplicity."[13] Reagan confessed that he had not been able to sleep for worrying about the danger to the Democratic Party.

He had good cause to worry, for it soon began to be evident than an endorsement of Cleveland's administration might cost the Democrats in Texas more votes than the total Democratic following of Clark. Early in March articles in the Populist *Advance* (which were echoed by about seventy other Populist papers) declared that there could be no harmony between the Hogg Democrats and the Cleveland Democrats.[14] Meanwhile, Populist "Cyclone" (James H.) Davis' new book, *A Political Revelation,* was being widely read. Davis charged the Democrats with deserting the cause of the people and sought to prove that Thomas Jefferson was in essence the first Populist. Harry Tracy, Thomas L. Nugent, Jerome Kearby, T. P. Gore (later United States Senator from Oklahoma), and R. J. Sledge were making converts to Populism every day. Reagan, the old veteran of political wars with Know-Nothings, Republicans, and Greenbackers, knew that the Populist movement was led by earnest and able men whose message on money, banks, and cheap interest held wide appeal.

Preceding the "Harmony Meeting" on March 19 and 20 in Dallas, Regular Chairman Baker called a conference of his Executive Committee, as did Matlock of his, each wing meeting separately at first to appoint members of a joint conference committee. As a first step in the later regular session of the full meeting Hogg and Reagan, the latter warily and reluctantly, accepted the Clark proposal to unite on the national Democratic platform of 1892. But almost immediately Clark and Reagan clashed on interpreting the money plank, Reagan bitterly denouncing President Cleveland for the repeal of the Silver Purchase Act in 1893. At the evening session, however, the report of the joint committee was adopted. Then, according to the reporter for the Dallas *Morning*

---

[13] *Ibid.*
[14] *Texas Advance* (Dallas), March 24, 1894. File in Arch. Tex. St. Lib.

News, "Every throat was screaming for the Governor, and Tal Buie gracefully led him to the front."[15]

The *News'* report also said that Hogg's "face was wreathed in smiles" as he began to speak. Hogg, however, knew that this was an occasion for labor, rather than for joy; somehow he must hold the "reunited" Democrats in line against the most serious threat to their control in Texas since 1874. Pledging his acceptance of the compromise as the best they could do, he urged Democrats not to feel "in the least humiliated by the concessions that the representatives of the party make to bring about harmony. . . . Those who differed from us are pledged not to propose to repeal or amend a single one of these [state reform] laws, and I have been taught to believe that a man is telling the truth when he makes me a pledge." Going as far as he could in defense of President Cleveland, Hogg pointed out that the President was under fire from Republicans and Populists. Aiming his final darts at the new foe, he declared the Populist leaders who had left the Democratic party were a "2 x 4 nomadic crowd," then added:

The Democratic party has a mission to perform. Republicanism means centralization, and Populism—what in thunder does that mean? The overthrow of law and order? The Democratic administration is on trial and we must stand by it, but we are not prepared to subscribe to the President's course every time he appoints a Republican to office, but in every effort to carry out the Democratic platform, why can't we say, amen? . . . Let the action of this day be a guarantee that not a Populist shall hold an office in Texas, nor any Republican from Texas disgrace the Halls of Congress. United we stand, not divided at all. . . . I want to say that, so far as I am concerned, if a measure is adopted by the Democratic convention by one vote, I will subscribe to the platform and will vote the ticket even if I dislike every man on it.[16]

Railroad Commissioner Reagan was thoroughly alarmed at the strength of the pro-gold forces. He agreed with Nugent's charge that the Dallas meeting had virtually ended in "a clear victory for Clark and his followers."[17] Reagan had never had much confidence in President Cleveland's knowledge of financial matters; in the summer of 1893 he had written the editor of the Dallas *Times-Herald,* James B. Simpson,

---

[15] Dallas *Morning News,* March 20, 1894.

[16] *Ibid.;* Winkler, *Platforms,* pp. 330 ff. The Texas Populists in June, 1894, stated they wanted the Railroad Commission but restated their belief that government ownership offered "the only complete and satisfactory solution of the railroad question." Dallas *Morning News,* June 21–22, 1894.

[17] *Texas Advance* (Dallas), March 24, 1894.

that Cleveland was "ignorant of financial matters."[18] Feeling that the growth of the goldbug organization in Texas called for strong measures, on April 10, 1894, Reagan delivered an anti-Cleveland address, giving the history of the silver-gold struggle in Europe and America and calling upon the Populists to join with silver Democrats to win the money fight for the deliverance of the South and West from Wall Street.[19]

By the middle of April the speech was being widely discussed. George Clark made a pro-Cleveland speech at Gonzales on San Jacinto Day, whereupon Reagan wrote the pro-Hogg editor of the Houston *Post:* "If anybody has to leave [the Party] let it be the President and those who like him agree with the Republican party on these great questions." Harry Tracy took his turn next, asserting that even Reagan's valiant stand for silver would not bring the Texas Populists back into the Democratic Party.[20] However, Reagan did not give up hope.

Finally facing the reality—that the efforts of George Clark[21] and Matlock to break the Hogg-Reagan-Chilton leadership had not abated—Hogg considered the list of aspirants for his office. The next two years would mark a transition, for obviously less reform legislation could be expected; the period must be controlled by a governor whom Hogg could trust to preserve the gains already made. E. M. House was already working for the nomination of Attorney General Charles Culberson,[22] whom Reagan had offered to support. Lieutenant Governor Crane could shift to the attorney generalship to continue the important legal battles. Hogg was still determined to send Horace Chilton back to the United States Senate, and the situation had been complicated by the inclination of Culberson's father to run for Coke's seat in the Senate rather than to stand again for his own seat in the House. Charles Culberson had gone to Washington to discuss the situation with his father, pointing out Hogg's desire for Chilton to have the Senate seat. One evening while Governor Hogg, General Hamby, and Colonel House were playing six-handed euchre with other friends at the Mansion, House received a telegram from Washington indicating that Dave Culberson

---

[18] Reagan to James B. Simpson, July 21, 1893, and Reagan to James E. Downs, March 16, 1894, J. H. Reagan Papers, 1847–1905, II, n.p.

[19] Reagan's speech of April 10 was printed in Austin *Daily Statesman*, April 13, 1894.

[20] *Texas Advance* (Dallas), April 28, 1894; Houston *Daily Post*, May 4, 1894; see also 14-page typescript in John H. Reagan Papers, Vol. II.

[21] For Clark's reply to Reagan see Austin *Daily Statesman*, May 14, 1894.

[22] Dallas *Morning News*, May 14, 1894; Robert L. Wagner, "The Gubernatorial Career of Charles Allen Culberson," unpublished M. A. thesis (the University of Texas, 1954), p. 41.

would not oppose Chilton and that Hogg and Chilton would be expected to aid Charles in the race for governor.[23] At this time Speaker of the Texas House John Cochran of Dallas, Comptroller John D. McCall of Austin, and U.S. Congressman Samuel W. T. Lanham of Weatherford—all Confederate veterans, all older and more conservative than Culberson—were already in the governor's race.[24]

When Charles Culberson returned to Austin he set about preparing for a series of early speeches to be made through the state, assuming that he had Hogg-Reagan-Chilton support since House had become his manager. For the break that came, House held Culberson largely responsible, later saying that Culberson was always independent and "not very communicative and he never told Hogg anything about his plans."[25] The Attorney General left for his first campaign speeches in North Texas without conferring with Hogg, a move that House declared was against his advice. What House did not record was that Reagan and Hogg had realized that House did not agree with them on free and unlimited coinage of silver and was, as Culberson's adviser, soft-pedaling the money issue; such a policy, Reagan and Hogg were sure, would send more hundreds of Democrats into the Populist camp. House did not accuse Hogg of breaking a promise to support Culberson, but said: "I wanted Hogg, of course, to support Charley Culberson, and yet, I understood fully, why he didn't do it."[26]

Meanwhile, various influential men, including W. A. Shaw, editor of the *Texas Farmer* at Dallas, Richard Wynne, a Fort Worth attorney, and leading Democrats among the German groups in South Texas, had begun encouraging Reagan to enter the race, and the Governor, in the light of his long-standing admiration for and friendship with Reagan, told a few mutual friends that he would quietly support the Commissioner if he did enter the race, but would shun public speeches on behalf of or against any of the candidates. Editor Shaw felt that it was important to provide the farmers with a candidate such as Reagan, whom they could trust, for Clark's rush to support Culberson was enough to

[23] Typescript "Memorandum of Conference, Edward M. House, George Bailey, and A. J. Rosenthal, Jr., in New York, November 7, 1922," Let. Biog. J. S. Hogg.
[24] Telegram from N. A. Stedman to Culberson, May 12, 1894. Edward M. House Papers, Yale University Microfilm of originals in University of Texas Library. Three days later Culberson in Fort Worth (Lanham's district) was writing House: "The Reagan movement is making some headway and between the two I have to work."
[25] "Memorandum of a Conference, Edward M. House, etc., November 7, 1922," Let. Biog. J. S. Hogg.
[26] *Ibid.*

turn many farmers against the Attorney General and candidates McCall and Lanham, like Culberson, tended to shy away from the national issues, including money. Something needed to be done to alert the Democrats to the danger of further defections to the Populists. Several leaders got the impression that Reagan wanted to be governor. After an unrecorded talk with Hogg, Wynne decided that he would make public speeches urging Reagan to run; the possibility of Reagan's entrance might force the other candidates to take a stand on silver, thus showing potential Populists that the reform wing had not forgotten this important issue.

On May 14, Wynne reported to Hogg: "I put the Old Roman's claims before the people the best I could on so short notice. . . . Will he accept. . . . We must not let him be beat—it would be a direct slap at your Administration in the face." Five days later he wrote that Lanham and Cochran were challenging Reagan to run and declaring he was too old.

It would be the very devil if we put the old man in and let him get beat. . . . I am looking for the first fellow I meet on the stump to ask me if you and I did not agree when you were in Fort Worth that I would put the old man in the race. . . . What shall I say? If I refuse it will be taken as a confession and if I should answer you know what I am compelled to say.[27]

Wynne's speech had indicated that Reagan ought to run but that he was tied down by a pledge to support another candidate. Culberson, in Waco at the time, magnanimously wrote Reagan that he wanted Reagan to consider himself free to do as he pleased; whether the letter was pure impulse or whether he had conferred with Colonel House or George Clark prior to mailing it and had obligated himself to stand by silver and gold parity is not known.[28] Other candidates also freed Reagan from any obligations to them.

Exactly why John H. Reagan, age 75, decided to enter the race remains a mystery. However, it is clear that he hoped his candidacy would, first, make sure that Clark would not be nominated and, second, perhaps also militate against any other gold Democrats. Culberson's delay in standing forth four-square for silver had perhaps worried him to the point of believing that someone must take an unequivocal stand.

[27] Wynne to Hogg, May 14, 1894, J. S. Hogg Let. Rec., XXX, 30; Wynne to Hogg, May 19, 1894, *ibid.*, XXX, 55–61. Among other things Wynne wanted Reagan's reply to Clark and Wynne's own speech at Mansfield distributed in large numbers.

[28] Charles A. Culberson to John H. Reagan, May 12, 1894, J. H. Reagan Papers.

On May 22, the Dallas *News* published the following from their Austin reporter:

... There is Ed House ... For several years he had played Pythias to Governor Hogg's Damon ... He was one of His Excellency's most trusted managers and lieutenants during the last campaign ... When the Governor waltzed over the State for a week with the Chief of the Tammany tigers, Mr. House was at his side. But Mr. House is not for the venerable Chairman of the Railroad Commission. ... He is a Culberson man dyed-in-the-wool and rock-ribbed. He is Chairman of the Culberson Campaign Committee ... This fact being known, the opponents of Judge Reagan point to it with great glee and chuckle over it. They say it is proof that Governor Hogg is going to keep hands-off and let the other fellows fight it out among themselves. They say further that if he does this, Judge Reagan's pole will never reach the persimmon. Governor Hogg is known to have a great friendship with Judge Reagan, but Governor Hogg has other friends to whom he owes just as much regard, and he is not prone to take up the cudgel for one friend against another.

The day this item appeared Hogg answered a letter from M. M. Crane, who had helped write the commission law. Crane had warned that the farmers seriously questioned the Dallas harmony action, thinking it a Clark, big-city deal. He was concerned at the apathy toward voting and called upon Hogg to sound the alarm: "A blast from you ... will do much in that direction." Hogg replied: "Reticence on my part I hope is yet proper. My trumpet shall be blasted if necessary."[29]

Culberson when working with George Clark on the Greer County case had found him genial and highly able and could not bring himself to distrust the man politically as Hogg and Reagan did. Actually, since House and Hogg did not see eye to eye on the silver issue, Culberson had hoped to stay away from the national issue, but Reagan had blasted that hope. Apparently the Attorney General had developed a case of political nearsightedness: he seemed at this time not to realize that the internal Party struggle over the money issue was actually a struggle for control of the Party in the national elections of 1896.[30] He was the more harassed when Shaw's *Texas Farmer* began to lampoon him as "Little

[29] J. S. Hogg to M. M. Crane, May 22, 1894, Gov. Let. Pr., 5, p. 565. Horace Chilton to J. S. Hogg, May 21, 1894, J. S. Hogg, Let. Rec., XXX, 58A, urged Hogg not to overlook what he could do for Chilton by way of early instructions from the big county of Harris. Such action, he declared, would "ring out over the State and strike dismay to the breasts of the 'watching and waiting steeds who stand in the dark'."

[30] James W. Madden, *Charles Allen Culberson*, xiii; Wagner, *op. cit.*, p. 18.

Lord Fauntleroy" and as one of Congressmen Dave Culberson's "Little Lambs," who came bleating for public support. Culberson also complained that Wynne, who followed him in speaking at Fort Worth, had tried to line up "the entire Hogg forces for Reagan." *"This undoubtedly is the scheme,"* he confided to House, "as they believe they can obtain a majority . . . and nominate him. . . . The most dangerous thing is the effort to make it a Hogg-Clark race over—with Reagan representing Hogg. This is perilous. . . . The race clearly is between Reagan and myself, and all my friends think I can win but we can tell best Wednesday after Reagan's Sherman speech."[31]

One result Wynne had hoped for when he publicly urged Reagan to run was partially achieved: Culberson was forced to decide and to announce where he would stand on the money issue. Speaking at Quanah on May 22 he endorsed free and unlimited coinage of silver at the ratio of 16 to 1—*provided* there was gold and silver dollar parity. He also complimented the Texas delegation in Congress for voting against repeal of the Sherman Silver Purchase Act. Then, as the depression grew worse, he took up the local issue of state governmental expenditures, advocating a halt for the time being to the geological survey and termination of the $20,000 appropriation for purchasing daily newspapers for members of the legislature. He declared his opposition to Colonel Lanham's proposal to decrease the membership of the legislature by one-half so the pay of the remaining members could be increased. In other words, Culberson intended to balance the budget.[32]

When Reagan opened his speaking campaign at Sherman on June 2, Culberson was being acclaimed by his friends for the May 26 decision of the United States Supreme Court upholding the State's contention that the Texas Railroad Commission Law was constitutional.[33] Commissioner Reagan's initial speech lauded the Hogg reform program, opposed using county convicts in competition with free labor, advocated stricter economy while still defending liberal appropriations for schools. He favored still lower transportation rates, a primary election law, and

---

[31] Charles Culberson to E. M. House, May 31, 1894, E. M. House Papers, Ramsdell Microfilm 109B, E. C. Barker History Center, Univ. Tex. Lib.; Rupert N. Richardson, authority on House, to R. C. Cotner, November 29, 1954, stated his belief that Reagan really wanted to become governor, not merely to clarify the money issue.

[32] Culberson's speech at Quanah, May 22, 1894, quoted in Dallas *Morning News,* May 23, 1894. An anti-Culberson speech by Speaker Cochran at Denton was quoted in the same paper. See also Wagner, *op. cit.,* p. 46.

[33] Austin *Daily Statesman,* May 27, 1894; *Reagan v. Farmers' Loan and Trust Co.,* 154 U.S. 362.

direct election of railroad commissioners.[34] He was able to make clear the fundamental character of the issues involved in the money question, both as he saw them from his own thinking on the subject and as he had experienced their political significance during his senatorial term in Washington. Reagan could talk to the farmers in a way that Culberson could not, because he understood their interest in increasing that circulating medium as one way of raising prices for their farm products. Indeed, the rumor spread by opponents that Reagan's nomination would receive the support of the Populists, although quite untrue, was actually an admission that he talked language the farmers understood.

Culberson was from Dallas, which marked him as something of a "city boy" to many farmers. He was also considered too friendly with Clark.[35] However, no one fought more aggressively than he did to defend the "Hogg Laws" and the Greer County case as inherited by Hogg and passed on from him to Culberson, and no one could have labored more devotedly to bring the Railroad Commission case before the Supreme Court to its successful conclusion. Nevertheless, rumors of his negotiations with the Clark faction kept circulating; the rumor mongers seemed to have forgotten that the Dallas harmony meeting had been held for the express purpose of bringing the factions together.

Reagan had waited so long to indicate his intent to run that some of Hogg's closest friends were already working for Culberson, among them Allison Mayfield (later to serve on the Commision), who was chairman of the Grayson County Culberson Club,[36] Judge Nathan A. Stedman of Fort Worth, and Judge John Bookout, Culberson's law partner at Dallas. Hogg believed—on the basis of his own experience—that the younger generation of progressive Democrats held the key to the success of the Party in Texas, but he would not oppose the "grand Old Roman" in his fight to protect silver and the interests of the West and South. Reagan had been an inspiration to Jim Hogg, the boy, by meeting adversity with courage, and had brought luster to James Stephen Hogg, the Governor, by retiring from the Senate to head the first Texas Railroad Commission. Almost immediately after Reagan's announcement to run, the Houston *Post,* which had extensive Southern Pacific interests, had requested him to withdraw from the race and remain at his job as

[34] Dallas *Morning News,* June 3, 1894.

[35] John Cochran to J. S. Hogg, July 14, 1894, J. S. Hogg Let. Rec., XXXI, 252–253. Culberson to House, May 24, 1894, E. M. House Papers, microfilm 109B, shows that Culberson expected Clark to vote for him.

[36] Wagner, *op. cit.,* pp. 42–45. Mayfield held an appointment in Attorney General Culberson's department.

chairman of the Commission;[37] here was proof that a powerful railway network had not found his Commission schedules in general "unreasonable" or his valuations of railway property unfair. Hogg decided that it was not yet part of political wisdom to interfere directly in the gubernatorial free-for-all, especially if he intended to get Chilton into the United States Senate. Furthermore, he knew he could trust both Culberson and Reagan to champion the Commission and—now that Culbersond had ceased his wavering on the money issue—to endorse the free and unlimited coinage of silver.

In mid-June the Governor, accompanied by a group of businessmen —some of them with railroad interests—left Texas for a tour of northern and eastern cities, where he was to explain his reform program. With a large element of the Clark forces supporting Lanham for governor and with the antipathy of the Dallas *News* and the Galveston *News* for "moss-back" John Reagan undiminished, one might suspect that the railroad interests had put their heads together to devise a scheme that, by taking Hogg out of the state during the crucial pre-Convention campaign, would help to defeat Reagan. House actually claimed credit for Hogg's departure, as a way to get him "to do nothing, which he did, because he was in something of a jam. . . . Before he got back to the State we had Reagan practically beaten."[38] However, there is other evidence showing that plans for the Governor to make a northern tour to explain his reform program had been first broached the previous winter by banker John N. Simpson of Dallas, who was also vice-president of the Missouri, Kansas, and Texas.[39] At that date, the outcome of the Railroad Commission test case was unknown and Reagan had declared as a supporter of Culberson. Texas railroad men and businessmen generally had become less critical of the Hogg program, and, since it seemed apparent the reforms had come to stay, they thought it well to request the Governor to explain the laws in the Eastern business and financial centers, to show that, contrary to some of the wild tales, honest and intelligent investors had nothing to fear from Texas laws. Undoubtedly, Hogg was glad to escape the campaign prior to the Convention, but House was wrong in claiming all the credit for the trip. In May, just about the time the Supreme Court upheld the constitutionality of the Commission but

[37] May 4, 1894. Cf. Houston *Post* May 25 and 26 replying to the Austin *Daily Statesman* in editorials.

[38] "Memorandum of a Conference, Edward M. House, etc.," E. M. House Papers.

[39] John N. Simpson to J. S. Hogg, May 19, 1894, J. S. Hogg Let. Rec., XXXI, 51.

ordered a restudy of rates, Hogg gave his final consent to the tour, which would include stops at Chicago, Cleveland, Buffalo, Albany, Boston, Providence, New York, Philadelphia, Washington, and St. Louis.

Shortly before Hogg left there was a plea from the Old Roman, who wrote: "Had a fine audience at Sherman. . . . It is believed you can in a quiet way secure Bexar [County—San Antonio] for me. Hope you may not leave the State now."[40] What Hogg actually thought and felt about the situation is simply not known with certainty, but the above letter indicates that Reagan did not expect Hogg to make a speaking tour in his behalf. However, Hogg knew Reagan's political canniness and toughness, the result of many battles, and it is also fairly probable he knew that interference by himself at this stage would be a fatal gesture, in terms of preservation of the reform program. Had he gone publicly all out for Reagan, only to have the final tide of Texas Democracy, disturbed as it was by inner and outer conflicting winds and currents, go against them both, all legislative gains of the past few years might have been canceled. Reagan was no man's lamb to be led to slaughter; at seventy-five he was in full possession of his faculties, and in many ways, abler than ever. His decision to run was dictated in part at least, by an intent to save the Democrats and his revered Texas from the Populist Party. Sooner and with more fearsome clarity than any others of the policy-guiding group, Reagan had seen that the silver issue was the yawning pit of danger, unless Democratic leaders declared themselves so clearly that the farmers understood the Populists were not the only group concerned for the farmer's welfare.

It is quite possible that Hogg knew Reagan could not win, and he may also have believed that the old man, despite the plea just before the Governor's departure, knew it too. However, Colonel House's mention of Hogg's being in "something of a jam" was not inaccurate; there were at least two complications, both of them involving dear friendships and political values in about equal proportions. Reagan might have made a greater governor than Culberson, for though the younger man was extremely able he did not have the seasoned wisdom of the Old Roman. Yet Culberson's years fitted him to the needs of the post, as Hogg had clearly seen. Here then was one of the complications. The seat in the U.S. Senate that Hogg wanted for Chilton was another. Chilton and the now deceased Sawnie Robertson had represented to Hogg, from the day of their boyhood meeting, the best minds and the highest integrity to be

[40] John H. Reagan to J. S. Hogg, June 4, 1894, J. S. Hogg Let. Rec., XXXI, 134; Dallas *Morning News*, June 18, 1894.

found in his own generation. Devoted friendship aside, the Governor believed that Chilton's presence in the Senate would lend Texas outstanding prestige and would also insure a strong, wise voice to carry on the national fight for free silver, for lower tariffs and for the other issues the "young" Texas Democrats espoused. Yet H. G. "Brock" Robertson of Dallas, Chilton's cousin and Sawnie's brother, was working for Culberson and arguing that if East Texan Reagan won the nomination old sectional feuds would be reopened to the extent that Chilton, also of East Texas, would be denied the senatorial post by the section-conscious legislature, on the grounds that his election would once more give too much power to the eastern region.[41] In such a situation, for Hogg to take a too decisive step too soon in either direction might set in motion a train of circumstances that could wreck the planning of many prior years.

Further, the tour was not an insignificant matter. Hogg had stipulated that he would not make any partisan political speeches, but the very fact that the governor who had been the candidate of the young, liberal Democrats would be talking about the program which he and a Democratic legislature had together evolved made an extremely telling partisan point in itself, and one that could be of major assistance in the issue-strewn national campaign that was taking shape for 1896. Finally, the fact that Hogg did make the tour was one more indication of two of his qualities that had been no small part of his political success: the ability to distinguish between the moment when a fight was the only possible recourse and the moment when compromise was more desirable; and the ability to trust his friends. Reagan and Culberson (now that Culberson had declared for silver, even with qualification) were in essence Exhibits A and B, respectively, of the efficacy of the reform program—Reagan whose work as head of the Railroad Commission, which was the crux of the program, had demonstrated the Commission's usefulness; Culberson, whose efforts had helped free the Commission from the perilous strait-jacket of injunction the opposition had imposed.

The strictly business and good-will nature of the tour seemed to be further guaranteed by the interesting mixture of Democrats, Republicans, and Prohibitionists making up the party that boarded the special cars with the Governor.[42] Mrs. Hogg was unable to make the trip, but

---

[41] Robertson to Hogg, May 14, 1894, J. S. Hogg Let. Rec., XXX, 30 ff.
[42] The Chicago *Herald* for June 17, 1894, listed the names. State officials included Governor Hogg, State Treasurer W. B. Wortham, and Dr. W. L. Barker, superintendent of the State Asylum at San Antonio; from Dallas came John N.

the Governor took his daughter Ima, nearly twelve years old. Speaking to a group of reporters in Chicago, the first city visited, Hogg stated that objectives of the Texans were 1) to repay the numerous visits of men from the North who had visited Texas, 2) "to show the North that the animosities of years ago" had disappeared and "that we are all men and brothers," and 3) to prove that "Texas is a vital and highly important part of the Union." He said that he would not discuss Cleveland or the Wilson tariff bill or "politics of any nature." There had been an agreement not to talk politics. Should he let a political opinion drop, he was sure it would result in his being "cribbed, cabined, confined in the sleeping car by the entire party"[43] while the others labored to convince him that his opinion was wrong.

The Texans stopped briefly in Albany, New York, where Joseph H. Choate, later ambassador to England and then president of the State Constitutional Convention, introduced Governor Hogg to the convention. He made a brief impromptu patriotic speech. During the visit to New York City the Texans were bombarded by businessmen with questions about Texas and its laws. The New Yorkers were also frankly curious about this man Hogg, who had been called names ranging from "rural dreamer" to "demagogue"—and many others less polite. They found that he was far from being a Populist. He evidenced a kind of frank and practical idealism in holding to the idea that no business, great or small, could endure unless it was founded upon the simple virtues of honesty, fair play, and justice. He told them that the new Texas laws were intended to insure that corporate and individual enterprises dealt fairly with the public; this did not mean that their enforcement was necessarily unfair to business. To the contrary, such laws were sound and practical not only for the public but also for business. It was apparent that he convinced many of his questioners that Texas legislation reflected

---

Simpson, manager of the Dallas Fair and vice-president of the M.K.&T., W. H. Gaston, banker, W. A. Shaw, publisher of the *Texas Farmer,* and G. M. Bailey, reporter for the Dallas-Galveston *News;* from Fort Worth, Mayor B. B. Paddock; from San Antonio, George W. Brackenridge, banker and benefactor of the University of Texas, and T. H. Franklin, attorney who had upheld the Texas penal code before the Supreme Court; from Austin, John Orr, merchant, and Walter Tipps, capitalist and manufacturer; from Waco, R. B. Parrott, capitalist, E. Rotan, merchant, and W. D. Lacy, capitalist; from Temple, W. A. Barclay, capitalist, and F. F. Downs, banker; from Sherman, F. C. Dillard, attorney; from Tyler, H. H. Rowland, banker; from Brenham, Heber Stone, banker and, until June 5, candidate for governor. Personal interview with Mrs. Margaret Barclay Megarity (Waco), May 23, 1951.

[43] Cotner, *op. cit.,* p. 356.

the need of the times for progressive solutions to existing problems. The business and railroad men who had arranged for the tour were encouraged by their reception.

The visit to New York was impressive to both father and daughter, although Ima confessed herself disappointed in some features of the city. Fabulous Broadway turned out to be narrower than Congress Avenue in Austin, and Macy's store seemed to her much less "stylish" than the Hatzfeld establishment in Austin, where her mother shopped. But the Fifth Avenue Hotel, where they were quartered, Delmonico's restaurant, and other famed places compensated by seeming "glorious enough."[44] The Texas delegation was much feted.

Many parties and banquets were given in their honor by New York business and social leaders, with complimentary bouquets being sent on all occasions. The phonograph and the electric piano were among the novelties demonstrated to the Texans, who were duly impressed.[45]

Governor Roswell Flower, also a Democrat, who had been away from Albany when the party stopped there, made a special trip to New York City later and arranged for the Texans to attend a singing festival of the Liederkranz Society in Madison Square Garden. Word had been passed around that two Democratic governors would be present. Accompanied by many friends and dignitaries, Flower and Hogg appeared upon the stage and were hailed by a standing and heartily cheering audience. The clean-shaven Southwestern governor towered like a giant beside the short, stocky New Yorker with tawny burnsides. After an enjoyable musical interlude , Governor Flower turned to his companion and asked, "Will you have a glass of champagne, Governor?"

"No, thank you," replied Governor Hogg, as the waiter stood by to receive the order, "I'll just take a glass of beer."

Many of the audience were watching the governors when the waiter returned bearing on his tray a small bottle of champagne and a huge schooner of beer. When Governor Flower took the champagne and the Texan began to drink from the foaming schooner, the audience arose and gave cheer after cheer for Hogg as he drank the favorite German beverage. This kept up until the schooner was drained.

Hogg now turned to his host and said in a low voice: "By Gatlins, Governor, this is no wine crowd, and a man in politics must remember the people he happens to be with."

[44] Ima Hogg, "Life in the Governor's Mansion," typescript, H.C.
[45] Version of reporter George Bailey in G. W. Bailey Notes.

"Oh, well," replied Governor Flower, laughing, "they are all Republicans, anyway."

In Boston, Hogg's speech to the Chamber of Commerce was titled "Political, Industrial, and Social Conditions in Texas."[46] As blunt as any Yankee, Hogg declared he had been informed that some people still had the notion that Texas was a "small state of ugly methods, of unrighteous laws, and of uncertain resources," although he realized that traveled people knew better. Not wishing "to reflect upon the knowledge of school children," he hoped he would be pardoned if he compared the size of Texas to fourteen average states in the East. Within the vast territory of Texas were lands as "rich and alluvial as the valley of the Nile; and others as poor and fruitless as the Sahara Desert." He told of "million-acre stock ranches, thousand-acre cotton plantations, leagues of wheat fields and miles square of sugar farms," and he intended to impress descendants of ship captains when he described the five-hundred-mile Texas Gulf Coast and the four good harbors being constructed by government and private enterprise.

He reviewed the great material progress that had been made since 1870. In that year the aggregate property values rendered for tax purposes were $170 million; in 1893 they amounted to $886 million. During that interval population had increased from 818,000 to 2,400,000. In 1870 there were 320 miles of railroads, in 1893, 9,250—equal to the mileage in the whole South in 1860. Some 1,800,000 acres were farmed in 1870, something over 9,000,000 in 1893. Cotton production had increased about six times, corn production about four times, and the wheat yield had risen from 415,000 bushels to 6,553,000. The number of factories had increased from 2,399 to over 4,000; in 1870 the factories represented a $5,284,000 capital investment, in 1893 their value was estimated at over $60 million, while the factory hands increased from 7,607 to over 25,000.[47] "Even the blessed school children in the last ten years have increased from 295,457 to 630,303," declared the Governor. He also pointed out that there were no mortgages on homesteads, which "condition of freedom" he believed would be a great factor in guaranteeing "the perpetuity of human liberty under a republican form of government."

[46] Cotner, *op. cit.*, pp. 356–373, quotes the speech delivered June 28; *Texas Farmer* (Dallas), July 21, 1894.

[47] Hogg's figures for wage earners reflected current unemployment; almost 35,000 were counted in 1890.

When he stressed the low tax rates, Bostonians must have wondered how a good school system could be financed for so many children from a 12½ cent ad valorem tax. Hogg explained that great benefits from the 20 million acres of remaining school lands were available to actual settlers at two dollars per acre, and that there was some income from leasing unsold lands. He also pointed out that Texas saw to it that the available funds were "prorated upon the per capita scholastic basis equally among the whites and blacks." Furthermore, each local school district had the right to supplement these funds through local taxation to improve their schools. He referred to the two normal schools, one for white and one for Negro teachers, and to the A. and M. College and "a first class university."

Coming to the heart of his talk, James Hogg said:

I know full well that false impressions have gone abroad in reference to five laws that have been passed during my administration. They are regarded by those who understand them and respect fair dealing and good government as the culmination of substantial justice and undoubted wisdom. They are the safeguards and bulwarks protecting the liberties and rights of an honest, frugal, patriotic people, fully capable of self-government. They are the foundations today of our State government relaid to meet the strange new conditions of the twentieth century now upon us. At the risk of taxing your time, I will briefly explain them to you.

They are:
1. The Railroad Commission law.
2. The Railroad Stock and Bond law.
3. The Alien Land law.
4. The Municipal Bond law.
5. The Corporation Land law.[48]

His explanation of the five laws was clear and succinct. Speaking of the Commission, he denied the charge that railroads could not get into court:

My observation is that railways, like men, can make friends or enemies, according to their deserts. Litigation to protect rights even should be the last resort after all reasonable efforts have been exhausted to accomplish the same end. Like the old Negro, most of them point to the courthouse and say, "Dar's whar I settle. Go dar," and like him, they lose the respect of juries and complain of prejudices. Let them put in motion a good example, and the juries and the courts and the State governments will meet them in friendship and justice more than half way.[49]

[48] *Texas Farmer* (Dallas), July 21, 1894.   [49] *Ibid.*

410

Hogg was frank about the stock and bond law and the efforts of Texas to end fictitious indebtedness. He said: "The law will never be repealed so long as Texans possess self-respect, independence, and the ability to control their own affairs." He had faith that the new bonds would soon go at a premium in any market of the world where safe, first-class securities were in demand. Furthermore, posterity would be spared "the degradation and desperation to which unjust, fictitious public obligations would drive them."[50] The Governor declared that he was sure the men of Boston knew that such laws as he had described were not leading Texas into communism, anarchy, or crime, but that these were hardy American solutions to problems which had loomed large to men who only recently had "emerged from the gloom of defeat in war to grapple with starvation for life's subsistence." The attention of every member of the Chamber of Commerce was held as he concluded:

From penury to plenty, from ash heaps to mansions, from rags to cloth, from ox carts to railroads, from bull-tongues to gang plows, from walking to riding, from starving to feasting, they have heroically striven, until now, in the full measure of their manhood and retrieved prosperity, they proclaim to the world—Peace! They throw open their doors to liberty-loving people everywhere, and invite them to come and share the blessings of their homes.[51]

In Providence (where the Governor and Ima were house guests of Governor Brown and his family) and in Philadelphia the good-will ambassadors from Texas repeated the story of the growth and opportunities of the Southwest. At Philadelphia, speaking to the Manufacturers Club, Hogg directed attention to the importance of an isthmian canal. General interest in the canal project had been mounting. Hogg had long foreseen the great economic and cultural development which would come to the Gulf region if such a canal were built, as well as the boon it would be to American shipping in general, particularly in view of the new trade treaties with Japan.[52] Hogg pointed out the importance of the Suez Canal to Britain, especially in giving Liverpool a great advantage over any Atlantic or Gulf port of the United States for trade with the Orient and Australia. Since Americans were still largely anti-

[50] *Ibid.*

[51] *Ibid.*; Cotner, *op. cit.*, p. 373; personal interview with Miss Hogg in Houston, June, 1954.

[52] Richard B. Hubbard, *The United States in the Far East: or Modern Japan in the Orient* (Richmond, B. F. Johnson Publishing Company, 1899), p. 195. Hubbard had been American Minister to Japan in Cleveland's first administration.

411

British, the Philadelphia audience was no doubt pleased when Hogg described the inevitable decline he believed would strike Britain when an isthmian canal became a reality. Complaining that Americans made the traffic but the English were hauling it, he said:

We produce the wealth and they get it through the method of transportation taxes. Thus feasting upon the fruits of our labors for these years, the people of that little island have fattened and gradually become our creditors and dictators in finance and commerce. [Hogg was not happy over the Cleveland-Morgan-London gold purchase plan to keep up the gold reserve] You may repeat the question and ask what is the cause of this unfortunate condition. For it there are many causes, but the overshadowing one lies in the negligence of the United States in not taking advantage of her situation and having her Atlantic and Gulf harbors placed in closer proximity to the markets of the world; or, to transverse the proposition, I may say the cause of it is mainly on account of Liverpool being nearer the markets of the world than any of the United States Atlantic or Gulf ports. . . . For every evil there is a remedy. . . . My answer is, cut and control the Nicaragua canal. . . . Why should not the seat of finance be changed from Lombard Street to some American point? Why should not the center of commerce be changed from England to the United States? The experiment is at least worth making, and in the work the United States government is due it to the people to keep both foreign and private hands off the enterprise. Let her assume it as a national measure of necessity to give freedom to commerce and justice to the American ships.[53]

The tour on the whole was a triumph. The Governor had enjoyed himself and, as always in a new situation, had consciously added to his store of knowledge and experience. As noted, he had, however, been troubled by the evidences of increasing strife between labor and management. The Pullman strike had begun a few days after the Texas party left Chicago, and Cleveland sent the federal troops to Chicago two days after Hogg's speech in Philadelphia.

By the time the party returned to Texas it was clear that Culberson would be the strongest single candidate for governor before the Democratic Convention, but a combining of votes in a shift to one or another of the other candidates could be embarrassing to him. Nevertheless, the superior organizing ability of Colonel House had snatched more than

[53] Cotner, *op. cit.,* pp. 374–376. Hogg said our shipping stood "as a spring shoot by the side of a forest oak, as a minnow by a whale, as a canoe by the *Great Eastern!*" Populists and Republicans also favored a Nicaraguan canal. See Winkler, *op. cit.,* pp. 333, 346.

one county from the hands of those who claimed it for another candidate.[54] Efforts were being made by all candidates not to alienate Reagan's supporters, in the event that his votes would shift.

Then came the incident of Hogg's "watch speech" on July 15 at the State Guard encampment, with the Dallas *News* seizing the opportunity to fracture its truce with Hogg.[55] The "sweetness and light" that had pervaded the attitude of some of the railroad interests during the northern tour were dispelled as they and the *News* renewed their hope that Hogg and Reagan would cease to be political influences after the Convention. However, the effects of the Governor's follow-up speech in San Antonio on August 1 gave pause again to that hope.

The State Democratic Convention assembled at Dallas on August 14. Because of numerous questions about the "watch speech," Hogg proudly hung the watch from a chandelier in the hotel lobby and left it there for some time so that all who wished to examine it might do so. House and Culberson came to Dallas with a tentative draft of a platform. When they asked Hogg to look it over, he was pleased with the program for Texas but pointed out that Reagan would not like the qualified statement regarding silver. There was still the danger that the progressive forces—or, as they were now being referred to, the liberals—would be split by differences over silver.

A united party was Hogg's immediate goal, but Reagan and Culberson still differed on the silver plank when the official platform was being drafted. The following account in Colonel House's own words describe Hogg's efforts at compromise:

I remember at the Dallas Convention which finally nominated him [Culberson], the battle he fought when by yielding a point he might have been nominated almost unopposed. It was a question of the wording of the platform regarding the coinage of silver at the ratio of 16 to 1. That was a never-to-be-forgotten day when at the Old Windsor Hotel, Governor Hogg, Judge Reagan and L. L. Foster sat in one room, and down the same corridor Culberson and I sat in another. Hogg was the mediator and tried to reconcile the differences between the two candidates. The difference was, briefly, that Culberson would agree to the free and unlimited coinage of silver at the ratio of 16 to 1 only provided it could be maintained at a parity

[54] E. M. House to E. F. Storer, July 6, 1896, Governor Culberson's Let. Pr., 1896. Cf. Dallas *Morning News* August 17, 1894. The standing of the candidates a month before the Convention, July 6, was: Culberson, 248; Reagan, 124; Lanham, 105; and McCall, 53—leaving 250 votes out of a total of 859 to be accounted for.
[55] See Chapter XIII of this book.

with gold. Reagan was insistent upon an outright declaration without any qualification. The negotiations lasted from early morning until late afternoon and in the end failed.[56]

While Reagan and Culberson haggled and Hogg tried to obtain the much-needed compromise, the Clark forces gained supporters for the Cleveland money plank of 1892. When the Convention by vote of 451 to 415 adopted the majority report praising Cleveland for using troops in Illinois and, with the single addition of "equal" before "coinage of both metals without discrimination against either metal or charge of mintage," reported word for word the national plank of 1892 on gold and silver, Reagan withdrew his name just before the nominations were to begin. He wanted to be free to oppose these planks. McCall also withdrew before the balloting started, and most of his and Reagan's votes shifted to Culberson. Culberson's nomination was assured on the first ballot, when he received 587 votes to 286 for Lanham. The nomination was then made unanimous.[57]

There remain many unanswered questions as to why Reagan ran and why he withdrew. The eminent Yale historian Charles Seymour, who became the editor of House's *Intimate Papers*, drew an interesting picture of House convincing Hogg that he should get Reagan to withdraw in order not to split the vote of "the liberal wing." Seymour explained Reagan's withdrawal largely in terms of House's own account of his last interview with Hogg. Tempers were no doubt a bit frayed from the prolonged negotiations. House, "of slight build and quiet manner, speaking in a monotone," is pictured as being "inflexible in his argument that liberalism in Texas depended upon the union of the Progressive forces and that Reagan must withdraw. It ended in Hogg going to Reagan, who magnanimously agreed to retire in order to avoid the split in the liberal group." Hogg and House were in agreement that "Texas never produced a nobler citizen than Judge John H. Reagan. He was honest, he was able, and he was fearless."[58]

[56] Quoted in Madden, *Culberson*, p. xxviii. House also reported on the economical management of campaigns in Texas before 1900. He stated that Culberson's Campaign Committee spent $1,500—most of it probably having been advanced by House—and that later Culberson repaid every penny.

[57] Wagner, *op. cit.*, p. 55, gives 440 as the first vote. Cf. Austin *Daily Statesman*, August 17, 1894. The article "Samuel W. T. Lanham," in Webb and Carroll's *Handbook of Texas*, II, 26, does not mention Lanham's 1894 race and withdrawal. He became governor in 1903.

[58] Charles Seymour, *Papers of Colonel House*, I, 30; Wagner, *op. cit.*, p. 19; Herbert Hoover, *The Ordeal of Woodrow Wilson* (McGraw-Hill Book Company, 1958), pp. 13–19.

However, Dr. Rupert Richardson, who has worked several years on a biography of House, wrote in answer to a question on the Seymour quotation:

I cannot reconcile his statements with what I know about the situation . . . Seymour's account of House's strategy in Texas must have been obtained

JIM GIVES CHARLIE GOOD ADVICE
Austin Daily Statesman
August 26, 1894

in a large degree from House himself and the exploit had grown through the years. House was a superb political strategist, but Seymour over-simplifies the story.[59]

Richardson also pointed out that House was not Hogg's adviser in 1894, but Culberson's. Hogg and House did not cease to be friends, but differences over monetary theory developed between them. House had evidenced the same sort of independence from the party leader which later would cause him trouble with Woodrow Wilson at Versailles and end their friendship. In any case, if House and Culberson had been more willing to compromise on Reagan's wording after Culberson's nomina-

[59] Rupert Richardson to R. Cotner, November 29, 1954. Cf. Smith, *House,* p. 28. There are several hundred Culberson letters on this campaign in the Texas State Archives. Seymour offered to check his sources, but no further reply has been received.

tion was assured, Culberson would not have been forced to spend so much time explaining his position on silver.

Before the Convention adjourned Hogg declared that, although the platform was not as specific as he wished, it was "broad and catholic enough for every Democrat in Texas to stand upon." He wanted it

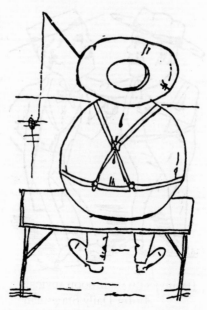

THE GOVERNOR OFF DUTY
Austin Daily Statesman
August 26, 1894

understood that when a properly called Democratic Convention wrote a platform he would stand by it, for such a platform was an indication to the world that differences had been settled. Speaking as the conciliator, the compromiser, the custodian of party unity, he continued:

The very fact that we differ is a potent factor in our good government. . . . If we are to preserve our liberties we must have free speech, we must have clash among us, we cannot all think the same. It is the views from the hustings and the views from the rostrum that bring about the very highest degree of all good results in a democratic form of government.[60]

[60] Dallas *Morning News,* August 18, 1894.

416

Then he did what he alone of all his group could do so well. Saying that one of his friends had come to him before the Convention and confided, "Governor, I hate to see you have to take any crow," Hogg exclaimed triumphantly:

My friends, what kind of dish have you got? [voice—crow, buzzard, by golly] I rejoice in the united Democracy. This is a good occasion for crow-eating and buzzard-eating. Get on the platform and stay there even if it wobbles a little. And if you can't stand on it get down under it like a yellow dog and follow in the trail and let someone else drive.[61]

The majority platform reflected an increase in the strength of the Clark pro-gold wing and a tapering off of the Hogg-Reagan-Culberson reform platform. The Clark faction had dominated the platform committee. Nevertheless, the Hogg administration received a hearty endorsement and the people were congratulated "on the reforms it has accomplished" and on the fact that the "disturbing question of railway legislation" was finally settled "in a manner alike just to the people and the railways."[62] Both factions had agreed to postpone until 1896 the money battle; the sparring for control had obviously not ceased, but a present truce was accepted as necessary in the face of their immediate concern—the defeat of the Populists.

Most of the pre-Convention differences were eased by the splendid reception given for Attorney General Culberson upon his return to Austin. The Governor, on being asked to speak, briefly urged united action for victory at the polls. Asking everyone to get out a "pile driver" and go to work hammering down the Populists, he said that he and Culberson were still part of the same silver and reform team and he hoped that Culberson's path would not be "so studded with brier patches" as his own had been.[63]

The Clark forces had been forced to eat crow of their own on some of the nominations. Martin M. Crane was the candidate for attorney general, Watt Finley the candidate for comptroller, both loyal Hogg men, and the nominees for Texas' courts of appeal included Thomas J. Brown, LeRoy G. Denman, and William L. Davidson—all Hogg appointees. The Governor was always immensely proud of the excellent records and ability of the men whom he had appointed to the bench during his two administrations. He was always pleased to show an

[61] *Ibid.*
[62] Winkler, *Platforms,* p. 340, Section 8.
[63] Austin *Daily Statesman,* August 22, 1894.

album in which he had collected their pictures, and in which he had inscribed as a little preface: "So long as the Bench keeps pure the Government will be safe."

Culberson, Hogg, Reagan, House, and a few others soon went off to Rockport to fish and to plan the final campaign against both Republicans and Populists. When Culberson took to the stump at Goliad at the end of August, he vigorously upheld the increased coinage of silver.[64] The Clark forces later charged him with jumping off the platform on this issue, but he was actually being consistent with his pre-Convention commitments as a bimetallist. The fight to beat the Populists was on in earnest, and Hogg was satisfied that Culberson would loyally continue the reform program.

[64] *Ibid.*, August 26, 1894.

CHAPTER XV

The Balance Sheet

THE PLATFORMS of Texas parties in 1894 interestingly served as partial evaluations of the Hogg administrations. The only direct criticism made by the "Reform" Republicans against Hogg concerned his failure to stop completely the long-condemned custom of leasing convicts for work outside the walls of the penitentiary. The "Regular" Republican platform did not mention the prison system but was highly critical of the reduction of the per capita appropriation for the state school fund from $5.00 in 1892 to $3.50 "or less at the present."[1] The lower figures reflected a decline in tax collections due to the depression, but did not mirror the Governor's efforts to provide funds from other sources to meet the expanding needs of 100,000 new students. Hogg himself agreed that the school situation was deplorable, but neither the public nor the legislators had acted upon his recommendations to provide more money in 1893.

One valid criticism to which the Governor might be held answerable was his failure to call a special session in 1894 for specific measures on the school tax and the balancing of the budget. The school situation grew worse with declining collections; according to *The Report of the Superintendent of Instruction, 1893–1894,* school funds had a deficiency of $659,468 at the end of the fiscal year, August 31, 1894. The seriousness of the depression in Texas is seen clearly in the fact that the arrears of interest on land sales and leases had reached $1 million by January 1, 1895.[2]

The Republicans denounced "in unmeasured terms" the Democratic administration for "invading and depleting the permanent school fund as an assault upon the noblest heritage by the fathers to the children of Texas." No mention was made of the fact that the Jester amendment, providing for transfer of a small percentage of the Permanent School Fund to the available funds, was an effort to support the schools more adequately and that the people had voted for the amendment. Both the

[1] Quoted in Ernest Winkler, *Platforms of Political Parties in Texas,* p. 346.
[2] Edmund Miller, *Financial History of Texas,* p. 370.

419

Cuney and the Clark platforms in 1892 had sharply criticized the financial results of the Jester measure. During the special session in 1892, however, Governor Hogg had expressed his own concern that the plan would not bring in enough money to provide a six-month term; in the 1893 session friends of education heeded Hogg's warning and introduced a bill to amend the Jester finance program. The bill died in committee. This failure to obtain legislation providing financial support adequate to assure the six-months' term was a great disappointment to James Hogg, for he understood from his own experience what handicaps were forced upon a child who did not receive the benefits of education of a high standard.

In practically every one of his major messages to the legislators Governor Hogg had reminded them of the need for the efficient administration of the public schools, and for a term lasting "at least six months." In the special message of March, 1892, he declared that, although this latter goal had been provided for by law, state and local taxation, action of school boards or trustees, and lack of income from other sources had kept the state from fulfilling its constitutional obligation. He frankly declared that increased taxation was necessary.[3] On January 12, 1893, he called attention again to the growing school population and to the need for careful evaluation of the tax structure if adequate school funds were to be available. This was not altogether popular talk during a depression, but he knew it was necessary and just. Furthermore, he never ceased to be the champion of the University of Texas as the "capstone" of the public school system, constantly encouraging its leadership in efforts to improve the offerings and standards at all levels of instruction. In one of his last public addresses as governor he reminded the people of Texas that he had asked the Twenty-fourth Legislature to consider his proposals for increasing tax values, but his suggestions were not followed.[4] Meanwhile, more thousands of children had come of school age, beginning their schooling under crowded conditions and with short terms.

The Populist platform of 1894 advocated that all children between the ages of six and eighteen have a six-months' term "and that each

---

[3] Message of March 14, 1892, quoted in Cotner, *Addresses of James S. Hogg*, pp. 164–165.

[4] Message to the Twenty-fourth Legislature, January 11, 1895, Texas *House Journal* (1895), pp. 24–26; J. S. Hogg, "The University of Texas: Cap-stone of Our Public Free School System," delivered at the University March 26, 1892, J. S. Hogg Misc.

race shall have its own trustees and control its own schools." Hogg declared that Populist speakers were trying to take the Negroes from the Republican Party "on account of a Democratic law" that the speakers described in confusing terminology:

They make the Negro believe that he has no right at all to trustees in school districts. Of course, they will arouse much prejudice over this question. If any intelligent man, however, will examine the school law . . . he will find that in those districts where white trustees are elected in which there are also Negro schools, the Negroes have the right to elect their own trustees, who are to cooperate with these white trustees in the supervision of colored schools. The only Negro member of the Legislature [N. H. Haller of Brazoria] voted for this law, while out of the seven or eight Populist members, not one of them objected to it on the ground that it discriminated against the Negro race.[5]

✓ In his "farewell" address of January, 1895, Hogg bluntly told the members of the legislature they had never complied with the constitutional requirement to provide funds adequate for a six-months' school term. During the second year of his first term state appropriations had increased $300,000 to provide a $5.00 per capita allotment—an increase of 50 cents per student, which ranked well by comparison with even the North Atlantic states. The depression had caused a $650,000 decrease in funds available, while the school population increased 25,000; therefore, in 1893–1894 the per capita apportionment slipped to $4.50 and then was down to $3.50 for 1894–1895, owing in large measure to delinquent collections and to an increase of 63,000 students. Hogg was more interested in correcting the deteriorating school situation than in any personal acclaim over an economically run government. He warned further that there would be 100,000 more children in school at the end of the next biennium in 1896, then reiterated what had been his stand since his first term.[6]

The proposition, narrowed down to the line of candor, is, that if the people ever expect to have an efficient system of free schools, they must prepare to

[5] Hogg's Rockdale speech, October 1, 1894, quoted in Cotner, *op. cit.*, pp. 427–428; the Populist platform, section 15, quoted in Winkler, *op. cit.*, p. 333. The Republicans added a resolution condemning the school law of 1893, which they interpreted as providing "that negroes living in counties under the district system shall not be trustees under that system."

[6] Hogg here was quoting his own words from his first message of 1891. Texas *House Journal* (1891), p. 109. See Cotner, *op. cit.*, p. 121.

pay for it. . . . If the people revolt at the situation, they alone have the power to change it. . . . The schools must become a failure or taxation to support them must be increased.[7]

The Republicans had also charged that Hogg would go out of office leaving a financial deficit, when he had come into office inheriting a surplus. The record of the state government paralleled that of the federal government in this regard: Cleveland and Hogg both faced this charge. To many persons the depression seemed a sufficient reason. Not foreseeing early in 1891 the serious effects of a non-existing depression, Hogg made the "mistake" of advising a reduction of tax rates at a time when taxes were relatively easy to collect. (It may be recalled that financial wizard Andrew Mellon made the same kind of mistake as Secretary of the U. S. Treasury in 1924.) In 1890 Hogg had it in his power to continue the tax rate—and possibly assure the six-months' school term—but the surplus was delusive; part of it, $248,000, was required to retire bonds issued during Reconstruction.

Official records disclosed warrants outstanding on January 4, 1895, in the amount of $687,669, and the Comptroller reported $1,380,000 as the amount of uncollected taxes for 1894. Hogg declared that, since the two tax-rate deductions had saved the people $1,305,000, they could now afford a tax increase if the imposition of the penalties for not paying promptly did not end the deficiency. By way of defending his record, he pointed out that $723,160 had been spent for new items not in appropriation bills previous to his administration, and much of the money had been used for new buildings, which remained long-run assets. He had vetoed $350,000 worth of needed projects when it had become clear that money would not be available for the essentials required by the public schools and fixed expenses. Then the legislature, not heeding his warning, had reduced taxes a second time. In conclusion, he said: "The fault, after all, lies in the ill-conceived and unnecessary reduction of taxes."[8]

When O. M. Roberts completed his summary of Texas history from

[7] Texas *House Journal* (1895), pp. 25–26. Except in a few cities the Texas schools were worse off in 1901 than in 1891–1895, as Hogg had predicted. Governor Culberson urged economies and increased taxes and did balance the budget, but low local support programs and the rapid increase in the number of scholastics spread too thin the income from the Permanent School Fund so that Texas ranked 37th in amount spent per student ($1.63) for 1901–1902. There was also less than a full six-months' term.

[8] Texas *House Journal* (1895), p. 26.

1845 to 1895, these events were fresh in his mind. His explanation of the deficit of the Hogg administration read:

√ Hogg's policy had been prominently directed to the establishment of certain reforms pertaining to corporations of all kinds and to alien ownership of lands in Texas, which diverted attention to some extent from the subject of finance—a subject that continually requires the most watchful care for the proper adjustment of income and expenditure annually by the government.[9]

It is worth noting that Comptroller McCall in his report at the end of 1894 also maintained that increased taxation was the only solution in a rapidly growing state which was increasing its public services. Of the charge of extravagance he said, "The present administration has not been extravagant in its expenditures and I do not think it possible that the state government can be conducted on a more economical basis" because of the rapid growth of Texas.[10]

✗ Hogg was sensitive about the charge that his administration was in debt. In his farewell message he set forth in detail what he felt were real credits for the permanent benefit of the people, and he also indicated such indirect savings as the reduced railway tariffs. In his October, 1894, Rockdale speech he had used the following recapitulation as of September 1, 1894, which was the beginning of a new fiscal year in Texas:

Receipts and cash on hand	$ 8,543,383.74
Disbursements, improvements, debt payment, and expenses	8,504,939.09
Registered warrants	435,114.84
Disbursements over cash and receipts	396,670.59
Credits:	
No. 1—By new buildings, etc.	1,228,210
No. 2—By extraordinary expenses	426,240
No. 3—By reduction of taxes	1,305,000
No. 4—By reduction of interest	7,200,000
No. 5—By reduction of railway charges	3,450,000
No. 6—By value of lands recovered (1,800,000 at $2 per acre)	3,600,000
	$17,209,450

[9] Roberts, *op. cit.*, p. 309. See also Louis J. Wortham, *A History of Texas,* V, 103.

[10] Austin *Daily Statesman,* December 14, 1894.

Over $6,500,000 of the foregoing items are taken from the official records, and are unquestioned from any source. The others are estimated from the best and most reliable statistics at my command, and have been placed within conservative limits. They are presented not in defense of my administration, for it has not been attacked this year from any responsible quarter.[11]

It should be pointed out that the "extraordinary expenses" were not blinds to any hidden action, for the itemization shows refunds paid for school lands, publishing constitutional amendments, expenses of the Greer County suit before the United States Supreme Court, aid to western counties trying to destroy certain wild animals, aid to cyclone sufferers, expenses of the educational department and of institutions transferred from the school fund to the general revenue account, etc. The first item which might be questioned was the credit for interest saved on $92 million worth of real estate mortgages; the Governor estimated that the reduction of interest from 12 to 10 per cent saved $1,800,000 for each of four years or a total of $7,200,000. This assumed that all of the debt was added, after the law was passed, at 2 per cent lower than it otherwise would have been. It is doubtful whether the change in rate affected existing contracts or whether all of them were at 12 per cent. Item 6 was optimistic; the ultimate return to the state consisted of about 1,300,000 acres of land, not the 1,800,000 of the printed estimate. However, the repossessed land was worth more than enough to pay the cost of the state government for an entire year. This was an accomplishment for which James Hogg merited special praise. From his attorney general days on, in the face of much opposition, he had continually insisted on the suits to regain this land illegally obtained by the railroads for sidings and switches.

Hogg found a certain wry amusement and consolation in the conflicting opinions expressed respectively by Republicans, Populists, and the State Labor Convention relating to his criticism of President Cleveland's use of federal troops in Illinois. The last plank of the "Regular" Republican platform read: "We deplore the communistic tendencies of Governor Hogg and his antagonism to that spirit of National unity which should pervade every State of this great Nation."[12] The Laborites denounced Cleveland's use of the army "to uphold organized capital and overawe organized labor, in defiance of the protest of the governor

[11] Quoted in Cotner, *op. cit.*, pp. 423 ff.
[12] Regular Republication Platform of 1894, Section 14, quoted in Winkler, *op. cit.*, p. 346.

of the State of Illinois and in contravention of the Federal Constitution and the guaranteed rights of sovereign States," and the delegates also pledged to oppose any man endorsing the President's action.[13]

The Governor had won appreciation from the Laborites in the early spring of 1894 during the difficulties over the contingent of "Coxey's Army" that came via Texas on its way from Los Angeles to Washington, D.C. When in the late winter of 1893–1894 Populist Jacob S. Coxey of Massillon, Ohio, a businessman and reformer, prepared to lead an army of jobless men to Washington in an attempt to induce Congress to issue legal tender currency to be spent on roads and other projects that would make work for the destitute, his appeal drew men from all over the country. The Los Angeles group, led by Lewis Fry, set out on foot on March 16, later boarding a freight train. Many townspeople along the way gave them food and encouragement. On March 21 the mayor of El Paso wired Governor Hogg, asking him to request the War Department to place the Fort Bliss garrison at the state's service to repel the "invasion." Hogg refused, characteristically assuring the mayor that Texas could enforce its own laws. On March 22, Fry and 700 men arrived in El Paso and were fed and allowed to camp around the city hall. The next evening they marched to the railroad tracks—where they waited for two days, because the railroads held back any trains that would have been useful to them. Finally, on Easter Sunday, March 25, they did board a Southern Pacific eastbound freight.

Near Sierra Blanca, some seventy miles out of El Paso, trainmen uncoupled the cars the men rode, leaving them in a region that was the nearest thing to a desert between the Rio Grande and the Pecos River. No food or water was available for many miles in any direction, and a few scattered Mexican families were the only human inhabitants of the area. Some of the men walked the twenty miles to Sierra Blanca to make their plight known. Governor Hogg, thoroughly aroused, told the railroad authorities that they must pick up and transport the men out of the state, since they had seen fit to bring them in; further, the railroads were to see to it that the men were provided with water and not made to suffer undue hardships. He also pinpointed his views on the subject to the newspapers:

You can truthfully say that neither the cormorant nor the commune can disgrace Texas while I am Governor. When a railroad company hauls tramps or unemployed penniless men into this State it cannot dump them

[13] Labor Party Platform of 1894, section 1, *ibid.*, p. 349; Dallas *Morning News*, September 25 and October 6, 1894.

into a barren desert and murder them by torture and starvation without atoning for it, if there is any virtue in the machinery of justice. Nor will I permit them to be shot down on Texas soil by any armed force whatever, no matter how much the Southern Pacific and the other enemies of the State may howl about the commune.[14]

He also let it be known that the Texas Rangers, keeping an eye on the "Army" and railroad property at the junction, would be withdrawn if the Southern Pacific did not provide transportation within a reasonable time. Meanwhile, the marooned group had almost nothing to eat, and the papers quoted the superintendent of the Frisco at St. Louis as saying, "There is no power on earth to compel us to operate our road if we do not want to."[15] Then the Southern Pacific agreed to carry the men back to El Paso if the Governor desired, but this was to be "purely gratuitous" and not a legal obligation. Hogg stood his ground that the railroads had brought the men in and should take them out. Popular opinion in general supported the Governor. The Central Industrial Council meeting at Dallas endorsed his stand in resolutions, and six residents of El Paso wired him that "the infamy of the Southern Pacific . . . is without parallel for barbarity."[16] El Paso citizens, partly from compassion and partly from a desire to keep the "Army" from returning to their city, shipped provisions and hired a special train of five coaches and two baggage cars which took the men to San Antonio, several hundred miles out of their way toward Washington. Fry wanted to visit Austin and march his men to the mansion to thank Governor Hogg, but Receiver Tom Campbell and the I.& G.N. moved them on eastward.[17] The six hundred men arrived at Longview packed in fourteen box cars; transferred to the Texas and Pacific, they arrived in Little Rock the last day of March, where they were described as orderly, sober, and serious men.[18] (Some of the group finally reached Washington weeks later—after Coxey had been arrested on May 1, for trespassing on the Capitol

[14] Austin *Daily Statesman,* March 29, 1894.

[15] Quoted in Donald L. McMurray, *Coxey's Army* (Boston, Little, Brown and Company, 1929), p. 135, n. 1; J. S. Hogg to General Manager, G.H.&S.A. Railway Company, March 27, 1894. Telegram ordering removal, quoted in Austin *Daily Statesman,* March 29, 1894, along with reply and Hogg repetition of notice—"will not multiply words on subject."

[16] Walter P. Webb and Bailey H. Carroll, "Coxey's Army," *Handbook of Texas,* I, 430.

[17] Austin *Daily Statesman,* March 31, 1894, indicated Hogg's hecklers would like to present the Industrial Army to Hogg, but the I.& G.N. would carry the men to Texarkana.

[18] New York *Times,* April 2, 1894.

grounds.) Once more the railroads had come off second in a needless contest with Hogg.

✓ The episode did not change Hogg's basic belief that Coxey's project was not the way to bring relief to the mounting numbers of unemployed. In a proclamation issued sometime later he said this publicly and pointed out to Texans that depression conditions were no better—and probably worse—outside of their own state. He urged the unemployed not to leave Texas to look for work, and especially not to abandon their families.

A number of Hogg's political opponents saw fit to praise him for his action in the Coxey matter, and at least one railroad official wrote to him—General Manager B. F. Yoakum of the Gulf, Colorado, and Santa Fe—and thanked the Governor for protecting the railroad property from the "army of commonwealers." He offered to help destitute men, making a distinction between honest unemployed and tramps in declaring that his line would not let the latter travel free.[19] The numbers of train hitch-hikers had been steadily increasing as the depression deepened, constituting a real hazard. Hogg agreed that genuine tramps should not be tolerated, but he also knew that men and women seeking honest employment were all too frequently being arrested upon vagrancy charges. He urged that those in misfortune who were honestly seeking work should be assisted in their desperate search for a way to earn a living, saying, "Food, not fines, will be the treatment of the law-loving, law-abiding element in this state when men commit no greater crime than traveling as tramps for lack of work."[20] In the depressions of 1857 and 1873 the frontier still offered homesteads to men who needed them and were willing to work for them—with free water, free grass, and free timber for fuel and houses and fencing. But now the frontier had largely disappeared; the search for it by the unemployed was mostly a forlorn hope. At the same time the industrial era had not yet reached that later peak whereby it would put to work millions of both skilled and unskilled men.

The last resolution of the Laborites' 1894 platform denounced the convict system of Texas (as the "Reform" Republicans had also done). Governor Hogg in his first message of 1891 had spoken at some length

[19] Yoakum to Hogg, May 19, 1894, J. S. Hogg Let. Rec., XXX, 57; Dallas *Morning News*, May 6, 1894; S. B. Maxey to J. S. Hogg, May 6, 1894, J. S. Hogg Let. Rec., XXXI, 5.

[20] Quoted in McMurray, *op. cit.*, p. 272; *Journal of the Knights of Labor*, October 18, 1893. See also B. F. Yoakum to J. S. Hogg, July 11, 1894, J. S. Hogg Let. Rec., XXX, 235–244.

427

on what he considered to be the evils of leasing convicts to private contractors for work outside prison walls,[21] and the Democratic platform of 1892 had reiterated the belief that such contracting was against "public policy." In 1885, George W. Cable had severely criticized the Texas prison system for its high death rate, which he associated with the state's desire to make money from leasing and contracting the prisoners; in 1879–1880, with a prison population of about 2,100, there were 256 deaths, almost 200 of them occurring at the contracting camps.[22] For 1888–1890, while Hogg was attorney general, the number of deaths was 183. Despite a doubling of the prison population since 1880, better management during Hogg's administration cut the deaths to 114 for 1891–1892, although they rose to 150 for 1893–1894. The heaviest toll was on the farms in South Texas, where heatstroke and pneumonia were high on the list of causes of death; the contract farms had the worst records of all. Through frequent visits, often unannounced, Hogg tried to assure better treatment and better food for the prisoners. He was also unstinting in his encouragement of efforts aimed at reformation of offenders and at better application of the parole system. While he was in office increasing attention was given to the teaching of trades that might help the released or paroled make a living in the newly industrial and more complicated urban society. Some reform of the leasing system was effected, although legislative failure to provide adequate space for the rapidly growing prison population worked against the effort. Too, the political influence of certain men who profited by the work-lease system should not be overlooked as one of the powerful deterrents to reform in this respect. The establishment of the Board of Pardon Advisers in 1893, at Hogg's urging, had speeded up the granting of deserved pardons: in 1891–1892, when Hogg was solely responsible (as the Texas Constitution specified) for investigation of the pardon requests, 116 were processed; in 1893–1894, with the assistance of the new Board, the number rose to 321.[23]

In the Rockdale speech Hogg said, "We have made and kept the penitentiaries self-sustaining," and this was borne out by Fiscal Agent R.

[21] Cotner, op. cit., pp. 127–129.

[22] George W. Cable, The Silent South (New York, Charles Scribner's Sons, 1889), pp. 162 ff. (1st ed., 1885); Herbert J. Doherty, Jr., "Voices of Protest from the New South, 1875–1910," Mississippi Valley Historical Review, XLII (June, 1955), p. 51; Arlin Turner, "George W. Cable, Novelist and Reformer," South Atlantic Quarterly, XLVIII (October, 1949), 539–545.

[23] Using the Board of Pardon Advisors, Governor Culberson pardoned 339 during 1895–1897.

Watt Finley's report. (Such a goal has often been seriously criticized by writers on the subject, both in Hogg's time and since; however, Texans still try to make prisoners pay their own way, as evidenced by the prison reorganization of 1952–1954, and the matter appears to be a problem that those concerned with social welfare will debate for a long time to come.)

Hogg's Rockdale speech was made after all of the political parties had met and leveled their darts at the Democrats—and after his own reform wing of the Democratic Party had been obligated to compromise to some extent on the silver issue in the reunited Convention. In it the Governor reviewed what he considered to be the outstanding features of his administration, and he appeared to be frankly enjoying himself, secure in his decision to retire to private practice. Relaxed and at ease, he adroitly made the speech serve at least three major purposes: 1) as a weapon in the coming election—the report of his stewardship by implication became a campaign speech for Culberson; 2) as a clarification of the Democratic Party compromise—the elucidation of the Democratic platform (and contrasting ridicule of the Populist platform) made clear the nature and the necessity of the compromise between the two wings of the Party; 3) as a battle call on the silver issue—the terms of the national-scale silver conflict brewing for 1896 were laid down unequivocally.

After the review of his administration's accomplishments he warned the people that if they wanted the reform program to stand and grow they must be alert. He believed that properly increased taxable values or the use of more effective means to force delinquents to pay taxes would bring in enough revenue to balance the budget. If the legislature should decide not to accept these methods, then he believed taxes should be raised. He declared there had not been the default of a cent; warrants were paid in turn as revenues were collected, and there had been no "scandal in connection with any institution or department, except in one instance (Land Office), and then on full investigation, legislative vindication had followed."[24]

In furtherance of a united Democracy and of Culberson's campaign, Hogg dwelt on the accomplishments of the national Democratic Party in working for the people's interest, mentioning the restrictions on foreign immigration, suits to regain lands illegally held by railroads and other private corporations, repeal of an "odious" federal elections law,

[24] *Proceedings of the High Court of Impeachment in the Matter of the State* vs. *W. L. McGaughey, Land Commissioner* (1893), pp. 169–178.

429

reduction of governmental expenditures and the number of federal employees, passage of a tax on incomes (later declared unconstitutional), and the lowered tariff, with some articles such as farm implements, cotton ties, and bagging for cotton and for grain placed on the free list. Saying that he had not always agreed with President Cleveland, he explained that reforms came slowly and that the great machinery of government is "heavy, sluggish, and almost unmanageable . . . This is a family row, and we need no outside meddlers to take part in it."[25] He warned that too much disagreement with Cleveland's work could destroy the genuine reforms of the national administration, and he listed a score of good measures passed during his administration, stressing the "great five," and adding:

Suppose the opposition to the five great laws I have discussed as the subsills on which the magnificent future of Texas must rest had succeeded in convincing a majority of the Democrats that my administration should be defeated, where would have been these governmental measures? Buried, buried deep down in oblivion, perhaps never to rise again. Then suppose the dissensions in our party are encouraged until the national administration is overthrown, must we not expect to receive as the fruits of our hasty, intemperate action the defeat forever of the great reform measures, to the establishment and maintenance of which our party and leaders are solemnly committed?[26]

Hogg chided the Populists, who claimed to be friends of the farmer, for opposing a tariff for revenue. Did they intend to pay the cost of government from direct taxes alone? He doubted this, since their fundamental principles declared that land, water, and air should be free. Further, since they held that no one should become an exclusive owner of any part of the land and no one should pay taxes on land, it was "queer" that some of their platforms advocated the single tax:

If land is to be free, and the improvements are not to be taxed, and they are opposed to a tariff for revenue, how would they run the government?

These things I can not understand. They are simply a conglomerated mess of moonshine thrown into the sights of unsuspecting voters by a cunning class of chimerical clackers filled alone with the essence of hope, to blind, dazzle, and mislead.[27]

[25] Cotner, *op. cit.*, p. 417.
[26] *Ibid.*, pp. 417–418. For Hogg's discussion of the "five great laws," see *ibid.*, pp. 402–403.
[27] *Ibid.*, pp. 419–420.

Taking up in detail the record of several Populists in Congress, Hogg declared that their measures would ruin the country if the new party came to power. He opposed Kansan Populist John Davis' proposal that the United States government should lend money to mortgage debtors at low rates of interest, and Kansan Clover's bill that would permit the federal government to lend states money for the people up to 50 per cent of the assessed valuation of their property, which, with another measure of Clover's, would involve over $15 billion. He instanced the bills by Omer Kem, Tom Watson, Thomas Hudson, and William Peffer for public charities, internal improvements, rain-making in the West, "and other extravagant measures of no material advantage to the people" which would "place the government in debt over $35 billions." This was about four times "all the money in the world." After a parting volley at the Populist propensity for printing paper money, Hogg asked the Democrats not to abuse the Populists:

Tell them that you will forgive them for trying to destroy the house built by patriots, in which they were cradled—the house in which the fathers sat to teach them better doctrines than free lands, no homes, no taxes, and a centralized government! . . . They mean well . . . in their better moments a heavy conscience swings terror over their souls.[28]

He declared his great respect for men of whatever party who, "out of pride and honor, . . . nerve and manhood" spoke openly and gave reasons for their convictions, whether they were in agreement with him or not; then he described the politicians for whom he had no respect:

But for the pinks of innocence, for know-alls, for word-slingers, for hat-smashers and smart alecks, who swing around political circles, idling their time away, leaving their wives and children at home to cultivate patches while they are off gallivanting in politics, or stay on street corners loafing, chewing tobacco, spitting at dirt daubers, whittling on white pine boxes, and "cussing" out the country, I have the profoundest contempt. If they would exercise a little more muscle, perspire a little more over the brow in honest efforts to make bread, and work their jaws less and exercise their reason more, their condition would be decidedly elevated.

Such fellows could not drive a wagon and team without running over every stump within range of the road. They could not operate a wind mill without bursting every joint of the machinery. Many of them could not set a mouse trap. Yet they go around telling you how to run the government. Argument and reason on such fellows fall like saw dust on ocean waves.[29]

[28] *Ibid.*, p. 421.　　　[29] *Ibid.*, p. 427.

Continuing his attack upon Populist proposals, the Governor charged that their efforts to lend school funds to individuals on land security would only benefit the large operators, because homesteads (200 acres) could not be mortgaged in Texas; furthermore, no plan had been outlined to pay for the railroad, telegraph, and telephone companies the Populists wanted the government to own. He suggested that "these modern philosophers on governmental economy should descend from the high flights of their maudlin sentimentality and alight among common, plain people, and explain to them the curiosities of their magic wand by which they are to effect such wonderful governmental reforms." He reminded the voters that these same philosophers when in their other guise as members of the Texas legislature had voted against making the stock and bond law effective immediately—and during the consequent ninety-day delay the various railway companies had rushed authorization of $40 million in bonds.

He urged all Populists who would to return to the Democracy—"the party of reform." Immediate relief or correction, however, of "the real and supposed wrongs," he warned, might not be possible:

After Democrats once leave the party they feel ashamed to return. . . . Lurking in the hearts of many men who left us two years ago is a spirit of conscious wrong; and if they would speak the truth openly and manfully they would confess it. They would retrace their steps, come back to the party of the fathers, and help perpetuate its power over the Federal government, and every town, city, county and State within it. If supported heartily and enthusiastically, I believe this great party will yet bring about every reform of the Federal government demanded by any upright, patriotic people. . . . Reflect and comment upon the tenets, principles, policies and declarations of all parties contending for supremacy in this government, and you must admit that the people's friend is the Democratic party.[30]

It was a particular source of pride to the outgoing governor, in the midst of the greatest challenge to Democratic supremacy in Texas since 1867, that the Populist leader, Judge Nugent, for whom Hogg expressed the "profoundest respect personally," had publicly stated:

If intrusted with the administration of State affairs, there will be no undoing of what has been accomplished by Governor Hogg's administration for the welfare of the people of the State. The commission law, the laws regulating the issuance of bonds by railroads, corporations, and by counties, cities, and towns, the law prohibiting perpetuities, by which corporations

[30] Cotner, *op. cit.*, pp. 417–418.

can no longer acquire and hold land above the needs of their business, the law against alien land ownership—all of these and other beneficial laws now upon the statute books must be adhered to and enforced. They are wise and just, and can not but conduce to the welfare, the happiness, and the prosperity of the people.[31]

Keeping faith with his pledge made at the Democratic Harmony Meeting, Hogg defended the majority platform, but felt free to emphasize the parts with which he most agreed. When he came to the so-called labor planks, 9 and 10, which had been much discussed and criticized, he said that he felt the most favorable construction possible to labor should be put upon them. He pointed out the specific words of Plank 9 that recognized "to the fullest extent" the right of labor to organize, and added, "Capitalists organize; professional men organize; business men organize; railroads organize; farmers organize; then why should not labor organize?"[32] He believed that any interpretation of the plank as an intention to prevent strikes was a very strained construction. He praised labor for its excellent record in Texas, stating that, "with a very slight exception," there had been not a dollar's worth of property destroyed or a human being injured as a result of a labor strike. He believed that as long as pools, associations, trusts, and business combinations existed, labor organizations of necessity must exist also. His own interpretation of the plank was that it authorized the legislature to create a board of arbitration to settle differences between railway corporations and their employees.[33]

Plank 10 called upon the legislature to strengthen the executive officers with all powers necessary to suppress lawlessness and give protection to human lives. Hogg held that this was not aimed at organized labor in any specific way, unless its members should be guilty of violent offenses under the Penal Code—in which case he would "enforce the laws as quickly against them as against others." He had found no disposition among the laboring men of Texas, organized or otherwise, to destroy persons or property or to violate the laws. To him the tenth plank represented an effort to strike at an evil which, during the years of his administration, he felt constituted the main weakness of the Penal Code —the lack of provision for suitable measures to suppress mob violence. Over and over again, in special message and regular message, Hogg had emphasized that the "wanton, cruel, inhuman execution of defenseless

[31] *Ibid.*, p. 407. Hogg quoted from Nugent's 1894 acceptance speech.
[32] *Ibid.*, p. 429.   [33] *Ibid.*

citizens and prisoners" was an outrage that must be done away with. On this October day at Rockdale he once more described lynchers and mobs as "bands of murderers" who should "have their necks broken," and as "cowardly, criminal outlaws" with no "respect for constitutional guaranties or the stability of government or the lives of human beings."[34]

The subject of lynching, perhaps more so than any other, seemed to bring together in passionate impact the several characteristics that constituted James Hogg's power as a reformer. His hatred for violence, his deep respect for, and belief in, the efficacy of law and constitutional government, his resentment of injustice meted to any man, his capacity for persistence, his compassion for human beings, his own personal wish for a kindly world where men could be friends and use their talents and reason according to their best lights—all combined to produce his burning abomination of mob action, which he then would denounce with all the power of another characteristic: his fluency in graphically descriptive, uninhibited speech. Were it necessary at this date to find further confutation of the worn-out charge of demagoguery so often made by his contemporary opposition, an assembling of his many remarks on lynching—particularly as applied to Negroes—would provide it. In Texas of the late nineteenth century this was not a popular reform subject with any sizable group among those upon whom he must depend for the power he was accused of desiring.

The great improvement in public order during the eight years of Governor Hogg's incumbency has been attested by Colonel House: "Governor Hogg did more than any executive in Texas to break up [the] habit of public killing."[35] A section of the Penal Code that Hogg was convinced contributed perniciously to "the habit of killing" was the chapter on manslaughter, which defined the offense as "voluntary homicide committed under the immediate influence of sudden passion arising from an adequate cause, but neither justified nor excused by law." His experience while prosecuting criminal cases as district attorney had shown him the delicate line a judge must walk in distinguishing manslaughter from murder in the various degrees. Any slip in his definition or in the charge to the jury setting forth the law applicable to a case made it likely that a bill of exception would be drawn up, and on appeal

---

[34] *Ibid.*, pp. 430–431.

[35] Charles Seymour, *Papers of Colonel House*, p. 22; Lewis Nordyke, "Lawful Murder in Texas," *Coronet*, XLIV (October, 1958), pp. 168–172. For Governor Hogg's forthright stand against "lynch law" see his special message of February 6, 1893, reprinted in *Addresses and State Papers of James Stephen Hogg*, pp. 331–334.

the Court of Appeals was bound to reverse the case. Tired of hearing that "murderers were less punished in Texas than thieves," Hogg had proposed at four different sessions of the legislature that the manslaughter chapter be removed and the following be substituted:

A change in the law of murder so that when a person of sound mind and discretion unlawfully and with malice aforethought kills a human being in this State, he shall be guilty of, and on conviction punished for, the first or second degree of that offense, according to the facts developed in the trial.

Qualify the law of self-defense so that when a person takes the life of another and relies on the "appearance of danger" for protection, the jury, not the defendant, must determine from all the evidence whether the "appearances" were sufficient to justify a prudent man in believing the "danger" in fact existed at the time the killing occurred.

Make every slayer who provokes the attack which results in the homicide, or who voluntarily engages in the combat, knowing that it would or might result in death or serious bodily injury to his adversary or himself, guilty of murder in the first or second degree, according to the facts of the case.[36]

Over and over again he had placed himself on record that there had never been and could never be "in sound justice and principle, any reasonable excuse for civilized people to permit technical complications to remain in the way of the conviction of men who are guilty of the highest crime" known in law. He had called for a revision of the jury system so as to remove most of the exemptions and disqualifications which were placing a premium on the use of ignorant and "professional" jurors. The City of Austin and Travis County, by the great improvement it had made along these lines, won his praise, as did District Attorney for Travis County James H. Robertson. Despite the Governor's pressure, encouragement, and praise, however, none of the legislatures had acted on this suggestion. Nevertheless, through Hogg's vigilance, the work of the Texas Rangers, and the increasing diligence of local enforcement officers, the reputation of Texas as a wild and lawless land was gradually changing. The old type of individual outlaw was being hemmed in.

[36] Message of January 21, 1891, Texas *House Journal* (1891), pp. 116–117. Hogg repeated his insistence on these changes in his messages of January 12, 1893, Texas *House Journal* (1893), pp. 28–29; and January 11, 1895, Texas *House Journal* (1895), pp. 35–36. Mary Louise Wimberly Barksdale, "The Gubernatorial Administration of James Stephen Hogg," Master's thesis (the University of Texas, 1932), pp. 116–118; Mizell F. Kennedy, "A Study of James S. Hogg, Attorney General and Governor," Master's thesis (the University of Texas, 1919), p. 153.

However, as Hogg had pointed out innumerable times since 1886, a new type of rapacious outlaw had developed, one much more difficult to handle through law enforcement—the unprincipled corporation. He was often accused of believing that the word "corporation" must invariably be modified by "unprincipled." The accusation was of course false; nevertheless, it is historically true that in the early days of their swift growth the new companies (each one naturally out to suppress as much competition as possible and to make all possible profit) in general indulged in practices that were not, to put it gently, in "the public interest." Like full-blooded, powerful wild horses, most of them had to learn the restraint of bridle and bit. The contest was sometimes in the open, sometimes underground and subtle. In the end, as the nineteenth century gave way to the twentieth and the years of the twentieth moved on, the forces of law, with regulatory powers to protect the public, would win, and even the corporations would find themselves more secure thereby from the piratic tendencies of their own brethren. Responsible officials of many states and of the federal government fought this battle. James Hogg, however, was among the very first to realize that it must be fought; he was also one of the most successful battlers, being completely unafraid and persistent as he saw to it that legal durable weapons were created which could then be wielded stoutly.

One of the most important efforts to protect the progressive program during the latter part of Hogg's administration was the preparation for the suit later to be brought against the powerful Standard Oil Company and the Waters-Pierce Oil Company of Missouri for violation of the Texas antitrust law. In 1889, while Hogg was attorney general, his attention had been called by George Rice of Marietta, Ohio, to certain practices of the John D. Rockefeller interests.[37] Making use of cheap river and ocean transportation to St. Louis, New Orleans, and Galveston, Rice had stayed in the oil industry race with Rockefeller and Henry Flagler and their expanding trust until they started price wars and enticed away dealers, having the advantage of railroad rebates and the special treatment which would come from being stockholders in railroads. Before Gould's death late in 1892, Rockefeller had been buying into railway lines, and he became even more powerful after 1893.

[37] The public testimony of George Rice may be read in *Report of the United States Industrial Commission* (Washington, Government Printing Office, 1899), I, 704–711; John T. Flynn, *God's Gold* (New York, Harcourt, Brace, and Company, 1933), pp. 316–318.

Through the Morgan banking house Rockefeller also became associated with steamship lines operating on the East and Gulf coasts. By 1894 it was apparent to men in the oil business that the expanding market for oil and kerosene in the Southwest was dominated by the Waters-Pierce Oil Company and Standard Oil working together; in Texas, however, Standard operated, not under its own name, but through Waters-Pierce.

After accumulating data for months about the operations of the five main divisions of Waters-Pierce in Texas, Attorney General Culberson decided that he had enough evidence to prove that Waters-Pierce and Standard were working together in such a way as to violate the Texas Antitrust Act approved in March, 1889. Waters-Pierce, obtaining permission to operate after the Act was passed, had put into the record that it was not a trust or party to a trust or combination in restraint of trade. In the numerous briefs prepared by Culberson and subsequently by succeeding Attorneys General Martin M. Crane and Thomas S. Smith, it was made clear that Waters-Pierce had been a party to the famous joint trust agreement of 1882 and to such of its continuing benefits, after it was supposedly ended in 1892, as the virtual monopoly of the Southwestern trade area. Competition was frequently eliminated by the following actions:

1. Rebating to customers who would discontinue handling products of rival concerns;

2. Lowering prices until rival had closed or sold out and then raising prices above the market price;

3. Operating the Eagle Refining Company after consolidation as though it were a real competitor to Waters-Pierce;

4. Controlling Waters-Pierce policies by trustees whose authority was acquired by transfer of stock to Standard Oil which made Waters-Pierce a part of a trust.[38]

There was ample evidence of restraint of trade as defined by the law: Attorney General Crane in 1896 declared that "99 per cent of the oil business of Texas, amounting to one-half million barrels annually" was handled exclusively by Waters-Pierce for their benefit and the benefit of the Standard Trust.[39] In preliminaries to the suit, which became known as *The State of Texas* v. *John D. Rockefeller et al,* indictments were obtained at Waco in 1894 against John D. Rockefeller, Henry M. Flagler, William Rockefeller, John D. Archbold, other Standard

[38] 19 *Texas Civil Appeals Reports* (1898) 1; 44 SW 936 (1898); 177 US 28 (1899).
[39] 36 *Texas Criminal Reports* 261 (1896).

stockholders and trustees, and officials and agents of Waters-Pierce, including Henry Clay Pierce, president, Arthur M. Finley, a vice-president at Galveston, J. P. Gruet, secretary, E. Wells, auditor, William Grice, agent at Dallas, E. T. Hathaway, agent at Denison, William E. Hawkins, agent at Waco, and others. Sheriff John W. Baker of McLennan County was expected to arrest these persons and have them ready for trial in the Fifty-fourth State District Court at Waco.[40] The Texas Antitrust Act was purposely worded to include out-of-state officers, trustees, principals, and agents and to provide for their trial and punishment if they violated the law.

Governor Hogg stepped into the picture to ask for extradition of John D. Rockefeller from New York and Henry M. Flagler from Florida. This was a novel request, but the Governor of Florida almost honored the one for Flagler. Article IV, Section 2 (paragraph 2) of the Constitution of the United States reads:

A Person charged in any State with Treason, Felony, or other Crime, who shall flee from Justice, and be found in another State, shall on Demand of the executive Authority of the State from which he fled, be delivered up, to be removed to the State having Jurisdiction of the Crime.

Congress in establishing the machinery to enforce this provision in 1793 repeatedly referred to "a fugitive from justice" or to the condition that a charged person "has fled."[41] Governor Flower of New York was told by his legal advisors that he was not obliged to grant the request of the governor of Texas, since Rockefeller had not "fled" Texas. Rockefeller's legal expert, Samuel C. T. Dodd, ridiculed the Texas sheriff who was awaiting word that he might bring the culprits out of New York; fully understanding that the import of the Texas action was an attempt to break up trusts and combinations in restraint of trade, Dodd sought to quiet Rockefeller's concern by saying that the Texans had "one of those crazy socialistic laws which are unconstitutional."[42]

Governor Henry L. Mitchell of Florida also finally refused the request for Flagler's return and in so doing was legally correct (as he still would be in the 1950's; even the Uniform Criminal Extradition Code is not mandatory, and reads, "The Governor of this State may also surrender . . . any person . . . charged in such other state . . . even though the ac-

---

[40] *John W. Baker, Sheriff* v. *William Grice*, 169 US 284 (1897).
[41] Edwin S. Oakes (ed.), *American Jurisprudence* (Rochester, Lawyer's Cooperative Publishing Company, 1939), pp. 247 ff.
[42] Flynn, *God's Gold*, p. 318.

cused was not in that state at the time of the commission of the crime, and has not fled therefrom."[43]) Governors have always exercised a large amount of personal discretion in the matter of extraditions, and it is of interest that Mitchell's first inclination was to honor the request. He issued a warrant for Flagler's arrest, but when informed that he was making a serious political mistake and his political future might hang in the balance he withdrew the order.[44] Dr. Sidney Martin in his *Florida's Flagler* wrote that it was Hogg's desire "to keep himself before the public" that made him become "active in a crusade to uphold the Sherman Anti-Trust law," adding that Hogg disliked "railroad builders too, for the railroads in Texas had fought him in a recent election."[45] Martin seems to have accepted too readily the point of view of the railroad-dominated Florida *Times-Union,* whose articles made these assertions. He overlooked two facts: that Hogg had already at this time announced his plan to retire from officeholding, and that Texas was initially prosecuting under its own law and not the Sherman Act.

Blocked in efforts to bring the principals of the "conspiracy" to trial, the State of Texas was obliged to begin with suits at Waco and Austin against the oil companies and the agents of Waters-Pierce, who usually turned out to be men who had served that company well for ten years or more, some prior to any known agreements between it and Standard Oil. After Hogg was out of office, E. T. Hathaway, division manager at Denison, was tried in the district court at Waco and convicted on December 2, 1895, for being a party to "a conspiracy against trade," being fined fifty dollars. The ubiquitous George Clark took part in his defense, arguing that the "equal protection" clause of the United States Constitution was involved, since the law was "inoperative and void as to persons resident beyond the territorial limits of Texas," that interstate commerce was involved—hence the case was not a proper one for a Texas district court—and that the agent was not overruled, as

[43] Adopted by Texas in 1951, Section 6, Article 1008a, *Texas Code of Criminal Procedure.* Seven states had not accepted the Uniform Act by April, 1955. Assistant Attorney General A. M. Le Croix and former Assistant Attorney General Gresham have been helpful on these technical points.

[44] Flagler's influence in Florida was reputed to extend to law changes.

[45] Sidney W. Martin, *Florida's Flagler* (Athens, University of George Press, 1949), p. 254; Hogg's speech at San Antonio, August 1, 1894, quoted in Cotner, *op. cit.,* p. 395. See also Ida M. Tarbell, *History of the Standard Oil Company,* (New York, McClure, Phillips, and Company, 1904), II, 151 ff.; Allan Nevins, *Study in Power: John D. Rockefeller* (New York, Scribner's, 1953), II, 233, 365 ff.; *Florida Times-Union* (Jacksonville), December 26, 1894; January 4, 1895.

was a motion to arrest judgment. The fine not being paid, Hathaway was incarcerated.

Before the Court of Criminal Appeals, Clark and his assistant Bollinger filed "a most able and elaborate brief." There were lengthy citations on the interstate commerce features, and Clark made efforts to have the whole law declared unconstitutional; however, the decisive points were that the indictment had failed to charge and the state to prove that the agent had "knowingly" been a party to any conspiracy. Hathaway was declared not guilty of knowingly conspiring and ordered released from prison on June 26, 1896, because "to hold a party responsible, as an agent for such a trust or conspiracy, the indictment must allege, that he knew of the conspiracy and its purposes."[46] Texas had tripped on the case because Attorney General Culberson's office had failed to charge that Hathaway had "knowingly" conspired. Any study of the history of the Texas antitrust law would have shown clearly how the original draft as it left the hands of Attorney General Hogg was amended on the floor to include the word "knowingly."

While trials against other division managers were pending, the Texas Antitrust Act was strengthened by amendments in 1895, one of which declared that the law was not to be "construed to prevent the organization of laborers for the purpose of maintaining any standard of wages." By exempting labor and agricultural organizations the Texas law plainly stated its intent; the Sherman Antitrust Act of 1890 was supposed to have had the same intent, but its wording was ambiguous, and not until Wilson's administration was it clarified. The Texas law also supplemented its specification of conspiracy in "restraint of trade" by these words: "or commerce, or aids to commerce, or to create or carry out restrictions in the full and free pursuit of any business authorized or permitted by the laws of this State."[47]

Trials of the other Waters-Pierce division agents, William Grice, William E. Hawkins, F. A. Austin, and others were carried over from one court session to the next. Grice made application before a federal judge for habeas corpus following the delays, and on December 9, 1896 (some six months after Hathaway's release) Sheriff Baker was ordered to appear before the United States Circuit Court, Fifth Circuit, at Waco and show true cause for detaining him. George Clark was emphasizing the right to an early trial. Hearings were set for Dallas in January, and on appeal the case of *John W. Baker, Sheriff, Appellant* v. *William*

[46] 36 *Texas Criminal Reports* 261 (1896).
[47] Texas *House Journal* (1895), pp. 38–39.

Grice, Appellee came before the October 1897, term of the Supreme Court of the United States.[48]

Meanwhile, Attorney General Crane had started a new case against Waters-Pierce Oil Company and its agents in the district court at Austin, requesting a judgment which would force the company to forfeit its charter and discontinue doing business in Texas for violation of the Texas Antitrust Act. On June 15, 1897, the jury held for the State of Texas and against Waters-Pierce, but in favor of the individual agents Hathaway, Austin, Grice, Keenan, and Fries. The court then ordered that Waters-Pierce Oil Company was henceforth "denied the right and prohibited doing any business within this State, and that its permit to do business within this State heretofore issued on July 6th, 1889, by the secretary of state of this State be, and the same is hereby, canceled and held for naught."[49] This judgment was upheld by the Court of Civil Appeals in March, 1898, and taken on appeal to the Supreme Court of the United States later that year. It is of interest that Rockefeller's lawyer, Samuel C. T. Dodd, frankly contended that the Texas antitrust laws of 1889 and 1895 made "penal all association of two or more persons for business purposes" and rendered it impossible for two or more persons associated to carry on business, although the right of association and to carry on business was "a liberty protected by the Fourteenth Amendment." In his argument, Dodd said:

Associations restrictive of competition were not void at common law, but that on the contrary combinations restrictive of competition have always been upheld by law, and the right to combine is to be classed among the most important and least questioned liberties of citizens.[50]

Commenting upon the possibility that state legislatures could "declare criminal contracts and associations restrictive of *competition*," including price-fixing or price-changing, he concluded with these words:

If the liberty which our Constitution guarantees does not protect the men who conduct the business of this country against such absurd and dangerous legislation, it is but a glittering generality, instead of a safeguard upon which the citizen may rely.[51]

[48] 169 U.S. 284 (1897); 79 *Federal Reporter* 627 (1897).
[49] *The State of Texas* v. *Waters-Pierce Oil Co.*, 177 U.S. 28 (1899).
[50] *Waters-Pierce Oil Company, Plaintiff in Error* v. *The State of Texas*, being a printed brief, No. 334, Supreme Court of the United States, October Term, 1898, in a bound Collection of Briefs of George Clark, Vol. I, University of Texas Library.
[51] *Ibid.*

441

Although Samuel Dodd and George Clark had fought a hard six-year legal battle in behalf of the old order—to uphold the mores of the period of consolidation that was "unrestrained" from 1873 to the time in 1889 when Kansas and Texas pioneered the first antitrust laws—Attorney General Crane's argument won on March 19, 1900, a Supreme Court decision that upheld the Texas law and the verdict of the Texas Supreme Court of Civil Appeals on three counts:

1. The right of foreign corporation to engage in business within a state other than that of its creation depends solely upon the will of such other state, except with respect to business of a Federal nature.

2. Forfeiture of permission to do business was not a violation of contract as the provision for forfeiture was a part of the obligation.

3. The Texas exemption of labor organizations by the law of 1895 did not repeal the act of 1889, because if it were ruled void it could not operate as a repeal of the former act.[52]

However, Henry Clay Pierce, Standard Oil, and the Waters-Pierce Oil Company were not to give up easily. Texas in 1900, with its rapidly expanding markets and new oil fields at Corsicana, was a land of rich promise. Spectacular later developments would then involve the new United States Senator Joe Bailey and citizen Jim Hogg.

When private citizen Hogg re-entered the fight against the oil trust in 1901 he may have wondered why he had been so optimistic in October, 1894, as he said the following to his Rockdale audience:

Standing now upon the threshold of my permanent retirement to private life, I am proud that my confidence in the justice of the people is strengthened by the magnanimity and cordial indorsement accorded to me within the past few months by all those who opposed me so bitterly in the past two campaigns. . . .

The dark clouds that lowered over Texas and cast a gloom upon the hopes of the people two or three years ago have passed away, leaving the bright sunshine of content in the hearts of a reunited Democracy, to shed its inspiring rays upon the feelings of every Texan, without reference to his political, social, or physical condition or complexion. To-day no abuse is heard from the leaders of Democracy, or Republicanism, or Populism, nor from the rank and file of either party, against these great laws; but with common acclaim they declare in favor of their support, maintenance, and faithful execution.

Then why should we not all be happy? Why should not I be proud? Why should not my loyal, faithful supporters through so many hot, trying ordeals

[52] 177 U.S. 28 (1899).

join in and share the glory that must crown our splendid State as a result of these magnificent laws? From lessons of the past, it is well to draw inspiration for the future, and in the spirit of good faith press on to a higher destiny. Texas is safe![53]

Governor Hogg deserved to go out of office a happy man, but among the malicious rumors spread during the 1894 campaign for Culberson was one persistent tale that Hogg had enriched himself while in office. This was of course a deliberate untruth, as all of his friends and many of his enemies could have testified. For James Hogg, a man without private means, the governorship had meant continual struggle to make ends meet. In 1894 he had sold, to meet current expenses, some of the property acquired in Tyler before he became attorney general—and he even had difficulty collecting what was owed him on the sale. When he looked at his $135 bank balance and then added up his personal bills early in January, 1895, he found that it would be necessary to extend his credit until he could get established in private practice.[54] Those who knew him best understood his deep concern for the security of his family, in the face of the fact that the inevitable financial drain of high but not adequately recompensed office had given him no chance to save money; they knew also that one of his major reasons for leaving public office was this desire to build up an estate to protect his loved ones. His excessive weight lessened his chances for a long life. He was entirely confident about his ability to do well in private practice, but he was aware that the situation brooked no delay. The story that he had somehow battened on the largess of the state was for a time a source of unhappiness to him, even though so easily proved untrue. Other than that, however, the end of the year 1894 found him serene and full of glad anticipation of the life ahead—in which he could test his abilities anew and above all have the time he had largely lacked during the past eight years to expand the opportunities for pleasure as a husband and father. In making plans for his future he discussed informally with District Attorney James H. Robertson of Austin the possibility of their forming a partnership if Hogg stayed in Austin. No decision was reached at this time.

Ten days before Christmas 1894, as Hogg started the preparation of his final official message, he wrote a gracious invitation to Governor-elect Culberson: "Should you so desire I shall be glad to confer with you on a general line of cooperation aiming at harmony of action and success

[53] Cotner, *op. cit.*, pp. 404–405.
[54] J. S. Hogg to S. W. Blount, January 9, 1895, J. S. Hogg Let. Pr., 12, p. 72.

of the work lying before you. . . . Come by the house, take dinner with me, rest up and talk over matters—with me 'dinner' means noon."[55] The message was the product of days and nights of careful writing. Near midnight of December 20, when it was all but finished, its author paused to write a letter to his long-time and dearly loved mentor, his sister Martha Frances Davis, then in Pueblo, Colorado. In it he allowed himself to dwell on his personal pride and satisfaction in the years just past. The storms of those years were scarcely recalled, and perhaps to this man, now so obviously at peace with the world, they had been, not storms in any exceptional sense, but merely the upheavals natural when men were striving to create a better world to live in:

My last message to the Legislature is about finished, Sallie and the children are all asleep, and in the quiet solitude of the night I am glad to say a few words to you. After rather an eventful career of eight years at the Capitol I am on the verge of permanent retirement to private life. Recently I have reviewed the record and checked up every branch and Department of the Government. Result: Every pledge of reform that I made as a candidate for Governor has been fully redeemed and now stands in the shape of accepted and acceptable law. Every institution has been operated economically, efficiently, without scandal, at reduced expense. Tonight I have the endorsement of the people and above all the support of a clear conscience. So I am willing, anxious to quit. To *you* I may say, I hope without the suspicion of immodesty, that the U. S. Senatorship was open to me without opposition from any source the next time. Not only did I decline to become a candidate at a time when all parties wanted me to run but I promptly announced

---

[55] J. S. Hogg to C. A. Culberson, December 14, 1894, J. S. Hogg Let. Pr., 12, p. 15. Culberson was not a majority victor in 1894; the observation that a combined vote might win led to the Populist-Republican fusion in 1896. A comparison of the votes indicates that 100,000 more votes were cast in that presidential election year and that the Populists standing alone had reached their peak in 1894. The Republicans came through on their agreement to help the Populist state ticket, but the Populists did not reciprocate in voting for McKinley.

1894 Governor		1896 Governor	Pres. Electors
Culberson (Democrat)	207,167	Culberson	298,643*	284,000
Nugent (Populist)	152,731	Kearby	238,325	76,750
Makemson (Reg. Repub.)	54,520	———	....	158,650
Schmitz (Ref. Repub.)	5,026			
Dunn (Prohibition)	2,196			
Total	421,640		536,968	519,400

* In this campaign the Negro leader William (Gooseneck Bill) McDonald worked for the Democrats. See *Report of the Secretary of State, 1894* (1894), p. 252; Martin, *The People's Party in Texas,* p. 243.

that under no circumstances would I accept the place. So my best friend Chilton became a candidate and will be elected next January without opposition. Thus my appointment of him has at last been approved (or will be) by the people, and this will finish the approval and endorsement of all my important public official acts as Governor. My period of public life is therefore "well rounded" and my cup of ambition is full. And speaking tonight in the fear of God I can say what but few men can truthfully state, that I am on friendly terms with every living creature in being that I know or ever heard of. My next start in life though in poverty will be a happy one, with prospects of success good all along the line.

The Administration to succeed me is cordial and friendly to me in every way possible. My Attorney General, Mr. Culberson, is to be the Governor. My Lieutenant Governor, Mr. Crane, is to be the Attorney General. My Treasurer, Mr. Wortham, is to succeed himself. My appointee as Financial Agent of the Penitentiaries—R. Watt Finley— is to be the Comptroller. My appointee as Temporary Land Commissioner, Mr. Baker, is to be the Land Commissioner. My appointee to fill a vacancy, Mr. Carlisle, is to succeed himself as State Supt. of Public Education. So are the Commissioner of Agriculture, the Adjutant General, the State Health Officer, the Superintendent and the two assistants of the Penitentiaries; many other officers under the new administration were my appointees to places and for years were associated with me intimately. Texas is my friend and I am, thank the Lord, the friend of Texas. . . .

While this letter sounds egotistical, self-laudatory, it is nevertheless permissible, I am sure, to you. I am so glad that I am able to leave office honorably, and fully satisfied, that I must tell *somebody* of it—who better than yourself? Yes, yourself, my Sister, to whom I could always go for a smile, for help and encouragement in the struggling days of my blundering youth.

Well, I am through, except to say that Sallie and the children are well and happy, and to send greetings to yourself, William and family.

May the Great God, in whom I trust, shower blessings on you all.[56]

When the day came in January, 1895, to inaugurate the man who would carry on the reform program, Hogg was pleased to introduce the "sterling, chivalrous, intellectual" Charles A. Culberson. Any suggestion of a temporary difference between the two men had vanished, and Culberson was especially grateful for the vigorous support Hogg had given him during the latter part of the campaign, when Populist Nugent threatened to gain control in the "black" counties through shifts of 20,000 to 30,000 Republican voters. Governor Culberson turned to the out-going Governor to say, with the utmost sincerity:

[56] J. S. Hogg to Martha Frances Davis, December 20, 1894, Fam. Let.

This great audience, I feel certain, will unite with me in tendering Governor Hogg on his retirement from office assurance of the high esteem in which he is held. His has been a useful and remarkable career. (Large of body and mind, great-hearted, generous and brave, devoted to the masses —his place in the affections of the people is securely fixed and the great impress he has left on our legislation is an enduring monument to his fidelity, his courage and his statesmanship.) Wherever his lot and his fortunes may be cast, the best wishes of the people will attend him for his continued success and happiness.[57]

[57] Quoted in Madden, *Culberson,* p. 63; Texas *House Journal* (1895), p. 44.

CHAPTER XVI

Citizen-Statesman

WHEN JAMES STEPHEN HOGG became a private citizen in January, 1895, he lacked about two months of being forty-four years old: rather young to have already had a major political career, yet old enough to lend some uncertainty to the outcome of the future accomplishment he most desired—the provision of material security for his wife and children. Nothing was certain on the January day when Mr. and Mrs. Hogg with their four children moved from the Governor's Mansion to the Misses Beggs' boardinghouse on Eighth Street. Their future dwelling place could not be chosen until Hogg made up his mind whether he would set up his practice in Austin or move to one or another of the towns that offered certain advantages to be carefully weighed. Given time, he would fulfill his dream to achieve material security for his children, but his first year out of public office was mainly a period of readjustment.

However, it is highly improbable that the concept of insecurity occurred to any one of the Hoggs on moving day. Though the matter of choosing the right combination to fulfill his purpose was of deep concern to James Hogg, he actually had complete confidence that he would be successful. Worry over possible later disappointments was not characteristic of him, as he himself pointed out in a letter written several years later to his daughter Ima: "As you may have observed in times gone by, I am of sanguine temperament and rarely get discouraged. I never suffer much from *disappointment.*"[1] His ability to persist, well-enough known to railroad men and others who had fought him that at times they must have felt they had got themselves in the tooth-grip of a mastiff that never would let go, would stand his own ambitions in good stead. (Some years later Will Hogg in writing to his sister, apropos of her coming home from New York for Christmas as her father wished her to do remarked: "Father has his heart set on your coming, and you know when 'Jym' is sot something is bound to give way."[2]) Since the head of

[1] James S. Hogg to Ima Hogg, February 18, 1900, Fam. Let.
[2] Will Hogg to Ima Hogg, December, 1902, Fam. Let.

447

the family showed no qualms about the future, it would not have occurred to Mrs. Hogg or any one of the children to doubt him. But there
was the problem of getting settled in a new home. Memories of life in
the Mansion kept coming to mind.

Just as the state of Texas was indisputably the better for Hogg's having inhabited the Governor's office for four years, so the Mansion was
better off for his residence there. As noted earlier, under the fastidious
and accomplished direction of Mrs. Hogg the dismaying disrepair of the
nobly built house (designed in 1855 by Abner Cook) had been remedied
as much as possible—which still left something to be desired, because
complete renovation would have cost much more than could be spent
during a depression.[3] The Mansion, during the Hoggs' four years in it,
was kept spotlessly clean and its grounds devotedly tended, for Sallie
Hogg was a famously efficient housekeeper. She was not sorry, however,
to be leaving the hard-to-keep house and the social duties entailed by
her husband's office.

Despite the increasing delicacy of her health, her skill in management
of the Mansion never flagged; both official and personal expenses were
kept down through hundreds of careful, small economies, although the
entertainments never seemed skimped and at times even had the appearance of lavishness. Nothing came out of the storeroom (stocked with
barrels of flour and sugar, hundred-pound cans of lard, smoked turkeys
and chickens by the dozen, and sides of bacon, as was the custom then)
without being checked by the mistress of the Mansion, who went about,
like a chatelaine of old, with a great bunch of keys during the hours
when she was supervising the servants in the myriad housekeeping
chores. Servants, whether white or colored, were sometimes hard to
keep; although most of them were devoted to the family, the demands
of an official household—superimposed on a personal household of four
rambunctious children—were taxing. Among the obligatory entertainments, the annual New Year's reception called for especially arduous
preparation. Help usually arrived in the shape of willing neighbors, extra servants, the cateress and her minions, a porter or two from the
Capitol, and young men who were always willing to help with the flower
and foliage decorations, wanting to be thought of as in the Austin social
swim. Under Mrs. Hogg's expert supervision, based on minute planning,
all would go smoothly, even when she was confined to bed and must

---

[3] The text that follows (to page 454) is based on Ima Hogg, "Life in the
Governor's Mansion, 1891–1895," typescript in H.C., *passim,* and on letters and
interviews with family friends of the period.

issue orders through a deputy—usually the extraordinarily capable housekeeper and friend, Grace. When Grace left the service of the Hogg family at Christmas time, 1894, the Governor and his wife wrote a letter testifying to their appreciation of her estimable qualities:

December 14, 1894

To Whom this May Concern:

The bearer of this, Miss Grace Bauer, has been in our service as housemaid for over three years and six months. During that time she has been honest, faithful, industrious and lady-like in all her conduct. We have never known a better or more deserving girl, and beg to commend her to the kind treatment of every one with whom she may be in anyway connected.

Respectfully
J. S. Hogg
Mrs. Hogg[4]

A familiar and very welcome figure at the New Year's receptions was Bob, the former Negro overseer of "Mountain Home," who had never lost his affection and admiration for "Marse Jeems." It was said that his father had been an important African chieftain, and Bob's noble bearing amply validated the story as, elegant in cutaway coat and striped trousers, he would sit in a corner of the reception room waiting to play his fiddle for the guests. His annual trips to Austin were the more gratifying to him because his wife, Easter, considered the "fiddle" a true instrument of the devil and forbade him to touch it at home; only in Austin could he fiddle to his heart's content.

There were many other receptions, and of course dinners, to honor visiting dignitaries and to emphasize special occasions. And nearly every Saturday night there would be a dance for young people, for it was seldom that the house did not harbor relatives or one or more glamorous young lady guests, daughters of old family friends, who would come for the various gala occasions of the year, and especially at Guard Encampment time when belles were chosen as "sponsors" of the various companies. The Governor had given up dancing some years before (appreciating that it was not quite seemly for one of his largeness of figure), and Sallie, who had formerly loved the pastime, would not now dance without her husband, but they both took delight in watching their guests gayly go through the paces of schottisches and polkas.

On Sunday evenings the family gathered around the piano to sing hymns and old-favorite songs. Guests were welcome to drop in, and

[4] J. S. Hogg Let. Pr., 12, p. 57.

many usually did—being especially well received by the Governor if they could play or sing. Mrs. Hogg had originally been the official pianist, but when her headaches grew worse young ladies of the neighborhood took over. Ima, whose musical talents had first been fostered by her mother and then by the highly considered Professor Ludwig from Russia, was also in demand.

The Mansion during the Hogg regime was much more than the official center of Austin social life. The hospitality dispensed was easy and generous, and friends and neighbors came often, because they felt themselves made so sincerely welcome by this family for whom life was intensely interesting, and always fun. (Testimony to this is found in many letters and diaries of the time. Mrs. L. Milton Brown, as a girl, a frequent visitor to the Mansion, in an interview of May 10, 1941, said she had never heard a cross word between James and Sallie, adding, "I don't think any family ever lived in the Mansion who had as much fun as Governor Hogg and his family.") None of it was easy for Sallie Hogg. Small and dainty in size, seldom weighing a hundred pounds, she possessed only slight endurance, but she enjoyed both the informal entertaining (because she liked people and especially because having friends about pleased her husband) and the formal (because she felt this was a duty she was bound to execute as well as possible to be a credit to "Mr. Hogg"—her affectionate name for him when others were present). The large receptions, which involved standing for hours, were ordeals for her, however, although she never complained and her smile and words to those who came along the receiving line were always modestly gracious. The Governor finally arranged to have a high stool placed behind her, so that she could sit on it at intervals, or at least lean against it. Somewhat shy and retiring among people she did not know intimately, she had nevertheless trained herself to meet the public with ease and dignity.

She was his confidante and adviser always; he trusted her intuition and judgment about people, and believed that a wife should be in every way a complete partner. His admiration for her charm was unbounded, and her skills at keeping the official and personal household functioning so smoothly on the minimum amount of money available never ceased to amaze him. She had an exquisite sense of dress, taking great care in her shopping for materials. All of her clothes and Ima's were handmade, and she would have felt disgraced had any machine-stitching gone into dresses or undergarments. The gowns her position required were fairly elaborate; these she had made by the best dressmakers Austin afforded,

450

not because she could not have done it herself (she was an accomplished needlewoman) but because the press of other duties did not leave time for it. She did, however, make much of her underwear and Ima's, and when a dress arrived not finished to her satisfaction she would rip out stitches and replace them herself. In every way possible she tried to use what strength she had to its best advantage, and thus seized whatever opportunities for resting she could find. The Governor enjoyed a drive on Sunday afternoons, and Sallie would gladly let him fill the carriage with the children and Sunday dinner guests while she stayed behind to relax in the unaccustomed quiet of the empty house. When friends came in of a weekday evening to play the popular six-handed euchre, she would beg off sometimes and go to bed.

She was a worrier about only two things: the virulent slanders directed at "Mr. Hogg," which, although they were actually a commonplace of politics, never ceased to outrage her, and the acrobatic tendencies of the three younger children (particularly after they had gone to a circus with their father). She was always sure they would incur at the least broken necks, but tried to believe her husband's hearty reassurances to the contrary. The Governor wanted the children to have every chance for healthy physical development, but even he made a new ukase after the day Tom, indulging in their favorite indoor game of whizzing down the long and highly polished stair banister, fell off midway and hung by his chin from the corner of a step, bleeding profusely. Tom was in trouble also for starting a fire too close to the wooden fence near the carriage house.

To the children, the Mansion period had been sheer delight. The commodious block of ground that surrounded the house was divided up into smaller plots of fascinating uses: a well-kept front lawn, a croquet lawn, a pool, flower beds, vegetable garden, and a space for fruit trees that included fig, peach, plum, and quince. Next to the stable in back was a large plot, used both as a running ground for the horses and as a playground for the children. Mrs. Hogg took charge of the flower garden, and the Governor enthusiastically made the vegetable garden and the fruit trees his provinces. The children hovered around all plantings, growings, and harvestings, helping when they were allowed. A victoria and a pair of beautiful, matched black horses (a gift to the Governor from his brother John) were kept for formal occasions; a three-seated hack or carryall was used for country driving, and the children had a small trap for their own shetland pony, Dainty, who was also used for riding and seemed to take mischievous pleasure in pitching a

451

rider off or whirling the trap so fast that everyone spilled out, but always without injury to anyone.

There were innumerable pets at various times, enjoyed by father as much as by children. On one of the Governor's trips to San Antonio a menagerie was being dispersed, and he arrived home with a large contingent of cockatoos and other exotic birds. A large cage was built at the north side of the Mansion, and the Governor, with one or all of the children, paid a visit here each morning before he went off to the Capitol. A red-headed parrot that he had bought from a Mexican near Austin would never stay in the cage; she was a privileged character, named Jane, and roamed the grounds and the house. At noon she would wait at the front door for the Governor's return for dinner; as he started up the walk from the gate she would begin flapping her wings and screaming "Papa, papa!" as she ran toward him. In the house she took up a perch on the back of his chair, listening intently to the conversation. If people laughed, she would laugh. (Ima, whose laugh was greatly admired by her father, served as a model, so that Jane's laugh might improve.) Each child had a dog, and there were also many cats, as well as the baby coons, possums, and squirrels that Mike, the naturalist of the family, was always finding wounded or sick and bringing home to nurse back to health.

The grounds of the Mansion were practically a neighborhood playground, and contests of some sort—running, jumping, competitive games—were always going on in good weather, Ima competing along with the boys. Will, eight years older than Ima, was aloof from these playtimes, although condescending to be interested in tales about them now and then. During part of the Mansion years he attended a boarding school near Tyler, run by Professor Orr, later going to Southwestern University in Georgetown, so that the other children saw little of him except on holidays in Austin and during the summers, which all of them generally spent blissfully on Grandfather Stinson's farm.

Good schooling for all the children was one of James Hogg's most earnest concerns. Life at the Mansion, however, was an education in itself. The children, except on rare very formal occasions, were permitted to sit at the dinner table with guests; they had been well and firmly instructed in listening and not being heard, and for these times they were fairly successful in subduing their usual high spirits. Guests might include an old friend from East Texas, a Chinese diplomat, a famous actor or actress of the Shakespearean companies often visiting Austin, or a governor visiting from another state, and the dinner-table talk, lively with arguments, was usually on a high plane. The children heard a great deal about the much-discussed books, plays, and music of the day, as well as national and local public affairs.

In spite of their father's many out-of-town trips and his sometimes necessary preoccupation with business when in Austin, the children apparently felt no deprivation, probably because he was always so willing as a companion whenever it was possible. As mentioned earlier, he enjoyed having at least one of them as companion on his trips, and Will, and later Ima, went with him on campaign sorties and on tours to the prisons and other state institutions. All of the children enjoyed his habit of talking to men who could tell him about things he was not himself expert in; he was always eager for new knowledge, and hopeful that his companions were learning too. He never inflicted corporal punishment; Mrs. Hogg had a little switch, however, with which she would flick errant legs at times. In general, discipline was by example and absorption, although now and then when something further might be needed, the Governor was equal to the occasion. When Tom one day showed off some lewd words recently learned from playmates, his father acquired some charcoal, held the child tightly while decorating his mouth inside and out, then told him to look at himself in the mirror: "You look all smutty, and that is the way you'll look to people when you use ugly words." Although the wise father often seemed not to notice a misdemeanor, sooner or later he would make a remark that showed the offender the error was known; such remarks were usually couched in impressive and sometimes even amusing language, not easily forgotten, but he never corrected any of them in front of other people, having great respect for their feelings and pride. His relationship with them, as revealed in his many letters to them and in theirs to him, was one of true comradeship and unreserved affection.

Now had come the day when, free from the press of official duties, he hoped to enjoy his family life to its full extent. It is probable, however, that both he and his wife must have experienced some uneasiness that his restless initiative and inability to refrain from some degree of activity as his brothers' keeper would sooner or later precipitate him again into situations that would require much of his time. Their one main anxiety was the state of Sallie's health. Never robust, for a number of years she had been really unwell and her serious illness at the time of Tom's birth in the late summer of 1887 (during Hogg's first term as attorney general) had left her suffering from severe headaches and a sense of great fatigue much of the time. Various doctors kept suggesting

453

trips to watering resorts. At her husband's urging she would hopefully make the trips, sometimes taking one of the children with her, but any gain would prove to be illusory after she had been back home for a few days. Hogg devoutly hoped that the quieter life she could now lead would help. He also planned, as soon as his business affairs were set, to find a country place that would give her greater benefits of quiet, and that would provide the children a vacation spot where they could roam fields and woods and be less bother to her.

After they all settled down temporarily in the comfortable establishment on Eighth Street, the first order of business for Jim Hogg was the choice of location for his law practice. The ties to Tyler were very strong, but now that his best friend Horace Chilton had gone to Washington as United States Senator the "Athens of East Texas" seemed less attractive, although he had many other friends there. He also considered Dallas, with its great distributing companies and wealthy connections in and out of the state. There also he had good friends, even though many business interests in Dallas had opposed him. However, after the death of Sawnie Robertson in 1892 the greatest personal attraction for him there had vanished. His friend Judge Thomas Franklin of San Antonio had recently suggested that he come to join him in a partnership, but Hogg delayed a reply while he reviewed the other possibilities, particularly Austin. If he located in the capital he would be able to keep an ear to the ground on matters political and financial; more important, Austin offered excellent educational opportunities for Will and the "little ones." In his eventual letter to Judge Franklin he wrote: "I think this [Austin] is the place on that account.[5]

From the start, his legal business was good. Hogg was pleased that Colonel House would have some matters for him to attend to when he could make a journey to New York, and he was retained by the Taylors of Georgetown to be their agent to sell securities for the Georgetown Railroad, known as the "Link Line," that ran between Georgetown and Round Rock, a junction with the I.& G.N.[6] During late February and March he was busy drawing up articles of association and powers of attorney for various companies and also arranging interviews with projectors of companies who sought eastern financial support. He drew articles of incorporation for the Texas Sugar Refinery, for example,

---

[5] J. S. Hogg to Thomas Franklin, February 15 and 28, 1895, J. S. Hogg Let. Pr., 12, pp. 249 and 329; J. S. Hogg to Harry Kuteman, February 15, 1895, *ibid.*, p. 246.
[6] St. Clair Reed, *Texas Railroads*, p. 314; J. S. Hogg to C. J. Jones, General Manager G.&I. Railroad, February 27, 1895, J. S. Hogg Let. Pr., 12, p. 322.

and articles of association for the Texas Equitable Coal Company involving some five thousand acres of land that had clay for bricks, and was retained to represent the Oasis Irrigation Company, involving thirty thousand acres of land. He became a legal adviser at three thousand dollars a year for the Texas Promotion, Deposit, and Fidelity Company. He arranged to assist a Rockport landowner in finding a buyer for fifteen thousand acres, and promised to keep in mind banker George W. Brackenridge's desire to sell twenty thousand acres of ranch lands.[7]

When rumors began to spread that the "people's idol" was doing business for the railroads, a number of Hogg's friends wrote him in some alarm. In his replies he suggested that they knew him well enough not to believe that he would knowingly do anything which would hurt the people or Texas. His dealings were scrupulously honest and open, and he did not traffic with enterprises he could not approve of. When he negotiated with a Cleveland, Ohio, investment firm, for instance, and praised the prospectus for the Gulf and Interstate Railway Company, organized to run from Port Bolivar (Galveston) to Beaumont, about seventy miles, to tap the pinelands of that region, he wrote: "Remember that bonds can not be executed in advance of the completion of the road as a whole or in sections, and then they must bear the Ry. Commission's approval as honest, legitimate securities."[8] The language of some letters marked the amateur salesman, but it indicated faith in the product to be sold. When his old friend M. H. Gossett wrote that the Texas Trunk Line was being sold by action of a federal receiver, Hogg acted to try to organize a group which would keep it under Texas control. He knew the road was in a bad way, with "rocks, reefs, gulches, and canyons ahead of it," but he drew up plans to make W. H. Gaston of Dallas—one of the original charterers—trustee and to use the Exchange National Bank of Dallas as the place of deposit for funds accumulated for the use of the trustee at the public sale. He arranged to be the legal adviser for the line at five thousand dollars a year for ten years, making it very clear in the contract that he was not obligated to appear in trial courts against the state or the Railroad Commission or to lobby for legislation.[9] How-

[7] See a series of confidential letters to E. S. Lacy (Chicago), George Sealy (Galveston), and Gov. David R. Francis (St. Louis), March 7, 1895, J. S. Hogg Let. Pr., 12, pp. 337–341.

[8] J. S. Hogg to Deitz, Denison, and Prior (Cleveland, O.), February 27, 1895, J. S. Hogg Let. Pr., 12, p. 311; J. S. Hogg to W. N. Brazzil, February 19, 1895, J. S. Hogg Let. Pr., 12, p. 291.

[9] J. S. Hogg to M. H. Gossett, March 5, 1895, J. S. Hogg Let. Pr., 12, pp. 331–332; J. S. Hogg to Hugh M. Wilson, Secretary of Railway Age, March 2, 1895,

ever, money was hard to obtain for the project, partly because of the unabated depression, and the Trunk Line became a part of the Southern Pacific System later in 1895.[10]

As the 1895 legislative session proceeded, Hogg cheered from the side lines Culberson's successful efforts to balance the budget and to continue the reform program. He was disappointed, but not surprised, when the Supreme Court of the United States ended the long-protracted dispute over Greer County by awarding it to the Oklahoma Territory and announcing that settlement of this last frontier would be administered under federal supervision. From time to time friends asked him to help them with legislation, and he always refused firmly. Answering one such request from Judge Clint of Dallas he reminded Clint that he had *"consistently,* constantly and stubbornly refused to even discuss any measure or bill pending before the Legislature. My aversion to the lobby or the 'Third House' is so deep and well known that I will not go where its members daily swarm. To avoid the appearance of evil I keep clear of them, and up to date have not read a bill before the Legislature nor expressed myself on one."[11]

Considering the general depression throughout the country, Hogg realized he might be overoptimistic about his ability to obtain capital for Texas enterprises, but he believed that investors, if told the facts concerning the astoundingly rapid growth of the Southwest, were bound to be interested. He was anxious to be off on a selling mission, but hesitated because of his wife's health. Her headaches and general fatigue had not decreased to the extent he had hoped; yet when local physicians were again consulted they found no cause to offer other than the fact that the care of two small and very active boys was tiring, even with sister Ima to help.[12] As the March days went by, Sallie noted how restless her husband was, and, knowing that the shift to private practice had not been easy after his long experience on the larger and more exciting stage of public life, she strongly encouraged him to make the trip. Prior to his departure he had concluded with Judge James H. Robertson a law partnership—to be known as Hogg and Robertson. On March 24,

J. S. Hogg Let. Pr., 12, pp. 326–328, asking that a correction be made in previous issue, which misquoted him on the stock and bond law.

[10] Reed, *op. cit.,* p. 322.

[11] J. S. Hogg to C. F. Clint (Dallas), March 18, 1895, J. S. Hogg Let. Pr., 12, p. 364.

[12] Tom M. Campbell to J. S. Hogg, September 6, 1894, J. S. Hogg Let. Rec., XXXII, 194; personal interview with Miss Ima Hogg, June, 1954.

his forty-fourth birthday, Hogg left Austin, planning to stop at St. Louis, Chicago, New York, and Boston.

On the trip Hogg renewed many acquaintances made on the 1894 tour; he found, however, that investment money was hard to come by. In New York he believed he was finally on the trail of some substantial capital—when word reached the city that Governor Culberson had vetoed a major railroad consolidation bill that involved competing lines in southeast Texas and the expansion of the Southern Pacific System.[13] Never too happy about the Texas policies against monopoly and consolidation, the New York negotiators felt their fears confirmed, and the deals fell through. Proud that his successor was courageously upholding the laws and the Texas Constitution, Hogg sent his congratulations to Culberson: "By gatlins, . . . I would approve . . . [the] action if all my financial arrangements got smashed by it."[14]

By the middle of May, Hogg was impatiently waiting for other final yes's or no's. Although many men seemed interested in his stories of the rapidly growing Southwest, money was still not freely available for new speculations. As he later wrote to his clients, he was frequently led to believe that he was "close to all of the money needed but something would pull it out of the way."[15] He urged clients to be patient and not too anxious to sell, saying that more time might bring better results. However, a letter written on May 8 by Sallie had disturbed him, and he made up his mind that if no decisions had come through by the first of June he would go home; although the letter seemed cheerful and contained one of her characteristic flashes of humor, he sensed a change from her usual tone:

Austin, Texas
May 8th 1895

Dear Papa

I went to see Dr. [Thomas D.] Wooten yesterday and had him examine my lungs and chest well. He says I have bronchitis and catarrhal affection —that my lungs are all right. Now take your time, I am perfectly satisfied, contented and not impatient at your long stay. I know you are doing your best to succeed and I *fully* appreciate it all. I heard Mr. Foster will start for New York tonight. Mr. A. Stedman has his place on the Commission.

---

[13] Texas *Senate Journal* (1895), p. 548; Dallas *Morning News,* April 27, 1895, for editorial opposing Culberson's veto.

[14] Quoted in Rupert Richardson, *Texas,* p. 362.

[15] J. S. Hogg to C. J. Jones, June 13, 1895, J. S. Hogg Let. Pr., 12, p. 404.

Politics are getting *hot here*. I am glad you are gone. If you were here they would say you were at the bottom of it all. The little boys are well. Dr. Wooten says it will not hurt me to go to Col[orado] some time in June. Willie and Ima are well and sweet to Mama. Willie shows me the tenderest care. Well goodbye. I will write a long letter next time. With a world of love-kisses.

Affectionately,
Sallie[16]

I got the checks

In Hogg's absence various newspapers and old enemies in Texas seized all opportunities to misrepresent him, apparently hoping to tear him down in public esteem as soon as possible. The San Antonio *Express* in early May properly praised Governor Culberson's accomplishments with the Twenty-fourth Legislature and pointed out that he was more popular with the people than previously, then found room for a comment on Hogg:

He [Culberson] took advantage of every opportunity in the past few months to make himself solid with the boys from the forks of the creek. The latter have come to the conclusion that the 24th Legislature was an aggregation of . . . tools of corporate greed and that the "young man upstairs" came . . . to the rescue and snatched the State from beneath the teeth of the cormorants. Governor Hogg, their idol of the past, has eliminated himself from their list by becoming a bond broker and promoter of railroad schemes. . . . They swear by Charley now.[17]

However, neither the *Express* nor any other paper with similar intent was successful in driving a wedge between Hogg and Culberson.

Back home, Hogg was distressed at the continued failure of the doctors to find the cause or a cure for his wife's general debilitation, which was definitely more marked than formerly. The old panacea, a change of scenery, was called into play once more. Sallie was sent off to join the children at her father's farm in East Texas. The following letter to Ima suggests that Hogg at this point had a watchful wait-and-see attitude about the benefits of the trip for his wife:

[16] J. S. Hogg Fam. Let. Dr. Wooten was also President of the Board of Regents of the University of Texas. Former Railroad Commissioner L. L. Foster is referred to.

[17] San Antonio *Express*, editorial, May 3, 1895, quoted in Robert L. Wagner, "The Gubernatorial Career of Charles Allen Culberson," Master's thesis (the University of Texas, 1954), pp. 94, 95–103; Texas *House Journal, First Called Session* (1895), p. 23; *Report of the Adjutant General of the State of Texas, 1895–1896* (Austin, 1896), p. 11.

My Dear Daughter,   June 13, [189]5

Your sweet little letter of the 2d has reached me from New York to which place it was directed. I left there on the first day of June and nearly suffocated during the four days travel in getting home. The weather is scorching hot here and I am rather miserable over it. The little brownies you sent me by former letter were cute and interesting and I missed the lioness your last one mentioned. Now it is too bad for you to be spending your time in writing and drawing with only bad pencils and inferior paper. Tell your Mother that I shall accept it as a great favor if she will get some nice material, for you certainly deserve it. From all I can learn you and your Mama will fatten up so we will hardly know either of you. Won't that be nice? No news. Love to all. Kiss all the family for me. Goodbye.

Your Papa[18]

Toward the end of June, Hogg traveled to East Texas to bring his family back, but it was decided to leave Mike and Tom on the farm, probably because Sallie showed little improvement. Hogg had great confidence in Dr. W. L. Barker, whom he had selected to direct the State Hospital at San Antonio, and after the return to Austin he took his wife to see him. Dr. Barker called in Dr. Adolph Herff, the able son of famous Dr. Ferdinand Herff, as a consultant. Dr. Herff's diagnosis was that Mrs. Hogg was in the early stages of tuberculosis; he strongly recommended that she rest more and get away from the intense summer heat. Arrangements were quickly made for her to go to Pueblo, Colorado, where she would stay with Martha Frances Davis and her physician son, William Davis, whose own tuberculosis had been arrested after his removal to Colorado. Mike and Tom would remain with Grandfather Stinson; Ima would accompany her mother.

Reports soon came from Pueblo that the invalid seemed to be improving in the new environment, and her own letters were optimistic and had regained some of the old sparkle. To the big man sweltering in Texas this was precious news. The law firm of Hogg and Robertson was steadily increasing in popularity, and James Hogg felt that it might not be long until he could realize his dream of a substantial house in the country. If Colorado proved to be the cure for Sallie's illness, his happiness would be complete.

The large amount of business the new firm did in its first year is illustrated in a story former Governor Dan Moody, whose law partner was John B. Robertson, the son of Hogg's partner, enjoyed telling. When Hogg asked James H. Robertson to become his partner in the winter of

[18] J. S. Hogg Let. Pr., 12, p. 408.

1895, Robertson was somewhat reluctant to abandon the security of the district judgeship to which Hogg had appointed him in 1891. Hogg, a long-time admirer of Robertson, feeling that he was exactly the man for a successful law team, offered him a fifty-fifty sharing plan. However, Robertson knew how little cash the ex-Governor had and believed he would be safer with a guarantee of a fixed salary; they settled for a guarantee of three thousand dollars, which was the salary carried by the judgeship—a tidy sum in 1895. At this point in the story, Moody's eyes would gleam as he said, "The firm did about a thirty-thousand-dollar business in the first year."[19] Robertson was soon quite willing to make a new contract with his partner.

Hogg continued to give attention to the fight for free and unlimited coinage of silver. The election of Horace Chilton to the United States Senate had been a victory for the silver forces, and Chilton had immediately been effective in giving direction to the pro-silver program, probably not realizing that Governor Culberson and Congressman Joe Bailey were not so pleased that Hogg's mantle fell so gracefully upon the new senator. Nevertheless, all of the Texas pro-silver men knew they could not afford disunity, and in April, 1895, the silver Democrats held a meeting in Austin to make plans for future moves. This meeting resulted in the immediate calling of two conferences by gold Democrats, one in Austin, composed of the gold-advocating members of the legislature, and the other in Waco.

The Waco meeting, held on May 9, projected a platform that was one of the clearest statements ever made by the proponents of a gold standard; it professed their willingness to "favor honest bimetalism and the use of both gold and silver as the money of the country and the largest coinage of silver consistent with the safety of our financial system and the preservation of an honest dollar worth 100 cents at all times and in all countries."[20] Among the leaders at the Waco meeting were George Clark of Waco, George Zimpleman and Lewis Hancock of Austin, A. L. Matlock of Fort Worth, W. E. Hughes of Dallas, David A. Nunn of Crockett, H. D. McDonald of Paris, Leo Levi of Galveston, D. C. Giddings of Brenham, and H. M. Whitaker, Cone Johnson, Theodore Woldert, and former Governor R. B. Hubbard, all of Tyler. All of them were old foes of the Hogg administration.

Democratic members of the legislature favoring free and unlimited

[19] Personal interview with Governor Dan Moody, April, 1951; interview with Ben Robertson, November, 1958.
[20] Dallas *Morning News,* May 10, 1895; Ernest Winkler, *Platforms,* pp. 350 ff.

coinage, encouraged by Reagan, Hogg, Culberson, and Chilton, issued a statewide call for a meeting to be held at Fort Worth on August 6, 1895. Hogg was scheduled to speak, and as the time approached he busied himself enthusiastically with preparations for his address and with messages asking other influential silverites to meet him at the conference. This was the first time since his retirement from public life that he had allowed himself to enter the arena; he was enjoying the prospect thoroughly, when, on the first of August a telegram arrived from Pueblo. Sallie Hogg had taken a turn very much for the worse, and Dr. Davis urged that he and the three boys come up at once.

On August 2, just before leaving, he wrote to his nephew Dr. Francis Baylor Hogg (who had gone to medical school in Galveston with Hogg's financial help) telling him of the bad news, in the forlorn hope that as a recent graduate he might have learned something new that could be brought to bear on the dreadful malady. Death came to Sallie Hogg on September 20, 1895.[21] When Hogg and his children left Pueblo to bring her body to Austin for burial, Mrs. Davis traveled with them, ready once more to assume the care of motherless children as she had done long ago when her own mother died.

The faded letter book shows no more entries until October 8, on which day Hogg wrote to his friend J. W. Blake, chairman of the Democratic State Executive Committee and of the Free Silver Democratic League, asking to be excused from an address he had been invited to make during "Free Silver Day" at the Dallas Fair, "for the reason that I cannot feel at ease or comfortable in any crowd in my present condition."[22] A letter of October 14 to his sister Julia is eloquent of his grief:

Dear Sister: In all the storms of an eventful life the severest shock that I ever received was the death of poor Sallie. Indeed, since Mother's death when I was twelve, I had never been called to witness the death of a relative. It is all over, except now and then—almost hourly—when memory recalls the past and with it my wife's suffering and death compared to her gentleness and virtues. Then my feelings overcome me. She never spoke an unkind word to me in her life and never had I to account to others for a word or act of hers. God knows if all men were so blessed the earth would be more like heaven. My ambition is to raise my children after her model. If I succeed the world will be much better for it.[23]

[21] Austin *Daily Statesman*, September 22, 1895.
[22] J. S. Hogg to J. W. Blake, October 8, 1895, J. S. Hogg Let. Pr., 12, p. 528.
[23] J. S. Hogg to Sister [Julia Ferguson], October 14, 1895, J. S. Hogg Let. Pr., 12, p. 530.

461

He did not know at this time how carefully his wife had tried to insure that he would have help in his efforts with the children. During the last weeks, when it became apparent to Sallie that she might not recover, she had had many long talks with thirteen-year-old Ima, preparing the child to take care of her father and Tom and Mike, and to build her own life to reflect the values that Sallie had lived by.[24]

A short while after the funeral Hogg decided that for a time at least it would be best to send Ima and the little boys away to school. Mrs. Davis (called "Aunt Fannie" by the children) went with the trio to San Marcos, where they were entered in Coronal Institute. Hogg took a suite (which now bears his name) at the Driskill Hotel in Austin, finding some solace in his busy practice and in the weekends he spent with the children, either joining them in San Marcos or having them come by train to Austin. His companionship with Will, who had just entered the University of Texas Law School,[25] was even closer than it had formerly been. It may have been at this time that the bar episode, one of the leading "Hogg-lore" items, took place. Hogg had heard a rumor that Will was a visitor to one of the more popular Congress Avenue drinking places. On a day when he and Will were driving in the carriage, Hogg drew up in front of the saloon involved, alighted, and prepared to enter the building. Will, knowing his father's self-restriction about not appearing in public drinking places, watched him incredulously, then begged him not to go in. Thereupon Hogg said mildly, "Where you go, I can go, for I should like to meet your friends." Will insisted that it was not proper for his father to be seen there—people still thought of him as the governor of Texas, who should set a standard of behavior. Hogg finally consented to drive on, and nothing further was said about the matter.

In the late fall of 1895 the silver campaign was intensifying. At the August convention in Waco, Congressman Joe Bailey had been made permanent chairman and young Cullen F. Thomas of Waco was selected as secretary. Commissioner Reagan, Wynne, Duncan of Tyler, J. S. Dougherty of Houston, and Hogg's brother-in-law, H. C. Ferguson of Denton, had been among the Convention leaders who charged President Cleveland and his following with attempting to:

overturn the established creed of the Democracy upon the financial question, and to place the business interests of this country within the control of

[24] Personal interview with Miss Ima Hogg, June, 1954.
[25] Austin *Daily Statesman*, September 26, 1895.

the concentrated money power and above the laws and will of the people; the proposed issue of $500,000,000 of gold bonds in time of profound peace, and the withdrawal and cancellation of $500,000,000 of greenbacks and National currency from circulation, and the substitution of National bank currency therefor, is a proposition so startling to the Democratic party as to cause just alarm.[26]

The Texas advocates of the gold standard were charged with organizing to defeat the will of the masses and to create discord within Democratic ranks in order to win the next election. Waco Resolution 9 was indicative of the growing bitterness resulting from the depression and the money issue:

We denounce as unwarranted the declaration of certain advocates of the gold standard in this State to the effect that the friends of free silver contemplate or desire the disruption of the Democratic party, or to take action independently of the organization of said party in this State, and conceive and express the belief that our only hope for financial reform in the interest of the masses of the people is by loyalty to the organization and precepts of the Democratic party.[27]

Banker J. W. Blake of Mexia, a "white blackbird" (the term applied to the few prominent bankers who were for free silver—the white metal), who, as chairman of the Free Silver Democratic League in Texas, had arranged with Texas State Fair officials for the "Silver Day" at the Dallas Fair, wanted Hogg to be present even though he had declined to be one of the speakers. Governor Stone of Missouri and William Jennings Bryan were scheduled to speak. There had been some delay in getting an affirmative answer from Bryan, but it was finally forthcoming when Dr. Charles M. Rosser of Dallas wrote him, saying that many of the Democratic leaders who would be delegates to the 1896 National Convention would be present at the Fair.

Bryan arrived in Dallas the last of October, and was a guest in Dr. Rosser's home. He was entirely outspoken about his desire to receive the Democratic nomination for President.[28] His return to Congress having

[26] Fort Worth *Daily Gazette,* August 7, 1895; Winkler, *Platforms,* pp. 353–357. See also Bailey's speech on the insufficiency of gold in *Congressional Record,* December 28, 1895, and a speech criticizing Ambassador Bayard and President Cleveland, *ibid.,* March 20, 1896.

[27] Fort Worth *Daily Gazette,* August 7, 1895.

[28] Charles M. Rosser, M.D., *The Crusading Commoner* (Dallas, Mathis, Van Nort and Company, 1937), pp. 19 ff.

been opposed by Cleveland,[29] Bryan was now speaking throughout the country on the silver issue, hoping that the silver forces might control the Convention and wrest control from the gold bugs, who were under the leadership of Cleveland, Secretary of the Treasury Carlisle, Senator David B. Hill of New York, and Senator William F. Vilas of Wisconsin.[30]

Just before his speech on "Silver Day," Bryan met for the first time James Hogg, Senator Chilton, Governor Culberson, T. M. Campbell, Richard Wynne, and J. W. Blake. He made a favorable impression on the friends of silver, but Hogg, Bailey, and Chilton still stood behind Richard Bland of Missouri, the leader of the silver bloc in Congress. However, by appearing in Dallas, Bryan had made himself known in the Southwest, and especially as a fighter for silver.

Bryan proceeded to wage a strenuous speaking campaign throughout the West and South, trying to line up delegates who would support him for President at the 1896 Convention in Chicago. He had concluded that, since it seemed likely no Southerner could be nominated, Southern Democrats would prefer a President from the West rather than risk another from the East. His conclusion was supported, at least in part, by a mid-1896 letter Hogg wrote in answer to one from his nephew in Colorado. Dr. Davis had written that the people of Colorado appreciated what Hogg was doing to line up silver delegates and, further, that his stand with Governor Altgeld against Cleveland had made him acceptable to many Colorado Democrats as a presidential nominee. Hogg answered:

Sectional timidity on the Southern side and political *audacity* on the other will for a long time make my chances for the Presidency too slim to even justify the remotest ambition in that direction on my part. Though not connected with the war I was *Born* in the South! This excuse by our own people is really a greater obstacle than any objection the Northern people would ever raise.[31]

Hogg had received other letters urging him to seek national office, but, as he told Dr. Davis, they were considered only "from the standpoint of pride and gratitude" and had not "stimulated the slightest hope." De-

[29] Richard L. Metcalf, *Life and Patriotic Services of William J. Bryan* (Chicago, Edgewood, 1896), pp. 163–166, 187.

[30] Horace S. Merrill, *William Freeman Vilas, Doctrinaire Democrat* (Madison, State Historical Society of Wisconsin, 1954), pp. 224–244.

[31] J. S. Hogg to Dr. W. B. Davis, July 1, 1896, J. S. Hogg Let. Pr., 13, pp. 208–209.

spite these sentiments such political interests were good for a man who was making a fourfold adjustment in this first year out of office: (1) the selection of a permanent town of residence, (2) the choice of a law partner, (3) overcoming the loneliness following the death of his wife, and (4) assuming full responsibility for rearing four children—Will, Ima, Mike and Tom.

None other than William J. Bryan wrote Hogg in February 1896:

I believe that you have all the qualifications necessary for president and there is no man whom I would rather support than yourself. Whether you secure the nomination or not remains to be seen, and whether you could be elected if nominated is still another matter. I write to you frankly because I know that your interest in democratic principles is greater than your ambition to be president, and therefore you would not stand in the way of the success of any more available candidate if at the convention you found that you could not be nominated. . . .[32]

This, of course, was a transparent bid for Hogg's support, for Bryan knew the influence the former governor could personally exert. In 1893, noting Hogg's firm and eloquent sugar bounty veto, he had written to thank him for the strong statement of the Democratic position. Hogg liked the earnest campaigning of "The Commoner," and found himself noting that "Silver Dick" Bland seemed to be taking Southern support for granted. As for Hogg's own interest in the Presidency, there exists no shred of evidence that it went any farther than expressed in the letter to Will Davis. He was no doubt gratified, as any man would be, to find himself discussed as a possible candidate, but it is clear that he meant what he said, on leaving the governor's chair, when he spoke of standing on the threshold of "my permanent retirement to private life."

A trenchant proof of his decision to live as a private citizen was established on May 29, 1896, when he purchased a roomy, two-and-a-half-story house standing on a generous half block of land at the northeast corner of Rio Grande and nineteenth.[33] The house commanded a view down the slope toward the Capitol and was near the University and the West Avenue home of Colonel House. Two rooms on the top floor were to be Will's domain while he was at law school; they were soon jammed

[32] W. J. Bryan to J. S. Hogg, February 24, 1896, J. S. Hogg Let. Rec., XXIV, 125–126. First published in Cotner (ed.), *Addresses of James Stephen Hogg,* p. 444, n. 1.

[33] Personal interviews with Miss Ima Hogg and Sterling Fulmore, Sr., June, 1954; Austin *Statesman,* March 4, 1906; Pat McKenna, "The Hogg Mansion," term paper (the University of Texas, 1955), H.C., pp. 3 ff.

with books on a variety of subjects (to Ima's awe) and there he studied nearly every night, often far past midnight. Aunt Fannie looked after the housekeeping and the children, who were overjoyed to be in a house of their own again. A new supply of pets was accumulated rapidly, including all sorts of barnyard animals, a splendid white horse, presented to Hogg by Governor Taylor of Tennessee (which Hogg permitted Ima, but not the little boys, to ride), and at one time a bear and a fawn. There were also the famous ostriches, Jack and Jill, often ridden by the children—but not by Hogg or any of his guests, as hostile newspapers later insisted in articles and in clever, lampooning caricatures. The dogs at Nineteenth Street and Rio Grande were usually hunting breeds, trained to accompany the various expeditions Hogg soon began to plan for himself and Mike and Tom. Hogg also renewed his interest in gardening, both flowers and vegetables now being his special care. In the flower garden he would find each day, if possible, a blossom for his lapel buttonhole; his wife had always placed a flower there, and to the end of his life he kept up the custom in her memory. There were also many fruit trees on the property, a great spur to his ambitions as a horticulturist.[34]

Almost before the house was in order after moving day, its proud and happy owner began issuing invitations to relatives and friends to "come down for a visit"—whether for "a day," "a week," or "several months." His pleasure in hospitality was having full rein; the presence of many guests served another purpose, too, in keeping him from dwelling too long on his loneliness without Sallie. Of the children at this time, Ima seemed to be his particular joy, although he never played favorites. She was becoming a charming young girl, with her blond hair and delicately tinted complexion, and her steadily developing musical talent. Hogg commented in a letter to his brother John, "she is the sunshine of my household."

The ex-governor continued to be deluged with invitations—to sponsor, to comment, to make an address. He stood off as many as he could; it was very evident that he wanted to stay home and enjoy his new home and his "new-found" family. To the silver fight, however, he felt thoroughly committed. A heavy barrage for party control was being laid down by both wings of the Democrats all through the spring of 1896. Deciding they could not win the primaries in June, 1896, the Texas gold bugs met at Dallas in April and voted to organize separately for sending

---

[34] Ima Hogg, "Life in the Governor's Mansion," *passim.*

a delegation to the National Convention and for putting up a slate of their own. This they did at Austin in June and at Waco in August, and George Clark was appropriately selected to head the gold delegation to Chicago.[35]

Hogg was thoroughly alarmed at these developments. The "Regular" Democratic organization was scheduled to meet at Austin on June 23–24, and Hogg made arrangements to go over the drafts of the platform and resolutions with Chairman Blake prior to the meeting.[36] As the Austin meeting opened, William F. Ramsey, of Cleburne, was temporary chairman; Senator Chilton's cousin, H. G. Robertson of Dallas, became permanent chairman. The delegates selected to attend the National Convention included Congressman Joe Bailey, Governor Culberson, Senator Chilton, John Duncan, J. W. Blake, John H. Reagan, and James S. Hogg. The delegation was instructed (1) to work for free and unlimited coinage of silver, (2) to oppose the issuance of interest-bearing bonds by the federal government in times of peace, and (3) to demand that the federal debt be diminished and fully paid off. An effort to praise Cleveland was voted down; Hogg and Reagan were in a nononsense fighting mood. That the defeat taken at the hands of the gold bugs in 1894 would not be repeated in 1896 was definitely indicated when the report of Reagan's platform committee was adopted.[37]

Despite the fundamental victories, something unforeseen happened at the Austin Convention which merited close attention from Hogg and Senator Chilton. During the recent session of Congress, Bailey's speeches in Washington on the tariff and on money and his blatant criticism of President Cleveland had kept him very much in a limelight, apparently not unnoted by Texans. When the count for delegates at large was taken, Bailey had more votes than Hogg, Culberson, or Chilton, respectively. Bailey's biographer, Sam Acheson, marked this as an open challenge to the Hogg-Chilton supremacy:

Bailey had made his first raid into the Hogg domain, and it had been successful. Instantly tongues were wagging; surely Bailey's ambition was now reaching beyond the bounds of the congressional district. It could be nothing less than a place in the United States Senate.[38]

Senator Mills' term would expire in 1899, and Chilton must stand for

---

[35] Austin *Daily Statesman*, June 24, 1896; Dallas *Morning News*, August 26, 1896; Winkler, *Platforms*, pp. 366–370, 389–391.
[36] J. S. Hogg to J. W. Blake, June 19, 1896, J. S. Hogg Let. Pr., 13, p. 172.
[37] Austin *Daily Statesman*, June 24 and 25, 1896; Winkler, *op. cit.*, pp. 370–376.
[38] Sam Acheson, *Joe Bailey*, p. 70.

reelection in 1901. Culberson was in line for the 1899 selection. Would Bailey risk a contest with Culberson or Chilton? John E. Thornton, the Dallas *News* correspondent, reported sometime after the Austin meeting that "Bailey said to me during the recent silver pow-wow that it would be useless for any man to deny that he would like to represent Texas in the American House of Lords."[39] The Austin incident had provoked talk and concern, but there was not yet an open rupture. Culberson, as governor, would head the Texas delegation to the National Convention; Hogg and Bailey were selected to go to Chicago early to make arrangements for the delegation, and Hogg urged Bailey to meet him at Texarkana so that they might make the journey together.[40]

The National Democratic Convention convened at Chicago on July 7, 1896. James Hogg was already busy helping to organize the silver majority, which was determined not to be deprived of nominating even the temporary chairman. Although the Texas delegation was pledged to Bland for President, Senator Chilton moved in caucus that the delegation sponsor William J. Bryan for temporary chairman, to give him an opportunity to be heard by the Convention; if Bland could not be nominated, Hogg and Chilton wanted Bryan's personality to be fresh in the minds of all delegates. (The Dallas *News* reporter, Colonel Bill Sterett, was quoted as saying that Hogg in caucus described Bryan as being "a most profound thinker, a most lordly orator, and a most beautiful man." The superlatives and the word "beautiful" were not customary in Hogg's vocabulary, however. Sterett was also quoted as reporting that after Reagan spoke in Bryan's behalf "several of Hogg's old reliables trailed in with bouquets for the Boy Orator of the Platte."[41]) Bailey challenged Chilton's motion, declaring that Bryan was unsound on free silver (an interesting remark, since Bailey himself had tutored Bryan four years before). He also held that Bryan was not a Democrat—having advocated government ownership of railroads and telegraphs and threatening to bolt if the free silver plank was not adopted. It is likely that Bailey's opposition was based partly on his resentment of Bryan as an oratorical rival; both men had large, unusual mouths and excellent speaking voices. Chilton's motion was not approved, but the Senator was empowered to deal further.

In the prolonged fight to prevent the national gold wing, which controlled the National Executive Committee, from electing forceful David

[39] *Ibid.*
[40] J. S. Hogg to J. W. Bailey, July 2, 1896, J. S. Hogg Let. Pr., 13, p. 213.
[41] Dallas *Morning News*, July 7, 1896; Acheson, *op. cit.*, p. 73.

B. Hill of New York as Convention chairman, John Duncan, Hogg's former law partner in Tyler, became a leader in the successful fight to substitute Senator John W. Daniel of Virginia. Texans knew Hill; Hogg had sized him up in 1892 and had originally preferred him to Cleveland. But now Hill had disappointed his Texas admirers by accepting the pro-gold policy. Richard Coke while still in the U. S. Senate once remarked: "Hill is a wonderful man. He's bigger than we thought when he first came to the Senate. And he'll not only fight, but by nature he's a desperado. If Hill had been brought up in Texas, I reckon he'd a' killed a dozen men by now."[42]

Very soon after Senator Daniel took the chair Hogg was recognized to introduce the resolution providing that each state delegation could name one member to each of the great committees: Credentials, Permanent Organization, Rules and Order of Business, and Platform. Furthermore, it was provided that all resolutions relating to the platform and all communications were to be referred "without reading or debate, to the Committee on Platform, and that the credentials of each delegation be delivered to the member of the Committee on Credentials from such delegation."[43] The Texas representatives on the four committees were J. W. Blake, John M. Duncan, W. W. Gatewood, and John H. Reagan —all personal friends of Hogg and champions of silver.

At the second morning session, after the opening prayer and while waiting for the Committee on Credentials to report, John Martin of Kansas moved that ex-governor Hogg be requested to address the Convention. When Hogg came forward, he called upon the Democrats to consider their great mission to serve the American people; further debate on internal differences must be abandoned in favor of decisions, reached in the spirit of friendliness in order to assure unity and victory over the Republicans:

The American people cannot in self-respect tolerate this great class-courtier; this masked coquetter, this great class-maker and mass smasher, this great bounty giver and poor-house maker, called the Republican party. Upon three grounds alone, to say nothing of other good and potent reasons, the people cannot and will not tolerate the return of the Republican party to power. . . . If we will unite, we can carry consternation, disaster and defeat into the Republican ranks. The three grounds . . . are these:

[42] For a sharp delineation of Hill's character see Alfred H. Lewis, *Richard Croker* (New York, New York Life Publishing Company, 1901), pp. 288–297.
[43] *Official Proceedings of the National Democratic Convention at Chicago, 1896* (Chicago, Logansport, Wilson, Humphries, and Company, 1896), p. 109.

First: It proposes to filter through the fingers of the rich men to the wageworker, under the pretext of taxation for revenue, the paltry stipends they receive.

Second: It proposes to give bounties from the public treasury to wealthy planters under the pretense of giving sugar to the poor.

Third: It proposes to belittle Americanism and to assert the inability of the people of this government to control themselves by yielding to the will of the crowned heads of other countries the regulation of our Federal finances.[44]

Elaborating these points, he inveighed against centralism, pools, trusts, and federal judges who, "with unconstitutional writs backed by federal bayonets," attempted to strike down labor organizations. At considerable length he went over the Texas opposition to the sugar bounty feature of the McKinley tariff, then discussed the need for careful tariff revision, since the Wilson-Gorman Act had not gone far enough and the income tax feature had been declared unconstitutional.[45]

He quoted from memory the 1896 Republican platform on money (the words he omitted are given here in brackets): "We are [, therefore,] opposed to the free coinage of silver except by international agreement with the leading commercial nations of the world, [which we pledge ourselves to promote,] and until such agreement [can be obtained] the existing gold standard must be continued [preserved]."[46] He then said he wanted to know why the Republican Party did not "come out like men and say that the gold standard is best for the American people" instead of hiding their real purpose. Dependence upon foreign nations created a big "if . . . mountain high. . . . Why humiliate the proud American spirit of our fathers by this false, this useless, this criminal confession, that our people are not able to run their own financial system without the consent of crowned heads?" In conclusion, Hogg called attention to the wavering Republican position; in 1892 their platform had declared that "the American people from tradition and interest" favored bimetallism, and they had promised to maintain "parity of values of the two metals."[47]

When Governor Altgeld of Illinois spoke, after emphasizing Mark Hanna's influence in the nomination of William McKinley at the Republican Convention, he followed Hogg's line of attack, saying that the

[44] *Ibid.*, pp. 115–116.

[45] *Pollock* v. *Farmers Loan and Trust Co.*, 158 U.S. 601 (1895).

[46] South Trimble (comp.), *Platforms of the Two Great Political Parties, 1856–1912* (Washington, n. pub., 1912), p. 101.

[47] *Ibid.*, pp. 114–121.

Republican Convention had declared in favor of "the present single standard of English gold, a standard which the London newspapers have complimented. They are delighted with it. An Englishman always feels good when he sees a prospect of getting more sweat and more blood out of the American people."[48] Altgeld considered the Republican tariff plank a "little dough to hide the hook." He also reminded the delegates that the people were in earnest and there must be no straddling on platform or candidate: "Gentlemen, it is not the time for compromise." (Altgeld was the man Hogg really wanted to carry the Democratic banner, and prior to the Convention had so informed him. Altgeld had replied that since he was not native-born he was ineligible.[49])

There was great concern over the outcome of the labors of the Committee on Platform and Resolutions. Bryan of Nebraska, Senator James K. Jones of Arkansas, and "Pitchfork" Ben Tillman of South Carolina would defend silver, and Senator Hill of New York, Senator Vilas of Wisconsin, and ex-Governor William Russell of Massachusetts would defend the pro-gold minority report.[50] At this point Hogg performed a significant service for Bryan, although the Texas delegation was still pledged to vote for Bland, at least on the first ballot.

The setting for Hogg's action was as follows. Not long before the Convention, Dr. Rosser of Dallas, who was not a delegate but would come to Chicago at Bryan's personal request, had gone to South Carolina, ostensibly to study the operation of that state's new liquor law under the State Dispensary System. Chilton and Culberson had given him letters of introduction to Senator Ben Tillman, since Rosser's actual mission was to enlist Tillman's support for Bryan. One evening Tillman and he dined with Governor J. G. Evans at the Mansion; Rosser came away feeling that Tillman was in earnest when he said, "Bryan is the biggest man among us; he is the wisest man in our party."[51] As it turned out, South Carolina instructed its delegation for Tillman, who was, however, free to use the votes for Bryan.

When the Committee on Platform announced the line-up for speeches, it appeared that Bryan was to speak first. This he preferred not to do. He wanted to follow Senator Hill, whom he designated as "the brains of the opposition." Rosser went to Hogg, not only because

48 *Ibid.*, p. 128.
49 J. S. Hogg to John P. Altgeld, June 1, 1896, Let. Pr., 13, p. 121.
50 Francis Simkins, *Tillman*, pp. 334–337; *Official Proceedings of the National Democratic Convention, 1896*, pp. 119 ff.
51 Rosser, *op. cit.*, p. 34.

he was a member of the Texas delegation, but because of his "intuitive as well as reasoning ability, . . . that rare quality common sense, and his associations were fruitful of ideals and purposes in consonance with those for which Bryan stood and labored." Rosser then said:

I found that Hogg was already considering Bryan as the best hope of Democracy, and would be pleased to be of any possible service. He soon conferred with James K. Jones, senior senator from Arkansas, who had charge of the discussion in favor of the majority Committee report, and found him enthusiastically favorable to Bryan. Fortunately for the success of the situation, Senator Jones had already been appealed to by Senator Hill not to be followed in the debate by Senator Tillman, of "Pitchfork" fame, with whom he had experienced unpleasant contacts in the Senate, and so the exchange desired by Mr. Bryan was more than agreeable to all parties concerned.

I am not sure that Mr. Bryan ever learned of that interview with Senator Tillman or the influence which Governor Hogg exercised upon Senator Jones as his friend. What I know of importance is that Senator Jones very wisely designated Bryan to close the debate and that Senator Tillman was most amenable to any arrangement that Mr. Bryan might prefer.[52]

That night Bryan and Rosser enjoyed a late supper at the Saratoga Restaurant. Despite the banners displayed at the Convention for Bland and the ardent manifestations for Governor Horace Boies of Iowa, Bryan was confident that the crowd would be for him the next evening after he had made what he promised would be "the greatest speech of my life . . . in reply to Senator Hill." Still later that night Rosser talked to a member of the Texas delegates, who considerably deflated his optimism. Governor Culberson in fact hurt Rosser's feelings by saying that the doctor looked "on Bryan as a tin god." Rosser also got the impression that Senator Chilton was not too favorably disposed toward his hero. (Rosser's impression was correct; even after the great address Chilton's keenly analytical mind considered Bryan a "political adventurer.") Rosser tried to win over Attorney General M. M. Crane by having him meet Bryan after breakfast the day of the speech.[53]

[52] Rosser, *op. cit.*, pp. 34–38. Cf. William J. Bryan, *Memoirs* (New York, John C. Winston Company, 1925), p. 111; Paxton Hibben, *The Peerless Leader: William Jennings Bryan*, pp. 183 ff.
[53] Rosser, *op. cit.*, p. 40. Tom Finty, Jr., correspondent for the Galveston *Tribune* listened to Rosser and sent out a story predicting Bryan's nomination "at a time when other correspondents refused to believe that it was possible." For

"Pitchfork" Tillman opened the platform speeches in his usual blunt way and at length, getting the silver forces off to a poor start. By the time Senator Hill had finished his excellent speech, the gold bugs were feeling fine. Remarks were audible from listeners in the gallery that some did not want to stay to hear "that crazy Populist, Bill Bryan from Nebrasky."[54]

Not long after Bryan began speaking, these and others had changed their minds in a way that made history. With no man present able to say exactly why, the enthusiasm mounted rapidly, until a near-hysteria was sweeping the hall time and time again after each such telling point as Bryan's reply to Senator Hill:

You come to us and tell us that we will disturb your interests; I reply to you that you have already disturbed our business interests and that you have made too limited in its application the term "business men." We hold that the country doctor or the crossroads lawyer is as much a business man as the corporation attorney of New York. We hold that the clerk behind the counter is as much a business man as his employer; we hold that the farmer who goes out in the morning and toils all day, and who goes out in the springtime and toils all summer, is as much a business man as the financial magnate who sits upon the Board of Trade to bet upon the price of grain.[55]

At the moment of his final graphic picture of mankind being crucified "upon a cross of gold," the whole Convention went wild. In the midst of the commotion Senator Daniel of Virginia, Governor Altgeld of Illinois, Governor Thomas of Colorado, James Hogg, and a few others huddled together for a quick consultation, and one of them was saying: "There is no doubt about it. Bryan is the man and we must nominate him by acclamation and do it now."[56] Arthur E. Sewall of Maine, who would become the second man of the Democratic ticket, urged that action be taken before the evening adjournment. Bryan preferred to wait for the regular order of business, believing that he had now nothing to fear from "Silver Dick" Bland, who would be handicapped by his age and the fact he was from a former slave state.[57]

Congressman Joe Bailey's part see Dallas *Morning News,* July 19 and August 20, 1896, J. W. Bailey Papers, Dallas Historical Society, Hall of State, Dallas, Texas.
[54] Rosser, *op. cit.,* p. 48.
[55] *Official Proceedings . . . 1896,* p. 228.
[56] Rosser, *op. cit.,* p. 49.
[57] William V. Byars, *An American Commoner* [Richard Parks Bland] (Columbia, E. W. Stephens, 1900), p. 233, says that the fact that Bland was from a former slave state was more important in defeating him than his advanced age.

Bryan's self-confidence was extraordinary; a passage in his book *The First Battle* tells, however, the role that James Hogg played in reinforcing his confidence during the famous speech:

Two faces stand out as in memory I look over the hall. Ex-Governor Hogg, of Texas, was a large man, probably 6 feet 2 or 3 inches tall and heavy. He wore no beard and his face was beaming with delight. He stood by the aisle at my left, and about the same relative position on my right stood Ollie James, a member from Kentucky, also a large man with a smooth face. As I turned from one side to the other, these two faces impressed me, . . . they were in full sympathy with the sentiments to which I gave expression.[58]

When the time came for nominations Congressman Bailey of the Texas delegation made one of the speeches seconding Bland's nomination. Out of the many candidates, Bland was in the lead for several ballots, then Bryan began to gain. Bailey was furious; Hogg was pleased. Bailey's ire increased to the point that he threatened to resign from Congress rather than support Bryan, since he considered him too close to the Populists. The Texas delegation, being under the unit rule, did not vote for Bryan until his nomination was assured. Dr. Rosser wrote:

It is certain that a majority of those composing the delegation were not merely favorable to Congressman Bland, but also opposed to Bryan. It was said that Governor James Stephen Hogg tried, after the Cross of Gold oration, to swing the Texas delegation to Bryan after the first or second ballot; but, as I now recall, he, alone, among the Texas delegates stood stoutly for the statesman who was about to come into his own.[59]

After the Convention, Hogg worked hard for Bryan, helping to offset the influence of the Clark-Cleveland forces, which were supporting John M. Palmer of Illinois and Simon B. Buckner of Kentucky; this "simon-pure" gold group was dubbed by the "Regular" Democrats "The Republican Aid Society." Joe Bailey still declared that he would not support Bryan and threatened not to stand for re-election to Congress. This worried Bryan; he did not know, however, the extent of the local Populist-Democratic feud with which Bailey had to contend in his home district or that friends of Bailey, without much difficulty, were convincing him that he should run again. When Bryan asked Hogg if he

[58] Bryan, *First Battle*, p. 115.
[59] Rosser, *op. cit.*, pp. 39–40. See also Allan Johnson and Dumas Malone, *Dictionary of American Biography* (New York, Charles Scribner's Sons, 1943), VI, 577–578.

should plan to speak in Texas to counteract the Bailey defection and the danger from Palmer, Hogg assured him that Texas was "safe—more than safe" and wisely urged him to spend his time elsewhere, "especially in Indiana, Illinois and Michigan."[60]

When McKinley won the election in November, the Democrats were dashed, but not discouraged. Citizen Hogg would still advocate free silver and give his staunch political support to Bryan. The two men had become firm friends; Bryan some years later revealed that, had he been elected in 1896, he would have asked Hogg to be his Attorney General.[61] And strange to relate, Congressman Bailey, who had made his first open break with the Progressive forces, joined Bryan in the odd fight they would carry on against imperialism in 1898 and 1900.

[60] J. S. Hogg to W. J. Bryan, July 24, 1896, Let. Pr., 13, p. 270.
[61] Interview with Miss Ima Hogg, April, 1958.

CHAPTER XVII

The Conservative Trend: Bailey Challenges the
Hogg-Chilton Leadership

JAMES HOGG continued to take solid pleasure in his status as a busy partner of Hogg and Robertson and as a private citizen. At first unable to find a suitable office on the Avenue, he had located at 105 West Eighth. Soon however, Hogg and Robertson were at 722 Congress Avenue. He was fortunate in being able to eat and have his cake at will; otherwise, it is possible that his status would not so well have satisfied him. The deluge of correspondence never slackened, and he kept a private secretary steadily busy. Requests came to him on every conceivable matter: political endorsements, pardons for criminals, job recommendations, donations both to causes and to persons. He was always being asked to attend such functions as barbecues, fairs, and reunions, with the further hope that he would address the gathering; these invitations he refused tactfully when he could. Moreover, the idea that he could be induced again to run for public office would not die. The most usual suggestion was a seat in the United States Senate, but all manner of other offices or ex-officio political posts were also brought up. Hogg would listen to none of the candidacy talk. Again and again he wrote such answers as this: "I unhesitatingly refuse to become a candidate or accept the [senatorial] office for I am financially unable to do so. My practice is good, and I am fast retrieving the losses caused by my eight years service."[1] Or, "To put it in a nut shell, I am too poor to hold the distinguished position of U.S. Senator. While I do not live for money, I feel that I owe something to the education and raising of my children."[2]

The house on Nineteenth Street was always gaining some improvement, inside or out. In the fall of 1897, Hogg purchased three lots adjoining his property, providing room for more of the horticultural experiments with which he was always fascinated. Whenever he traveled, he

[1] J. S. Hogg to W. A. Shaw (Dallas), June 14, 1895, J. S. Hogg Let. Pr., 12, p. 414.
[2] J. S. Hogg to Richard Coke, April 27, 1896, J. S. Hogg Let. Pr., 13, pp. 5–6.

476

often brought home seeds from fruit he had eaten at a hotel or restaurant; melon seeds from New York's Waldorf Hotel, for instance, did famously in his garden. He also acquired several hives of bees, concerning which he wrote to a friend, "I shall either raise plenty of honey, or get stung every day in the experiment." One of his few laments was that Texas summers were increasingly less easy on him, and, when he could no longer find coolness even on the side gallery of the house that had been well positioned to catch any breeze, he would go north in search of coolness, as he did in the summer of 1897, when he and Ima spent some weeks at a lake-shore hotel in Chicago.

It was on one of his northern trips during these years that he wrote to Mike and Tom a letter which well illustrated a philosophy he had been living ever since the events of his late boyhood had shown him the bitter perils of sectionalism:

I am the guest of Mr. Glidden of Lowell, Mass. His wife and Mr. Cummings and several other Boston and Lowell people stay most of the time with us. They are all intelligent, good, patriotic, and hospitable people. I only wish that you two nice boys could see these people as I have. Some day you must do so. Then you will not have *sectional prejudice*—the most inexcusable of all prejudice. When people hate each other on account of the sections in which they live they do so from ignorance. You boys must become broad and sensible enough not to be guilty of such a wrong.[3]

In the fall of 1897, Will Hogg opened his own law office in San Antonio. The firm of Hogg and Robertson in Austin had steadily prospered, and the former governor was justifiably proud of this success; however, at the start of Will's venture he remarked to a friend, "Should he succeed, my pride will be more gratified than it has ever been by any successful act of my life."

Although Hogg steered warily around the many direct requests for his aid in this and that political matter, he was of course always available for counselings with his old friends, such as Reagan, Chilton, and Culberson. Colonel House was a near neighbor, and, although the financial issues of Culberson's 1894 campaign had somewhat dissipated the former intimacy between Hogg and House, a pleasant friendship still stood. Hogg knew, however, that House had not been enthusiastic over Bryan in 1896 and had not enjoyed his nomination—further, that he had no interest in a future nomination for him. Hogg bided his time, hoping that House could be converted when necessary.

[3] J. S. Hogg to Mike and Tom Hogg, August 26, 1896, Fam. Let.

In April, 1898, when the war with Spain developed over Cuba, the *Maine*, and the Philippines, both Hogg and Bryan volunteered for duty. Bryan was the Colonel of a Nebraska regiment, but saw no combat duty other than that of fighting mosquitoes in a southern camp. The army found no place for Hogg, which is not surprising considering his 275 pounds and his 47 years of age.

Fortunately, the war was over in a matter of weeks. Meanwhile, Hawaii had been annexed in July, 1898, and Hogg was on a peaceful mission across the Pacific. During the State Guard encampment he had become well acquainted with a number of army officers stationed at San Antonio. Many of them were going to the west coast for assignment overseas. When an invitation was extended to the ex-Governor to join in the official raising of the Stars and Stripes over Hawaii, it was proudly accepted. Arrangements were made for Ima, now a beautiful "Gibson girl" of sixteen, to accompany her father. (Pictures taken aboard ship show Hogg clowning with Brigadier General Charles King and Major General H. C. Merriam, who would go on to the Philippines; the two officers somewhat resemble pygmies in contrast to the huge Texan.[4])

On the trip Hogg gave free rein to his enthusiasm concerning the expansion of American trade, as he realized what great stimulus the war had given to the building of an isthmian canal, a project long close to his heart. He did not wish to see the United States embark upon the kind of imperialism which had made England disliked and feared around the world, but he did favor expansionism in the Western Hemisphere. He did not agree with Bryan's stringent stand against imperialism, and by no means wanted this issue made the main one for the 1900 Democratic platform, believing that silver again must be at the top of the standard.

By the time Hogg was back in Texas, the snarl in Hogg-Bailey relations that had been developing for some time was taking on serious proportions. In the latter part of 1897 and early 1898 both Hogg and Culberson had been willing to support Attorney General Martin Crane for the office of governor. Culberson wished to run for the United States Senate and had sought and received Hogg's support for his candidacy against Senator Mills. In later years Crane would complain that Hogg did not get out and work for him, but in his complaint he did not adhere to the actual time sequence of events or mention his own reluctance

---

[4] Robert Cotner (ed.), *Addresses of James Hogg*, picture opposite p. 468.

in the early stages of the campaign to be known as having Hogg's blessing.[5]

During the past year the swing toward conservatism in the Texas legislature—despite the commendable continuance of the reform program by Culberson—plus increased taxes, the strict economy necessary to put the government back in the black-ink column, and the growing strength of the cities had all been adding up to considerable opposition to straight-out Hogg men. Office seekers outside the favored circle could be counted on to chafe under the tendency of Hogg and his friends to reward loyal allies. Hogg considered Crane a truly worthy ally, but Colonel House would not give his support to Crane, having decided that the tendency to elevate attorneys general to the governorship should not be allowed to become a set custom.[6] Hogg would have helped his friend despite House's opposition. Word came to him, however, that Crane wanted to stand on his own record, and somewhat hurt by this attitude, Hogg remained relatively inactive during the pre-Convention stages of the campaign. The inactivity, nevertheless, was also a part of the ex-governor's political theory. In a significant letter, Hogg explained to Judge Edward Gray of Dallas why he did not publicly campaign for Crane:

In view of the political prominence into which I have been thrown by my several campaigns, it would be easy for me, by any action I might take, to convey to the public the idea that I aspire not to political honors, but to the odious, unAmerican position of political boss. Of all the terms most offensive to my sensibilities are those of "boss," "Warwick" and "czar." I hate them so intensely that I wish to perform no act during my private life which will give the slightest excuse to any man to lie on me in this particular. I never tried to run a ward, or a precinct, or a county in which I lived, and never attempted privately to make out a ballot for a voter. Now for me to undertake to force my convictions upon the public as to whom I prefer for the governorship would be, indeed, to self-stamp myself with a brand obnoxious to my sense of propriety, and against my convictions of what a "back number" should do under any circumstances. I know it is difficult to give to you and my other friends a satisfactory explanation of the motive which actuates me in seeking political obscurity, or in taking this position in the present campaign. I must take my chances, however, upon the con-

[5] Personal interview with Judge Joseph L. Lockett in his office in Houston, July, 1953. Lockett had recently graduated from the Texas Law School and was employed by Hogg and Robertson.

[6] Smith, *House*, pp. 28–29.

currence of your better judgment with me in this course as the wisest and safest to be pursued.[7]

Congressman Bailey, who had grown extremely restless about his secondary role in Texas politics and was seeking the means for a position of dominance, had decided to support his conservative congressional colleague Joseph Draper Sayers of South Texas for governor instead of Crane.[8] When Colonel House, who was directing both Culberson's and Sayers' campaigns, skillfully lined up in early primaries the known support for Congressman Sayers (who was also quite acceptable to the Clark wing) Crane misjudged the trend, grew alarmed, and withdrew from the race. This was a serious blow to the progressive wing of the party.

Bailey was ardent in his support of Culberson for Mills' seat in the Senate, but Hogg, unusually skeptical, interpreted this as Bailey's bid for Hogg's support against Chilton in 1900. In February, Hogg had bluntly announced, "You may say that I am for Governor Culberson this year and for Senator Chilton two years from now."[9]

The war with Spain gave Bailey a welcome new issue; by late summer he had launched on a crusade against colonialism, putting himself in line with Bryan and Cleveland in their opposition to annexation of overseas territory. Just when it looked as if the State Democratic Convention meeting at Galveston in early August would have no great issues, since Culberson would be practically unopposed for the Senate and Sayers by this time faced no serious gubernatorial conflict, Bailey and Hogg collided head-on over instructions concerning the peace treaty between Spain and the United States. Bailey was assisted by Robert Henry of the Waco area, who had been instructed, among others, to support the Bailey contention of no expansion.[10] Congressman Bronson Cooper and Thomas H. Ball indicated they would support the rising new leader. In opposition, Culberson, though asking freedom for Cuba, urged retention of Puerto Rico and at least a coaling station in the Philippines; Crane, Chilton, and Thomas Watt Gregory (later to serve in Woodrow Wilson's Cabinet) spoke in similar vein.

[7] J. S. Hogg to Edward Gray, February 1, 1898, J. S. Hogg Let. Pr., 14, pp. 138–139.

[8] Walter P. Webb and H. Bailey Carroll (eds.), *Handbook of Texas,* II, 576; James L. Tenny, "The Public Services of Joseph Draper Sayers," typescript in Arch. Univ. Tex. Lib.

[9] Dallas *Morning News,* February 11, 1898.

[10] For Bailey's speech at Plano see *ibid.,* July 27, 1898.

Hogg, however, outdid his friends. Reminding the Convention audience of the expansion record of Anglo-Saxon people, he declared, "Even Monroe put his hand upon his hip pocket and looking Spain square in the face, told her he wanted to purchase Florida. . . . What has come over the American people that they don't want to expand any more? Do you want to tell Congressmen to expand? For me, I do!" He was, however, willing to confine expansion to the "Western continent"—which for him included Hawaii. Without much regard for the population figures of the Orient, he said sweepingly that if, after his generation was gone, the next generation felt crowded and wanted to expand over the Pacific—"then by Gatlins, let them do it!"[11] He was satisfied to agree that the Philippines should not be retained, but believed that their people should be protected against other foreign powers.

As it turned out, Bailey had not chosen the popular view, but he delivered a thoughtful speech, more interesting today because of its prophetic character. He pleaded that the flag not be carried to areas unprepared for self-government, as the United States government "derives its just powers only from the consent of the governed."

The time will come when this war fever cools, when the noise of these fifes and drums has died away, when men cease to feel and begin to think: the people will wonder at the nightmare which possesses them and at the cowardice of some of their Representatives and Senators in Congress.[12]

When asked by an interrupting delegate if he would haul down the flag, Bailey replied:

I would haul it down in any land where the Constitution cannot follow it. I know I am right, and if you doubt it now, you will not doubt it in the time to come when in the presence of standing armies and warlike navies the citizen is dwarfed, state's rights are annihilated, and the Republic has become as imperial as the most devoted follower of Alexander Hamilton could have wished to make it. . . . I do not know how you will vote, but as for me and mine, we'll vote for the Old Republic.[13]

Henceforth, Bailey would be known as the opponent of "colonialism,"

[11] Galveston *Daily News*, August 3, 1898. Cf. J. S. Hogg to W. J. Bryan, July 6, 1898, J. S. Hogg Let. Pr., 14, p. 501, asking for a confidential statement on the war issues.

[12] Galveston *Daily News*, August 3, 1898. Dallas *Morning News*, August 12, 1898, quotes from a similar speech at Ladonia on August 11. Cf. Samuel F. Bemis' famous chapter, "The Great Aberration of 1898," *A Diplomatic History of the United States* (New York, Henry Holt and Company, 1931), pp. 463–475.

[13] Galveston *Daily News*, August 3, 1898.

of annexation of any territory incapable of self-government, or of the addition of any lands which would "demand an increase of the standing army." His minority report was tabled 721 to 334.[14]

Bailey's biographer declared that:

[this] rout seemed to darken his entire political future. The vote in the convention, in fact, saw his fortunes at the lowest ebb; in the first test of strength with the Hogg forces on an issue of state and national importance, he had lost. The heroes of the convention were Hogg, Chilton, Crane—not Bailey. Even Culberson, now safely on the road to the Senate, had not deemed it expedient to stay with him.[15]

But Bailey's own district listened to his arguments and returned him to Congress, where he teamed up with Bryan in opposing expansion. Bryan had it within his power to block ratification of the treaty with Spain in the Senate, but he did not do so. It must be concluded that Bailey shared Bryan's desire to see the treaty ratified in order to make an issue of imperialism in 1900; as Democratic minority leader in the House, Bailey could have put up a fight on the appropriation of the $20 million called for by the treaty to pay Spain for the Philippines, but he preferred to assert his belief that the House of Representatives was now obligated to approve the money. On February 28, 1899, a few days after President McKinley had signed the Treaty of Paris, a Democratic caucus took the ironic action of adopting an anti-expansion manifesto, which followed almost to the word the plank that Bailey had introduced at Galveston.[16] In helping to vote the money to pay for the Philippines, Bailey had once more defied Hogg and the Democratic majority in Texas, which had instructed him to oppose annexation of the Philippines.

Bailey's ambitions to enter the Senate in 1901 were now clear. Perhaps he recalled what happened to Mills and decided the time was not ripe for a Texan to obtain the speakership, even if the Democrats won the congressional elections of 1900. In the spring of 1899 Bailey lectured his Democratic colleagues in the House for not supporting his contention that no member of Congress, even the ex-Confederate Joe Wheeler of Alabama, should be allowed to hold his seat while holding

[14] Ernest Winkler, *Platforms*, p. 404.
[15] Sam Acheson, *Bailey*, p. 119.
[16] *Ibid.*, pp. 126–127; Hibben, *Bryan*, p. 222. See also Charles S. Olcott, *Life of William McKinley* (Boston, Houghton Mifflin and Company, 1916), II, 110–111. 110–111.

a commission in the armed forces: "No man is more popular with the Democratic masses than the Constitution, a reverence for which has been the chief article of our faith."[17] With this parting lecture, Bailey set out for Texas to try to control the Texas delegation to the next national convention and to make long-range plans to contest Chilton's re-election to the Senate. Senator Chilton recognized the showmanship of Bailey's tactics, noting in his diary the increasing references to the American flag, the Constitution, "home and mother"—and wondering when Bailey's opposition to him would break into the open.[18]

Adopting strategy that House had used to advantage, Bailey, a year ahead, began lining up all the counties which were likely to pledge delegates to him and arranged for their conventions to be called early in April, 1900. He planned well, and he was also clever in stressing his north Central Texas (Cooke County) residence in contrast to the East Texas background of Senators Chilton and Culberson (who succeeded Mills in 1899), arguing that the blacklands region and West Texas should be represented. He was stretching a few points here, since Culberson, though coming originally from East Texas had long been a Dallas resident. Bailey was promising patronage to a new group of political aspirants if they would assist in overthrowing the Hogg-Chilton-Reagan dynasty.[19]

Hogg, meanwhile, had been hoping that Colonel House might be changing his mind about Bryan. In the late fall of 1898 he had encouraged Mr. and Mrs. Bryan to bring their daughter Grace, who had not been well, to Texas, saying that the climate might help her. The Bryans were his guests for a few days, then, as had been arranged, they moved into a house on West Avenue next door to the Colonel.

There was much visiting back and forth through the hedge separating the properties on West Avenue. At first House seemed enthusiastic about Bryan, openly admiring many of his traits, but the improved estimate was only temporary. Looking back on those days, House recorded: "I was amazed to see how lacking he was in political sagacity and common sense. Mrs. Bryan was much more practical than he. She was open to advice and suggestions. But I honestly believe that Bryan never

[17] *Congressional Record, 55 Cong., 3 sess.,* Vol. 32, p. 2935; Acheson, *Bailey,* p. 126.
[18] After Bailey contested Chilton's return to the Senate, Chilton charged him with using demagogic methods. See Diaries of Horace Chilton, Book 5, pp. 244–254, Arch. Univ. Tex. Lib. Used by permission.
[19] Acheson, *Bailey,* pp. 130 ff.

altered an idea after he had formed an opinion of it. It was his weakness and his strength."[20]

Hogg knew that Bryan and House would clash on the silver issue, but he felt it possible that "The Commoner" could win House over notwithstanding, and thus have the great assistance of the Colonel's skill in party campaign organization. The Austin visit was helpful in any case to Bryan, for Hogg saw to it that he met influential Democrats, such as young Cullen Thomas of Waco, who was rising fast in the Party, and Colonel William L. Moody, the famed Galveston financier who would be a delegate to the National Democratic Convention. Hunting expeditions furnished the background for Bryan's relaxed comradeship with these new friends, and Hogg thoroughly enjoyed his role as genial entrepreneur.

Still concerned about keeping Bryan and the silver issue in the Democratic limelight, Hogg was pleased to obtain, through his friend and former staff member Fred Feigl, an invitation to address Tammany Hall in 1899 at its Fourth of July celebration. (Feigl had been editing the *Tammany Times* for several years.) In the off-election year many of the Tammany leaders, among them Boss Croker, who was in Europe, former President Cleveland, former Senator David B. Hill, and Bryan, were conspicuously absent. However, it was well known that Joseph J. Willett of Alabama was scheduled to spark a boom for Judge Augustus Van Wyck, Mayor of New York, for President, and Hogg had decided to use the occasion to call the Democrats back to first principles and to indicate that the South still wanted Bryan.

The Associated Press account reported that Governor Hogg received a hearty ovation and that his introductory remarks were well received by the Tammany men. Then he launched into "a philippic which set the house in an uproar. The applause began when he asserted that the next year the Democratic party would declare for the free and unlimited coinage of silver at the ratio of 16 to 1. Men who had appeared to be half asleep woke up with a start and joined in the applause." Among other things, Hogg said:

We will again declare for the unlimited free coinage of silver and gold on an equal basis at the government mints at the ratio of 16 to 1, so that

---

[20] Quoted in Arthur D. H. Smith, *Mr. House of Texas*, (New York, Funk and Wagnalls Company, 1940), p. 32; Hibben, *Bryan*, p. 224. Cf. Charles Seymour, *The Intimate Papers of Colonel House* (Boston, Houghton Mifflin Company, 1926), I, 39. It is believed by some that House, in looking backward, overlooked a favorable interest in Bryan which he undoubtedly displayed.

484

the people of South and West, as well as those of North and East may have a sufficient supply of metal money to meet their growing demands.

We will declare against the English gold standard, which American flunkyism has fastened upon this government. We will denounce the endless financial chain of monometallism, which in its circular motion draws without limit bonds from the government and money from the people.

We will declare against the Republican protective tariff, which enriches the few at the expense of many and breeds trusts to menace every man.

We will demand a graduated income tax as the best means of equalizing the burdens of government in peace and which paralyzes the strong arm of American workmen in their struggle for subsistence.

We will declare for the suppression of trusts and for levying high federal taxes upon their interstate shipments with suitable forfeiture penalties.

We will denounce the growing spirit of imperialism which threatens the stability of our republic and tell the foreigners upon the eastern hemisphere that while in war we are united until victory graces our flag, yet that in peace we would not have their territory nor their citizenship, but in good faith our congressional pledges shall be kept.

We will renew our pledges to the Cubans that they shall have independence, and when they knock at our door for admission conditions being suitable for the solemn action, we will welcome them into the union as a State.

We will demand the construction, the ownership, the operation and the maintenance of the Nicaraguan or other isthmian canal by the government to the end that our commerce may become free from foreign domination.

On a platform embracing these unequivocal declarations, the grand old party of our national government in its purity will go to the next campaign, confident of triumphant success.

In this great contest we want the aid of united Tammany—the greatest local political organization on earth. We want you to close up ranks, to settle your local differences, if they exist, and to go arm in arm with the stalwart breadwinners of the South and West to victory next year under the leadership of the chivalrous, the dauntless, the matchless great American—William Jennings Bryan.[21]

This speech did not go unheeded, although biographers of Boss Croker do not mention this meeting. Several newspapers played up the event, among them the Minneapolis *Journal*, which on July 5 cartooned Hogg as a Texas steer, carrying a tail-clinging Bryan into the "heart of Tammany." Furthermore, word of the effect of the address was cabled to Croker, and by the time he returned in August he had decided to place the votes of Tammany behind a second try for Bryan. The influential political sheet, *The Verdict*, for September 18, issued a full-page color

[21] Dallas *Morning News,* July 5, 1899.

A TEXAS STEER.

How he carried Bryan into the heart of Tammany.

Minneapolis Journal, *July 5, 1899*

A PAINFUL SURPRISE FOR POOR RICHARD.

Washington Star, *July 6, 1899*

cartoon of Hogg which portrayed him as "The Bryan of the Lone Star State."

During the winter of 1899–1900 Bryan was again in Austin. Some of the Republican and anti-Bryan papers, continuing the subtle art of belittlement and ridicule, enjoyed the kind of copy they could get out of Austin. The January 1, 1900, issue of the Chicago *Times-Herald* ran such a story, which was reprinted in the Indianapolis *Journal* under the headline "Happy Days for Bryan":

As has been set forth in previous despatches, ex-Governor Hogg is getting up many unique forms of entertainment for his guest, the peerless leader, W. J. Bryan. The two statesmen have shot ducks and caught panthers, and learned to ride ostriches. The people of this city have, in fact, come to look for something new every day. It seems that Mr. Bryan's friends have privately informed Governor Hogg that the peerless leader must in some way be made to forget how much Lincoln reminds him of himself. They were becoming alarmed at his condition. He would, according to these zealous guardians, awake at night, sit up in bed, and exclaim: "Ah, I have had a beautiful dream in which I saw Lincoln and heard his voice, and I could not believe that it wasn't me. Lincoln in 1860. Me in 1900!"

Governor Hogg has, therefore, been asked to try to make the peerless leader think of something else, and he is doing his best in this direction. On Monday last the ex-Governor and the peerless leader played leap-frog for three hours in the former's back yard, but after the game the great Nebraskan arose and said: "This is fine sport. It reminds me of when Lincoln was a young man and was the champion of his township. Lincoln in 1860. Me in 1900."[22]

Hogg, as an experienced newspaper man and political campaigner, knew the value of having the public hear something about Bryan daily. Not until 1908 would the Dallas *News* support Bryan, but Tom Finty, Jr., who was soon to become political editor of the *News,* has told how reporters in 1900 contributed to dispatches such as the above, and how Hogg, "a man of richly flavored personality and gargantuan humor," was "in on" these jokes. According to Finty, when Bryan objected to the "preposterous positions they were putting him in," Hogg, sitting beside him, appeared equally indignant, "even more solemnly shocked than Bryan." A few hours later Hogg would be closeted with the newsmen, planning some new installment of "the grotesque roles in which

[22] Mark Sullivan, *Our Times* (New York, Charles Scribner's Sons, 1926), I, 272.

Bryan was being put."[23] While Hogg did not always approve of the precise methods of the newsmen, he relied upon the public to enjoy the jokes; above all, Bryan was not being ignored. While hostile Texas newspapers might figure that references to Lincoln would hurt Bryan in parts of the South, they would probably help in the North, where most of the tales were being repeated.

Early in February, 1900, Bailey finally issued an open challenge to Senator Chilton by asking him to enter into a series of joint debates before the people of Texas, who thus would be able to "fairly decide" between the two, and in this way, even with the limited current primary election laws, the contest would approach "the election of a Senator by a direct vote of the people." Chilton doubted if a joint campaign would "be productive of useful results; yet because you invite it, I am disposed to join you in making a list of appointments." He was at the time concerned with bills needing immediate attention in the Senate, but expressed a willingness to "devote the month of May to joint debates, distributed over the State."[24] Bailey had already planned speeches to be delivered in March; just before he left Washington for that purpose, he told Chilton to let him know later when they would get together in May. It is at least probable that Bailey realized that the campaign would be practically settled before May, largely owing to his foresighted, skillful planning of early primaries in certain counties.

In his opening address at Cameron—on Hogg's birthday, March 24— Bailey charged Senator Chilton with being an exponent of the "Republican" doctrine of expansion, favoring a big navy, sponsoring private operation of the projected Nicaraguan canal, and having accepted the "Cleveland heresy" of free raw materials in the tariff.[25] Continuing these charges, Bailey went into North and West Texas. Years of depression and drought had made Republicans of many West Texans, and both Democrats and Republicans among the cattlemen were interested in tariff protection for wool, hides, and meat.

Friends wrote Chilton urging him to get into the race before it was too late. The first of the selected counties to hold primaries early in April pledged for Bailey. Hogg, Finley, and others quickly offered to help,

[23] *Ibid.*

[24] J. W. Bailey to Horace Chilton, February 3, 1900, and Horace Chilton to J. W. Bailey, February 4, 1900, J. W. Bailey Papers, Dallas Historical Society.

[25] Dallas *Morning News,* March 25, 1900; Acheson, *op. cit.,* pp. 138–139. See Winifred Kupper, *The Golden Hoof* (New York, A. A. Knopf, 1945), p. 140.

but Chilton, not yet recovered from a severe case of grippe, seemed to have little heart to plan a real campaign. When he reached Texas in mid-April he was still so unwell that his doctor ordered him to rest for at least five weeks. By April 17 some thirty counties, largely in West Texas, had pledged themselves to Bailey. After consultation with his doctor and his political allies, much to Hogg's distress, Chilton announced his retirement from the race.[26]

Hogg had already been in the field as the citizen champion of a new set of reforms, seeking no office for himself but hoping to elect a reform legislature and to bestir his old friends to be on guard to protect Chilton's interests when the 1901 legislature would meet to select the senator. Despite Chilton's retirement, Hogg went ahead with his plans to continue speaking on the series of amendments to the Texas Constitution he was advocating.

As soon as Chilton's decision was announced, Waller Baker of Waco telegraphed Hogg, "Your friends will elect you United States Senator if you will allow them." Hogg replied, "It will take a lifetime as a private citizen for me to pay my debts to the people of Texas, and I cannot incur further liabilities along that line. Thanks."[27] The exchange of telegrams appeared in the newspapers on April 19, the day that Hogg was scheduled to be in Waco for his first address on the amendments.

Both his friends and his enemies were waiting to hear what he would say. In spite of the publicized refusal to Baker, it was not difficult for alert political noses to smell a "deal" in Chilton's retirement. Bailey was especially skeptical, having been warned by some of Hogg's old enemies that it was never safe to drop one's guard when battling with the ex-Governor. Many men were surprised, a few were relieved, and a good many were still disbelieving when Hogg began his speech thus:

Ten years ago today I opened my first campaign at Rusk as a candidate for Governor. I now commemorate that event by entering upon another campaign, clear of political ambition, with the hope alone of benefiting the people of my native State.[28]

He then reviewed the benefits which had come to the railways and to the people through the Railroad Commission and the stock and bond law, reminding them that in this year of 1900 no railroad in Texas was

[26] Dr. C. A. Smith to R. N. Stafford, quoted in the Dallas *Morning News,* April 18, 1900; N. W. Finley's speech for Chilton at Dallas, *ibid.,* April 14, 1900.
[27] Quoted in Dallas *Morning News,* April 19, 1900.
[28] *Ibid.,* April 20, 1900.

in the hands of a receiver. He asked that the people "add the capstone" to the work already done by adopting a constitutional amendment embracing three principles:

1. That no insolvent corporation shall do business in this State.
2. That the free pass system over the railways of Texas shall forever terminate.
3. That the use of corporate funds in politics and to support a lobby at Austin shall be prohibited.[29]

For convenience he called these proposals, as grouped into an amendment, "Resolution Number One," under which designation he hoped the people would "discuss it, read it, study it, know it," and instruct their senators and representatives in the legislature to submit it as an amendment to the Texas Constitution for adoption at an election in 1901.

The proposed amendment was read in detail, and Hogg explained the meaning and reasons for each section. He called attention to the new federal bankruptcy law of 1898, pointing out that railway corporations had been exempted from its provisions.[30] Such a situation, he affirmed, made it necessary for Texas laws to cover "this ground by defining what is an insolvent corporation and making it the duty of the State to wind it up." Answering railroad lobbyists who would contend that the proposal was harsh and unjust, he quoted the federal law, which declared a person insolvent "whenever the *aggregate* of his property . . . shall not, at a fair valuation, be sufficient in amount to pay his debts"; creditors were given immediate right of action. Hogg believed his proposal was liberal in that a corporation would be insolvent "only when its other indebtedness added to its 'stocks and bonds' shall *exceed* its property valuation from *seventy-five to three hundred per cent*. And it gives the insolvent company a full year in which to correct its delinquencies." Continuing, he said:

The Federal government is not criticized for this act by which creditors may swoop down on their embarrassed citizen debtors, but Texas, indulgent old Texas, is held up to scorn by stock-jobbers and inflationists everywhere when she proposes to deal with the frauds of her corporate creatures by this exceedingly liberal rule. And she can stand the criticism![31]

[29] Cotner (ed.), *op. cit.*, pp. 452–454. The full speech is reprinted pp. 452–472.
[30] See Charles Warren, *Bankruptcy in United States History* (Cambridge, Harvard University Press, 1933), pp. 134–143.
[31] Cotner, *op. cit.*, p. 459; Dallas *Morning News*, April 20, 1900.

Hogg was concerned about the increasing stock issues and the number of consolidation bills about to be presented for approval by the Sayers administration. He pointed out that the 9,702 miles of Texas roads had submitted a tax valuation value of $73,603,406, while the Railroad Commission had valued them at $141,069,801, despite the fact that their outstanding bonds and stocks aggregated $358,218,541.[32] Hogg also maintained that all the old roads constructed before the stock and bond law of 1893 went into effect were insolvent and had been for years:

This statement can not fail to engender bitter feeling, but it is true. Any man is too obtuse, too blunted to human sensibilities to understand the approach of a nightmare if he can not see ahead the stubborn, relentless opposition which this position must arouse if the people, for the protection of their interests and the establishment of justice, should become alive to their duty in this campaign.[33]

He went on to show how the Commission rate structure was connected to railroad evaluations and freight rates and the constant difficulty of injunctions and Supreme Court decisions. He called attention to the "last leading case," *Smyth* v. *Ames* (169 U.S. 466) in 1898, which was without dissent. Hogg quoted the decision:

"We hold that the basis of all calculations as to the reasonableness of rates to be charged by a corporation, maintaining a highway under legislative sanction, must be the fair value of the property being used by it for the convenience of the public. And in order to ascertain that value, the original cost of construction, the amount expended in permanent improvements, the amount and market value of its stocks and bonds, the present as compared with the original cost of construction, the probable earning capacity of the property under particular rates prescribed by statute and the sum required to meet operating expenses are all matters for consideration and are to be given such weight as may be just and right in each case.[34]

This decision was an alarm bell, in that Hogg believed it was but the precursor to a ruling that Commission rates must be high enough to pay, not only railway operating costs, but also the interests on bonds and

---

[32] Texas Railroad Commission, *Eighth Annual Report* (1899), pp. 136–137, 173.

[33] Cotner, *op. cit.*, p. 459. Hogg had recently read an article by the Wall Street financier Henry Clews in the *Railway Age* which characterized the speculative construction transactions of the past twenty years "as direct frauds upon the public." Cf. Henry Clews, *Twenty-eight Years in Wall Street* (New York, Irving Publishing Company, 1888), p. 479.

[34] Cotner, *op. cit.*, pp. 461–462.

some dividends to stockholders. Thus he said he spoke "from the look-out" to warn the people of Texas to take care of themselves.

Governor Sayers did not agree with Hogg's diagnosis; consolidations continued to be approved. In a subsequent publication, *Railroad Consolidations in Texas, 1891–1903,* Sayers argued that Hogg had nurtured the consolidation program by approving the M.K.& T. reorganization in 1891.[35] Hogg's new thesis, namely that heavily indebted roads should not be able to consolidate with well-managed and reasonably financed lines until the former had paid off or scaled down their debts as a way to enable the Railway Commission to justify lowering freight rates, was ignored.

Treating next the lobbying section of his amendment, Hogg said that, although he would not deny to any man or set of men the right to be heard in the protection of their interests, corporations which used funds to support a permanent professional lobby in Austin, with its parade of "Knights of Congress Avenue" who came to Austin before the legislative session and remained until it closed, should be stopped in their efforts "to thwart the people's will." He also argued that the use of funds for political purposes was an unreasonable expense to the stockholders as well as to the public. He was opposed to allowing Texas railroads to make reports, as they had done before the days of the Commission, lumping $14 million as "miscellaneous expenses"—almost half of their gross receipts for the year. After the Commission had been established, a new category of "general expenses" had shown up, averaging annually over $2 million, and not itemized. Hogg called for more detailed reports which would show up the amounts spent for lobbying and for other political purposes:

It is not the object and should never be the purpose for which corporations are created or permitted, that they may collect money through the use of public franchises for the purpose of prostituting political parties or corrupting legislative bodies to defeat the public will.[36]

On May 4, Hogg spoke in Denison, near Bailey's home town of Gainesville. He would not be led into a clash with Bailey's friends over the issue of imperialism, although he did express regret that the Texas Democratic platform of 1898, recommending freedom for the Philip-

[35] Joseph D. Sayers, *Railroad Consolidations in Texas, 1891–1903,* (Austin, n. pub., 1904), pp. 5–61. See railroad map facing p. 155.
[36] Cotner, *op. cit.,* pp. 471–472.

pines under American protection, had not been followed by President McKinley, with the result that difficult problems of subduing, governing, and final disposition of the Islands now plagued America.[37] During the address he announced that he intended to talk for the amendments right up to the June meeting of Democrats in Austin, where delegates to the national convention would be selected.

While Hogg was on the tour Congressman Bailey arrived in Austin, ostensibly to "watch the fight over Imperialism." Subsequent events indicated that Bailey was also 1) trying to line up the anti-Hogg forces in Austin, 2) planning strategy for the Democratic Convention, and 3) being of considerable assistance to President H. Clay Pierce in the efforts of the Waters-Pierce Oil Company to continue doing business in Texas, despite the U.S. Supreme Court decision of March 19, 1900, validating the Texas Antitrust Law and declaring that the Waters-Pierce Company as an agent of Standard Oil must forfeit its license and go out of business in Texas.[38]

The entirety of Bailey's reasons for being interested in the future of the Waters-Pierce Oil business may never come to light. It is possible that his immediate interest stemmed from the fact that his friend David R. Francis of St. Louis, a former governor of Missouri and Cleveland's Secretary of the Interior (1896–1897), led Bailey to think that Waters-Pierce was a fine business which was being "pushed around" in Texas for political reasons. Francis had learned that H. Clay Pierce of St. Louis needed a good Texas lawyer and might pay well for services rendered.[39] Bailey needed money. Prior to the time he became interested in dislodging Chilton, he had begun purchasing lands and blooded horses in Texas and Kentucky. Barnett Gibbs, who left the Democrats in 1896 and was the People's Party candidate for governor in 1898, had entered into an involved deal, by which Bailey got Gibbs' six-thousand-acre farm near Dallas and Gibbs received David Francis' twenty-one-thousand-acre ranch in West Texas, as well as four thousand dollars cash from Bailey, who also executed a much larger mortgage. By this time Bailey's stock farm in Kentucky was in poor financial condition, and he needed to raise five thousand dollars.

Francis brought Bailey and Pierce together, but Bailey always maintained that he rejected the offer to become Pierce's attorney, saying: "If you want to abide by the law, you won't need a lawyer. Go down there

[37] Dallas *Morning News,* May 5, 1900.   [38] 177 U.S. 28 (1900).
[39] Statement made at the Waco Democratic Convention, August 8, 1900, quoted in Dallas *Morning News,* August 9–10, 1900; Acheson, *Bailey,* pp. 140–143.

and tell the Democratic officers that you will be willing to abide by the law, and they will be glad to have you resume business in the state." Bailey apparently tried to sell some horses to meet his debts, but he also seems to have known that if he did not succeed in selling, or getting a price he wanted, he could borrow the money from Pierce. As it turned out, time was too short to make a good horse deal, so he signed a "demand loan" for $3,000 on April 25, 1900. Bailey's biographer has said that this transaction, through the whole of the bitter investigations of 1907, remained "the weakest point in the whole case against Bailey. . . . If Bailey had had the least feeling of wrongdoing, would he have signed his name to such a paper and handed it over to a stranger? Even a simpleton would be more circumspect with a bribe. . . . Would he [Bailey] have signed a note, if it were a fee?"[40]

In any event, on May 1, 1900, Bailey, Pierce, and others concerned were in Austin together. Bailey talked with Governor Sayers about the efforts of "their opponents . . . to control the delegation" to the National Convention and then he told Sayers of his advice to Pierce about ways to get back into business in Texas. Bailey interpreted Sayers' remarks about seeing to it that "the laws are obeyed" as not ruling out his plan. The matter was referred to Attorney General Thomas Smith, who was a personal and political friend of Sayers, Bailey, and Hogg. Smith pointed out that it was not merely a matter of "promising to be good," but that the old company must go out of business in Texas. Then he suggested that Waters-Pierce "go and purge itself," return with "clean hands," and take an oath to obey the Texas Laws—whereupon they might receive a welcome like "any other legitimate business." A newly organized company could obtain a new charter or license. In other words, if the new Waters-Pierce "subscribed to the affidavit that they are not in truth a part of the oil trust" they could meet the law and be relicensed.

Pierce went to Waco on Bailey's advice, and the company's Waco attorneys, including George Clark, tried to get County Attorney Cullen Thomas to agree to a reduced cash settlement in the civil suit and to drop the criminal indictment. Thomas refused. In some of the negotiation over fees, the "compromise" talk seems to have involved considerable financial pressure. Thomas resisted, asserting that he was not permitted to split fees with the defendant's attorneys but must collect his legal percentage on the total judgment collected from Mr. Pierce and

---

[40] Acheson, *op. cit.*, p. 143.

the company. These negotiations were not generally known to the public until August, a few days before the Democratic Convention in Waco.[41]

Returning to St. Louis, Pierce got a new charter from the State of Missouri, declaring the old company dissolved. On May 23, Pierce and the chief attorney for the company were back in Austin telling Attorney General Smith and reporters that his company had reorganized, was not controlled by Standard, and "always complied with the laws of every state." Before the last day of May a new license was issued, and Waters-Pierce continued to operate in Texas.

When the Democrats assembled for their meeting in Austin on June 20, rumors had been circulating about Bailey, among them that the Gibbs ranch deal was his pay for helping Waters-Pierce. Bailey himself seemed not aware of the rumors. With no opponent in sight, he was delighted that his friends seemed to have a clear majority at the Convention. This majority wanted to instruct the Texas delegates to the National Convention in Kansas City to pledge independence for Cuba and "the same treatment" for the Philippines.[42] The Hogg forces were furious at this, for it constituted a revision of the platform of 1898 and would indicate that Bailey rather than Hogg called the tune in Texas; Hogg did not want to close the door to possible annexation of Cuba, and he sought a protectorate over the Philippines. Furthermore, the Baileyites made clear that they intended to use their strength to keep Hogg off the list of delegates. When Robert Stafford, a close friend to Jim Hogg, proposed a minority report repeating the 1898 platform Bailey answered him personally in scathing terms. In a direct slap at the influence of the former governor, Bailey stormed that three conventions had been dominated by personalities; "if there were an anti-Bailey party" he called upon the delegates "to crush it out." Stafford's proposal was snowed under by a tabling vote of 707 to 165.[43]

Hogg, apparently realizing that he could do little at the moment to counteract the dominance of the Bailey and Sayers conservative wing, stayed out of the open fight, preferring to spend his time building up sentiment for his amendments, which would come up in August at the Democratic meeting to be held in Waco. Neither he nor Clark was a delegate to the National Convention. However, Hogg knew when he

[41] Waco *Daily News*, August 6–10, 1900. See also Dallas *Morning News*, May 2 and 23, 1900, and Bailey's testimony January 21, 1901, in Texas *House Journal* (1901), pp. 146 ff.

[42] Winkler, *Platforms*, p. 417; Dallas *Morning News*, June 21–22, 1900; Acheson, *op. cit.*, p. 145.

[43] Austin *Daily Statesman*, June 21–22, 1900; Winkler, *op. cit.*, pp. 416–418.

went to Kansas City as a visitor that he would not be overlooked by national leaders of the Party.

The Convention convened in Kansas City on July 4. The Texas delegation was once more a pro-silver group and included a few of Hogg's friends—John Duncan, James Swayne, and W. L. Moody—but it was controlled by such rising young pro-Bailey Democrats as Bronson Cooper of South Texas, Tom Ball of East Texas, and the poker-playing young man from the far southwest, John Nance Garner. Following the opening prayer on the morning of the second day the Convention chairman announced that the Committee on Platform was not ready to report, then said he understood Governor Hogg was present, whereupon a motion was voted unanimously to invite Hogg to address the Convention.

Hogg, although saying he was "disinclined to make a speech at all," wasted no time in launching into a frank warning to the deliberating Committee that they had better not sidestep old principles of democracy —freedom of speech, freedom of the press, freedom of conscience, the preservation of personal rights, and equality of all citizens before the law:

I am waiting, waiting with the Democrats of this Convention for the report of the Committee on Platform and Resolutions. I want to see that document and to know whether the Democrats . . . are ready to fluke or fight. In common with you I want to know if we are to become a party of dodgers or a party of freemen, striking for liberty and the success of our cause. I desire to know if we are to dodge the issues of 1896 and trail after the Republicans; or, are we to meet all issues and go into the contest for victory in the interests of the masses of this country? Are we to be independent freemen or the truculent peons of the British government? I, for one, long for the time when Americans can be Americans without going abroad for political aspirations or for tutelage in their political affairs! It has been over 100 years since we became emancipated from England. It has been but a few years since we began to walk back under the yoke of England; and I want to see this Convention stand up for the liberty of Americans against English domination everywhere.[44]

Referring to the sharp debates in the Senate over the unratified first Hay-Pauncefote treaty of 1900 and Secretary Hay's effort to clear the way for building a canal across Panama, he reminded his audience that President Cleveland had upheld the Monroe Doctrine in the Brit-

[44] *Official Proceedings of the Democratic National Convention at Kansas City, Mo., 1900* (Chicago, McLellan Publishing Company, 1900), p. 96.

ish-Venezuela boundary dispute, in that instance standing up to the British. Hogg charged that the Republicans had been taken in by the British negotiator and had drawn up an unacceptable draft of a treaty governing the building of a canal:

We must not have entanglements with England or any other nation. We should avoid difficulties with all people. We prefer peace, but will exercise the right to attend undisturbed to our own affairs upon this American continent, and if our Committee on Platform and Resolutions come in here to evade a single issue that we presented in 1896, I ask you to vote it down. . . . If the Democrats of this country are presented with a platform of principle such as we had in 1896, changed to suit the conditions of today, we will march to victory under the gallant, matchless Bryan next November.[45]

In spite of the fact that he spoke as a visitor and not a delegate, Hogg's influence was never greater in the Democratic Party than when he proceeded to outline in great detail a platform which he declared would be acceptable to the people. This included:

1. Unlimited free coinage of silver at the established and honest ratio, 16 to 1, "to the end that the people of the South and West, as well as those of the North and East, shall have a full supply of metal money to meet their growing demands."

2. A graduated income tax.

3. A specific declaration not alone against combinations and conspiracies against trade, but against trusts.

4. A declaration against the importation of foreign labor.

5. A tariff for revenue only to support honest and economically administered government.

6. A pledge that Cuba shall be free as promised and that the Philippine Islands shall stand upon an equality with Cuba.

7. The Constitution shall follow the flag in Puerto Rico.

8. The acquisition of territory upon the Eastern Hemisphere by conquest or by any other method on the part of the United States government is a menace to American tranquility and independence and should be denounced.

9. A denouncement of imperialism: "We are ashamed of Uncle Sam when he goes across the waters to join John Bull, the German Emperor, and the Czar of Russia to despoil and divide old China in the pursuit of plunder. In thunder tones let our party declare against imperialism in every form."

[45] *Ibid.*, p. 97.

498

10. An unequivocal condemnation of "government by injunction, which is being fastened upon us by the Federal Courts [and] is a violent attack upon the Bill of Rights."[46]

After a prolonged tirade against the Republicans for double-talk on silver in 1896 and then fastening "an English policy" of gold on the country, he charged them with yielding again to England in the draft of the canal treaty on the matter of protection after the canal was built. The treaty should not be accepted. In the strongest language Hogg had ever used to denounce the Republican "octopus . . . of broken promises," he concluded:

For these and other reasons I say that it is a party of makeshifts, a party of false promises, a party of cowardice, a party that will lead these people to hell unless they are checked. . . . If we will incorporate in our platform suitable principles, as we did in 1896, without reaffirming or distinguishing between one plank and another, and go to the American people on the issues, we will in the year 1900 repeat the victory of 1800 by electing the second Jefferson to the Presidency of the United States.[47]

A careful reading of the platform as later submitted to the Convention by Ben Tillman of South Carolina indicates one or all of three things. Either Hogg was, like Jefferson in 1776, so steeped in the political thinking of his day that he could voice the innermost longings of the majority, or he had some influence on the Platform Committee through Ben Tillman if not through Tom Ball, or he had been kept informed of the progress of the Committee and was purposefully preparing the Convention to accept the platform. No item he mentioned was overlooked in the platform, although he would have preferred silver to imperialism as the foremost issue.

The platform condemned the law under which Puerto Rico was being governed and the Supreme Court decisions on tariff and tax matters by which the islanders were being "impoverished." The Philippines should have peace and an opportunity for self-government under the sort of protection the United States had afforded South and Central America. Some other items were introduced for the first time: 1) direct election of United States senators, 2) creation of a Department of Labor, 3) statehood for Arizona, New Mexico, and Oklahoma, 4) ter-

---

[46] *Ibid.,* pp. 97–99.

[47] *Ibid.,* p. 100; Dallas *Morning News,* July 6, 1900. See early letter to E. M. House, July 6, 1898, J. S. Hogg Let. Pr., 14, pp. 503–504, opposing annexation of the Philippines, but supporting the retention of Cuba in order to "control the Caribbean Sea and Gulf of Mexico."

ritorial government for Alaska and Puerto Rico, 5) extension of the Chinese exclusion law to include the same classes of all Asiatic races, 6) an intelligent system of improving the arid lands of the West, storing the waters for the purpose of irrigation, and the holding of such lands for actual settlers.[48]

The pro-gold East was concerned over the extent to which the West and South had called the tune at the Convention, indicative of the all-out effort the agrarians were making to regain control of the national government. A cartoon in *Harper's Magazine* pictured the embattled East protected by the wall of the gold standard, which was being stormed by "wild Indians" from the West led by Bryan and Eugene Debs; on the page opposite, Hogg was pictured sitting serenely on his home ground wrapped in his own blanket and smoking his own peace pipe.

Once more Hogg tried to enlist the organizing genius of Colonel House for Bryan, knowing that if the camp-meeting quality of the election of 1896 was repeated the result would be defeat; organization was essential amid the complications of the 1900 political scene. House still refused to work for Bryan, and when he quietly voted the Democratic ticket he expected defeat, for the Democrats were divided and confused. Hogg helped Bryan in late October and early November by making a speaking tour in Indiana and Illinois. The Republicans stayed by their party and won. Bryan, however, increased his vote over 1896, and Hogg did not desert him, recognizing that he was the best vote-getter the party had and that he had stood firm on the silver issue.

Two incidents of the 1900 campaign illustrate certain of the characteristics that made Hogg unforgettable to his contemporaries, whether they were his partisans or not. The town of Seguin in the South Texas county of Guadalupe was an important center of a large German-American and Anglo-American population, divided about evenly into Republicans and Democrats. Party leaders there decided to invite a speaker from each party to debate the issues of 1900. The Democrats invited Jim Hogg; the Republican leader, Eugene Nolte, invited the promising young William H. Atwell, who was making a name for himself as an orator.[49] Atwell did not know that his forensic opponent was to be the former governor, whom he admired. The speakers were escorted by their respective hosts to Senator Joseph Dibrell's office, where

[48] South Trimble (comp.), *Platforms of the Two Great Political Parties,* pp. 106–113.

[49] William Hawley Atwell, *Autobiography,* pp. 12–14.

Atwell was somewhat jolted to discover the identity of his opponent. He recorded later that Hogg in a kindly way said, "Bill, let's make this a 'jint' debate." Atwell, though alarmed at the prospect of tackling the governor, agreed. Hogg then framed the question: "Resolved, that we shall turn loose the Philippines"; he would take the affirmative for an hour, then Atwell would have an hour, and the Governor might have a rejoinder.

During his affirmative, Hogg worked up to a high point, stirring the audience with this statement: "The Republicans wish to retain thirteen hundred islands [actually over 7,000] in the far Pacific, and yet they do not even know the names thereof, and if my young Republican friend can name thirteen of them, I will concede this debate."

Atwell later confessed in his *Autobiography* that he did not know the names—nor did he believe that Governor Hogg knew them:

I thought fast and furious, and when my time came, I, too, worked up toward the answer to this very dangerous question, and when I reached that point, I named Luzon . . . by reason of my brother having been a soldier there during the Spanish-American war . . . and twelve other Spanish names, which I had remembered as belonging to different brands of cigars. At the conclusion of Hogg's speech, Mrs. Dibrell had presented him with a large bouquet of beautiful roses. When I closed, after giving the information . . . as to the names of the islands, he arose and came across the stage where I had taken my seat and divided the roses with me, saying, in a low tone of voice, "Here is to the champion liar, who cannot be caught." This particular episode was written up afterwards in the *Saturday Evening Post*, under the head of "Christening the Philippines."[50]

The second incident concerned an exchange of letters. Shortly after the National Convention, Editor Shaw of the *Texas Farmer* wrote to Hogg expressing his uneasiness both about the way Bailey was running around the country with the oil trust men and about the rumors of land deals. The fairness of Hogg's reply is the more remarkable in the face of the fact that Bailey had just ended Chilton's chance to return to the Senate:

I have such a high regard for men in general and especially those who hold high public positions in this country that it would take more than rumor or a combination of suspicious circumstances to convince me of the corruption of any man in office who has borne a reasonably good private reputation for honesty. The air seems to have grown full of rumors about

[50] *Ibid.*, p. 15.

Mr. Bailey in connection with that Waters Pierce Oil Trust, but so far I have not been led to give the slightest countenance to them. More than this, I should regret exceedingly, for the sake of my own native State and of the people who have honored him, if after sifting the matter to the bottom, the slightest taint should be left upon his character. It is so common with political opposition to grow into personal malignity and blind malice, that I am led to hope that this recent proposed crusade upon the character of Mr. Bailey will find the truth consistent with his good integrity and that the whole thing will evaporate as a mist before the shining sun. If those who are working to ascertain the truth should find in fact that he has been guilty of promoting that trust in any way, so as to fasten it upon Texas, I should feel humiliated that such is the result. At the same time, if such is the truth, those who possess the facts to support it should not hide behind rumor or injure him but should expose the case openly, manfully, so that the public may not be misled by it. So far as I am concerned, I should have nothing to do with it unless the truth is positive, or being circumstantial, leads to the conclusion of his guilt beyond a reasonable doubt. In either event I am unprepared to say what course I should take now. There are plenty of men, if he is culpable, to do him full damage to the point of prosecution without my joining in the crusade also. For the sake of our State, however, I do hope that a calm dispassionate investigation will disclose the truth to be that Mr. Bailey has not dishonored either his name or the people who have honored him by any such conduct as has been recently charged against him.[51]

[51] J. S. Hogg to W. A. Shaw, July 9, 1900, J. S. Hogg Let. Pr., 16, pp. 376–377.

CHAPTER XVIII

Hogg in Partial Eclipse: the Rise of Senator Joe Bailey and John Nance Garner

CITIZEN JAMES HOGG was using every opportunity to keep alive the spirit of reform and to make friends for the "Hogg Amendments." Soon after his return from the National Democratic Convention, he went to Galveston to attend the meeting of the State Bar Association. He always enjoyed the Bar meetings, which provided the chance to renew old friendships, but as he listened to James L. Autry's paper entitled "The Business Corporation in Texas: Its Formation if Domestic, Its Admission if Foreign" he was highly disturbed. Autry cited the recent example of the new charter granted Waters-Pierce to show that the legal formalities had the effect of continuing "the immense business of the defendant in all of its details and ramifications without jar or friction." Autry concluded that the permit "could not have been properly denied," although the state's officers could have delayed their action.[1]

Hogg was not content to let this thesis go unchallenged. He complimented Autry on his paper, but held that the charter should not have been granted. The business of the company in Texas should have been wound up, and in case of forfeiture the properties should go, not necessarily to the donors, but to those "who were entitled to it, creditors and others." He called the granting of the new charter a farce and a travesty upon justice, for the contracts were not changed, the agents were not changed; the company "didn't even change the mules which were drawing its wagons; . . . it did not change its books or accounts; it did not change its name; it did not change the instrumentalities under which it was declared a trust. If our trust laws are to be held under such precarious conditions as that we had as well wipe them out." Questions developed:

Mr. W. S. Searcy of Brenham: The old concern had closed business, and this was a new concern.

[1] Galveston *Daily News,* July 26, 1900.

Governor Hogg: No, sir; the concern did not go out of existence. It voluntarily changed its clothes. It did not change its domicile; it did not change its stock; it did not change its contracts, nor any of the instrumentalities by which it oppressed the people of this State as a trust. . . .

Prof. W. S. Simkins of The University of Texas: The declaration of that company being a trust was because of its contract—

Governor Hogg: No, sir; because of its operations. . . .

Prof. Simkins: . . . I can not see to save my life, why, because the new corporation marshals itself under the same name, it should be condemned before it does an act contrary to law.

Governor Hogg: I said that that corporation is a trust and that it has not been punished. The decree of the court was not enforced.[2]

Hogg would not agree that the laws of Texas were ineffective, but insisted that they had not been enforced, citing the example of the fifty-dollar-a-day penalty for every person belonging to the trust. The money had not been collected prior to or after granting a new charter. He charged that the president of the company, "a confessed criminal, stalked into the State Capitol, treated with the state officials, unwhipped of justice. That is what holds our laws in contempt."[3]

The next day Attorney General Thomas Smith arrived at the meeting and asked permission to discuss the legal aspects of granting the new charter to Waters-Pierce. He reminded the group of his long-standing friendship with the former governor but declared that Mr. Hogg was not talking law. In rejoinder Hogg made the point that he had not mentioned the attorney general the day before but had referred to the duty of the secretary of state. Smith then defended Secretary Hardy, who had acted upon his recommendations, to which Hogg replied that the secretary of state was there "to scourge back corporations which the laws of Texas forbid to do business in this state." He maintained that the oil company was not authorized to do business in Texas; the decree of the Supreme Court said it was not. Had Smith advised the secretary of state not to grant the permit because the new company was a fraud and subterfuge, and had they gone into court and the court found that the company was not a subterfuge, "we would at least have had a decree of the court to guide us in legislation hereafter." Concluding, Hogg drove his shafts home. He declared that it was difficult to re-educate corporation lawyers who had been trained to discover and employ technical defenses; while he had frequently been criticized for his lack

[2] *Ibid.*, July 26–27, 1900; quoted in Cotner, *op. cit.*, pp. 479–480.
[3] *Ibid.*, pp. 481–482.

of legal learning, he had learned enough to be able to teach his critics something in common sense, if not in law. He would never agree that in Texas "it is impossible to enforce the laws against the strong, while the penitentiary is full of the weak."[4]

Fresh from this clarification of his stand on law enforcement, Hogg went to the State Democratic Convention held August 8–10 at Waco. As the delegates assembled, the negotiations of County Attorney Cullen Thomas and Mr. Pierce's attorneys in May were being aired, with charges and countercharges. The local papers had printed several lengthy statements from the men involved, and partisan feeling ran high. Tom Ball and others were ready with a resolution defending the integrity of Secretary Hardy, Attorney General Smith, and Congressman Bailey; John Duncan, Hogg's former Tyler partner, was equally ready to introduce the resolution censuring the actions of the same three.

Bailey, greatly alarmed as he realized that the commotion might jeopardize his chances to be approved for the Senate by the Convention he had worked so hard to control, was anxious to tell his story. When he obtained the floor he reviewed the high points of his conversations with Pierce in the past spring:

Bailey: Mr. Pierce, I don't believe the people of Texas ought to and I do not believe the people of Texas will tolerate the methods of the Standard Oil Company. I would rather go back to the tallow candle than do it.

Pierce: Mr. Bailey, you are still laboring under the same impression that all the people in your State are under. We are not a part of the Standard Oil Company. . . . The Standard Oil Company has never owned a controlling interest in our company.

Bailey: If that is true then you go down to the State of Texas and tell our Democratic officers that that is true. They want to know that you are no part of the trust, and that you will abide by our laws, and you will have no trouble in being relicensed to transact business.[5]

When Pierce offered to employ Bailey as his attorney, Bailey said he replied:

"No, Sir; you haven't got money enough to hire me. [Cheers] I would not be employed for such a purpose. If you want to abide by the law you won't need a lawyer." . . . He took my advice. He came here, took an oath he

[4] Galveston *Daily News,* July 27, 1900.

[5] Dallas *Morning News,* August 9, 1900. Cf. Ralph and Muriel Hidy, *Pioneering in Big Business, 1882–1911: History of the Standard Oil Company,* pp. 486, 639–646.

would uphold the majesty of our law, begging permission to conduct his business in conformity with the law.[6]

After referring to Attorney General Smith's ruling that the effect of the Supreme Court decision was to put the company out of business in Texas after May 31, Bailey said, "I happened to be at the capital at that time [May 1] and talked with the Attorney General." Then he told Pierce that "he had to make up his mind to obey Texas laws." He suggested that Pierce go to Waco, pay the penalties, and seek a new charter.

At this point he was interrupted by Colonel Donovan of Colorado City: "Mr. Bailey, did you not at that time recognize the fact that you were negotiating with a criminal who was under indictment in the State of Texas?" When sharp words from Bailey followed, Donovan started belligerently for the platform but was stopped by some of the delegates. Continuing his defense, Bailey spoke of his long friendship with Governor Francis and how he trusted his word "implicitly"; when Francis said that Pierce would obey Texas laws, "that was enough for me." Therefore, Bailey went to Waco and told County Attorney Thomas that he believed Thomas "ought to settle" with Pierce, "being sure that he pays a penalty that shall vindicate the authority of the State of Texas. Who says that is wrong?"

> Voice: "Me."
> Bailey: "Who? Who?"
> Another voice: "An idiot."
> Bailey: "No, he is not an idiot. He is a scoundrel. [Cheers, hisses, great uproar, but despite its length denies he needs sergeant-at-arms] I detain you too long. I know that nobody believes [these charges], and I did not think it necessary to prove my innocence, but I did think that I owed it to my friends to make them a plain, honest statement of the truth so that hereafter nobody should misstate.[7]

When Bailey finished speaking, there was great applause. Then came calls for Hogg.

Hogg went straight to the point: "The material question presented by the repermission of the Waters-Pierce Oil Company to do business in this state is: Shall Texas, or the trusts control? [Wild cheers]"[8] The gist of his brief remarks was that he doubted if the action of the secretary of state should be accepted in itself as enough to override Texas laws and the Supreme Court decision. With all respect to Attorney General Smith,

[6] Dallas *Morning News,* August 9, 1900.
[7] *Ibid.*   [8] *Ibid.*

506

he said he believed Smith was mistaken in his advice. After a long effort, Texas officials had finally had a hold on "the tail of a slimy serpent and they should not [again] let it get hidden in the tall grass. The public deserved to be protected and the laws enforced."[9] He refrained from referring to Bailey's activities, but continued to hold the state's officers guilty of haste and careless action.

Hogg was followed by former Attorney General Martin Crane, who had initiated the suit against Waters-Pierce. He pointed out that the company had never stopped its work for one day and that the permit had been granted without so much as a change of name; he firmly believed that the new Missouri charter was evidence of fraud. He said that he had been advised that the commotion was a mere personal fight between J. W. Bailey and J. S. Hogg and that he should keep out. He would, however, like to know whether the Democratic Convention had "met to demonstrate which is the biggest man, Jim Hogg or Joe Bailey, or had it met for the purpose of mapping out a policy of government which must be enforced in this country in order that it may remain a country of the free?"[10] Crane was understandably defending his own record, but, like Hogg, he felt that Bailey had brought the painstaking work of several years to naught and that the present Texas officials had been duped or pressured, or had been careless in their duty.

The speeches dragged out, and a Dallas *News* reporter called it the "most acrimonious and bitter fight in the history of the Democratic party since the day when Richard Coke dethroned Edmund J. Davis." A closer parallel was the "Car-Stable" Convention of 1892, because, as in that convention, the issue was whether Hogg's reform amendments should be accepted or rejected. Bailey now seemed allied with Clark as the defender of big business, and Bailey had a larger Democratic following than Clark ever had in 1892.

Thomas Smith, smarting under the attack, excoriated Hogg's record. He charged that Hogg, while governor, had issued pardons to "two men convicted of violating the antitrust laws of Texas and that he had relicensed more trusts than all of the governors for a decade."[11] (The pardon records in the State Archives throw no light on the first charge, while the agents of Waters-Pierce Oil Company who were convicted

[9] *Ibid.*

[10] *Ibid.* For reference to Crane's part in the Southern Pacific "unjust discrimination" suits and the collection of $25,000 in fines see Texas *House Journal* (1901), p. 148.

[11] Dallas *Morning News,* August 9, 1900.

were subsequently released, through a reversal of judgment by the higher courts. The second charge is even more baffling, since the secretary of state and the attorney general routinely carried the responsibility for relicensing.) Smith also called attention to the so-called "Southern Pacific Compromise Cases" in which he declared citizen Hogg was "the attorney for Colis P. Huntington."

No information has been located in the files of the Hogg and Robertson firm or in the Southern Pacific Archives in Houston to support Smith's statement that Hogg was retained to assist Huntington's interests in these cases. His well-known rule was not to take cases against the State of Texas. Further, the following excerpts of letters from Crane and Hogg to the Railroad Commissioners speak for themselves. Crane wrote to Chairman Reagan late in January 1899: "Any sort of compromise would . . . magnify Judge McCormick's position as a rate maker." A few days later Hogg wrote to each of the Commissioners: "If you compromise those cases upon any condition short of absolute surrender, . . . then you must expect to meet the common criticism often heard, that you are too weak to cope with the Railways."[12]

The speeches dragged on in acrimony. Finally, when all possible steam had been let loose, the Convention chose to avoid censuring or condoning by formal action. Everybody was anxious to get away for some interval of relaxation before the important night session, when the question of accepting the platform, with or without the Hogg amendments, would occupy the limelight.

A headline writer for the Dallas *News*, prematurely interpreting Bailey's escape from formal censure to mean that the Bailey forces were going to run roughshod over the Hogg opposition, worded his summation thus:

THE KING IS DEAD! LONG LIVE THE KING![13]

Hogg disliked kings, and he was far from dead. Long before the evening session began, the galleries of the hall were jammed, largely with Waco people who hoped Joe Bailey would put Hogg down in a way Clark had never been able to do. Twenty-five boxes were filled with ladies, who came as spectators to the political arena. Bailey recognized the danger of letting Hogg address even a hostile audience, but he was

[12] Martin M. Crane, *Report of the Attorney General, 1897–1898* (1899), p. 5; Texas *House Journal* (1901), pp. 144–148; J. S. Hogg to John H. Reagan, L. J. Story, A. Mayfield, January 31, 1899, J. S. Hogg Let. Pr., 15, pp. 315–317.
[13] Dallas *Morning News*, August 10, 1900.

helpless, since the rejection of the minority platform report in committee had forced the issue to the floor of the Convention. Subduing his edginess, he took his seat on the platform with Reagan, Smith, and Hogg.

The three proposals advanced by Hogg were: 1) no free passes (railroad workers excepted); 2) no corporation money in elections; and 3) termination of insolvent corporations. In lieu of these three amendments, and in an effort to win, the Bailey majority had written into the proposed platform a weak anti-free pass clause, exempting sheriffs, constables, marshals and their deputies, and employees of railroads. The majority and the minority each would have one hour and a half to give their arguments. Unfortunately, Hogg had spoken in Waco a few weeks before, and, no doubt, some in the audience did not wish to hear him again. Others, however, came purposely to harass him. When Hogg was introduced someone yelled, "Give him three seconds!" at once the hall was resounding with "howls, cheers, hisses, and jeers." He tried to begin:

"Are you afraid to hear a question discussed?"
"Is it possible—" he was forced to pause.
"When free speech becomes suppressed—(more uproar)
"It won't take long," he pleaded. (Calls for Bailey—Odell, etc.)
"Gentlemen, (Hogg looked over the front rows) I know you are drunk."
A Delegate: "Mr. Chairman, I move to table the gentleman from Travis."[14]

Alarmed at the turn of events, some of Hogg's foes tried to restore order. Chairman Robert E. Prince of Navarro recognized his fellow delegate George Jester, who asked for quiet but got nowhere. Meanwhile, Hogg was like an old lion at bay. As the howling increased, it looked to some as if he might be compelled to give up. Then, thoroughly angry, he began throwing out a barrage of remarks, which were audible above the cat-calls and boos to at least some people at the front of the hall:

I see a lot of lop-eared scoundrels here who don't want to hear free speech. A man who is cowardly enough, who is base enough not to hear a speech is not a Democrat and is a fool besides. (Cheers and great confusion) I will stay here until I have been heard. I rise to speak for the people of Texas whom you are representing. The issue ought to concern you who are hollowing as the henchmen of corporations. (Cheers) I speak for your posterity, you cowardly scoundrels. (Cheers) I speak for those who are at home

[14] *Ibid.*

509

while you are here trying to tear down the institutions by your villainy tonight. (Cheers) I have faced a mob when the mob had the nerve to face me and I never shrank from death and no lot of white-livered curs can suppress my voice in a Democratic convention. (Cheers) There sits over there (turning to the rows of seats to his right) a cowardly whelp who would take a position in a convention to try and cry down a gentleman. (Fights break out—pandemonium) [15]

At this point Sheriff Tom Bell and the sergeants-at-arms by laboring for over five minutes managed to get a degree of order, while Hogg stood erect, glaring at the crowd. His face was flushed and his hands were clinched:

"Cowards," he exclaimed.

"No bully, no group of bullies, can drive me away from here," he shouted to a friend who had come down to the footlights.

"There is a fellow over there that I am going to stay with if it takes until tomorrow night."

Then came a strange lull—followed by a storm of cries for Hogg to proceed. Hogg sensed at once that he was finally master. Composure almost completely regained, he said:

I want to say that those of you who are opposed to me and act like gentlemen, I respect you. Those of you who undertake to howl me down I have no respect for and the man who will try it is a white-livered, cowardly cur. . . . I have come to speak to this convention, and by gatlins, I am going to do it.

He referred to his "two honorable opponents" on the platform and asked that they receive attention when they should speak. Declaring that the amendment concerning insolvent corporations involved what he believed to be $200 million of fictitious railroad values, he said any man who was not interested or concerned was "a fool and a knave." Then he added: "My friends, if you want to make up and have me withdraw the ugly expressions, withdraw your taunts and your jibes and your sauce and we will make peace."

From the audience: "Go on." "All right,—"

Hogg: "Now then, I am in a good humor. I hope there are no hard feelings, boys."[16]

The uproar had lasted more than twenty minutes. As he launched into his main speech there was no more trouble, and he held the floor

[15] *Ibid.*   [16] *Ibid.*

510

for about an hour. To many among the audience this was the greatest speech of his life. To Hogg it was the greatest strain he had ever been under, and the fact that it had happened at a convention of the Democratic Party, in which he so long and implicitly had placed his faith, inflicted a spiritual wound that took long to heal. Those closest to him believe that he overstrained his heart that night, and they saw many lingering effects of the physical and mental ordeal. But before he finished speaking, he knew that he had made many friends for his amendments. Furthermore, he had demonstrated that a private citizen could propose amendments without seeking any rewards through public office.

Tom Ball was the first to answer him. He argued that the legislature had sufficient power to pass laws on all of these subjects if it wished to do so and needed no instructions on how to proceed. He declared that everybody knew that Texas, rather than the corporations, was in control. He called Hogg's suggested penalty of forfeiture of charter if a corporation sent a lobbyist to Austin "iniquitous. . . . It would end the right of free petition and free speech."[17] When interrupted by a voice, asking if he denied that a legislature had ever been bought, Ball defended legislators as honorable men. He then went on to express doubt that Hogg's definition of insolvency would stand up in court. In a more sarcastic and personal tone, D. W. Odell of Cleburne declared that Hogg's speech and "eulogy of himself was as tragic and pathetic as any he had ever seen." He charged Hogg with spreading "old slime and slander," and thought that the stock and bond law was enough to corral the railroads. He accused Hogg of not trusting Governor Sayers and the legislature to know what Texas needed by way of new legislation.[18]

Anything could happen now. It was an hour past midnight when the vote was taken on substituting the Hogg amendments for Plank 10 of the majority platform. When the vote was counted at 1:35 A.M. the Hogg amendments had carried—561¼ votes to 401¾. Smiling, Hogg arose and thanked the delegates for their action. Adjournment was at 1:45. Hogg had won the first round of the battle, but the 1901 legislature would decide whether or not the people could vote on the amendments.

When the noticeably conservative legislature assembled in January, 1901, there was still no opponent to Bailey for the Senate seat. Hogg continued to refuse to run against him—or for any public office; he

---

[17] *Ibid.*   [18] *Ibid.* Cf. Texas *House Journal* (1903), pp. 5–6.

preferred to remain the citizen-statesman, taking the long look and trying to plug the holes in the dyke of reform as they appeared. The immediate outlook was not encouraging: Bailey's friend from Waco, Robert Henry, became the speaker of the House. But not all was smooth sailing for Bailey. Early in the session Representative David McFall of Austin introduced a resolution calling for an investigation "to ascertain if Mr. Bailey is a proper man to send to the United States Senate." His remarks also included a declaration that the relicensing of the Waters-Pierce Oil Company was "a fraud upon the State of Texas."[19]

Young John Nance Garner, serving his second term from Uvalde, headed the caucus of Bailey men who went to the Senate aspirant for instructions on how to handle the resolution. Bailey said that he did not want the investigation voted down, but that the words "By David Mc-Fall" should be added after "it is charged" in the resolution. Hearings were conducted for several days. Barnett Gibbs came down from Dallas to detail the peculiar land deal with Bailey and Francis. Bailey took the stand to repeat the statements made at Waco, "so that no honest man can misunderstand the transaction and no scoundrel can ever again successfully misrepresent me." He declared he would have taken a fee for his work had he known how prolonged the case would be:

I am a lawyer and I sincerely believe that I will never be such a political coward as to fear to defend any business when I think their rights are assailed unjustly, or with unnecessary severity. Neither am I such a fool as to really want to keep a legitimate business out of the State, or such a demagogue to pretend that I do.[20]

Attorney General Smith also put in an appearance, defending himself against Hogg's earlier charge of mistaken legal judgment and exonerating Bailey from the implication of improper influence.

On January 23, just forty minutes before the balloting for United States Senator was scheduled to begin, the House voted 87 to 25 to accept the investigating committee's report that no evidence of legal or moral wrong had been presented to reflect upon the state's officials or Bailey. At noon the first ballot for United States Senator showed Bailey had received 137 of the 141 votes cast by the House and Senate. Only 15 members had not voted.[21] Senator-elect Bailey thanked the legisla-

[19] Texas *House Journal* (1901), pp. 47, 137; Dallas *Morning News,* January 12, 1901.

[20] Texas *House Journal* (1901), January 21, 1901, pp. 145 ff.

[21] *Ibid.,* pp. 191, 205. Acheson, *Bailey,* p. 151, gives the total vote as 110, giving only the House vote.

tors and left for Washington, hoping that the oil charter negotiation was a dead issue. But he knew that the Hogg and Reagan forces would not forget the way he had defeated Senator Chilton.

Although the legislature had been instructed to submit the "Hogg Amendments" to the people for their approval or disapproval, the first month of the 1901 session passed with little action in this direction. The delay was partly explained by the amount of time given to the Bailey investigation, but Hogg knew that corporation lobbyists were also responsible. Finally he asked to be permitted to address the legislature on Joint Resolution No. 1. When a reply seemed slow in coming, he decided to arrange a public speech at the Hancock Opera House. However, the ambitious young compromiser John Garner, who was impatient for the passage of a redistricting bill which would enable him to carve out a new district in Southwest Texas and assist his early election to Congress, felt that Hogg was getting unduly rude treatment, especially as he sought no public office. In fighting trusts and demanding that insurance companies invest in Texas larger amounts of the premiums collected, Garner was upholding the reform pattern, although he was not pro-Hogg; he and a few others decided, perhaps realizing that it might be the better part of political wisdom to keep Hogg off the popular forum, to grant him permission to speak before the Committee on Constitutional Amendments at 4 P.M. on February 5. Garner introduced the motion inviting him to speak; in so doing he reflected the instructions his constituents had given him.[22]

Hogg was pleased to accept the invitation. When he appeared before the Committee he reviewed the reasons that had prompted him to propose the amendments. He then reminded his audience of legislators that Plank 10, upon which Democrats had been elected, called for submission of the joint amendment to the people. He said he knew that the session was still young and he had "every confidence that the matter would be submitted to the people," but since he must leave Austin soon on business he felt obliged to answer the ten major "arguments or approaches" of the opposing lobbyists who were "swarming around the capitol."

As everyone knew—though the full significance of the event had by no means yet registered—on January 10, 1901, the Lucas oil gusher at Spindletop had come in. Hogg and his friend (and fellow Democrat) James Swayne of Fort Worth were forming a syndicate to handle land

[22] Bascom N. Timmons, *Garner of Texas* (New York, Harper & Brothers, 1948), p. 22.

leases and oil business in the booming area about Beaumont. Hogg had engaged to travel outside the state within the next few weeks, "to be gone for an indefinite time." Prior to his departure, he felt he should "in this public way renew the campaign to support the amendment," so that when he returned he could follow it up, "after its submission," until the people finally adopted or rejected it.[23]

To anyone who lived through the first frenzy of the oil boom in Texas, it is probably remarkable that any man involved in it should still find time to give attention to such matters as reform legislation. However, that able but sometimes cynical writer about the New South, C. Vann Woodward, misinterpreted Hogg enough to call him a deserter from the ranks of the reformers. Professor Woodward ignored the evidence of what Hogg was really doing, and wrote:

Texas reverted to the control of a succession of conservative governors. Former Governor Hogg, firebrand of 1890, was touring Northeastern states in 1898 seeking to convince capitalists that Texas was the safest possible place for investment and corporate enterprise. A few years later he was amassing a fortune as an oil-company promoter.[24]

The implication is clear that he thought Hogg had joined the malefactors of great wealth and had forgotten the people. Material for study of Hogg's continuing role as a citizen-statesman was not readily available to Woodward. Contemporaries of Hogg—men who had clear evidence of Hogg's never-ceasing endeavors to see that the public was treated justly—made statements which have misled later investigators. Heretofore, neither historians nor local critics have taken sufficiently into account the rich variety of things, both of the world and of the spirit, that the big man's curiosity was eagerly capable of including in his life, nor his unusual steadfastness of purpose.

His speech to the Committee in Austin was long and faithfully reasoned. He believed that the people should be warned about the subtle effects of the railroad consolidation bills going through the legislature, declaring that their result was to entwine the spurious stocks—in 1892 worth three to nine cents on the dollar—with the Commission-regulated, bona fide stock of new lines. As the old lines absorbed the new with relatively light debts, "they have new resources for the support and

[23] Cotner, *op. cit.*, pp. 485–486; personal interview with Patillo Higgins in San Antonio, July, 1952; Beaumont *Daily Enterprise*, January 10, 1901.
[24] C. Vann Woodward, *Origins of the New South*, p. 370. In his account of lynching, Woodward cited a case at Paris, but failed to show Hogg's efforts to assure legal proceedings.

payment of their illegal heavy burdens. By this process they are insidiously, firmly, fastening these two hundred millions of frauds forever on the people of this State." Hogg wanted Texas to move into the third era of the "Railway Age," the Fair Period, and leave behind the Free Period and the Fraud Period in which the "princes of feenance" had flooded the country with watered stocks and bonds:

My confidence in human nature has never been shaken. I believe in the inherent honesty of man. Acting upon the rule that ninety-five per cent of the people whom I meet are honest, in all my varied dealings up to this day I have never been disappointed in this estimate. With free passes coming to you through the mails and from the hands of your personal friends and in various other ways, I know that it would be exceedingly embarrassing for you to refuse them. My purpose is not to add to this embarrassment, but simply to say to these people who assert that passes are not given to influence members of the Legislature, that the public mind, which is poisoned with a suspicion to the contrary, should be relieved of all doubt on the subject. . . . It is left to you, gentlemen, as the representatives of the stalwart Democrats of Texas, to pass on and over all environments and obstacles to the goal of duty, and, regardless of personal considerations, see that the people's will shall be obeyed![25]

The lobbyists were delighted to know that Hogg was leaving the state; they hoped that the oil game would become so fascinating that he would forget all about his promise to follow up his educational program. Some overlooked his pledge to combat frauds: "I tender to the people who have always honored me my personal, professional and political resources in the contest to the end.

After Hogg withdrew, the debates began. Some men in the legislature, among them young Garner, honestly felt that the acceptance of all of the proposed reforms at once was too drastic and that the railroads would retaliate. Garner was especially disturbed because his own district, although near the Gulf of Mexico, had no good water outlet and was still bidding for more railroad building. One of his biographers wrote, "Actually, he thought it was just possible that Texas was more dependent upon the railroads than the railroads were on Texas."[26] At one stage of the debate, Garner declared: "I am not for making a po-

---

[25] Cotner, *op. cit.*, p. 499.

[26] Timmons, *Garner*, p. 22. When I wrote Garner (after he had retired as Vice-President) requesting some additional information on these events, he returned my letter, but had written on the margin: "Too busy living in the present to go into the past."

litical punching bag out of the railroads. I think we can find a way to take care of the buccaneers without hampering the developers." He vigorously objected to Hogg's "package" proposal and balked at what he described as Hogg's "take-all-or-take-nothing-attitude."[27]

Speaker Robert Henry, who had been elected by the pro-Bailey majority, suggested that someone was needed to give an objective view of the issues. Garner, who had become known "as an oiler of troubled water," was selected. A press report of Garner's views read:

He is instructed by the people of his district to vote for the amendments, but he is personally opposed to them. He argues the party mandate is binding and said that before he would violate instructions laid down by his constituents he would resign. Asked, "What would you do first, violate your oath to support the federal constitution or violate the instruction of your people?" Mr. Garner replied that the proposed amendments were not a violation of the federal constitution; if he thought they were, he would resign rather than vote for them.[28]

Another reporter stated that Garner's speech pleased both sides and "was a great piece of oratorical and argumentative diplomacy." When the vote on submitting the amendments to the people was taken, Hogg's proposal met defeat, despite the platform instructions. But Hogg was not giving up; he would propose the amendments again when the next legislature convened.

The year 1900 had not been an easy one for Hogg personally, with the increasing revolt against his leadership that climaxed in the nightmarish experience at Waco. The refusal of the legislature to submit his amendments to the people must have been a great disappointment to him; however, Texas had not heard the last of those proposals. He expected better results from the work of two young leaders, Tom Connally and Pat Neff, who decided to back a progressive program for Texas. Hogg continued to criticize some pro-railroad and pro-business aspects of the administrations of Joseph D. Sayers and Samuel W. T. Lanham. Hogg regretted that Colonel House had seen fit in 1902 to back Lanham, the last of "the Confederate governors," instead of Hogg's boyhood chum, Tom Campbell. However, at the Democratic convention Campbell had come to the forefront of the progressive forces by successfully inserting a straight-out prohibition of "the employment of children under twelve years of age in factories using machines," instead of the weak recommendation that the legislature pass a law "for

[27] Timmons, *op. cit.*, p. 23.   [28] *Ibid.*

the protection of children of tender age from overwork." The completed platform called for the submission to the people of amendments to provide a system of state banks and to end the free-pass abuses. Hogg encouraged Judge Alexander W. Terrell in his efforts to enact uniform primary and general election laws in 1902. He also encouraged Tom Connally in his successful efforts to make Pat Neff speaker of the House in 1903.

Meanwhile, James Hogg was about to enter the last major period of his varied career; it would extend his horizons widely and bring great satisfaction to his enormous and genial capacity for exploring and enjoying life. His active participation in national politics would subside, but he was never to lose interest in the political developments of his much-loved native state or of the world at large. His two major concerns were the welfare of his children and the search for a way to guarantee to Texans and Americans the better life which could come from the increasing production of the natural resource—oil.

CHAPTER XIX

The Hogg-Swayne Syndicate and the Texas Company

WHEN ON THE MORNING of January 10, 1901, the Lucas gusher roared in at Spindletop, near Beaumont, spouting more than 75,000 barrels of oil a day, the news had very much the same effect upon the world as the discovery of gold in California had had a half century earlier. Once more the planet was offering largess for the taking, and men began flocking from the ends of the earth to the Beaumont-Houston area. Thus dramatically, the "oil century" had opened. The Gulf coast would soon be the scene of a great industrial boom, and in a little longer time the whole of Texas as Jim Hogg's generation had once known it would undergo a subtle change.

As the east coast enjoyed the first industrial boom in the first half of the nineteenth century and the west coast experienced a boom from virgin resources and overseas trade in the second half, so the Gulf coast after 1901 was laying the foundations for a prolonged development based upon the new oil and gas potential of the Southwest and lands bordering the Gulf of Mexico and the Caribbean Sea. Just as the early beginnings of manufacturing in coastal New England became the magnet of capital and then financed a network of railroads centering in the Boston-New York region, so in time the pipelines would come from West Texas, Oklahoma, and Kansas to refineries about Port Arthur and Houston. Coal would cease to be the determining factor in the location of industry, and the Gulf South, as far north as Jim Hogg's boyhood iron-laden lands about Rusk, would experience prosperity. The black stuff gushing from the soil would make Texas of importance to every state in the Union and to countries overseas that in 1900 perhaps had not even known its name.

To most of the men who reached the area in the next few months— their rush sometimes resembling the passage of steel filings to a magnet —the larger implications of what had happened were far from clear, but there were a few who understood, among them a former mayor of Toledo, Ohio, Samuel "Golden Rule" Jones, who was quoted by the *Literary Digest* as observing:

518

It is fortunate for the oil trade that it is not illuminating oil. If it were, it would paralyze the whole industry. Its advent, however, means that liquid fuel is to be the fuel of the twentieth century. . . . I believe this is the real beginning of the era of liquid fuel in the United States.[1]

Ever since 1859, when the Drake well in Pennsylvania came in at seventy feet, the search for oil in the United States had been increasingly intensified. In Texas the existence of oil and gas seeps in various regions had been known for a long time, but little had been done about them, since both capital and proper technical equipment for deep boring were unavailable. In 1892, Patillo Higgins, a brickmaker of Beaumont, began to assemble land, part of which he later named Gladys City, and, through his Gladys City Oil, Gas, and Manufacturing Company, to promote a search for oil. On a northern trip some time earlier, seeking to learn the secrets of making better bricks, he had seen Pennsylvania and Ohio kilns being fired with oil or gas, fuels that gave a more even and easily regulated heat than the log wood he had been using. The result was a finished brick of greatly improved quality. Back in Beaumont, he was determined to find gas and oil, believing that the salt domes and certain smells of the Gulf region indicated its presence in abundance.[2]

In 1893 he and his partner, George W. Carroll, hired Walter B. Sharp, a twenty-three-year-old drilling contractor, who had been experimenting with various kinds of well-drilling equipment since he was eighteen, to make test wells on Spindletop, a low mound on part of the Higgins land. At about four hundred feet Sharp bogged down in quicksand, and it was apparent that the treacherously shifting sands underlay most of the mound. Higgins, though temporarily thwarted, did not lose his faith in the region but had no more money for further experiment then. Sharp moved over to Sour Lake, fifty or so miles from Beaumont. At Sour Lake, long-famed locally as a health resort because of its mineral springs, Sharp had moderate success in drilling and for a time operated his own small refinery, using wood for fuel and turning out eight different grades of oil. When the depression of the mid-1890's hit, all oil production slowed; Sharp finally went back to itinerant water drilling, moving back and forth from Texas to North Carolina and making a fair

---

[1] *The Literary Digest,* XXII (February 9, 1901), 3; Beaumont *Daily Enterprise,* January 10, 1901; *The Citizen* (Houston), "The Spindletop Edition," January 11, 1951; Stewart Schackne and N. D'Arcy Drake, *Oil for the World* (New York, Harper & Brothers, 1950), p. 97; *The American Review of Reviews,* XXIX (January, 1904), 56; Everette L. DeGolyer, "Anthony F. Lucas and Spindletop," *Southwest Review,* XXXI (Fall, 1945), 83 ff.

[2] Personal interview with Patillo Higgins at his home in San Antonio, July, 1952.

living. Sometime after 1897 he and his brothers John and James turned up in Corsicana, the blackland region where a small oil boom was going on. With their improved rotary rigs, they were kept fairly busy.[3]

In 1897 a first-class oil refinery had been built at Corsicana by Joseph Stephen Cullinan, a recent arrival from Pennsylvania who had received his schooling in the oil business by working a dozen years for the Standard Oil Company. In 1895, at the age of thirty-six, he decided to organize his own Petroleum Iron Works. Making a trip to Texas, he arranged to buy 50,000 barrels of as yet unproduced oil and with the backing of John Galey and James Guffey, pipe and castings manufacturers of Pittsburgh, planned to build his refinery at the new Corsicana field. For some reason Galey and Guffey later withdrew their support; Cullinan, needing additional capital to complete his commitments, in 1897 formed a partnership with two Standard officials, Henry C. Folger and Calvin N. Payne, under the name of the J. S. Cullinan Company (the predecessor of the Magnolia Petroleum Company).[4] Waters-Pierce, controlled by Standard, agreed to distribute the products of the six-still refinery. Standard had hitherto paid relatively little attention to basic production, preferring to control refining and sales of oil and kerosene, but the increasing oil activity in Texas was no doubt an important factor in the efforts of H. Clay Pierce to get Waters-Pierce reinstated there in 1900— with or without the help of Joe Bailey.

Cullinan, tall, handsome, and vigorous, prided himself on being a good judge of character. On meeting Walter Sharp, he was at once impressed with the ability, intelligence, resourcefulness, and good humor of the six-foot redhead. Sharp had by now become thoroughly expert with cable tools and rotary-rig methods of drilling and had begun to develop, following out a suggestion from George Broughton, agent of the American Well Works Company in Dallas, a way of using mud to drill through caving sands.[5] Experimenting further with the method, he was bringing it to a degree of perfection that would serve the oil industry magnificently. By 1897 Sharp had drilled twelve-hundred-foot water

[3] Personal discussions with Mrs. Walter B. Sharp. Mrs. Sharp and her son, Dudley, have been the prime movers in making possible the new Pioneers in Texas Oil Collection at the University of Texas. Stories by and about many of the oilmen in Southeast and North Texas have already been preserved on tape recordings.

[4] *The Magnolia News* (Dallas), April–May, 1951, pp. 1–4; Marquis James, *The Texaco Story* (New York, The Texas Company, 1953), pp. 12 ff.

[5] E. H. Happel, Secretary City Assessor (Dallas) to Walter B. Sharp, July, 1897, Walter B. Sharp Letters, II, 49, Pion. Tex. Oil Col.; personal interview with Dr. William Owens, Columbia University, 1958.

wells in Alabama. In 1900 he went out to California to observe the oil boom at Bakersfield, returning with more faith than ever in his own improved equipment.

Meanwhile, Cullinan, searching for new uses to which oil might be put, had found that a sprinkled coating of oil worked well to keep down the thick dust of the streets and tried out the innovation successfully in Corsicana and Dallas. And on Christmas Day, 1898, he lighted fires under the boilers of the first oil-burning locomotive in Texas, which then proceeded to make the run on the "Cotton Belt" from Corsicana to Hillsboro.[6]

Technical advances continued. Drillers such as Al and Curt Hamill, who learned the mud process from the Sharps, Jim Savage, and Bill and Jim Sturm, were continually improving their methods and had begun to use heavier machinery at Corsicana. When Guffey and Galey, who were supplying from Pittsburgh large amounts of pipe and multiple castings to various oil fields, decided to back Anthony Lucas in his second try to bring in an oil well at Beaumont, they recommended the Hamill brothers to him as drillers. Lucas (born Luchlich in Dalmatia in 1855) had been trained in engineering in Europe. Coming to the United States in 1879 to visit a relative, he decided to stay, anglicized his name, and became naturalized. Around 1900 he was considered an outstanding authority in salt-dome structures, having pioneered in prospecting for them from California to Louisiana. Reaching the Beaumont area in 1899, he took a lease on some of Higgins' land—including part of Spindletop mound—and supervised the drilling of a few small wells, all of them unsuccessful. His scant capital was soon exhausted, and reports made on the area by geologists and other oil experts were unfavorable and discouraging.

However, in 1900 Lucas decided to try again, and eventually won Guffey's and Galey's support in obtaining leases from Higgins. With the technical advances, rotary drilling with mud, heavier machinery, the multiple castings supplied from Pittsburgh—plus good advice from the University of Texas field geologist Dr. William B. Phillips[7] and the persistence of Guffey, Lucas, and Higgins—the stage was set for the climax in the search for oil. The well, started at the end of October,

---

[6] Frank Cullinan Interview, Pion. Tex. Oil Col., Tape Recording No. 151; James, *op. cit.*, p. 12.

[7] From *Spindletop*, by James A. Clark and Michel T. Halbouty, pp. 109–110. Copyright 1952 by James A. Clark and Michel T. Halbouty. Reprinted by permission of Random House, Inc., p. 37.

1900, was finally pushed down through the formerly frustrating quick-sands to over 1,160 feet. On the morning of January 10, 1901, opera-tions had been shut down because the bit on the rotary drill needed changing. Just as the bit was being lowered, the well broke loose, roaring like a cannon shot; the subterranean treasure was hurled far above the derrick in an abundance that had never been dreamed.

On January 11, Walter Sharp (just recovered from a short illness) looked over the Hamills' equipment, musingly watched the spouting of the black geyser, then walked the few yards to his old drill pipe that had been protruding from the ground since the 1893 try. Laconically, he told a reporter that "heavier machinery spelled success."[8] Within a few days he had five rigs working at Spindletop. When he heard that over 4,000 railroad tickets had been sold in New York and Ohio to men heading for Beaumont, he wired his friend Ed Prather in Dallas to get his hands on as much money as possible and come at once, so that they could set up a leasing business. Sharp owned land at Sour Lake. When James Hogg arrived at Spindletop, Sharp was among the first men he talked to.

For years Hogg had hunted and fished and looked into railroad mat-ters along the Gulf coastal plain, so that he knew the area around Beau-mont well. In 1899 he and his partner, Judge Robertson, had bought the Gaines Plantation near West Columbia in Brazoria County for $15,784.[9] This appears to have been purely a land speculation, with little or no thought of oil or gas, for immediately after the purchase Hogg began to search diligently for purchasers. However, the land still had not been sold when the fabulous stories of Spindletop brought thousands of specu-lators and spectators to South Texas. One version of how Jim Hogg happened to become interested in oil development is related in a letter from O. B. Colquitt:

[8] Beaumont *Daily Enterprise,* January 12–15, 1901; Walter B. Sharp to Mrs. Sharp, January 24, 1901, Walter B. Sharp Letters, II, 6, Pion. Tex. Oil Col.

[9] J. S. Hogg to Ima Hogg (Eldorado, Schleicher County, Texas), July 9, 1900, J. S. Hogg Let. Pr., 16, p. 374; *ibid.,* July 13, p. 394; *ibid.,* July 17, p. 407; Walter P. Webb and H. Bailey Carroll, *Handbook of Texas,* I, 208; *ibid.,* II, 882. See also Ira H. Evans to James S. Hogg, March 23, 1901, J. S. Hogg Let. Rec., XXXIV, 187 E.

THE HOGG-SWAYNE SYNDICATE

O. B. COLQUITT

DALLAS, TEXAS

July 12, 1923

Geo. M. Bailey
Houston, Texas

Dear Sir:

. . . .

Relative to what I said about my probably being the cause of Hogg becoming interested in the oil business. I probably am not except incidentally.

My brother Will and I sunk one of the first producing wells for oil in Corsicana—he says we sunk the 4th producing well in the state and at the time the Lucas Gusher was found on Spindle Top Hill we had 6 wells in Corsicana making from 10 to 30 barrels per day, each.

Soon as I read on Sunday morning in the Dallas News an account of the Lucas Gusher coming in on Friday (the day before) I bought me a ticket for the first train to Beaumont, arriving there early Sunday morning. I remained there several days and made a purchase of a small tract of land out right, and returned to my home by way of Austin. Going up Congress avenue to Billy Wolf's barber shop, I met Hogg standing at the foot of the steps leading to his office which was up stairs in the same building. I stopped and chatted with him and he asked me where I had come from and I told him about the wonderful oil gusher and the chance to make some money by getting down there early and buying some leases or some lands, and urged him to go. But he said he was practicing law and didn't have any money to risk in such a venture. But I urged him that it would not hurt him to go down and see the sight any way but insisted that he should get in on some leases early. I was sure he would never see an oil well to beat it and I felt certain that there was a great chance for him to get rich. I urged him so strongly to go, that he finally said if it was like I represented it he might run down and take a look at it.

I went on to the capital [sic] and attended to some business I had with Gov. Sayers, and on my way back to the hotel I met Hogg again and he told me he had been thinking about what I had said to him. But he added that he never placed much faith in the boost of the well the newspapers had given it as he thought there might be a lot of "gas" about it, but that he had made up his mind to take my advice and go over to see what he could do, or at least look into the situation.

I went to my home in Terrell and remained there for a few days—about a week—and returned to Beaumont. On my return there as I went to the hotel from the train I found Gov. Hogg sitting on the porch of the old Crosby hotel. He saw me coming and got up and walked to meet me and told me he had no idea it was as big a thing as it was even after I had told him, but that I was the cause of his coming to Beaumont. He told me he had bought him some leases and was figuring then on considerable acreage in connection with some other friends; that he had already turned some leases and made some good profits, and he was about the most enthusiastic booster I found down there. He later went into the Hogg-Swayne syndicate.

This is the basis for my remark—whatever it may be worth to you.

Yours Truly,

O. B. Colquitt.[10]

In March, 1901, Hogg obtained an option to buy from the New York and Texas Land Company another tract, known as the Patton Place, which consisted of over 4,100 acres in the Martin Varner and Josiah H. Bell Leagues in Brazoria County. The price was $30,000, or just over $7 per acre.[11] He learned after buying the land that a lighted match would start brief fires from gas fumes escaping from the earth where artesian water bubbled up. Soon his letterhead showed these artesian wells, along with cattle, goats, and vegetables.

Before completing the purchase, Hogg arranged for a group of New Yorkers to visit the Gaines Plantation and the Patton Place (the latter now renamed Varner Plantation), with a view to making a contract with them to drill on his land. Believing that his old floor leader, Representative James Swayne of Fort Worth, who had had some oil experience, could help with the New Yorkers, especially as Buckley B. Paddock, former mayor of Fort Worth, had arranged the itinerary, Hogg had gone to Beaumont to visit him. Eventually no deal was made with the New Yorkers, and Hogg decided to bide his time. The purchase of Varner was completed on May 23, 1901.[12]

In April, Hogg went back to Spindletop (the "Big Hill"), which Guffey and Galey now controlled by virtue of their having backed the Lucas well. He saw many old friends there, including attorney George O'Brien, a former member of the Texas legislature, and an associate briefly with Higgins in contracting with Walter Sharp to drill for oil in 1893, and lumberman John H. Kirby, who had allied himself with Boston financial interests to obtain hundreds of acres of pine timberlands which became holdings of the Houston Oil Company.[13] Hogg also

[10] O. B. Colquitt to George M. Bailey, Let. Biog. J. S. Hogg, pp. 257–259.

[11] Ira H. Evans, president, the New York and Texas Land Company (Austin) to J. S. Hogg, March 23, 1901, J. S. Hogg Let. Pr., XXXIV, 187 E, 187 L; personal interview with Francis H. Evans, son of the Land Company's agent, March 24, 1958, on way to dedication of Hogg-Varner State Park.

[12] Personal interview with Miss Hogg, July 31, 1955; B. B. Paddock Papers.

[13] *The American Lumberman* (Staff), *Timber Resources in East Texas: Their*

talked with Patillo Higgins and George Carroll; Higgins' great faith in the underground resources of the Spindletop area had become legendary. No longer considered the slightly pathetic local dreamer, he was now known as the man who could infallibly show others, by his own brand of "moundology" and "creekology," where oil could be found. Soon he would be an honorary member of the new Beaumont Stock Exchange.[14]

The time sequence of the formation of the Hogg-Swayne Syndicate is not clear, since most of the earliest records have been lost. However, since Hogg spoke of his impending business trip when he addressed the legislative committee in early February, Swayne and he must have determined on the company prior to that. Sometime in early 1901 Swayne pointed out to Hogg that in view of the continuing rush to Spindletop (there were soon fourteen producers, some fifteen wells were being drilled, and many new rigs were being constructed preparatory to drilling) they needed capital to acquire more land. Judge Robert E. Brooks, A. S. Fisher, and William T. Campbell were invited to join the Hogg-Swayne Syndicate. The company, apparently, was not incorporated, since a careful check of the files of the secretary of state failed to reveal any record. Hogg understandably did not like the connotation of the word "corporation." However, there is ample evidence that the Syndicate was active early in 1901, principally engaged in the buying and selling of leases and in drilling and production on its own account.[15] On the last of May, when the Kiser-Kelley well about a mile north of the mound area was abandoned as a duster (a dry hole), prices for lands off the dome fell from $50,000 to $2,000 an acre in a matter of hours. The day after, prices of sites on the dome skyrocketed when Heywood No. 2 blew in, spouting a geyser over two hundred feet into the air.[16]

Andrew Mellon of Pittsburgh, who had engaged in oil and pipeline competition with Rockefeller in Pennsylvania and New York, knew that Standard Oil faced legal handicaps in Texas and that Waters-Pierce

---

Recognition and Development by *John H. Kirby* (Chicago, The American Lumberman, 1902), pp. 179–187.

[14] Ed Prather Interview with James Howard at Alexandria, Minnesota, August, 1952, typescript in Pion. Tex. Oil Col.; personal interview with Patillo Higgins, July, 1952.

[15] James, *The Texaco Story*, p. 15.

[16] Personal interview with Patillo Higgins, July, 1952; Clark and Halbouty, *Spindletop*, pp. 107 ff.; W. Scott Heywood, "Autobiography of an Oil Man," *Oil*, I (June, 1941), 31–34.

was still looked upon with suspicion there. He was doing well with his aluminum business (not yet as profitable as it would be after 1914), but he saw a chance to get ahead in the oil game in the face of Standard's handicap. He was prepared to put money into oil production through the development of the J. M. Guffey Petroleum Company (later Gulf) if the climate for investment in Texas proved satisfactory. He finally did invest, and before long the Guffey company laid a pipeline to Port Arthur and was building docks and ships to handle its oil.

In 1897, J. M. Page had bought fifteen acres on the eastern side of the Spindletop mound, for $450, part cash and the balance in two years.[17] Swayne had recently been trying to get Page to join in the formation of a $2-million corporation, allowing him $500,000 (over $30,000 an acre) for the land, not knowing that Lucas had leased it and that the control of mineral rights was now in the Guffey Petroleum Company. Finally approaching Guffey, the Syndicate was able to obtain mineral rights in the fifteen acres and in a well just going down, for what seemed then a high figure—$180,000. Page also received $105,000 for the surface rights. W. T. Campbell and Hogg then tackled the doubtful titles and pending lawsuits, and when these were practically all cleared up the total cost of the Syndicate's rights had come to around $310,000 or better than $20,000 per acre. In a short time, however, an acre on the mound was selling for over $40,000.[18] Guffey later recounted: "Northern men were not very well respected in Texas in those days. Governor Hogg was a power down there and I wanted him on my side because I was going to spend a lot of money."[19] Mellon and Guffey were also right in believing that Hogg would welcome them as competitors of Standard Oil.

The five partners, Hogg, Swayne, Campbell, Fisher, and Judge Brooks, had scraped together $40,000 to make the original plunge. When prices for land on the mound shot up and no one would sell, Hogg, concerned about the indebtedness, suggested that they offer to

[17] Clark and Halbouty, *op. cit.*, p. 108.

[18] *Ibid.*, pp. 105–107. Deed Records of Jefferson County, Beaumont, Texas, Vol. 53, p. 140, show the re-lease of the Page Tract in the Veatch Survey by J. M. Guffey Company to James W. Swayne, July 5, 1901. Carl C. Rister, *Oil! Titan of the Southwest* (Norman, University of Oklahoma Press, 1949), p. 62 n. 17. For the Tyrrell adjustment see Deed Records of Jefferson County, Vol. 38, pp. 544–545 and Vol. 54, pp. 474–476.

[19] Harvey O'Connor, *Mellon's Millions* (New York, John Day Company, 1933), p. 101.

sell small blocks and get out of debt. Their first sale of two and one-half acres brought $200,000! The Texas Oil and Development Company bought one-twentieth of an acre for $50,000, and Judge Brooks and some friends paid $15,000 for a twenty-fourth of an acre. The remainder of the tract was now clear of debt, and Hogg felt better as men still rushed to purchase quarters, sixteenths, and even thirty-seconds of an acre, paying part in cash and the rest in oil. However, he was somewhat skeptical about the oil payment part of the agreements: what if the price of oil per barrel became less than the cost of a cup of drinking water? In a short time, that development took place.

When the purchasers of the small holdings ("doormats") formed additional companies and further subdivided their land, the prospect of orderly development in the tract was doomed. Before long three hundred wells had been put down.[20] The lowering of pressures, due to the close spacing of the wells, demonstrated for all time the need for developing group or state regulation to assure a spacing necessary for prolonged maintenance of sufficient gas pressure to lift the oil to the surface. This was not generally understood in 1901, and actually was not effectively impressed on the independents until a special session of the Texas legislature in 1931. The Syndicate retained half of the Hogg-Swayne tract, which by the end of 1901 had become one of three conspicuous small areas of "jammed-up derricks," the other two being a five-acre spot in the Keith-Ward tract and George Carroll's Yellowpine tract.

Clark and Halbouty in their dramatic story of Spindletop make the following terse summary:

Whatever caused Guffey to sell the Page lease, whether it was to get Hogg into the field or as protection against Standard and political goodwill assurance, it was a monumental mistake. The resulting frenzied drilling program ruined the hill economically. It caused prices to drop to 3 cents a barrel, and hundreds of unnecessary holes dissipated the reservoir energy, resulting in the early end of flush production. Because they held 90 per cent of the leases on the hill proper, Guffey and Company suffered far more than anyone else from the Hogg-Swayne plan.

Guffey blamed Lucas, but the Mellons blamed Guffey for the tragic error. The error was tragic, that is, for Guffey and those who had the other eighty acres on the hill. It was the Hogg-Swayne deal, however, that caused

[20] For pictures of the derricks see brochure by American Petroleum Institute, *Spindletop, a Texas Titan* (New York, A.P.I., Department of Information, 1951), p. 12; Clark and Halbouty, *op. cit.,* pp. 84–85.

the drilling boom that gave hundreds of men the opportunity to learn the oil business from the ground up. Furthermore, it was the demand for oil built up during the period of overproduction, plus the sudden cessation of gushers, that inspired the mad search for other domes.

Had Lucas succeeded in his efforts to cover the dome with leases, or if the Page lease had not come under the syndicate's control, it is likely that there would have been no uncontrolled drilling boom. There would have been no Hogg-Swayne, Keith-Ward, or Yellowpine districts on the hill.

It was these three "districts" that gave the hill its tremendous boom. Without them there would have been no cause to drill hundreds of wells, where a handful would have sufficed. Without them the money would not have been forthcoming to finance the Spindletop University of Roughnecks and Roustabouts. . . .

Within a few months wells were so thick in the "districts" that they looked like three newly filled toothpick holders. Between the "districts" were great open spaces with no more than one well to every acre or two. Patillo Higgins looked on the sight and said the old hill looked like an onion patch. That was what the workers called it thereafter.[21]

Disastrous fires had plagued the field from the beginning—oil storage facilities lacked covers; there was careless use of fire in houses, restaurants, and saloons nearby; men new to the oil fields smoked and carried lighted lanterns in the midst of runaway gas; and sparks blew into the open oil tanks from nearby train engines. The Hogg-Swayne Syndicate soon joined with such outstanding operators as George Carroll, Ed Prather, George A. Hill, Frank Andrews, A. D. Lipscomb, and Walter Sharp in an attempt to prevent fires and other kinds of waste. On August 30, 1901, when forty gushers were flowing, over sixty individuals representing themselves, fifty oil companies, and two supply concerns adopted eleven rules formulated to cover the known dangerous contingencies:

1. No lodging house, boarding house, restaurant, nor cooking stove in use shall be permitted to remain within a distance of 150 feet of any drilling or producing well, and all such shall be removable to a distance of 500 feet, at the discretion of the Executive Committee.

2. No smoking shall be done within 100 feet of any producing well or pool of oil.

3. No lantern, torch or candle shall be taken within 20 feet of any open tank.

4. The inspector and watchman shall always be notified two hours in

[21] Gerald Forbes, *Flush Production: The Epic of Oil in the Southwest* (Norman, University of Oklahoma Press, 1942), pp. 13–25.

advance of the spouting of any well, so that adjacent fires can be outed and other precautions taken.

5. No well shall be permitted to flow unnecessarily nor except for substantial reasons, and then only so long as is necessary. [It was no longer thought prudent to shoot 6-inch streams of oil over a hundred feet in the air for the benefit of train loads of sight-seekers and buyers, when it endangered the field, and the oil spray was coating the town and making it a tinder box.]

6. Drillers and contractors, operators and others, shall extinguish all fires in their boilers or other places or have a man in readiness to do so at a moment's notice, when any well within a radius of 300 feet—or in the discretion of the inspector, within a radius of 500 feet—is about to come in, is being bailed or agitated.

7. All contractors shall require that no workman carry matches while at work in the field.

8. All sluice tanks shall be filled or leveled by the owner on ceasing to be used for drilling.

9. All land owners whose property abuts on the ditches to be cut for safety drainage shall take the utmost precaution to keep same open and unobstructed.

10. All wells shall be safely cased in or bricked in promptly after the well is brought in.

11. No land owner shall permit any saloon to be maintained on his land within 1000 feet of any oil well, nor shall any saloon in the vicinity sell liquor more intoxicating than beer.[22]

Carroll immediately petitioned for a writ of injunction to be issued against all defendants, meaning all operators in the field, commanding them to desist from all things complained of and to obey the rules. Such an injunction was granted the end of September, 1901, and the inspector was made a special bailiff to enforce the provisions. A Beaumont Stock Exchange was established, later superseded by a more effective one in Houston. It was hoped that 1902 might be less hectic and more profitable for the men who had staked their life earnings in the oil game.[23]

By the end of 1901, or soon thereafter, 214 producing wells were being operated in the Beaumont area by 100 companies; 28 wells had

[22] Charles A. Warner, *Texas Oil and Gas since 1543* (Houston, Gulf Publishing Company, c. 1939), pp. 42–43.

[23] Warner, *op. cit.*, pp. 43 ff. Ed Prather Interview with James Howard, August, 1952; personal interviews with Mrs. Walter B. and Dudley Sharp since 1949. Walter B. Sharp died from the after-effects of fighting a fire in 1912. Cf. James, *The Texaco Story*, p. 32.

been abandoned. In 1900, 836,000 barrels of oil had been produced from the wells at Corsicana and elsewhere in Texas; the total production for 1901 was over 4,393,000 barrels.[24] Something had to be done to find new uses for oil and its potential by-products, because the price of crude oil was going down to 3 cents a barrel. Of the 214 Beaumont area wells, 120 were on the Hogg-Swayne tract of fifteen acres in the total Spindletop field of 200 acres; not yet understanding the importance of preserving gas pressures to obtain the longest flow, the Syndicate had been willing to sell small blocks just large enough to hold derricks and some equipment. Something of the frenzy of the times may be gathered from an extract from a somewhat exaggerated article by geologist Robert T. Hill.

Thousands of acres of . . . land 150 miles from Beaumont have sold for as much as $1,000 per acre. Land within the proved field has sold for nearly $1,000,000 per acre; $900,000 having recently been paid for one acre. No sales were made for less than $200,000 per acre. Spindletop . . . may be justly assessed at a valuation of $500,000 an acre, or $100,000,000. Two years ago it could have been bought for less than $10 an acre.[25]

James Hogg had certainly landed in the midst of a domain of Arabian Nights' tales and business headaches: a woman garbage collector sold her former pig pasture for $35,000, and blocks of land 25 x 34 feet brought $6,000 to $40,000 each at the top of the boom. Stories now spread that Hogg was many times a millionaire.[26] Actually, he and the Syndicate still needed a more effective marketing agent and money for expansion; Hogg had his West Columbia lands, held stocks of various kinds, but had little cash. When he became a director of a Beaumont bank in 1902, he was involved in new problems that caused him to lose money; Will Hogg, who had joined his father's law firm in Austin, observed some irregularities in the bank's operation, and at once James Hogg demanded that the bank justify the confidence of the depositors, even though the directors might have to meet the deficiency.[27] Will, in writing to his sister Ima (then studying music in New York) about the reports of fabulous wealth, said: "All this stuff about James Stephen

[24] Warner, op. cit., p. 86.

[25] Robert T. Hill, "The Beaumont Oil Field, with Notes on Other Oil Fields of the Texas Region," Journal of The Franklin Institute (August–October, 1902), p. 27; Rister, Oil!, p. 61.

[26] Clark and Halbouty, op. cit., pp. 92, 80–93.

[27] Personal interview with Miss Hogg, July 31, 1955, tape recording in H. C.; Will Hogg to J. S. Hogg, August 23, 1904, J. S. Hogg Let. Pr., XXXV, 227–228.

making millions is the veriest rot and makes me tired. He will do well if he gets out with comfort."[28]

Hogg's earlier trips into the Houston-Port Arthur region to study railroads now stood him in good stead as he considered the problem of transportation. He realized the advantages which would accrue from having storage and shipping facilities at Port Arthur, some fifteen miles away; it was the terminus of the Kansas City Southern Railway, which John W. "Bet-a-Million" Gates had built to Port Arthur when he ran into trouble with the Kountze interests at Sabine Pass, stockholders in the rival Gulf, Colorado, and Santa Fe.[29] The Hogg-Swayne tract was only about two miles from the Neches River and only a mile from either the Kansas City Southern or the Texas and New Orleans. The main transportation problem would be licked if tank cars or barges were obtainable. However, a pipeline to Port Arthur might be necessary, especially if the Syndicate went ahead with plans to build its own refinery. Oil tankers were coming into Port Arthur before the end of 1901, but the oil had to be desulphurized to prevent explosion. When asked if he thought the Texas Railroad Commission had authority to take an interest in providing adequate cars to handle the oil traffic, Hogg replied that he did. The railroads generally were trying to make all possible cars available and were furnishing others as rapidly as they could be made in the new Beaumont factory or elsewhere.[30] While some tank cars may have been "lost" on purpose, it was not the usual practice.

By the summer of 1901 the Guffey Petroleum Company, backed by Andrew and Richard Mellon, had a stock value of $4,500,000. When the need for their own refinery was apparent, the Gulf Refining Company of Texas, with a capital of $750,000, was organized. Early in 1902, Guffey persuaded the Mellons to float a $5-million bond issue, of which the Mellon bank took half and the Old Colony Trust of Boston took $1,500,000.[31]

Hogg and Cullinan, observing these developments, were pleased that there would be another purchaser besides Standard and British companies. When Cullinan was in Austin during the summer of 1901 he and Hogg had become better acquainted. Hogg and Swayne had known for some time that they needed the experienced help of a real oil man such as Cullinan; his Texas Fuel Company could also assist in marketing

[28] Will Hogg to Ima Hogg, January 18, 1902, Fam. Let.
[29] Richard Overton, *Gulf to Rockies,* pp. 249, 354 ff.
[30] St. Clair Reed, *Texas Railroads,* pp. 434, 446, 760.
[31] Clark and Halbouty, *op. cit.,* p. 136.

the Hogg-Swayne oil. Cullinan was interested in the Syndicate's offer to become half owner in the Texas Fuel Company by putting up $25,000 worth of Syndicate properties.[32] (The Standard Oil men who had backed Cullinan's Corsicana refinery were not in the Texas Fuel Company, which was capitalized at only $50,000.) However, before anything more came of the Syndicate's offer, Arnold Schlaet, manager of oil and carbon black interests of the H. G. Lapham and Company investment firm, paid a visit to Texas.

Schlaet had come to New York from Germany in 1875, when he was fifteen, and had risen to a position of great responsibility with the Lapham Company. In Texas he discussed Cullinan's need of a selling agency in the East and agreed to put $25,000 into the Texas Fuel Company if Cullinan would manage the Texas offices. Buying oil cheap in Texas, they could sell at a profit in the North and abroad. Cullinan believed Standard Oil was vulnerable at the production level, and he wanted to create a producing company in which he could use the talents of Walter Sharp, but Schlaet opposed going into production as being too risky.[33] When the Texas Fuel Company finally received its charter in January, 1902, Schlaet and Cullinan were listed as the principal stockholders.

Meanwhile, the Hogg-Swayne Syndicate was still making money, but most of the acreage on the mound was disposed of and the crude oil which they would receive in part payment was heading for the low price of 3 cents a barrel. Expansion, including a pipeline to Port Arthur and a refinery, seemed an absolute necessity. The partners decided that Hogg should go East to try to find big money; should he fail, then he and Campbell would go to England on further quest. The idea appealed to Hogg, who was more than a little tired of the fires, rain, and quagmires of the oil fields, and the incredible disorder that accompanied the growth of a sleepy village of nine thousand to a roaring boom town of thirty thousand, including a disproportionate number of riff-raff.

George Carroll, later a benefactor of Baylor University, remarked that he would prefer never to have made a nickel from oil than to have had Beaumont deserve the reputation attached to the "Deep Crockett" district. Nothing in print equals the frank and lively descriptions of gamblers, saloons, vaudeville, knifings, and other bloody incidents portrayed in the basic social document, *Oil Field Medico*, which was

[32] James, *The Texaco Story*, p. 16.
[33] *Ibid.*, pp. 17 ff.

written by a young doctor, George Parker, recently graduated from Virginia Medical College.

The Syndicate realized that the land sales business was bringing only a small return in comparison with the potential of an integrated organization that would include producing wells and overseas sales outlets. However, such a development would require capital and a type of oil knowledge that the Syndicate members lacked; therefore, selling out on top of the boom, while all was well, might be the wisest course. In December, 1901, Hogg and W. T. Campbell set out for New York. They had something to sell: on September 27, Hogg-Swayne No. 3, drilled by Walter Sharp, had come in. Four more wells would come in by February 1, 1902, before they left for Europe.[34]

The house on Nineteenth Street had been more or less deserted for some time. Mrs. Davis, now nearly seventy, had gone back to Colorado in early 1901 when her son was taken ill. Her very determined and uncompromising mode of child-training had not been too successful with the three younger children; Mike and Tom especially had been unhappy. None of them ever complained, but apparently Hogg finally sensed the depressing effect she had on them; at any rate, he found tactful reasons to account for her remaining in Pueblo. An elderly housekeeper took kindly charge for a time after that. During the summer Hogg decided that Ima, who had studied at the University of Texas for two years, should have the chance to develop further her musical talents. In the fall she left for New York, and the boys entered Carlisle Military Academy at Hillsboro, Texas. Hogg had missed them all greatly, but he found solace in the fact that they were getting the education he so much wanted them to have.

The reunion with Ima in New York was joyful. Hogg stayed at the Waldorf-Astoria, and Ima spent with him as much time as her busy music program would permit. She was usually invited to the many evening dinners and some of the other functions arranged for him, not only by the business men he hoped to interest in oil, but also by such men as former Secretary of the Navy William C. Whitney, who respected Hogg's position in the Democratic Party. Whitney's generous offer that they should share his box at the Horse Show was accepted. One evening Ima joined her father at dinner in the home of John W. Gates. New York was a beehive of bankers, brokers, and business organizers,

---

[34] Warner, *op. cit.*, pp. 40–46; Rister, *op. cit.*, p. 71.

with people still talking about J. Pierpont Morgan's genius in organizing the United States Steel Corporation. Not yet twenty, Miss Hogg was intrigued by the glamor of Peacock Alley and stories about Morgan's power and connections with the Rockefeller interests. Hogg renewed his acquaintance with General Nelson Miles, who gave the Governor a beautiful white greyhound, thinking the dog should have the run of a plantation. A few years later, Miss Hogg met the General and he inquired about the greyhound. "Oh, he's the most wonderful rabbit dog," she replied. In describing the General's reactions, she said: "Well, that was the worst thing I could have said to General Miles . . . because the dog was supposed to be a great hunter."[35]

Hogg hoped to interest John W. Gates in putting up money, because he knew Gates believed in the future of Texas. The two had met back in the 1870's when the young Northerner first came to Texas to sell the skeptical ranchers on the virtues of barbed wire. During the summer of 1901 Hogg had discussed with him the Hogg-Swayne need for a refinery and the possibility of locating it in Port Arthur. Gates was unschooled and given sometimes to flagrantly ungrammatical speech, but his mind was quick and active, his personality warmly pleasing. His American Steel and Wire Company had become a part of the billion-dollar United States Steel Corporation organized by J. P. Morgan in 1900, but Gates resented the treatment he had received from Morgan. A large stockholder in the Kansas City Southern railroad and other properties, he had money for investment in 1901, and Hogg knew it.[36]

Despite the good will and friendliness evident in New York, nothing substantial materialized for the Syndicate. Hogg was back in Texas by January 10, 1902. During the train's brief stop in Hillsboro, Mike and Tom, trim in their Carlisle uniforms, boarded the train to greet their father enthusiastically. It had been a rather lonely Christmas for the boys, although Will had done what he could for them. In Austin, Will tried to persuade his father to leave the oil business to others, for he believed that Hogg was driving himself too hard and should be satisfied to give more time to the legal affairs of Hogg, Robertson, and Hogg. As a further inducement, Will offered to look after his father's wardrobe

[35] Personal interview with Miss Hogg, July 31, 1954, tape recording in H. C.; Mark D. Hirsch, *William C. Whitney, Modern Warwick* (New York, Dodd, Mead & Co., 1948), pp. 584 ff.

[36] Lloyd Wendt and Herman Kogan, *Bet a Million! The Story of John W. Gates* (Indianoplis, Bobbs-Merrill Company, 1948), pp. 192–195.

and other needs if they could room together. Apparently the idea was appealing, for Hogg wrote Ima on January 12:

You know Will was always disposed to pet and spoil me anyway. As I fatten up and *get old,* this disposition grows in him. . . . We will probably take board at the Driskill, although I am inclined to have the upstairs of my Brush building, on [Congress] Avenue, fitted up for this purpose. What do you think best for us to do? You know I respect your opinion more than I do my own—*when you give it seriously.* Will and I will take noon dinner at Mr. House's today.[37]

But ten days later he was back in Beaumont to report to his partners on the New York trip. Amidst the rush he took time to write his daughter on stationery of the Citizens National Bank: "In all probability I will leave here for England, via the Waldorf-Astoria, within the next day or so. Hope to see you enroute."[38] Delayed a few days, he went to Varner Plantation, where he found that a fine artesian water-well was spouting a stream twenty feet into the air. It was expected to double the value of the plantation, and it revived his hopes for oil there. Optimistically he wrote Ima:

The oil prospects are good. It may yet turn out to be a *gusher* of oil. As it is we have three veins of flowing oil, in paying quantities. These make the field a fine one. But we want a gusher, and we intend to have it—*if* we can *get it;* and we believe we can. . . . Beaumont is a veritable boom. It eclipses everything of the kind that ever occurred in Texas.[39]

Despite some of his earlier pronouncements about British imperialism and absentee ownership of lands, Hogg was ready to try to tap British investment capital. He had been keenly disappointed that American financial interests did not respond to his glowing but substantially accurate accounts of the potential future of the Hogg-Swayne Syndicate.

On the Cunard liner *Saxonia,* he spent considerable time reading such books as Frederic Harrison's *Oliver Cromwell* and a life of William Pitt, because he "needed to study England's institutions and great men." He told Ima that "little Willie" (280 pounds) Campbell was "the ladies man aboard," while their secretary, "Don Alfonso de" Aldridge, was "the Cavalier." Although Campbell was seasick, he managed to get to Divine Services; the "Cavalier was too thin to vomit." Hogg reported

[37] J. S. Hogg to Ima (311 W. 82 St., New York), January 12, 1902, Fam. Let.
[38] J. S. Hogg to Ima, January 22, 1902, Fam. Let.
[39] J. S. Hogg to Ima, January 26, 1902, Fam. Let.

CUNARD R.M.S. "SAXONIA."

Feby. 11, 1902.

Dear Ima: At this writing 6:30
Tuesday evening, the third
day of our voyage, I am glid-
ing along to wards London at
the rate of 370 miles a day, in
good health and excellent spirits. Reading
is my past time. I leave
just Saturday like of

Oliver Cromwell.
It is the well known,
unquestioned, conviction
in view that God guided
his conquest for the cause
of humanity. His faith in
Christ led him to know
God, to believe in God,
to pray to God, and to look
to God for direction in all
his efforts in behalf of
human liberty.

Jim Hogg to Ima (excerpts)

his own good appetite and his frequent wish that Ima could have made the trip, remembering what good company she had been on the trip to Hawaii. He sent a copy of the ship's "Programme," showing that "Mr. J. S. Hogg" was chairman of the Saturday night program to benefit the Seaman's Orphanage, Liverpool, and the Home for Aged Mariners in New York. In this same letter (see accompanying facsimile excerpts) Hogg revealed his interest in serious study, in philosophy, in religion, and in ethics.[40]

When the "innocents abroad" arrived at Liverpool, agents of Alferd Suart, a Britisher whom Hogg had met in New York, expedited their trip to London. On February 19, Mr. Suart and Mr. Roche, the latter the man through whom the Hogg-Swayne group had obtained a refinery site in Port Arthur, and Lord Deerhurst, who had business interests in America, called on them at the Cecil Hotel. Suart, an engaging young man, had earlier invited Governor Hogg and Miss Hogg to be his guests if they came to England. Now he took charge and moved the Texans to his home at 29 Great St. Helen's, E.C. London. Hogg described for his daughter the evening of February 19 at No. 42 Princes Gate:

I dined with Lord and Lady Deerhurst at their home and got a *glimpse* into English society. It was an elaborate affair, with every seat filled by a titled man or woman. The long table was decorated with fragrant flowers, ferns and palms. The sixteen courses were in all respects elegant in order and exquisite in *cuisine*. In all respects it was an event well worthy my longest recollection. How I missed you! In fact I miss you wherever I go. So you must excuse me for this boyish weakness, as I so much need you to keep *me straight!* I am to meet our Ambassador and others at a stilted dinner next Tuesday evening. After that I am to meet the King. "Little Willie" and Don Alfonso De Aldridge are great companions and afford me much pleasure. In London they feel at home, as Mr. Campbell is a native, having left here when a boy, and Don is like the famous goat—at home anywhere. We are going to make him cut his hair, part it on the side, turn out his side-whiskers and wear a plug hat! Then he'll be "Hinglish yer Know!" So far the fog obscures everything from clear sight, but we are promised better weather.[41]

On March 1, Hogg reported that Suart had put "several country places" and carriages at their disposal. "Since our arrival we have dined

[40] J. S. Hogg to Ima, February 15, 1902, Fam. Let.
[41] J. S. Hogg to Ima, February 20, 1902, Fam. Let.

out nearly every evening. In fact I am worn out by the good treatment from the Englishmen." Referring again to the conversation at the Deerhurst dinner as "vibrate with wit and humor," he listed the guests, including American Ambassador and Mrs. Joseph Choate, Mr. and Mrs. Bradley-Martin, Lord Cecil, Ambassador Metternich of Germany, Countess Galloway, Lord Claude Hamilton, Countess Knox, Lady Caledon, Mrs. Lawson, Lord and Lady Oranmore and Brown, and "Lady Shimelan—ishingawitchamary, etc, etc." Mrs. Choate, "the talented, sweet American lady was by my side." He enclosed a copy of *Vanity Fair,* that described the guests at the dinner "in honour of Governor Hogg (of Texas)." He had been to lunch with Lord Claude Hamilton and had enjoyed a ride on the Great Eastern Railway of which his host was director.[42]

As usual, Hogg was having a good time in new surroundings, but he was also impatient to attend to business and go home. Campbell counseled patience, explaining that Europeans were always leisurely about rushing into big business deals; they could not be rushed into hasty decisions. To fill the time between scheduled interviews or while waiting for some group to debate his project, Hogg availed himself of opportunities to travel, visit the museums, and in other ways broaden his knowledge of England. He was a weekend guest at Lord Deerhurst's country estate, where he was delighted to see the farming operations. Deerhurst had business interests in America, and Hogg hoped to work with him in selling the Syndicate or in selling oil and its by-products. With his usual quick comprehension, it was not long before he had learned a great deal about the British. When invited to speak, Hogg publicly expressed his admiration for British contributions in the fields of international law, justice, and democratic government.

Ambassador Choate, whom Hogg had met first in Albany in 1894, arranged for him to receive an invitation to an official presentation to the King; but after Hogg considered the incongruity of his great bulk enveloped in the prescribed presentation costume—knee breeches, silk stockings, low-quartered shoes, full-shirt front, low-cut vest, "cutaway" coat, and plug hat, the coat, pants, and vest to be of black velvet—he sent his regrets. A reporter got wind of the matter, and a story appeared in the New York *Journal* and other American papers about this staunch American who would not "bend a knee before a British King." This episode did not go unnoticed in Texas, and the popular version inspired

[42] J. S. Hogg to Ima, March 1, 1902, Fam. Let.; *Vanity Fair* (London), February, 1902; *London Times,* February 22, 1902, p. 15.

a song, composed by Ida Pender Pierson and published in Chicago under the title "Governor Hogg in London." The words follow:

> Now in London all was ready,
> And arrangements were complete,
> Governor Hogg in all his glory,
> Great King Edward was to greet.
>
> The Ambassador was saying,
> "You must look your very best;
> In the regulation costume,
> At the court you must be dressed.
>
> "You must wear a sword and buckler,
> Breeches fastened at the knee."
> Hogg was filled with consternation,
> "Then a pretty sight I'd be."
>
> He said, "Rigged in all those gewgaws,
> I will not attend the ball,
> I'll dress like an American,
> Or I'll not appear at all.
>
> "I'll not imitate your fashions,
> Nor will revolutionize
> Your dress and your English customs,
> Nor them do I criticize."
>
> Chorus:
> We're glad he's an American,
> And belongs to Uncle Sam.
> Though he's in another country,
> He's a soldier and a man.

Hogg was chagrined when the newspaper story got back to England, for he had later met King Edward informally at a garden party and liked him. The sincerity of his embarrassment and his regret that the misrepresentation of his action had been so widespread is shown by a long letter to Ima in which he expressed his desire to "maintain his own self-respect as an American gentleman as well as to show his respect for foreign customs." He declared that no person had ever been "treated better" than he by the British. However:

. . . many institutions and customs here are entirely foreign to my habits, education and tastes, but I am no critic of them. So long as they suit those who must support and endure them no visitor can with propriety condemn them. In official circles the ancient superstitions haunt the pathway of a gentleman as he *meanders* the red tape lines to pay his respects to officials. In social circles the customs are very much like those of the first class at Austin and in New York.[43]

While in England he never tired of observing the varied aspects of British life. When he had the time he would travel over the city observing the sights from the top of a "skyscraper" or double-deck bus. Mindful of Ima's interest in the trip, he once summarized for her his observations of the people who had flocked by the thousands in holiday attire to enjoy Regent's Park. He described them as "bright, light-hearted, merry, well-dressed, clean and pretty." Meditating upon their innocent plays, rope-dancing, and other wholesome recreations, he reminded his daughter of the importance of the "bread-winners—the *plain people,* who after all are the foundation—the mudsills—of all good government."[44]

On March 6, Lord Hamilton and his solicitor were finally ready "to discuss Texas oil." There is no information on what transpired during a luncheon at the Employers Liability Assurance Cooperation, Hamilton House, on the Thames Embankment, other than that the group was joined by a Mr. Whatley and that Hogg discussed the use of oil as locomotive and ship fuel.[45] About this time William Caudy and young Suart were also willing to talk business. However, by the middle of March business was "very slow," and Hogg confided that he was discouraged by the outlook. While Campbell remained optimistic, Hogg wrote: "*I doubt it!* At all events the experiment if it should fail will only retard, but not injure us."[46] Even a weekend at Brighton Beach did not dispel a growing homesickness, and he was also unenthusiastic over a trip to Paris.

On March 20, 1902, in a confidential letter to his daughter, Hogg unburdened his disappointment over the failure of his mission to sell the Hogg-Swayne Syndicate. He and Campbell had learned that "to build air castles in the sky is a childish, unmanly pastime full of alloy and

[43] J. S. Hogg to Ima, March 5 and 14, 1902, Fam. Let.
[44] J. S. Hogg to Ima, April 1, 1902, Fam. Let.
[45] *Ibid.,* P. S. enclosure, *London Times,* February 15, p. 10, and March 6, 1902, p. 4.
[46] J. S. Hogg to Ima, March 14, 1902, Fam. Let.

chimerical irredescence[*sic*]." While nothing material had been lost, they must pay the penalty for it and "go back home crest-fallen, ashamed." Then, typically, he rebounded: "Backs to the past; faces to the future; we press on! Anew, we start—the dauntless, happy twain— Willie and Jym!" Campbell added this note:

> Your poetic Papa has very eloquently informed you that
>   We fell ———
> Hit the ground hard ———
>   Got left ———
> but we are not discouraged—only
> feel sorry for these Britishers.[47]

On his birthday, March 24, James Hogg took stock of himself. The business outlook was somewhat better. He had turned down invitations to dine with friends; then, he wrote, he had "appropriately" attended the play *Ulysses* and enjoyed the "*reverie* of undisturbed time to *meditate*":

And of all the joyous reflections that illumined my heart on yesterday none was brighter, more lustrous and pleasure breeding than the trickling thoughts that fell from the cataract of my brain, as crystal drops into the Soul, to enliven my convictions and hopes that there is a God, and a better world for those who live a righteous life! Amidst the vicissitudes of a checkered career, from orphanage in boyhood, I know I have, at times, done wrong, but never wantonly, wilfully. Looking back I have little to regret. Looking forward I have unshaken hopes that in *you* and my three boys I shall enjoy much pride and undefiled pleasure in Old Age.—With Constancy of Love, Your Father, J. S. Hogg[48]

As was his custom in times of great stress, James Hogg confided in "Sister Frank"—Mrs. Davis. He reported that on March 29 he had closed a trade, subject to some modifications and ratification by his associates in Texas. An English company was to be formed to take over the "Spindletop land (with five gushers) and pipe line." The Hogg-Swayne Syndicate would receive $6 million. Evidently Hogg owned one-eleventh of the Hogg-Swayne holdings; his part from the trade was to be $135,000 cash and $400,000 in stock. He confided that if the company succeeded the stock would be very valuable, but if it did not, the "cash will quite well satisfy me as the result of my venture at Beaumont; especially when taken in connection with other unsold holdings I have

[47] J. S. Hogg to Ima, March 20, 1902, enclosure from Campbell, Fam. Let.
[48] J. S. Hogg to Ima, March 25, 1902, Fam. Let.

there and at Columbia. . . . I have never coveted riches. My desire is to have a safe income."[49]

Actually, several important details of the contract of sale were tentative, and the deal was still in the option stage and not closed. If the British did not create a company and complete the bargain in thirty days, the Syndicate would receive a forfeit of $25,000 cash, which was on deposit. Meanwhile, the possibility of carrying the Hogg-Swayne holdings abroad had created more interest in them in New York. Just when Hogg in England was most discouraged, new possibilities were opening up in the United States. The advantages of merging Cullinan's Texas Fuel Company and the Hogg-Swayne Syndicate became more attractive.

Hogg's earlier letters about music, plays, and people had started Ima "dreaming" about bringing the two young brothers over for a grand tour. Hogg nipped the budding plan quickly:

Now, Ima, that dream of yours won't work. I shall not indulge those boys in a "trip to England." I should not do so if I had the wealth of Carnegie. I never saw a "well travelled young man" that was worth kicking out of the back door! *My boys must work their way!* When they win their expense money they can travel with more pleasure and greater intelligence and benefit. Keep it before them that it is manly in them to succeed; that it is unmanly in them to spend the "Old Man's" money *except for an education and necessities while going to school,* if he should be fool enough to let them have it. Your influence over them will make fine men out of them. Of course I shall be glad to take you anywhere, if I have to make the boys work to defray the expenses. In other words, you shall have *carte blanche,* as you have always had and never abused.[50]

When Hogg returned to New York toward the end of April his attitudes toward Great Britain were somewhat changed. Association with the land which had furnished the poet James Hogg and the philanthropist Quintin Hogg filled him with pride. He remembered the British Captain Edward Chichester and his friendly act when Commodore George Dewey was in Manila Bay during the war with Spain. He was proud of the settlement of disputes with Britain by arbitration. He joined the ranks of that increasing number of Americans who became more friendly toward England in the fateful days when navies converted to oil burners and the rise of the German navy forced Britain to seek more diligently our friendship and alliance.

[49] J. S. Hogg to Sister (Mrs. Davis), March 30, 1902. See also J. S. Hogg to Ima (confidential), April 1, 1902, Fam. Let.
[50] J. S. Hogg to Ima, April 1, 1902, Fam. Let.

Back home, Hogg gave an interview, which appeared in the New York *Herald,* testifying to the alertness of the English trade experts and scientists who had made the "most thorough investigation and exploration of the oil fields of Texas." He referred to the "many mysterious, investigating, quiet working men in and around Beaumont" and at Columbia, Sour Lake, and Saratoga, and at Jennings, Louisiana, who had concluded that "practically speaking the quantity is inexhaustible." He had been surprised by what he saw the English doing with oil. Hogg perhaps did not fully comprehend that it had been in large measure the runaway production on the Hogg-Swayne tract which had suddenly made oil such a cheap fuel that trains and ships were rapidly shifting to equipment using oil. New outlets for oil were being found and a new demand had been awakened.

They . . . are making extensive preparations for the use of it as fuel in all parts of England. For instance, I saw one railway there with sixty engines converted to use fuel oil, and the president of the company informed me that they expected to have several more of them by the end of this year. . . . [Even] paying high transportation charges from Beaumont to London they find oil much cheaper and more satisfactory for steam purposes than coal. As everyone knows, the Englishman is a thorough, painstaking and independent thinker. . . . He has concluded that Texas oil as a fuel will save him a great expense.[51]

Crude oil was being used in preparing a substitute for linseed oil that could be sold at 15 cents a gallon instead of the linseed price of 50 to 75 cents. Someone had made a fine leather oil; someone else had combined oil with lignite to make briquettes, which were used as a substitute for coal in smelting iron ore and could also be used for heating and cooking in a specially built new stove. Hogg regretted the impatience of Americans and their lack of confidence in the oil properties, "which must in time become the greatest sources of their own regrets." He counseled Texans to sell lands or interests in oil production only for "reasonable prices," always withholding some from sale to take advantage of the future increases in prices which were bound to come.[52]

The Hogg-Swayne Syndicate had begun building their pipeline from Beaumont to Port Arthur early in 1902. The right-of-way had been obtained and construction had begun, when Cullinan, banker George M. Craig of Port Arthur, and Gates approached the Syndicate partners

[51] New York *Herald,* May 2, 1902. The *London Times,* March 3, 1902, tells of using Russian oil to run fire engines.
[52] New York *Herald,* May 2, 1902.

about possible joint activity. Apparently, Hogg's glowing accounts to Gates in December had been more effective than he knew, but it is probable that the long and genial relationship between the two men—each an adventurer in his own way—was the largest factor in Gates' decision. It would help Cullinan, a Pennsylvanian, to be associated more closely with Hogg and other prominent Texans, and it would be helpful to the Texans to have the benefits of the invaluable experience of "Buckskin Joe" Cullinan and the financial support of Mr. Gates and his railroad.

The Syndicate had just paid a nice profit to James Roche, the Englishman who introduced Hogg to friends in London. Roche had taken options on 1,000,000,000 barrels of oil at 3 cents and a tentative lease for a forty-acre refinery site at Port Arthur. As part of the now-discussed Cullinan-Sharp-Hogg-Swayne deal, these properties would be turned into the newly formed Producers Oil Company, with Walter B. Sharp in charge of drilling operations.[53] The Hogg-Swayne group would receive a half interest. The Texas Fuel Company had earlier arranged to buy more lands and tanks and was ready to complete the pipeline to Port Arthur, if a way could be found to take care of commitments "aggregating more than $600,000."[54] The forces compelling expansion or sale were powerful; both the Texas Fuel Company and the Hogg-Swayne group needed more capital.

A merger to pool both the physical and the personnel resources of Cullinan's Company and of the Syndicate would be, with Gates' financial help, an eminently sensible move. The Texas Company was chartered April 7, 1902, as a $3-million corporation under the laws of Texas.[55] Obviously, this was an undervalued company with combined holdings, since Hogg and Campbell had been negotiating to sell the Hogg-Swayne Syndicate alone at a value of $6 million. Whether the news of the formation of the Texas Company leaked to Britain is undetermined; in any case the English option was not used.

On May 1, 1902, formal announcement was made that the Texas Company was operating from offices in Beaumont and New York. Cul-

[53] Personal interviews with Mrs. Walter B. Sharp and Dudley Sharp (in 1958, Assistant Secretary for Air) in Houston and Austin, April, 1951, and May, 1952. The debate over the invention of the rotary-bit drill continues. See Clark and Halbouty, *Spindletop,* pp. 146 ff.; Ed Prather interview with James Howard, 1952, and Ed Prather Interview, Tape Recordings Nos. 151–152, Pion. Tex. Oil Col.

[54] James, *op. cit.,* p. 17.

[55] Original Charter No. 11314, The Texas Company, April 7, 1902, Office of the Secretary of State, State Capitol, Austin.

linan was president, Arnold Schlaet, who represented the Lapham interests, became vice-president, and Campbell and Judge Brooks represented the Hogg-Swayne interests on the board of directors. Hogg had insisted on a clear understanding with Cullinan and Gates that the main offices should never move out of Texas—consistent with his long dislike of absentee ownership. Apparently the agreement was not put in writing. It is not known why he did not stipulate that the item be made part of the charter; if he did try, he may have been talked into leaving it "a gentleman's agreement."[56]

The Texas Company was formed for the purpose of:

owning and producing petroleum oil, gas and other minerals, with the right and authority to contract for the lease and purchase of the right to prospect for, develop and use, coal and other minerals and petroleum; also the right to erect, build and own all necessary oil tanks, cars and pipes necessary for the operation of the business of the same; also the right to storing and transporting oil and gas, brine and other mineral solutions and to make reasonable charges therefor, to buy, sell and furnish oil and gas for light, heat and other purposes, to lay down, construct, maintain and operate pipe lines, tubes, tanks, pump stations, connections, fixtures, storage houses, and such machinery, . . . as may be necessary to operate such pipes and pipe lines between different points in this State; to own, hold, use and occupy such land, and rights of way, easements, franchises, buildings and structures as may be necessary to the purpose of such corporation.[57]

Corsicana was declared to be the home office, indicating that Cullinan, the president, spent considerable time there; branches were listed for Beaumont, Port Arthur, Sabine Pass, Galveston, Houston, and "other places as may be lawfully admitted." By 1905 meetings of the board were usually convened at Beaumont or Houston. The nine directors for the first year included the two New Yorkers, L. H. Lapham and Arnold Schlaet, evidencing their large holdings; John W. Gates and J. C. Hutchins, who listed Chicago as home base; four of the Texans, Roderick Oliver, W. T. Campbell, R. E. Brooks, and E. J. Marshall. J. S. Cullinan was given large powers as director and president of the company. Will Hogg served long enough as a director in 1913 to learn that the company had grown from the $3-million incorporation of 1902 to over $36 million. Deaths among the original stockholders, including J. S. Hogg and John Gates, were then giving the New York in-

---

[56] Personal interview with Miss Hogg, July, 1954; Clark and Halbouty, *op. cit.*, p. 150; Warner, *op. cit.*, pp. 45–46; Rister, *op. cit.*, p. 70.

[57] Quoted from the original charter, issued April 7, 1902.

terests greater control, a factor that would soon cause even Cullinan serious concern. When Gates' widow sold her stock, it became apparent that Cullinan had lost control of the direction of the company and that the offices would be moved to New York. Accordingly, he and Will Hogg withdrew from the company in November 1913.[58]

In 1902 wild rumors prevailed about the Texas Company, including one that called it a combination with capital and power far exceeding that of the Standard Oil trust. Actually, the new company still needed cash; hoping that the combined activities would strengthen their bargaining powers, Campbell and other agents of the company went to England in the summer of 1902. Hogg did not go abroad again. The efforts did not fare much better than the earlier trip of Hogg and Campbell, for British and Dutch oil interests were now concentrating on Sun and Shell oil companies. Other difficulties the new group encountered included the fact that the great flood of oil, for which relatively few uses had yet been found, tended to keep prices down, and that Waters-Pierce continued to be the southwestern purchasing and distributing agent for Standard. There was also frequent litigation, much of it involving the Hogg-Swayne interests. However, the Texas Company and the Producers Oil Company had invaluable assets: the high character of the men associated together, the technical experience of Cullinan and Sharp, the financial resources of Gates and Lapham, the shrewdness of sales agent Schlaet, and the legal talent and public relations value of Campbell and Hogg.

The new pipeline when finished connected with the docks and the Texas Company's $150,000 refinery in Port Arthur, which would soon become the greatest oil port in the world. Fifteen steel tanks were built at Garrison and twelve at Nederland, where the pipeline had rail connections and loading platforms. There were also tanks at Port Arthur (one earthen tank held over 100,000 barrels) and at Amesville, Louisiana, where an expanded sales program was teaching the sugar planters how to use oil instead of coal for fuel in grinding cane and in refining operations. It took about three barrels of oil to do the work of a ton of coal and there was a potential market for a million and one-half barrels annually. At a dollar a barrel delivered, oil could cut the fuel cost almost in half. The fluctuating price for oil at Spindletop during 1902 actually created an average of just over 20 cents a barrel.[59]

The Texas Company was now equipped to handle and sell large

[58] Personal interview with Miss Hogg, July, 1954; James, *op. cit.*, p. 36.
[59] James, *op. cit.*, p. 21.

amounts of oil—if the supply held out. The gas pressure at Spindletop continued to dwindle alarmingly, and soon after the company was formed, the Independence Oil Company decided it would stop supplying oil for 3 cents a barrel as per its contract with Cullinan's old company. When the Texas Company lost a suit to force continuance of sales to them from the Independence, the way was unhappily opened for all of Cullinan's contracts there to be canceled. Hogg and Cullinan turned to Walter Sharp for help. Sharp, bringing in Howard Hughes and Ed Prather, quickly organized the Moonshine Oil Company, using Cullinan or Texas Company money. Sharp used his patented process of injecting air into oil wells and causing them to flow again. It is said that the price was half the oil produced. But the Texas Company needed more oil.

Producers Oil Company was expected to furnish one million barrels at a price fixed at 25 cents per barrel. This might have been a good deal for Producers and might have solved the oil shortage for the Texas Company, but late in the year the new wells stopped flowing. Sharp decided to try restoring pressure by using his process for "blowing" with compressed air, but salt water invaded some of the Spindletop wells and the production of the field dropped from 62,000 barrels a day to 20,000. By the end of 1903 it was down to only 5,000 barrels.[60] After that the field rested for twenty years, until deeper drilling became a reality.

The Texas Company, with waiting pipelines, docks, barges, refinery, and asphalt plant, still needed oil badly. The Sour Lake area in Hardin County had seemed promising for some time, but test drilling had not been done since Sharp's early venture there. Sour Lake had long been famous as a health resort (Sam Houston had used its mineral springs). James Roche, the quick-witted Englishman, held an option on 865 acres there, including the old resort hotel; the Texas Company took an option at $20,000 cash on his tract offered for $1,000,000, the option to be exercised within a short time limit.[61] Trying to attract as little attention as possible, Sharp drilled two test wells; the results were kept secret. A third drilling was made northeast of the hotel—and at 780 feet it became clear to Sharp that he had a gusher.

---

[60] James, *op. cit.*, p. 21. Appreciation is expressed to the Public Relations Office of the Texas Company at Houston for permission to look over their manuscript history of the company. For convenience references in this book are to Marquis James, *The Texaco Story* (New York, The Texas Company, 1953).

[61] James, *op. cit.*, p. 23; Rister, *op. cit.*, p. 70, n. 6; Warner, *op. cit.*, p. 83.

It was decided to wait for a stormy night to test the well. When such a night arrived on January 8, 1903, Cullinan came out to watch. When the well came in, it was gushing oil high into the sky and over the trees. Could the discovery be kept secret? As the storm increased in fury, Sharp capped the well. In the morning all traces of oil had been washed away, and resort visitors were none the wiser. A hurried meeting of the Texas Company board was called. When Cullinan suggested that the meeting be held at the Sour Lake Hotel, Gates recalled Hogg's uncomplimentary description of the ramshackle frame building and the odorous lake (called Ponce de Leon Springs by "Dr. Mud," its promoter), which was stagnant, the foot-deep water showing gas bubbles. Hogg had also mentioned the "bath house," surrounded by high boards that protected the human visitors seeking cures from the razorbacks which also enjoyed the muddy resort. Therefore the directors' meeting was held at Gates' suite in the Royal Ponciana at West Palm Beach, Florida. Although Gates and Schlaet disagreed on procedure, Cullinan was instructed to exercise the option. Contracts were made to sell oil at 60 cents a barrel, a price that indicated the increasing scarcity at the time. In less than a month the new well had made the Texas Company $150,000, even though the spot price at Sour Lake had quickly dropped to 12 and 10 cents a barrel.[62]

To take up the option, which was dangerously near to expiration, the Texas Company needed to raise the agreed-on total cost of a million dollars. Schlaet and Lapham, always unwilling to see Gates become a controlling stockholder in any project, had seen to it that he held only "certificates of interest" ($90,000 of some $450,000) in the company. Gates now proposed either that he and some friends would put up $590,000, taking new stock being issued by the company, or that he would raise the whole million, allowing others to buy $400,000 worth as the subscribers were located. His suggestions stimulated the Lapham group to subscribe $350,000. Thus the company remained a closely knit organization, with only 138 stockholders as late as 1905. When Hogg's old friend, James Autry, then general counsel for the company, and Hogg and Campbell got through checking the option, their discovery of a flaw in the title saved the company $100,000.[63] The Sour Lake gusher

[62] Warner, *op. cit.*, p. 192, says the Sharp well produced 325,000 barrels. *Oil Investor's Journal*, IV (January 3, 1906), 9; Clark and Halbouty, *op. cit.*, pp. 154–155.

[63] James, *op. cit.*, p. 23.

started a new boom, and before long Sharp's drillers were getting oil at Saratoga and Batson in Texas and at Jennings, Louisiana. During 1904 the Jennings field would almost equal the Spindletop field of 1901.

In 1903 the Texas Company and affiliates produced almost 4 million barrels of oil, or about 4 per cent of the total United States production; in 1904 their production was over 5½ million barrels, the percentage of total production rising to 4.7 per cent. In the spring of 1903, soon after its first birthday, the company paid out $165,000 in dividends; a year later dividends were $180,000, but profits had been $794,250, making a substantial reserve available for future expansion. Dividends became an annual occurrence without a break. No small amount of credit belonged to Arnold Schlaet, who from his little office on Bridge Street in New York looked after sales. The name "Texaco" apparently originated from Schlaet's cable address, although an asphalt salesman, George M. Brown, is also credited with using the word in 1902 when advertising a product in St. Louis. In any case, the word became the company's registered trade mark in 1906.[64]

The Port Arthur refinery was ready to make kerosene for lamps and cooking stoves by the end of 1903. Then a technical difficulty arose: the new oil made inferior kerosene, hardly satisfactory for lamps. The chemists at the refinery then evolved "gas oil," which was used to "enrich" artificial gas used for lighting and cooking and could be used in the new heating stoves. Another product was naphtha, also used for cooking stoves, and for torches and certain industrial engines, and as a paint solvent. Gasoline was still largely a waste product, although the gasoline engine was beginning to be used in the new automobile.

Hogg had been enjoying the surge of events and people, and most of all the prospect that Texas would now move to the forefront of states industrially and culturally. However, the general lawlessness of the oil centers disturbed the big man who had tried all his life to enforce the laws of his native state, and he had been gradually withdrawing from the frenzy of the Beaumont region. His own group of associates were remarkable for their integrity, intelligence, and high principles, but this was rare in the midst of the stampede of adventurers drawn from all over the world. Longing again to have the children more often near him, he was sure that neither Beaumont nor Port Arthur was a beneficial environment for them, the gamut of undesirable conduct in the oil

[64] *Ibid.*, p. 24.

fields in general running from complete lawlessness to an amazing display of ostentation and arrogance.

Ima had now and then come to Port Arthur to enjoy a pleasant round of parties at holiday time, but was usually soon away to Austin or to Varner Plantation, and then back to her music studies in New York. From there she looked in from time to time on Mike and Tom at Lawrenceville Academy in New Jersey. Will was working faithfully for the law firm in Austin, assuming his father's legal responsibilities with care. He still felt, as he had earlier, that the oil business was too strenuous for "James Stephen" and looked forward to the day when the older man would come back to take over again his full share of duties in the law partnership.

The Varner Plantation had been Jim Hogg's greatest satisfaction in the last two years, especially when the children were there. Earlier, he had taken pleasure in the little house outside the city limits of Austin which he moved to shortly after Ima's first departure to study in New York, but the rush of events had kept him from establishing a full sense of continuity with it. Varner was to him the fulfillment of a long-cherished dream. Here was the country estate he had longed for ever since the loss of "Mountain Home"; here he could indulge his love for farming and here he could be the expansively hospitable lord of the manor; here also was a home always available to his children, a solid root for them in the soil. Nearby West Columbia had been the first seat of government of the Republic of Texas (from September to December, 1836), and Sam Houston was inaugurated President there on October 22, 1836; the region therefore had also a symbolic appeal to the man who felt such firm ties of loyalty with his state.

In the summer of 1902, when the decline in Spindletop activity became alarming, he created the "Hogg Subdivision" out of 160 acres of the Varner tract. The 160 acres were then divided into 5-acre plots, some of which he sold and some of which he gave to friends. One plot was presented to James H. Robertson, his law partner, for "ten dollars and for the further ample consideration of the services said Robertson has rendered me in my private affairs during our partnership, as well as for the deep sense of respect, affection, and love that I cherish for him as a citizen, partner, and friend." Another plot he recorded as a grant in the name of A. F. Lucas, "for a valuable consideration in the way of an expert opinion . . . which I accept in full as adequate, and for the further consideration to the people of Texas by the discovery of petroleum near Beaumont [Spindletop]."[65] Hogg had apparently hoped to enlist the expert's attention to the Hogg Subdivision. About the same time he had approached Lucas in regard to buying or taking an option on a large Mexican area, where it was thought sulphur could be developed by Lucas' drilling methods. Sharp had been scouting the Tampico area and noted that a large number of British and Standard agents were active in the region. Apparently, the restrictions upon Standard's operations in Texas had encouraged activity in Louisiana and Mexico.

Hogg's faith in the oil possibilities at Varner never flagged. In 1901 he had gone in with the Equitable Mining Company to drill on the Arnold tract at West Columbia. A showing of oil came up at 480 feet, but the test well was abandoned after a blowout at 620 feet; a second test well at first produced 1,000 barrels a day, then soon ceased to flow. During 1902 and 1903 three more wells were drilled and abandoned, the deepest going down 1,300 feet. In 1904, Hogg apparently tried to interest the Guffey and Gulf interests in moving over to West Columbia; he invited the Mellons to visit him at Varner, but pressure of business in Pittsburgh forced them to decline.[66]

Some commentators have been critical of Hogg for dealing with the Eastern financial interests; among the most recent is James A. Tinsley, who maintained that a "progressive" must become contaminated by such associations and alleged that Hogg's zeal for reform was lessened. Tinsley also charged that Hogg contributed to saddling Texas with a colonial economic status dependent on the Eastern magnates.[67] In this, Professor Tinsley seems to have wholly missed the point. Mellon's Gulf Refining Corporation was one of the few successful challengers of Standard, and Hogg had welcomed Mellon's enterprise from the beginning on that basis. To keep the oil business from becoming a Rockefeller monopoly, the Pittsburgh-Cleveland, Mellon-Rockefeller rivalry had been a healthy development, and further, it worked to the advantage of Texas producers.

Hogg had more than one purpose in encouraging Gulf. He had not been successful in interesting the Texas Company in drilling on his place. This fact may have made the Mellon-Gulf group reluctant to

[65] George M. Bailey, "A Country Home," typescript, G. W. Bailey Notes.
[66] L. M. Hoge, agent, J. M. Guffey Petroleum Co., to J. S. Hogg, August 23, 1904, J. S. Hogg Let. Rec., XXXV, 230; Warner, *op. cit.*, p. 200.
[67] James A. Tinsley, "The Progressive Movement in Texas," Ph.D. dissertation (the University of Wisconsin, 1953), pp. 46–49.

drill. No evidence has been found that Hogg ever doubted Cullinan's avowed purpose to keep Texaco a truly Texas company, in no way tied in with Standard. But if Hogg had doubted or considered the possibility, would it have been illogical to turn to Standard's competitor and to have given Guffey and Galey and Mellon, who it should be remembered had granted Hogg his opportunity to get a lease close to Lucas' well at Spindletop, a chance to unearth the fabulous amounts of oil which Hogg believed underlay his West Columbia lands?

When historians and economists refer to a "colonial economy" of the South,[68] they often do not explain the reasons for it, including the stocks and bonds held in Britain or Holland. The Civil War and its aftermath had either destroyed or taken out of the South its working capital. Southerners for a long time had to make the best bargains they could if they were to create a modern economy balanced between agriculture and industry. In 1894 Governor Hogg had pleaded with the financiers of Boston, New York, and Philadelphia to hasten the day when the United States in general would cease to swim in the "colonial economy" controlled from London. When Hogg realized, after the discovery of abundant oil, what a tremendous potential the Gulf coast had, he knew that sufficient capital to finance the development necessary to secure that potential did not exist in Texas. And when Easterners gave his projects the cold shoulder, he went to England to look for money, in spite of his long opposition to alien control or ownership. Of all his actions at this time, that one could be the most difficult for students to understand. Yet, given the situation, his action was in the nature of the only expedient left, a last resort, which Hogg, finally, was not forced to utilize. He was never too enthusiastic about the idea, although he was always grateful that he had been given the opportunity to extend his mental horizons and wipe away to some extent one of the few prejudices he had ever allowed himself. Hogg also came to understand that European financing of railroads had speeded their building in a vast new country which desperately needed transportation for development but which was short on capital. He was probably the most gratified of all the Syndicate group when it turned out that their particular situation was to be saved by Americans after all, and the more so because he

[68] Tinsley, *op. cit.*, pp. 50–53; C. Vann Woodward, *Origins of the New South,* Chap. XI, especially pp. 310–311 quoting *Manufacturers' Record,* XXXVII (June 7, 1895), 285. Cf. Francis B. Simkins, *A History of the South* (New York, A. A. Knopf, 1953), Chapter XXIX, "The Industrial Paradox"; Walter P. Webb, *Divided We Stand* (Austin, Acorn Press, 1944), pp. 83–99, 128.

believed that his stipulation relative to the location of offices would keep control of the Texas Company in Texas, among Texans who believed in the state and its future.[69] The Texas Company was fighting for its life. Selling oil in Louisiana met Waters-Pierce competition. Competition with Standard was met in Philadelphia by selling products directly from door to door twice a week instead of once.

In 1904, Hogg saw several indications, despite Texas Company dividends, that the oil boom was slowing down and the oil business entering a new phase. Among other things, the legal and financial center of the oil business was shifting from Beaumont to Houston, and mine leases in Mexico were not selling as fast as earlier. Cullinan wrote Hogg in June, 1904, that of the Eastern stockholders in the Texas Company only Schlaet showed up at the stockholders meeting.[70] Campbell had not been there to represent the Hogg-Swayne interests. Neither Cullinan nor Hogg realized that in time Schlaet would work to shift the home office and stockholders' meetings to New York. Production in the various fields of the Texas Company, after a good summer at Batson, fell off in the fall of 1904. However, the Crowley, Louisiana, stock had paid Hogg a 10-per-cent dividend in July, and Will Hogg had had an offer from a broker for about half of the Crowley stock but was waiting for a rise in price.[71]

During the year Hogg had spent more and more time at Varner and away from the law office in Austin, leaving the bulk of work to Robertson and Will. Will sensed that Robertson felt overworked—even Will himself was now away much of the time, making trips in reference to oil business in Louisiana and Beaumont. Jim Hogg in 1902 had brought Robertson into the oil business, but the former Judge did not like the venture and got out as soon as he could. In July, 1904, Will wrote his father after a trip to Louisiana: "If you only knew how much we need some one *away* from Columbia, you would not complain at me. Perhaps after a while you will agree that it was a good thing that I did not bury myself too at Columbia."[72] He hoped his father would take Ima and the boys north to avoid the possibility of malaria, adding the persuasion of a reminder that the Democratic Convention would convene

[69] Personal interview with Miss Hogg, July 31, 1955; Frank Cullinan Interview, Pion. Tex. Oil Col., Reel 152.

[70] J. S. Cullinan to J. S. Hogg, June 3, 1904, J. S. Hogg Let. Rec., XXXV, 13.

[71] Will Hogg to J. S. Hogg, June 6, 1904, J. S. Hogg Let. Rec. XXXV, 270; J. S. Hogg to Will Hogg, March 19, 1904, J. S. Hogg Let. Pr., 23, pp. 14–15.

[72] Will Hogg to J. S. Hogg, July 22, 1904, J. S. Hogg Let. Rec., XXXV, 105–106.

at St. Louis. (In the spring Colonel and Mrs. House had invited Hogg and Ima to join them on a summer tour of Europe. It is possible that the Colonel knew Hogg would probably never be too busy to speak for Bryan and against the gold standard, and considered it a good idea to get him out of the country in this election year. Hogg declined the invitation.) Will was also concerned lest Hogg get too deeply involved in a drilling venture at West Columbia and suggested that he not go ahead unless he disposed of enough National Oil and Pipe Line bonds to assure that he would not go into debt.[73]

The election contest, between Theodore Roosevelt for re-election and Judge Alton Parker, both from New York and both supporters of the gold standard, was only one confusing factor in Southwestern prosperity. In October, 1904, Higgins Oil and Fuel Company paid only $1.50 per share, or 1½ per cent, and frankly told stockholders: "Our production in the Spindle Top and Sour Lake fields continues to decrease and our wells at Batson also show some falling off in the last thirty days." They were already buying from Jennings "at a low price."[74] Crowley stock had paid Hogg $875 on 875 shares in July—a 10 per cent dividend—but National Oil and Pipe Line in October wanted the bondholders to vote to cut semiannual dividends from 10 to 5 per cent. When a gusher was reported at Humble, Will believed it would start a scramble for stocks and urged his father, if that happened, to sell out the holdings in the National. Horace Chilton, on the other hand, had informed Hogg that "Beaumont was getting pretty dull. The reaction from the boom is getting more and more apparent."[75]

Taking stock of the situation, Hogg finally decided to give up his law connections in Austin. A decision about location had to be made. Residence at Austin would be difficult, since Varner was too far away for proper attention to the fairly extensive land cultivation and stock raising, involving considerable investment, which was then under way. There might be drilling for better wells. Will also was ready for a change. He had considered the possibility of withdrawing from the firm and returning to San Antonio, but he had recently received from St. Louis encouragement of his desire to learn the banking business. James Hogg was under friendly pressure from pro-Bryan Democrat

---

[73] Will Hogg to J. S. Hogg, June 27 and 29, 1904, J. S. Hogg Let. Rec., XXXV, 54, 65.

[74] Higgins Oil and Fuel Company to J. S. Hogg, October 27, 1904, J. S. Hogg Let. Rec., XXXV, 444–445.

[75] Horace Chilton to J. S. Hogg, July 19, 1904, J. S. Hogg Let. Rec., XXXV, 105–106.

W. L. Moody, the banker, to consider a location in Galveston, where Moody promised personal and financial support. When Hogg decided to decline the Galveston offer, Will agreed with him: "I expect Houston is the place for you. I have heard of the failure of the Galveston folks to take hold as they should."[76] Of course, Galveston was still suffering from the great storm of 1900.[77]

After a family conference, James Hogg decided to withdraw from the firm of Hogg, Robertson, and Hogg in Austin and to locate his new law practice in Houston, where he could give more time to law, to Varner, and to the younger boys. Financing the oil development at Varner would be a big problem, and Will turned his steps toward St. Louis, where he hoped to learn the lessons of successful finance. Father and son were arranging a careful long-term program of development for their own holdings, with or without the Texas Company, in which they nevertheless remained substantial stockholders. Although his business interests were still complex and pressing, Hogg looked forward to days less hectic than the Beaumont period.

[76] Will Hogg to J. S. Hogg, November 29, 1904, J. S. Hogg Let. Rec., XXXV, 518, and 527 for letter of December 5.

[77] See John Edward Weems' *A Weekend in September* (Henry Holt and Company, New York, 1957) for a full account of this catastrophe.

CHAPTER XX

Hogg Stays with the People

JAMES STEPHEN HOGG was not only a pioneer in the early period of the Progressive Movement, but also an early and influential participant in the twentieth-century phase of the movement. Yet he relinquished his official leadership when the people of Texas were ready to bestow upon him even higher office. In 1895, when he could have had the United States Senate seat vacated by his friend Richard Coke, Hogg chose to decline public office and urged the selection of Horace Chilton. One of his outstanding contributions to Texas political history was his example as a former prominent officeholder voluntarily turning civilian. Even in this nonpolitical status, however, he continued to wield political influence. While never seeking public office after 1895, he remained a constant thorn in the flesh of men who chose to be blind to the interests of the public. Hogg continued to speak out for reform, never losing hope that through education the mass of the people could secure better government, by and for themselves, as opposed to careless government, by and for special interests. In May of 1896 Hogg wrote a friend in Sulphur Springs, G. R. Kirkpatrick, explaining his position: "My cup of ambition is full, but I shall stay with the people and help them out."

To the end of his life he sponsored measures to outlaw the system of permanent lobbyists, which had become an accepted feature of the Austin scene. He believed, however, that every citizen had a right to appear before the legislature to discuss any measure pending, and that every private or municipal corporation had a right to send its attorneys or agents before committees to discuss the merits of any bill affecting its rights. In a speech at the Opera House in Austin on March 11, 1903, Hogg was specific:

This class of service is clearly distinguishable from the sneaking, button-holding, sleeve-touching, arming, champagne-smearing influence which professional lobbyists attempt to use upon the legislators. Above all, the free-pass dispenser and free-lunch giver, who carries his roll of greenbacks in his overcoat pocket to foot the bills "incurred for his personal influence" among the members, is the most contemptible.

556

It will be a glorious day in Texas when in obedience to the will of the people, our representatives shall be free from such contaminating influences. If tonight I were in the paradise of heaven I should look with grief upon these conditions in Texas. If tonight I were in the seething crater of perdition I should look with pity upon the conditions as they are now in Texas, which, if continued, will make Texas hell itself.

Let us have Texas, the Empire State, governed by the people; not Texas, the truck-patch, ruled by corporate lobbyists.[1]

As the time approached for the 1904 presidential nominations, Hogg had watched unhappily the widespread acceptance by Democrats of the Gold Standard Act, which had been passed in 1900 during McKinley's administration. Knowing Hogg's affinity for William J. Bryan and unlimited coinage of silver, agents of Judge Alton B. Parker of New York came to Hogg and offered him a post in the Cabinet if Hogg would ditch Bryan and work for Parker's nomination. Loyal to Bryan, Hogg frankly told his visitors that he was not open to "bribery."[2] He did not know whether Parker had authorized such an offer or not, but he was opposed to the Judge in any case because he surmised that he was a gold-standard man, although so far the issue had been so neatly dodged that Hogg dubbed him the "lock-jawed judge." Ex-Governor Sayers, Governor Lanham, and Colonel House supported the pro-Parker Texas delegates, a combination which Hogg realized was unbeatable; therefore Hogg did not attend either the State Democratic Convention at San Antonio that selected the delegates or the National Convention at St. Louis. When Parker, after his nomination, announced his support of the gold standard,[3] Hogg could say, "I told you so."

In an address before the State Democratic Convention at Houston in August he denounced Parker's tactics of "nailing an extra plank to the platform after it was too late for the National Convention to help itself," and also congratulated Theodore Roosevelt for "the part he took in smashing the greatest transportation trust that was ever known" (Northern Securities case) and for starting the Panama Canal.[4] Then, reopen-

---

[1] Robert Cotner (ed.), *Addresses of James S. Hogg*, p. 513; J. S. Hogg to Richard M. Wynne, March 21, 1904, J. S. Hogg Let. Pr., 23, pp. 19–20; Tinsley, "Progressive Movement in Texas," Ph.D. dissertation (the University of Wisconsin, 1953), p. 56. For Hogg and Terrell's revival of the reform movement, see Charles Chamberlain, "Alexander Watkins Terrell," Ph.D. dessertation (the University of Texas, 1957), pp. 461 ff.

[2] J. S. Hogg to E. G. Senter, April 27, 1904, J. S. Hogg Let. Pr., 23, pp. 62–63; J. S. Hogg to John M. Duncan, June 3, 1904, J. S. Hogg Let. Pr., 23, p. 114.

[3] Ernest Winkler, *Platforms*, pp. 465–470; Houston *Post*, August 6, 1904.

[4] Cotner, *op. cit.*, pp. 526 and 526 n 10.

ing his war on corporate consolidations, Hogg drew a dark picture of the insidious measures nursed along by lobbyists in Texas for the purpose of railroad consolidation and undermining the Railroad Commission and the stock and bond law. After the speech, he received the silent treatment from the daily newspapers, and—in regard to the "insidious measures" he warned about—his opponents were (in Hogg's words) as "silent as the mists on a waveless sea"[5]; however, his attacks on Parker and especially his complimentary remarks about Roosevelt set off fireworks.

He was perfectly sincere in his praise of Roosevelt, and he had warned various Democrats—House among them—that the man who had taken over the reins of the national government on McKinley's tragic assassination had at the same time taken a firm hold on the American people by means of his fresh and vigorous approach to matters that had been smothered in shilly-shallying for several past administrations. Hogg considered the Republican President to be in the forefront of the progressive movement at the national level, diligently working in the public interest. After Parker (who was actually a nonentity to the majority of people) had lost to Roosevelt, Colonel House wrote to Hogg from New York:

Today, in the shadow of our great defeat, I want to take my hat off to you, for you are the only man I know that understood the hold that Theodore Roosevelt has upon the American people. I knew that Parker had no chance . . . but I did not anticipate such a crushing defeat. I hope that there is yet a future for our party but just now its light does not break in upon me.[6]

Hogg had a remedy: put the Democratic Party back in the role of presenting a progressive program which met the needs of the people. He had admired Roosevelt's handling of the great coal strike of 1902, and he knew that the Republicans were getting ahead of the Democrats in appealing to labor. Mark Hanna was the exceptional industrialist when he expressed a willingness to experiment with collective bargaining and urged his fellow businessmen in 1900, after McKinley had talked of the

[5] *Ibid.*
[6] E. M. House to J. S. Hogg, November 9, 1904, J. S. Hogg Let. Rec., XXXV, 481. Bryan wrote the same day wanting to talk with Hogg about the campaign of 1908. On January 1, 1905, Bryan wrote: "I find that Parker's defeat has strengthened you in Texas." J. S. Hogg Let. Rec., XXXVI, 1. William R. Hearst had tried to obtain Hogg's support against Parker.

"full dinner pail," to provide wage increases. Hogg had always believed that President Cleveland bungled the Democrats' relationship with organized labor in his handling of the Pullman strike.

Hogg's own reasonable attitude toward labor had frequently been made clear during his terms as attorney general and as governor—and he had often been labeled "communist" by his enemies therefor. When the publisher of the Houston *Labor Journal,* Max Andrew, shortly after the Houston meeting invited Hogg to speak at the large Labor Day rally to be held at La Porte, he added, "Since the recent State Convention, more than ever before, do the laboring masses recognize your nearness to them as a friend and champion."[7] The evaluation is the more interesting in the light of Hogg's recent hobnobbing with British royalty and nobility and his association with "oil magnates." Surely here was a man who, in Kipling's phrase, could walk with kings and not "lose the common touch."

The audience assembled at La Porte on September 5 was estimated by the newspapers as numbering more than 10,000. Hogg saw fit to elaborate on the theme expressed in the Democratic national platform: "Capital and Labor ought not to be enemies. Each is necessary to the other. Each has its rights, but the rights of labor are certainly no less vested, no less sacred and no less unalienable than the rights of capital."[8] Early in the address he stressed that every man who aspired to a political office and every man "who goes through the gateway of public favor to office, must take off his hat to labor. . . . Labor takes in all classes of men who earn their bread, whether by brain or brawn, and I would hate to see the day in Texas when any distinction is made save by reason of merit."[9]

Hogg was in the mood to answer questions, and in his answers he did not hesitate to uphold representative government and to oppose the impractical idea that hundreds of pages of proposed legislation could be handled by the current new idea of "direct legislation." Hogg's prac-

---

[7] J. S. Hogg Let. Rec., XXXV, 179, dated August 11, 1904. *The Journal of the Knights of Labor,* October 18, 1894, in speaking of the treatment of unemployed in Texas quoted Hogg: "Food, not fines, will be the treatment of the law-loving, law-abiding element in this State when men commit no greater crime than traveling as tramps for lack of work." William P. Hobby, managing editor of the Houston *Post,* on August 28, 1904, asked for an advance copy of the Labor Day speech. See James A. Clark, with Weldon Hart, *Tactful Texan, a Biography of Governor Will Hobby* (New York, Random House, 1958), pp. 9, 11, 16–18.

[8] Winkler, *Platforms,* pp. 465 ff.

[9] Quoted in Cotner, *op. cit.,* p. 514.

tical attitude may explain why "initiative" in legislation, like "referendum" and "recall," has not been used to any large extent.

Discussing the strike problem, he said he believed that most strikes involved men working for corporations and resulted from actual or threatened reductions of wages, from the unjust increase of daily hours of labor, or from wanton, arbitrary discharges. These conditions, he suggested, were due to the indifference or neglect of duty on the part of those state governments which failed to hold corporations to strict accountability in living up to charter obligations:

And right here, begin the strikes. Labor is abused; corporate wrongs are unseen, or overlooked; innocent women and children suffer; stalwart men grow resentful, intolerant, as day by day their losses cut deeper into their frugal savings.[10]

He emphasized that the public had an interest in strikes involving men working for corporations, especially as the corporations were created by the state and given certain governmental functions which individual citizens could not exercise. Corporations sometimes acted as if they had no fear of the restraining hand of the government that had given them life and placed them "in power over man."

Hogg ventured eight recommendations for lessening the need for strikes in Texas:

1. All public service corporations should be restrained from issuing any stocks or bonds in excess of reasonable value of their properties.

2. All such corporations should have to file an itemized list of assets with the Railroad Commission and with the Secretary of State.

3. The Railroad Commission will check the validity of the report before passing it on to the Secretary of State.

4. Tax assessors and boards of equalization should use the information as prima facie evidence in arriving at fair values for taxation.

5. Except for company officers and employees these corporations shall issue no free passes, free tolls, or reduced rates, etc.

6. No two such corporations which are or may become competitive may in any way consolidate business or management. [Hogg was ten years ahead of the interlocking directorate clause of the Clayton Antitrust Act.]

7. Such corporations should not be chartered for more than thirty years and any new charter will be subject to the sole discretion of the council or legislature having control of the subject.

8. That a board of arbitration, to be composed of, say, the Secretary of State, the Commissioner of Agriculture, and the Adjutant General, or

[10] *Ibid.*, p. 516.

President of the University, shall be created and given power to investigate and settle all strikes by the employes of corporations in this State.[11]

He admitted that labor might still need a weapon; if so, he recommended less use of the strike and more use of the ballot. He believed that the proper kind of state official would protect labor's legitimate interests and declared no weapon "more powerful than the ballot of a free man intelligently cast, honestly counted."[12]

That the speech was full of the political wisdom of the mature statesman and perhaps more expressive of Hogg's great heart than any other he ever made is testified to by these extracts:

A patriot has more difficulty in protecting his country in times of peace while the people are slumbering in the cradles of harmony than in defending it in time of war when they are shocked by battle's carnage into life and action.

The statesman looks down through the eyes deep into the hearts of countless posterity to learn their interests and hopes in government and works to accommodate them, as well as to help the living.

The politician keeps his eye on public office and schemes to get it.

With the ballot's monkey-wrench, the laborers should tighten the taps of governmental machinery so that no loose laws may fly about to hurt them.

Teach your children to obey the commands of God, to love good government and struggle to make it better.

Send your children to school. Educate them. Teach them that this government is theirs, but that if they expect to keep special privilege freebooters from stealing it they must be vigilant in their political affairs.

The colossal power of wealth may thwart the will of the people in some States, but it can not do more than foil the people for a season in Texas.

Intellect's calcium light turned onto the rugged brain walls of an unlettered man often exposes crude inscriptions of the profoundest philosophy there.[13]

On October 12, Legislative Day at the 1904 State Fair in Dallas, Governor Lanham of Texas, Governor Jeff Davis, of Arkansas, and James Hogg were the speakers before 5,000 people assembled in the Music Hall. Lanham's speech emphasized the prosperity of Texans

[11] *Ibid.,* p. 521. [12] *Ibid.,* p. 512. [13] *Ibid.,* pp. 523–524.

and the harmony existing within the Democratic Party. When Hogg's turn came he at once expressed concern over the amount of "harmony." He called admiring attention to Lanham's veto of the Southern Pacific consolidation bill in the last legislative session—a veto that saved the people $5 million—but now Lanham was again under great pressure from the lobbyists; Hogg called upon the Governor not to give in. He declared that if the Rock Island and Texas Central were permitted to consolidate, the Rock Island would make $10 million. Hogg maintained that he wanted to leave his own children free of the bonded railroad debts which the lobbyists were trying to fasten on them through the unconstitutional consolidations. He hoped the people could see the difference between politicians and lobbyists, and he wanted the latter— scoundrels he called them, men who would change the stock and bond law and destroy the alien land law and continue corporation rule— ousted from Austin.[14]

Yes, there was too much harmony for comfort, Hogg declared. He described Frank Andrews, the new chairman of the State Democratic Committee, as a "gentleman of breeding, reason and education, loyal to his past, loyal to his duty, but . . . [one whose] first duty for the past ten years had been to the Southern Pacific Railroad as the chief lobbyist at Austin. By gatlins, that is so."[15] After applause, he said that Andrews was no enemy but a personal friend, but he was a "greater friend to his client than he is to me or to you." Under these circumstances Hogg had thought it more important that he tell this story to the people of Texas than that he accept any invitations to campaign for the national Democratic ticket in some Northern state. Publicly he called upon Governor Lanham to stand up for Texas and to keep the state from getting into the hands of the corporations as had Missouri.

Hogg did a further daring thing; he challenged Governor Jeff Davis. The Arkansas Governor's speech had been a rabble-rouser, denouncing Republican efforts to revive the federal elections or "Force Bill" and declaring that President Theodore Roosevelt was not interested in the "corn-field negro" of the South but did these things to win Negro votes in the closely contested elections in New York, Ohio, Indiana, and Illinois. Davis may have believed such sentiments were popular in Texas because Senator Joe Bailey speaking at Brownwood in September had said: "No wonder Roosevelt eats with Booker. He wants the Negro vote

[14] Dallas *Morning News,* October 13, 1904.

[15] *Ibid.;* Houston *Post,* October 12, 1904; J. S. Hogg to James Hayes Quarles (Fort Worth), August 13, 1904, Let. Pr., 23, p. 172.

in the North. I believe more in the purity of the Anglo-Saxon race than I do in the principles of democracy."[16] Jeff Davis added that he doubted T. R. was contemplating any real move to bring about "social equality," then thundered, "If they tried it in Arkansas there would be a lot of dead niggers."[17]

These remarks were more than Hogg would take from even a visiting Democrat. He frankly told the Governor of Arkansas that he was not welcome if he intended to try to bring his brand of campaigning into Texas:

We don't want any race issue in the Southland, my friends. I am here, a native born, loving my race as every man loves his race, but I never want to see a race issue raised in this country. Anyone who starts it should never be encouraged. We have got the negroes among us and I don't want to build up the prejudice of my children against them and let them be murderers of the black race. I don't want the young men of this country to understand that they are to make any attack upon any human being unless it is by due process of law. There is no danger of social equality in Texas. . . . This race sentiment has been stirred up by those people down East who want to blind you with prejudice so they can get the federal treasury in their hands. . . . Whenever you see a mean negro in Texas you will find him mighty close to a mean white man.

The Governor of Arkansas is a good fellow, but I don't want him or any other man to build up race prejudice in Texas. Whenever it is done, those who curry the prejudice will be the sufferers.[18]

Negroes were in the country to stay, he said. Economic and political justice were their immediate concerns, rather than social equality. Only white men were trying to raise a racial issue for selfish purposes and he wanted them exposed for what they were—frequently the lobbyists for special interests and men who went around signing up old Confederate officers for public office in order to use them as fronts.

Hogg pointedly reminded Lanham that he was probably the last Confederate soldier who would serve as governor of Texas and urged him to "put on his spurs, get in the saddle and ride the corporations out of control in this State."[19] Recalling to the audience that this was Legislative Day at the Fair, Hogg pointed out that the Governor could not

---

[16] Houston *Post*, September 7, 1904.

[17] Dallas *Morning News*, October 13, 1904.

[18] *Ibid.* See also J. S. Hogg to Governor Culberson, June 29, 1896, Let. Pr., 13, p. 194, recommending a Tillotson College professor, E. L. Blackshear, a Negro, for the presidency of Prairie View Normal.

[19] Dallas *Morning News*, October 13, 1904.

563

fight all of their battles; he needed the assistance of a reform legislature. Texas must not "be manacled" by the corporations. As in his own campaign battle of 1892, Hogg wanted men elected who ran on a platform which "would do justice to corporations, but would not let them do injustice to Texas."

The keenness of his feeling about the "party peace and harmony," which he believed was stifling debate and intelligent exposure of abuses, was so great that he made a remark which must have stung the ears of many a Democrat. He declared that a "Democratic lobbyist"—who after election to the legislature put the interest of his special business clients ahead of the interests of the constituents who had voted for him in good faith—must be unseated: "Vote him out if you have got to put a Republican in his place."[20] These were strong words from a former Democratic governor in the presence of two Democratic governors. How much Hogg's unpulled punches at Houston, La Porte, and Dallas had to do with what happened on election day, less than a month later, cannot of course be estimated, but the people of Texas did send to Austin, for the first time in several years, a reform legislature.

Hogg's reply to Governor Davis on the race question was quoted from Little Rock to Boston. Three letters of the many Hogg received in reference to his remarks are of special interest. One was written by G. W. Jackson, the Negro president of the Central Texas Negro Fair Association at Corsicana: "Thank you for that humanitarian stand taken on the race question, which has no right to exist in this Country." He also appreciated Hogg's pointing out that white people were raising the issue; as far as the colored people were concerned, "We don't want the race question. We don't ask for it. We oppose it in every form. It is thrust upon us without our consent." Once more he thanked the former governor for putting his "stamp of disapproval" upon the whole affair.[21]

The other two letters came from Boston. Their author was Edward Atkinson, who was an influential Democrat and a liberal. A wealthy textile manufacturer, he had written books on economics, and was considered by some men rather too much of a zealot. Not content with what Hogg had done, Atkinson wanted him to do more. The first letter complimented Hogg on his speech and seemed to dangle before him the possibility of presidential preferment in 1908. Atkinson concluded: "You can lead Texas . . . to become the Empire State, the controlling

---

[20] *Ibid.*
[21] G. W. Jackson to J. S. Hogg, October 16, 1904, J. S. Hogg Let. Rec., XXXV, 400–401.

State in maintaining Constitutional principles and defending equal rights without distinction of race. The more backward the negro may be the more his right to an equal opportunity should be defended." The second letter offered a prescription by means of which Hogg could gain national recognition as an effective advocate of common human (and Constitutional) rights:

> Your position has taken possession of my imagination. No man ever had such an opportunity as you have to step right to the front *as a leader of the nation,* and that merely by doing your duty to your own State. You, the successor of Sam Houston, the leader of a people more democratic, more possessed with the spirit of individualism than almost any other in this country, wresting your State free from the old aristocratic caste and class system of the Atlantic Cotton States, coming right to the front as the head of a great national party, breaking both sectional parties into fragments; no solid South, no solid North, one great nation, standing by the Constitution, adhering to the principle of human liberty, of equal rights and of equal opportunities for each and all backward and forward races. If you could catch a spark of the vision as it stands in my mind, you would become rightly one of the foremost men in the whole nation.[22]

Hogg thanked Atkinson for his sentiments, apparently remaining untempted by his suggestions. Government and politics still fascinated him, but to his broad-visioned friends who often tried to change his mind about permanent retirement from public life he always replied that they must not look to him but find new and younger leaders.[23]

After the elections Hogg turned his attention to plans for his move to Houston. Always, however, in the background of any other activity was his interest in Varner. In the redecoration of the noble old house Ima's good taste had been given full authority; his part was to concentrate on plans to make himself known as a progressive farmer, stockman, and experimental horticulturalist. His pleasure in offering hospitality to all guests who crossed on the Brazos ferry was unbounded, and Houston Williams, one of the Negro servants, had special instructions on how to extend a gracious and genial welcome. As "lord of the manor," Hogg was reviving memories and accomplishing a major ambition: long ago

[22] Edward Atkinson to J. S. Hogg, November 21–22, 1904, J. S. Hogg Let. Rec., XXXV, 500–502, 506–507; Broadus Mitchell, *The Rise of Cotton Mills in the South* (Baltimore, Johns Hopkins Press, 1921), p. 117; Harold F. Williamson, *Edward Atkinson: The Biography of an American Liberal* (Boston, Old Corner Bookstore, 1934), pp. 236–237, 294.

[23] J. S. Hogg to T. F. Nash, October 31, 1904, is typical. J. S. Hogg Let. Pr., 23, p. 239.

he had seen his father and mother extend hospitality without stint to such men as Sam Houston and the young John Reagan, and now he had restored the family to prosperity and position in the best tradition. It is probable he never realized that he was a much kindlier man than Joseph Lewis Hogg had ever been, and that his vision of effective democracy encompassed new aspects that his ancestors might not have understood.

By the fall of 1902 Varner had been put under the able management of Joseph Fain, Dutchman, while the vegetable gardener was a Swede. At that time about a quarter of the plantation, one thousand acres, was being cultivated by a working staff of twenty-five Negroes. In 1902, during Aunt Fannie's visit there, English peas and strawberries were shipped early for the Christmas markets, and by mid-December 25 carloads of winter vegetables were also shipped.[24] The pastures were being cropped short by the 250 goats that Hogg had bought primarily "to clean up the place." The 50 head of "fine cattle" would soon be increased, while 16 mules provided the power for pulling plows, cultivators, and wagons. There were geese and chickens and turkeys, although Will cautioned against doing too much with livestock and birds, urging more attention to building up a fine pecan grove.

During 1904, Hogg put some of his oil profits into further improving his cattle. Having seen the sturdy white-faced Herefords on the High Plains, he considered purchasing some. Always a man to take expert advice, he appreciated the candor of one of his correspondents in Amarillo, who warned him that cattle from those plains would not thrive, perhaps not live, in the muggy coastal heat if transferred in midsummer. Therefore he sought cattle acclimated to the Gulf plain, which he obtained from Robert Justus Kleberg, the man whom he had appointed to be the first chairman of the Texas Livestock Commission, and who had helped to isolate the tick which caused Texas fever. He purchased 200 choice two-year-old Shorthorn heifers and 8 Hereford bulls to be shipped from the King Ranch. Will had been inclined to delay the cattle venture, feeling that his father was getting too much involved in the plantation, but after he learned what fine cattle had been received he sent congratulations and remarked that the animals were probably worth twice what Kleberg had charged.[25] Will was still concerned, however, lest the long

[24] Mrs. Martha Frances Davis to Hermilla Hogg Kelso, December (n.d.), 1902, Fam. Let.
[25] Will Hogg to J. S. Hogg, July 22, 1904, J. S. Hogg Let. Rec., XXXV, 105–106; Robert J. Kleberg to J. S. Hogg, August 13, 1904, *Ibid.*, p. 190; Tom

summers in the mosquito-infested low country prove unhealthful for his father. Hogg was determined to make the place more than pay its own way. He was very proud when the project attracted enough attention to cause the Houston *Post* in August, 1904, to publish a long report on the rehabilitation of Varner and the experiments in diversified farming that were providing jobs for thirty men.[26]

Ima, Mike, and Tom spent part of the summer in 1904 in Massachusetts, and their father's letters to them were full of his pride and satisfaction in Varner, and the characteristic musings that he enjoyed passing on to them, more in the manner of one comrade to another than of father to offspring. The letter of July 22, 1904, is typical.

The Spanish Flies made their appearance recently in myriads, schools, platoons—army style—to attack the alfalfa. Usually they ruin a hay crop. Most farmers are at a loss to "handle" them. As you may know . . . I am often bored by very ignorant men. But I have always indulged them patiently. I have always believed that in every head there is a good idea hidden like the jewels of the Ocean; that when intellect's calcium light is turned onto the rugged brainwalls of an unlettered man it often exposes crude inscriptions there of the profoundest philosophy; that most every man means well and wants to aid others. About a week before these pests came, I was "held up," so to speak, by one of these unlettered fellows. In the course of his incoherent remarks he suggested that *hot water* was *good* for Spanish Flies! Thus I caught the idea; got the nugget—the suggestion with a *thought* in it. So when the flies came I sent my men with scalding water after them. Within a few hours they were all dead, and I save the alfalfa! It is the simplest, most effective, and the least expensive remedy that has ever been applied to these enemies to the farmer.

In this there is a great lesson, which is, above all, that we must listen to all persons when they wish to talk—to give their opinions; not that we should gulp down—swallow—take for certain, that which they say; but that we should listen so as to pick out the good from the bad and profit by it, intellectually, if not in more ways.[27]

The affectionate relationships of the Hogg children to one another constituted a direct testimony to Jim Hogg's success as a father. The closeness that had prevailed in the family before Sallie Hogg's death had not been lost, even with the many separations. Will and Ima had in the past few years carried on an extensive correspondence, sometimes

Lea, *The King Ranch* (Boston, Houghton Mifflin Company, 1957), II, 497 ff., 722.

[26] J. M. Lewis, "Jim Hogg, Agriculturist," Houston *Post*, August 27, 1904.
[27] J. S. Hogg to Ima Hogg, July 22, 1904, Fam. Let.

567

gay, sometimes serious, but always full of the mutual respect they bore each other. Will knew how much his sister had helped achieve the family feeling he reveled in, and as her twenty-first birthday approached he could not refrain from letting her know how proud he was of what she had done, especially in regard to Mike and Tom, whom she had kept reasonably free of homesickness when they were away at school in Lawrenceville, New Jersey, and mothered in a subtle way on the summer vacations sometimes spent in New England. She and Will had always enjoyed teasing each other, establishing thereby a kind of *lingua franca* of relationship.

A letter of Will's prior to Christmas in 1902 was typical: "Prepare to become a comfortably rich woman. Your land at Columbia has healthy prospects of proving gusher territory. Drilling near here, adjoining your estate, is progressing rapidly and James Stephen 'would not be surprised to see 'em gush by Christmas.' Don't begin to spend money on your prospects, just now." The he urged her to come home. "You will be *permitted* to shoot at a duck or two in the company of your three brothers, that is if you be good and proper-like. I am your legal adviser and attorney."[28] In 1903 Will reported that their father had attended Governor Lanham's inauguration. "James Stephen was there and had more fun than anybody." There had been anxiety over the delayed arrival of a new dress suit, but everything turned out all right and Will was proud of his father's appearance. "I really like to see him *in dress.*"[29]

Early in 1905 cards were received by Hogg's numerous friends announcing the formation of his new law partnership in Houston with Edgar Watkins and Frank C. Jones, under the firm name of Hogg, Watkins, and Jones. Houston was having growing pains, stimulated by the possibility of rivaling Galveston as a port, and there was much debate over the best way to become a great port. One dream saw New Orleans being rivaled if the grain and meat traffic of the plains as far north as Denver and Kansas City could be sent by rail along the shortest and fastest routes to the Gulf. Hogg was interested in all of these developments, and especially in the idea that when, in ten years, the Panama Canal would be finished, Houston should have a ship channel ready to handle the new trade possibilities, including shipments of cotton to Japan.

Development of heavy industry in the Houston-Rusk-Beaumont region was another tantalizing possibility. The consulting geologist for the

[28] Will Hogg to Ima Hogg, December (n.d.), 1902, Fam. Let.
[29] Will Hogg to Ima Hogg, January 25, 1903, Fam. Let.

Southern Pacific, E. T. Dumble, who had been the state geologist when Hogg was governor, had suggested in 1902 that an oil and lignite combination was well adapted to the making of pig iron from the East Texas ores. "It was under your administration as Governor and through your cooperation that the facts were gathered which gave the lignite industry of Texas its start and proved its utility. While our wonderful oil deposits may temporarily retard the development of the lignite this may be increased ... by a combination of the two."[30] He hoped Hogg would start the experiment. New Birmingham, Texas, had failed in the depression of the nineties, but there was a new era ahead for iron and steel development in Texas, even if it should be necessary to import iron ore from South America.

Since the distance from Houston to Varner was too long for a daily trip back and forth, Hogg kept a suite at the Rice Hotel. In the evenings he frequently attended civic meetings or discussed with friends the future of Houston, the nation, and the Democratic Party. He still maintained several business ventures in Mexico, including a horse ranch just below the border,[31] and he was actively continuing his earlier efforts to improve American relations with Latin-American states. His new law venture was eminently successful. In short, James Hogg was happy and in the thick of events as he had always been. He was still a comparatively young man—he would be fifty-four in March 1905—and could look forward to a future full of adventure in a world that was steadily providing events of ever-increasing interest.

On January 26, 1905, the train in which he was returning to Houston after a day or so in Varner collided with a string of box cars as they were being switched.[32] The sudden impact threw many passengers forward, against seats or on the floor. Hogg was thrown violently down and instantly felt great pain in his neck. However, the injury seemed only minor at first, but when the pain did not diminish, he consulted Dr. Joseph Mullen, an eye, ear, nose, and throat doctor, who found evidence of serious injury and subsequent abscess.[33] During the next months delicate operations were performed, including one to relieve a large swelling which developed inside the throat, like an interior carbuncle. The newspapers expressed concern for his life, and even his

[30] E. T. Dumble to J. S. Hogg, May 2, 1902, J. S. Hogg Let. Rec., XXXIV, 196–198.

[31] J. Frank Dobie and Raymond Dickson developed some of their ability to tell Mexican and cowboy stories and folk tales while working on the ranch.

[32] Houston *Post,* January 27, 1905.

[33] Personal interview with Miss Hogg, June, 1955.

old enemies among the editors softened their tone and praised him for the foresight of his accomplishments as governor. During the dreary days and many restless nights of his prolonged illness Ima was his faithful attendant.[34] Often his heavy breathing in the night kept her awake, listening, hoping, praying, and if she were asleep any change in his breathing—even his turning over—usually awakened her.

His strong constitution and indomitable will little by little came to his aid; by mid-March he was greatly improved and able to enjoy the signs of spring at Varner. When an invitation came for a banquet honoring Theodore Roosevelt at Dallas on April 5, he decided to accept and to make the brief address requested. He knew that many Democrats would never quite understand why he would make so much effort to honor any Republican, but Hogg liked the man and had something to say to this great American champion of the Progressive Movement who loved the West and who was bringing to fruition the canal Hogg had long dreamed about.

The program had scheduled Hogg's address to follow the President's. When Hogg's turn came, he seemed very much his old self as he rose:

I came here, several hundred miles, after a protracted, serious, spell of sickness in order to testify my appreciation of the man who . . . liberated Texas from commercial tyranny. A man who . . . made it possible for our commerce, so great, so wonderful, and of such boundless possibilities, to reach a market of 300,000,000 people without traveling 9,000 miles out of the way.

Yes, it is a pleasure to me as a Texan, rising above partisan prejudice, to come here to meet the great President, who had the manhood to strike back the dough-faced pirates who have fettered commerce for over 100 years. That's Americanism, not politics. . . .

I came to pay my respects to him for other reasons. He is the first President to obey the will and the sentiment of the American people absolutely, fearlessly, regardless of his own environments. An instance, in point, is his taking the first step to strike down the Northern Securities Company. He was the first one to lead out to suppress the trusts of this country that are now throttling commerce and destroying individualism. . . . And, if there is the spirit of Andrew Jackson that has descended to find place again in the bosom of any man in the last seventy years, it is in Theodore Roosevelt. . . . And when Texans stand up to welcome the great Democratic President,

---

[34] Personal interview with Miss Hogg, June, 1955; W. J. Bryan to J. S. Hogg, February 5, 1905, J. S. Hogg Let. Rec., XXXVI, 13, told Hogg he was needed for "party service."

we are proud to have the Republicans to help us. [Laughter and applause][35]

After mentioning that Roosevelt was a rare student of his country's history, Hogg referred to his cowboy days:

He has been upon the plains, under the blanket, to study the dry regions of the great West, to see the necessity of irrigation. Did you ever know a man who was raised upon the plains, or who had spent his young manhood there in the saddle, that was not opposed to monopoly in every form? He is for the greatest individual freedom consistent with human rights in obedience to the Constitution of the country. . . . Mr. President, we want to say to you, sir, that . . . the representatives of every class of people in our State, . . . [are] ever ready to do honor to a servant of the people who will obey their will. . . . I must say no more. Good night.[36]

Suddenly the President rose and walked over to Hogg, shook hands with him and thanked him for what he had said. Both Democrats and Republicans joined in the applause and cheers.

A few days later Hogg was asked to speak before the Good Roads Convention at Houston about John H. Reagan, who had died in March. Hogg reminded his audience how Reagan, from his prison at Fort Warren in 1865, had warned Southerners that they must not alienate the good will of the Moderates in the North and had also counseled Texans to grant limited suffrage, civil rights, and fair treatment to the colored people or run the risk of playing into the hands of the vindictive Radicals. At the time many Texans thought Reagan had been forced to write the letter, and when he came home many shunned him. But when the "military satrap," General Charles Griffin, offered him the Texas governorship, Reagan "turned and spurned it."[37] Hogg was visibly moved when he recalled aloud from his memory the scene in the fields near Palestine when Reagan stood "between two plow handles" and spoke words of encouragement to an orphan boy. He was "always a gentle, good, kind neighbor," and never "on the wrong side of politics. If he blundered, he was manly enough to correct it, and seldom did he blunder" in "political thought or action." Like Roberts and Lubbock, Reagan lived to a great old age; Hogg attributed this to the fact that in middle life these men had been forced to start over; they had rejuvenated their constitutions by physical labor, inhaled new atmosphere, and got a new lease on life:

[35] Dallas *Morning News,* April 6, 1905; Cotner, *op. cit.,* pp. 526–527.
[36] *Ibid.,* p. 528.   [37] *Ibid.,* p. 530.

So I believe that every one who follows a profession ought to go back to nature and scour himself out. It prolongs life, it rejuvenates life, it stimulates the constitution that has perhaps been worn out years before, and I think that the example of John Reagan, Governor Lubbock, and Governor Roberts ought to be thought of by every professional man, merchant and business man in this country. You can live much longer by working a few years at menial labor. I am telling you what I ought to have done, and what I would do if I had time. These men did not do that from a matter of choice, but as a matter of necessity.[38]

Speaking of Reagan as an example for men, Hogg paid tribute to the qualities that went into the Old Roman's greatness:

The first law of that man was to behave himself and obey the law. The law-abiding citizen is an honorable gentleman, he is respectful to other people. He discussed politics without partisanship, and when he took a stand he did it independent of the thoughts of others. He was careful never to give an opinion until he had formed a judgment. He would investigate every question of public concern that came up, and having investigated it, he had the sidelights of his own reason thrown upon his judgment. That made him a statesman, that made him a great man, that stamped him in the eyes of Texas forever.[39]

Returning to Varner, Hogg was hopeful that his health would continue to improve. He was greatly pleased to learn that in trying to provide a "unified strong and well-integrated" railroad commission law the legislature of Wisconsin, responding to Governor La Follette's recommendations, left the drafting to experts who "modeled it after the best features of the Texas and Iowa laws."[40] Hogg must have felt more than vindicated in his early insistence upon the right to appoint the first commissioners so as to assure a good beginning, when Progressives in Wisconsin pointed with pride to what they considered a distinctive feature of their new commission—the members were appointed, were of known ability, and brought it great prestige.

Will came down to the plantation, and there were long talks about the future. These were precious days to Hogg as he rode over the estate with his daughter and his oldest son, trying to instruct them about his business and about their property and how to develop it for themselves and for the benefit of the people of Texas. During these talks plans were formulated for a long-range program to enlist the people of Texas in a

---

[38] *Ibid.*, p. 531.   [39] *Ibid.*

[40] Robert Maxwell, *LaFollette and the Rise of the Progressives in Wisconsin* (Madison, State Historical Society of Wisconsin, 1956), p. 76.

fund-raising campaign to improve the institutions of higher learning. It was hoped that such a project would not only educate the people to the needs of the public schools and colleges, but also stimulate elected representatives to give more attention to the legislation required to provide better educational opportunities.

These hopes were realized, though not fully within Hogg's lifetime. A few years later the "Hogg Organization" succeeded in raising over $150,000 through the assistance of the University Alumni Association.[41] In 1912 "Hogg Memorial Day" for the improvement and strengthening of public sentiment for education was observed throughout the state. The president of the State Teachers Association, J. F. Kimball, of Temple, stressed the need for adequate local schools accessible to all children and for a type of training which would create within children the desire for a "complete education." He concluded by saying that the Memorial Day was the first organized state-wide effort in Texas to inculcate "the value of higher education in the minds of all the children. ... It is peculiarly fitting that it should bear the name of the great Texas commoner, Governor Hogg. In my childhood he was my father's friend and neighbor, and of him I well remember hearing my father say that he was only a common man, but raised to the n-th degree."[42]

Will could not stay long away from his work in St. Louis, but Ima continued to learn from her father and plan for a better Varner. During August and September, 1905, father and daughter spent several weeks in Manitou, Colorado, in the hope that Hogg would be benefited. The altitude proved to be very bad for him; Ima summoned Will to help them make the journey back to Texas. For some time afterward Hogg was very ill again, and once more letters and telegrams of appreciation and encouragement poured in. On warm days Hogg and various of the children might be seen in a four-seated spring wagon, driving over the Varner lanes and fields, but progress was slow, and it became evident that his heart was impaired. In the summer of 1904, Hogg had been somewhat concerned about the chance of a heart attack, referring to it somewhat jokingly as "Fat Man's Fear."[43]

Drilling had been going on sporadically at Varner, with no more suc-

[41] Sidney E. Mezes, "The Organization for the Enlargement by the State of Texas of its Institutions of Higher Education," in Edwin D. Shurter (ed.), *Addresses on Education* (Bulletin of the University of Texas No. 234, Austin, 1912), pp. 7–9.

[42] *Ibid.*, pp. 11–12, reprints J. F. Kimball, "An Address to the People of Texas," given April 11, 1912, and on pp. 13–14 reprints T. U. Taylor, "Jim Hogg."

[43] Interview with Miss Hogg, July, 1954.

cess than earlier. Hogg was still convinced that substantial amounts of oil would eventually be found, and, determined to protect his children, he stipulated in his will that the Varner properties should not be disposed of by the executors—except as a last resort—for at least fifteen years. He believed that in time the need for oil would force development at West Columbia, but in the meanwhile he wanted the children secured against the attractive offers which might be presented to them by companies that sought to control the region but were not ready to drill. In these provisions of the will, Hogg was eminently wise. This area would be developed after 1917, and, during World War I, would become famous as the West Columbia Oil Field.

In November, 1905, Hogg was invited to address a meeting of state officials in Dallas. The invitation came at a time when he seemed better, and he decided to accept, particularly since the four potential candidates for the governorship, including Tom Campbell, would also make speeches. Hogg had endorsed Campbell and was anxious to see him elected, believing that he would ably carry the banner of reform. When he reached Fort Worth, he was suddenly too ill to continue the journey, and was put to bed in a hotel. The meeting was ready to assemble in Dallas; realizing her father's great disappointment in not carrying out his promise to speak, Ima arranged for him to make a recording to be carried to Dallas. Thus the audience heard the voice of Jim Hogg, lacking its long-known physical vigor but speaking firmly of the sort of measures he had never ceased to advocate for the good of Texas:

Mr. Toastmaster and Gentlemen:

In a recent nocturnal voyage on the watery waves of despair, I drifted over the vortex of eternity, but was wafted back by the breath of Fate. To Him I stood ready and willing to render a final account, with no fear of my place in the great beyond. As to Texas, I felt there was yet much political work to be done, in which every patriotic citizen should take part. Before leaving her, I should like to see:

Rotation in office permanently established;

Nepotism forbidden;

Equality of taxation a fact;

Organized lobbying at Austin suppressed;

The free pass system honestly, effectively abolished;

Oil pipe lines placed under the commission's control;

Insolvent corporations put out of business;

All bonds and stocks of every class of transportation limited by law;

Corporate control of Texas made impossible; and

Public records disclose every official act and be open to all, to the end that everyone will know that, in Texas, public office is the center of public conscience, and that no graft, no crime, no public wrong, shall ever stain or corrupt our State.[44]

Hogg was again a very sick man. When he was finally able to leave Fort Worth, he wanted to go to Austin—the scene of political triumphs and the resting place of his wife. In his old suite at the Driskill, which had continued to be officially known as the Hogg Suite, he received friends, old and young. Railroad Commissioner Allison Mayfield and his daughter, Mary, found him one day sitting alone. Because he appreciated their visit so much he autographed a photograph and gave it to Mary, who gave it in 1950 to the Texas State Historical Association, an organization of which he was one of the earliest members. Austin was more like home than any other place. Political animosities had faded. Men and women and little boys and girls came to call; former employees at the Mansion and Capitol came to pay their respects. Once more he seemed to rally as he responded to the love and interest of his friends.

In the evenings he frequently read the Bible. The story is told that one day a chapter he was reading so impressed him that he picked up a hotel menu left in his room and penned on it the following in his bold distinctive handwriting:

A people without the Bible are savages. A people with the Bible, and desecrate it, are barbarians. A people who strive to obey the Bible commandments live in the sunlight of heaven with God's blessings to comfort them in this life and to guarantee eternal happiness in the life to come.[45]

He seemed aware that he was not going to get well, but he did not say this to the children. Because in recent years he had not been an active member in his local church, he was concerned lest Tom and Mike might not understand his broad but firm religious convictions. Earlier he had

[44] Cotner, *op. cit.*, p. 532; Charles Culberson to Will Hogg, October 27, 1905, J. S. Hogg Let. Rec., XXXVI, 163–164. A copy of this "Manuscript to the People of Texas" was placed in the cornerstone of Saint Anne's Catholic Church in Houston by the Most Reverend C. E. Byrne, Bishop of Galveston. Houston *Chronicle,* March 27, 1939. For pipeline regulation and the Hepburn Act see Arthur M. Johnson, *The Development of American Petroleum Pipelines: A Study in Private Enterprise and Public Policy, 1862–1906* (Ithaca, Cornell University Press, 1956), pp. 219–224.

[45] The Driskill Hotel menu was dated December 19, 1905. Scrapbook of Mrs. Hermilla Hogg Kelso (formerly of Fort Worth). James Stephen Hogg to E. C. Dickinson, December 16, 1905, Let. Wr. Sup., reported that doctors wanted him to stay out of the office until spring, 1906.

sought his daughter's assistance in training the boys—after she wrote asking if he approved of her inclination to become an Episcopalian:

. . . As to the Episcopal Church: If it is your choice and you so desire I could have no objections to your joining it. Tom is thinking of joining the Methodist Church. Your Mother and her people all belonged to it. Mine were of the Baptist persuasion. Let your own conscience and better judgment be gratified on this question and I shall be satisfied. Be good and write me fully.[46]

Hogg was eager for assurance that his children were guarding their spiritual welfare, and he counted on Ima to serve as an example for the younger boys:

The attention and kindness shown you everywhere, and especially in Austin, where you are so well known, shed floods of light of pleasure into my heart. And you deserve it all. With your acquaintances and large circle of friends in Texas, won by your own exemplary character and excellent behavior, you have nothing to dread in the future; provided that you do not change radically in your disposition and habits. With you or away from you I have every reason to be grateful to God for such a girl. One thing I do hope and that is you may go to Church a little oftener.

Affectionately your Father,
J. S. Hogg[47]

In numerous letters Hogg exhorted his daughter to watch over the spiritual development of Mike and Tom.

In February, 1906, he was improved enough to go back to Varner, where he spent a happy few weeks. Will was anxious to have him go to Battle Creek or to Rochester for treatment, and finally won his consent to try Battle Creek. Will and Ima would accompany him. They went first to Houston, where Hogg wanted to spend a few days at the home of his law partner Frank Jones. He enjoyed seeing Jones and told him, now that the trip was planned, "I feel now as if I am going to get well."

On Friday night, March 2, Texas Independence Day, Hogg was cheerful. He mentioned to Jones that at his death he wanted no monument of stone, but, instead:

Let my children plant at the head of my grave a pecan tree and at my feet an old-fashioned walnut tree. And when these trees shall bear, let the

---

[46] J. S. Hogg to Ima, May 29, 1902 and December 9, 1905, Fam. Let. See Chapter I.

[47] J. S. Hogg to Ima Hogg, December 9, 1905, Fam. Let.

pecans and walnuts be given out among the plain people so that they may plant them and make Texas a land of trees.[48]

When Ima was distressed that he should talk so, he said, "I am going to get well and shall be with you many years." At midnight he retired and so far as anyone knew slept soundly. About 8:30 the next morning Jones paused at the door of Hogg's room; hearing him breathing as in restful sleep, he left orders with the servants that his guest should not be disturbed. At 11 o'clock Ima went to the door and called: "Time for you to get up, Papa." There was no response.[49]

The news of the death of James Stephen Hogg was flashed quickly over the state. All newspapers carried long accounts of his services to the people, citing evidences of his foresight and statesmanship, and editors everywhere expressed sympathy for the children. When memorial services were held in Austin, Dallas, Tyler, and elsewhere, column after column was devoted to the speakers and to recounting the story of his life.[50] James H. Robertson and Colonel House made the arrangements for placing his casket in the Senate Chamber to remain in State from Sunday afternoon until the funeral services. On Monday afternoon, March 5, 1906, James Stephen Hogg was buried, as he had requested, beside his wife in Oakwood Cemetery, Austin.

All over Texas during March, especially during the week of his birthday, Jim Hogg's friends gathered to pay tribute to his memory. In Dallas, the principal speaker was a Republican, William H. Atwell, Hogg's young opponent and "champion liar" in the debate on imperialism in 1900. (He became a great federal judge.) In Tyler, Hogg's former law partner, John Duncan, delivered a thoughtful evaluation, including the following word portrait that deserves to endure along with the portraits by William Huddle and Robert Joy:

Endowed with a giant mind, set in a giant frame, his very port and presence evidenced a superior intellectuality, and that honesty, sincerity and firmness which characterized his every act and utterance of life. No man, not even a foe, could come within the radiance of that countenance, beam-

---

[48] Texas Education Agency, *Centennial Handbook, Texas Public Schools, 1854–1954* (Austin, 1954), pp. 22–23.

[49] Edgar Watkins, "Sketch of James Hogg," Interv. Fol., pp. 20–25; Frank C. Jones to Ima Hogg, June 29, 1935, Interv. Fol.; Houston *Post* and Houston *Chronicle* March 4, 1906.

[50] Houston *Post,* March 3–28, 1906; Dallas *Morning News,* March 4–28, 1906; Austin *Daily Statesman,* March 3–27, 1906; Houston *Chronicle,* March 4–14, 1906; *East Texas Register* (Carthage), editorial by Miss Margie E. Neal, March 9, 1906.

ing with intelligence and good humor, nor look into the clear depths of those frank, blue eyes, without being wonderfully impressed with the force, candor and originality of the man.[51]

The wise Horace Chilton remarked prophetically about his best friend:

Time will take care of his name, but let us never forget the practical side of his life and the advice he gave to those who must take up the work that Fate decreed should drop from his hands. . . . The only true memorial which a people he dearly loved can make to this wise and constant friend is to keep his creed before them as a guiding star.[52]

James Stephen Hogg had stood for law enforcement in the midst of a lawless era, resulting from the Civil War and its Reconstruction aftermath and from the influence of a frontier and a thousand-mile border which attracted the criminal and the hunted of two nations. Hogg had joined with his brothers in opposing Carpetbag rule and the corruption of the Grant administration. He had opposed the grasping practices of some railroads which were never satisfied in their efforts to pay dividends on inflated stocks and bonds. Realizing that the Office of the Attorney General could not get ahead of this game, he pressed for the creation of an effective railroad commission. He wanted this agency to pass upon the validity of new issues of stocks and bonds; in time he came to advocate that it should exercise jurisdiction over pipelines. He did not limit his close scrutiny to railroads. Through his efforts Texas had the second state antitrust law in the country, preceding the national act by a year. Through his foresight in initiating these measures, prosecuted by a succession of attorneys general, the state of Texas regained over a million acres from the railroads. Continued pressure on the Waters-Pierce Oil Company eventually brought Texas in 1909 the payment of a fine of $1,808,483 for violation of the antitrust law.[53]

These were among the accomplishments of Hogg for the people of Texas. Later politicians and statesmen, imbued with his political philosophy, continued his work. As Hogg had hoped, Thomas Campbell be-

[51] John M. Duncan, *James Stephen Hogg,* a pamphlet, H. C. The Houston *Post,* March 26, 1906, reported the memorial services in the First Presbyterian Church of that city. For Horace Chilton's address see Dallas *Morning News,* August 14, 1906.

[52] Cotner, *op. cit.,* p. 29; other quotations in Mary Louise Wimberly Barksdale, "Gubernatorial Administration of James Stephen Hogg," Master's thesis (the University of Texas, 1932), pp. 132–135.

[53] Richardson, *Texas,* p. 372; Ralph and Muriel Hidy, *Standard Oil,* p. 686.

came the next Governor of Texas, and, as if to erect a new kind of monument to the departed statesman, the legislature, under the stimulation of Campbell's administration, passed the anti–free-pass bill. In 1907 Hogg's Austin law partner, James Robertson, succeeded in obtaining the enactment of the insurance law that bears his name, which required life insurance companies to invest in Texas securities at least 75 per cent of the reserves set aside for insurance policies written for Texas citizens—the capstone of Hogg's first efforts as attorney general. In 1908 only about $1 million of the $40-million reserve was invested in Texas, but as a result of this law Texas would have an increasing amount of capital for investment. The Progressive reform climate of the era of Presidents Theodore Roosevelt and Woodrow Wilson was the lengthening shadow of the earlier leaders of reform in the states. Governor Hogg deserves to be recognized as a worthy colleague of such progressive governors as Altgeld of Illinois, Roosevelt of New York, La Follette of Wisconsin, and Wilson of New Jersey.

Despite Hogg's busy life and the masses of professional mail, he always had taken time to read and hear the complaints and longings of the "plain people," as well as of the "important people." His gentleness, often unsuspected by men who knew only his external appearance, brought him many friends among the children of Austin and elsewhere. Soon after his death the editor of the Houston *Chronicle* received the following letter:

To the Editor of *The Chonicle:*

Since the death of Gov. Hogg my mama has read me many nice sentiments expressed by other people about him, and will you please give room for what I know about this good, kind-hearted gentleman. I was truly sorry when I heard he was dead. While he must have been a great man for his state and people, he never overlooked small things as well. Two or three years ago I wrote him a letter and in just a few days I received a reply (of which I will send you a copy), and you can imagine my joy at getting such a nice letter from the ex-governor of our state, and, Mr. Editor, will you kindly give it room in your valuable paper, as I would like other boys to read my letter I prize so highly. I am, respectfully, your little friend, Freddie Hughes. Houston, Texas.

Hogg's "such a nice letter" to the little boy follows:

My Dear Little Friend:

Out of the thousands of calls on me for contributions, presents and assistance, I find none so unique, terse and boy-like as yours; which simply asks me to send you a goat. I wish I had one here now to express to you, but

I have none. Down on my plantation, several hundred miles from this place, I have some goats and I will describe them to you. There are big goats, and little goats, he goats, and she goats, white goats, black goats, red goats, blue goats, grey goats, yellow goats, speckled goats, long-horned goats, short-horned goats, one-horned goats and mooly goats, Angora goats, Spanish goats, fine goats, common goats, all kinds, classes and colors of goats, and each and every one of them is a book-eating, tree-skinning, briar-cleaning, snake-stamping, bucking goat, used for the purpose of clearing up the woods, brambles and thickets around the premises. Now, the first time you hear that I am in Houston, I want you and your brother to call on me at the Rice hotel, so that you can explain to me whether or not one of these malicious goats which you call for would get your father into trouble with his neighbor. I warrant you are a nice boy, and I hope to make your acquaintance. With sincere regards, I am,

Your Friend,
J. S. Hogg[54]

February 21, 1903

Among the many testimonies of the benefits Governor Hogg secured to his state, the improved University of Texas must be counted one of the most enduring in the enormous geometrical progression of its spreading influence on the people of Texas. Hogg's veneration for education and his abiding faith that *only* through education could the public learn the duties and responsibilities of citizenship and give the informed "consent of the governed" that would assure good government came early to the aid of the University, when it was a struggling and largely disregarded young institution. As Leslie Waggener wrote in his note of appreciation to Hogg during the 1890 campaign:

. . . I wish to thank you most heartily for the outspoken endorsement you gave the University in your speech at Rusk. So far as I know you are the first prominent statesman of Texas, who, in a campaign speech, has had the boldness to speak an earnest word in behalf of the State University; and if you are elected Governor, you will be the first one who has committed himself before hand to the adequate and proper maintenance of this institution since its organization.[55]

In many other direct and indirect ways (not the least of them being the recovery of the "switches and sidings" lands from the railroads for the benefit of the Texas school system) public education in Texas owes immeasurable debt to this man and to his children. During his first

[54] Houston *Chronicle,* March 6, 1906.   [55] Cotner, *op. cit.,* p. 27.

administration he cooperated with the president of the University in arranging an evening on the campus, so that the legislators and other visitors might see the plant and the students and thus come to know the needs of "the cap-stone of our public free school system." The audience for his speech on this occasion included many of the students:

Hereafter the great battles to maintain the liberties of the people must be fought in the forum of reason. It is well for the great army turned out year by year from the public schools to understand the cause of its training. Linked together with the common schools are inseparably connected the Normal School, the Agricultural and Mechanical College and the State University. In courses of study there is no clash. In their operation consistency and harmony prevail. To their advancement the hopes, the pride and the money of the people lend succor.

While here to-night to testify our appreciation of the University in its splendid achievements, we should not forget to acknowledge our respect for the wisdom of the fathers who laid its foundations, and to express our gratitude to the people for their generosity in its support.

Young men, you can never forget the causes that led Texans to popular education without injustice to a sense of patriotism. You cannot forget the obligations you are due the masses for the splendid educational advantages afforded you without smothering those sentiments intermingled with the pure principles of elevated manhood.

The people are proud of the University; for here the poorest boy, side by side with those more favorably situated, can, at trifling cost, acquire a finished education. They are proud of the men whom they have educated at public expense. In return for their liberality and confidence, they expect no more than a defense of their rights and liberties under the banner of justice. So long as they are not disappointed the University will prosper, for its richest nourishment must be found in their affections.[56]

With the passing of time Hogg's influence in Texas politics has continued to be dynamic. Practically every candidate has either referred to his connection with Jim Hogg or stated that he wished to carry on his work, even if Jim Ferguson and some of those who ran subsequent to the administrations of Pat Neff and Dan Moody did not appear to understand what Hogg had stood for. Fortunately, in 1905, Cadwell W. Raines, who had been appointed librarian of the Texas State Library by Governor Hogg, and encouraged by him to build up the historical records, gathered together many of his important speeches and published them in a substantial volume. In time these books became

---

[56] James S. Hogg Misc., March 26, 1892; quoted in Cotner, *op. cit.*, Appendix H.

scarce and it became more difficult for the average man to check on the accuracy of a "quotation" used by the office seekers.

In March, 1951, Governor Allan Shivers declared the ensuing year to be officially designated the James Stephen Hogg Centennial Year.[57] In the rotunda of the Capitol, along with portraits of all the other Texas governors, is a new and excellent likeness of Governor Hogg by Robert Joy of Houston. The portrait, a duplicate of one Miss Hogg has in her River Oaks home, was given to the people of Texas. As a part of the many celebrations of the Hogg Centennial Year, the University of Texas through the new University Press issued a revised edition of *The Addresses and State Papers of James Stephen Hogg* and made a copy available to each high school in the State. It was a fitting tribute to the man who was a champion of education to the end that "the rights and liberties of the people" would be preserved, and whose son, Will, ably defended the cause of higher education. Miss Hogg, while a member of the Houston School Board, had also made her contribution to education, working diligently to improve the public schools of a rapidly growing city.

In 1951 the officials of the State Fair set aside October 12 as James Stephen Hogg Day. James Pinckney Hart, Chancellor of the University of Texas, delivered the principal address on "What James Stephen Hogg Means to Texas." Among other things he said:

To Governor Jim Hogg, who thought clearly and spoke bravely, the Constitution was a guide for rough weather as well as smooth sailing. And it may be noted that while he suffered the abuse that all public officials must endure, even his political enemies respected his integrity and the people of Texas loved him for his uncompromising honesty. Texans have boasted with good reason of their material resources. All about us today in this great State Fair are exhibits which give graphic demonstration of the agricultural, commercial, and industrial wealth we have attained. But our greatest asset has been and always should be the character of the people who live here. So long as the people of Texas can produce leaders like James Stephen Hogg, we can face the future with confidence.[58]

James Hogg supported and made more meaningful the political doctrine of sovereignty of the people. He was opposed to annexation of the Philippines and advocated their liberation, but he declared that Ameri-

[57] Senate Concurrent Resolution 23, Texas *Senate Journal* (1951), p. 207.
[58] Reprinted in *Southwestern Historical Quarterly*, LV (April, 1952), pp. 439–447. See George Fuermann, *Reluctant Empire: The Mind of Texas* (Garden City, Doubleday and Company, 1957), pp. 54, 67.

582

can civil liberties and the duties of citizenship should follow the flag in this hemisphere in Puerto Rico and Hawaii. Well aware of the lethargy of the people in the mass, and alert to the dangers of mob action, Hogg worked fearlessly and honestly to inform the people how they could make government serve their needs. His enemies expected him to build up a political machine to keep himself in power, but he had vigorous dislike for this method of political action and always counseled against it—knowing full well that when the reaction came, the opposition would then be able to wipe out a reform program, root and branch. This personal unwillingness to create a machine is an often overlooked characteristic of the true progressive, and was one of the many distinctive qualities of Hogg that emphatically denied the charge of demogoguery.[59] Hogg was able in his lifetime to build a strong legal foundation for the corporate age in the Southwest. However, as the great corporate structures were erected in the early days of the twentieth century, some of the blueprint was not followed. Nevertheless, Governor La Follette and Governor Wilson studied it and benefited therefrom. When Wilson visited the Fair at Dallas in October, 1911, just prior to becoming a candidate for the Presidency, he appropriately called attention to Hogg's record and pronounced him a forerunner of the Progressive Movement.[60]

After 1917, the wisdom of Hogg's stipulation in regard to Varner became apparent. A little later his faith in the existence of abundant oil in the West Columbia region was justified—and spectacularly so when, on January 15, 1919, the Tyndall-Hogg No. 2 well marked the finding of a prolific new oil-bearing sand.[61] In 1921 the West Columbia field produced over 12 million barrels; in 1947 the production was still over 2 million. Will's teasing notation to his sister in 1902—"prepare to become a reasonably wealthy woman"—became an exaggerated understatement, and the financial security that James Hogg had unceasingly hoped to provide for his children was attained many times over.

One of the acid tests of the true goodness and greatness of a man is

[59] Richard Hofstadter, *The Age of Reform* (New York, Knopf, 1955), pp. 267–268; Robert S. Maxwell, "LaFollette and the Progressive Machine in Wisconsin," *Indiana Magazine of History*, XLVIII (March, 1952), 55–70; George Mowry, *The California Progressives* (Berkeley, University of California Press, 1951), pp. 138–139, 292; Herbert Gambrell, "James Stephen Hogg: Statesman or Demagogue?" *Southwest Review*, XIII (Spring, 1928), 338–366.

[60] Dallas *Morning News*, October 29, 1911. Ray S. Baker, *Woodrow Wilson*, III, 294–296, omits references to this speech. See Arthur S. Link, "The Wilson Movement in Texas, 1910–1912," *Southwestern Historical Quarterly*, XLVIII (October, 1944), 176.

[61] Warner, *Texas Oil and Gas*, p. 201.

the steadfastness with which his example is followed by those closest to him. No public figure has better stood this test than has James Stephen Hogg, in the persons and endeavors of his three sons and his daughter. In the use of their wealth they not only followed Jim Hogg's example; they also manifested the qualities which were a part of their inheritance from their parents and which they developed to a peak of gracious public service.

There can never be a full accounting of Will Hogg's benefactions; much of what he did both for individuals and for public causes was under the severe injunction of secrecy to those who aided in the distribution.[62] The State of Texas, the University, the City of Houston, and uncounted individuals were among the benefactors of his financial and other gifts, as well as of the enthusiasm of his creative planning for such endeavors and causes as civic forums, museums, and other useful projects. Through the family organization established after the end of World War I to administer the estate, his brother and sister sponsored innumerable projects. After Will's death in 1930 (while vacationing in Europe with his sister) a request of his will that a major portion of his estate be set aside for a purpose to be specified by his brother Mike Hogg as executor, with the assistance of his sister, was carried out in the establishment of the Hogg Foundation for Mental Hygiene, administered through the University.

After the deaths of Mike (1941) and Tom (1949), Miss Hogg carried on both the business and civic responsibilities of the family tradition. In 1958 on Jim Hogg's birthday, March 24, she presented the Varner Plantation to the State of Texas as a state park and museum—a singularly percipient and appropriate gift, for it was at Varner that her father found most happily, except for the absence of his wife, that sense of home he had craved since boyhood. On the broad gallery of the house, surrounded by guests and his children, or sitting alone in the afternoon to relax in a chair and sip a glass of lemonade, he would look out over the trees and the fertile good land. There he was at peace. The house was readied for its presentation to the state by a complete restoration and redecoration "in the spirit of the series of eventful changes which the various owners of the plantation" had known since Stephen Austin granted the land to Martin Varner in 1824, and it was Miss Hogg's desire that the gift be dedicated not only to her "father's

---

[62] John A. Lomax, *Will Hogg, Texan* (Austin, University of Texas Press for The Hogg Foundation, 1956), pp. 35–42.

memory, but to those valiant Texas pioneers of each successive period whom he held in high esteem." [63]

The principal address at the dedication was delivered by Governor Price Daniel, who said:

Much of our State government as we know it today can be traced to the program of Jim Hogg. . . . This honest, sincere and firm man left an indelible mark on the pages of Texas history. . . . He put Texas on the road to progress and good government. . . .

Just as he believed in the future, Governor Hogg believed in preserving the history of Texas. He encouraged the division of the Department of Insurance, Statistics and History, out of which division developed the Texas State Library. By appointment of Judge C. W. Raines to supervise the statistical and historical work, he stimulated the collection and preservation of Texas' priceless records. . . . Texas will soon begin the erection of a State Library and Archives Building to provide a permanent home for our priceless archives and historical records. This achievement, like so many others in the past half century, develops from a pattern drawn by Governor James Hogg for the welfare of the people of Texas.[64]

Thus the people of the state which Jim Hogg served so well have gone on receiving the benefactions of his generous spirit. Of all of these, perhaps the most symbolic of him are the trees that have grown from the pecans and walnuts given out in February of each year through the Department of Horticulture of Texas A. and M. College, in accordance with his request the night before he died. Miss Hogg, too, distributes the seed to friends and callers who will promise to plant them and tend them well. Among the trees at "Mountain Home" the boy Jim Hogg could always find spiritual solace and new strength. In asking that his monument be "a land of trees," he was giving to the people of Texas the best legacy he knew.

Another legacy, more far-reaching in its effects upon the lives of Texans, was his contribution to government for the welfare of the entire citizenship. During the brief span of time from 1870 to 1906, Hogg had grown from the youth who attacked President Grant's corrupt administration through his Longview and Quitman *News* to the mature Demo-

---

[63] Ima Hogg, "The Gift of Varner and Its Purpose" (distributed at the dedication in West Columbia, March 23, 1958), H. C.

[64] From the press release of the Address of Governor Price Daniel, Varner-Hogg State Park, West Columbia, March 24, 1958. Full text may be obtained from the Governor's Office.

cratic leader who would publicly praise the great progressive Republican President Roosevelt as a statesman meeting most of his standards for political leadership. In an era of rapid centralization of power in Washington, Hogg labored to make state government effective and strong. He stood up to check the tide of federal encroachments upon states' rights, even to "the extent of opposing acceptance of federal money for state enterprises and state institutions."[65] When his own party, as Hogg observed, strayed from Democratic principles, he, like young Theodore Roosevelt and Charles E. Hughes in the Republican Party, did not desert and join the Populists, but stayed to reform his party from within. Hogg opposed government ownership of corporations, but he was equally opposed to corporate ownership or control of government. Hogg questioned the notion that either bankers or mine owners had a monopoly on a satisfactory knowledge of the intricacies of money, or the fiscal system, with the result that Hogg remained a champion of William J. Bryan rather than Cleveland and Parker.

Hogg was a sincere defender of the rights and liberties of the people. When he became a private citizen and a man of wealth he used his own time and money to give leadership to the reform movement until such a time as the conservative reaction to the dangers of Populism subsided and the time was ripe for the transfer of progressive leadership to the custody of his boyhood chum, Governor Thomas Campbell.[66]

Hogg is generally recognized as one of the four great statesmen in Texas. Stephen F. Austin, from New England and Spanish Missouri, made it possible for Texas to be settled by men dedicated to progress and to constitutional government. Sam Houston, from Tennessee, preserved the Republic of Texas, and, aided by such men as Joseph Lewis Hogg, brought her eventually into the Union as the Lone Star State. John H. Reagan, also from Tennessee, worked for the Interstate Commerce Act and then accepted Governor Hogg's appointment as the first chairman of the Texas Railroad Commission. The native son, James Stephen Hogg, inaugurated an outstanding reform program which placed Texas in the forefront of the Progressive Movement.

[65] Eugene C. Barker, "Foreword" to Cotner (ed.), *Addresses and State Papers of James Stephen Hogg*, pp. v–vi.
[66] The Cambell Papers are in the possession of a grandson, William Cambell, of Austin.

Index

Abbott, Jo: 161–162
Abilene, Texas: 120
Acheson, Sam: 467, 482
Acker, Walter: 103
Adair, W. A.: 60–61
Adams, Charles F.: 126, 241
Address proceedings: 111
Advance (Dallas): 396
Agassiz, Louis: 59
Alcoholism: 347–348
Aldridge, "Don Alfonso de": 535–543 *passim*
Alien Land Law: background of, 137, 261, 265, 294; and anti-British feeling, 341–342, 342 n. 39; unenforceable, 268; re-enacted, 283; newspaper opposition toward, 324
Alliance. *See* Farmers' Alliance, Southern Alliance, Northern Alliance
Altgeld, John P.: 387, 391, 470–471
Americanism: 570
American Revolution: 7–8
Anarchists: 172, 194
Anderson, John: as church trustee, 218; and Negro vote, 218
Andrew, Max: 559
Andrews, Frank: 528, 562
Andrews, Widow: 105
Anti-British feeling: 341–342, 411–412
Antitrust. *See* Trusts
Archbold, John: 437–438
Arthur, J. J.: 375
Ashby, Harrison S. P. (Stump): opposes Hogg, 256; as Populist, 258; as chm. Populist convention, 264; as chm. Populist state exec. com., 265
Ashe, Sam: 203
Asher, W. G., Jr.: 148, 150–153
Askew, H. G.: 375
Atkinson, Edward: 564–565
Attorney general, office of: importance of, 100–104; duties of, 117,

124–125, 337, 337 n. 29; report of, 153; as route to governor's office, 479
Atwell, William H.: 237–238, 577
Austin, Stephen F.: vii, 586
Austin, Texas: in 1886, 105; rapid transit in, 126; city charter of, vetoed, 333–336; Board Water and Light Commissioners of, 334; bond issue questioned, 335–336; Hogg addresses Culberson rally in, 417–418; as educational center, 454; Sunday in, 451
Austin *Capitolian*: 266
Austin *Daily Statesman*: 136, 183, 214 n. 53, 216, 394 n. 7
Austin *Evening News*: 267 n. 50
"Austin Manifesto": pro-Hogg Alliancemen, 248; opposes Tracy dictation, 254–255; Macune quoted on, 255. *See* Farmers' Alliance
Australian ballot: 265, 561
Autry, James J.: 503, 548

Bahn, G. A.: 378–379
Bailey, George: pro-Clark reporter (1892), 382; and Hogg's "liver and lights" speech, 380–382, 384 n. 65; notes for biography, 384; eastern tour, 407 n. 42
Bailey, Joseph Weldon: and Populist opponent, 307; criticizes Cleveland's gold policy, 462–463, 463 n. 26; opposes Bryan for president, 474; supports Bryan, 475; defies Hogg leadership, 481–482; opposes territorial expansion, 480–482; supports J. D. Sayers, 480; and Waters-Pierce oil cases, 442, 494–498, 501–502, 505–511, 520; opposes Sen. Horace Chilton, 460, 467, 480, 482–483, 489–490; seeks political leadership, 503–513 *passim*; right of, to be senator ques-

587

INDEX

613

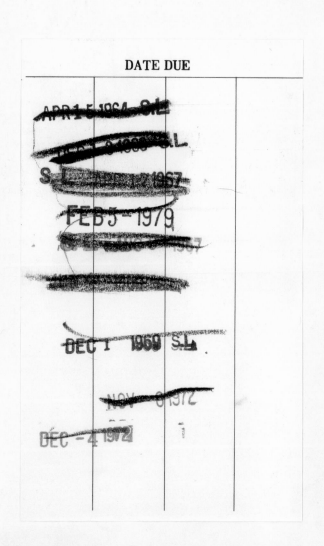

DATE DUE